# Contemporary Psychology and Effective Behavior

## Seventh Edition

**Charles G. Morris**
The University of Michigan

HarperCollins*Publishers*

**Cover Photograph:**
Kelly/Mooney Photography.
**Cover Background Photograph:**
Adamsmith Productions, West Light.

**Library of Congress Cataloging-in-Publication Data**

Morris, Charles G.
    Contemporary psychology and effective behavior/Charles G.
Morris.—7th ed.
      p. 624
    Rev. ed. of: Contemporary psychology and effective behavior/
James C. Coleman, 6th ed. c1987.
    ISBN 0-673-38954-5
    1. Psychology.  2. Adjustment (Psychology)  I. Coleman, James C.
(James Covington).  Contemporary psychology and effective behavior.

  II.  Title.
BF121.M596  1990                     89-28177
158--dc20                          CIP

3   4   5   6-VHJ-94  93  92  91

# Preface

THIS revision of *Contemporary Psychology and Effective Behavior* has been especially challenging since previous editions have been so well received by faculty and students. For example, as I sat down to write this preface, a 1989 review of the last edition crossed my desk in which the reviewer noted that the Sixth Edition ". . . is one of the better adjustment books I have seen. . . . [It] is an easy-to-read and well-organized book. It is reader friendly. . . . The flow of ideas is good. In effect, it is a carefully crafted book" (Geoffrey Maruyama, *Contemporary Psychology,* August, p. 763). What, then, could be improved in this new edition of the text? Well, quite a lot, as it turns out!

## The Research Perspective

There has been a concerted effort in this edition to give greater emphasis to research studies. In-depth descriptions of contemporary research studies have been added to every chapter, along with briefer descriptions of many others. Throughout the text there are more case studies and human interest stories to demonstrate important principles and concepts in real-life situations. Numerous self-tests and questionnaires have also been added to enliven the discussion of important concepts.

The Seventh Edition has also been extensively updated. As one measure of this effort, more than 200 of the references cited in the bibliography are new to this edition (many of them dated 1988 and 1989, with several others still in press as of this writing). Almost 40 percent of this edition's bibliography is new.

## Summaries

The chapter summaries have been completely rewritten. More extensive than in previous editions, each provides an overview of all key points in its chapter.

## Glossaries

The running glossary has been extensively revised: it is now devoted exclusively to technical terms, and many of the definitions have been rewritten. And for the first time, there is an alphabetical glossary at the end of the text to assist students as they work through the text and review for exams.

## A Separate Self-Discovery Journal

A very popular and useful element in the Sixth Edition was the Self-Discovery exercise that closed each chapter. These exercises are now collected in a separate *Self-Discovery Journal,* along with a number of similar self-exploration activities. All are designed to accomplish two purposes: (1) to encourage individual self-awareness, and (2) to help students understand how the material in a given chapter applies to their own lives. There are three exercises in every chapter. The material moves from fairly structured exercises that often have definite closure, to the more personal, open-ended, exploratory work that was the singular strength of the original Self-Discovery exercises.

## A Major Reorganization and Revision

The organization of the book has also changed significantly. The first seven chapters now cover the core concepts that form the heart of any course on the psychology of adjustment. The last seven emphasize the adjustive challenges of developmental tasks over the life span, with an extended discussion of adulthood.

### Part One—Adjustment and the Individual

Chapters 1 and 2 lay the foundation for understanding human adjustment. A major effort has been made to make Chapter 1 more engaging and interesting through the use of new human interest stories, examples, and case studies, and by tightening the chapter's organization. The concept of adjustment (both adaptive and maladaptive) is now introduced in this chapter. New also is an in-depth discussion of research on the perceived vs. real dangers of various hazards.

Chapter 2 has been extensively reorganized and rewritten. A case study is presented at the start of the chapter and is then analyzed from the perspective of each theoretical model as the chapter progresses. For each model, new material explores how that model views healthy adjustment and evaluates the model's strengths and weaknesses.

### Part Two—Stress: Its Nature, Effects, and Management

Building on this foundation, Chapters 3 through 7 discuss the basic principles of adjustment: the nature of stress, typical reactions to stressful events, coping more effectively with stress, maladaptive reactions to stress, and formal and informal therapies. New research covers such topics as the effects of stress on the immune system, urban stress, the stressfulness of AIDS, Type A personality and cardio-vascular disorders, learned helplessness, social support and health, thought suppression, the prevalence of psychological disorders, and the genetic predispositions underlying some psychological disorders. Throughout these chapters, there is greater emphasis on such topics as perceived control, physiological reactions to stress, and the diathesis-stress model of disorders. The discussion of disorders has been revised to reflect DSM-III-R.

## Part Three—Adjusting to Challenges over a Lifetime

The second half of the book examines in greater detail the most common adjustive challenges that arise during the course of life. Chapters 8 and 9 provide an overview of life-span adjustment: Chapter 8 examines common adjustive demands on infancy, childhood, and adolescence, while Chapter 9 focuses on adjustment in adulthood. Throughout, I have made a concerted effort to link these chapters to the first part of the book, by showing how major developmental tasks require the adjustment and adaptation techniques discussed in Chapters 1 through 7 and by deleting material peripheral to understanding life-span adjustment. Used throughout the last half of the book are the methods of effective coping discussed in Chapter 5, to demonstrate how people can reduce the stressfulness of inevitable adjustive challenges that arise in the course of living.

New material is included on the stressfulness of various childhood events (including a questionnaire that allows readers to try to predict the results of current research), physical and cognitive changes throughout adulthood, Gould and Levinson's studies of adjustment in adulthood, the mid-life transition, changing social relationships in adulthood, and adjustment in later adulthood.

## Part Four—Interpersonal and Social Aspects of Adjustment

Following the overview in Chapters 8 and 9, Chapters 10 through 14 examine much more closely those areas of adult life that are the most frequent sources of major adjustive challenges: interpersonal relations (Chapter 10); love, marriage, and other intimate relations (Chapter 11); human sexuality (Chapter 12); work and leisure (Chapter 13); and living in groups (Chapter 14). New material is included on interpersonal attraction, effective listening, mate selection, the effect of employment of married women, the effects of divorce on couples and their children, AIDS, homosexuality, and specific techniques for coping with stress in the workplace.

As in previous editions, the closing Epilogue completes the circle by returning to the discussion of the importance of values to human life and adjustment, a discussion that appears in the first chapter and reappears throughout the book.

## Acknowledgments

I continue to be indebted to the many distinguished scientists and writers and their publishers who granted me permission to quote from their works. I am also grateful to many people who contributed generously of their time to make this edition even better than the last. Thanks go to those professionals who reviewed the Sixth Edition and the manuscript for this new edition and who offered recommendations for improvement. I have benefitted greatly from their suggestions.

Professor David Andrews
*Indiana State University*

Professor Marsha Beauchamp
*Mt. San Antonio College*

Professor Karen Border
*Berkshire Community College*

Professor Frederick Brown
*Pennsylvania State University*

Professor Jeffrey Goodpaster
*Gateway Technical School*

Professor Sara Gutierres
*Arizona State University*

Professor Nancy Harken
*California State Polytechnic University, Pomona*

Professor Charles Harris
*James Madison University*

Professor William Heckel
*Robert Morris College*

Professor Barbara Hermann
*Gainesville College*

Professor Joseph Horvat
*Weber State College*

Professor Marilynn Jackson
*Howard Payne University*

Professor Clint Layne
*Western Kentucky University*

Professor H. John Lyke
*Metropolitan State College*

Professor Geoffrey Maruyama
*University of Minnesota*

Professor Salvador Macias, III
*University of South Carolina at Sumter*

Professor Nanette Manning
*Southeastern Community College*

Professor Ronald Murdoff
*San Joaquin Delta College*

Professor Terry Pettijohn
*Ohio State University, Marion*

Professor Fred Robbins
*Daytona Beach Community College*

Professor Joan Rykiel
*Ocean County College*

Professor John Sample
*Slippery Rock University*

Professor Michael Sperling
*Fairleigh Dickinson University*

Professor Robert Tomlinson
*University of Wisconsin-Eau Claire*

Professor Deborah Weber
*University of Akron*

Professor Mary Wheeler
*Western Carolina University*

Special thanks goes to Sandra Byers, of the University of New Brunswick, for her essay on Sex Roles and Gender Identification in Chapter 8, "Development and Adjustment in Childhood and Adolescence." Her contribution was a welcome addition on an important subject and enhanced the chapter overall.

## New Authorship: *Instructor's Manual/Test Items* and *Student Study Guide*

I am also grateful to those who have worked on the ancillaries for the text. The completely revised *Instructor's Manual and Test Bank* was prepared by Professors Jeanne L. O'Kon and Dale McColskey of Tallahassee Community College. The completely revised *Student Study Guide* was authored by Professors Joan Rosen and Lois Willoughby of Miami Dade Community College.

Finally, thanks go to the professional staff at Scott, Foresman. In particular, my thanks to Gail Savage, who listened to all of my ideas and then gently guided my efforts in the most productive directions while politely ignoring some of my more bizarre proposals. The book is much stronger as a result of her contributions.

C.G.M.

# To the Student

**T**HIS book has been written with you in mind. It is a book about the psychology of adjustment—the personal meanings of psychology. In it you will find information relating the findings of psychology and other disciplines to your life.

Several objectives have guided my preparation of the Seventh Edition of *Contemporary Psychology and Effective Behavior*. First, I wanted this book to be scholarly and up-to-date but not dry. I also wanted this text to be helpful without being a rigid and inflexible "how-to" book. I have attempted to make explicit the idea that adjustment is an active process that extends throughout the life span. Adjustment is not simply a matter of adapting to one's environment once and for all, but a continuing endeavor through which we shape our lives and our selves. Finally, I have tried to make you feel as though I am addressing you directly and personally. And it is my hope you will use material from this book to increase the understanding and satisfaction you get from life.

## EFFECTIVE STUDY TECHNIQUES

*. . . Much study is a weariness of the flesh.*

Ecclesiastes XII, 12

Effective study is an active process. It does not mean passively reading some material; it does not mean cramming for exams; and it does not mean endless hours spent in a frustrated search for understanding. Rather, effective study involves actively "digging in" and mastering course material; it involves steady progress; it involves more efficient use of your study time and, possibly, a reduction in the time you devote to study. In short, effective study can reduce the "weariness of the flesh" and replace it with an exhilarating sense of competence, pleasure, and mastery.

## Where to Study

Choosing appropriate study areas is the first step in an effective study program. Ideally, a study area should be free from distractions, well lit, and quiet.

Eliminating distractions is both a subtle and an obvious process. Some of the obvious distractors include telephone calls, friends or family stopping to chat, and so forth. The subtle distractors are often more numerous, but they can just as easily interrupt a study session. These subtle distractors can be a newspaper or magazine within easy reach, hobby materials such as records, photographs, and piles of unfinished projects in the study area. Even a textbook from another course can be a distractor. As you study for a particular course, the sight of another textbook reminds you how far behind you are in another course, and you begin to worry and daydream and become distracted. Once you become attuned to these distractions, you can eliminate them and improve your study skills.

Seeking a quiet and well-lit study area is equally important. A radio blaring in the background, a stereo playing next door, and the sounds of an interesting conversation are but a few of the factors that can disturb a study area.

Many students erroneously believe that a radio playing softly in the background improves their study skills. Unfortunately, this belief is not supported by scientific data. If anything, the use of a radio increases the time spent in a study session because of the distracting, noise-producing characteristics of the radio.

Finally, a study area should be used only for studying, not for any other activity. This implies that you should not study while lying in bed. If you choose a desk to be your study area, you should only study while at the desk. Socializing should be conducted elsewhere. Talking on the telephone or listening to the stereo should be performed away from the desk. And when you find yourself daydreaming, you should get up and move away from the desk. In short, establishing a specific study area ensures that you will be mentally attuned to study when you sit in your study area.

## When to Study

Two principles govern suggestions for deciding when to study. The first principle is that, for learning textual material, *continuous practice is better than massed practice*. We retain more information when we attempt to learn it in small, manageable packets than when we attempt to learn a great deal of material all at once. This implies that all-night study sessions just prior to an exam are less effective (and more exhausting!) than continuous, regular study sessions.

The second principle is an old one, repeatedly confirmed by research—*practice improves retention*. Reviewing course material on a regular basis facilitates the learning process. Adhering to a regularly scheduled study program has major benefits for remembering and retaining course material.

## How to Study: The SQ3R Approach

The SQ3R method was devised to increase your involvement with text material. Although the SQ3R system appears to be somewhat involved and complex, it can significantly increase your comprehension and understanding of the material, and so your ability to apply the material throughout the course.

The SQ3R method has five parts: Survey, Question, Read, Recite, and Review. Let us examine how to use each of these steps to help you increase your study efficiency.

**Survey.** Briefly survey the chapter; look at the chapter title, section headings, and so forth. Your aim here is not to go into detail but to develop a general idea of the structure and focus of the chapter.

The text is designed to help you with this step. You will notice that a chapter outline is placed at the beginning of each chapter. Look over this outline as you survey the chapter. Also, examine the chapter summary to get some idea of the material presented in the chapter. Remember, your goal in this part of your study is to become acquainted with the material to come.

**Question.** As you survey the chapter, write down several questions about the material you are about to learn. These questions should be relatively detailed and should cover the chapter. Portions of the outline may be written as questions.

The purpose of asking questions is to increase your involvement with the material and to give some purpose to your studying. By formulating questions, you are not simply reading the material, but you are trying to find answers to important issues. Also, you will focus on the more important material without becoming overwhelmed by details.

The text can help you formulate questions. The major headings of the chapter are printed in color and are excellent sources for generating questions. Additionally, key terms are printed in **boldface type,** and definitions for these terms can be found in the page margins.

**Read.** Now that you have formulated some questions, read the material in order to answer the questions. Write down the answers to the questions you have posed. It is important to read actively and with involvement, for this increases your understanding of the material. If you become tired or distracted, stop reading until you can devote your entire energies and attention to reading. Remember, your job here is not just to cover a number of pages but to "dig in" while you read.

**Recite.** Recitation is the part of the SQ3R method that most people find difficult (or embarrassing) to carry out. Look at your questions and try to answer your questions *aloud*. Listen to your responses. Are they complete? Are they correct? If not, reread the appropriate section and try again to answer your question. This form of rehearsal increases the likelihood that you will retain the material.

If you find it difficult to carry out this portion of the SQ3R method by yourself, enlist the cooperation of other members of your class. Form a small group and meet on a regular basis. Ask questions of each other, and answer these questions. Prepare short lectures on the material. (Be sure to stay on target and not let extraneous material enter into your study sessions.) If you make a mistake, briefly review the material and state aloud your corrected answer.

**Review.** On a regular basis, look over your notes. Answer the questions you have posed to yourself. Try to summarize the major points in the chapter. By making this rehearsal an active and a regular process, you again increase your chances of retaining the material.

In closing, I hope that you will benefit from the suggestions on improving your study skills. I also hope that reading this book will be as exciting, challenging, stimulating, and rewarding for you as preparing this new edition has been for me.

# Overview

# Contents

## CHAPTER 4   REACTIONS TO STRESSFUL EVENTS   104

## CHAPTER 5   EFFECTIVE METHODS OF COPING WITH STRESS   138

## CHAPTER 9 DEVELOPMENT AND ADJUSTMENT IN ADULTHOOD 296

## CHAPTER 12  SEXUAL ATTITUDES AND BEHAVIOR  422

EPILOGUE

# 𝒯he 𝒬uest for 𝒱alues  524

# Adjustment and the Individual

# The Human Dilemma

*It was the best of times, it was the worst of times, it was the age of
wisdom, it was the age of foolishness, it was the epoch of belief, it was
the epoch of incredulity, it was the season of Light, it was the season of
Darkness, it was the spring of hope, it was the winter of despair, we had
everything before us, we had nothing before us . . . in short, the period
was . . . like the present period . . . .*

*A Tale of Two Cities* (Dickens, 1859)

*I*N many respects you and I are living in "the best of times." Most people
have never before had such opportunities for enjoying life to its fullest. The
average person in the United States is better fed, housed, clothed, and educated
than anyone else in history. Machines—powered by electricity instead of human
labor—remove much of the drudgery from everyday living. We can enjoy the finest
literature, music, and art. We can travel farther in less time than our ancestors could
possibly have imagined. We can participate in sports and other leisure-time activities
once available only to the very rich. Through motion pictures, television, cable
networks, and other video systems, we can be entertained by spectacles that would
have astounded ancient kings. Modern achievements in medicine have made us
among the healthiest people of all time and have greatly increased our life expectancy.
Humans have already walked on the moon, and still greater achievements are ahead.

Reminders of our good fortune are easy to find as exemplified in the newspaper
headlines of one recent week.

Infant Mortality Rate Edges Down
Unemployment Drops to New Low
New Hope for Victims of High Blood Pressure
Experiment Provides Hope for Arthritis Treatment
Skywalks and Tunnels Bring New Life to the Great Indoors

The stories behind the headlines during that week were just as remarkable.

Robert S. entered the hospital a week ago suffering from cardiac artery disease. Friday
night his heart stopped beating and he was put on a heart-lung machine. Saturday morning
he received an artificial heart as a "bridging device" until a human heart transplant became
available. This morning, just five days after receiving his artificial heart, he was talking,
eating, and walking around his room.

Norman P. was sipping coffee in the study of his home when his computer terminal noted
an irregularity at the rolling mill of the steel company where he worked, an hour's drive
away. He called up on the screen a diagram showing the operation of the mill's seven
finishing rollers, and discovered that one set of rollers was pinching the steel too thin.
Norman typed a command and watched on his screen as the computer at the mill adjusted
the rollers, bringing the thickness of the sheet metal back into line.

*The paradox: increased opportunities, even happy circumstances, can trigger stress caused by a greater number of roles, responsibilities, and complexities.*

Our ancestors would have been astounded to read or hear about stories such as these, stories that suggest you and I are truly living in "the best of times." However, a closer look indicates that all is not going exactly as we might hope and expect. In some respects these are also "the worst of times." Poverty, illiteracy, unemployment, job burnout, high divorce rates, and fear of nuclear disaster are part of everyday life. Crime has become so widespread that we hesitate to help a stranger in apparent distress, and we think twice before we go outside at night, even in our own yards (see Insight, p. 6).

These and other serious problems of modern living are also reflected in the daily news. The same newspapers that carried upbeat headlines and articles also recently contained these headlines.

Attorney General Lists War on Drugs as Top Priority

Left at Airport Gate? Hope for the Best

Study Shows Substantial Increase in Child Abuse, Neglect Cases

Riots Ensue After Police Attempt to Enforce Curfew

Jets Screech; Residents Cry "Enough"

12 Indicted in Mailing of Child Pornography

# *Insight*

---

## The Paradoxes of Our Time

**The Paradox of Technology.** While modern technology has enabled us to land people on the moon and return them safely to earth, it has not enabled us to solve many critical problems on earth, some of which have been caused or aggravated by technology itself.

**The Paradox of Communication.** Via communication satellites and mass media, we have developed highly advanced communication facilities and techniques; yet "communication gaps" prevent or distort our understanding of each others' ideas and motives.

**The Paradox of Affluence.** The United States is the most affluent nation in the world and in history; yet in 1987, 32 million people were living below the government-set poverty line, school programs and urban renewal programs are being cut back due to lack of funds, and each year the already mammoth national debt grows larger.

**The Paradox of Equality.** In a society based on the principles of freedom, equality, and justice for all, we find widespread group prejudice and discrimination with limited opportunities and unequal justice for the poor and the "different."

**The Paradox of Defense.** The security our costly military defense system should provide is offset by the spiraling arms race, the proliferation of nuclear weapons, and the increase in the number of "super-powers."

**The Paradox of Values.** In a society founded on principles which have brought unprecedented well-being and opportunity to a majority of its citizens, we find a sizable number of youth and adults feeling alienated and dehumanized.

As with these recent newspaper headlines, many of the stories during that week conveyed equally disturbing messages about modern living.

Robert S. was standing on a street corner Friday about 9:30 p.m. when a small, blue two-door car pulled up, the window rolled down, and a tall man shot Mr. S. in the chest with a small caliber gun. The victim told police he did not know the suspect or why anyone would shoot him.

Merrie B. lost her 32-year-old son in the fiery crash of an airliner a year ago. "Some days I sit here, and the tears just flow and I'm not sure why I'm crying. It's not something you can live with. I haven't adjusted at all. Every day I think of all the things he would be doing."

One in seven Vietnam veterans suffers from post-traumatic stress disorder, a rate seven times that estimated by a government study earlier this year.

On a less dramatic level, each of us is affected every day by the stress of modern living. For example, at times it seems as though the pace of life has increased to a frenzy; for many of us there's a great deal of truth in the saying, "The faster I go, the behinder I get!" As we rush about, we encounter endless problems: freeways are clogged, there is seldom a parking place when we need it, and even our cars seem to break down more often than they used to. Making decisions is increasingly difficult as we face an ever-larger number of choices: thousands of colleges to attend,

*The automobile has given us great freedom and made far-away places accessible— except when everyone is trying to go to the same place on the same road at the same time.*

hundreds of ways to invest our savings, a vast array of potential careers (with more appearing every day). Sometimes it is even difficult to relax: there are dozens of TV channels or radio stations to choose from at any given moment and more magazines and books to read than one could fit into several lifetimes.

If this is indeed a Golden Age, then it is also an Age of Stress: our unprecedented progress has brought with it unprecedented problems. Yet progress and problems have always coexisted. Both were present during the period of the French Revolution, as Charles Dickens so vividly described in the passage that opens this chapter; progress and stress coexisted during the height of civilization in Greece and Rome; and they coexist in the world today. Since progress and stress go hand in hand, each generation must learn how to cope effectively with the stress of everyday living. The best course of action lies not in trying to stop or even reverse change, but rather in guiding change and in developing new ways of adjusting to the unique problems and challenges of today's world (see Insight, p. 8).

## THE PROCESS OF ADJUSTMENT

**adjustment:** the process of meeting environmental demands and modifying the world around us to better meet our needs in the future

**adjustive demand:** life event that requires changes in an individual's thoughts or behaviors

**Adjustment** is the process by which any organism (1) attempts to meet the demands placed upon it by the environment and (2) attempts to structure its environment to enhance survival, understanding, and growth. Notice the two parts to this definition of adjustment: adjustment is reactive—we respond as best we can to events in the world around us. Adjustment is also proactive—we try to alter and modify our environment so it will better meet our needs in the future. Adjustment is therefore a process through which we try to cope with **adjustive demands** in the world around us, and at the same time try to influence and change the world we will encounter in the future. For example, if we find ourselves in a college class that is

# *Insight*

## Progress and Expectations

Three decades ago, psychologist Hadley Cantril (1958) wrote:

*As more and more people throughout the world become more and more enmeshed in a scientific age, its psychological consequences on their thought and behavior become increasingly complicated. The impact comes in a variety of ways: people begin to feel the potentialities for a more abundant life that modern technology can provide; they become aware of the inadequacies of many present political, social, and religious institutions and practices; they discern the threat which existing power and status relationships may hold to their own development; they vaguely sense the inadequacy of many of the beliefs and codes accepted by their forefathers and perhaps by themselves at an earlier age.*

*The upshot is that more and more people are acquiring both a hope for a "better life" and a feeling of frustration and anxiety that they themselves may not experience the potentially better life they feel should*

*be available to them. They search for new anchorages, for new guidelines, for plans of action which hold a promise of making some of the dreams come true. (pp. vii-viii)*

Cantril is suggesting that life today is more stressful than it was one hundred or two hundred years ago in part because we have made such extraordinary progress. A century ago, hardship, disease, and discomfort were expected as a normal part of life. People simply accepted these problems as unavoidable and endured them as best they could. However, we have come to expect more out of life—a higher standard of living, instant cures for disease, greater comfort, less hard work, more time for leisure. When these expectations are not always met, it is understandable that people become frustrated, angry, and disillusioned. If Cantril is correct, then it would follow that as we make further progress in the future toward an even more ideal way of living, we will become even less satisfied with the world in which we then find ourselves! Do you agree?

too difficult, we attempt to cope with the situation as best we can; but we also take steps to assure that we will not make the same mistake again.

## Adaptive and Maladaptive Adjustment

Of course, not all efforts at adjustment are equally effective. To the extent that our coping behavior meets the demands of the situation, satisfies our needs, and is consistent with the well-being of others, then we can say that it is **adaptive.** To the extent that our behavior does not achieve these goals, it is **maladaptive.** Let's look more closely at these three criteria of adaptiveness.

**Does the action meet the adjustive demand?** Some actions do not resolve the underlying problems but merely provide temporary relief from symptoms. For example, Louise G. has been taking a prescription tranquilizer for four years to help her cope with the stress of her job as a lawyer in a high-powered law office and the demands of being a wife and a mother of two school age children. For several years John and Sharon's marriage has been in trouble; although Sharon wants to see a

**adaptive:** behavior that effectively meets adjustive demands, satisfies our needs, and contributes to the well-being of others

**maladaptive:** behavior that does not meet adjustive demands, does not satisfy our needs, or does not contribute to the well-being of others

marriage counselor, John refuses to do so and insists that they are simply having "minor problems," "going through some rough times," and that everything will be fine shortly. These kinds of maladaptive responses to stress provide temporary relief from stress, but by themselves they do not resolve the underlying problem. As a result they may actually make the situation worse and make it even harder to cope effectively in the future. For example, Lorraine W. found that a glass of wine helped her to break through her shyness at parties and at social events connected with her business. After a while she found that a glass of wine could also help her cope with the stress after a busy day of meetings and tight deadlines. Not long after, she began drinking two glasses of wine at night, then three glasses. Eventually she was no longer able to control her drinking even though it endangered her health, her career, and her social life. For adjustment to be effective, it must meet both the immediate and long-range requirements of the situation.

**Does the action meet the individual's needs?**   Sometimes an action meets the demands of a situation but fails to meet the individual's needs. Marie wants to be a physicist but surrenders to her parents' wish that she go into nursing. Her decision temporarily relieves the pressure she feels from her parents, but it leaves her own needs unsatisfied. Far from being an effective adjustment, such a decision likely will create inner conflict and feelings of frustration that later on will cause more difficult problems of adjustment for her. Adaptive adjustment must meet not only the requirements of the situation but also the immediate and the long-term needs of the individual.

*Adjustment skills are most important when stress is greatest and no options seem acceptable. Certainly in such situations the challenges—and the costs—are the most difficult.*

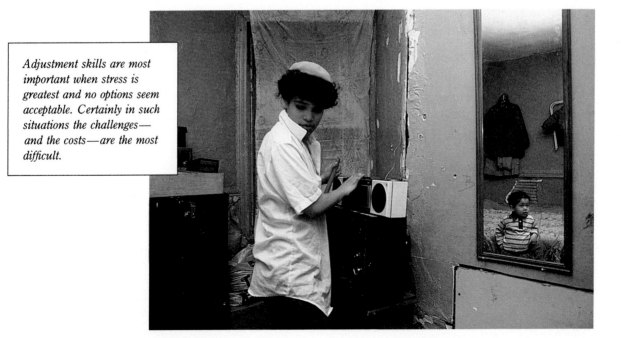

**Does the action contribute to the well-being of others?**    Adaptive coping behavior should contribute to the well-being of others as well as the integrity and well-being of the individual. George M. discovers that he is not the favored candidate for promotion to vice president of his company. George invites the company president to lunch, and during the course of the meal hints that his competitor may have acted unethically when negotiating for some important contracts several years earlier. In fact, George has no reason to believe that the favored candidate ever acted unethically in his business dealings. If we attempt to meet our needs at the expense of other people, our coping behavior is likely to be self-defeating in the long run.

Unfortunately, examples of maladaptive adjustment are easy to find in today's world: Americans' use of vast numbers of tranquilizing drugs, sleeping pills, and sleeping aids each year, and our yearly consumption of billions of dollars worth of alcoholic beverages, are signs of maladaptive adjustment. Other examples include the difficulties that people have in establishing and maintaining satisfactory long-term relationships with others, the marked increase in suicide among our youth, and the alarming increases in crimes of violence.

Adjustment needn't be maladaptive. In fact, one major goal of this textbook is to demonstrate possible ways to adjust effectively to the stresses of modern life. However, it is important to realize from the outset that adaptive adjustment does not arise from increased technological know-how. It comes instead from a better understanding of ourselves, of other people, and of the way in which we are affected by (and affect) the environment in which we find ourselves. In the next portion of the chapter we will explore briefly each of these sources of understanding and the ways in which they can lead to more adaptive ways of coping.

## The Search for Understanding

*We have been as confused about ourselves, often—as uncertain about what our human nature is and what it requires of us—as an acorn would be if it were not sure whether its proper destiny was to be an oak or a cabbage.*

    *The Mind Goes Forth* (Overstreet & Overstreet, 1956, p. 240)

As human beings, we have a number of unique talents that provide the opportunity to adapt extremely well to a great variety of stressful situations. (1) We are self-aware: that is, we are able not only to be aware of ourselves as unique individuals but also to reflect upon, review, and reevaluate aspects of our own experiences. (2) We have tremendous capacities for learning, reasoning, and imagining, which in turn give us almost unlimited flexibility for coping with new and changing situations. (3) We can think and communicate about absent or even imaginary objects, events, and concepts; in turn, this ability has enabled us to develop sciences from which we

# Psychology in Action

## The Hazards of Modern Living

Below you will find a list of thirty hazards of modern living. Later in this chapter we will discuss at some length the risks posed by these hazards. You will find that discussion much more interesting if you take a few minutes now to think about each of these activities and technologies, and then to rank them in terms of the risk of dying (across all U.S. society as a whole) from each of them. Assign "1" to the item that represents the greatest risk to people across the U.S. as a whole, "2" to the next riskiest item, and so on until you reach the least risky item, to which you should assign the number "30."

| | | | |
|---|---|---|---|
| Alcoholic beverages | ____ | Motor vehicles (including collisions with bicycles and pedestrians) | ____ |
| Bicycles | ____ | Mountain climbing | ____ |
| Commercial aviation | ____ | Nuclear power | ____ |
| Contraceptives (IUDs, pills) | ____ | Pesticides | ____ |
| Electric power (electrocution, mining, etc.) | ____ | Police work | ____ |
| Fire fighting | ____ | Power mowers | ____ |
| Food coloring | ____ | Prescription antibiotics | ____ |
| Food preservatives | ____ | Railroads | ____ |
| General (private) aviation | ____ | Skiing | ____ |
| Handguns | ____ | Smoking | ____ |
| High school & college football | ____ | Spray cans | ____ |
| Home appliances | ____ | Surgery | ____ |
| Hunting | ____ | Swimming | ____ |
| Large construction (dams, bridges, etc.) | ____ | Vaccinations | ____ |
| Motorcycles | ____ | X rays | ____ |

can gain greater understanding of ourselves and how the world works. (4) We can make value judgments about what is good and what is bad; unlike other organisms, we can choose our goals and the means for achieving them. (5) There seems to be almost no limit to the ways in which we can modify the environment for our own ends (see Insight, p. 12).

These various properties of human beings—reflective self-awareness and the abilities to learn, reason, imagine, communicate, make value judgments, and modify the environment—make possible a high degree of **self-direction.** Compared to other animals, we can rely to a greater extent on our mental abilities as we attempt to cope effectively both by continually modifying our behavior to meet the demands of new situations and by shaping the environment to better meet our needs. However, this capacity for self-direction comes at a cost: it places a heavy demand upon us to acquire information about ourselves and our world because the goals we strive for and the methods we select to achieve them are determined by what we conceive ourselves to be, by what we think we can become, and by the ways we picture the opportunities and limitations of the world around us.

**self-direction:** using ones mental abilities to devise effective methods of adjustment

11

# *Insight*

It is worth reflecting on the fact that you and I must learn how to adjust effectively to the problems we encounter. Branden (1965) pointed out that, "Given the appropriate conditions, the appropriate physical environment, all living organisms—with one exception—are set by their nature to originate automatically the actions required to sustain their survival" (p. 2). We humans are the exception: we have few built-in adjustive behavior patterns and so we must learn how to adjust effectively to the problems that face us.

In contrast, most species in the animal world rely largely upon coping behaviors that do not have to be learned but which can be extraordinarily effective. For example, the night moth has sensors under each wing that can detect the presence of a bat more than one hundred feet away. The sensors cause the wing nearest the bat to beat faster, and as a result the moth automatically turns and flies away from the bat without thinking about or even understanding what it is doing. Sharks and cockroaches also rely heavily on built-in adaptive

behaviors which have helped to assure their existence for hundreds of millions of years. Even the dinosaur, considered to be much less intelligent than we are, survived for more than 150 million years while the human race appears to be in danger of extinction after only about two million years.

However, instinctive adaptation in non-humans has some serious drawbacks. The less fit simply perish or are destroyed according to the "law of the jungle." Although such a situation is adaptive for animals in the wild, it is not a policy that most people would find acceptable in the civilized world. Moreover, built-in adaptive responses are seldom effective in the face of rapid or widespread change. For example, thousands of plant and animal species have already been destroyed as a result of their inability to adapt quickly enough to the changes we humans have made in the environment during just the last few decades. Rapid change that requires immediate adaptation leaves most instinct-bound animals in a dangerous position.

**Self-understanding.** Our unique capacity for self-direction brings with it the responsibility for acquiring a good deal of information about ourselves. Most people would consider it sheer folly to attempt to climb a mountain peak without a good sense of their physical condition, their level of skill, and their limitations. Yet many of these same people expect to go successfully through life without knowing much about themselves. For such people, living becomes simply a matter of muddling through, of making costly and needless mistakes, and wasting much of their potential. They prepare for the wrong occupations, choose incompatible mates, and bring up children with the naive hope that good intentions will be sufficient. If we are to direct our behavior in more adaptive ways, we must clear up this confusion and gain an accurate view of what and who we are. Toward this end, much of this book is devoted to helping you gain greater understanding of yourself—both the qualities you share with other human beings and the qualities that make you a unique individual (see Insight, p. 14).

**Understanding others.** Self-understanding is not by itself sufficient to lead to effective adjustment. We also need information about the groups to which we belong, the ways in which we are affected by them, and the ways in which we can contribute

*Challenges can be stressful—sometimes frightening, dangerous, and seemingly insurmountable—but they can also surprise, strengthen, and enlighten us.*

to their well-being and progress. A large part of modern life involves relationships with other people. Our behavior affects the people around us just as their behavior affects us. If other people share our needs and our personal qualities, then our efforts to cope effectively may also contribute to their well-being. But if they have different needs or goals, then what is best for us may not be best for them. In such cases, adaptive coping requires that we take account of both our needs and the needs of others as we try to respond to adjustive demands. This means that we must have some insight into the nature of the people around us—a topic that will concern us repeatedly throughout this book.

**Knowledge of the environment.**    Finally, if we are to cope more effectively with the problems of modern living, each of us must learn more about the world in which we live. We must learn about the ways in which our environment influences our behavior—including its potentials for meeting our needs, and its pitfalls and dangers—and the skills we will need for coping. We need especially to become more aware of the long-range effects of our actions on the environment. These topics, too, will be explored throughout this book.

# *Insight*

## Three Key Questions

Understanding oneself means trying to find the answers to three key questions: Who am I? Where am I going? How do I get there?

### Who Am I?

We can understand much about ourselves by understanding the characteristics common to all men and women, for we are all members of the human species. Each of us, however, is also unique, and therefore we also have to understand the ways in which we differ from others. Adequate self-knowledge can prove very beneficial: we can gain insight into some of the irrational forces that shape our behavior, and gain an accurate appreciation of our own capabilities and aptitudes. Equipped with a better understanding of ourselves, we can plan more appropriate courses of action, make better decisions, and use our resources more effectively to make our lives more productive and satisfying. On the other hand, a blurred sense of who we are is likely to make it difficult for us to plan and decide effectively.

### Where Am I Going?

As we acquire knowledge about ourselves, we are in a better position to set realistic goals for ourselves. Goals focus our energy and effort, help determine what skills and abilities we need to develop, and provide a basis for deciding between alternative courses of action. Long-range goals are particularly important since they give coherence and continuity to life. Some goals, of course, are more realistic than others in view of each person's unique personal resources and opportunities and in view of the satisfactions they are likely to produce. Pursuit of unrealistically high goals leads to failure and frustration. Pursuit of goals that are too low leads to wasted opportunities and dissatisfaction. Pursuit of "false" goals leads to disillusionment and discouragement.

### How Do I Get There?

This question concerns skills and competencies—the means by which we hope to achieve our goals. Although the specific skills required will vary with the circumstances, several general competencies appear basic for reaching one's goals. (1) Physical competencies: the practice of good physical health measures and the use of medical resources to keep one's body functioning efficiently. (2) Intellectual competencies: the acquisition of essential information about oneself and one's world; proficiency in learning, problem solving, and decision making. (3) Emotional competencies: the ability to love and be loved and to deal effectively with fears, anxieties, anger, and other problem emotions that we all experience. (4) Social competencies: the ability to deal effectively with other people and to build satisfying interpersonal relationships.

Besides such general competencies, we also need to equip ourselves to meet specific challenges that we are likely to experience. Although we cannot foresee all the problems we will face, there are certain adjustments that most of us almost certainly will have to make: obtaining an education, preparing for rewarding life work, building a fulfilling marriage, bringing up children, finding a personalized philosophy of life, coping with the illness and deaths of friends and family members, and growing old. We can increase the probability of success if we know what difficulties may be involved and what information and competencies we will need in dealing with them. The last half of this book is devoted largely to a consideration of these and other common adjustive demands that occur throughout the life cycle.

The *Self-Discovery Journal* manual that accompanies this text contains a series of exercises that are intended to help you begin to develop answers to these three key questions. These exercises should help you apply important concepts in the text to your own life, and help you use the chapter material to gain greater insight into yourself. Completing these exercises should result not only in a better understanding of the text but also in a greater degree of self-awareness. I recommend strongly that you take the time to work through the self-discovery exercises as you read the corresponding chapter in the text.

### The Search for Values

*Thus we envision the possibility of an evolutionary leap to a
transindustrial society that not only has know-how, but also has a deep
inner knowledge of what is worth doing.*

*An Incomplete Guide to the Future* (Harman, 1976, p. 112)

**values:** deeply-held,
enduring beliefs about what
is desirable and undesirable

This passage highlights the fact that effective coping requires more than simply gathering information. It also requires that each of us develop a set of **values**—deeply-held, enduring beliefs about what is good and bad, desirable and undesirable. While information concerns what is or what could be, values concern what ought to be. Values help us to answer such questions as: Why this action rather than another? What kind of life is good or bad for human beings in general and for me as an individual? What makes this goal good and that one bad? Hadley Cantril (1958) has compared values to a "compass" which shows us the direction—how we should act and why. Whether or not we have thought through our values or are even clearly aware of them, our behavior reflects our values. Even if we forfeit the chance to plan for ourselves and instead "take life as it comes," we are making a choice and in this sense making a value decision.

Old values daily give way to new ones, yet finding and agreeing upon these new values is not an easy task. There is a bewildering array of conflicting and changing values offered by contemporary society, and the values that prove satisfying and fulfilling to one person may not appeal to another. As we will see in Chapter 11, a growing number of couples are choosing to live together and even raise families without first getting married; yet other couples find this choice completely unacceptable. Some business people welcome computer technology, while others believe that computers depersonalize and dehumanize business relations. Some people believe that abortion is legally and morally acceptable, while others believe abortion is murder.

If we choose values which are not in keeping with either the needs of our own nature or the realities of the world, they will work against us. Although we are free to act against the requirements of our nature and our world, we are not free to escape the consequences. Therefore, throughout this book you will find not only information about yourself and others and the adjustive demands you are likely to face, but also a consideration of values and the role they must play in your efforts at coping with the life challenges you encounter.

## THE ORIENTATION OF THIS BOOK

Today, people look increasingly to modern science—particularly to psychology—as a dependable source of information that will help them in their search for understanding. We also take the view that a sound approach to human behavior should be based in part on scientific findings. As you read further in this book, you will see many examples of ways in which the findings of modern science can help us to arrive at a greater understanding of ourselves and of others. However, we do not assume that science is infallible, nor do we assume that science can provide all the answers we need to cope with modern life. In the search for values, particularly, each of us must go beyond science and draw upon additional sources of insight and guidance. So in this book we will use scientific findings as far as we can, but we will not expect the impossible of them. While we will view science as a dependable source of information about human beings, we will remain free to utilize information from other sources as well.

## A Scientific Approach

**psychology:** the science of behavior and mental processes

**Psychology** is the science of behavior and mental processes. Like all scientists, psychologists seek to describe, explain, predict, and gain a measure of control over what they study. This means that psychologists first attempt to *describe* various aspects of behavior. Consider, for example, several of the assertions made earlier in this chapter: the rapid pace of modern living is a source of stress; self-understanding contributes to effective adjustment; use of alcohol to escape from stress is maladaptive. Each of those assertions is based on data collected by psychologists and others in their effort to describe important aspects of human behavior.

However, facts such as these are only the beginning of the scientific process. Once you confirm, for example, that rapid change is a source of adjustment problems, the next question is Why? How can you *explain* the relationship between rapid change and problems of adjustment? As you will see in Chapter 3, one explanation is that people prefer to live in a stable, coherent environment; rapid change brings with it ambiguity, lack of structure, chaos, and lack of understanding. Thus, rapid change requires adjustment to a new (and less desirable) environment.

Once you have developed an explanation for why rapid change is stressful, you should be able to *predict* behavior. For example, if our explanation is correct, then you would predict that any ambiguous situation is likely to create problems of adjustment for people. You would also predict that in times of rapid change people who experience a great deal of ambiguity will find the changes more stressful than people who don't experience a great deal of ambiguity.

Finally, if your explanation is correct, you should be able to *control* behavior to a degree: for example, in a hospital setting you might be able to reduce the stress experienced by some patients if you were to reduce the ambiguity of the situation in which they find themselves. Similarly, you might be able to reduce the stress you are experiencing in a situation by taking steps to reduce the ambiguity of that situation as much as possible. (You will get more out of the following discussion if you have filled out the questionnaire on the hazards of modern life; see Psychology in Action, page 11.)

This example of ambiguity and stress shows how psychological research can contribute to greater understanding of ourselves and others, and how this in turn can suggest ways in which we might cope more effectively with adjustive demands.

*Many hazards are potentially devastating, but if we foresee the risks we often can adapt our behavior accordingly.*

Let's look at another example of the way in which psychological research can contribute to greater understanding and more adaptive adjustment.

**Hazards: perception versus actuality.**   We have spoken a great deal in this chapter about the hazards of modern living—drugs, terrorism, violence, crime, health problems, and the threat of a nuclear accident. These are all real hazards, all representing risks to each of us, and all contributing to the problems of living in the late twentieth century. However, it has been suggested that the extent to which we worry about each of these hazards doesn't correspond very well to the real threats involved—that is, we tend not to worry very much about some extremely grave threats, while we worry a great deal about other hazards that are relatively harmless (Wildavsky, 1979; Kasper, 1980). Neither of these behaviors is very adaptive: it makes little sense to worry needlessly about things that aren't really very dangerous, and it is suicidal to be unconcerned about hazards that represent a real threat to our survival.

Do people really worry needlessly about some hazards of modern life and not worry enough about others? To answer this question, Christoph Hohenemser, Robert Kates, and Paul Slovic (1983) asked a group of college-educated adults to rate nearly one hundred hazards on "the risk of dying (across all U.S. society as a whole) as a consequence of this activity or technology." When they compared the perceived risk of each hazard with its real threat to human life, they found that indeed there was no relationship between the two: some very dangerous activities were rated quite low in risk, while other relatively safe activities were seen as very dangerous (see Table 1.1). Thus, Hohenemser and his colleagues described an important fact about human behavior: people overestimate the threat of some hazards of modern life and underestimate the threat of other hazards.

Why should this be? Are people simply misinformed about the dangers of various hazards? Are people irrational and illogical? Or is there some other explanation for the judgments? Paul Slovic, Baruch Fischhoff, and Sarah Lichtenstein (1985) set out to discover answers to these questions. In a series of experiments involving college students and college-educated adults, they confirmed the earlier finding that people's judgments about the risk of dying from various hazards bore virtually no relationship to the actual risk of each hazard. As you can see from Table 1.1, people greatly overestimated the risk of dying from such things as nuclear power, police work, fire fighting, hunting, spray cans, mountain climbing, and skiing. At the same time, they greatly underestimated the risk of dying from X rays, swimming, electric power, home appliances, and surgery. (You can determine the extent to which you over-estimated or underestimated the threats of these hazards by comparing your answers to the questionnaire on page 11 with the experts' rankings in Table 1.1.)

However, Slovic et al. went beyond simply describing this aspect of human behavior and attempted to *explain* why people over- and underestimate the risks of certain hazards. By administering detailed questionnaires to several new groups of subjects, they discovered that when people such as you and I are asked to judge the risks of various hazards, we consider much more than just the likelihood that a particular hazard will cause death. We also worry about whether it might be difficult to reduce the risks associated with the hazard and to prevent accidents from occurring altogether. We worry about whether the consequences of the hazard are almost certain to be fatal and whether there would be any way to reduce the number of fatalities from the hazard. We worry about whether the hazard is likely to have catastrophic effects (killing many people at once, perhaps across the whole world, perhaps affecting future generations as well). It turns out that all of these consid-erations are vastly more important to us than simple mortality statistics when we try to assess the risk of a given hazard.

**Hazards: applying research.**  Let's see how these research findings help us to understand the fact that the public greatly overestimates the risks of nuclear power and greatly underestimates the hazards associated with producing electric power. To most of us, nuclear accidents appear uncontrollable and difficult to prevent; moreover, they are likely to be fatal to those involved and also likely to result in catastrophes. Most of us don't just worry about nuclear accidents, we dread them. In contrast, few of us have the same feelings about conventional electric power; despite the fact that electric power is actually extremely hazardous, most of us believe that injury or death from electric power is easier to prevent. If an accident does occur, electric power seems less likely to result in fatalities, and it rarely causes catastrophes. While we may worry about electric power, few of us truly dread it. As a result, we tend to underestimate the associated risks.

Now that we have a better understanding that people worry about some things more than others, it should be possible to do a better job of predicting what kinds of hazards people will worry about. For example, you might predict that people overestimate the risks associated with genetic engineering and terrorism, and worry less than they should about the risks of home power tools, boating, and lack of exercise.

**TABLE 1.1   Risk of Dying in Any Given Year from Various Activities and Technologies as Ranked by the Public and Experts**

| Experts | Hazard | Public |
|---|---|---|
| 1 | Motor vehicles | 3 |
| 2 | Smoking | 4 |
| 3 | Alcoholic beverages | 6 |
| 4 | Handguns | 2 |
| 5 | Surgery | 10 |
| 6 | Motorcycles | 5 |
| 7 | X rays | 21 |
| 8 | Pesticides | 7 |
| 9 | Electric power | 20 |
| 10 | Swimming | 24 |
| 11 | Contraceptives (IUDs, pills) | 15 |
| 12 | General (private) aviation | 11 |
| 13 | Large construction (dams, bridges, etc.) | 12 |
| 14 | Food preservatives | 18 |
| 15 | Bicycles | 19 |
| 16 | Commercial aviation | 17 |
| 17 | Police work | 8 |
| 18 | Fire fighting | 9 |
| 19 | Railroads | 23 |
| 20 | Nuclear power | 1 |
| 21 | Food coloring | 25 |
| 22 | Home appliances | 29 |
| 23 | Hunting | 13 |
| 24 | Prescription antibiotics | 26 |
| 25 | Vaccinations | 30 |
| 26 | Spray cans | 14 |
| 27 | High school & college football | 27 |
| 28 | Power mowers | 28 |
| 29 | Mountain climbing | 16 |
| 30 | Skiing | 22 |

Our new understanding also means that it should be possible to control our own worries more effectively. For example, if we overestimate the risk associated with some hazard (perhaps swimming or skiing), one reason might be that we find the hazard not simply dangerous but a source of dread. In such a case, the best way to reduce our worry would not be to gather statistics about how safe the activity really is; rather, the most effective approach would be: (1) determine the extent to which the risks associated with the hazard can be reduced and an accident prevented; (2) determine whether the consequences are in fact likely to be fatal and whether the likelihood of a fatality can be minimized should an accident occur; and (3) discover whether in fact an accident is likely to have catastrophic effects.

The studies of perceived risk are only one example of the way in which science has helped us to understand human nature and human behavior. You will see many

*We depend daily on the multitude of petroleum-based products. Still, the paradox of technology warns us that we must accurately anticipate the risks accompanying any industry, or suffer the consequences.*

more examples of this sort as you read further in this book. However, science does not provide all the answers we will need if we are to cope effectively with the pressures of modern living, and it is to this that we turn in the next section of the chapter.

## A Humanistic Approach

Psychology and allied sciences have no monopoly on understanding human behavior. There is little scientific information about such vital experiences as hope, faith, concern, love, alienation, and despair. In literature, art, religion, philosophy, and autobiographical accounts we often find poignant and authentic descriptions of experiences meaningful to all of us. In fact, over the centuries we have accumulated a vast store of "nonscientific" information about the nature, behavior, mistakes, and grandeur of human beings. To ignore all this information would be to run the risk of dehumanizing ourselves. So, throughout the text we shall not hesitate to draw upon the humanities—literature, art, history, religion—and related fields for insights into human behavior.

In addition, science often presents us with new and challenging problems that are difficult to solve without going outside of science itself. For example, the research by Slovic and his colleagues tells us how we might reduce a person's worries about a particular hazard, but *should* we attempt to influence people's worries and fears? Science alone offers little to help answer such questions, and so we will draw upon other disciplines—not just to provide you with a richer understanding of human nature, but also to guide us toward a set of values that can shape our behavior, our goals, and the direction of our lives.

### Belief in the Individual's Dignity and Growth Potential

The preamble of the Ethical Principles of Psychologists (1985), as formulated by the American Psychological Association, begins as follows:

> Psychologists respect the dignity and worth of the individual and strive for the preservation and protection of fundamental human rights. They are committed to increasing knowledge of human behavior and of people's understanding of themselves and others and to the utilization of such knowledge for the promotion of human welfare. (p. xxviii)

Implicit in this statement is a belief in each individual's growth potential, and in the individual's ability to play an active role in building the kind of life he or she chooses, while also contributing to a better future for humankind.

This does not mean that personal effectiveness and growth can be achieved by simply reading a book, nor does exposure to research findings about human behavior and well-being ensure that we can or will make use of such information in our own lives. Change, adjustment, and adaptation are difficult tasks that require far more than simply being better informed. Despite widely publicized research findings pointing to the harmful effects of smoking cigarettes, for example, they are still widely used in our society. Modern psychology can provide dependable information about ourselves and our world, but the mastery and effective use of this knowledge is up to the individual. In short, we are each responsible for our own growth.

### LOOKING FORWARD

In the remainder of this book, we shall attempt to show how the findings of contemporary psychology—together with other relevant sources of information—can help you to better understand yourself and others, to improve your personal and career competence, and to develop your resources for effective living. In Chapter 2 we will explore the fundamental characteristics shared by all human beings. Are we rational beings or are we basically irrational? Are we driven by unconscious forces outside of our awareness, or are we in control of our behavior? To what extent is our behavior shaped by the environment in which we find ourselves?

Then, in Chapters 3-5 we will explore the sources of stress in our lives, the way each of us responds uniquely to that stress, and some ways of coping more effectively with common stressful events. We will examine the effect of frustration, conflict, pressure, and change on our ability to cope and adapt effectively. We will look at factors that influence the severity of stress, and explore the reasons some people are less affected by stress than are other people. We will examine the ways in which stress can be beneficial, as well as the ways in which it can be harmful. In the process, you will learn to identify the way in which you uniquely respond to stressful events and the warning signs that tell you that you are approaching the limits of your ability to cope. Finally, we will discuss numerous techniques for coping more effectively with stress, for bringing the reactions to stress under control, and for using stress for personal growth. Here you will have the opportunity to learn how you can cope more effectively with common stressors in your own life.

In Chapters 6 and 7 we will look closely at what happens when things go wrong, when people's efforts to cope with stress are ineffective and behavior becomes maladaptive. Then we will turn our attention to the ways in which professional counselors and therapists provide help when normal coping abilities are exhausted.

In the remainder of the book, we will examine some of the most common sources of stress that people encounter in the course of their lives. In Chapter 8 we will discuss the most important changes that take place during childhood and adolescence. At each point in the life cycle, we will look closely at several of the most important developmental tasks that each person must accomplish, at the ways in which these tasks require adjustment and adaptation, and at the ways in which their accomplishment leaves the individual better equipped to cope with and adapt to future life challenges. We will discuss the characteristics of family life that contribute to healthy development as well as those that interfere with healthy development. You will also have an opportunity to discover how well you understand the stressfulness of various

*Often new experiences make us aware of unfamiliar aspects of our characters. As we learn, cope, and adapt, our sense of self-esteem often grows stronger.*

events in the lives of school-age children. In Chapter 9 we will continue our exploration of developmental tasks, challenges, and accomplishments through the adult years. We will examine such things as the development of intimacy in early adulthood, the choice of a job, the mid-life crisis, menopause, the impact of retirement, the importance of families throughout adult life, and finally the prospect of death and dying. In the process we will uncover some of the myths about old age that are widely held to be true.

In Chapters 10-14 we will take a much closer look at several of the most important areas of adult life. Each area can contribute greatly to the stress of living, but each also can provide great satisfaction and fulfillment. In Chapter 10 our focus will be on interpersonal relationships. We will look first at the ways in which interpersonal relationships develop from the first encounter through increasing degrees of intimacy. We will look at various kinds of maladaptive interpersonal relationships as well as at some ways to build more satisfying relationships with others. In Chapter 11 we will turn our attention to various aspects of intimate relationships such as love, the reasons why people marry, and how people choose mates. We will also study the most frequent sources of stress in marriage, the causes and effects of divorce, and the promise and the problems of remarriage. Finally, we will look at alternatives to marriage: cohabitation and singlehood. In Chapter 12 we will examine sexual attitudes and behaviors. We will learn more about masturbation, premarital sex, marital sex, extramarital sex, and homosexuality. We will also look at the human sexual response, at sexually transmitted diseases, and at sexual dysfunctions. In Chapter 13, we will turn our attention to the world of work. We will look at the reasons why people work, how they choose an occupation, and what happens when they change occupations. We will also explore job satisfaction and job stress, burnout, and the stress of unemployment. Finally, we will look at leisure and the ways in which it complements work during the adult years. In the final chapter, Chapter 14, we will examine the challenges of living in groups. We will consider the rewards and costs of group membership, the pros and cons of social influence and ways to resist influence, fear of public speaking and "stage fright," and the psychological effects of crowding.

We conclude the book with an Epilogue in which we will re-examine the importance of human values and the role they play in guiding us toward a better future for ourselves and for our world.

## SUMMARY

The advances of modern science and technology have led to unprecedented progress and problems. While we live in an affluent society with seemingly endless opportunities for personal growth, we are also beset by seemingly endless problems. We live in the best of times and the worst of times, in a time of progress and a time of anxiety, in a Golden Age and an Age of Stress. Therefore, we must learn to cope effectively with the problems of modern living and with their effects on us.

*Adjustment* is the process by which an organism attempts to meet the demands placed upon it by the environment and to structure and alter the environment to enhance survival, understanding, and growth. Adjustment is an interactive process in which the individual influences and is influenced by the environment. Not all

*Adapting well to life's stresses is a skill, not an inborn ability, and, like all skills, can be learned. Adaptive skills promote greater understanding of yourself and the world around you.*

adjustment is equally effective or adaptive. Adjustment is *adaptive* to the extent that it (1) meets the immediate and long-range *adjustive demands* of the situation, (2) satisfies our immediate and long-range needs, and (3) is consistent with the well-being of others.

Though examples of *maladaptive* adjustment are easy to find, adjustment need not be maladaptive. However, better adjustment will not come through more technological know-how. Rather, it comes from exercising *self-direction*: applying our uniquely human capacities of self-awareness, reasoning, imagining, and making value judgments in order to achieve greater self-understanding, as well as a better understanding of other people and of the environment in which we find ourselves. Each of us also must develop a set of *values* that will help us to decide which goals and behaviors are desirable and which are undesirable.

In the quest for understanding and values, this book relies heavily upon the findings of modern science—particularly psychology. *Psychology* is the science of behavior and mental processes. Like all sciences, its goals are to describe, explain, predict, and control what it studies. Throughout the textbook we will see that psychology does indeed contribute greatly to our understanding of ourselves, of other people, and of our interaction with the environment around us.

However, science is not the only source of insight into human behavior, and it provides little guidance in the development of personal values. Thus, this book also draws upon the humanities for the contributions they can make to our understanding of behavior and values. Finally, we approach the study of human adjustment with a firm belief in the dignity and growth potential of the individual. Though this book presents dependable information about adjustment and coping, the mastery and use of this information is up to you.

## KEY TERMS

adjustment (7)

adjustive demand (7)

adaptive (8)

maladaptive (8)

self-direction (11)

values (15)

psychology (16)

# The Quest for Understanding

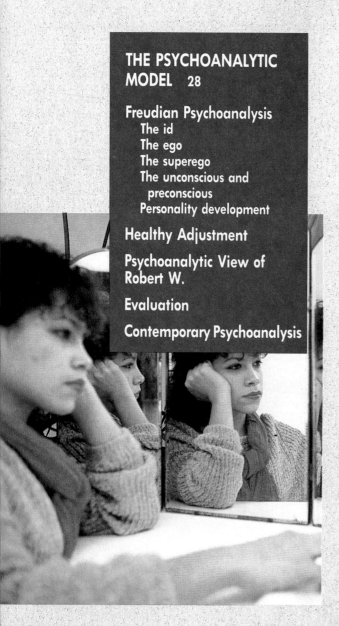

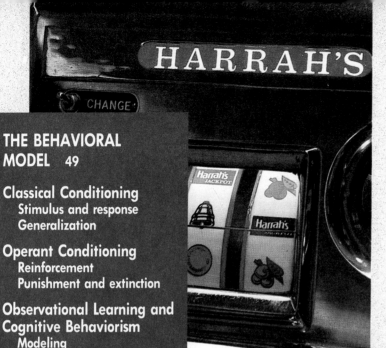

*Every person is in certain respects*
*  a. like all other people,*
*  b. like some other people,*
*  c. like no other person.*

*Personality in Nature, Society, and Culture*
(adapted from Kluckhohn & Murray, 1961, p. 53)

*T*HE last chapter emphasized the importance of understanding the ways in which each of us is unique, the ways in which individuals are more like some people than others, and the ways in which each of us is like everyone else in the world. In this chapter we will begin this quest for self-understanding by examining three quite different models of human nature, each offering something different about the ways in which people are alike and the ways in which they differ. We will begin with the psychoanalytic model (see Psychology in Action, p. 29).

## THE PSYCHOANALYTIC MODEL

**psychoanalytic model:** view that all human behavior is heavily influenced by unconscious factors such as needs, instincts, wishes, and conflicts

According to the **psychoanalytic model,** much of our behavior stems from motives, drives, needs, wishes, and conflicts that are hidden from view. This dark side to human nature exerts a profound influence on behavior and often overwhelms conscious intentions. As a result, according to this model, people often act in irrational and impulsive ways that even they cannot fully understand. Hammarskjold (1964/1974) expressed this sense of incomprehension in the following poem.

Sleepless questions
In the small hours;
Have I done right?
Why did I act
Just as I did?
Over and over again
The same steps,
The same words:
Never the answer.

This rather pessimistic view of human nature grows primarily from the observations and writings of Sigmund Freud. However, in the years since Freud's death in 1939, many other psychoanalytic writers have modified and extended his ideas in new and different directions. We will look first at Freud's version of the psychoanalytic model, then describe briefly some of its more contemporary versions, which significantly extended Freud's original theories.

# Psychology in Action

## The Case of Robert W.

This is an introduction to Robert W. Read this case with care, because during the course of this chapter you will see how several different models of human nature cast a somewhat different light on Robert's personality. Here are the facts.

*Robert W. is the oldest of three children. He has a brother two years younger than he and a sister five years younger. Robert's mother and father both graduated from high school. Robert's father holds a fairly responsible white-collar position with a large manufacturing firm; Robert's mother was a housewife until three years ago, when she took a clerking job in a lawyer's office to help pay for Robert's college expenses and the upcoming expenses of his brother and sister.*

*At age nineteen, Robert is a college sophomore. Although he has not yet declared a major, he is leaning toward business and accounting because it is "practical" and because he feels he can get a good job following graduation.*

*Robert feels relatively close to his mother, whom he describes as warm and affectionate. On the other hand, he describes his father as somewhat formal and cold,* although he is certain that his father loves him. Robert notes that his father is the disciplinarian in the family and sets high standards for the children. When the standards are not met, the children receive a stern lecture on the importance of achievement and personal responsibility.

*Robert's performance in high school and college has been generally above average. However, he often experiences severe stomach pains prior to exams. In grade school and high school, these pains would become so intense that his mother would take him to the doctor for a checkup. However, each checkup revealed that he suffered from no physical illness.*

*Robert has a small number of friends whose company he enjoys. He dates relatively frequently, but he has no steady girlfriend. His hobbies include jogging, listening to music, and reading. On the whole, Robert regards himself as "relatively normal and well-adjusted."*

As you will see, each model of human nature contributes something different to your understanding of Robert and, ultimately, to your understanding of yourself as a human being.

## Freudian Psychoanalysis

Freud's pioneering work extended over a period of fifty years, during which he studied hundreds of patients undergoing psychotherapy. Ultimately, Freud concluded that behavior results from the interaction of three key subsystems within the personality: the id, the ego, and the superego.

**id**: biologically-based portion of the personality composed of primitive needs and drives such as sex and aggression

**The id.**   The **id** contains primitive drives—such as hunger, thirst, aggression, and sex. Some of these drives are constructive, contributing to the survival of the individual and of the human species; hunger, thirst, and sex are all examples of constructive drives. Other basic drives are destructive, causing people to destroy, to tear down, to kill; aggression is a good example of a destructive drive. Together, according to Freud, these two kinds of drives provide all the energy for behavior. Like a river, energy from the id may flow one way or another, into one activity or another, but in the final Freudian analysis everything we do is driven by energy derived from the id.

**pleasure principle:** pursuit of immediate pleasure regardless of reality or morality

The id operates according to the **pleasure principle:** it strives for pleasure and comfort, and for the avoidance of pain or discomfort. In this pursuit of pleasure, the id is completely selfish and unconcerned with either reality or morality. In this sense the id is like a spoiled child who wants something and wants it immediately, no matter how unrealistic or selfish the demand may be, no matter what the consequences may be for other people.

**primary process:** gratification of an instinctual need by fantasy

By itself the id is not only selfish but also relatively powerless: if it can't get satisfaction through reflex action (such as sneezing or coughing), its only alternative is to generate images and wishes related to need gratification—something Freud called the **primary process.** If someone angers you, and you spend the following few minutes imagining all the clever things you could have said or done in response, then you are engaging in a form of primary process thinking. Primary process images and wishes often reveal your needs, and may even satisfy them for a brief time, but such images and wishes alone are not fully satisfactory, if you are thirsty or hungry, eventually you must find a source of real water and real food or you will die. This search for effective ways of meeting needs in the real world is the responsibility of the ego.

**ego:** reality-based portion of the personality that mediates between the demands of the id, the superego, and the real world

**reality principle:** pursuit of instinctual gratification through the real world

**The ego.**    According to Freud, the **ego** is not present at birth, but begins to develop soon afterward. Its primary job is to mediate between the demands of the id and the realities of the external world. The ego tries to meet id demands in a realistic and effective way that will help ensure the individual's survival. For this reason, Freud states that the ego operates according to the **reality principle.** The ego may have to block the energy of the id temporarily, or redirect it slightly, but eventually the ego must find some way to satisfy the id's needs in the real world. As it goes about its job of dealing with the realities of the external world and exercising

*Freud argued that people must contend with three subsystems of personality: the id, the ego, and the superego. Each person is driven by energy derived from the id, meets demands through the ego, and regulates behavior through the superego.*

# Psychology in Action

Just before midnight on February 4, 1982, thirty-year-old Steven Callahan was sailing alone across the Atlantic when his small sailboat sank. He spent seventy-six days in a life raft engaged in a desperate struggle for survival. The following excerpts from his book *Adrift* (1986) illustrate vividly the nature of primary process thinking.

*(Day 17) My body knows what it needs. For hours on end fantasies of sweet ice cream, starchy baked bread, and vitamin-rich fruits and vegetables water the mouth in my mind, though my real mouth long ago gave up its vain attempt to salivate. Not an evening passes without dreams of food . . . . (Day 27) I spend an increasing amount of time thinking about food. Fantasies about an inn-restaurant become very detailed. I know how the chairs will be arranged and what the menu will offer. Steaming sherried crab overflows flaky pie shells bedded on rice pilaf and toasted almonds. Fresh muffins puff out of pans. Melted butter drools down the sides of warm, broken bread. The aroma of baking pies and brownies wafts through the air. Chilly mounds of ice cream stand firm in my mind's eye. I try to make the visions melt away, but hunger keeps me awake for hours at night . . . . (Day 46) Food dreams become more real than ever. Sometimes I can smell the food; once I even tasted a dream. But it is always without substance . . . . (Day 63) I stand, wobbling, my brain stuffed with im-ages of food and drowned by dreams of drink. They are all I can think about . . . . (pp. 81, 108, 144, 187)*

However, throughout his ordeal, Callahan also used secondary process thinking in an heroic effort to assure his survival.

*(Day 15) I'm continually faced with hard decisions. Each time I fish, I risk damaging the spear gun and the raft. If that happens and I'm not rescued in short order, I may die. On the other hand, I may die if I don't fish enough. Every time I decide on taking action, I run through the possible results to try to rationally decide on the best thing to do . . . . (Day 23) I must work harder and longer each day to weave a world in which I can live . . . . The important thing is to keep calm. The small details of the repair will determine its success or failure. As always, I can only afford success. Don't hurry. Make it right . . . . (Day 37) Doing just enough to hang on will no longer do. I must keep myself in the best shape possible. I must eat more . . . . I must get the other still to work and keep it working . . . . For hours I try to think of a way to seal the leaking still . . . . I must find an effective solution . . . . (Day 40) Each day now I set my priorities, based on my continuing analysis of raft conditions, body condition, food and water . . . . (pp. 74, 76, 96–97, 113, 115–116)*

control over id demands, the ego uses various higher mental processes such as thinking, planning, reasoning, decision making, reality testing—what Freud called the **secondary process** (see Psychology in Action, p. 31).

If your behavior were controlled only by the id and the ego, you could survive and prosper for a while, but you would be totally selfish: your only concern would be meeting your own needs, regardless of the needs of other people. You would steal food and water to satisfy your hunger and thirst, rape to satisfy your sexual and aggressive needs, and attack anything or anyone that got in your way. Obviously, civilized society could not survive if everyone acted this way. Thus, according to Freud, a third subsystem of personality becomes necessary—the superego.

**secondary process:** rational processes used by the ego such as planning, reasoning, decision making

**superego:** culturally-based portion of the personality responsible for conscience, ethics, and moral standards

**The superego.**    The **superego** develops as the individual learns the rules, regulations, and moral values of society. For the most part, the superego corresponds to "conscience": it is concerned with good and bad, right and wrong. The superego tries to compel the ego to avoid immoral or illegal behavior, even though the behavior might satisfy basic needs; civilized human beings don't steal food to satisfy their hunger, don't rape people to satisfy their sexual and aggressive needs, and don't kill people who get in their way. Instead, they limit themselves to behaviors that are civilized, moral, and legal—behaviors that meet their needs without threatening the well-being of others.

**The unconscious and preconscious.**    At this point, you may doubt that Freud's model relates at all to your own behavior. It's hard to imagine the great "seething cauldron" of urges and desires that Freud contended lies within the id; even more difficult is believing that these urges and desires form the basis of everything we think and do. Freud would respond by pointing out that all the primitive impulses of the id, and many of the operations of the ego and superego as well, are part of the vast **unconscious** part of the mind. Because the id's needs are so primitive, they are kept forever beyond awareness, even though indirectly they affect every thought and action. Freud believed that the conscious (those things of which we are aware) and the **preconscious** (things not presently in awareness, but which can be brought to awareness if desired) represent only small portions of the human mind. In contrast, the unconscious—like the submerged part of an iceberg—is massive and of tremendous importance in determining who and what we are, what we think about, how we feel, and how we act, even though we are not normally aware that it even exists (see Figure 2.1).

**unconscious:** portion of the mind that cannot be brought to awareness under normal circumstances

**preconscious:** portion of the mind that can be brought into consciousness after a moment's reflection

**FIGURE 2.1**

The subsystems of the personality, according to psychoanalytic theory, can be depicted as an iceberg, of which only the tip rises above the water. Similarly, only a small part of the mind—the very tip of the iceberg—is conscious. The largest part of the mind, including all of the id (the largest subsystem of the personality) remains unconscious.

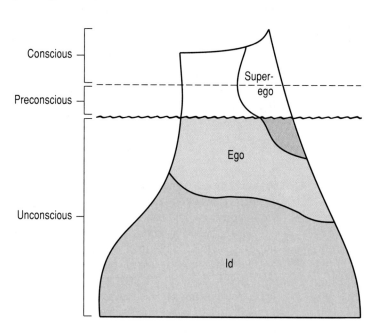

Although writers and dramatists have long portrayed the influence of unconscious motives on behavior, Freud was the first to study this phenomenon systematically. In book after book, he described in great detail behaviors that he interpreted to reflect unconscious motives: dreams in which "forbidden" desires appear; slips of the tongue; the way people "forget" things they do not want to remember; and a range of abnormal behaviors, such as unrealistic fears and uncontrollable compulsions (see Psychology in Action, p. 34).

Freud's notion of the unconscious has been so widely accepted that most of us routinely accept that to some extent we are only partially aware of the motives behind our behavior. Rebecca McCann (1932/1960) makes this point in a poem titled "Inconsistency."

> I'm sure I have a noble mind
> And honesty and tact
> And no one's more surprised than I
> To see the way I act!

At times, other people may understand our motives more accurately than we ourselves can. Thus, it may be apparent to others—but not to us—that we continually lean on others, or that we prevent people from getting too close to us, or that we constantly try to build ourselves up by belittling other people. Similarly, we may show off, wear expensive clothes, even marry for reasons unclear to us but which are more understandable to others. Although we may offer good reasons to justify our behavior, at times most of us will concede that these explanations are only "part of the story." Nevertheless, as we will see throughout this book, there is considerable controversy among psychologists concerning the precise role of unconscious processes in human behavior (see Insight, p. 36).

**Personality development.**    Freud also wrote a great deal about how each of us develops during the course of a lifetime. Not surprisingly, Freud's ideas about human development are closely tied to the development of the id, the ego, and the superego. He also emphasized the early years of life: in Freud's view, personality development is essentially complete by about age seven. Virtually everything significant to an adult's behavior is a reflection of early life experiences. Let's look more closely at Freud's theory of human development.

*The oral stage.* Freud argued that different areas of the body become sources of pleasure and gratification at various points in life. The area around the mouth, for example, is especially important during the first year of life. Much of the child's gratification at this age comes from eating, sucking, swallowing, and putting things into the mouth. Because of the mouth's special importance during a child's first year, Freud termed this period the **oral stage** of development.

**oral stage:** first stage in development, during which pleasure is centered on the mouth

During the oral stage, the child learns to differentiate "me" from "not-me," self from others. In the process the child begins to discover the difference between wishes and reality. For example, the hungry child soon learns that simply imagining or wishing for food is not the same as eating real food. In short, during the oral stage, the child begins to develop an ego.

# Psychology in Action

## Freudian Interpretation of a Dream

Freud (1920/1966) stated that dreams provide a rare opportunity to gain insight into a person's personality because id impulses are expressed more openly, with less distortion, during sleep when the ego's guard is relaxed. The following excerpt demonstrates the way Freud used surface dream content (what he called "manifest content") and the reactions of his patient to the dream to shed light on the unconscious wishes of the dreamer (the dream's "latent content").

*The Dream*
*A lady who, though she was still young, had been married for many years had the following dream:*

> *She was at the theatre with her husband. One side of the stalls was completely empty. Her husband told her that Elise L. and her fiance had wanted to go too, but had only been able to get bad seats—three for 1 florin 50 kreuzers—and of course they could not take those. She thought it would not really have done any harm if they had. (p. 122)*

### Freud's Interpretation

Upon questioning, Freud discovered that the dreamer's husband had recently told her that Elise L. had become engaged. Also, the previous week the dreamer had paid an extra fee to buy theatre tickets early in order to be sure of a seat at a performance; but when she arrived with her husband, she found that one side of the stalls was almost empty. Her husband had teased her about being in such a hurry. Also, the previous day her sister had been given 150 florins by her husband and had rushed out to buy some jewelry. Working from these clues, Freud (1920/1966) offered the following interpretation of her dream.

*We cannot help being struck by the fact that periods of time occur at several points in the information she gave us about the dream, and these provide a common factor between the different parts of the material.*

*She took the theatre tickets too early, bought them over-hurriedly so that she had to pay more than was necessary; so too her sister-in-law had been in a hurry to take her money to the jewellers and buy some jewellery with it, as though otherwise she would miss it. If, in addition to the "too early" and "in a hurry" which we have stressed, we take into account the precipitating cause of the dream—the news that her friend, though only three months her junior, had nevertheless got an excellent husband—and the criticism of her sister-in-law expressed in the idea that it was absurd of her to be in such a hurry, then we find ourselves presented almost spontaneously with the following construction of the latent dream-thoughts, for which the manifest dream is a severly distorted substitute:*

*"Really it was absurd of me to be in such a hurry to get married! I can see from Elise's example that I could have got a husband later too." (Being in too great a hurry was represented by her own behaviour in buying the tickets and by her sister-in-law's in buying the jewellery. Going to the play appeared as a substitute for getting married.) This would seem to be the main thought. We may perhaps proceed further, though with less certainty, since the analysis ought not to have been without the dreamer's comments at these points: "And I could have got one a hundred times better with the money!" (150 florins is a hundred times more than 1 florin 50.) If we were to put her dowry in place of the money, it would mean that her husband was bought with her dowry: the jewellery, and the bad tickets as well, would be substitutes for her husband . . . . We have . . . discovered that the dream expresses the low value assigned by her to her own husband and her regret at having married so early . . . . (The dreamer) agreed to the interpretation indeed, but she was astonished at it. She was not aware that she assigned such a low value to her husband; nor did she know why she should set such a low value on him. (pp. 123–25)*

*According to psychoanalytic theory, deprivation or over-indulgence of gratification at any one stage of development can result in fixation. Some would argue that chewing gum is a form of oral fixation.*

**anal stage:** second state in development, during which pleasure is centered on the anus

**The anal stage.** The process of ego development continues during the second year of life, the **anal stage** of development. During this time, the child gets pleasure from stimulation around the anus and from withholding and releasing feces. The child's pleasure, however, is not shared with his or her parents, who hope that the child will quickly learn to use toilets in an appropriate manner.

**phallic stage:** third stage in development, during which pleasure is derived especially from the genitals

**The phallic stage.** Beginning in the third year, the child enters the **phallic stage** of development. Freud believed that during this stage the center of physical pleasure moves from the anal region to the genitals. During this stage of development, many children first discover the pleasures of masturbation. Also during the phallic stage, children develop an intense attraction for the opposite-sex parent and wish that they could replace the same-sex parent. For example, boys develop an attraction to their mothers and hope to replace their fathers in the mother's affection and attention. Freud, noting the similarity between this process and the Greek legend of Oedipus — who unknowingly killed his father and married his mother, named the psychological process that occurs during the phallic stage the **Oedipus complex.**

**Oedipus complex:** child's desire for the opposite-sex parent and wish to replace the same-sex parent

# Insight

## Are People Often Unaware of Their Real Motives?

The following classic demonstration by Erickson (1939) has often been used to suggest the possibility that people's behavior may be dominated by motives of which they are partially or totally unaware.

*During profound hypnosis the subject was instructed to feel that smoking was a bad habit, that he both loved and hated it, that he wanted to get over the habit but he felt it was too strong a habit to break, that he would be very reluctant to smoke and would give anything not to smoke, but that he would find himself compelled to smoke; and that after he was awakened he would experience all of these feelings.*

*After he was awakened the subject was drawn into a casual conversation with the hypnotist who, lighting one himself, offered him a cigarette. The subject waved it aside with the explanation that he had his own and that he preferred Camels, and promptly began to reach for his own pack. Instead of looking in his customary pocket, however, he seemed to forget where he carried his cigarettes and searched fruitlessly through all of his other pockets with a gradually increasing concern. Finally, after having sought them repeatedly in all other pockets, he located his cigarettes in their usual place. He took them out, engaged in a*

*brief conversation as he dallied with the pack, and then began to search for matches, which he failed to find. During his search for matches he replaced the cigarettes in his pocket and began using both hands, finally locating the matches too in their usual pocket. Having done this, he now began using both hands to search for his cigarettes. He finally located them but then found that he had once more misplaced his matches. This time however he kept his cigarettes in hand while attempting to locate the matches. He then placed a cigarette in his mouth and struck a match. As he struck it, however, he began a conversation which so engrossed him that he forgot the match and allowed it to burn his finger tips whereupon, with a grimace of pain, he tossed it in the ash tray. . . .*

*This behavior continued with numerous variations. He tried lighting a cigarette with a split match, burned his fingers, got both ends of one cigarette wet, demonstrated how he could roll a cigarette, kept stopping to converse or tell a joke, and so on. Several cigarettes were ruined and discarded. When he finally got one going successfully, he took only a few good puffs with long pauses in between and discarded it before it was used up. (pp. 342–45)*

---

Freud asserted that the Oedipus complex applied equally to males and females (Freud, 1931/1961; Rychlak, 1981). However, some later psychoanalytic theorists proposed that the myth of Oedipus applies only to males, and a related myth, that of Electra, applies to females. In the Greek legend, Electra goaded her brother, Orestes, into killing her mother. Although Freud resisted the notion of a separate **Electra complex,** the term has become a part of later psychoanalytic tradition.

According to Freud, the phallic stage is particularly important for personality development. The child's growing attachment to the opposite-sex parent leads to fear of punishment from the same-sex parent; and this in turn produces anxiety. To reduce the anxiety, most children identify with their same-sex parent, they take on the characteristics of their parent, adopt their beliefs and values, perhaps even mimic their ways of dressing, walking, and talking. A boy attached to his mother but fearing his father resolves this conflict by identifying with his father. Similarly, a girl attracted

**Electra complex:** version of the Oedipus complex that occurs in females to her father reduces her anxiety by identifying with her mother. Such identification provides an ideal opportunity for the development of sexual identity. It also contributes to the formation of the superego, since one way for the child to avoid punishment is to adopt the moral standards and values of the same-sex parent.

***The latency and genital stages.*** Following the resolution of the Oedipus (or Electra) complex, the child enters a period of latency during which sexual needs appear to fade into the background; during this period, the child concentrates primarily on learning social and educational skills. The **latency stage** lasts until puberty, when physical maturity and the ability to reproduce usher in the final, **genital stage** of development. During this final phase of development, genuine caring and love for others first appears, as we will see in Chapter 8.

**latency stage:** fourth stage in development, during which sexual instincts are largely missing

**genital stage:** fifth and last stage in development, during which adult sexuality and genuine love for others appear

Assuming no major problems arise in any of the stages, most children progress more or less smoothly through the stages, ultimately becoming healthy, well-adjusted adults. However, a number of factors can inhibit progress through the psychosexual stages. For example, a child in the oral stage who is not encouraged or allowed to experience and enjoy the pleasures of feeding may not receive enough gratification of oral needs, and so may not learn that at times it is both safe and appropriate to depend upon others to provide for the gratification of some needs. In contrast, a child may be overprotected and overfed, and so may learn to become overly dependent on others.

**fixation:** concentration of mental energy in an infantile stage of development

Both deprivation and overindulgence can result in what Freud called **fixation.** The fixated child invests a great deal of mental energy in the psychological processes and behaviors characteristic of a particular stage of development and, as a result, has less energy to progress successfully through later stages. For example, according to Freud's theory, a person fixated at the oral stage of development might become an obese adult, overly dependent on others, and passive. Someone else might show oral fixation by being unusually gullible—willing to "swallow" or "take in" whatever other people say. Another person might be biting, sarcastic, and argumentative—all forms of oral aggression. If fixation occurs in the anal phase, according to Freud the adult consequences might be the stinginess and miserliness exemplified by the Charles Dickens character, Scrooge. Alternatively, the person might be disorderly, messy, destructive, and given to explosive outbursts. Fixation at the phallic stage, according to Freud, can lead to excessive vanity, promiscuity, and flirtatiousness on the one hand, or to feelings of worthlessness, shyness, and inadequacy on the other.

## Healthy Adjustment

For Freud, a well-adjusted individual is one who maximizes gratification while also minimizing punishment, fear, anxiety, and guilt. In other words, if you are a healthy person, you are able to satisfy the needs of the id in the real world without offending the superego (which would lead to feelings of guilt) and without offending other people (which would lead to punishment). Since it is the ego's job to mediate between the demands of the id on the one hand, the real world and the superego on the other, you can see that for Freud the hallmark of effective adjustment is a strong, effective ego. A strong ego should allow a person to control impulses, to deal with the world intelligently and effectively, and to behave in moral and legal ways. In contrast, a weak ego will either be unable to control id impulses, ineffective in dealing with the real world, or unable to deal with the harsh demands of the superego.

### Psychoanalytic View of Robert W.

On page 29 you were introduced to Robert W. Based on that description, Freud would have concluded that in general Robert appears to be relatively well adjusted. He has done above average work in high school and college, has chosen a career and is working to prepare himself for it, has good relationships with his parents, apparently enjoys being with friends, and has a number of hobbies that add variety to his life.

That Robert is much closer to his mother than to his father, and that he experiences his father as "somewhat formal and cold," suggest he may not have fully resolved the Oedipal rivalry between himself and his father. However, he apparently has made some progress in resolving the Oedipus complex: for example, his high motivation and achievement orientation seem to come from identification with his father, as do his interests in accounting and business (though he seems unaware of this influence on his choice of careers). He also seems to have adopted his father's very high standards.

Unfortunately, Robert's superego (the aspect of his personality that sets these high standards) is at least as demanding as his father's—apparently intolerant of less than outstanding performance. Thus, in a situation where Robert's performance might be less than perfect (for example, on examinations), he becomes anxious, fearful, and experiences stomach pains. We also might speculate that Robert feels some hostility toward his cold but demanding father; if so, his stomach pains may reflect the tremendous effort his ego is making to keep his anger under control when he is being evaluated and judged by someone in authority.

In summary, according to the psychoanalytic model, much of Robert's behavior can be attributed to experiences early in his life (Oedipal conflict, identification with his father) as well as to unconscious determinants (an overly strict superego, anger toward his father). Since Robert is unaware of both his early life experiences and the unconscious determinants of his behavior, he cannot understand fully the reasons why he behaves as he does.

### Evaluation

Freud's psychoanalytic model has impacted tremendously on twentieth-century thinking about human nature. His was the first complete theory of human personality ever developed. It gave credence to the notion that human beings, to some extent at least, are dominated by primitive biological drives and by unconscious passions, wishes, desires, and motives. It made people more aware of the tremendous importance of the early years of life and of the special needs of children during infancy. Freud's model provided an explanation not only for the most creative and constructive accomplishments of the human race, but also for the darker side of human history that is otherwise so difficult to comprehend. As we will see in Chapter 7, his theory also led to a form of therapy that has helped countless people to lead more productive and enjoyable lives. A testimony to the power of Freud's intellect is that fifty years after his death, his theory continues to spark creative thinking about the complex nature of human beings.

However, Freudian theory has been subjected to many criticisms, as well. No doubt Freud painted a bleak picture of human nature, and—to some people—it is too bleak. Portions of Freud's theory were also blatantly sexist (Gilligan, 1982). Moreover, although Freud supported his theory by describing the lives of his patients, there is no way of knowing how accurately he reported those facts, how much he might have distorted them (intentionally or unintentionally) to better fit his theory, and how selectively he picked the cases he reported (Sherwood, 1969). In addition, from a scientific point of view, it is extremely difficult to determine exactly what Freud meant by some of his terms (such as "fixation" or "Oedipus complex" or "unconscious"); it is equally difficult to predict what will happen under given circumstances—for example, we have seen that anal fixation might lead to an extremely neat and tidy person, or to the exact opposite (Masling, 1983, 1985). Finally, Freud's unyielding emphasis on the importance of id impulses in understanding all behavior seems to leave a great deal of human behavior unexplained, as we will see in the next section of the chapter.

## Contemporary Psychoanalysis

In the years since Freud's death, his followers have significantly modified his theory. His daughter, Anna Freud (1946), suggested that perhaps too much attention had been given to the unconscious wishes and desires of the id, and not enough to the ego and its links to the outside world. Her interest in the ego led her to emphasize the ways the ego satisfies id impulses. She also emphasized interpersonal relationships, mastery of life's problems, and environmental influences on behavior.

Heinz Hartmann (1958) went one step further, suggesting that the ego serves many important functions that have little or nothing to do with the id. Thinking, remembering, perceiving, learning, and communicating are all important aspects of everyday life; through these processes people interact with and master the world around them—quite apart from obtaining gratification for the id. According to Hartmann, the unconscious id and the conscious ego are equally important aspects of human nature, and neither exists simply to serve the other.

Erik Erikson (1963, 1968) extended the Freudian model by describing in some detail the ways in which the ego develops during the course of an individual's life. Where Freud emphasized the ego's role in satisfying id impulses, Erikson believed that relationships with other people are an important aspect of ego functioning. We will look more closely at Erikson's version of the psychoanalytic model in Chapters 8 and 9.

Most recently, Heinz Kohut (1971, 1977) has proposed even more drastic revisions in the psychoanalytic model. According to Kohut, unconscious impulses are of little or no importance in understanding human behavior; similarly, the Oedipus complex has been greatly overemphasized. In Kohut's view, far greater attention should be paid to an individual's ambitions, ideals, goals, skills, talents, empathy, and healthy adaptation to life.

Relative to classical Freudian psychoanalysis, these contemporary versions of the psychoanalytic model show a greater respect for the adaptive functions of the ego, a greater appreciation of the rational and constructive aspects of human nature, and a greater emphasis on interpersonal relationships. The next section will explore a different model of human nature, one that emphasizes even more strongly the positive, rational, and constructive side of human nature.

## THE HUMANISTIC MODEL

*For this is the journey that men make: to find themselves. If they fail in this, it doesn't matter much what else they find.*

*The Fires of Spring* (Michener, 1949, p. 488)

**humanistic model:** view of human nature that emphasizes self-direction and strivings toward growth and fulfillment

In many respects, the **humanistic model** of human nature differs from the psychoanalytic model as much as possible. Humanistic psychologists emphasize the importance of uniquely human powers such as reflection, reasoning, judgment, self-awareness, rationality, and creative imagination. Although many humanists acknowledge that unconscious and irrational motives exist, they prefer to stress the importance of conscious planning and rational choice in human behavior. Consider this statement from Abraham Maslow (1968), an influential humanistic psychologist.

> Perhaps we shall soon be able to use as our guide and model the fully growing and self-fulfilling human being, the one in whom all his potentialities are coming to full development, the one whose inner nature expresses itself freely, rather than being warped, suppressed, or denied. . . . It is as if Freud supplied to us only the sick half of psychology and we must now fill it out with the healthy half. Perhaps this health psychology will give us more possibilities for controlling and improving our lives and for making ourselves better people. Perhaps this will be more fruitful than asking "how to get *unsick*." (p. 5)

Humanistic psychologists also emphasize that each person, by virtue of particular learning and personal experience, is unique. This uniqueness compels everyone to discover who they are, what sort of person they want to become, and why. Only in this way can they fully develop their potential as self-directing human beings. As you will see, the humanistic outlook has influenced significantly contemporary thought about human nature and behavior.

### Rogers' Person-centered Humanism

Carl Rogers (1951, 1961, 1977, 1980) played a major role in developing the humanistic model. Rogers believed that people are rational, that they are aware of what they are doing and why, and that they are not helpless victims of past experiences.

*The actualizing tendency in each of us directs us toward fulfillment, improvement, and growth.*

**actualizing tendency:** striving toward growth and fulfillment of inborn potential

**Actualizing tendency.** Rogers argued that human behavior can be explained in terms of one basic motive: the **actualizing tendency.** Human beings strive to grow, improve, express themselves, fulfill themselves as human beings, enhance their lives, become more competent, develop all their capacities. They move forward toward actualization despite difficulties and setbacks. They persist in becoming whatever is in their nature to become, even if the environment is hostile (see Psychology in Action, p. 42).

Rogers also maintained that human beings, left to their own devices, are quite capable of directing their behavior toward greater actualization. Behaviors that contribute to actualization will be experienced as genuinely satisfying, and consequently people will seek and maintain such behaviors. In contrast, behaviors that do not contribute to actualization will not be experienced as satisfying, and people will tend to avoid them. In other words, it is possible to trust your own experiences to guide you toward activities and behaviors that will contribute to your fulfillment. Consider these comments from Jim M., an accomplished tennis player:

> I started playing when I was seven, and I knew right away that this was *it,* this was for me. Every chance I got I played tennis. I loved it—nothing made me happier than being on the court playing tennis, hour after hour. I would ride by bike to the courts early Saturday morning and hang around until I found someone who needed a partner; I'd play as long as they wanted, then look around for someone else. When it got too dark to see the ball, I'd finally bike home. I tried playing baseball and basketball and golf, but they weren't as exciting or satisfying as tennis. They just weren't *me.*

# Psychology in Action

## Portrait of an Artist: Victor S.

The struggle to actualize inborn potential despite discouragement is portrayed vividly in this brief excerpt written by a young man, Victor S., during his junior year in college.

*I believe myself to be competent in the field of art, especially graphic design. I can visualize images in my mind and easily transpose them to paper, clay, or whatever the medium be. Looking back on the development of this talent, much of the credit for encouragement can be attributed to my parents. However, with this encouragement there was much discouragement as well.*

*Since I did have a talent for art, I was always encouraged by my parents. It started with blocks, finger paints, coloring books and crayons, and erector sets. My parents seemed quite proud that I was such a creative child as well as quiet and easy to manage. Give me a coloring book and crayons and I was occupied for days. These forms of artistic creativity were basically activities for both boys and girls, thus my parents approved wholeheartedly.*

*As I grew older, it became evident that I was more interested (as well as more talented) in graphic designing. I was permitted (and much encouraged) to pursue this as long as it was done in a masculine manner. I was allowed to draw and paint, but was not permitted to weave or do needlepoint. This was very frustrating. It is usually necessary to do designs in more than one medium to see if the design is actually good or not. Since weaving and needlepoint lend themselves well to this, it seemed a logical assumption to me to use them. My parents, however, felt differently.*

*Since the materials for this expression were restricted, I became frustrated. I began to wonder whether or not I was any good at graphic designing. I began to doubt my abilities and my parents acted on this doubt. They thought that to discourage these "inappropriate" outlets but keep me happy, I should find new outlets; they felt that to get rid of the problem I should direct my talents to more practical uses. In high school I shifted from art courses to mechanical drawing courses and, finally, in college to architectural drawing courses. I am good in architectural drawing, but I do not have the passion for it that I had for graphic designing. I have finally decided that I do not want to be an architect, but I no longer feel adequate going back to graphic designing. I neglected it through most of high school and two years of college. If I go back to it, I will be behind everyone else. I gave up part of myself to become something I'm not, and I'm frustrated and confused. I stopped nurturing my talent, and now I am afraid to see if I still have any.*

It is important to realize that for Rogers, human nature is basically good, constructive, and cooperative. Human beings are not inherently destructive, selfish, or hostile. Thus, in marked contrast to Freud, Rogers believed that there is nothing to fear in allowing people to seek out and express their inborn nature. In Rogers' opinion (1961), destructive and hurtful behaviors do not reflect inner human nature, but rather result from society's attempt to control and distort the normal, healthy actualization process.

I am quite aware that out of defensiveness and inner fear individuals can and do behave in ways which are incredibly cruel, horribly destructive, immature, regressive, antisocial, and hurtful. Yet one of the most refreshing and invigorating parts of my experience is to work with such individuals and to discover the strongly positive directional tendencies which exist in them, as in all of us, at the deepest levels. (p. 27)

**Self-concept and self-actualization.**    According to Rogers, one important consequence of the actualizing tendency is that we learn to distinguish the *self*, or what each of us refers to as "me" or "myself," from everything else around us. In other words, early in life each of us learns that some events belong to the external environment (such as clouds, trees, and other people), while other events are part of our self (such as skills, abilities, values, needs, and goals). Moreover, we also form an image or idea of our self; Rogers called this the **self-concept.** Examples of self-concepts include: I am intelligent, I am overweight, I am confident, I am shy, I need other people, I am a high achiever, I am unattractive, I am unimaginative. (The first chapter of the Self-Discovery Journal that accompanies this text is intended to help you explore various aspects of your self-concept. If you haven't yet taken the time to work through that exercise, you might find it instructive to do so now.)

**self-concept:** image or beliefs about oneself

Just as most of us strive to maintain and enhance our inborn capacities, according to Rogers we also try to maintain and enhance our image of ourselves, our self-concept. This **self-actualizing tendency** leads us to behave in ways that are consistent with our self-concept and to resist evidence that our self-concept might be inaccurate. For example, it you think of yourself as "intelligent," you may interpret an "A" on a test as a sign of your intelligence; however, if you think of yourself as "unintelligent," you might conclude that it was an easy test, or that you were just lucky. In these ways we try to maintain our self-concepts even in the face of contradictory evidence.

**self-actualizing tendency:** striving to enhance and maintain one's self-concept

**Congruence and incongruence.**    What happens if a person's self-concept isn't accurate? What if someone who is actually intelligent and creative comes to consider himself or herself unintelligent and uncreative? Rogers believed that this is an unnatural state of affairs, though he also thought it occurs quite often. Rogers believed that under optimal circumstances, inborn nature and self-concept would be in **congruence** — in agreement, consistent. In that case, the actualizing tendency and the self-actualizing tendency would both lead toward the same behaviors and experiences, and so work together to shape an individual's life in a healthy way. Under these circumstances, a person could fully trust that all experiences will lead toward greater fulfillment.

**congruence:** according to Rogers, condition in which one's self-concept is consistent with one's inborn nature

However, quite often other people have different ideas about the kind of person each of us should become, about our capacities and our potentials. You saw this vividly in Victor's account of his struggle to express his artistic abilities despite his parents' interference (see Psychology in Action, p. 42). Victor was aware of this conflict between his own nature and how other people perceived him, what other people wanted him to become.

> My whole life I have been seen by my family and friends as having certain tendencies and predispositions. Their labels practically forced me to behave in ways that they expected of me. I was guided and pushed, sometimes forcibly, into categories that others assumed were where I belonged.

**incongruence:** according to Rogers, condition in which one's self-concept is inconsistent with one's inborn nature

In Rogers' terms, Victor was experiencing **incongruence** — a discrepancy between his inborn capacities and his self-concept.

Why would someone surrender to such pressures, give up being who he or she truly is, and become instead what other people suggest? Listen to Victor.

> Some people are able to stand up to the world and retain more of themselves than others. When so many people seemed to see me similarly, instead of holding fast to my own perceptions and trusting my own experiences, I adopted other people's perceptions and conformed to their will. Insecurity and fear of rejection made me accept their idea of who I am. I gave up part of myself because I cared about what other people thought of me. I wanted to be liked, I wanted to be loved, I wanted to be respected and accepted.

**conditional positive regard:** situation in which the love and affection of others is conditional on our behaving as they wish us to behave

In other words, Victor learned that the love, affection, and caring of other people (what Rogers called **positive regard**) was **conditional** on his behaving as others wanted him to behave. He believed that if he acted the way *he* wanted to act, in a way that felt right to him and that reflected his real nature, he would lose the love and acceptance of his parents and friends. As a result, he began living his life as others wanted him to live it. In living out someone else's dream, he was no longer being true to himself. He had come to believe that he was worthy in the eyes of others only under certain conditions, that he would be prized and valued only if he became what others wanted him to become even if that was not his true nature. He came to think of himself in ways that did not correspond to what he really was, and so he could no longer trust his experiences to guide his life.

## Maslow's Humanistic Psychology

Another humanistic psychologist, Abraham Maslow (1968, 1969, 1970, 1971), has greatly expanded the understanding of actualization tendencies by studying the lives of such extraordinary persons as Abraham Lincoln, Eleanor Roosevelt, Thomas Jefferson, and Ludwig van Beethoven. The cornerstone of Maslow's model is his belief that human beings have a number of inborn needs or motives, and that these can be arranged in a **hierarchy of needs** from the most basic biological needs to the need for self-fulfillment or self-actualization, which represents the highest development of the human personality. Maslow's hierarchy has five levels of needs:

**hierarchy of needs:** Maslow's suggestion that needs can be arranged in order from the most basic deficiency needs to higher level growth needs such as self-actualization

1. *Physiological needs*—basic bodily needs such as the needs for food, water, sleep, and sex.
2. *Safety needs*—needs for structure, order, security, stability, protection, predictability, and freedom from fear, anxiety, and threat.
3. *Love and belongingness needs*—needs for acceptance, warmth, affection, belonging, loving, and being loved.
4. *Esteem needs*—including needs for adequacy, worth, recognition, prestige, acceptance, status, and self-respect.
5. *Self-actualization*—needs for personal growth, becoming what one has the potential to become, and actualizing one's potentials.

**deficiency motivation:** domination of behavior by physiological and safety needs

According to Maslow, the four lower levels of the hierarchy concern **deficiency motivation:** if these lower needs are not filled, the person will become motivated to fill them. People who have not eaten in a long time are likely to become driven

**FIGURE 2.2**

According to the findings of Maslow (1969, 1971) so-called lower level needs—such as needs for food and security—tend to dominate our behavior. When lower level needs are met, however, our behavior tends to be dominated by "higher" level needs, such as various forms of actualization strivings.

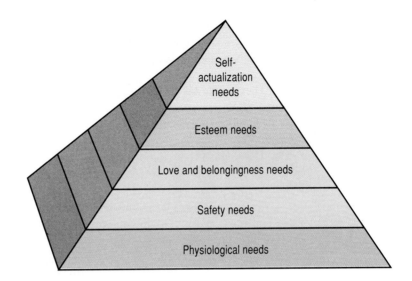

**growth motivation:** domination of behavior by needs for love and belongingness, esteem, and self-actualization

**unconditional positive regard:** situation in which the love and affection of others is unconditional and independent of a person's behavior

to find food; all their thinking and behavior is likely to be devoted to finding food. Steven Callahan's experiences when adrift in the Atlantic Ocean for months (described in the Psychology in Action, p. 31) illustrate dramatically the effect that unfilled physiological needs can have. Also, the presence of danger or feelings of anxiety or fear will trigger behavior directed at increasing safety. The absence of friends and family, or being rejected by others, causes people to strive to fulfill their needs to belong and to be loved. Feelings of incompetence or inadequacy, or criticism and lack of recognition by others, leads people to behave in ways that will satisfy their esteem needs. In contrast, the highest level of Maslow's hierarchy reflects **growth motivation:** striving to actualize oneself, to become what each person is uniquely capable of becoming, and to fulfill one's potential as a human being. Maslow's growth motivation corresponds quite closely to Rogers' self-actualizing tendency.

According to Maslow, needs lower in the hierarchy are more powerful and potent than needs higher up—they tend to command your attention and efforts until you satisfy them. Thus, unless your physiological and safety needs are reasonably well met, your behavior will be dominated by these needs. However, once deficiency needs are gratified, you are free to devote your energies to meeting needs on higher levels. This notion of an ordered hierarchy of motives has profound implications for understanding human adjustment.

## Healthy Adjustment

For Rogers, the key to healthy adjustment is avoiding incongruence. This, in turn, will most likely occur when parents and others express **unconditional positive regard.** Children and adults must understand that they will be valued and prized as human beings regardless of their behavior, that positive regard is never conditional on behaving as others wish. Under such circumstances, Rogers believed that people's

**fully-functioning person:**
according to Rogers, a person who is well adjusted, mature, and fully open to experience

self-concepts would be congruent with their inborn potentials, that their images of themselves would correspond to their real nature. Moreover, he contended that such persons would be **fully functioning persons** with the following characteristics:

1. They would be open to experience, they would be aware of all their experiences without the need to be defensive. Their self-concepts would be congruent with their inborn capacities, and would change if necessary in response to new experiences.

2. They would trust themselves and their feelings and would guide their lives by the nature of their own experiences rather than by the judgments of others. They would do what "feels right."

3. They would have unconditional positive regard for themselves—they would value and prize and accept themselves unconditionally—and they would express unconditional positive regard toward others.

4. They would respond to situations with unique and creative adaptations when appropriate, and would be likely to seek out new experiences and new challenges. They would also live fully in each moment since each moment is a new experience, different from what has gone before and what will come afterward.

5. They would have a sense of freedom, a sense of being in control of their own lives, of being responsible for their own actions, and being able to choose the course of their lives.

6. They would live with others in the greatest possible harmony because they would prize and value others unconditionally.

In Rogers' words (1959):

> It should be evident that the term the "the fully functioning person" is synonymous with optimal psychological adjustment, optimal psychological maturity, complete congruence, (and) complete openness to experience. (p. 235)

Well-adjusted individuals, according to Rogers, will perceive themselves and others as they really are. They will seldom experience great inconsistency between the way they see themselves and the way in which other people see them. If they encounter new experiences or adjustive demands, they are likely to deal with them realistically and appropriately without experiencing undue anxiety or threat and without the need to distort or deny their experiences or to "go on the defensive."

For Rogers, becoming a fully functioning person is an ideal toward which everyone should strive, even though it is unlikely that anyone will ever achieve the ideal. Moreover, Rogers (1961) also pointed out that:

> . . . for me, adjectives such as happy, contented, blissful, enjoyable, do not seem quite appropriate to any general description of this process I have called the good life, even though the person in this process would experience each one of those experiences at appropriate times. But the adjectives which seem more generally fitting are adjectives such as enriching, exciting, rewarding, challenging, meaningful. This process of the good life is not, I am convinced, for the faint-hearted. It involves the stretching and growing of becoming more and more of one's potentialities. . . . It means launching oneself fully into the stream of life. (pp. 195-96)

In other words, from Rogers' perspective healthy adjustment does not correspond to quiet contentment. Rather, it means living life fully, seeking and responding to new challenges, constantly striving toward the ideal of becoming fully functioning.

Maslow also has added to the understanding of healthy adjustment. For him, the well adjusted person is one whose deficiency motives are satisfied well enough that his or her behavior is motivated primarily by self-actualization needs. Most people never reach this state, and so self-actualization needs are relatively unimportant in their day-to-day lives. However, there are exceptions, and Maslow as well as other researchers (for example, Seeman, 1984) have identified and studied a number of such self-actualizing persons. As noted earlier, Maslow based his research on the biographies of extraordinary human beings such as the psychologist and philosopher William James, the theologian Martin Buber, the musician Pablo Casals, the chemist George Washington Carver, the abolitionist Harriet Tubman, and others including Albert Einstein, Albert Schweitzer, and Benjamin Franklin. Most other researchers have studied less well-known people using a 150-item questionnaire (the Personal Orientation Inventory, or POI) designed by Everett Shostrom (1963, 1964, 1974, 1976) that measures various characteristics that are thought to characterize people who are relatively high in self-actualization. The research has demonstrated that growth-motivated people are able to perceive reality more efficiently; can tolerate uncertainty better; are more spontaneous and creative; are more accepting of themselves and others; are more problem-centered and less ego-centered; have deeper than average relationships with other people; have a philosophical, unhostile sense of humor; and feel kinship with and concern for all humanity. In short, Maslow's self-actualizers turn out to be quite similar to Rogers' ideal "fully-functioning individuals." However, Maslow also noted (1963) that such people have their imperfections: some are vain, some are temperamental, others are ruthless, boring, stubborn, or irritating.

## Humanistic View of Robert W.

You might gain a clearer understanding of Rogers' and Maslow's ideas by considering how they would view Robert W. From the humanistic perspective, Robert's opinion of himself as "relatively well-adjusted" is an important piece of information, giving us reason to believe that he is in no apparent distress. His hobbies and social activities also suggest that his actualizing tendencies are present and play a role in shaping his life. However, Rogers would point out that Robert's goals in life seem to be related more to parental wishes and training and less to his own desires and capabilities than would ideally be the case if he were fully self-actualized. In particular, Rogers would note that Robert's desire to complete a business and accounting program may be more related to his father's emphasis on success and achievement than to Robert's own desires. Robert's mother seems to accept Robert for what he is (unconditional positive regard), but to some extent his father may accept and value him only if he performs well in school (conditional positive regard). To the extent that Robert has failed to choose a course of life for himself and make his own decisions, he is not living a life that fully expresses his inborn capacities.

Maslow might add that while Robert's physiological needs appear to be well satisfied, he seems to be preoccupied with meeting safety needs: he gets stomach pains when he is being evaluated, his choice of major is determined primarily because it is "practical," and he leads a quiet, relatively protected lifestyle that assures structure, order, stability, and predictability. Belongingness, love needs, and esteem needs are not much in evidence, being unimportant factors in his behavior. Also, Robert does not seem concerned with self-actualization.

Compared to psychoanalytically oriented theorists, both Maslow and Rogers would be more concerned with Robert's uniqueness, his effort to become what he is uniquely capable of becoming. Neither of them would concentrate on Robert's early life experiences or on possible unconscious determinants of his behavior. Their focus would be on the "here and now," what Robert has become, and what he is capable of becoming.

## Evaluation

The humanistic model of human nature has profoundly affected twentieth-century psychology. Humanistic psychologists have drawn attention to the importance of psychological health; they have opened the possibility that studying sickness may not provide much insight into wellness, human virtues, or the positive and healthy side of being human. Moreover, as we will see in Chapter 7, Rogers' "person-centered therapy" has been widely used in the fields of counseling and psychotherapy and has improved the lives of hundreds of thousands of people. The humanistic perspective has also contributed to the recent upsurge in sensitivity training and encounter groups. Shaping contemporary thinking about education, this perspective led to increased recognition of human beings as naturally inquisitive and eager to learn, especially if they can see the relevance of what they are learning, if they can learn from direct experience, and if they can learn in an environment free of threat. Finally, Rogers' theory has triggered a great deal of research on the nature of the self-concept and changes in the self-concept during the course of psychotherapy.

On the other hand, humanistic theorists have drawn their share of critics (Maddi, 1989). For example, although Rogers stresses the importance of "inborn potential," he is very vague about it beyond describing it as a kind of "genetic blueprint." Rogers and Maslow have both been criticized for underestimating the influence of unconscious forces and for trusting whatever people say about themselves. Still, other critics believe that the humanistic model is too positive about human nature; these critics point out that aggression and destructiveness are too much a part of human nature to be regarded simply as the result of inadequate upbringing; nor can they be excluded from a hierarchy of important human motives. Finally, in some cases people have become fully-functioning adults apparently without experiencing unconditional positive regard, and despite the fact that their physiological and safety needs often were not met; we will consider one such case in Chapter 8 (see Insight, p. 50).

In the next section we will look at a third and final model of human nature, which differs markedly from both the psychoanalytic and humanistic models.

## THE BEHAVIORAL MODEL

We have seen that the psychoanalytic and humanistic models of human nature differ markedly in many respects, but on one point these two models are in complete agreement: to understand human behavior one must look inside the person, since the important causes of behavior lie out of sight within each person. The **behavioral model** disagrees sharply with this basic assumption. One of the earliest behaviorists, John B. Watson (1919), asserted that if psychology wishes to be the *science* of behavior, then like any other science it must limit itself to the study of events that can be observed and measured directly. He argued against a science based on hidden processes such as id impulses, the ego, the self-concept, and so on. Moreover, Watson believed it is not necessary to refer to hidden processes to explain behavior. Starting from this basic position, Watson urged psychology to shift its focus from invisible psychological processes to visible behavior which can be directly observed and measured. In taking this position, Watson opened up a new and valuable approach to the study of human behavior, now known as **behaviorism.**

All behaviorists agree that most behavior, whether adaptive or maladaptive, is heavily influenced by learning. Moreover, all behaviorists agree that the social and environmental context in which learning takes place is an important determinant of behavior. For example, if people wear funny hats, become intoxicated, and sing "Auld Lang Syne" at New Year's Eve parties, the explanation for their behavior is

**behavioral model:** view that most human behavior, whether adaptive or maladaptive, is learned

**behaviorism:** belief that psychology, as a science, should focus on observable behavior rather than unobservable mental processes

*Adaptive and maladaptive behavior are influenced by learning and the environment in which we live.*

# Insight

not to be found in unconscious processes and id impulses, but rather in the rewards they have received in the past for such behavior. If these same people do not engage in similar behavior when they are attending religious services, this need not be explained by something as vague as a superego, but rather by the fact that people learn to behave differently in a place of worship than at a New Year's Eve party.

Understandably, the emphasis behaviorists place on learned behavior has led them to concentrate on discovering how learning comes about. They have described three different processes through which behavior can be learned: classical conditioning, operant conditioning, and observational learning.

## Classical Conditioning

**classical (respondent, Pavlovian) conditioning:** a learning process in which a response is transferred from one stimulus to another after multiple pairings of the stimuli

Watson was intrigued by the concept of **classical conditioning** discovered some years earlier by the Russian physiologist Pavlov. Although Pavlov worked with dogs, Watson believed that Pavlov's findings could be used to explain some kinds of human learning. In classical conditioning, sometimes called *Pavlovian* or *respondent conditioning,* an individual learns to transfer a response from one stimulus to another. For example, if a child reacts with terror at the sight of dogs but shows no fear of teddy bears, through classical conditioning it is possible to link the fearless response to dogs so that in the future the child will show no fear of dogs or teddy bears. In the next few pages we will see how this occurs.

**Stimulus and response.**    Let's start with a simple example: imagine you want to teach someone to blink when you sound a bell. Prior to conditioning, you know that a very mild puff of air to the eye will produce a blink, while the sound of the bell will not produce eye blinking. In this situation, the puff of air is called the **unconditioned stimulus:** it elicits the desired response (called the **unconditioned response),** in this case the eye blink. The sound of the bell is the **conditioned stimulus**—a neutral stimulus at the start of conditioning, since it does not cause the desired response. During conditioning, the bell is sounded just before the puff of air is delivered to the eye. This pairing of the conditioned stimulus (sound of the bell) and the unconditioned stimulus (puff of air) is repeated. Eventually, when the bell is sounded by itself without the puff of air, the eye blink occurs. In other words, the person has learned to give the eye blink response (now called the **conditioned response**) to a new (conditioned) stimulus: the sound of the bell.

**unconditioned stimulus:** stimulus that always elicits the desired response before new learning begins

**unconditioned response:** the desired response that is elicited whenever the unconditioned stimulus occurs

**conditioned stimulus:** stimulus that does not initially elicit the desired response until new learning has occurred

**conditioned response:** a new response that comes to be elicited by the conditioned stimulus after association has occurred

How might this simple example apply to more complex human behaviors? In a classic experiment, Watson and Rayner (1920) used classical conditioning to show how some kinds of maladaptive behaviors might be learned. Using Albert—an eleven-month-old boy who was fond of animals—as a subject, they showed how an irrational fear or phobia could be learned through classical conditioning. Their procedure was simple. An experimenter stood behind Albert while the boy was playing with a white rat. Whenever Albert reached for the animal (conditioned stimulus), the experimenter struck a steel bar with a hammer. The sudden loud noise (unconditioned stimulus) elicited a fearful reaction (unconditioned response) from Albert. After several repetitions of this procedure, Albert became upset and fearful (conditioned response) at the sight of the rat (conditioned stimulus) even when the loud noise was not made. In fact, his fear transferred not only to the white rat, but it also spread to include other furry animals and objects. In short, Albert had developed a phobia of furry objects through classical conditioning.

**generalization:** tendency to give a learned response when in the presence of different but similar stimuli

**Generalization.**    This dramatic demonstration of the development and **generalization** of an irrational fear suggests that other types of maladaptive behavior might also be learned through classical conditioning. Indeed, as you will see in Chapter 6, there is a good deal of evidence showing that this actually occurs. However, classical conditioning underlies more than learning maladaptive behavior. Many emotional reactions to various objects appear to be learned through classical conditioning. For example, if you watch television ads carefully you may notice how often the advertiser first presents a pleasant or amusing scene (unconditioned stimulus) and then shows the name of the product (conditioned stimulus); the expectation is that after numerous repetitions, you will react positively (conditioned response) to the sight of the product or its name. Perhaps it is necessary only to mention such names as "Bartles & Jaymes," "Lite Beer," "Oscar Meyer," and "Fruit of the Loom" for you to appreciate the power of such classical conditioning.

These same processes can be used to teach people more adaptive behavior. In the case mentioned at the start of this section, if a child fears dogs but does not fear teddy bears, it would be possible to associate playing with teddy bears and seeing pictures of friendly dogs until the child shows no fear of the pictures. Then the child could be put in the same room with a quiet, caged dog and allowed to play with teddy bears until all signs of fear have disappeared. Eventually the child could be moved closer to the cage, then the cage could be opened, and finally the dog could be let out without the child showing signs of fear. In fact, Chapter 7 will examine in some detail a version of psychotherapy called "systematic desensitization" that proceeds in this way.

However, behaviorists have discovered that classical conditioning is not the only way in which adaptive and maladaptive behaviors can be learned, as we will see in the next section.

## Operant Conditioning

You can probably remember many times in your life when you learned to behave in certain ways because you were rewarded or punished for your behavior. Perhaps you learned to clean up your room or to look both ways before crossing the street because you received praise for doing these things; maybe you learned to eat dinner with a fork because you were scolded for eating with your fingers. According to the behaviorist B. F. Skinner (1953, 1958, 1971, 1974), these are all examples of **operant conditioning**—the future likelihood of a behavior changed as a result of its consequences. Of course, the likelihood that a behavior will occur again depends a great deal on the kind of consequences that follow it.

**operant conditioning:** a learning process in which the likelihood of a behavior changes as a result of the consequences of that behavior

**reinforcer:** any consequence that strengthens or maintains a behavior that precedes it

**positive reinforcer:** any event whose presence increases the likelihood that a behavior will occur again in the future

**Reinforcement.**   If behavior is strengthened by its consequences, then the consequences are called **reinforcers.** There are two kinds of reinforcers. A **positive reinforcer** adds something rewarding to a situation. Some positive reinforcers are quite obvious: if you are paid to do a job, being paid is a positive reinforcer for completing the job. Children are frequently reinforced with candy, food, or special treats of various kinds. Other positive reinforcers are more subtle: a smile or an embrace from a loved one, praise, a pat on the back, recognition. Perhaps you have noticed that the trash containers at many fast food outlets have the words "Thank You" printed in large letters across the front; every time you put your trash in the container, you see the message and receive some subtle positive reinforcement.

*Reinforcement can be positive or negative, but it also can be intermittent. Playing the slot machine is an effective form of intermittent reinforcement which may lead to compulsive gambling despite its inconsistent rewards.*

**negative reinforcer:** any event whose reduction or removal increases the likelihood that a behavior will occur again in the future

**Negative reinforcers** also reinforce or strengthen behavior, but they work by reducing or removing an unpleasant or "aversive" stimulus from the environment. If you are speeding on the highway and see a police car at the side of the road, your slowing down may be negatively reinforced if the police car does not pursue you. The likelihood of your driving slower in the future is increased (negatively reinforced) by the removal of an unpleasant event (your momentary fear of being ticketed for speeding). If you have a headache which gets better or disappears entirely when you take a particular medicine, you are more likely to take that medicine in the future when you have a headache. The likelihood of using the medicine in the future is increased (negatively reinforced) because the medicine reduced or removed an unpleasant condition (your headache).

Both adaptive and maladaptive behaviors can be learned through operant conditioning. If you learn that jogging or meditation reduces tension, you are more likely to go jogging or to meditate when you feel tense and irritated. However, for the same reasons, another person may learn to drink alcohol, take tranquilizers, or throw a tantrum. This is because *any* behavior that is reinforced is more likely to occur in the future in the same situation, even though in the long run some behaviors are more effective than others at solving the underlying problem (in this case, reducing tension).

**intermittent (partial) reinforcement:** providing reinforcement only some of the time that a desired behavior occurs

Interestingly, reinforcement need not be consistent or continuous to be effective. In some situations, **intermittent** or **partial reinforcement** can be particularly powerful in strengthening and maintaining behavior. For example, a person may win at cards, the slot machines, or the state lottery very irregularly and inconsistently. Nonetheless, these intermittent reinforcers are so powerful that some people become compulsive gamblers.

**Punishment and extinction.**    We have seen that some behaviors are strengthened or reinforced by their consequences: these behaviors, whether adaptive or not, are more likely to occur in the same situation in the future. However, on other occasions behavior is weakened or eliminated as a result of its consequences. If you are caught speeding or shoplifting, the resulting **punishment** reduces the likelihood that you will behave that way again in the future. Similarly, a child may have television privileges suspended as punishment for some undesired act. In each of these cases, operant conditioning occurs: the future likelihood of a behavior is reduced by punishing it when it occurs.

**punishment:** any event whose presence reduces the likelihood that a behavior will occur again in the future

In fact, behavior can be weakened if it is followed by no consequence whatsoever. This procedure, called **extinction,** is embedded in the popular instruction "Just ignore her and she'll stop." Since the individual receives no reinforcement, the undesirable behavior should gradually weaken and disappear. This is an important concept: according to the behavioral model, behavior will not persist unless reinforced in some way, even though it may not be immediately obvious what the reinforcer is. A child who persistently lies, steals, or destroys things, despite being ignored and perhaps even punished, must be getting some kind of reinforcement for that behavior, otherwise the behavior would stop. As we will see in Chapter 7, the most important step in changing some kinds of "bad habits" is to identify the subtle reinforcers that are maintaining the undesirable behaviors.

**extinction:** gradual disappearance of a learned behavior when reinforcement is withheld

Note also that learning can take place without the awareness of the learner. You needn't be aware of what TV advertisers are doing for their ads to change your behavior. Similarly, in one laboratory study (Sasmor, 1966) the experimenter monitored tiny muscle movements and reinforced changes in the tension in the muscle. All of the subjects said they were aware that they were being reinforced more often as time went on, but none of them was able to identify the behavior that was causing the reinforcement. In other words, they were being conditioned without being aware of what they were being taught.

Although conditioning can occur without awareness, there are many circumstances under which learning occurs much more rapidly when people *are* aware. For example, DeNike & Spielberger (1963) engaged each of their subjects in casual conversation; after a short while, they began saying "good" or "um hum" every time the subject used plural nouns. At the end of the experiment they asked the subjects whether they were aware of what was happening. Those subjects aware of the experimenters' actions had dramatically increased their use of plural nouns; subjects who were unaware made virtually no change in their use of plural nouns. As we will see in the next section, results of studies such as this have led many contemporary behaviorists to look more closely at some of the mental processes that seem to underlie human learning.

*The consequences of an action may or may not reduce the likelihood of the behavior. Yet if punishment is the consequence, as in the case of stealing, the future likelihood of the behavior may be reduced.*

## Observational Learning and Cognitive Behaviorism

So far we have been discussing learning that results from first-hand experience: in classical conditioning, you are repeatedly exposed to the simultaneous pairing of the conditioned and unconditioned stimuli; in operant conditioning, you are reinforced or punished for your behavior. However, there are many other cases in which most of us learn simply from watching others. For example, a clerical worker may notice a co-worker's careful attention to detail. If the co-worker is praised or receives a salary increase or a promotion, the observer may learn to be more attentive to detail as well. Children also learn from watching others: Through observation, they pick up many of their parents' mannerisms and habits (both good and bad); they learn to dance and play games and act a certain way in school primarily by observing how others behave. They learn how to act when driving a car by watching the way their parents act in the same situation.

**observational learning (modeling):** form of learning in which an individual learns by watching someone else

**Modeling.**    In all such cases, behavior changes as a result of **observational learning** or *modeling:* individuals observe others and, when the conditions are appropriate, imitate or perform similar behaviors. As Bandura (1977b) notes, observational learning is an important kind of learning.

> Learning would be exceedingly laborious, not to mention hazardous, if people had to rely solely on the effects of their own actions to inform them what to do. Fortunately, most human behavior is learned observationally . . . : from observing others one forms an idea of how new behaviors are performed, and on later occasions this . . . information serves as a guide for action. Because people can learn from example what to do, at least in approximate form, before performing any behavior, they are spared needless errors. (p. 22)

As psychologists have studied the process of observational learning, it has become clear that it is not simply a matter of imitation or "monkey see, monkey do." Rather, a whole sequence of internal, mental processes seems to be involved: you must first pay attention to the modeled behavior, then process and retain the information observed, and finally, be motivated to perform the learned behavior at some later time (Posner, 1982; Woodward, 1982). By using terms such as "attention" and "motivation" and asserting that observational learning can occur without any immediate change in behavior, contemporary behaviorists have diverged sharply from traditional behaviorism. As you will see in later chapters, a great many contemporary **cognitive behaviorists** have begun to look closely at internal psychological processes such as thoughts, emotions, and feelings. To get just a flavor of this "new look" in the behaviorism model, let us look briefly at the way some contemporary behaviorists believe that **expectancies** can affect behavior.

**cognitive behaviorism:** contemporary version of behaviorism that acknowledges the importance of some unobservable mental processes in learning

**expectancies:** predictions about future events based on previous experience

**Expectancies.**    As most of us engage in everyday behavior, we make active attempts to predict what will happen if we behave in various ways; that is, we form expectancies. We examine a situation, compare it to similar situations, and estimate the likelihood of various outcomes. For example, a manager may disagree with an employee, then compare the present situation to previous situations of this sort, and so estimate the chances of resolving the disagreement in various ways. If the manager has successfully resolved similar disagreements in the past by saying, "I understand your position, and I respect it, but in this case I prefer that we do things this other way," then saying something similar might work in this situation, as well. The manager's expectation about what might happen in the future influences present behavior.

We can also form expectancies by watching for cues in the behavior of other people. A friend who nods understandingly when you start talking about your personal problems leads you to expect that further disclosure will be accepted, and you adjust your behavior accordingly. On the other hand, if your friend stares out the window, does not pay attention to you, or seems impatient, you may conclude that further disclosure will not be eagerly received and change the direction of the conversation (Mischel, 1981).

Two important points emerge from this brief overview of expectancies. First, some contemporary behaviorists have begun to show renewed interest in mental processes such as attention, memory, and expectation—internal processes that cannot be observed directly but that nonetheless apparently play important roles in human behavior. Second, many contemporary behaviorists believe that everyone plays an active role in initiating and regulating personal behavior. Most of us actively choose and shape our behavior, although influenced by factors outside of ourselves (such as reinforcements and stimuli). We also are able to control to a great extent the way in which those factors will affect our behavior. In these respects, modern behaviorism has become more similar to the psychoanalytic and humanistic models than once was the case.

## Healthy Adjustment

"Healthy adjustment" is not as central in the behavioral model as in the psychoanalytic and humanistic models. However, most traditional behaviorists probably would agree that adjustment is healthy or effective to the extent that: (1) a person's behavior leads to a great deal of reinforcement and little or no punishment; (2) a person's behavior changes appropriately in response to changes in the environment; and (3) a person exercises a good deal of self-regulation without the need for external, environmental control. Conversely, someone who receives a great deal of punishment, behaves in rigid and inappropriate ways, and is unable to exercise self-control is not coping effectively.

## Behavioral View of Robert W.

A behaviorist would begin by assuming that most of Robert's behavior has been learned on the basis of prior experience. For example, his achievement behavior appears to have been learned by observing the model set by his father. Also, his father repeatedly emphasized the importance of achievement in his lectures to his children. In addition, his achievement efforts have been reinforced with above average grades and probably praise and attention as well. Robert's stomach pains may be the result of learning: by acknowledging his complaints, his mother may have unintentionally reinforced them and made it more likely that he would experience stomach pains in the future when under stress. Furthermore, Robert's focus on business and accounting seems to be related to his expectation that important sources of reinforcement (well-paying job, security, etc.) will become available once he finishes his college program.

To a far greater degree than either the psychoanalytic or humanistic models, the behavioral perspective focuses on observable behavior. Though Robert's experiences earlier in life have shaped his behavior patterns, those behaviors will not be changed by tracing them to their origins in childhood or adolescence. Rather, if change is needed or desired, new learning will have to take place under carefully controlled and supervised conditions. At the same time, the behavioral perspective gives reason to be optimistic: any behavior that has been learned can be unlearned. Thus, behaviorists are inclined to believe that anyone can be helped to lead a more effective and well-adjusted life through carefully designed learning experiences. We will examine a number of behavioral approaches to psychotherapy in Chapter 7.

### Evaluation

Like the psychoanalytic and humanistic models, the behavioral model has also profoundly affected the development of psychology in this century. The behavioral emphasis on observable behavior and the importance of careful laboratory research has been generally well received, particularly in America. A tremendous amount of research has accumulated over the past half century, describing in detail how various behaviors can be learned. The behavioral model also lends itself well to practical applications; as a result it has been applied to almost every imaginable setting: to classrooms, television advertising, animal training, psychotherapy, the training of athletes, prison, management, child rearing, the work setting, even international arms negotiations. As we will see in later chapters, the renewed attention to cognitive processes has made the behavioral model even more valuable to those who wish to understand human behavior.

Behaviorism, however, like the other models we have examined, has its share of critics. Many psychologists object that, in some of its extreme versions, behaviorism reduces people to being little more than machines pushed and pulled this way and that by events in the environment. Moreover, some critics assert that behaviorism overlooks much that is distinctly human—passions, values, hopes, fears, thoughts, ideas, loves, hates, goals, plans, dreams, and other such important aspects of human existence. Finally, while behaviorism may provide insight into understanding specific behaviors, some critics object that it doesn't provide a sense of the "big picture," of the way the pieces of the puzzle fit together coherently for a particular person.

## CONFLICTING VIEWS OF HUMAN NATURE

To help you pull together and organize what you have learned about each of the models, this final section of the chapter will compare the position each model takes on some long-standing debates about human nature: Are human beings basically good or evil? Are people basically rational or irrational? Is human behavior the result of determinism or free will?

### Good or Evil

Throughout history, some people have asserted that human beings are basically selfish and self-seeking; others have denied it. Some have seen human beings as competitive by nature; others have seen them as cooperative. While some have maintained that human beings are hostile and cruel, others have described humans as inherently friendly and kind. All these assertions are part of a larger question: is human nature basically good or evil?

**Human nature as evil.**    The view that human beings are basically "evil" receives substantial support from history and human experience. The chain of war, violence, assassination, and cruelty evidenced by the human race reaches from the most ancient times to today's headlines. Each week brings new reports of terrorism. Each year, hundreds of thousands of children are beaten or burned by their parents; tens of thousands die from their injuries. In the United States alone, more than half a million women will be raped next year—and the list goes on. Not surprisingly, the view of human nature as basically evil has greatly influenced much of Western thought.

**Human nature as good.**   Despite humanity's deplorable record, a number of thinkers have asserted forcefully that people are basically friendly, cooperative, and loving. According to this view, aggression and cruelty result from a distortion of essential human nature; if people are allowed to live "naturally," much of the evil in the world would disappear.

**Human nature as neutral.**   Such contrasting views of the good or evil of human nature have led many other social scientists to conclude that human beings are neither good nor bad by nature. Instead, human beings are highly educable creatures with the potential to develop in either direction. In this view, whether people become selfish, cruel, and warlike or self-sacrificing, kindly, and peaceful depends largely upon the conditions in which they grow up. While most of us admittedly have the capacity for selfish and cruel behavior, we clearly have the capacity for love and goodness as well.

*In the dispute over whether humans are basically good or evil, some social scientists claim that human nature is neutral. This view asserts that people have the potential to become either good or evil. They learn their values from their environment.*

**The three models.** Each of the three models we have studied in this chapter takes a different position regarding whether human nature is essentially good or evil. Freud clearly believed that deep down inside, people are selfish, uncivilized, impulsive, demanding, cruel and destructive. He expressed this in *Civilization and Its Discontents* (1930/1955).

> . . . men are not gentle, friendly creatures wishing for love, who simply defend themselves if they are attacked, . . . a powerful measure of desire for aggressiveness has to be reckoned as part of their instinctual endowment. The result is that their neighbor is to them not only a possible helper or sexual object, but also a temptation to them to gratify their aggressiveness . . . to seize his possessions, to humiliate him, to cause him pain, to torture and to kill him. . . .
>
> Anyone who calls to mind the atrocities of the early migrations, of the invasion of the Huns or by the so-called Mongols under Jenghiz Kahn and Tamurlane, of the sack of Jerusalem by the pious crusaders, even indeed the horrors of the last world-war, will have to bow his head humbly before the truth of this view of man. (pp. 85–86)

In contrast, humanistic psychologists clearly believe that human beings are basically good, as reflected in this passage from Carl Rogers (1961).

> One of the most revolutionary concepts to grow out of our clinical experience is the growing recognition that the innermost core of man's nature, the deepest layers of his personality, the base of his "animal nature," is positive in nature—is basically socialized, forward-moving, rational and realistic. . . . the basic nature of the human being, when functioning freely, is constructive and trustworthy. (pp. 90–91, 194)

Finally, most behaviorists and even some contemporary psychoanalytic theorists tend to believe that human beings are inherently neither good nor evil. People are born with the capacity to learn various behaviors. Some learn to behave in constructive and socially desirable ways, while others learn to behave in destructive and hostile ways. Human nature is neutral, but experience causes some people to become "good," while others become "evil."

## Rational or Irrational

The human race has not only been indicted for being selfish and cruel, it has also been characterized as irrational and irresponsible. In every age there have been those who scoffed at the much-celebrated gift of reason. At the same time, others have spoken highly of human rationality and the human ability to govern according to reason.

**Human nature as irrational.** The view that human beings are irrational creatures has a long history, and modern laboratory research has confirmed that, at least under some circumstances, people behave in irrational ways. For example, in Chapter 1 you saw that people often over- or under-estimate the risk of environmental hazards even though in most cases they know the true dangers of those hazards. Psychologists have also discovered that people in some decision-making groups are so concerned with preserving group unity that they make disastrous decisions, sometimes costing thousands of human lives; that people have become physically ill after being "infected" by an imaginary epidemic; that people can be influenced by others to report things that do not exist; that people will behave in ways completely contradictory to their beliefs and values if asked to do so by someone in authority, even if their behavior may injure another human being; and that people participating in a study of a mock prison can become so confused that they come to believe they are in a real prison! In these cases and many others, people certainly behave in apparently irrational ways. In fact, they often are amazed afterward at their own behavior.

**Human nature as rational.**    From earliest times reason has also had its champions. The ancient Greeks exalted reason as the highest human virtue. The Roman aristocrats emphasized human rationality and prided themselves on their pragmatic approach to social problems. Although faith in human rationality has been severely tested in recent times, it has by no means been destroyed. Many modern diplomats, philosophers, and scientists believe in natural tendencies toward common sense and reason. Also, there is a good deal of research in psychology that lends support to this view of human beings. For example, the same experiments that provide examples of people acting irrationally also demonstrate that, under the same conditions, at least some people are capable of acting quite rationally. Some decision-making groups are stunningly successful at making extremely complex decisions; not everyone responds irrationally to rumors, panics, and imaginary epidemics; many people stand firm in the face of pressures to conform to erroneous judgments; and many people refuse to behave in ways that are contradictory to their beliefs and values even if requested to do so by a person in authority.

**The three models.**    Although Freud took the position that human beings are basically irrational creatures driven by forces that are forever beyond their awareness, many contemporary psychoanalytic thinkers and humanistic psychologists believe that human beings are capable of reflection, reason, and rational planning and choosing. Consider this comment from the humanistic psychologist Carl Rogers (1961).

> Man's behavior is exquisitely rational, moving with subtle and ordered complexity toward the goals his organism is endeavoring to achieve. The tragedy for most of us is that our defenses keep us from being aware of this rationality. . . . (pp. 194–95)

Most behaviorists, on the other hand, would say that there is no inherent tendency for human beings to behave in either rational or irrational ways. Some people may learn from their experiences to behave in ways that seem to be rational, while others may learn to behave in ways that appear to be irrational. Since behavior is always explainable, it always "makes sense," given the individual's experiences. Therefore, in this limited sense, it might be said that all behavior ultimately is "rational."

## Free or Determined

In everyday life, most people operate on the assumption that they are free to make decisions and choose their behaviors, at least within certain limits. Most of us see ourselves as continually weighing alternatives and choosing among them. However, many philosophers, theologians, and scientists have questioned whether this freedom of action is real or illusory—whether most of us are active and responsible agents with some measure of free will, or whether we are puppets whose behavior is actually determined by forces beyond our control.

**The assumption of determinism.** The great dramatic tragedies of Aeschylus and Sophocles reflect the ancient Greek belief that men and women are, in the final analysis, the pawns of fate. A sense of inevitability permeates their actions, leading to consequences from which individuals cannot escape. Despite the "illusion" of freedom, human beings are at the mercy of past experiences and present environmental conditions.

Each of us could find examples in our own lives suggesting that freedom of action may be illusory. New Year's Eve resolutions are notoriously ineffective: despite our best intentions and, perhaps, concerted efforts, we often find that undesirable behavior is remarkably resistant to change. Anyone who has been overweight can attest to the difficulty first of losing weight, then of keeping it off. Smokers, fingernail biters, alcoholics, child abusers, gamblers, and impulse shoppers also represent people whose behavior seems to be beyond their control.

**The assumption of freedom.** On the other hand, very few people fully believe in strict determinism in the affairs of their own lives. Most people probably would agree with the psychologist Shibutani (1964).

> Each person believes that he is able to exercise some measure of control over his own destiny. He is capable of making decisions and of selecting among alternative lines of action. It is this widespread belief that provides the basis for the doctrine of "free will" and for the concept of moral responsibility (p. 233).

The American political and legal systems are also based on the assumption that most of us are capable of self-determination. The entire legal system is based on the assumption that, unless someone is criminally insane, he or she knows what is legal and illegal, and can be expected to behave within the limits of the law. Also, when we assign credit to others for their actions, the assumption of freedom usually underlies our judgment. Skinner (1971) stated:

> We are not inclined to give a person credit for achievements which are in fact due to forces over which he has no control. . . . The amount of credit a person receives is related in a curious way to the visibility of the causes of his behavior. We withhold credit when the causes are conspicuous. . . . We give credit generously when there are no obvious reasons for the behavior . . . (especially) when there are quite visible reasons for behaving differently. . . . (pp. 41–43)

For example, if someone runs into a burning building to rescue a complete stranger, he or she tends to get a great deal of credit. However, imagine how different your reaction would be if the rescuer then said of the victim "Well, heck, he owes me $100 and I want to be sure he's around long enough to pay me back."

**The assumption of reciprocal determinism.** The debate over free will versus determinism may never be resolved. However, many contemporary psychologists are

*Our actions and perceptions affect the environment just as the environment influences our behavior.*

choosing a third alternative that emphasizes the interaction of the individual and the environment. This assumption of **reciprocal determinism** has been well summarized by Craighead, Kazdin, and Mahoney (1981).

> The existing psychological evidence does strongly support the notion that environmental events exert control over behavior. However, there is equally strong evidence illustrating that behaviors exert control over environments . . . . The influence process is reciprocal in that it works both ways. Environments influence behavior; behaviors influence environments.
>
> This reciprocal determinism between behavior and environment has tremendous significance for human performance and the issues of personal freedom, responsibility, and choice. Since environments are a function of behavior, the individual can take an active role in self-determination. (pp. 186–87)

For example, you may discover that it is easier to concentrate without interruptions when studying at the campus library than when studying in your dormitory room. Armed with this knowledge, you are better prepared to assume control over your behavior: when you need to study, you can increase the effectiveness by studying in the library. Similarly, common advice to people who have trouble getting to sleep is, "Don't get into bed until you feel tired. If you find yourself feeling restless, get out of bed and go to another room until you feel tired again." In this way, over time, being in bed will become associated with feeling tired and sleepy, rather than restless and alert. For the same reason, studying while sitting on your bed is likely to be less effective than studying at a desk or in another setting regularly associated with alertness and concentration.

While acknowledging that human behavior is heavily influenced by the individual's background of experience, scientists who emphasize reciprocal determinism are impressed with the importance of self-awareness: people's ability to reflect upon and reinterpret past experience, and their ability to imagine new possibilities different from anything they have experienced previously. According to this view, people are capable of modifying the environment, and so taking an active role in shaping their destiny (Bandura, 1977, 1982a).

**The three models.**    Freud clearly believed everything people do, think, or feel is determined; even apparent slips of the tongue or brief moments of forgetfulness have a cause (a personal meaning). Contemporary psychoanalysts are generally less dogmatic on this point, but most tend to lean toward determinism.

Humanistic psychologists take the opposite position: People are essentially free to exercise control over their own destinies. Although they are affected by their inheritance and past experiences, they can always select from alternative courses of action. Thus, they are responsible for their own behavior.

Behaviorists, like psychoanalysts, believe that human behavior is determined. As Skinner (1953) put it: "The hypothesis that man is not free is essential to the application of the scientific method to the study of human behavior." Most behaviorists, however, support the notion of reciprocal determinism; they believe that while the environment influences behavior, behavior also affects the environment. In operant conditioning, for example, environmental events (reinforcements, punishments, cues) clearly affect behavior, but in turn behavior operates on and changes the environment. Similarly, people develop expectancies based on their experience; those expectancies affect their subsequent behavior and the environment in which they find themselves in the future.

We have come a long way in this chapter. Let's pause here to take stock of where we are. We have seen considerable disagreement on the question of human nature. Some scholars believe that all human beings are basically good, others that all people are basically evil, and still others take a more neutral position. While some scholars believe that all human beings are rational, others believe they are inherently irrational. Also, some assert that all human behavior is totally determined by past experiences and present environmental conditions, others argue that each person exercises some degree of free will and choice in his or her own behavior, while still other psychologists believe there is a reciprocal influence between each person and the environment.

We have also seen that each of the three major models of human behavior—the psychoanalytic model, the humanistic model, and the behavioral model—makes somewhat different assumptions about human nature, about the ways in which you and I are like all other people (see Table 2.1).

Although there are many variations on the three major models of human behavior that we have reviewed, the basic models remain relatively distinct and are to some extent contradictory. Like the blind men feeling different parts of the elephant and each describing it as a different animal, each model emphasizes certain aspects of the human experience and helps us understand part of the puzzle of human nature.

**TABLE 2.1  Human Nature as Seen by Differing Models of Behavior**

| Model | Good/Evil | Rational/Irrational | Free/Determined |
| --- | --- | --- | --- |
| Psychoanalytic | Evil | Irrational | Determined |
| Humanistic-Existential | Good | Rational | Free |
| Social-Learning | Neutral | Depends on learning | Reciprocal determinism |

*Distinguishing characteristics of the psychoanalytic model:*
1. importance of unconscious processes;
2. focus on early childhood events;
3. key role of personality structures in behavior.

*Distinguishing characteristics of the humanistic-existential model:*
1. importance of self-report and self-perception:
2. focus on present events and experiences;
3. key role of choice, growth, and self-actualization.

*Distinguishing characteristics of the social-learning model:*
1. importance of environmental events in shaping behavior;
2. focus on observable behavior with some interest in cognitive events;
3. key role of the effects of learning.

For this reason, this book will not be limited to any one model, but instead will utilize concepts from many different theoretical orientations to help illuminate human behavior.

## SUMMARY

This chapter examines in detail three different models of human nature. According to the *psychoanalytic model,* much human behavior can be attributed to *unconscious* impulses, wishes, and conflicts. According to Freud, for example, unconscious *id* impulses provide the energy for all behavior. The id operates according to the *pleasure principle:* it pursues pleasure without regard to reality or morality; if necessary it can use wishes and images (the *primary process)* to provide gratification. The *ego* develops after birth and serves to help satisfy the id's needs in the real world (the *reality principle).* For this purpose the ego relies on *secondary process* thinking, such as planning and reasoning. In addition, the *superego* develops to assure that id impulses are satisfied in socially acceptable ways. Although the id impulses, and much of the ego and superego as well, are unconscious, other portions of the ego and superego are *preconscious,* which means they can be brought to awareness.

For Freud, human development occurs in a series of stages. During the *oral stage,* the mouth is the most important source of pleasure. In the *anal stage,* the primary source of pleasure shifts to the anus. During the *phallic stage* the genitals become the main source of pleasure. Toward the end of the phallic stage, children become attached to their opposite-sex parent; in boys this is called the *Oedipus complex,* and in girls it is called the *Electra complex.* Fearing punishment, children

*Each stage in life offers new challenges and provides an opportunity to grow toward greater self-understanding.*

renounce their sexual impulses and enter the *latency stage.* With the arrival of puberty and a reawakening of sexual impulses, the young adolescent enters the final stage of development—the *genital stage.*

From the Freudian perspective, healthy adjustment corresponds to having a strong ego that can maximize gratification of id impulses while minimizing punishment, fear, anxiety, and guilt.

Freud's model has profoundly affected the way psychologists think about human behavior. It has drawn particular attention to how people do not always understand the reasons behind their actions and to the importance of early experiences in shaping people's lives. However, some psychologists find Freud's model too bleak. Moreover, at least some portions of his theory are sexist. Finally, scientific evaluation is difficult for many of the most important aspects of his theory. Recent psychoanalytic theorists have attempted to address some of these weaknesses by placing greater emphasis on the positive, rational, constructive side of human nature, as well as on interpersonal relationships.

The *humanistic model* emphasizes the importance of growth and fulfillment throughout life. According to Carl Rogers, an *actualizing tendency* causes each person to strive to express his or her unique, inborn potential. In addition, as people develop they acquire a *self-concept,* and the *self-actualizing tendency* causes them to strive to express and confirm this image of themselves as well. If a person receives *unconditional positive regard* from others, their self-concept and inborn potentials are likely to correspond closely (be *congruent),* and the two actualizing tendencies will work together toward the same end. Such a *fully functioning* person will be optimally well adjusted. However, optimal adjustment is an unreachable ideal toward which people strive: since everybody at one time or another receives *conditional positive regard* from others, the normal state of affairs is for the self-concept and inborn capacities to be *incongruent,* for the two actualizing tendencies to be somewhat incompatible, and for the person to be less than fully functioning.

According to another humanistic psychologist, Abraham Maslow, human behavior reflects a number of inborn needs or motives that can be arranged in a *hierarchy,* ranging from *deficiency motives* (such as physiological, safety, love and belongingness, and esteem needs) to *growth motives* (self-actualization). Only when deficiency needs are satisfied is a person's behavior likely to be dominated by growth motivation and a striving toward self-actualization.

The humanistic model draws attention to the importance of understanding psychological health and human virtues, and to the possibility that people are naturally inquisitive and growth-oriented. On the other hand, some critics believe that the humanistic model underestimates not only the importance of unconscious determinants of behavior but also the role of such human motives as aggression and destructiveness. As with the psychoanalytic model, many important aspects of the humanistic model have proven difficult to evaluate scientifically.

The *behavioral model* differs from both the psychoanalytic and humanistic models in that it emphasizes observable behavior and minimizes the importance of any invisible psychological processes. Behaviorism proceeds from the assumption that virtually all important human behavior is learned through experience. Some learning occurs through *classical conditioning,* in which a response that occurs in the presence of one stimulus is transferred to a new stimulus. The original response is called the *unconditioned response* and occurs in the presence of the *unconditioned stimulus.* By associating the unconditioned stimulus with a different, *conditioned stimulus,* a new *conditioned response* can be acquired. Many emotional reactions appear to be learned in this way.

Behavior can also be learned through *operant conditioning:* behavior that is followed by a *positive reinforcer* or a *negative reinforcer* is more likely to occur in the future; in contrast, behavior that is followed by *punishment* or that is ignored is less likely to occur in the future. Although some operant conditioning can occur without awareness, there are many circumstances in which learning occurs more rapidly if the learner is aware of what is happening.

Still other behaviors can be learned through *observation* or *modeling. Cognitive behaviorists,* in particular, have emphasized that through direct experience as well as observation and modeling of others, people learn *expectancies* which permit them actively to choose and shape their own behavior.

For behaviorists, people are well adjusted if their behavior leads to far more reinforcement than punishment, if their behavior changes appropriately in response to changes in the environment, and if they are to a considerable extent capable of self-regulation.

A great deal of carefully controlled research has demonstrated that external events can play a significant role in directing and shaping behavior. The behavioral model has also been applied to understand and change a wide variety of maladaptive behaviors. However, some critics believe that behaviorism reduces human beings to little more than machines and that it underestimates the importance of thoughts and emotions, many of which seem to lie at the heart of the human experience.

The several models take somewhat different positions on a number of long-standing debates about human nature. The psychoanalytic model, stressing the evil and irrational side of human nature, proceeds on the assumption that all behavior (from the most trivial to the most profound) is determined. In contrast, the humanistic model, emphasizing the virtuous and rational aspects of human behavior, assumes that to a great extent people are free to behave as they wish. The behavioral model assumes that people are inherently neither good nor evil, neither rational nor irra-tional. Some people learn to behave in ways that are good while others learn to behave in ways that are evil; similarly, some people learn to behave in rational ways, while others learn to behave in irrational ways. The behavioral model, however, assumes that behavior is determined, though most behaviorists also believe that behavior in turn can operate on and change the environment *(reciprocal determinism)*.

## KEY TERMS

psychoanalytic model (28)
id (29)
pleasure principle (30)
primary process (30)
ego (30)
reality principle (30)
secondary process (31)
superego (32)
unconscious (32)
preconscious (32)
oral stage (33)
anal stage (35)
phallic stage (35)
Oedipus complex (35)
Electra complex (36)
latency stage (37)
genital stage (37)
fixation (37)
humanistic model (40)
actualizing tendency (41)
self-concept (43)
self-actualizing tendency (43)
congruence (43)
incongruence (43)
conditional positive regard (44)
hierarchy of needs (44)

deficiency motivation (44)
growth motivation (45)
unconditional positive regard (45)
fully-functioning person (46)
behavioral model (49)
behaviorism (49)
classical (respondent, Pavlovian)
    conditioning (51)
unconditioned stimulus (51)
unconditioned response (51)
conditioned stimulus (51)
conditioned response (51)
generalization (51)
operant conditioning (52)
reinforcer (52)
positive reinforcer (52)
negative reinforcer (53)
intermittent (partial)
    reinforcement (54)
punishment (54)
extinction (54)
observational learning (modeling) (56)
cognitive behaviorism (56)
expectancies (56)
reciprocal determinism (63)

# Stress: It's Nature, Effects, and Management

# Problems of Adjustment

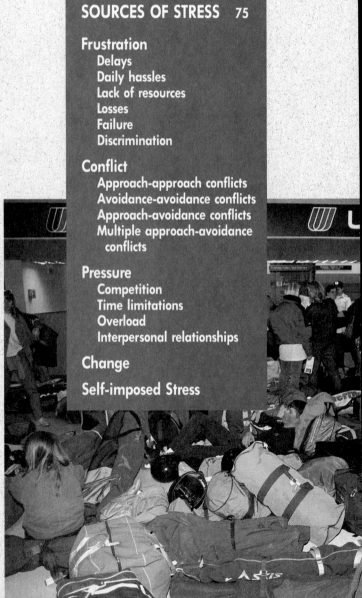

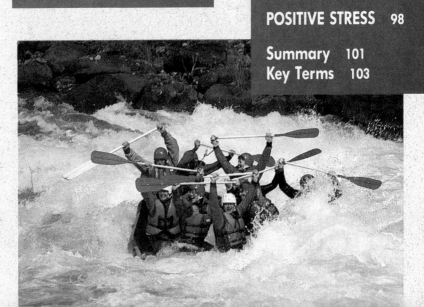

*I have to get away for a while. There's just too much pressure. I feel like my job is on the line, so I have to be careful at work not to make any mistakes or to offend anyone. I'm taking some night classes so I can improve my education and maybe get a better job, but that just adds more pressure. Even at home I'm tense and stressed out most of the time; I yell at the kids and don't do as much to help as I should. It's gotten to the point where I can't even get a good night's sleep. I've got to get out from under the stress, or I'm going to explode.*

$\mathcal{M}$OST of us have experienced occasional moments like these, times when we felt absolutely overwhelmed and worried that we were reaching the limits of our ability to cope. As a result of such experiences, we understand in a general way what "stress" means. For example, even people who have never studied psychology probably understand what it means to be "stressed out" and to need to "get out from under the stress." Stress is simply a fact of life. Sometimes people deliberately choose to engage in activities causing stress, such as mountain climbing, hang gliding, and competitive sports. Many other stresses (such as competition and conflict between people) are so widespread in our society that we tend to take them for granted. But what exactly is stress? What causes it? Why are some situations more stressful than others? And why are some people more likely than others to be bothered by stress?

The next several chapters explore the answers to these and other questions about stress. This chapter focuses on the types and sources of stress and the factors making stress more or less severe. The next chapter examines the various ways people react to stress. Chapter 5 focuses on coping effectively with stress, while Chapter 6 examines ineffective methods of coping that some people use when they experience severe stress. Finally, Chapter 7 discusses the kinds of professional assistance available when the task of coping with stress becomes overwhelming. The following section begins with a closer look at the nature of stress.

## THE NATURE OF STRESS

**stress:** adjustive demand that requires change or adaptation

**Stress** is any adjustive demand that includes a state of tension or threat and that requires change or adaptation if an individual is to meet his or her needs. Beginning in infancy and continuing through adolescence, adulthood, and old age, all of us constantly cope with stress. Infants and toddlers may cry from a bruised knee or from being picked on by the neighborhood bully. School children may become upset when told that games must be played according to rules or that much of each school day they must memorize seemingly endless strings of facts and rules. Adolescents may rage against parents who grant them the independence they seek, but rarely

*Life changes are inevitable, and even if they are welcome, they are stressful when they occur.*

at a pace they desire. Although young adults may be aware that they are making decisions that will affect the rest of their lives, they are unsure about whether their decisions are right or wrong (or even how to tell the difference). Middle-aged adults may feel constrained by their marriage, their occupation, their children, or their aging parents. Elderly adults may become frustrated at increasing physical disability and at being cast aside as useless by a society that overvalues youth. In other words, as people grow and develop and their lives change, the sources of stress change. As Lamott (1975) stated, stress remains at all stages of life, and stems from a variety of sources.

> Whether emotional or physical, natural or man-made, public or private, stress exerts an influence on our lives . . . [and] more than any other factor . . . determines the point at which we find ourselves sliding down the slope from health. . . . Stress is not unique to Americans, but given our way of living, one would not be far off to call it the "American disease." (pp. 8–9)

## Stressors

Sources of stress abound in contemporary life. In some cases, stress arises from unpleasant, uncontrollable, or unpredictable events. For example, the loss of a home through fire, earthquake, or flood can be a source of stress. The loss of a job or a loving interpersonal relationship can also be a source of stress, as can taking on new, increased responsibilities at home or at work. More typically, daily we all confront delays, losses, pressures, conflicts, and other conditions that place demands on us. For some people, even the routine pressures and worries of modern life are a constant source of stress. All these various environmental sources of stress are called **stressors.**

**stressors:** sources of stress outside the individual such as delays, losses, job demands

## Perceptions

Moreover, the *perception* of threat can produce stress even in the absence of an actual environmental stressor. A student may experience stress from imagining terrible things that may happen if he or she fails to get an A on an exam. The athlete or businessperson who competes intensively may experience stress in situations that others would not find particularly stressful. The teenager who would "die of embarrassment" if he or she did not wear the latest fashions might also experience stress. In other words, the presence of an actual environmental stressor is not essential for a person to experience stress.

## Coping

Coping with some stressors is relatively easy. If food is available and we are hungry, we eat. When we meet an individual who isn't friendly and outgoing, we can walk away and soon forget the unpleasant encounter. However, coping with other stressors is difficult. Major surgery, divorce, and serious financial difficulties are examples of such severe stressors.

Capacities for dealing with stress differ as well. Some people appear to be able to tolerate extremely unpleasant situations with little apparent effect. Others fall to pieces at the slightest provocation. People also differ in the ways they respond to stress. Some individuals respond by developing physical symptoms such as high blood pressure or ulcers. Others have trouble sleeping or become withdrawn. Stress can also affect people's day-to-day activities. Some people under stress do not function as well at work or have trouble studying and preparing for classes. Still others are difficult to get along with because they become irritable. Some individuals develop effective mechanisms for coping with their stress, while others develop severely maladaptive reactions.

In the next section we will explore the most common causes of stress. We will then examine why some instances of stress are more severe than others, and why some people experience more stress than others in the same situation. Much of our discussion and many of our examples will concentrate on the negative aspects of stress, often termed **distress.** However, we will also see that some stress is a necessary part of life and some kinds of stress can actually give rise to joyous experiences. These positive aspects of stress, termed **eustress,** will be examined at the end of the chapter.

**distress:** negative stress; stress that has a detrimental effect

**eustress:** positive stress; stress that has a beneficial effect

## SOURCES OF STRESS

Four key environmental sources of stress are frustration, conflict, pressure, and change. Of course, elements of all four may be present in the same stressful situation but, for simplicity, we will discuss them separately. Then we will look at self-imposed stress, stress that comes from within ourselves.

### Frustration

**frustration:** result of being unable to satisfy needs or desires

**Frustration** results from the blocking of needs and motives, either by something that prevents or hinders the achievement of a desired goal or by the absence of an appropriate goal object. Overly restrictive parents can be a source of frustration to an adolescent who wants to go to a school party, while a traffic jam would be a source of frustration to a person in a hurry to get somewhere. Failing to find an open gas station can be extremely frustrating to a motorist whose car is low on gas. Environmental obstacles such as accidents, hurtful interpersonal relationships, and the deaths of loved ones can also be sources of extreme frustration. Even personal characteristics such as physical handicaps, insufficient skills, or lack of self-discipline can cause frustration. Some of the more common frustrations that often cause stress include delays, hassles, lack of resources, losses, failure, and discrimination.

**Delays.**    In our time-conscious culture, we seem to value every minute, but with our crowded urban centers and high degree of interdependence, delays are inevitable. We apparently are forever standing in line or waiting in traffic. In our complex, technological society, even preparation for a career can take long years of intensive study.

*Systems break down, plans fall apart, and the resulting frustration is a common source of stress.*

In addition, delays in acquiring material possessions are made more frustrating by the constant barrage of advertising that stimulates our desire for things we cannot presently afford, and perhaps never will be able to afford. A recent study, for example, reported that in the early 1950s, thefts increased significantly in cities and states where television had just been introduced compared to cities and states where television had not been introduced (Hennigan et al., 1982). The researchers cited other research which demonstrated that early television shows tended to concentrate on white, employed males in the middle and upper social classes leading comfortable lives with a large number of possessions. They concluded that the introduction of television was responsible for the increase in larceny and explained that many lower class viewers "may have felt resentment and frustration over lacking the goods they could not afford, and some may have turned to crime as a way of obtaining the coveted goods" (p. 474).

**Daily hassles.** Another source of frustration is what Lazarus calls "daily hassles" (Lazarus, 1981; Lazarus et al., 1985).

> . . . the irritating, frustrating, distressing demands and troubled relationships that plague us day in and day out . . . such as misplacing or losing things, not having enough time for one's family, filling out forms, planning meals, concern about weight, and unchallenging work. (Lazarus & DeLongis, 1983, p. 247)

Though each of these annoyances may be minor in itself, taken together they can add a great deal to our levels of frustration and stress.

**Lack of resources.** Although most of us have the basic necessities of life, probably few of us are completely satisfied. We all might like more money to buy and do the things we want—perhaps to buy a new car or to travel. Many people also feel they lack the educational, occupational, or social opportunities essential for realizing their potentials.

Personal limitations can be particularly powerful sources of frustration in our competitive society. Physical handicaps that reduce our attractiveness or place serious limitations on our activities can be a source of stress. Similarly, the inability to obtain outstanding grades in college may severely frustrate a student who wishes to pursue a professional career.

In a recent study, Bernstein and Crosby (1980) set out to discover how a lack of resources affects people. They asked more than 500 college students to read short stories about other people—some of whom were deprived of things they wanted—and imagine how those people felt, and then describe those feelings. The researchers discovered that resentment, dissatisfaction, disappointment, unfairness, anger, and unhappiness were judged to be highest when people are deprived of something they want and feel they are entitled to have, when they believe it was once feasible to have the object, when they feel responsible for not having it, and when they see little likelihood that they will have it in the future.

**Losses.** The loss of something we value is frustrating because it deprives us of a resource for meeting our needs. Loss of money or time may mean forgoing a cherished dream. Loss of friendship or love may deprive us of satisfactions we have come to depend upon and may threaten our self-esteem. Losses are especially frustrating because they are often beyond our control; once they have occurred usually there is nothing we can do about them.

**Failure.**   Even if we did not live in a highly competitive society, we would be bound to fail occasionally. Competition simply increases the frequency of failure and the consequent frustration. Athletic teams do not win all the time, and people who wish to become movie or television stars or achieve high political office rarely achieve their dreams. Even when we do well in light of or own abilities, we may experience frustration if we have not done as well as we hoped to do or as well as someone else did in the same situation.

**Discrimination.**   Many people experience frustration when they are denied opportunities simply because of their sex, age, religion or race. Women, the elderly, Jews, Catholics, blacks, Native Americans, Hispanics, Orientals—all of these groups have been and continue to be targets of discrimination. One consequence of discrimination is frustration: people experience frustration when denied opportunities, when their needs and desires and dreams remain unfulfilled despite their personal qualifications.

In all these cases, frustration occurs when something we want, need, or deserve is unavailable or when our wishes are thwarted. Whether an environmental event temporarily interferes with our goals or wishes (as when a delay on the subway prevents us from getting home on time) or permanently frustrates us (as when an accident leaves us disabled), the effect is the same: more stress.

## Conflict

**conflict:** simultaneous arousal of two or more incompatible motives

Another source of stress is **conflict.** Conflict exists when an individual experiences two or more incompatible motives simultaneously. For example, you might like to visit some friends for the Thanksgiving holidays, but the trip involves a long and tiring car ride. You are motivated to make the trip, but you are also motivated to stay home. These motives are incompatible, since you can't do both things simultaneously. Another conflict may be when you have a job offer attractive in terms of salary, but unattractive in terms of location. You can't accept the salary without also accepting the location, so you experience conflict. We may also experience conflicts selecting a suitable major in college, selecting the right person with whom to share our lives, and selecting the kind of life style that will prove most fulfilling.

Psychologists usually distinguish between four types of conflict: approach-approach, avoidance-avoidance, approach-avoidance, and multiple approach-avoidance. These are depicted in Figure 3.1 and discussed below.

**approach-approach conflict:** conflict produced when a person must choose between two or more desirable alternatives

**Approach-approach conflicts.**   As the name implies, **approach-approach conflicts** involve competition between two or more desirable alternatives. You are drawn toward, or want to approach, each of the alternatives, but you can only select one of them. On a simple level, you may have to decide between two desirable courses of action—for example, choosing between a hot fudge or a butterscotch sundae,

**FIGURE 3.1   Types of Conflict**

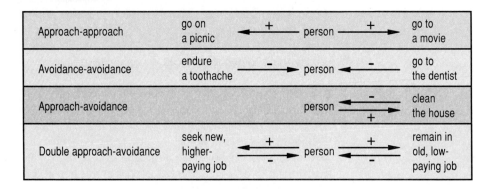

choosing which of two excellent films to see, or deciding which good book to read. On a more complex level, you may have to choose between many desirable courses of action—for example, selecting from among many interesting college courses meeting at the same time, or choosing from many attractive places for a vacation. To a large extent, "plus-plus" conflicts result from the inevitable limitations on our time, space, energy, and personal resources. We cannot be in two places at once, nor do we have the time and energy to do all the things we would like.

Although approach-approach conflicts can be difficult to resolve, they do not ordinarily upset us greatly because both options are pleasant and we may have an opportunity to obtain the other alternative at a later time: we can often "have our cake and eat it too." However, this is not always the case. Sometimes—as when a young person is torn between preparing for a career in law or medicine or between present and future satisfactions—decision making may be very difficult and stressful, since selecting one option may forever rule out the second option.

**avoidance-avoidance conflict:** conflict produced when an individual must choose between two or more undesirable alternatives

**Avoidance-avoidance conflicts.**   In an **avoidance-avoidance conflict** we are caught "between the devil and the deep blue sea" and must try to choose the lesser of two evils. The unskilled young person may have to choose between unemployment and a disagreeable job. A middle-aged person may have to choose between a loveless marriage and an unpleasant divorce. These "minus-minus" conflicts can cause serious adjustment problems because we would rather not make either choice—each will result in an undesirable situation. In these cases, it is not unusual for people to delay making a choice while hoping the conflict will resolve itself or that other, more desirable alternatives will become available.

**approach-avoidance conflict:** conflict produced when a goal has both positive and negative features

**Approach-avoidance conflicts.**   An **approach-avoidance conflict** consists of strong tendencies to approach and to avoid the same goal. You might want to marry, yet at the same time you might fear the responsibilities and loss of personal freedom that marriage could involve. You might want to ask someone a personal question, but at the same time fear they will think you are being nosy. In these cases, the same goal has positive as well as negative aspects, and you are torn between going ahead and avoiding it (see Insight, p. 81).

*Parenthood presents a variety of conflicts. Disciplining children is difficult, but lack of discipline may hurt a child more in the long run.*

Figure 3.2 illustrates an interesting feature of approach-avoidance conflicts that was first described by John Dollard and Neil Miller (1950). Often, when you are some distance away from your goal, the tendency to approach is stronger than your tendency to avoid. However, as you move closer, your tendency to avoid the goal grows stronger until finally it is just as strong as your tendency to approach. At this point, you are likely to stop approaching the goal and to waver back and forth (vacillate). In fact, in the conflict depicted in Figure 3.2a the person will never reach the goal unless something is done to increase the approach tendency, decrease the avoidance tendency, or both (as in Figure 3.2b). Rather, the person will vacillate while trying to decide which way to go.

Most of us can recall times we have confronted approach-avoidance conflicts of this sort. For example, at some point in your life you probably spent hours or days "getting up the nerve" to call someone on the telephone: you decide "I'm really going to do it this time"; you pick up the telephone and start dialing, you "lose your

**FIGURE 3.2 Approach-avoidance Conflict**

3.2a: Representation of a simple approach-avoidance conflict. When the goal is far away, the tendency to approach is stronger. However, as the goal becomes nearer, the tendency to avoid becomes stronger. Where the two cross (indicated by the dotted line), the two tendencies are equal and the person vacillates.

3.2b: In the second example, the approach tendency is always stronger than the avoidance tendency. Thus, the person will reach the goal.

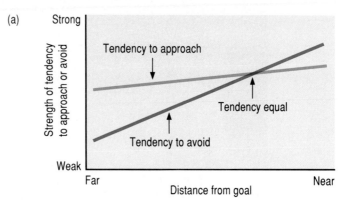

(a)

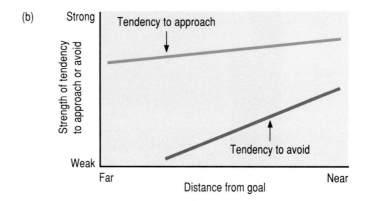

(b)

nerve" and hang up. Perhaps you've watched people try to decide whether they are going to dive into a pool of chilly water: they dip in one toe, make a halfhearted rush to the edge of the pool only to come to an abrupt halt and back away, stand on the edge of the pool, lean forward, then quickly catch their balance and walk off. Perhaps you have decided to accept a job offer, but as you approach the post office to mail your letter of acceptance you hesitate, then put the letter away so you can think about the decision a bit more. Unless something happens to tip the balance in these situations, the conflict can continue indefinitely.

**multiple approach-avoidance conflict:** conflict produced when an individual must choose between two or more goals, each of which has positive and negative features

**Multiple approach-avoidance conflicts.** **Multiple approach-avoidance conflicts** arise when you are simultaneously attracted and repelled by more than one goal. For example, you may be faced with a choice between an excellent new job (which unfortunately is located in an undesirable part of the country) and your less desirable present job (which is located in a very desirable part of the country). You may have to choose between buying the house of your dreams that will cost more than you can afford or a less-than-ideal house that is more suited to your budget. This is the most common form of conflict, since we are often faced with more than one choice in a situation and most choices typically have both good and bad features.

# Insight

## Pressure

pressure: adjustive demand that requires an organism to speed up, intensify, or change behavior

**Pressure** is yet another external source of stress. Pressure refers to anything that forces us to speed up, intensify, or change our behavior. As the end of the semester draws near, we may find that we have too much to do in too little time. We experience pressure to speed up, work harder and longer, and cancel or postpone various activities that detract from studying. We may find ourselves falling behind schedule on a long trip with miles left to travel, darkness approaching, and a car full of children wailing "Are we *there* yet? When are we going to get there?" Examples of pressure are so numerous, we can't possibly discuss them all; we can, however, look more closely at a few common sources of pressure that are probably familiar to everybody.

**Competition.** In our highly competitive society, we compete for grades, athletic honors, jobs, marital partners, and everything else we might want. At times the strain of sustained competition may seen endless. In school, we are expected to study hard and get good grades. At work, a person may be under pressure to advance and make more money. In general, people are encouraged to be ambitious and to "think big," to do more, earn more, achieve more, sell more. . . . The result is pressure: we have to speed up our activities, make a greater effort, and focus our energies more intensively. This in turn leads to stress.

How fishermen blow their own minds

**Time limitations.**   At times it may appear that life is primarily a battle with the clock. There are deadlines for handing in term papers, due dates for bills and payments, appointments to be kept, parking meters to be fed, closing times for stores, and time limits on exams. Some days it seems that everything is either too late, overdue, expired, or closed! As we will see, some people are more concerned than others about beating the clock, but to some extent time pressure is a factor adding to the stress of everyone's life.

**Overload.**   Closely related to time pressure is the problem of overload. You have five telephone calls to return, there are three people waiting to talk to you, an unfinished report is sitting on your desk, and you still haven't finished your shopping for an important birthday party tonight. You start to get a sinking feeling as you realize you can't possibly do everything at once. The result is pressure and stress.

Some people routinely experience overload as a result of their jobs. Emergency room physicians, stock and commodity traders, air traffic controllers, waiters and waitresses all work at a feverish pace because they often have more to do than they can possibly accomplish. A decisive factor regarding whether to enter these careers must be an ability to tolerate high levels of pressure (and the resulting high levels of stress) for long periods of time.

**Interpersonal relationships.** Although many of our deepest needs are satisfied through interpersonal relationships, these relationships can also place difficult pressures upon us. Marriage requires adjusting daily to an intimate relationship with another person, developing a mutually satisfactory approach to problems, and resolving conflicts. Relationships with people outside our families can also be sources of pressure. Our friends may need our help at inconvenient times; organizations to which we belong may need long hours that we cannot easily spare; community groups may make demands upon us as concerned citizens. All these demands add to the pressures that complicate our lives.

## Change

All life involves change. People grow up, change jobs or careers, face the death of parents and friends, undergo illnesses, and adjust to innumerable other major and minor changes as they go through life. In addition to these nearly universal life changes, the world around us is also changing at a dizzying rate. More than a decade ago, the National Education Association questioned fifty distinguished leaders and world citizens about their views of the modern world. In summarizing the results, Shane (1976) reported that, "Without exception, the respondents recognized that not only the U.S. but the world as a whole is passing through the greatest tidal wave of transition in history" (p. 253). However, most people strive to achieve an orderly and coherent world in which to live; they prefer to avoid ambiguity, lack of structure, chaos, and events that seem beyond their understanding. As a result, rapid change is a source of considerable stress for many individuals and groups in our modern world.

Holmes and his colleagues (Holmes & Holmes, 1970; Holmes & Rahe, 1967) suggested that change from whatever source, whether desirable or undesirable, is stressful because it disrupts an individual's life. They concluded that by measuring the number of significant changes in a person's life in a given period of time, they could estimate the amount of stress the person has experienced. Their Social Readjustment Rating Scale (SRRS) is designed to do just that (see Table 3.1, p. 84 for the entire scale).

In developing their scale, Holmes and Rahe began by asking people to indicate the amount of readjustment required by several dozen common life events. Each event was then given a number designating its severity in terms of **Life Change Units** (LCUs). For example, death of a spouse was assigned 100, divorce 73, and personal illness or injury 53 LCUs. Holmes and Rahe suggested that by adding the number of LCUs it should be possible to assess the severity of stress a person has experienced over a given period of time.

As you might expect, in the Holmes and Rahe scale the most stressful events are unpleasant ones. However, note that some of the stressful events on the scale are actually pleasant. For example, outstanding personal achievement is assigned 28 LCUs; a vacation receives 13 LCUs. In other words, within limits the critical fact is not whether a life change is pleasant or unpleasant, but whether the life change requires change and adjustment. Some pleasant events (such as going on vacation) can cause just as many adjustive demands and be just as stressful as some unpleasant events (such as minor violations of the law).

**Life Change Unit (LCU):** quantitative measure of the stressfulness of events on the Social Readjustment Rating Scale

**TABLE 3.1    The Social Readjustment Rating Scale**

| Events | Scale of Impact (LCUs) | Events | Scale of Impact (LCUs) |
|---|---|---|---|
| Death of spouse | 100 | Change in responsibilities at work | 29 |
| Divorce | 73 | Son or daughter leaving home | 29 |
| Marital separation | 65 | Trouble with in-laws | 29 |
| Jail term | 63 | Outstanding personal achievement | 28 |
| Death of close family member | 63 | Spouse begins or stops work | 26 |
| Personal injury or illness | 53 | Begin or end school | 26 |
| Marriage | 50 | Change in living conditions | 25 |
| Fired at work | 47 | Revision of personal habits | 24 |
| Marital reconciliation | 45 | Trouble with boss | 23 |
| Retirement | 45 | Change in work hours or conditions | 20 |
| Change in health of family member | 44 | Change in residence | 20 |
| Pregnancy | 40 | Change in schools | 20 |
| Sex difficulties | 39 | Change in recreation | 19 |
| Business readjustment | 39 | Change in church activities | 19 |
| Change in financial state | 38 | Change in social activities | 18 |
| Death of close friend | 37 | Mortgage or loan less than $10,000 | 17 |
| Change to different line of work | 36 | Change in sleeping habits | 16 |
| Change in number of arguments with spouse | 35 | Change in number of family get-togethers | 15 |
| | | Change in eating habits | 15 |
| Mortgage over $10,000 | 31 | Vacation | 13 |
| Foreclosure of mortgage or loan | 30 | Minor violations of the law | 11 |
| Gain of new family member | 30 | | |

Source: Holmes & Holmes, 1970

While the SRRS has attracted a good deal of attention, it is not without critics. We have seen that there are many sources of stress. Significant life changes such as those on the SRRS are only one source of stress, and so the SRRS by itself can provide only a crude estimate of the stress that any person may have experienced over a period of time. Moreover, Lefcourt et al. (1981) have suggested that positive events (such as marriage or marital reconciliation) may be less stressful than negative events with roughly the same number of LCUs (such as personal injury and being fired). In addition, Brim and Ryff (1980) have suggested that the SRRS excludes lots of important, but less dramatic, stressful life events such as being "trapped" in an unsatisfactory marriage, dealing with adolescent children, and trying to balance career and family obligations.

Finally, as we will see shortly, it is important to consider the ways in which important life events are perceived and the meaning of those events for the person experiencing them; for example, some people may find getting divorced less stressful than getting married, although divorce has more LCUs than marriage on the SRRS. (See Psychology in Action, pp. 86–88, for an improved life-stress scale that attempts to respond to these criticisms.)

The SRRS also fails to account for stress due to technological change in the world around us. The past three decades have seen the introduction of microcomputers and video cassette recorders, laser surgery and microwave ovens, cellular telephones and cable TV, space stations and the landing of astronauts on the moon. The tax laws keep changing, prices keep rising, and the number of choices we face when buying products seems to increase every year. Moreover, the rate and pervasiveness of change today are different from anything our ancestors experienced. Just trying to keep up with these changes can be a source of considerable stress. Too much change and we are in danger of "overloading" our adaptive circuits, something Toffler (1970, 1980) called **future shock**.

**future shock:** stress produced by rapid, accelerating technological, social, and cultural change

## Self-imposed Stress

So far we have explored stress arising from environmental events or stressors. However, in some cases people impose stress on themselves in the absence of real stressors. Psychologist Albert Ellis has suggested that many people experience unnecessary stress because they have irrational beliefs about themselves and other people (Ellis & Harper, 1975). Because these beliefs are irrational and unreasonable, they are the source of considerable stress even in the absence of environmental stressors. Following are some of the most widespread of these irrational beliefs.

*It is essential to be loved or approved by almost everyone for everything I do.* Ellis does not mean that we should not want to be loved or approved by others. Rather, he is referring to the irrational belief held by some people that they must always be loved and approved by everyone important to them. For such people, any sign of disapproval is a source of stress.

*I must be competent, adequate, and successful at everything I do.* Some people believe that if they are not excellent at everything, then they are total failures. Their confidence is tied to their accomplishments: if they succeed, they believe that they are worthwhile as human beings; if they fail, they believe they are worthless. Therefore, any sign of failure is a threat and is likely to cause considerable stress.

*People behaving badly are bad people who deserve to be blamed and punished.* According to this view, people acting inappropriately or making mistakes deserve to be blamed for their errors: if a person's behavior is undesirable or immoral, then the person is not worthy of respect. People sharing this belief must be constantly on guard to ensure that they never behave badly or make a mistake, lest they too become unworthy and deserving of blame and punishment. The result is a great deal of unnecessary stress.

*It is disastrous if everything doesn't happen as I would like.* Some people believe it is the end of the world if things don't work out as they wish. As a result, they feel unhappy, upset, and generally miserable if things go badly or if they are frustrated. One way people avoid these unpleasant feelings is by attempting to ensure that everything will always happen as they want it to happen. However, this is an unrealistic, impossible goal that simply increases stress.

*People have little or no control over unpleasant emotions.* According to this belief, people are depressed, angry, or upset by events that are outside of their control. If someone says we are incompetent or inconsiderate then we have no choice but

# *Psychology in Action*

## The Life Experiences Survey

The following questionnaire was developed by Irwin Sarason and his colleagues at the University of Washington as an alternative to the Holmes & Rahe scale (Sarason, Johnson, & Siegel, 1978). It lists a number of life events people likely will experience in the course of a year, but space is provided for you to add other events that were especially important in your life in the past year. For each event, indicate whether the event had a beneficial or detrimental effect on you and how strong the impact was. Thus, this questionnaire attempts to take into account individual differences in life experiences and that similar events may be experienced differently by different people.

If you would like to assess the impact of recent changes in your own life, for each event on the list which you experienced in the past year circle the number that best represents the impact of the event on your life at the time it occurred. For example, if an event had an extremely negative impact on your life at the time it occurred, circle the number "−3" to the right of the item; if an event had a moderately positive impact, circle "+2"; and so on. If an event didn't occur at all in your life during the past year, don't circle any number for that item. Space is provided at the end of the questionnaire for you to list a few additional events that impacted on your life in the last year but that do not appear elsewhere on the questionnaire.

When you have finished, add up all the positive numbers that you circled; this is your *positive life change score*. Do the same for the negative numbers you circled to get your *negative life change score*. Then add the two totals to get a *total life change score* (ignore the negative sign on the negative life change score). For example, a positive change score of 8 and a negative change score of 6 would add up to a total change score of 14. For comparison, in one group of college students studied by Sarason and his colleagues in the mid-1970's, the average total score was between 16 and 17; about two-thirds of the students had total life change scores between 6 and 27, which is a moderate amount of life change.

| | extremely negative | moderately negative | somewhat negative | no impact | slightly positive | moderately positive | extremely positive |
|---|---|---|---|---|---|---|---|
| 1. Marriage | −3 | −2 | −1 | 0 | +1 | +2 | +3 |
| 2. Detention in jail or comparable institution | −3 | −2 | −1 | 0 | +1 | +2 | +3 |
| 3. Death of spouse | −3 | −2 | −1 | 0 | +1 | +2 | +3 |
| 4. Major change in sleeping habits (much more or much less sleep) | −3 | −2 | −1 | 0 | +1 | +2 | +3 |
| 5. Death of close family member: | | | | | | | |
| a. mother | −3 | −2 | −1 | 0 | +1 | +2 | +3 |
| b. father | −3 | −2 | −1 | 0 | +1 | +2 | +3 |
| c. brother | −3 | −2 | −1 | 0 | +1 | +2 | +3 |
| d. sister | −3 | −2 | −1 | 0 | +1 | +2 | +3 |
| e. grandmother | −3 | −2 | −1 | 0 | +1 | +2 | +3 |
| f. grandfather | −3 | −2 | −1 | 0 | +1 | +2 | +3 |
| g. other (specify) | −3 | −2 | −1 | 0 | +1 | +2 | +3 |
| 6. Major change in eating habits (much more or much less food intake) | −3 | −2 | −1 | 0 | +1 | +2 | +3 |
| 7. Foreclosure on mortgage or loan | −3 | −2 | −1 | 0 | +1 | +2 | +3 |
| 8. Death of close friend | −3 | −2 | −1 | 0 | +1 | +2 | +3 |
| 9. Outstanding personal achievement | −3 | −2 | −1 | 0 | +1 | +2 | +3 |

### The Life Experiences Survey   (continued)

| | extremely negative | moderately negative | somewhat negative | no impact | slightly positive | moderately positive | extremely positive |
|---|---|---|---|---|---|---|---|
| 10. Minor law violations (traffic tickets, disturbing the peace, etc.) | −3 | −2 | −1 | 0 | +1 | +2 | +3 |
| 11. *Male*: Wife/girlfriend's pregnancy | −3 | −2 | −1 | 0 | (+1) | +2 | +3 |
| 12. *Female*: Pregnancy | −3 | −2 | −1 | 0 | +1 | +2 | +3 |
| 13. Changed work situation (different work responsibility, major change in working conditions, working hours, etc.) | −3 | −2 | −1 | 0 | +1 | +2 | +3 |
| 14. New job | −3 | −2 | −1 | 0 | +1 | +2 | +3 |
| 15. Serious illness or injury of close family member: | | | | | | | |
| a. father | −3 | −2 | −1 | 0 | +1 | +2 | +3 |
| b. mother | −3 | −2 | −1 | 0 | +1 | +2 | +3 |
| c. sister | −3 | −2 | −1 | 0 | +1 | +2 | +3 |
| d. brother | −3 | −2 | −1 | 0 | +1 | +2 | +3 |
| e. grandfather | −3 | −2 | −1 | 0 | +1 | +2 | +3 |
| f. grandmother | −3 | −2 | −1 | 0 | +1 | +2 | +3 |
| g. spouse | −3 | −2 | −1 | 0 | +1 | +2 | +3 |
| h. other (specify) | −3 | −2 | −1 | 0 | +1 | +2 | +3 |
| 16. Sexual difficulties | −3 | −2 | −1 | 0 | +1 | +2 | +3 |
| 17. Trouble with employer (in danger of losing job, being suspended, demoted, etc.) | −3 | −2 | −1 | 0 | +1 | +2 | +3 |
| 18. Trouble with in-laws | −3 | −2 | −1 | 0 | +1 | +2 | +3 |
| 19. Major change in financial status (a lot better off or a lot worse off) | −3 | −2 | −1 | 0 | +1 | +2 | +3 |
| 20. Major change in closeness of family members (increased or decreased closeness) | −3 | −2 | −1 | 0 | +1 | +2 | +3 |
| 21. Gaining a new family member (through birth, adoption, family member moving in, etc.) | −3 | −2 | −1 | 0 | +1 | +2 | +3 |
| 22. Change of residence | −3 | −2 | −1 | 0 | +1 | +2 | +3 |
| 23. Marital separation from mate (due to conflict) | −3 | −2 | −1 | 0 | +1 | +2 | +3 |
| 24. Major change in church activities (increased or decreased attendance) | −3 | −2 | −1 | 0 | +1 | +2 | +3 |
| 25. Marital reconciliation with mate | −3 | −2 | −1 | 0 | +1 | +2 | +3 |
| 26. Major change in number of arguments with spouse (a lot more or a lot less arguments) | −3 | −2 | −1 | 0 | +1 | +2 | +3 |
| 27. *Married male*: Change in wife's work outside the home (beginning work, ceasing work, changing to a new job, etc.) | −3 | −2 | −1 | 0 | +1 | +2 | +3 |
| 28. *Married female*: Change in husband's work (loss of job, beginning new job, retirement, etc.) | −3 | −2 | −1 | 0 | +1 | +2 | +3 |
| 29. Major change in usual type and/or amount of recreation | −3 | −2 | −1 | 0 | +1 | (+2) | +3 |

## The Life Experiences Survey   (continued)

| | extremely negative | moderately negative | somewhat negative | no impact | slightly positive | moderately positive | extremely positive |
|---|---|---|---|---|---|---|---|
| 30. Borrowing more than $10,000 (buying home, business, etc.) | −3 | −2 | −1 | 0 | +1 | +2 | +3 |
| 31. Borrowing less than $10,000 (buying car, TV, getting school loan, etc.) | −3 | −2 | −1 | 0 | +1 | +2 | +3 |
| 32. Being fired from job | −3 | −2 | −1 | 0 | +1 | +2 | +3 |
| 33. *Male:* Wife/girlfriend having abortion | −3 | −2 | −1 | 0 | +1 | +2 | +3 |
| 34. *Female:* Having abortion | −3 | −2 | −1 | 0 | +1 | +2 | +3 |
| 35. Major personal illness or injury | −3 | −2 | −1 | 0 | +1 | +2 | +3 |
| 36. Major change in social activities, e.g., parties, movies, visiting (increased or decreased participation) | −3 | −2 | −1 | 0 | +1 | +2 | +3 |
| 37. Major change in living conditions of family (building new home, remodeling, deterioration of home, neighborhood, etc.) | −3 | −2 | −1 | 0 | +1 | +2 | +3 |
| 38. Divorce | −3 | −2 | −1 | 0 | +1 | +2 | +3 |
| 39. Serious injury or illness of close friend | −3 | −2 | −1 | 0 | +1 | +2 | +3 |
| 40. Retirement from work | −3 | −2 | −1 | 0 | +1 | +2 | +3 |
| 41. Son or daughter leaving home (due to marriage, college, etc.) | −3 | −2 | −1 | 0 | +1 | +2 | +3 |
| 42. Ending of formal schooling | −3 | −2 | −1 | 0 | (+1) | +2 | +3 |
| 43. Separation from spouse (due to work, travel, etc.) | −3 | −2 | −1 | 0 | +1 | +2 | +3 |
| 44. Engagement | −3 | −2 | −1 | 0 | +1 | +2 | +3 |
| 45. Breaking up with boyfriend/girlfriend | −3 | −2 | (−1) | 0 | +1 | +2 | +3 |
| 46. Leaving home for the first time | −3 | −2 | −1 | 0 | (+1) | +2 | +3 |
| 47. Reconciliation with boyfriend/girlfriend | −3 | −2 | −1 | 0 | +1 | +2 | +3 |
| 48. Beginning a new school experience at a higher academic level (college, graduate school, professional school, etc.) | −3 | −2 | −1 | 0 | +1 | (+2) | +3 |
| 49. Changing to a new school at same academic level (undergraduate, graduate, etc.) | −3 | −2 | −1 | 0 | +1 | +2 | +3 |
| 50. Academic probation | −3 | −2 | (−1) | 0 | +1 | +2 | +3 |
| 51. Being dismissed from dormitory or other residence | −3 | −2 | −1 | 0 | +1 | +2 | +3 |
| 52. Failing an important exam | −3 | −2 | −1 | 0 | +1 | +2 | +3 |
| 53. Changing a major | −3 | −2 | −1 | 0 | +1 | +2 | +3 |
| 54. Failing a course | −3 | −2 | −1 | 0 | +1 | +2 | +3 |
| 55. Dropping a course | −3 | −2 | −1 | 0 | +1 | +2 | +3 |
| 56. Joining a fraternity/sorority | −3 | −2 | −1 | 0 | +1 | +2 | +3 |
| 57. Financial problems concerning school (in danger of not having sufficient money to continue) | −3 | −2 | −1 | 0 | +1 | +2 | +3 |

*Other recent experiences which have had an impact on your life. List and rate.*

| | | | | | | | |
|---|---|---|---|---|---|---|---|
| 58. ___ *death of Pet* ___ | −3 | (−2) | −1 | 0 | +1 | +2 | +3 |
| 59. _____ | −3 | −2 | −1 | 0 | +1 | +2 | +3 |
| 60. _____ | −3 | −2 | −1 | 0 | +1 | +2 | +3 |

to feel hurt, depressed, and upset. It follows, then, that if we feel unhappy, depressed, or hurt, there is nothing we can do about it. As a result, we are likely to spend our lives often feeling unhappy and upset, and these negative emotions contribute to the stress we experience.

*If something unpleasant might happen in the future, I must dwell on it and worry about it as much as possible.* Certainly unpleasant things do happen: sometimes people forget their lines when speaking in public; sometimes hotel reservations get lost; sometimes tax audits result in additional taxes and penalties. In each case, it is prudent to take steps to reduce the chances that disaster will strike, but once those precautions have been taken, further worry is unlikely to be productive. However, some people become overly worried and upset about what might go wrong; they imagine the worst, become preoccupied by the possibility that something terrible might happen, and in the process they make a potentially difficult situation even more stressful than necessary.

*It is better to avoid dealing with problems and to take the easy way out.* According to this irrational belief, the easiest way out is likely to be the best way out; if we avoid facing and dealing with problems, then perhaps they will disappear or solve themselves. Unfortunately, few serious problems solve themselves, and the easiest way out is not always the best. Avoiding problems tends to perpetuate the problems, making them into continuing sources of stress.

*The effects of past experience cannot be overcome.* People who share this view believe that because something was once, it must always be. If they have been unpopular in the past, they must always be unpopular; if they have been passed over for promotion in the past, they will continue to be passed over; if they have had marital problems in the past, their marriage must always be troubled. People who share these beliefs spend little time and energy seeking better solutions to problems or developing new skills and competencies. As a result, they unintentionally prolong stressful situations.

*It is catastrophic if I do not find the perfect solution to my problems.* It is unlikely that there is a perfect or ideal solution to most of life's problems. Therefore, people who fail to do anything about their problems until they discover a perfect solution are likely to wait for a very long time and experience a great deal of unnecessary stress.

As Ellis suggests, to a great extent people create their own problems and stresses by thinking in irrational ways. Added to the frustrations, conflicts, and pressures occurring in the external environment, these irrational beliefs increase the stress with which people must cope.

Ellis is not alone in seeing irrational thoughts as a basis for a great deal of unnecessary distress. Beck (1976) looks for the roots of depression in distorted thinking. In his view, depressed people often dwell on their bad experiences and overlook the good things. They also assume that their failings result from their own shortcomings, even in those cases when they were not at fault. Freud, too, pointed out how irrational beliefs (usually stemming from childhood) can create much adult misery. For example, many children in our society develop the mistaken belief that to be loved by their parents, they must be superachievers. As adults they torment themselves when they believe that they are not "the best." Psychologists counseling college students sometimes encounter this problem when bright, capable students become extremely depressed because their grade-point average drops from a perfect 4.0 to a less-than-perfect 3.95.

So far we have discussed the most important sources of stress in most people's lives. However, why are some situations more stressful than others? Why do some people find a situation very stressful while other people in the same situation experience little or no stress? The next section of the chapter considers these questions.

## FACTORS INFLUENCING THE SEVERITY OF STRESS

Some stress is minor and inconsequential, while other stress poses a serious threat to our well-being and survival. In cases of mild stress, adjustive action is usually simple and the individual is only slightly threatened. In moderate stress, proportionately greater demands are imposed on us, and adjustive action may be difficult. In cases of extreme stress, our adaptive capacities are likely to be overtaxed, and physical or psychological breakdown may occur. Thus, we may think of the severity of stress as a continuum varying from mild through moderate to excessive stress.

The severity of stress in any situation is determined primarily by three factors: (1) the characteristics of the adjustive demand; (2) the characteristics of the individual; and (3) the social support available to the individual. Let's examine each of the factors in more detail.

### Characteristics of the Adjustive Demand

Earlier in the chapter, we noted that life events require different amounts of readjustment. For example, postponing a trip to the movies is less stressful than breaking off an engagement. Similarly, failing the bar exam is likely to be more stressful than performing poorly on a surprise quiz. In addition to these inherent differences between various events, however, the severity of stress is also influenced by the number, duration, predictability, and imminence of the adjustive demands that confront us at any moment.

**Number.**    As the number of adjustive demands increases, so does the severity of the stress a person experiences (Holmes & Rahe, 1967). For example, consider the situation in which an individual must cope with a promotion, increased responsibilities at work, a deteriorating marriage, and a burglarized apartment. If these events occurred one at a time, the individual might have more adequate resources for dealing with them. However, if they occur simultaneously, the individual might be unable to cope effectively.

**Duration.**    The duration of the adjustive demand clearly affects the severity of stress. If we have a minor disagreement with a friend, the dispute usually lasts no more than a few hours or days and it is simply a small problem. However, should the dispute go on months or even years, as in the case of bickering marital partners, the stress can become quite severe. Similarly, we might be able to function reasonably

*Every job has its own particular type of stress, and that stress includes both physical and emotional manifestations.*

well in a short-term crisis situation at work or at home, but if the crisis becomes a routine part of each day, our ability to deal with the adjustive demand may diminish.

**Predictability.**   Our ability to deal successfully with stress is also related to our ability to foresee or predict future events. For example, a natural catastrophe such as an earthquake strains our adjustive capacity in part because it is so unexpected. On a more individual level, unpredictable events such as an automobile accident can have devastating effects because we cannot anticipate them.

However, some adjustive demands can be predicted. Individuals who plan for future stress usually find themselves better able to cope with the stress that does arise. For example, workers who plan for retirement by developing hobbies, good health habits, and sound financial planning usually find retirement much more enjoyable and less stressful than individuals who shift from work to retirement without any advance preparation (O'Brien, 1981).

**Imminence.**   Anticipating an adjustive demand is itself stressful, particularly as the event comes closer in time. Thinking about one's forthcoming marriage or the arrival of a child is less stressful six months before the event than one week before the

# Psychology in Action

## The Effect of Exam Anxiety on Grandma's Health

Examination time can be a source of considerable stress, as reflected in this delightful excerpt from an article by John J. Chiodo of Clarion University.

I entered the ranks of academe as well prepared as the next fellow, but I was still unaware of the threat that midterm exams posed to the health and welfare of students and their relatives. It didn't take long, however, for me to realize that a real problem existed. The onset of midterms seemed to provoke not only a marked increase in the family problems, illnesses, and accidents experienced by my students, but also above-normal death rates among their grandmothers.

In my first semester of teaching, during the week before the midterm exam, I got numerous phone calls and visits from the roommates of many of my students, reporting a series of problems. Mononucleosis seemed to have struck a sizable portion of my class, along with the more common colds and flu.

A call from one young woman awakened me with the news that her roommate's grandmother had died, so she (my student) would be unable to take the exam. I expressed my condolences, and assured the caller that her roommate would not be penalized for such an unexpected tragedy.

Over the next few days I received many more calls—informing me of sickness, family problems, and even the death of a beloved cat. But the thought of three grandmothers passing away, all within the short exam period, caused me a good deal of remorse. but the term soon ended and, with the Christmas break and preparations for the new semester, I forgot all about the midterm problem.

Eight weeks into the second semester, however, I was once again faced with a succession of visits or phone calls from roommates about sick students, family problems, and, yes, the deaths of more grandmothers. I was shaken. I could understand that dorm meals and late nights, along with "exam anxiety," might well make some students sick, but what could account for the grandmothers? Once again, though, other things occupied my mind, and before long I had stopped thinking about it.

I moved that summer to a large Midwestern university, where I had to reconstruct my teaching plans to fit the quarter system. I taught three classes. By the end of the first midterm exams two of my student's grandmothers had died; by the time the year was over, a total of five had gone to their reward.

I began to realize the situation was serious. In the

---

event. As the following passage from Mechanic (1962) illustrates, the same is true of students approaching exam time.

> As the examinations approached and as student anxiety increased, various changes occurred in behavior. Joking increased, and while students still sought social support and talked a great deal about examinations, they began specifically to avoid certain people who aroused their anxiety. Stomach aches, asthma, and a general feeling of weariness became common complaints, and other psychosomatic symptoms appeared. The use of tranquilizers and sleeping pills became more frequent.
>
> When the examinations are nearly upon the student, anxiety is very high, even for those rated as low-anxiety persons, although students do fluctuate between confidence and anxiety. Since studying is difficult, the student questions his motivations, interest, and ability in the field. (pp. 142, 144)

(See the Psychology in Action on pp. 92–93 for a somewhat different perspective on the stressfulness of exam time.)

### The Effect of Exam Anxiety on Grandma's Health   (continued)

two years I had been teaching, 12 grandmothers had passed away; on that basis, if I taught for 30 years 180 grandmothers would no longer be with us. I hated to think what the universitywide number would be.

I tried to figure out the connection. Was it because grandmothers are hypersensitive to a grandchild's problems? When they see their grandchildren suffering from exam anxiety do they become anxious too? Does the increased stress then cause stroke or heart failure? It seemed possible; so it followed that if grandmothers' anxiety levels could be lowered, a good number of their lives might be prolonged. I didn't have much direct contact with grandmothers, but I reasoned that by moderating the anxiety of my students, I could help reduce stress on their grandmothers.

With that in mind, I began my next year of teaching. On the first day of class, while passing out the syllabus, I told my students how concerned I was about the high incidence of grandmother mortality. I also told them what I thought we could do about it.

To make a long story short, the results of my plan to reduce student anxiety were spectacular. At the end of the quarter there had not been one test-related death of a grandmother. In addition, the amount of sickness and family strife had decreased dramatically. The next

two quarters proved to be even better. Since then, I have refined my anxiety-reduction system and, in the interest of grandmotherly longevity, would like to share it with my colleagues. Here are the basic rules:

- Review the scope of the exam.
- Use practice tests.
- Be clear about time limits.
- Announce what materials will be needed and what aids will be permitted.
- Review the grading procedure.
- Review the policies on makeup tests and retakes.
- Provide study help.
- Make provision for last-minute questions.
- Allow for breaks during long exams.
- Coach students on test-taking techniques.

I have been following these rules for 13 years now, and during that time have heard of only an occasional midterm-related death of a grandmother. Such results lead me to believe that if all faculty members did likewise, the health and welfare of students—and their grandmothers—would surely benefit.

## Characteristics of the Individual

Situations that one person finds very stressful may be only mildly stressful or not stressful at all for another. Some people relish the opportunity to talk with strangers at a party, while others react with tongue-tied panic in the same situation. The differences are due to three factors: situations mean different things to different people, people's past experience with and perceived control over situations differ, and some people are more easily stressed than others. Let's look at each of these individual characteristics and their effect on the severity of stress.

**Meaning of the situation for the individual.**   We saw earlier that one of the criticisms of the SRRS scale is that the same stressor may have very different meanings for different people. Even though a stressor has a particular LCU value, its impact will differ depending on how each individual perceives it. For example, pregnancy carries 40 LCUs on the Holmes & Rahe scale. However, pregnancy is likely to have

*Childhood games frequently get out of control, someone gets hurt, and the happy playfulness dissolves into confusion and stress.*

a different impact on the woman than on her husband, and it certainly has a different impact on a couple who is eager to have children than on a couple who does not want more children. Being fired carries 47 LCUs, but its impact is likely to be much greater on the person with no other job options than on the person who has been dissatisfied with the job and who has other job opportunities. As we saw earlier, the life stress scale on pages 86–88 is designed to emphasize that a particular stressor can mean quite different things to different people.

However, the matter is even more complex: the same event may have *multiple* meanings even for a single person. If you hope to be promoted to a new job and you receive a bad performance evaluation from your present supervisor, you are likely to experience a good deal of stress. However, if you have mixed feelings about being promoted—perhaps it would mean a move to another city or you are unsure of your ability to supervise other people—you may actually feel both relieved and distressed: you don't like to be evaluated poorly, but now you don't have to face the prospect of being promoted in the immediate future. Therefore, any fully adequate life stress questionnnaire would need to take all these additional meanings into consideration when rating the stressfulness of events.

Complicating matters further is Freud's assertion that people are not always aware of all the additional meanings that events may have for them. What if you don't fully realize, for example, that a poor performance evaluation will be terribly threatening to you? In this case, if you receive such an evaluation you are likely to experience a great deal of stress without fully understanding why. Also, the stress you experience is likely to be far greater than anyone would have expected based on your answers to the SRRS or similar self-report measures (Paulhus, 1984, 1986). In other words, not only do stressful events mean different things to different people, but we may not always be aware of all the ways in which an event may affect us.

**Prior experience and sense of control.**   Prior experience also affects the severity of stress in new situations. For instance, familiar situations are less likely to be stressful than unfamiliar situations; if the situation is familiar, the person at least has some guidelines for attempting to deal with it. Consider the problems facing an individual going to a job interview. If this is the person's first interview, the situation may seem overwhelming. It can be difficult to know how to dress, how to behave, and what to expect. For these reasons a person without prior experience in job interviews will more likely find the situation stressful than someone who has had numerous interviews, even if those interviews were not always successful.

Of course, success in coping with similar situations in the past is a tremendous help in reducing the severity of stress when the situation occurs again (Hunt, 1964; Murphy & Moriarty, 1976). White (1976) suggested that successful coping leads to a sense of competence, which contributes to feelings of confidence and self-esteem in similar situations in the future. In situations where we feel competent to act, where we have a sense of control, we are likely to experience less stress than the person feeling less competent and having less sense of control. In contrast, when we feel helpless in a situation, our ability to cope effectively with the situation diminishes as well (Bandura, 1982b).

The relationship between control over an event and the stressfulness of that event was explored in a series of experiments by Martin Seligman and his colleagues (Seligman, 1975; Maier, 1987). In a typical experiment, they would expose an animal to mild shock that could be turned off by pressing a bar or turning a wheel. In such a situation, the animals quickly learned what to do to terminate the shock. By itself, this is not especially surprising! However, while the first animal was learning, a second animal was hooked up to the same shock machine so it was shocked every time the learning animal received a shock. The only difference was that this second animal could do nothing to end the shock; it had to wait for the first animal to press the lever or turn the wheel. In other words, both animals received exactly the same number of shocks during the course of the experiment; however, one animal could stop the shock and the other animal could not.

The experimenters found that the two kinds of animals behaved quite differently in future experiments: animals unable to control the shock in the first experiment seemed to be unable to learn that they could control shocks in future experiments; when put in a setting where they could terminate shocks by pressing a bar or turning a wheel, they never learned what to do. Moreover, the animals didn't even try to escape from the setting; they just passively endured the shock until the experimenter turned it off. These animals also became generally less aggressive and more sub-missive when around other animals, they developed more ulcers, and they suffered more weight loss than the animals able to control the shock. In short, the animals unable to control the shocks seemed to experience more stress than those that could control the shock, and their stressful experiences had a long-term effect on their ability to cope effectively in the future.

Interestingly, another set of experiments shows that our ability to control a stressful situation is not as important as our *belief* or perception that we have control over the situation. David Glass and Jerome Singer (1972) created a situation in which people were exposed to loud, unpredictable bursts of urban noise. Some people were told the noise was unavoidable; other people were told they could throw a switch to stop the noise. As measured by various bodily reactions, the subjects who had access to the switch but didn't use it nonetheless experienced much less stress than the subjects without such a switch. In other words, their *belief* that they could control the noise reduced the stressfulness of hearing the noise, even if they never exercised the control! Moreover, these same subjects tolerated frustration much better in a follow-up experiment than did the subjects with no control over the noise. From these and other experiments, we can conclude that individuals believing that stress is to some extent under their personal control are less likely to be affected by stressors and are more likely to cope effectively with those stressors than individuals believing that stress is outside their control (Geer, Davison & Gatchel, 1970; Phares, 1984).

A study by Suzanne Kobasa (1979) demonstrates nicely how past experience, a sense of competence, and a sense of control can combine to increase a person's stress tolerance. Kobasa studied a group of executives exposed to equally stressful life events over a three-year period (as judged by the Holmes & Rahe scale). One group became ill as a result of their experiences, but the second group (whom she called "hardy executives") did not, even though they had apparently been exposed to just as much life stress. What accounted for the difference?

The hardy executives seemed to have a clearer sense of their own values, goals, and capabilities, and they tended to become actively involved with their environment. They also interpreted the events in ways that helped to minimize the stress they experienced; the events had a different meaning for them than for the less hardy executives. The hardy executives also believed that they determined, to a large extent, whether the consequences of the events would be good or bad. While they may or may not have been able to do anything about the occurrence of the stressors, they *felt* that they controlled the impact that the events would have on their lives and the lives of their families. By interpreting the events in a less stressful way and by relying on a sense of personal competence and control over the situation, the hardy executives were able to reduce significantly the severity of the stress they experienced.

**Personality characteristics.** Meyer Friedman and Ray Rosenman (1974) have identified two different life styles that appear to influence the severity of stress different people experience. One style, **Type A,** is characteristic of the individual who is rushed and hurried. Speech is quick and abrupt. Walking and eating are done quickly. The Type A individual finds it difficult to relax and do nothing, is competitive even in noncompetitive situations, is overly concerned with not having enough time to complete tasks, and is impatient with others and intolerant of slowness. Moreover, many Type A individuals are quick to become hostile and aggressive (Booth-Kewley & Friedman, 1987; Matthews, 1988). We will discuss in the next chapter the effect of this life style on people's health.

**Type A behavior:** life style characterized by an emphasis on speed, competitiveness, and aggressiveness

The Type A individual corresponds to our image of the hard-driving, achievement-oriented, and status-conscious individual. In contrast, the **Type B** individual is easy-going, relaxed, patient, and tolerant. The Type B individual does not boast about accomplishments, feels little time pressure, does one thing at a time, and generally takes things less seriously than does a Type A person (Rosenman, Friedman, Strauss, Wurm, Jenkins, & Messinger, 1966; Yarnold & Grimm, 1982) (see Psychology in Action, p. 97).

**Type B behavior:** life style characterized by tolerance, relaxation, and lack of time pressure

## Type A versus Type B Personality Test

The following questions can help you to determine whether you are more like a Type A or a Type B personality. Answer each question by writing a number from the following list in the space provided next to each question:

**5** Very true of me          **4** Usually true of me          **3** Sometimes true of me

**2** Seldom true of me          **1** Never true of me

<u>4</u> I often try to do several things at the same time.
<u>3</u> I often interrupt people when they are talking or try to hurry them by finishing their sentences for them.
<u>3</u> I find it irritating when someone does a job slowly or inefficiently.
<u>2</u> While people talk to me, I often think of something else (such as solving a problem) while I listen to them.
<u>2</u> I usually become uncomfortable when I don't have anything to do.
<u>3</u> I get frustrated when people take a long time getting to the point they are trying to make.
<u>3</u> I tend to do most things quickly (walking, eating, speaking).
<u>2</u> I get impatient when things move slowly (traffic jams, long lines).
<u>1</u> I find it hard just to relax and do nothing.
<u>5</u> I usually set deadlines and schedules for myself.
<u>3</u> When I play games (cards, board games), it is more important for me to win than to have fun.
<u>2</u> When I am emphasizing a point, I become tense and tend to raise my voice.
<u>2</u> I prefer that people around me do things as quickly and efficiently as possible.
<u>3</u> I accentuate key words when I speak.
<u>4</u> I am a hard-driving and competitive person who values achievement and success.

When you are done, add up the numbers you entered for the fifteen items. Your total score should be between 15 and 75. A score of 60 or higher suggests that your lifestyle corresponds closely to a Type A lifestyle; a score of 30 or lower suggests that your lifestyle is quite a lot like that of Type B persons. A score between 30 and 60 suggests that your lifestyle is a moderate blend of Type A and Type B styles.

Interestingly, some recent research shows that differences between Type A and Type B individuals are evident even in children as young as three years old. In one study (Brown & Tanner, 1988), teachers of 144 children enrolled in a preschool program were asked to rate the children on the extent to which they showed Type A behavior. The children were then taught a relaxation exercise, after which they played a mildly stressful memory game. Throughout the experiment, the children's blood pressure was monitored. Type A children showed normal blood pressure during the relaxation exercise; they seemed to be just as relaxed as the other children during this game. However, during the memory game, their blood pressure became much higher than that of the non-Type A children, suggesting that the Type A children found the memory test more stressful than did the other children. Brown and Tanner are now following the children in an effort to determine whether the

Type A children grow up to become Type A adults, and to see whether it is possible to change their Type A life style in view of the detrimental effect it may have on their health later in life.

## Social Support Available to the Individual

In the last decade it has become increasingly clear that relationships with other people can help us by buffering the effects of stressful situations (Cohen & McKay, 1984; Kessler et al., 1985; Cohen, 1988). People having close relationships with others seem to be able to withstand stressful events better than those without such social support. The death of a family member can be less stressful if family and friends gather around to provide emotional support, to help us make the necessary decisions, and to share our grief. Loss of a job can be made more tolerable if we can count on the emotional support of family and friends. Simply the support of family and friends is often enough to help us weather difficult times, but friends also can provide suggestions and encouragement, tactful and sympathetic advice, agreement with our thoughts and feelings, and an opportunity to "ventilate" our feelings and concerns in a safe environment. Brown and Harris (1978), for example, studied a group of women experiencing significant stress. Almost 40 percent of the women without some kind of close, intimate social relationship became depressed; only 4 percent of the women able to draw upon social support became depressed.

However, the apparent relationship between social support and effective coping may not be a matter of simple cause and effect. While it certainly makes sense that social support can ease stress, it is also possible that people who can effectively manage their stress are also more likely to maintain durable and gratifying inter-personal relationships. In studies of both cases, the data would show that people with strong social relationships experience less stress, but the explanation of the data produced by each study would be quite different. For example, one woman who sought therapy was undergoing a divorce and was deeply depressed. All she seemed able to experience was hopelessness and anger. She also had very few lasting relationships with friends, but she was isolated because when she became upset she would either lash out at her friends or withdraw from them. During the divorce, in fact, her two closest friends offered their support, but she withdrew from them saying that she "had to handle it alone."

In this case, and in many others, social support, coping resources, and personality style are tightly interwoven: people need social support to help them through difficult times, but their personality and coping styles sometimes prevent them from keeping friends or from making use of those who do come to their aid. For example, in one recent study of adolescent girls, the researchers found that girls who had unsatis-factory relationships with their mothers—and who could therefore benefit most from close friendships outside the home—also were the girls who found it most difficult to develop such close friendships (Gold & Yanof, 1985).

## POSITIVE STRESS

We have focused so far on the negative side of stress, but, as we noted at the beginning of the chapter, not all stress is harmful or negative. Some stress can be useful and beneficial. In fact, to say "no" to all forms of stress is to say "no" to life.

As Hans Selye (1980) put it, "Complete freedom from stress is death" (p. 128). Positive stress, or *eustress,* can take a variety of forms. For example, active participation in sports or exercise programs, vacations and trips, and mastery of new academic or practical skills can be sources of eustress. In fact almost any adjustive demand can be a source of eustress, as long as it is approached with a sense of zest, anticipation, and competence.

Marvin Zuckerman (1978, 1979) has discovered that there are some people who actively seek out dangerous and risky situations, new experiences, and other sources of stimulation. Such "sensation seekers," as he calls them, seem to thrive on change, thrills, novelty, and challenges that others would probably find stressful. For example, they enjoy such risky activities as flying, parachute jumping, and mountain climbing; they would rather get lost exploring a strange city than use a guide; they look forward to changing jobs from time to time to avoid getting into a rut; they seek out friends who are somewhat unpredictable and unstable, and enjoy heated arguments even if people become upset by them. Clearly, people who are high in sensation seeking probably would not experience the same degree of stress in many situations as would most people; in fact, they might find many potentially stressful events (such as changes in living conditions and work responsibilities) exhilarating (see Psychology in Action, pp. 100–01).

Naturally, eustress, like distress, is a personal matter. Getting an opportunity to meet new people can result in eustress or distress, depending on the personal characteristics of the individual involved. Moreover, positive stress is not necessarily an unmitigated blessing. Too much positive stress can place significant adjustive demands upon the individual and lead to stress reactions such as headaches, ulcers, and difficulty sleeping (Evans & Bartolome, 1980). When an individual experiences

*Eustress is positive stress in a person's life. The challenges are real, and the benefits include a growth in self-esteem.*

# Psychology in Action

## Sensation Seeking Scale

Each of the items below contains two choices, A and B. Please indicate for each item which of the choices most describes your likes or the way you feel. In some cases you may find items in which both choices describe your likes or feelings. Please choose the one which better describes your likes or feelings. In some cases you may find items in which you do not like either choice. In these cases mark the choice you dislike least. Do not leave any items blank.

It is important you respond to all items, with only *one choice*, A or B. We are interested only in your likes or feelings, not in how others feel about these things or how one is supposed to feel. There are no right or wrong answers. Be frank and give an honest appraisal of yourself.

1. A. I would like a job which would require a lot of traveling.
   B. I would prefer a job in one location.
2. A. I can't wait to get into the indoors on a cold day.
   B. I am invigorated by a brisk, cold day.
3. A. I often wish I could be a mountain climber.
   B. I can't understand people who risk their necks climbing mountains.
4. A. I dislike all body odors.
   B. I like some of the earthy body smells.
5. A. I get bored seeing the same old faces.
   B. I like the comfortable familiarity of everyday friends.
6. A. I like to explore a strange city or section of town by myself, even if it means getting lost.
   B. I prefer a guide when I am in a place I don't know well.

7. A. I would not like to try any drug which might produce strange and dangerous effects on me.
   B. I would like to try some of the new drugs that produce hallucinations.
8. A. I would prefer living in an ideal society where everyone is safe, secure and happy.
   B. I would have preferred living in the unsettled days of our history.
9. A. A sensible person avoids dangerous activities.
   B. I sometimes like to do things that are a little frightening.
10. A. I would like to take up the sport of water-skiing.
    B. I would not like to take up water-skiing.
11. A. I would like to take off on a trip with no pre-planned or definite routes, or timetable.
    B. When I go on a trip I like to plan my route and timetable fairly carefully.

**hyperstress:** overstress; stress that exceeds the person's ability to cope

**hypostress:** understress; insufficient stress resulting in boredom

stress, whether eustress or distress, that exceeds the individual's ability to cope effectively, psychologists speak of overstress or **hyperstress.** Clearly, overstress should be avoided. On the other hand, too few adjustive demands can lead to understress, **hypostress.** The individual who is not sufficiently challenged in life may suffer from a lack of self-realization and from boredom. As Selye (1980) has put it, "Our goal should be to strike a balance between the equally destructive forces of hypo- and hyperstress, to find as much eustress as possible, and to minimize distress" (p. 141).

In this chapter we have seen that stress can arise from a number of sources and that the stressfulness of any particular situation will differ from person to person depending on characteristics of the adjustive demands, characteristics of the person, and the social support available to the person. In the next chapter we will look at the most common reactions to stress and the effects that stress can have on us.

## Sensation Seeking Scale   (continued)

12. A. I would not like to learn to fly an airplane.
    B. I would like to learn to fly an airplane.
13. A. I would like to have the experience of being hypnotized.
    B. I would not like to be hypnotized.
14. A. The most important goal of life is to live it to the fullest and experience as much of it as you can.
    B. The most important goal of life is to find peace and happiness.
15. A. I would like to try parachute jumping.
    B. I would never want to try jumping out of a plane with or without a parachute.
16. A. I enter cold water gradually giving myself time to get used to it.
    B. I like to dive or jump right into the ocean or a cold pool.
17. A. I prefer friends who are excitingly unpredictable.
    B. I prefer friends who are reliable and predictable.

18. A. When I go on a vacation I prefer the comfort of a good room and bed.
    B. When I go on a vacation I would prefer the change of camping out.
19. A. The essence of good art is in its clarity, symmetry of form and harmony of colors.
    B. I often find beauty in the "clashing" colors and irregular forms of modern paintings.
20. A. A good painting should shock or jolt the senses.
    B. A good painting should give one a feeling of peace and security.
21. A. People who ride motorcycles must have some kind of an unconscious need to hurt themselves.
    B. I would like to drive or ride on a motorcycle.
22. A. I prefer people who are calm and even tempered.
    B. I prefer people who are emotionally expressive even if they are a bit unstable.

Source: Zuckerman, 1978

In order to score this Sensation Seeking Scale, give yourself one point for each answer that matches this key: 1A, 2B, 3A, 4B, 5A, 6A, 7B, 8B, 9B, 10A, 11A, 12B, 13A, 14A, 15A, 16B, 17A, 18B, 19B, 20A, 21B, 22B. For comparison, in a large group of university students who took this test in the 1970s, half of the students scored 14 or less on this scale; the other half scored above 14. The top 10 percent of the students (those highest on sensation seeking) scored 18 or higher; the lowest 10 percent of the students (those lowest in sensation seeking) scored between 0 and 9. Refer to the text for a discussion of the differences between people who are high and low in sensation seeking scores.

## SUMMARY

*Stress* refers to adjustive demands that include threat or tension and that require change or adaptation. Stress is a fact of life at all ages, though the kinds of environmental events that can give rise to stress (*stressors*) change as people grow older. Stress can arise either from a real threat or from a perceived threat in the absence of an actual stressor. Some stress (*distress*) is undesirable, but other kinds of stress (*eustress*) can have a beneficial effect.

There are five common sources of stress: frustration, conflict, pressure, change, and self-imposed stress. *Frustration* occurs when something a person wants, needs, or deserves is unavailable or when a person's needs or desires are blocked. Delays, daily hassles, lack of resources, losses, failures, and discrimination are all common sources of frustration that give rise to stress.

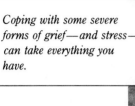

*Coping with some severe forms of grief—and stress— can take everything you have.*

*Conflict* is another common source of stress. When two or more incompatible motives are aroused simultaneously, a person is in conflict. In some cases (called *approach-approach conflict*), people are attracted to two desirable objects or goals simultaneously. Although this kind of conflict is common, it is usually not a source of great stress since quite often it is possible to "have our cake and eat it too." *Avoidance-avoidance conflicts* are usually more stressful. In these situations, people must choose between two undesirable objects or goals; whatever their choice, the outcome is guaranteed to be unpleasant. In *approach-avoidance conflicts,* people are drawn toward an object or goal that has both desirable and undesirable features. They are torn between approaching and avoiding the object, and may get to a point where they waver back and forth: first approaching, then moving away, then approaching again in an endless cycle of indecision. Finally, *multiple approach-avoidance conflicts* arise when people are simultaneously attracted to more than one object, each of which has both good and bad features.

*Pressure* is yet another common source of stress. Pressure can arise from competition with other people, from having too little time to do everything that needs to be done, from overload, from demanding interpersonal relationships, and from change.

Another source of stress is change. Although most people prefer living in a stable and predictable world, life changes are inevitable and unavoidable. Several questionnaires attempt to assess the stress that arises from life changes, sometimes measured in *Life Change Units* (LCUs); though these questionnaires provide a rough estimate of some kinds of life stress, all of them are open to criticism.

Stress can also arise from irrational beliefs about ourselves and others. In such cases we unnecessarily impose stress on ourselves in the absence of any real stressor. A number of psychologists have detailed the ways irrational thoughts can form the basis for a great deal of unnecessary self-imposed stress.

The severity of stress in a situation is determined in part by characteristics of the stressor. In particular, adjustive demands are likely to be more stressful if they are many in number, of long duration, unpredictable, and imminent.

Individuals differ in the extent they experience stress in any particular situation. In part, these individual differences are due to the fact that the situation may mean different things to different people: an event that one person finds threatening another person may find exhilarating. Moreover, prior experience with and perceived control over the stressful situation can modify the extent to which it is experienced as stressful. If a situation is familiar, and if the person believes that he or she has some degree of control over it, the situation is less likely to be experienced as stressful. Finally, some individuals (such as *Type A* personalities) are more likely than others (such as *Type B* personalities) to experience a wide variety of situations as stressful.

The extent to which a person has close relationships with other people can also modify the effect of a stressful situation. Family and friends can be a valuable source of comfort and can help to buffer the effects of stressors. Unfortunately, many people most affected by stress also have great difficulty maintaining interpersonal relationships.

Not all stress is harmful or undesirable. Some stress can be positive and beneficial. Moreover, some people actively seek out and enjoy stressful situations that others would avoid. Thus it is important for each of us to strike a balance in life between too much stress (called *hyperstress*) and too little stress (called *hypostress*).

## KEY TERMS

stress (72)

stressors (74)

distress (74)

eustress (74)

frustration (75)

conflict (77)

approach-approach conflict (77)

avoidance-avoidance conflict (78)

approach-avoidance conflict (78)

multiple approach-avoidance
  conflict (80)

pressure (81)

Life Change Unit (LCU) (83)

future shock (85)

Type A behavior (96)

Type B behavior (96)

hyperstress (100)

hypostress (100)

# Reactions to Stressful Events

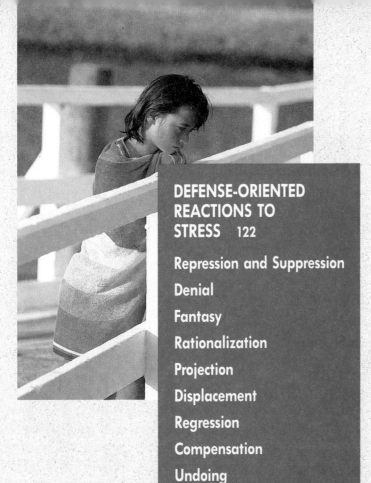

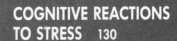

*Any kind of activity sets our stress mechanism in motion, though it will largely depend upon the accidental conditioning factors whether the heart, kidney, gastrointestinal tract, or brain will suffer most. In the body, as in a chain, the weakest link breaks down under stress although all parts are equally exposed to it.*

*Stress Without Distress* (Seyle, 1974, pp. 45–46)

*A*N employee of a large company begins to experience chest pains; shortly thereafter, she suffers an emotional breakdown. A student suddenly finds that he is unable to recall material that he studied and remembered the day before. An airport firefighter is finding it increasingly difficult to sleep; he feels anxious much of the time and is occasionally overwhelmed by feelings of guilt. An otherwise healthy farmer in South Dakota suffers a mild heart attack. An elderly adult male enters a hospital with no known illness, yet he dies four days later.

What do these people have in common? They are all experiencing reactions to stress. Six months earlier, the employee was transferred to a new supervisory position that she did not feel capable of handling. The forgetful student is taking an important midterm examination and has just discovered that he has no idea how to answer the first question on the test. The firefighter was one of the first people to reach the scene of an airplane accident in which more than 100 people were killed; though a year has passed since the night of the accident, he still cannot manage to drive past the scene on his way to and from work. The farmer is deeply in debt due to several years of severe drought. He has just come from a meeting with the officers of his local bank who told him that, unless the situation changes, they will have to call in his loans and foreclose on his mortgage. The elderly hospital patient lost his wife several weeks earlier; they had spent more than fifty years together, and he had been overcome by grief and loneliness in the weeks since her death.

Each of these cases illustrates that stress, from whatever source, involves costs to the individual. If the stress is neither prolonged nor severe, the effects may hardly be noticeable. If stress persists or is unusually severe, eventually the effects will be apparent in one way or another. In this chapter we will explore the ways that people react to stress, beginning with physiological reactions (see Table 4.1, p. 107).

## PHYSIOLOGICAL REACTIONS TO STRESS

Several of the examples at the beginning of this chapter showed that psychological stress can cause physiological disorders such as illness, and even death. This idea may seem surprising at first. In our culture, people often think of the body and mind as separate entities. In other words, most people look for biological causes for

**TABLE 4.1  Curing the Anxious Worker: Money Goes a Long Way**

A wide range of employees now claims that on-the-job pressures cause mental problems. Many of them now take claims to state courts—and win sizable monetary awards. Some actual cases:

| Occupation | Work-related Stress | Mental Disability |
|---|---|---|
| Advertising Manager | Overworked, supervisor requested early retirement | Anxiety, depression |
| Assembly-line Worker | Keeping up the pace | Schizophrenia, anxiety |
| Claims Director | Job pressures | Psychiatric illness |
| Custodian | Claustrophobia when cleaning boiler | Nervous condition |
| Fireman | Frequent exposure to danger | Psychoneurotic injury— cardiac neurosis |
| Foundry Technician | Fear of radiation exposure | Anxiety neurosis |
| Guidance Counselor | Job pressures, students' criticism of work | Severe depression |
| Insurance Underwriter | Increase in job duties | Mental breakdown |
| Policeman | Viewed job as demeaning | Anxiety, depression |
| Secretary | Witnessed scene of boss's suicide | Shock |
| Telephone Repairman | Resentment of younger and female supervisors | Paranoid personality |

Source: National Council on Compensation Insurance, *Newsweek:* June 2, 1986

biological events, and psychological causes for psychological events. For example, we may conclude that we contracted the flu because we were tired; in this case, a physiological event (the flu) is seen as having physiological causes (fatigue). In contrast, we may conclude that we feel anxious because we are eager to do well at something; in this case, a psychological event (anxiety) is seen as having psychological causes (a desire to do well).

However, this neat separation of body and mind isn't very realistic. Anyone who has ever experienced his or her face burn with embarrassment or anger knows that psychological states can profoundly affect the body. Anyone who has consumed too many soft drinks or cups of coffee can attest to the effect of caffeine on feelings of anxiety and nervousness. In fact, biological and psychological events interact: psychological stress can have biological consequences, and biological stress can have psychological consequences. Accordingly, we may contract the flu not because we are tired, but because we are depressed or upset about something. Conversely, we may become depressed or upset because our body is fighting off an infection or because we are physically exhausted or fatigued.

## General Adaptation Syndrome

**General Adaptation Syndrome (GAS):** series of physical responses to both physical and psychological stress

The Canadian physiologist Hans Selye (*sell-yay*) shed a good deal of light on the way in which psychological and physiological events interact when people are under stress. Selye (1976) asserted that organisms respond to *all* kinds of stress in similar ways. He called this response the **General Adaptation Syndrome (GAS).** According to Selye, stress produced by an infection does not differ substantially from stress produced by frustration, conflict, or pressure. In all these cases, and others as well, Selye suggested that the body responds to stress in three major stages: alarm and mobilization, resistance, and exhaustion. Let us examine each of these in more detail.

**Alarm and mobilization.**     The body's first reaction to any kind of stress is to organize itself to cope with the adjustive demand. Selye called this the **alarm and mobilization reaction.** When an organism is faced with a physical challenge or a life threatening emergency, physical changes occur that are designed to speed up the body's physical reactions and to increase strength. Cortisol is released into the bloodstream and moves quickly throughout the body; in less than one minute, our entire body is alert and preparing to respond to the stressor. Meanwhile, epinephrine and norepinephrine are dumped into the bloodstream and carried throughout the body. Norepinephrine causes the heart to beat faster, respiration to increase, and blood pressure to rise. Epinephrine causes greater flow of blood to muscles, a slowing down of digestion, and the release of blood sugar from the liver as the body makes sources of energy more readily available. All of these physiological responses have a common purpose: to prepare the body for physical exertion in response to the stressor. In other words, when faced with a physical stressor, the body gets ready to fight as powerfully as possible or to flee as quickly as possible.

According to Selye, these alarm and mobilization reactions also occur when the source of stress is psychological. For example, faced with the need to speak before

**alarm and mobilization reaction**: first stage of the General Adaptation Syndrome, characterized by the mobilization of defenses to cope with stress

*Your body's physical responses to stress are closely related to what Hans Selye called the General Adaptation Syndrome, which any organism experiences when faced with danger.*

a large group, many people experience the pounding heart, dry mouth, and sweaty palms characteristic of the alarm and mobilization stage of the GAS. In other words, regardless of whether the source of stress is physical or psychological, when an individual is under stress the initial reaction is the same: preparation for extreme physical exertion.

If you stop and think about it, this phenomenon is really quite extraordinary. Preparing yourself physically is reasonable when faced with an oncoming car, a growling dog, a house fire, or some other physical danger; in these cases the alarm and mobilization reaction is entirely appropriate. However, as we will see, these same reactions are often quite inappropriate when the source of stress is psychological: faced with the prospect of speaking before a large gathering, taking a difficult exam, or asking for a promotion, a pounding heart, dry mouth, and sweaty palms don't help much; in fact, they often make the situation worse.

There is another reason the alarm and mobilization response is often not very helpful when the source of stress is psychological. The physical reactions occurring during the alarm and mobilization phase can be quite powerful: the body prepares for swift, powerful physical exertion that may make the difference between life and death. This is appropriate for major physical challenges or threats, which usually last for only a short time. However, severe psychological stress can persist for months or years; during this time, it is not unusual for the body to remain in a state of alarm and mobilization. As we will see later in the chapter, this puts a tremendous load on the cardiovascular system and can be devastating to our overall health and well being. The human body simply is not designed to be exposed for long periods of time to the powerful biological changes that accompany alarm and mobilization.

**resistance:** second stage of the General Adaptation Syndrome, in which physical and psychological resources are used to combat continued stress

**Resistance.** If the stressful situation continues, the individual enters the **resistance** phase of the GAS. Here the organism tries to find some way of dealing with the stress while resisting psychological or physical disorganization. However, coping resources are limited; therefore, if the body's resources are already mobilized in response to one stressor, they are less available for coping with other stressors. People who are ill, for example, simply do not have the resources to cope as effectively as they normally would with frustrations, conflicts, pressures, and other sources of psychological stress. Conversely, you may be surprised to learn that people coping with sustained or severe psychological stress are less able to resist infections and diseases. Research data show that people experiencing psychological stress are also more likely to suffer from tuberculosis, arthritis, diabetes, leukemia, herpes, cancer, colds, stomach disorders, back pain, mononucleosis, and a variety of other diseases (Levy, 1982; Fox, 1983; Jemott & Locke, 1984; Sarason et al., 1985).

**immune system:** complex mechanism which the body uses to protect itself against infections and diseases

In the last few years, scientists have studied these effects and discovered that stress suppresses the body's **immune system** (Maier, 1987; Glaser & Kiecolt-Glaser, 1988; Kiecolt-Glaser & Glaser, 1988). The immune system is responsible for identifying and destroying foreign materials such as viruses and bacteria in the body. Exactly how it works is still a mystery, but when a foreign substance is detected, the body rapidly increases the number of certain white blood cells, which play a central role in the attack on the foreign substance. All kinds of stressful events have been shown to reduce or suppress the immune system response; a significant amount of life change, the pressure of competition in college, being deprived of sleep, experiencing profound grief, and severe depression all can make us more vulnerable to infections and diseases.

Some examples may help you to grasp this important link between psychological stress and lowered disease tolerance. A number of laboratory studies with animals have shown that animals under stress are much more prone to infection and to the growth of tumors. For example, Sklar and Anisman (1979) implanted some mice with tumor cells. Some of the mice were subsequently exposed to inescapable shock, others to escapable shock, and still others to no shock at all. In Chapter 3 we saw that inescapable shock is more stressful than escapable shock. Therefore, we would expect stress to be highest in the mice that could not escape the shock.

The researchers found, indeed, that the animals exposed to inescapable shock developed larger tumors than either of the other two groups. Were these results due to the effect of stress on the immune system? Apparently, this is true according to recent research demonstrating that rats able to escape from electric shocks showed no change in their immune system, while rats unable to escape developed impaired immune system functioning and were more susceptible to disease and infections (Laudenslager et al., 1983).

Would the same results be found in humans? While these same experiments cannot be repeated on human beings, other research evidence indicates that stress does suppress the human immune system. For example, in 1979 the nuclear reactor at Three Mile Island released a significant amount of radioactivity into the environment. People who still live near the reactor are displaying numerous signs of stress, including higher blood pressure and a higher incidence of both major and minor illnesses. Their urine shows elevated levels of cortisol, epinephrine, and norepinephrine—three substances released during the alarm and mobilization reaction to stress. Blood tests show that their immune systems have indeed been suppressed (Schaeffer & Baum, 1984; Gatchel, Schaeffer, & Baum, 1985).

In another study, Roger Bartop and his colleagues in Australia (Bartop et al., 1977) studied several dozen people during the weeks and months after the deaths of their spouses. The researchers found that within just a few weeks, the immune systems of the survivors were impaired. Other research shows that anyone experiencing unusual stress at home, in college, or on the job, and who reacts to that life stress with anxiety or depression, is likely to be more vulnerable to various kinds of illnesses due to suppression of the immune system (Jemott & Locke, 1984).

Conversely, other research indicates that reducing stress can bolster the immune system. Kiecolt-Glaser et al. (1985) studied forty-five elderly residents living in retirement homes. One third of the residents were visited regularly by students teaching them techniques for relaxing. Another third of the residents were visited just as often by the students, but were not taught relaxation techniques. The final third of the residents were not even visited. The data showed clearly that the first group—those taught relaxation techniques—improved their immune system activity. In other words, learning how to relax and reduce stress made them more resistant to infections and diseases.

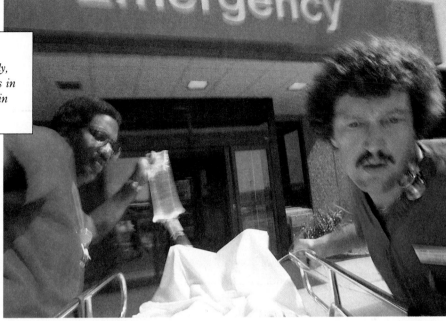

*Because of the physical effects of stress on the body, prolonged periods of stress in a person's life can result in serious illness.*

**Exhaustion.**    People may stay at the resistance stage of the GAS for months and years at a time, spending day after day ready for physical confrontation and becoming increasingly vulnerable to other kinds of stressors. Predictably, the physical cost of resisting stress increases continually as the coping methods used during the stage of resistance begin to falter. Even a brief period of stress can have long-lasting effects, as Selye (1976) found in his pioneering studies.

> Experiments on animals have clearly shown that each exposure leaves an indelible scar, in that it uses up reserves of adaptability which cannot be replaced. It is true that immediately after some harassing experience, rest can restore us almost to the original level of fitness by eliminating acute fatigue. But the emphasis is on *almost.* Since we constantly go through periods of stress and rest during life, just a little deficit of adaptation energy every day adds up—it adds up to what we call aging. (p. 429)

Faced with prolonged or repeated exposure to severe stress, it becomes necessary to use more extreme measures to cope if we are going to survive. However, each new effort further taxes our dwindling resources. Eventually, **exhaustion** may set in and quick intervention may become necessary. Otherwise, our condition may continue to deteriorate and we may die, as in the case of the elderly widower described at the beginning of the chapter. We now know, for example, that prolonged stress can lead to serious, even fatal, cardiac problems. One study gathered data about the lives of thirty-nine subjects who had suffered fatal heart attacks (Rahe & Lind, 1971). In almost every case, there had been a sudden rise in the number and

**exhaustion:** final stage of the General Adaptation Syndrome, characterized by the use of extreme measures to cope with stress

intensity of life-changes during the six months prior to their deaths (see Psychology in Action, p. 113).

So far in this chapter, we have seen that stress from whatever source produces a number of physiological effects, including changes in the cardiovascular system, respiratory system, and other physical systems. In most people, these changes disappear when the stressors are reduced or eliminated. In some individuals, however, prolonged or severe stress produces a permanent change in an organ system. These people suffer from **psychophysiological disorders**—biological disorders produced by psychological stress. In the next section we look more closely at these common disorders, or "diseases of adaptation," as Selye has called them.

**psychophysiological disorders:** physical disorders produced by stress

## Psychophysiological Disorders

Recent research has shown that a wide variety of physiological disorders, formerly understood as strictly physical in nature, may in fact arise directly or indirectly from prolonged or severe life stress. The more common psychophysiological disorders include the following.

- *Gastrointestinal reactions,* such as peptic ulcers, ulcerative colitis, and irritable bowel syndrome
- *Respiratory reactions,* including asthma, bronchial spasms, and hyperventilation
- *Musculoskeletal reactions,* including backache, muscle cramps, and teeth-grinding
- *Skin reactions,* including hives, itching, and excessive sweating
- *Cardiovascular reactions,* including migraine headaches, hypertension (high blood pressure), and rapid heartbeat
- *Immune reactions,* including rheumatoid arthritis, systemic lupus erythematosus, and chronic active hepatitis

These disorders formerly were called "psychosomatic disorders." The term *psychosomatic* was intended to connect the mind ("psyche") and the body ("soma") to show that each influenced the other. Unfortunately, the term evolved to suggest that a patient's sufferings were "imaginary." That, of course, is not the case: people with psychophysiological disorders such as asthma, hypertension, and ulcers have clearly defined medical problems that are definitely not "all in their minds." To avoid the negative connotations associated with the word "psychosomatic," the term "psychophysiological" is now used for these disorders.

Psychophysiological disorders not only produce significant discomfort for millions of people, but they can be life-threatening as well (Hull, 1977). The United States Centers for Disease Control (1980) estimates that among the ten leading causes of death, 50 percent of the deaths can be traced to stress and maladaptive life styles. For example, 330,000 Americans each year suffer sudden cardiac death—representing one out of every five deaths; approximately 20 percent of those people were exposed to severe psychological stress in the twenty-four hours preceding their death. Moreover, approximately 50 percent of patient visits to general practitioners involve a psychophysiological stress-related disorder, and these visits clearly place a significant burden on the health care system as well as on the finances of the

## Voodoo Death

Most of our stresses are relatively mild, and most of our responses to stress are correspondingly mild. However, in unusual cases, very stressful conditions can lead to death. Consider the following cases.

*A Brazilian Indian condemned and sentenced by a so-called medicine man is helpless against his own emotional response to this pronouncement—and dies within hours. In Africa a young man unknowingly eats the inviolably banned wild hen. In discovery of his "crime" he trembles, is overcome by fear, and dies in 24 hours. In New Zealand a Maori woman eats fruit that she only later learns has come from a tabooed place. According to her culture, her action has profaned her chief. By noon of the next day she is dead. In Australia a witch doctor points a bone at a man. Believing that nothing can save him, the man rapidly sinks in spirits and prepares to die. He is saved only at the last moment when the witch doctor is forced to remove the charm (Richter, 1957, p. 191).*

As these reports show, stress can be so severe that it can lead to physical deterioration and death. The remarkable aspect of these studies is that these severe emotional states seem to be set off by such apparently "minor" events as a bone pointed in the victim's direction.

From the perspective of the GAS model, one hypothesis is that the severe effects reported in these cases resulted from extreme autonomic arousal. That is, the physiological arousal was so intense that the individual rapidly entered the disorganization and exhaustion phase which, in turn, led to death.

A somewhat different hypothesis is that the individuals "condemned" to die simply gave up hope. That is, believing that they were about to die, they developed a sense of helplessness and hopelessness (Seligman, 1975). These feelings, in turn, helped produce biological changes that led to their eventual deaths.

Of course, a piece of fruit or a bone is not itself stressful. However, these objects become stressful when they are perceived and reacted to in negative ways. Thus, in examining the reactions to stress, it is important to be aware of and pay close attention to the perceptions and experiences of the individual.

patient. Thus, it is tremendously important to understand the causes of psychophysiological disorders.

**Preconditions.** In general, psychophysiological disorders are most likely to arise when three conditions are met: (1) sustained exposure to stress, which arouses emotional tension; (2) failure to cope adequately with the stress, resulting in continued emotional arousal over a long period of time; and (3) organ vulnerability. The first two points should not require additional comment, but "organ vulnerability" may be a new concept for you. Let's look a bit more closely at this idea.

Researchers have known for some time that people differ in the way they respond physiologically to prolonged or severe stress. Thus, one person may respond to stress with headaches; another person may respond with an upset stomach; still another may respond with increased blood pressure. This is called **organ specificity:** stress affects only some organs, and the particular organ system affected usually differs from one person to another.

Why should this be so? Faced with the same stressful situation, why does one individual develop peptic ulcers, another high blood pressure, and still another back-

**organ specificity:** tendency for different people to react to stress with different physical disorders aches? One suggestion is that prior injury, illness, or diet makes one organ system weaker and more vulnerable than others. Another suggestion is that organ specificity is inherited; according to this view, each of us is born with the tendency to react biologically in different ways when exposed to stress. A third suggestion is that psychophysiological reactions are learned through imitation or selective reinforcement (see Chapter 2 for a discussion of these basic learning processes). For example, a child who has avoided unpleasant events in the past because of stomachaches may learn to respond to stressful situations in the future by developing an upset stomach.

Recently, a fourth explanation for organ specificity has attracted a great deal of attention. According to this view, certain "personality types" react to stress with specific emotions that are likely to affect one organ system more than another. For example, in Chapter 3 you learned about Type A individuals who are hurried, impatient, hard-driving, and likely to become hostile or aggressive. A significant amount of research data shows that having a Type A personality significantly increases the risk of coronary heart disease (Rosenman et al., 1975; National Institute of Health,

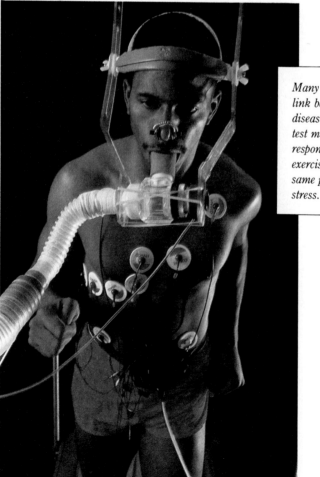

*Many doctors find a strong link between stress and heart disease. A standard stress test measures the body's response to strenuous exercise, which often has the same physical impact as stress.*

1981; Friedman & Booth-Kewley, 1988). In addition, one carefully controlled study (Friedman et al., 1984) demonstrated that reducing Type A behavior led to a reduction in recurring heart attacks. However, there has been a great deal of controversy recently about which aspect of the Type A personality is responsible for the link to heart disease. Some researchers believe that the key ingredients are a sense of urgency combined with constant activity, and a tendency to control or deny anger while keeping it bottled up inside (Spielberger et al., 1985; Wright, 1988). Other researchers suggest that anger and hostility alone account for the relationship between Type A behavior and high risk of coronary heart disease (Matthews, 1988; Dembroski & Williams, in press). Despite their disagreements, all these researchers agree on one point: certain personality types are predisposed toward greater risk of coronary disease.

Still other researchers have identified a "Type C" personality, characterized by passivity, helplessness, compliance, conformity, and lack of emotional expression (especially lack of hostility or anger). Evidence indicates that such people will more likely contract cancer and have poorer prospects for cure when it is discovered (Temoshok, 1988).

Although considerable disagreement exists regarding the exact causes of psychophysiological disorders, millions of people suffer from them. In the next section, we will review three of the most common types of psychophysiological reactions to stress: peptic ulcers, headaches, and hypertension.

**peptic (gastric) ulcer:** a pathological condition of the stomach brought about by excessive stomach acid

**Peptic ulcers.**    Estimates project that one in every ten Americans will develop a **peptic** (or **gastric**) **ulcer.** The incidence of such ulcers is two to three times higher among men than women. The ulcer is caused by an excessive amount of stomach acid, which eats away the lining of the stomach, leaving a craterlike wound. Although diet, disease, and other organic conditions can lead to peptic ulcers, emotional states such as anxiety, anger, and resentment also can stimulate the flow of excess stomach acid.

Some of the most useful knowledge of ulcers comes from a historic study reported by Wolf and Wolff (1947). In this study, the researchers reported on the case of Tom, an individual whose surgery left him with a "window" to his stomach. When Tom was subjected to experiences that elicited strong negative emotions, his stomach became engorged with blood and increased its production of acids. When the emotional arousal stopped, his stomach gradually returned to normal. If, however, his stomach lining was continually exposed to increased acid production, an ulcer occurred.

Laboratory studies confirm this link between stress and stomach ulcers. Jay Weiss (1968) exposed some rats to electric shocks that they could terminate by turning a wheel; other rats received the same shocks but could not turn them off. As we saw in Chapter 3, the rats with no control over the shocks should have experienced greater stress than the rats that could control the shock. As a result, the rats with no control developed more severe ulcers than did the other rats during the course of the experiment. In a similar fashion, it has been found that air traffic controllers (who can't directly control the airplanes for which they are responsible) are twice as likely to suffer ulcers than are the pilots who actually fly the planes

(Cobb & Rose, 1973). Finally, a recent review of many research studies concluded that high levels of anxiety (but not high levels of anger or hostility) are associated with a greater likelihood of ulcers (Matthews, 1988).

**Headaches.**    An estimated fifty million Americans suffer from recurrent headaches, with the incidence being higher among women than men (Raskin, 1988). Although headaches can result from a wide range of biological conditions, most headaches are related to high levels of emotional tension and anxiety or to high levels of depression (Matthews, 1988). There are two quite different kinds of stress-related headaches: tension headaches and migraine headaches.

**muscle contraction headache:** most common form of headache characterized by "bands" of pain around the head

**Muscle contraction headaches** (tension headaches) occur as "bands" of pain or tightness around the head. As the phrase "tension headache" implies, it is thought that the headaches arise when the muscles surrounding the skull contract and cause the constriction of blood vessels in the head.

**migraine headache:** severe, intense headache, often accompanied by nausea and vomiting

**Migraine headaches** are a particularly severe form of headache marked by throbbing or piercing pain often on just one side of the head. The intense pain may last for hours or days and may be accompanied by dizziness, nausea, and vomiting. Often people with migraine headaches become unusually sensitive to light, sound, smells, and touch; occasionally they may see bright spots of light in the visual field. Migraines cost an estimated $50 billion each year in lost work time and medical treatment.

Various events have been shown to trigger migraine attacks: hormonal changes, allergies, certain foods or drinks, and bright lights have all been shown to play a role in many cases of migraine. However, the most common cause of migraine attacks is psychological stress. In a recent study by the National Headache Institute, for example, nearly 70 percent of the migraine sufferers reported that their attacks often occur when they are relaxing after a period of unusually severe psychological stress.

For many years, it was thought that migraine attacks were caused by the constriction of blood vessels in the brain. However, research in the past two years has shown that the cause is actually a major chemical imbalance in the brain. Migraine sufferers are found to have unusually high levels of serotonin in their brains; serotonin is a brain chemical that plays a major role in controlling sleep and emotional arousal. Exactly how psychological stress causes unusually high levels of serotonin, and how serotonin causes migraine attacks, is not yet known.

**Hypertension.**    Of the various organ systems, the circulatory system is perhaps the most sensitive to emotional stress. As we have seen, under stress the heart beats faster and with greater force, and blood pressure mounts. Usually, when the stress or crisis passes, the body resumes normal functioning and blood pressure returns to normal. However, under sustained exposure to emotional stress, high blood pressure may persist. While organic factors such as diseases of the kidney and diet can contribute to high blood pressure (Benson, 1975), emotional stress plays a key role in about 90 percent of the cases.

**hypertension:** chronically high blood pressure

More than twenty-five million persons in the United States suffer from chronically high blood pressure or **hypertension,** and most of these people don't even know they have it. Unlike most other psychophysiological disorders, there are usually no symptoms to signal high blood pressure, although in severe cases some persons complain of headaches, tiredness, insomnia, or occasional dizzy spells—symptoms that are often easy to ignore. As Mays (1974) has described the situation:

> In most instances . . . the disease comes as silently as a serpent stalking its prey. Someone with high blood pressure may be unaware of his affliction for many years and then, out of the blue, develop blindness or be stricken by a stroke, cardiac arrest, or kidney failure. (p. 7)

High blood pressure is an insidious and life-threatening disorder. It is a primary cause of more than 60,000 deaths each year, and it is thought to play a major role in another million or more deaths each year from strokes and heart attacks.

To this point, the focus has been on physiological reactions to stress. In the remainder of the chapter, we turn our attention to psychological reactions to stressful events. We begin by looking at emotional reactions to stress.

## EMOTIONAL REACTIONS TO STRESS

Stressful events usually cause a wide range of emotional reactions. In the cases discussed at the beginning of this chapter, we saw examples of anger, fear, anxiety, depression, grief, and loneliness—all emotions that frequently are caused by stress. The connection between stress and emotions is so strong that one large-scale study of coping used self-reported "emotional upset" as an index of stress (Pearlin & Schooler, 1978). In addition, two major stress researchers (Goldberger & Breznitz, 1982) actually *define* stress in terms of its emotional effect: in their view, stress is "all that is unpleasant, noxious, or excessively demanding." Losing a job, for example, is likely to result in depression, frustration, and anger; it may also result in anxiety about being unable to pay the bills or being unable to find another job. Even routine, daily hassles can lead to anxiety or frustration. In this section of the chapter, we will look more closely at the most frequent emotional reactions to stress.

### Fear and Anxiety

**fear:** feeling of threat or danger from a specific object or event

**anxiety:** generalized feelings of fear and apprehension

**worry:** commonly used term to describe the simultaneous experiences of fear and anxiety

The term **fear** is generally used to describe a response to a specific, known danger, while the term **anxiety** is used to describe generalized fear or dread in the absence of a specific danger. According to this distinction, a frightened individual usually knows what he or she is afraid of and what can or cannot be done about it, whereas an anxious individual senses danger but is not certain about its exact nature, or what action he or she can take to deal with it. Often fear and anxiety go together. Fear is a response to the clearly perceived aspects of the dangerous or stressful situation, and anxiety is a response to the less predictable or certain aspects of the situation. For example, an individual approaching marriage may experience fear concerning financial problems and new responsibilities and at the same time feel vaguely anxious and apprehensive about whether this is really the "right" person, whether the marriage will succeed. **Worry** is the term commonly used to describe the simultaneous experiences of fear and anxiety.

A certain amount of worry is probably an inevitable by-product of modern living. Most of us feel vaguely apprehensive about possible accidents, failures, setbacks, losses, or other poorly defined future possibilities. However, chronic worry can have a number of negative effects. First, chronic anxiety can keep us physiologically mobilized for emergency action when no appropriate action is evident; as we have seen, this can lead to psychophysiological disorders. Second, as we will see shortly, anxiety beyond a moderate level can cause us to narrow our perception and to think less logically; we become more rigid, less inventive, and try to protect ourselves through the use of defense mechanisms. This means that we are less able to face our problems objectively and to work effectively toward solutions. Third, chronic worrying deprives us of much of the enjoyment of living. We are continually concerned with the negative and dangerous aspects of living rather than with the positive and enriching ones. Often a chronic worrier will worry about things that never happen, then be taken unawares by the stresses that do occur.

## Anger

Anger is a normal response to frustration and interference. In some situations, anger can lead to appropriate and constructive behavior. For example, anger aroused by unjust treatment may be used constructively in working for social reforms. On a more personal level, expressions of anger may help another person realize his or her inconsiderate behavior. The expression of anger in a nonthreatening, constructive fashion that respects the self-worth and dignity of the individual and is directed toward the problem can be both appropriate and effective.

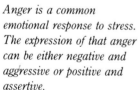

*Anger is a common emotional response to stress. The expression of that anger can be either negative and aggressive or positive and assertive.*

**aggression:** expression of anger with the intent to harm or injure another person

More commonly, however, anger leads to destructive **aggression.** Aggression is hostile behavior intended to harm other people. Intention is a key element in aggression. If we say something in anger that unintentionally hurts the feelings of another person, we have not behaved aggressively. If we say something knowing the person will be hurt, then we are being aggressive. Aggression is rarely an effective response to stress: it often leads to ill-considered actions that may be regretted later. Also, aggression against another will likely generate a counterattack in return, and the stressfulness of the situation will continue to increase for everyone involved.

## Guilt

*Of all the forms of mental suffering, perhaps none is as pervasive or as intense as the ache of guilt.*

*Guilt and Human Meaning* (Gelven, 1973, p. 69)

Most of us experience a sense of guilt when violating ethical or moral principles in which we believe—either by doing something we consider wrong, or by failing to do something we consider required. Guilt is characterized by feelings of being bad, evil, and unworthy, usually intermixed with remorse, self-recrimination, and anxiety.

To understand guilt feelings it is useful to remember that: (1) values concerning right and wrong are learned, (2) these values are then applied to one's own behavior, and (3) we also learn, often by hard experience, that wrongdoing leads to punishment. Thus, when we behave in ways that we consider unethical or immoral, we not only experience self-devaluation but also some degree of anxiety. Because we feel responsible for the wrongful act, we blame ourselves and often engage in severe self-recrimination. The intensity of our guilt will depend mainly on how serious we consider our misdeed to be and whether we can make amends for it.

### Grief, Depression, and Loneliness

Grief, depression, and loneliness are similar responses that arise when important sources of interpersonal contacts or other pleasurable events in life are not available to us. We feel grief, for example, when friends or family members are taken from us by death. We become depressed when important relationships or other sources of pleasure are lost to us. We feel lonely when we are cut off from the joys of closeness and friendship that others can provide us.

*Grief* is commonly associated with the discouragement, dejection, and gloomy thoughts characteristic of depression. It is also a universal reaction to bereavement, found even among some animals. We experience grief when we suffer severe loss.

Such grief is especially apparent with the death of a family member, but other losses also can lead to a sense of grief (see Insight, p. 121).

*Depression,* the feeling of being dejected, discouraged, and "down in the dumps," is usually accompanied by low initiative, listlessness, and some degree of self-devaluation. Depression is often accompanied by loss of appetite, sleep disturbances, and a low sex drive. Most of us have probably felt depressed at one time or another as a result of a disappointment in love, an accident, a failure, or the death of a loved one. In fact, there are literally hundreds of thousands of Americans who show mild depression. However, even in mild form, depression can lead to feelings of despair and can markedly reduce personal effectiveness and joy in living. I will have much more to say about depression in Chapter 6.

*Loneliness* is a painful feeling of emptiness and deprivation arising when people are cut off from the pleasures of close interpersonal relationships. Widowed and elderly persons, such as the man described at the beginning of this chapter, are perhaps most likely to suffer acutely from loneliness, but loneliness is a problem that affects young and old alike. People can feel lonely even in the midst of a crowd.

It is important to distinguish between aloneness and loneliness (Ivanhoe, 1977). There are many occasions when we are subjected to short or long periods of aloneness. While such occasions may be unpleasant, aloneness is often desirable. In fact,

*People don't suffer the emotional emptiness of loneliness as long as they are not cut off from emotional contact with other living beings.*

# *Insight*

## Are There Built-in Patterns for Coping with Tragedy?

It appears that there may be built-in responses to severe personal loss that follow much the same pattern regardless of the specific nature of the loss.

In a pioneering study, Cholden (1954) delineated three typical stages in the responses of newly blinded persons: (1) a period of shock; (2) a period of depression or mourning involving feelings of dejection, self-pity, and hopelessness; and (3) a period of readjustment involving changes in life plans designed to salvage what the person could from the tragedy.

Parkes (1972) found a similar pattern in the reactions of amputees and women suffering bereavement. Typically, the first reaction was one of shock and numbness accompanied by a strong tendency to deny or screen out the reality of what had happened. This was followed by anxiety, depression, and the so-called pangs of grief. Finally, the persons gave up hope of recovering what they had lost and began to make the necessary readjustment to life.

These patterns appear to operate with a minimum of learning and are characteristic of most people undergoing such personal tragedies.

many individuals strive to preserve their periods of aloneness or solitude. It is important to realize, however, that these people choose aloneness and know that they can choose to end it. In contrast, loneliness is thrust upon us and cannot as easily be overcome.

## Learned Emotional Associations

The various emotional responses to stress that have been described are universal: they are part of what it means to be human. However, each of us differs regarding the kinds of situations that trigger these emotions. That is, each of us learns to associate particular emotions with specific stressful events. You may have learned to associate a particular person, object, or event with fear or anxiety, while another person has learned to associate that same person or thing with anger or sadness. For example, most people learn that parent-child relations are accompanied by love, warmth, and mutual caring. However, abused children learn from their experiences that parent-child relationships in general are threatening and anxiety-provoking. Later, when they become parents, their own children will trigger feelings of fear and anxiety rather than love and affection. As Kempe and Kempe (1978) point out:

> The fear . . . lives on in abusive mothers and fathers; that is why, in relating to them, we must be so ready to cope with their rather primitive and seemingly irrational reactions to comparatively simple situations. Their quick and intense responses to any kind of rejection, real or imagined, illustrate this underlying fear. (p. 14)

In terms of the models that were introduced in Chapter 2, a behaviorist would contend that many learned emotional reactions result from classical conditioning: in the example of an abused child, fear is a conditioned emotional response to the parent-child relationship (the conditioned stimulus). A social learning theorist and a psychoanalytic psychologist would add that many emotional reactions are also learned through modeling or identification. If your parents found you to be a source of fear and anxiety, you may also come to believe that children are to be feared even though you have not yet had any experiences with children of your own.

## DEFENSE-ORIENTED REACTIONS TO STRESS

**defense-oriented responses:** self-deceptive responses to stress that protect one's feelings of adequacy and worth or alleviate unpleasant emotions

So far we have seen that stress can cause powerful physiological and emotional reactions. In the face of these potent responses, at times all of us use self-protective, defensive responses to soften failure, alleviate anxiety, repair emotional hurt, and maintain our feelings of adequacy and worth, while we seek ways of coping more directly with the source of our stress. These **defense-oriented responses** to stress are particularly likely to arise during the resistance stage of the GAS. Even though they involve some measure of self-deception and reality distortion, they are normal and useful responses to stress as long as they are not used so much that they interfere with our ability to meet and cope with life's problems. In the next section of the chapter, we will look more closely at the various kinds of defensive reactions to stress that are available to us.

### Repression and Suppression

**repression:** defense mechanism in which anxiety-arousing desires or intolerable memories are kept out of consciousness

**Repression** refers to the process of excluding threatening or painful thoughts and desires from consciousness. Although we are no longer aware of the repressed material, it is not really forgotten: it remains in our unconscious where it continues to have an effect on our behavior. For example, it is not unusual for soldiers who have undergone an especially traumatic combat episode to be brought to an aid station suffering from amnesia. Although they may be nervous, depressed, and show other signs of their ordeal, the intolerable combat situation is completely screened from consciousness. Thus, they are protected from overwhelming stress until time and other conditions have desensitized them to the point where they can recall the event without serious psychological disorganization. The repressed experience eventually can be brought into conscious awareness through psychotherapy or by means of hypnosis or certain drugs.

A more common version of repression occurs when we block sexual, aggressive, or selfish wishes from consciousness because we consider them immoral. By so doing, we ward off guilt and maintain our sense of self-esteem. For example, nearly all children at some point wish that their parents, brothers, or sisters were dead. This is not because children are evil; they simply do not have effective strategies for toning down strong emotions, so when they are angry they have very powerful aggressive fantasies. If you try to remember having similar thoughts, you will probably be unable to do so. You probably repressed such wishes once you became old enough to "know better." Similarly, some people repress competitive feelings as adults because they do not like to see themselves as competitive; nevertheless, their actions often betray their real feelings as they try to "one up" friends or colleagues without being aware of it.

**suppression:** defense
mechanism in which
thoughts or desires are
consciously excluded from
immediate awareness

It is important to distinguish between repression and **suppression.** Repression operates without our being aware of it; the repressed material is kept out of consciousness, as is our awareness of even using repression. However, as we saw earlier in this chapter, at times we may consciously decide to avoid thinking about something—as a way of coping with strong emotions, for example. This illustrates suppression: we are aware of blocking out unpleasant thoughts or desires, and if necessary we can describe those thoughts or desires. The firefighter described at the beginning of this chapter was very much aware that avoiding the scene of the airplane accident helped him to *suppress* the unpleasant memories and emotions associated with that horrible experience. However, he was completely unaware that he also harbored unconscious feelings of guilt and shame over the fact that he had been powerless to help the victims, and that he had been terrified for his own safety when he first arrived on the scene. These feelings were so overwhelming and threatening that he completely *repressed* them and was unable to become aware of them without the assistance of a psychotherapist.

Repression and suppression are important means of coping with the potentially disorganizing effects of extremely stressful experiences. In fact, in varying degrees, repression or suppression enter into most other defensive reactions, as well. However, in some situations, suppression and repression screen out stressful experiences that could better be met by realistically facing and working through the experiences. We cannot solve a problem that we do not see (see Table 4.2).

**TABLE 4.2   Summary Chart of the Defense Mechanisms**

| | |
|---|---|
| **Repression** | ■ Preventing painful or dangerous thoughts from entering consciousness |
| **Suppression** | ■ Conscious exclusion of thoughts from immediate awareness |
| **Denial** | ■ Refusing to perceive or face unpleasant reality |
| **Fantasy** | ■ Gratifying frustrated desires by imaginary achievements |
| **Rationalization** | ■ Attempting to prove that one's behavior is "rational" and justifiable and thus worthy of the approval of oneself and others |
| **Projection** | ■ Placing blame for difficulties upon others or attributing one's own unethical desires to others |
| **Displacement** | ■ Discharging pent-up feelings, usually of hostility, on objects less dangerous than those which initially aroused the emotions |
| **Regression** | ■ Retreating to earlier developmental level involving less mature responses and usually a lower level of aspiration |
| **Compensation** | ■ Covering up weakness by emphasizing some desirable trait or making up for frustration in one area by overgratification in another |
| **Acting Out** | ■ Reducing the anxiety aroused by forbidden desires by permitting their expression |
| **Undoing** | ■ Counteracting "immoral" desires or acts by some form of atonement |
| **Emotional Insulation** | ■ Reducing ego involvement and withdrawing into passivity to protect oneself from hurt |
| **Intellectualization** | ■ Suppressing the emotional aspect of hurtful situations or separating incompatible attitudes by logic-tight compartments |

## Denial

**denial**: defense mechanism in which the individual refuses to perceive unpleasant or threatening aspects of reality

Another defense mechanism allowing us to restrict experience is the **denial** of realities. We evade many disagreeable realities simply by ignoring or refusing to acknowledge them. We turn away from unpleasant sights, refuse to discuss unpleasant topics, ignore or deny criticism, and refuse to face many of our real problems. Very few of us, for example, accept the full inevitability of death. Even if we act as if we were quite resigned to the idea, the vision of our own death is usually mercifully vague. In some cases we may feel, "This just isn't happening to me."

Denial can protect us from the full impact of a traumatic experience. For example, in a study of stroke, lung cancer, and heart disease patients, Levine and Zigler (1975) found that denial was commonly used as a means of coping with the threat of impaired functioning, disability, and, in some cases, impending death. In fact, denial is often the first reaction people have when they learn they are dying. By ignoring or denying an unpleasant reality, we protect ourselves from a great deal of stress, but at the same time we may fail to become aware of many realities necessary for effective adjustment (see Psychology in Action, p. 126, for a look at the role of illusion in coping with cancer).

## Fantasy

**fantasy**: defense mechanism in which the individual escapes from the world of reality to a world of imagination

Besides screening out unpleasant aspects of reality, we may use **fantasy** to imagine things as we would like them to be. We may fantasize being the "conquering hero," a great athlete, a renowned scientist or artist, a person of immense wealth, or some other remarkable figure who performs incredible feats and wins the admiration and respect of all. James Thurber used this theme in his popular "Secret Life of Walter Mitty."

Fantasies are certainly not always defensive reactions to stress. They can be used to enrich our experience and to provide pleasure, as when we daydream about exciting adventures. They can also be used as part of problem solving, as when we imagine an outcome we would like and then actively pursue making that fantasy a reality.

Defensive fantasies, however, can be maladaptive when they capture so much of our attention that we begin to live primarily in our own fantasy world. Very lonely people wishing they could establish relationships with others sometimes drift into their own worlds, receiving more gratification from their fantasies than from reality. While this may be an adaptive response in the short run, if it persists it can prevent the person from making the effort to establish real interpersonal relationships; thus, it can lead to even greater loneliness and alienation in the long run.

## Rationalization

**rationalization**: defense mechanism in which the individual thinks up "good" reasons to justify his or her actions

**Rationalization** is a defensive response to stress which justifies our behavior by imputing logical, admirable, or at least acceptable motives to it. If we decide to go to a movie instead of studying for an examination, we can usually think up various reasons to justify our decision: after all, we only live once; everyone needs a change

*Fantasizing becomes maladaptive when someone uses it as a way to escape the stresses of everyday life.*

of pace; the relaxation will help us think more clearly; and so on. Often people try to justify cheating by pointing out that others cheat, that there is no virtue in being taken advantage of, and that in life people look the other way as long as you are successful. By rationalizing, we can usually justify almost everything we have done, are doing, or propose to do and hence can soften somewhat the effects of failure, guilt, and irrational behavior.

Rationalization is also used to defend against the disappointment of frustrated desires. A common example of such rationalization is the "sour grapes" reaction. In Aesop's fable, the fox was unable to reach a cluster of delicious grapes and decided he did not want them anyway because they were probably sour. Similarly, if we are turned down for a job, we may decide the job probably would have been dull anyway. The opposite of the sour grapes type of rationalization is the "sweet lemon" reaction—not only is what we cannot have not worth having, but what we do have is remarkably satisfactory: now that I think about it, I like things just the way they are; it is better to be poor than rich, because money is the root of all evil.

Rationalization is a very complex mechanism often difficult to detect, since it frequently contains some elements of truth. However, there is a good chance that we are rationalizing when we: (1) hunt for reasons to justify our behavior or beliefs, (2) cannot recognize inconsistencies that others see, and (3) become emotional when others question our behavior.

# Psychology in Action

## Coping with Cancer

To many psychotherapists *illusion* is a bad word. In their view, staying in touch with reality is the hallmark of mental health, and people who cherish too many illusions, especially about important things, are not truly well adjusted.

Shelley E. Taylor (1983) takes a strikingly different view. "Far from impeding adjustment," she says, "illusion may be essential for adequate coping" (p. 1171).

Taylor reached this conclusion after a two-year study of women with breast cancer. The women who coped best with the stress of disfiguring surgery, painful follow-up treatment, and fear of death proved to be those who constructed comforting illusions about themselves and their illness. Taylor defined illusions as beliefs based on an overly optimistic view of the facts, or as beliefs with no factual basis at all.

The helpful illusions grew out of the women's attempts to do three things: to understand the causes of their cancer and its significance in their lives; to gain a sense of mastery over the disease in particular and their lives in general; and to restore their self-esteem in the face of a devastating experience. Here are some of Taylor's findings (1983) on each of these points:

1. Although the causes of cancer are not fully understood, 95 percent of the women nevertheless believed that they knew why their cancer had occurred. Some blamed the stress of an unhappy marriage. Others mentioned birth control pills, heredity, or diet. The women's erroneous belief that they had pinpointed the reason for their illness seemed to make them feel better psychologically. It may have helped them to feel that they were not at the mercy of a capricious fate. Whatever the reason, even highly improbable explanations—like having been hit in the breast with a Frisbee—seemed useful.

Moreover, many women took comfort from the belief that having cancer had in some ways made their lives better. "I have much more enjoyment of each day," said one. "You find out that things like relationships are really the most important things you have—the people you know and your family—everything else is just way down the line," said another (p. 1163).

2. Having cancer is a very sobering experience that can make people feel powerless. To counter that feeling, two thirds of the women expressed the conviction that if they thought the right thoughts and did the right things, they could prevent the recurrence of cancer. As one woman put it, "I think that if you feel you are in control of it, you control it up to a point. I absolutely refuse to have any more cancer" (p. 1163).

3. Numerous studies show that undergoing a major stressful experience often lowers self-esteem, even if the victim is blameless. That may explain why the women tried to feel better about themselves by drawing comparisons with others whom they chose to regard as less fortunate. "I think I did extremely well under the circumstances," said one woman, remarking that there are "some women who aren't strong enough, who fall apart and become psychologically disturbed" (p. 1165).

It is clear that illusions promoted the adjustment of the women in Taylor's study. However, relying on illusions would seem to be a very risky way of adjusting: if the illusion is shattered, then the person's sense of well being should collapse as well. For example, imagine that a woman suffers a recurrence of cancer despite following a rigorous diet, or practicing positive thinking in the firm belief that it would keep her well. What happens to this woman's ability to cope?

Oddly enough, the women in Taylor's study did not seem to be too troubled when their theories turned out to be wrong, their self-protective measures useless. Of course, they were disheartened by their failing health. However, their adjustment seemed none the worse because they had embraced an illusion and seen it fall to pieces. What they usually did then was simply take a new approach to coping, try to control another aspect of their lives, or seek to bolster their self-esteem in a new way.

To remain continuously in close touch with unrelieved reality is sometimes too much to bear. At such times, Taylor suggests, the well-adjusted people may be those who allow themselves to nurture their illusions and "are ultimately restored by those illusions" (p. 1168).

## Projection

**projection:** defense mechanism in which the individual attributes his or her unacceptable desires and impulses to others

**Projection** is a mechanism through which we blame others for our mistakes and shortcomings or ascribe to others our unacceptable motivations. A husband feeling guilty about his extramarital affairs may place the blame on his unsympathetic wife or on "women who lead him on." The boy punished for fighting protests, "He hit me first—it was his fault." If an individual loses a job because of difficulties with other employees, he or she is quick to project the blame onto their former colleagues who "have it in for them." A student who delays writing a term paper until the last possible minute may believe that the poor grade on the paper was due to unclear instructions by the professor, inadequate library resources, or too many problems at home. In all these cases, projection serves as a means of defending the worth and adequacy of the self (Sherwood, 1981, 1982).

## Displacement

**displacement:** defense mechanism for redirection of emotions to objects other than those which initially aroused the emotions

**Displacement** allows us to discharge hostility toward a person or object other than the one actually eliciting it. A common subject for cartoons is the meek employee who has been mistreated by a domineering supervisor. Instead of expressing any hostility toward the supervisor, the employee goes home and yells at his spouse for no apparent reason. She, in turn, takes out her hostility on their young son, who displaces his anger by kicking the family dog.

Displaced hostility may take other forms. One is blaming problems on a scapegoat who cannot fight back. Among the ancient Israelites, the priest symbolically heaped all the sins of the people upon an unblemished goat—the scapegoat. Then the goat was driven into the wilderness to die. In Hitler's Germany, the Jews were blamed for the country's ills, and pent-up feelings of frustration and hostility were discharged against this group. Many cases of prejudice are thought to reflect such displacement of hostility.

## Regression

**regression:** defense mechanism in which the individual retreats to the use of less mature responses in attempting to cope with stress and maintain self-integration

**Regression** is the use of reaction patterns that have been long outgrown. For example, a woman who sought help from a therapist for a public-speaking anxiety found her ability to talk in front of people gradually improving. Previously she had been so frightened even of speaking with groups of friends at parties that she had begun staying at home on weekends. During the course of the therapy, however, she had a bad experience in which she forgot her note cards before a talk and simply "froze" in front of an audience. In an instant, it seemed, all her therapeutic progress was lost: she retreated to her home and refused any more offers to speak. In the face of stress, she regressed to an old solution to her fears.

Not surprisingly, in the face of severe stress or new challenges an individual may retreat to a less mature level of adjustment. We might expect regression to occur because newly learned reactions frequently fail to bring satisfaction. In looking for other, more successful methods of adaptation, it is only natural to try out discarded patterns that had previously brought satisfaction.

## Compensation

**Compensation** is used to defend the individual against feelings of inadequacy by emphasizing or developing a more desirable trait. Compensatory reactions take many forms and may have considerable adjustive value. For example, a physically unattractive youth may develop a pleasing demeanor and become an interesting conversationalist. As a consequence, physical unattractiveness is no longer a major obstacle to social acceptance and success.

Unfortunately, not all compensatory reactions are desirable or useful. Children who feel insecure may show-off to get more attention and increase their status. The boy feeling inferior and unpopular may become the local bully. The person feeling unloved and frustrated may eat too much. Some people attempt to convey confidence by bragging about their own accomplishments; others do it by criticism or innuendos in an attempt to cut other people down.

People who seem so taken with themselves that others do not seem to matter are often assumed by those around them to be "stuck up" or overly self-loving. In reality, many such people develop their attitude as a defense against their own feelings of worthlessness and low self-esteem. People who must tell you how great they are may actually be trying to convince *themselves*. It is almost as if they could believe they really are worthwhile if only they could convince you.

## Undoing

**Undoing** is a mechanism designed to negate or atone for some disapproved thought, impulse, or act. It is as if the individual wants to use an eraser to clear the paper and start over. Apologizing for wrongs against others, penance, repentance, and undergoing punishment are some of the common forms of undoing. For example, an unfaithful husband may have a sudden impulse to bring his wife flowers; an unethical business executive may give unusually large sums of money to some charitable organization; and the rejecting father may shower his child with gifts to show how much he "really" cares.

Sometimes undoing can be a highly appropriate strategy. If you realize that you have hurt someone and would like to make amends, you can sometimes make both the person and yourself feel better by making some kind of reparation. However, sometimes undoing can become a substitute for forethought. When that happens, people find themselves forever making up for things they have already done instead of initially avoiding the inappropriate behavior.

## Emotional Insulation

In **emotional insulation,** we reduce our degree of emotional involvement in potentially hurtful situations. Since we all undergo many disappointments in life, we usually learn to keep our hopes and anticipations within bounds until a hoped-for event actually occurs. We are careful to avoid premature celebrations or to let our hopes get too high. For example, a student applying to a very competitive law school may not let herself get too enthusiastic until she is accepted into the program.

*Overindulgence is one way to compensate for frustrations and feelings of inferiority or inadequacy.*

Under conditions of long-continued frustration, as in chronic unemployment, many people lose hope and become resigned and apathetic. These individuals protect themselves from the hurt of sustained frustration by further reducing their involvement—they no longer care, and hence they deprive the stressful situation of much of its power to hurt them.

Up to a point, emotional insulation is an important mechanism for defending ourselves from both unnecessary and unavoidable pain. However, life involves calculated risks, and most of us are willing to take our chances on active participation. Although we may get badly hurt on occasion, we have the resilience to recover and try again. Emotional insulation provides a protective shell preventing repetition of previous pain, but in so doing it also prevents the individual's healthy, vigorous participation in living.

People who have "loved and lost" sometimes make use of emotional insulation. They protect themselves from future rejection and loss by making themselves invulnerable or hardening themselves to tender feelings. The disadvantage of this strategy is that it prevents them from ever really enjoying intimacy with another person. In protecting themselves against life's lows, they eliminate one of life's greatest highs. One client who had chosen this strategy in response to some significant losses as a child often became furious at her therapist for little or no reason. As the treatment progressed, the therapist recognized that the woman became most angry shortly after a session during which she had revealed something important about herself. The therapist interpreted this to the patient as an example of her defense against intimacy: as soon as she felt close, she tried to drive the therapist away. By repeatedly examining her relationship to the therapist, she was able to begin to see how she was avoiding intimacy for fear of loss and rejection. The process was long and arduous, but with time the woman made significant progress in developing more intimate relationships with people generally.

### Intellectualization

**intellectualization:** defense mechanism by which the individual achieves some measure of insulation from emotional hurt by treating the situation as an abstract problem to be analyzed

In **intellectualization,** people avoid the anxiety and emotions normally accompanying a stressful event by treating the situation as an abstract problem to be analyzed. Someone may soften the grief over your mother's death by intimating that she lived to be over seventy years of age. People soften failures and disappointments by pointing out that "it could have been worse."

Intellectualization may be utilized under extremely stressful conditions as well as in dealing with the milder stresses of everyday life. Bluestone and McGahee (1962) found that this defense was often used by prisoners awaiting execution. "'So they'll kill me; and that's that'—this said with a shrug of the shoulders suggests that the affect appropriate to the thought has somehow been isolated" (p. 395). Other prisoners may feel as though it is happening to someone else, and they are watching impersonally from a distance.

In the preceding discussion, we have examined the major defense mechanisms that people use in coping with the stresses of life. It is worth repeating that although all the defense-oriented responses to stress involve a degree of self-deception and distortion, they can serve a valuable purpose: by protecting us from the full force of a stressful situation, they can pave the way for more task-oriented behavior, as we will see in the next section in which we examine cognitive reactions to stress (see Psychology in Action, pp. 132–33).

## COGNITIVE REACTIONS TO STRESS

Chapter 3 stated that while some people may experience a situation as stressful, other people in the same situation may experience little or no stress. We saw that one reason for these individual differences is that the "same" situation often means quite different things to different people. When faced with a potentially threatening situation, then, one of the first things each of us does is appraise the situation to determine whether it is in fact stressful, positive, neutral, or irrelevant. The psychologist Richard Lazarus (1981; Lazarus & DeLongis, 1983; Lazarus & Folkman, 1984) calls this process **primary appraisal.**

**primary appraisal:** judgment of the stressfulness of an event

Suppose, for example, you are taking a class on the psychology of adjustment, and the professor suddenly announces a pop quiz. Some students will immediately appraise this as a stressful situation. If you have not been keeping up with the work or if you have little faith in your ability, you will likely appraise the situation as potentially harmful or threatening. If, on the other hand, you feel confident and

competent and have read the material, you may appraise the situation as an opportunity to apply your knowledge and display your expertise. In both of these cases your initial cognitive appraisal of the situation—the way you understand it and its consequences for you—has an enormous impact on the extent to which you experience it as stressful.

**secondary appraisal:** judgment of the most appropriate coping strategies for dealing with stress

Once a situation has been appraised as stressful, the next step is what Lazarus calls **secondary appraisal:** the person evaluates possible coping strategies and chooses the strategy likely to be the most effective. To continue the example of the unexpected quiz, if you appraise the situation as threatening, you may consider acting ill to excuse yourself from the exam; you may quickly glance at the chapter summary in your text; you may remind yourself that the quiz is only 5 percent of your course grade. All of these are possible ways of coping with the stressful event; your secondary appraisal determines which, if any of them, you will use to manage this particular stressor.

After a coping strategy is selected and utilized, you then reappraise the situation to determine whether it is still stressful. If the situation remains stressful, you are likely to try different coping strategies, appraise their effects, and if necessary consider still further ways of coping. In other words, stress triggers a series of cognitive reactions: appraisal, initial efforts to cope, reappraisal, additional efforts to cope, reappraisal, and so on until the stress is relieved.

# Psychology in Action

## Reactions to the Stress of AIDS

The full range of reactions to stress can be seen in the way different people react *to acquired immune deficiency syndrome* (AIDS). AIDS was first identified in 1981. Since that time, its incidence has doubled every six months. Over 80 percent of those diagnosed with AIDS die within two years.

Not surprisingly, in the population at large the fear of AIDS has reached epidemic proportions. For example, even though the threat of contracting AIDS by transfusions is less than one in a million, people have become so afraid that many have refused even to give blood (Batchelor, 1984). This illustrates the kind of irrational thinking that often occurs under stress, since a person can no more catch AIDS by giving blood than by pricking their finger with a sewing needle. AIDS has also bolstered irrational stereotypes and prejudices against high-risk groups such as homosexuals and Haitians. As one writer has noted, the level of prejudice and hysteria elicited by the AIDS epidemic suggests that "paranoia and political idiocy are far more contagious than AIDS" (Krauthammer, 1983, p. 20).

Within high-risk groups (such as homosexuals, Haitians, intravenous drug users, and hemophiliacs), the psychological stress is much greater, of course. Uncertainty about the causes and symptoms of the disease can be excruciatingly stressful. No one knows how long the disease takes to develop, and so people in high-risk groups do not know if their past behavior could already have exposed them to the disease. Further, the symptoms are so varied that any sign of illness can provoke intense anxiety. In San Francisco, for example, some public health experts believe that half the gay male population has been exposed to AIDS. Joseph et al. (1984) noted the remarks of one high-risk male:

*All I need to do is lie in bed half asleep, becoming aware that I have a sore throat and suddenly it's all there: my heart starts racing, I'm drenched in sweat, and I'm dealing with the possibility that I'll be dead in a year (p. 1300).*

Homosexuals are particularly likely to experience stress from the threat of AIDS. In addition to the problems already mentioned, the AIDS epidemic feeds insecurities and guilt about being homosexual. Even though many homosexuals have come to terms with most of these feelings, the emergence of AIDS is bound to reactivate many old doubts and worries.

AIDS has also reactivated discrimination against gays in housing and employment. As a result, many homosexuals say that they feel as if they are contaminated, like lepers. Researchers in one study at the University of

In the opening chapter of this book, we discussed at some length the fact that human beings are capable of a high degree of self-direction because they can use uniquely human cognitive abilities to cope with stress. Self awareness, the ability to reason and imagine and communicate, the ability to make value judgments—these cognitive skills allow us to rely on our mental abilities to cope with stress not only by modifying our own behavior but also by shaping the environment to better meet our needs. This is such an important aspect of human reactions to stress that the next chapter is devoted entirely to its consideration.

However, before we continue it is important to note that when we are under stress, we may be less able to use cognitive processes. Low levels of stress actually help most people to think better: they are better at remembering, they think more effectively, they are better at solving problems, and so on. However, as stress

**Reactions to the Stress of AIDS   (continued)**

Michigan discovered that many homosexual men:

> . . . *were concerned about passing a soft drink can from person to person or . . . kissing relatives in greeting. Altruistic behavioral changes such as no longer donating blood often saddened respondents as it heightened their sense of estrangement and stigmatization within general society (Joseph et al., 1984, p. 1302).*

Within high-risk groups, the stress of AIDS is heightened still further by grief over the loss of friends and acquaintances. In the gay community in San Francisco, for example, virtually everyone has had a friend die of AIDS, and many have lost more than one friend. To make matters worse, the social support people typically receive while mourning is frequently not available to homosexuals grieving for lovers, since family and heterosexual friends are often uncomfortable about homosexual relationships.

Even though AIDS itself attacks the immune system, there is growing evidence that the *stress* of having AIDS may further suppress the immune system (Bridge, Mirsky, & Goodwin, 1988). In other words, when AIDS patients need to strengthen their immune system, the system may be further weakened by the stress of uncertainty, insecurity, guilt, discrimination, loneliness, grief, and the ultimate realization that AIDS is both a deadly and an uncontrollable disease.

The combination of these factors makes coping with AIDS extremely difficult. Some people respond with denial, as did two of the respondents in the Michigan study: "Doctors can't even agree with one another; you can't tell me they know what they're doing"; "Look, if going to bathhouses made you get AIDS I would have been dead years ago. I figure I'm just not going to get it" (Joseph et al., 1984, p. 1302). Others respond by becoming extremely well informed about AIDS; some of these people go on to use the defense of intellectualization to distance themselves from the real threat of the disease. Others attempt to cope by changing the nature of their sexual activities, thus, hopefully, reducing the likelihood that they will be exposed to AIDS. Still others turn to support groups within the gay community.

Virtually everyone uses different techniques for coping. One homosexual remarked, "What have I changed? I've changed everything a hundred times. I've also unchanged everything a hundred times. And then, I start over somewhere else" (Joseph et al., 1984, p. 1302). In short, the strategies people use to cope with the stress of AIDS are the same as those used by anyone who is trying to cope with a major, life-threatening disaster.

increases beyond a certain point, thinking processes begin to change: attention narrows so the person is aware of less information; it becomes more difficult to concentrate and to think logically; memory and judgment deteriorate; thinking becomes more rigid; and the efficiency of problem solving and decision making tends to decrease.

These effects are particularly noticeable on complex, difficult tasks—exactly those situations where we most need to use our thinking skills to deal with the source of the stress. Our adaptive efficiency may also be impaired by the emotions that typically accompany severe stress. For example, acute stage fright may disrupt the performance of a public speaker. Test anxiety may lead to poor performance despite adequate preparation. In a sudden catastrophe, intense fear may cause an individual to panic or freeze.

In this chapter we have seen that stressful events cause people to react in complex ways: they respond physiologically, cognitively, emotionally, and defensively, and these different responses interact with and reinforce one another. We have also seen that severe stress can take a heavy toll because of these various reactions. Nonetheless, people can and do learn to cope effectively and efficiently with the stresses of everyday living. In the next chapter, we will look at some of the ways of coping more effectively with stress, and I will suggest some ways to use stress for growth—not destruction.

## SUMMARY

Psychological stress can have a profound effect upon the body. Physiological reactions to stress are part of what Hans Selye called the *General Adaptation Syndrome* (GAS). According to Selye, reactions to stress (from whatever source) occur in three major phases: alarm and mobilization, resistance, and exhaustion. During *alarm and mobilization,* the body prepares for vigorous physical activity if that is required in coping with the source of stress. Among other things, the heart beats faster, blood pressure rises, and energy is made readily available. While these changes are appropriate when people are confronted with physical danger, the same changes are much less helpful when the source of stress is psychological: prolonged psychological stress puts a tremendous load on the body and can lead to severe disorders, even death under certain circumstances.

*It is important for each of us to discover a stress relieving method and to fall back on it whenever stress is persistent.*

If stress persists, the second phase of our reaction is called *resistance*. Here the individual tries to deal with the stress. However, the more coping resources that are used in dealing with one stressor, the fewer resources are left for dealing with other stressors. In particular, psychological stress can actively interfere with the body's *immune system* and leave the person more vulnerable to infections and diseases. Reducing stress has been shown to increase the effectiveness of the immune system in fighting off diseases.

If stress persists, eventually the individual enters the stage of *exhaustion*. Unless something is done to stop the stress, permanent damage or even death may occur.

Some people under severe or prolonged stress suffer from *psychophysiological disorders*. *Peptic ulcers*, asthma, backaches, hives, *tension headaches* and *migraine headaches*, and *hypertension* (high blood pressure) are among a long list of physiological disorders more likely to occur when an individual is exposed to severe or prolonged stress. Different people exposed to the same kind of stress will differ in the particular disorder they are likely to develop. Such *organ specificity* is thought to be due to some combination of prior injury or illness, heredity, learning, and personality type.

In addition to physiological reactions, stress virtually always triggers emotional responses, as well. *Fear* and *anxiety* are often experienced together as *worry*. While worry can be an appropriate response to some kinds of stress, chronic worrying can have a variety of negative consequences. Anger can be expressed constructively, as a nonthreatening response to stress that deals directly with the issues, or as *aggression*, destructive behavior that is intended to harm others.

Another frequent emotional reaction to stress is guilt, which arises when we feel personally responsible for some wrongful act. Grief, depression, and loneliness are also frequent reactions when we lose important sources of pleasure or when important people in our lives are no longer present. It is necessary to distinguish between aloneness or solitude (which is often a matter of choice) and loneliness (which is usually not a matter of choice).

While these various emotional reactions are universal, each of us learns which emotions are most appropriate in which kinds of situations. Thus, one person may respond with anxiety or fear in a situation that another person finds depressing. Abused children, for example, learn to respond with anxiety and fear rather than with love and affection to the parent-child relationship.

All of us at one time or another also make use of *defense-oriented responses* to stress. These reactions can be adaptive if they help to insulate us from some of the effects of stress and thus make it possible for us to cope more effectively with the sources of stress. They are maladaptive if they interfere with our ability to cope with life's problems. Two of the most important defense-oriented reactions to stress are *repression* and *suppression*. Repression involves completely excluding threatening or painful thoughts and emotions from consciousness; repressed material continues to influence our behavior even though it is unconscious. Suppression involves consciously blocking awareness of unpleasant thoughts or wishes; in this case, however, we can still gain access to the thoughts and wishes if we try to do so. *Denial* involves ignoring or refusing to acknowledge disagreeable realities. *Fantasy* allows us to imagine a more pleasant world without as much stress. *Rationalization* allows us to justify inappropriate behavior or to defend against disappointments. *Projection* allows

us to blame others for our mistakes or to attribute to others our unacceptable desires. *Displacement* allows us to redirect hostility toward new targets. *Regression* involves behaving in a relatively immature way. *Compensation* allows us to substitute or emphasize more desirable traits and thus to overcome feelings of inadequacy. *Undoing* involves negating or atoning for some undesirable thought or action. *Emotional insulation* refers to reducing our emotional involvement in threatening or stressful situations. *Intellectualization* allows us to deal with a stressful situation by treating it as an abstract problem to be analyzed.

Cognitive reactions to stress are extremely important, since it is through the use of cognitive abilities that human beings are uniquely able to cope with and deal with stress. When confronted with a stressor, a person first makes a *primary appraisal* of the dangers and possibilities inherent in the situation. If the situation is appraised as stressful, a *secondary appraisal* is used to determine possible coping strategies to manage the stress. A reappraisal of the situation occurs after attempting to use a strategy to determine whether further steps are needed to bring the stress under control. Chapter 5 is devoted in large part to a detailed discussion of secondary appraisal. It is important to note that stress also makes it more difficult than usual to use cognitive abilities to cope: under stress, attention narrows, concentration declines, thinking becomes rigid, and the efficiency of problem solving decreases. Thus, at the time when we are most likely to need our cognitive skills, they are not fully available for our use.

## KEY TERMS

General Adaptation Syndrome
    (GAS) (107)
alarm and mobilization reaction (108)
resistance (109)
immune system(109)
exhaustion (111)
psychophysiological disorders (112)
organ specificity (113)
peptic (gastric) ulcer (115)
muscle contraction headache (116)
migraine headache (116)
hypertension (116)
fear (117)
anxiety (117)
worry (117)
aggression (119)
defense-oriented responses (122)

repression (122)
suppression (123)
denial (124)
fantasy (124)
rationalization (124)
projection (127)
displacement (127)
regression (127)
compensation (128)
undoing (128)
emotional insulation (128)
intellectualization (130)
primary appraisal (130)
secondary appraisal (131)
acquired immune deficiency syndrome
    (AIDS) (132)

# Effective Methods of Coping with Stress

139

*Sitting in a dentist's chair is stressful, but so is exchanging a passionate kiss with a lover—after all, your pulse races, your breathing quickens, your heartbeat soars, and yet, who in the world would forego such a pleasurable pastime simply because of the stress involved? . . . Our aim shouldn't be to completely avoid stress . . . but to learn how to recognize our typical response to stress and then try to moderate our lives in accordance with it.*

*On the Real Benefits of Eustress* (Selye, 1978, p. 60)

$\mathcal{I}$N the quote above, Selye is repeating a point that I have made over and over again in the last two chapters: some kinds of stress are beneficial, other kinds of stress are harmful, but stress of one sort or another is an inevitable part of living. It comes along with our successes as well as our failures, our moments of happiness as well as our moments of despair. Effective adjustment does not mean eliminating all stress from our lives. Rather, it means learning how to keep stress within acceptable limits and learning how to cope more effectively with stress.

In this chapter, we will focus on various ways of responding more effectively to stress. First, we will consider some techniques for coping effectively with the physiological, emotional, and cognitive reactions that so often accompany stressful events. Then, we will explore some effective techniques for coping directly with sources of stress. Finally, we will consider the ways stressful situations can be used for personal growth. Throughout our discussion, we will see that the ways each of us responds to stress depend upon factors such as the nature of the stressor, the characteristics of the environment, our frame of reference, our motives, and our competencies.

Most of us can usually meet adjustive demands without undue difficulty. In other cases, we may be only partially successful. In still other cases, we may fail completely and our physical and mental well-being may be jeopardized as a result. Sometimes we respond effectively to stressful situations with little or no conscious planning. In other cases we may be partially aware of our efforts to cope. In still other cases, our attempts to cope with stress may be thought out and carefully planned. We begin our discussion with a look at some ways of coping with the immediate effects of stress.

## COPING EFFECTIVELY WITH REACTIONS TO STRESS

In Chapter 4, we saw that stressors can have a profound effect upon us physiologically, emotionally, and cognitively. Often it is necessary to control stress reactions before trying to deal with the source of the stress itself. For example, if you are

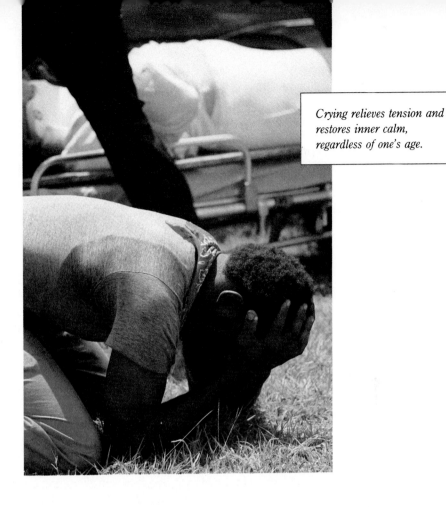

*Crying relieves tension and restores inner calm, regardless of one's age.*

experiencing a throbbing headache, experiencing great anxiety, or if you find yourself unable to think clearly and plan effectively, you are unlikely to do a very good job of identifying and dealing with the source of your stress. Therefore, before you attempt to deal with the source of stress, you should take steps to cope with your responses to the stressful situation. In this section of the chapter, we will explore effective ways of coping with physiological, emotional, and cognitive stress responses. Keep in mind the fact that just as these three stress reactions interact with each other, so too do the strategies people use in coping with them. Dealing effectively with cognitive reactions to stressful events, for example, will often relieve some of the physiological and emotional reactions, as well. Similarly, reducing emotional reactions to stress may help a person to think more clearly, and this in turn may also serve to lessen stress.

## Built-in Coping Mechanisms

**built-in coping mechanisms:** predominantly unlearned patterns such as crying and laughing that can be used to relieve stress reactions

When people are experiencing stress, certain coping reactions begin to operate automatically, rather than as a result of deliberate choice. These **built-in coping mechanisms** are helpful in reducing tension and anxiety, repairing psychological damage, and restoring psychological equilibrium—all steps which pave the way toward more deliberate and carefully determined coping measures. The following are among the more common and important of these built-in coping mechanisms.

**Crying.**   Crying is a remarkably effective way of relieving emotional tension and pain. This reaction is commonly seen in the behavior of children who have been frustrated or hurt. Although children are often taught that "grown-ups don't cry," crying is not uncommon among adult men and women and serves as an important means of relieving tension and hurt, and of restoring inner equilibrium. For example, crying is an important part of the "grief work" that a person experiences while recovering from the loss of a loved one.

**Talking about problems.**   Another built-in way of relieving emotional tension is by discussing a problem. This mechanism is so simple and so widely used that its value is often overlooked. Nearly everyone probably has encountered individuals who enjoyed recounting in gory detail their accidents, operations, or other traumatic experiences. Similarly, people who have survived catastrophes—such as major fires, floods, and earthquakes—often show a compulsive need to tell others about their experiences. Repetitive talking about a stressful experience often helps the person to become desensitized to it and to cope more readily with it. Discussing a problem—gaining relief through putting disturbing feelings into words and gaining an understanding of a situation—is also an important part of most psychotherapy.

What if no one is available to listen? Then talking to oneself is a good substitute. Although we miss the comfort and caring of another person in this case, talking to oneself can put matters into perspective. It can also encourage us to be as compassionate and rational with ourselves as we would be with a friend facing similar problems. In fact, a recent study shows that talking to oneself is one of the most widely used techniques for dealing with stress (Horton, Gewirtz, & Kreutter, 1988).

**Humor.**   Trying to view personal problems with a sense of humor is also an effective way of reducing tension. Humor helps many of us to keep things in perspective, to accept inevitable pain and setbacks, and not to take ourselves too seriously. Humor in the form of stories or jokes can also serve to relieve aggressiveness and anger.

**Sleep and dreams.**   Many people cannot sleep when they are under stress. However, when sleep is possible, it often has a healing function. People who have undergone highly traumatic events, such as combat experiences, often have nightmares in which they reenact their experiences. Such nightmares often desensitize these individuals to the traumatic event and help them understand and accept their experiences. Sleep is also an effective built-in method of coping with less stressful situations. For example, some researchers placed preschool children in full sight of some tempting rewards, but told them not to touch the rewards until an adult returned to the room (Mischel & Ebbesen, 1970). Faced with this difficult and frustrating situation, some of the children simply went to sleep until the adult returned!

Crying, talking, laughing, and sleeping can be helpful ways of coping with stress reactions. However, by themselves they are rarely effective in relieving all the effects of stress. In the next portion of the chapter, we will examine some other ways of coping with specific stress reactions.

## Coping with Physiological Reactions to Stress

Imagine you have just finished an extremely stressful day. Perhaps you had two long exams and a term paper due; or perhaps you had several important meetings with clients and then a key strategy session with your supervisor. Whatever the cause of the stress, your muscles are tense; your head aches; you have a knot in your stomach; and you feel exhausted. As we saw in Chapter 4, these are all common physiological reactions to stress. There are two effective ways of dealing with these and many other physiological stress reactions: relaxation and exercise.

**Relaxation.**    How often have you heard the familiar refrain: "You're tense and uptight. Relax." The instruction seems simple enough: "Relax," as though this were the most natural thing to do in stressful situations. It would be wonderful if we could simply throw an internal switch from the position marked "Tense" to that marked "Relaxed," but this simply is not possible. In fact, such a naive attitude about relaxation leads some people to rely on alcohol or drugs to quickly achieve a state of relaxation. Actually, relaxation is an extraordinarily valuable skill that, like any other skill, must be learned through practice.

How does one go about relaxing? Early in this century, physiologist Edmund Jacobson noticed that muscle tension often accompanied reports of people who felt "tense" (Jacobson, 1934). He concluded that if people were to relax their muscles, they would report *feeling* relaxed, as well.

Jacobson was the first person to develop a specific, nonpharmacological approach to **relaxation training** by using muscle relaxation. Through his research, Jacobson (1938) found that systematically tensing and relaxing various muscle groups aided muscle relaxation. He also found that it was important for people to pay attention to the various sensations produced by the tensing and relaxing of the muscles. In this way, the relaxation achieved by his procedures was aided and supplemented by internal feelings of tension and relaxation. His trainees eventually learned to achieve deep levels of relaxation. Unfortunately, Jacobson's procedures never became very popular, primarily because the procedures were very long and time-consuming, requiring over fifty sessions of training.

However, interest in relaxation training was renewed when Joseph Wolpe (1958) discovered that he could shorten Jacobson's procedures considerably and achieve virtually the same results. Wolpe found that six twenty-minute sessions supplemented by twice-daily home practice could help people achieve deep relaxation levels. Wolpe's modification of Jacobson's procedures spurred other psychologists to try to learn more about relaxation. Their findings have confirmed the suggestion that relaxation training can indeed result in lowered levels of physiological arousal and subjective anxiety (for example, Paul, 1969).

Several aspects of relaxation training appear to be important. First, achieving a deep state of relaxation is a learned skill, not an ability that you either have or don't have. Anyone can, with practice, learn the skill of relaxation. As with any other

**relaxation training:** specific learned techniques that help an individual attain a relaxed state

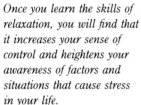

*Once you learn the skills of relaxation, you will find that it increases your sense of control and heightens your awareness of factors and situations that cause stress in your life.*

skill, consistent practice will increase your effectiveness at achieving and maintaining a state of relaxation when it is needed.

Second, in the long run, relaxation training is more beneficial than the drugs that people commonly use to achieve relaxation. When people use alcohol, marijuana, or tranquilizers to achieve a state of relaxation, they recognize that their relaxed state is brought on by the drug, not by their own efforts. On the other hand, relaxation that people can attribute to their own efforts is both longer lasting and more beneficial, in part because it provides a sense of control over the situation; and as we have seen in previous chapters, having a sense of control greatly reduces the stressfulness of a situation (Davison, Tsujimoto, & Glaros, 1973).

Finally, relaxation training can increase people's awareness of the situations producing stress. Through training, it is possible to become more sensitive to various levels of tension and relaxation and to use this heightened awareness to identify the factors responsible for most stress.

Relaxation is such an important skill that I have provided detailed instructions for learning one effective way to relax (see Psychology in Action, pp. 146–47). Of course, there are many other ways of achieving a state of relaxation. According to psychiatrist Paul Horton and his colleagues, some of the most popular techniques for relaxing are listening to music, watching TV, reading, prayer or meditation, and going for a walk (Horton, Gewirtz, & Kreutter, 1988). It may seem strange to think of these as learned strategies for relaxing and managing stress, but that is just what they are. Either from direct experience or from observing others, you may have learned that some of these techniques can help you to control some of your reactions to stress.

The technique you use is not particularly important: each person relaxes in a different way. The important point is to develop some technique that allows you to achieve a state of relaxation whenever you find yourself trying to cope with stress. Toward this end, you might find especially useful a book by Peggy Gillespie and Lynn Bechtel titled *Less Stress in 30 Days* (1986). The authors are experienced stress-reduction professionals who describe an effective step-by-step program for reducing stress.

Of course, relaxation is not a cure-all for harmful stress, but it is one of the most beneficial components in an effective stress-management program.

**Exercise.** Exercise is another useful technique for controlling the physiological effects of stress. Whether our activity is with others, as in group sports, or by ourselves, exercise can provide release from the stresses and tensions that develop during the day.

Exercise helps release tensions in several ways. First, vigorous exercise actually reduces or eliminates some of the physiological effects of stress. Second, the time spent exercising reduces the time spent in stressful situations. This "time off" also provides an opportunity to think of potentially useful strategies for dealing with the underlying problem that is causing the stress. Finally, exercise contributes to physical fitness. As fitness increases, physical resources for dealing with adjustive demands increase, as well.

As with relaxation, exercise is only useful when done regularly. Many experts advise exercising three times per week as an aid to maintaining health. The most effective way to assure this amount of exercise is to deliberately set aside time for exercising. The participation of a friend in an exercise program can also increase the chances that you will continue in the program, and it may make the process of exercising significantly more enjoyable, as well. Unfortunately, not everyone benefits from exercise. Some compulsive overachievers interpret exercise as yet another competitive challenge: they try to run longer and play harder than anyone else; they work so hard at exercising and training that the activities become simply more sources of stress and strain in their lives. In such cases, professionals often recommend that the person start with relaxation or meditation; then, when the stress is under control, the individual can start a program of relaxed, enjoyable exercise.

**Coping with specific disorders.** In addition to relaxation and exercise, there are ways to cope with some of the specific physiological reactions to stress.

1. *Ulcers.* For people prone to ulcers, the best long-term treatment is reducing the level of stress. In the short-run, physicians can prescribe dietary changes and medicines that reduce stomach acid and coat the walls of the stomach. These steps are often effective in reducing the damage from excess stomach acid.

2. *Headaches.* It is often useful to keep a diary of events that trigger headaches and then to try to avoid those things in the future—for example, chocolate, red wine, and cheeses trigger migraine attacks in some people. Another approach is to learn to control muscle tension in the head and neck. By relaxing the muscles in these areas, it is often possible to reduce the severity of headaches. Some migraine

## Learning How to Relax

Relaxation is a skill that anyone can learn. Like other skills, relaxation is best learned in the proper setting using the proper techniques.

First, prepare a relaxing setting. Find a comfortable chair (preferably a recliner), a wide couch, chaise lounge, or bed in which to practice relaxation. Second, remove all distractions. Make sure that you will not be bothered by phone calls, visitors, television, stereo, radios, and so forth. A darkened, quiet room is ideal. Loosen all tight clothing. Since you will probably want to close your eyes during relaxation training, remove contact lenses if you wear them.

The relaxation instructions I have presented here assume that you will record them on a tape recorder. If you do not have access to a tape recorder, someone can read them to you. Or, you can memorize the sequence and practice relaxation alone. While it does not matter whether the instructions are tape recorded or memorized, it is important to take your time while going through the exercises. It should take you about twenty minutes to complete this relaxation program.

A final rule for relaxing: Make time to practice relaxation. Don't let old ways and worn phrases such as "I just don't have the time" stand in the way of learning this useful skill.

Now settle back as comfortably as you can and listen to what I'm going to be telling you. If you listen closely, you'll be able (with enough practice) to learn to relax the various muscles of your body and to enjoy the accompanying feelings of relaxation, pleasantness, and calm.

Clench your left hand into a fist. Just clench your fist tighter and tighter, and study the tension as you do so. (Five-second pause.) And now, let go. Try to let go entirely of the tensions in your left hand. Let your fingers become loose. Notice the contrast between the degree of relaxation in your hand now and the degree of tension that you created in your left hand just a moment ago. (Ten-second pause.) As we go through these various procedures and I ask you to let go of a given muscle group, see if you can let go all at once rather than gradually releasing the tension. Almost throw the tension out of

your muscles as well as you can. This is something you'll get more of a feel for as we proceed.

Now clench your right hand into a fist, study the tension, and pay close attention to what that feels like. (Five-second pause.) Now let go. Let go and see if you can keep letting go a little bit more, even though it seems as if you've let go as much as you possibly can. There always seems to be that extra bit of relaxation. Just keep letting go of your right hand and your left hand as well, just relaxing as best you can. (Ten-second pause.)

Now, bend both hands back at the wrists, pointing your fingers at the ceiling, so that you tense the muscles in the back of your hand and in your forearm. Study the tension. (Five-second pause.) And now let it go. Let it go and keep letting go to the best of your ability, becoming more and more relaxed. (Ten-second pause.) Once again, bend both hands back at the wrists, fingers pointing toward the ceiling. Study the tension, notice what it feels like, pay close attention to it. (Five-second pause.) And now let go. Notice and enjoy the contrast between tension and relaxation. (Ten-second pause.) Now clench both your hands into fists and bring them toward your shoulders so as to tighten your bicep muscles, the large muscle in the upper part of your arm. Study that tension. (Five-second pause.) Now let go, letting your arms drop down again to the chair, relaxing once again. Even as you think of letting go, you can feel the tensions leaving your muscles. (Ten-second pause.)

Now concentrate on your forehead. I would like you to wrinkle up your forehead. Wrinkle the muscles in your forehead and study the tension. (Five-second pause.) Now smooth it out; relax those muscles. Don't tense them any more. Smooth out and relax your forehead as best you can, noticing the difference between tension and relaxation. (Ten-second pause.) I would like you now to close your eyes tightly so that you feel tension around your eyes. Notice what that feels like. (Five-second pause.) And now relax. Relax, allowing your eyes to remain lightly closed if that's comfortable for you. And notice once again the difference between the tension you created before and the relaxation that you are creating

## Learning How to Relax   (continued)

now. (Ten-second pause.) Now I would like you to press your lips together. Press your lips together so that you feel tension around the mouth and the chin and the cheeks. (Five-second pause.) And now let go. Let go of the tension as best you can. Let go all at once, and enjoy the contrast between tension and relaxation. (Ten-second pause.)

Now I would like you to shrug your shoulders. Bring both your shoulders up as if to touch your ears. Feel the tension in your upper back and your neck. (Five-second pause.) And now let go. Let your shoulders drop down. Feel that relaxation. Just let go of those tense muscles. (Ten-second pause.) Perhaps you are feeling some different sensations at this time—a tingling feeling or sensations of warmth. Whatever it is you're experiencing, just enjoy it; go along with it. Let yourself enjoy the feelings that accompany relaxation.

Now press your head back against the couch. Study the tension; pay close attention to it. (Five-second pause.) And now let go. Let your head come back to a resting position and relax the muscles in your neck. (Ten-second pause.) Now bring your head forward and try to bury your chin into your chest. Notice the feeling. (Five-second pause.) Now relax. (Ten-second pause.)

Now I would like you to take a deep breath and hold it. Study that tension; feel the growing discomfort. (Five-second pause.) And now exhale and breathe normally once again. (Ten-second pause.) Let each exhalation become a signal to let go generally, to let your muscles become more and more relaxed. (Ten-second pause.)

I would now like you to arch your back so that you're sticking your chest out and the arch of your back is leaving the chair somewhat. Study the tension. (Five-second pause.) Now let go. Let your back drop down once again. And relax once again. (Ten-second pause.) Now I'd like you to tense your stomach muscles as if someone were going to punch you in the stomach. (Five-second pause.) Now relax them. Let your stomach become softer once again. Relax those muscles. (Ten-second pause.) Now I'd like you to tense the muscles in your buttocks by trying to lift yourself out of your chair. Tense those muscles.

Study the tension. (Five-second pause.) And now let go; relax those muscles. (Ten-second pause.) Notice once again the contrast between the tension and the relative relaxation you experience when you're no longer tensing those muscles, when you're letting go and trying to let go even further.

Now I'd like you to extend your legs and lift your feet so that your thighs are tensed. Feel the tension in your thighs; notice it, study it. (Five-second pause.) And now let your feet drop down. Let your legs become looser and more relaxed. (Ten-second pause.) I would like you now to bend both feet back at the ankles in the same fashion as you did with your wrists before. Your toes are pointing back toward your face. (Five-second pause.) And now let go; let go of that tension. (Ten-second pause.)

I'm going to review with you briefly the various muscle groups that we've covered. As I call out the name of each group, just think of releasing the tension in those muscles. Think of letting go a little bit more if you can. Relax your hands. (Five-second pause.) And your forearms. (Five-second pause.) Your upper arms: the biceps, the triceps. Your entire arms down to your fingertips. Let them become more relaxed. (Five-second pause.) Relax your shoulders, the muscles of your face, your forehead, your cheeks, your mouth, your jaws, and your neck. (Five-second pause.) A wave of relaxation spreading downward from your head, coming now into your chest and down into your stomach. (Five-second pause.) And relax your calves, your thighs, and your feet. (Five-second pause.) Let your entire body become more relaxed. (Five-second pause.)

Let yourself relax like that for a while, and in a moment I will have you open your eyes once again. (Two-minute pause.) I'm going to count from five to one, and as I count, you'll begin to stretch and gradually arouse yourself. At the count of one, let your eyes open, be wide awake and refreshed, alert, and probably a little more relaxed than when you started. Five . . . four, stretching . . . three . . . two, take a deep breath . . . and one . . . eyes open, wide awake, refreshed, and relaxed.

sufferers also find that by redirecting the flow of blood to their fingers, they can reduce or eliminate headache symptoms.

Prescription drugs can also be effective in alleviating headaches until a more direct approach to the underlying source of stress can be taken. Many new drugs taken at the first signs of a migraine, for example, can reduce the likelihood of a full-blown attack. While many drugs for treating migraines have some undesirable side effects, new drugs are being tested that apparently have few if any important side effects. For migraine sufferers it is also often helpful to maintain regular schedules of eating, sleeping, and exercise; changes in schedules (for example on weekends) are often found to be associated with the onset of migraine attacks. Of course, with any prolonged or severe headache it is important to consult a physician to assure that the headache is not a sign of a more serious problem.

3. *Hypertension.* Fortunately, hypertension is both simple to detect and relatively easy to control by changes in diet, weight loss, medication, and stress-reduction techniques. The most effective long-term solution, of course, is to alleviate the sources of stress. If hypertension becomes a chronic problem, medication frequently becomes necessary.

## Coping with Emotional Reactions to Stress

We saw in Chapter 4 that stressful events can trigger a variety of powerful emotional reactions including fear and anxiety, anger and hostility, guilt, grief, depression, and loneliness. Up to a point, these and other emotions convey important information about ourselves and our environment. For example, fear and anxiety alert us to potentially dangerous or threatening situations. However, when the emotional reactions are inappropriate to the situation or when they are so extreme that they are overwhelming, then it is time to do something about them. In this section, we will explore various ways of dealing effectively with the most common emotional reactions to stress.

**Fear and anxiety.**    Fear and anxiety are normal experiences. However, many people consider it a form of weakness or even cowardice to feel fear and anxiety—let alone express such feelings. It is often especially difficult for males in our society to admit their fears and anxieties because the stereotyped role of the male is a strong, confident provider under whose protection his family can feel secure. Recognizing fear and anxiety as normal aspects of the human situation is a first step in dealing with these emotions.

A second step is to distinguish between realistic and unrealistic fear, anxiety, and worry. Is our worry elicited by a real danger or does it reflect a pervasive feeling of inadequacy and inferiority? Is it proportional to the actual degree of danger, or is it exaggerated? Is it rational or irrational? Of course, it is not always easy to distinguish between realistic and unrealistic fears and anxieties nor is it easy to determine whether a given individual is overly prone to fear and anxiety when dealing with the everyday problems of living. However, an awareness of this distinction between realistic and unrealistic sources of emotional stress, coupled with an approach to

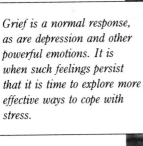

*Grief is a normal response, as are depression and other powerful emotions. It is when such feelings persist that it is time to explore more effective ways to cope with stress.*

fear and anxiety as reactions to be recognized and understood rather than denied and hidden, are important steps in dealing with these emotions.

Since fear and anxiety may stem from a feeling of inadequacy in the situation, one effective way of dealing with them is through the development of needed competencies. Obviously it is not possible to know ahead of time all the kinds of stress we are going to encounter from day to day, but we can foresee at least some stressful events and prepare ourselves for them. With specific preparation for marriage, vocation, parenthood, and old age, for example, we are much more likely to maintain a constructive, task-oriented approach in meeting the problems we encounter. Knowing what to expect and what to do about it can make us feel confident instead of fearful, even in a very demanding situation.

We can also modify our emotional responses to particular situations. For example, we shall see in our discussion of psychotherapy in Chapter 7 that it is quite possible to learn to conquer even the most powerful fears.

Taking action in a fear-producing situation may also be effective. Fear often leads to a paralysis of action, and paralysis to an intensification of the fear. Action (almost any action) can break this vicious circle and lessen feelings of fear, even when it does not lessen the actual danger. The performer usually loses stage fright once the action begins, as does the athlete once the contest is under way.

**Anger and hostility.** Unexpressed or indirectly expressed anger and hostility are common in our society and often lead to irrational behavior, psychophysiological disorders, and unhappiness. As with other emotions, competence in dealing with anger and hostility begins with an understanding and acceptance of our feelings rather than denial or moral self-condemnation. If we view hostile feelings as dangerous or immoral, we may resort to some defense mechanism to keep those feelings out of consciousness, or we may turn our hostility inward and engage in self-recrimination for having such feelings. These ways of dealing with anger only aggravate the problem.

One "safety valve," emphasized by Singer (1976), is fantasy: "Sometimes, for instance, it is more sensible in the long run just to think and fantasize about an activity than to go ahead and do it" (p. 32). Most of us probably have fantasy lives in which we act out our hostile feelings toward those we feel treat us unfairly. Fantasies of this type can reduce our anger and hostility to a point where we can cope with them in more rational and effective ways.

Feshbach and Weiner (1982) have outlined several other methods for dealing with anger, all of which emphasize the cognitive control of emotions and all of which have proven helpful in regulating anger and aggressive behavior. These methods include reacting with a response which is incompatible with anger, empathizing with the person causing the anger, and downgrading the importance of the situation.

As we learn to accept our own anger and hostility, it is important to learn to accept such emotions in others, even when they are directed toward us. Perhaps the most important method of dealing with overt anger and hostility from others is to be prepared for them and surrender the notion that everyone should love and appreciate us at all times (Ellis & Harper, 1961; Goldfried & Sobocinski, 1975). Although reacting angrily to the seemingly unjustified anger of another person may offer some satisfaction, this is a form of self-indulgence that seldom pays off. Two people overcome by mutual anger and determined to retaliate for past offenses only feed and perpetuate their hostility. In essence, they create a vicious circle of anger, retaliation, and more anger.

In such situations, it is often helpful to remember that anger can result from a variety of frustrating and self-devaluating conditions, including rejection. If we can pinpoint specific behavior on our part that is eliciting the other person's anger, we often can make appropriate changes and establish a more harmonious relationship. If, despite our best efforts to reason with or placate other people, they remain angry and hostile toward us, it may be useful to view their anger as a problem for them rather than as a threat to our own self-esteem and worth.

**Guilt.**    Some people attempt to cope with their guilt by engaging in exaggerated self-condemnation and even self-hatred. The result is usually severe self-devaluation and depression (Murphy, 1978). Often such reactions reflect immature, rigid, and unrealistic moral standards, which may lead to feelings of failure and self-recrimination. In other instances, people resort to self-defense mechanisms such as projection, placing the blame for their misdeeds on others and defending themselves from guilt and self-devaluation. Neither of these approaches is conducive to effective behavior or personal growth.

Normal guilt can usually be dealt with more constructively through confession of guilt to oneself or others, a sincere effort at reparation, and a willingness to accept forgiveness. The individual must then look to the future instead of dwelling on the past. This sequence usually leaves the individual better able to avoid the same mistake on subsequent occasions. For some, the opportunity for confession, the provision for reparation, and the assurance of forgiveness are met through religious practices. For others, the resolution of guilt is a more individual matter.

**Grief, depression, and loneliness.**    As we saw in Chapter 4, three stages seem to be involved in **grief work,** or mourning: (1) an initial stage of shock or numbness accompanied by a strong tendency to deny or screen out the reality of what has happened, (2) a second stage involving anxiety, depression, and so-called pangs of grief, and (3) a final stage of giving up hope of recovering what has been lost and beginning to make the necessary readjustment to life (Parkes, 1972).

grief work: the processes associated with mourning and the recovery from loss

The process of grief work ordinarily lasts from a few weeks to several months, depending upon the individual and his or her method of coping. Using denial or tranquilizing drugs to avoid grief may offer some immediate, if temporary, relief. However, this tends to prolong the grief work that is necessary if the person is to adjust adequately to his or her new life situation. Grief is an extremely stressful emotion and people often try to protect themselves from the unpleasantness of grief work (Ramsay, 1977). As a result "the 'normal' reactions of shock, despair, and recovery are often distorted, exaggerated, prolonged, inhibited, or delayed" (p. 132). Grief work may also be prolonged and complicated by guilt and depression, particularly when the bereaved person has **ambivalent feelings** toward the deceased.

ambivalent feelings: simultaneous existence of contradictory emotions toward the same person

Depression sometimes seems to be based upon **learned helplessness:** an individual learns as a result of past experience that there is no effective way of coping with the stress situation, and so he or she loses hope and stops fighting. In an experiment with animals, for example, dogs were given electric shock in a situation from which they could not escape. Later the dogs failed to escape even though the situation had been changed to allow for escape (Seligman, 1975). Similarly, past experiences can lead people to perceive stressful situations in a limited and self-defeating way. As a result, they fail to see ways in which they could cope more effectively (Abramson, Seligman & Teasdale, 1978; Abramson, Gardner & Seligman, 1980; Peterson, Schwartz & Seligman, 1981).

learned helplessness: state in which an individual believes that he or she is helpless to cope with adjustive demands

According to the learned helplessness model, the most effective way of coping with depression is to learn to anticipate as many stressful situations as possible and to realize that in *any* situation there are choices of actions, some of which are more adaptive and effective than others. Of course, it is not possible to predict or control every stressful event we are likely to encounter; some such events are unexpected and completely beyond our control—relatives and friends die suddenly, unexpected failures occur, loved ones unexpectedly disappoint us. However, as we will see throughout this chapter, it is possible to prepare ourselves for coping with many of the more likely and predictable sources of stress—job pressures, financial problems, interpersonal conflicts, difficult decisions, and so on. Knowing what to expect and what to do in these situations can help to reduce unnecessary feelings of helplessness and depression.

As for loneliness, the first step is to accept that sometimes we are going to feel lonely. The second step is to use this experience as an opportunity to get to know ourselves better and to draw upon potentials never before realized (Moustakas, 1961). Deeply lived loneliness can lead not only to greater self-acceptance but to increased compassion for and relatedness to others. This process has been referred to as "creative loneliness." The third and essential step in dealing with loneliness is to build truly meaningful, loving, and enduring relationships with others. This often requires not only relating on an individual level but developing a concern for, involvement in, and commitment to the human enterprise.

**Social support.**    As we saw in earlier chapters, social support can provide a buffer against stress (Kessler, Price, & Wortman, 1985). In fact, being with someone else is the single most popular way for people to cope with stress (Horton, Gewirtz, & Kreutter, 1988). Other people can support us and provide reassurances when we are under stress; they can agree with our appraisals of the stressful situation, help us set more realistic goals, and point out positive features of the situations in which we find ourselves. They can also allow us to vent some of our emotions such as anger, fear, and frustration (Wortman, 1984). In all these ways, social support can make us feel more comfortable emotionally when we are in a stressful situation.

Some recent research shows that the benefits of social contact go far beyond simply *feeling* better. An impressive array of evidence shows that social isolation is as great a threat to health as is cigarette smoking, high blood pressure, and obesity (House, Landis, & Umberson, 1988). Recent, long-term studies in the United States, Finland, and Sweden show consistently that when other health risk factors are held constant, people with few close social relationships are more likely to become ill or to die over a ten or twelve year period; this is especially true for men, though to a lesser extent it also is true for women. Moreover, laboratory studies have shown that the presence of a familiar member of the same species can reduce the incidence of ulcers and hypertension in rats, mice, and goats under stress; being petted by humans, or simply having a human present, has been shown to reduce the physiological effects of stress on dogs, cats, horses, and rabbits; and the presence of other people in intensive care units has been shown to reduce the effects of stress on patients.

At times, however, social support can be counterproductive. In the short run, it may be comforting to have someone agree with you, support you, and commiserate with you. However, in the long run it is sometimes more helpful if people around us point out our errors and discourage us from acting in ways that may not be in our best interest, rather than always agreeing with us. This is true even though at the moment their disagreement and lack of full support may add to our stress. In addition, there are times when support can become intrusive and lead to more stress rather than less. We can all remember times when we preferred to deal with our problems alone, without interference from others; at times like these, expressions of concern or interest from others can become just another source of stress. So social support is a mixed blessing, helpful at times as a buffer against stressful emotions, but detrimental at other times.

## Coping with Cognitive Reactions to Stress

**stress inoculation:** cognitively oriented approach to coping with stress, consisting of educational, rehearsal, and application phases

As we saw in Chapter 4, in addition to physiological and emotional reactions, stress triggers a variety of cognitive reactions, many of which provide short-term relief from stress but interfere with long-term solutions. One of the ways people can cope more effectively is to develop a variety of cognitive skills that can be drawn upon in times of stress. In this section, we shall focus primarily on **stress inoculation** (Meichenbaum, 1977). Stress inoculation training has been used to help people cope with a variety of stress reactions by changing the cognitive component of the stress response. In fact, recent research has shown that stress inoculation is among the most effective techniques for reducing the pain, discomfort, and anxiety that often accompany unpleasant medical procedures such as spinal taps and tooth extraction (Ludwick-Rosenthal & Neufeld, 1988). As we shall see, stress inoculation is a three-part process involving (1) education, (2) rehearsal, and (3) application.

In the first (educational) phase of stress inoculation training, an individual is given a framework for understanding his or her response to stressful events. For example, a person who has difficulty controlling angry outbursts under conditions of stress might be given information on how emotional responses develop. Similarly, the person panicking at the sight of snakes and rats might be asked to pay greater attention to the "internal dialogue" accompanying those responses. Some of these internal responses might include thoughts of disgust related to the snakes and rats, thoughts of panic, thoughts of being overwhelmed by anxiety, a desire to flee the situation, fears of social embarrassment, or fears of "going crazy." In stress inoculation training, the emphasis is on increasing the individual's awareness of the personal reactions and experiences that occur during a stress response. In other words, the individual is "educated" about and becomes more aware of his or her responses to stress.

**cognitive self-statements:** statements that can be used to recast a stressful situation in a more effective and productive way

During the second (rehearsal) phase of stress inoculation training, the person learns how to use **cognitive self-statements** to control reactions to stress. The individual is taught to reassess the situation and his or her reactions to it, and to cast these in a more positive light. For example, a woman experiencing uncontrollable anger in stressful situations might reassess those situations by saying to herself, "This could be a difficult situation, but I can handle it," or "Try not to take this too seriously. Keep your sense of humor." She might also say to herself, "There is no point in getting mad. Just stay calm." Or, she might think, "I'm not going to let this get to me."

Self-statements can also be useful as a way of monitoring stress reactions and shifting to a more effective coping strategy. The angry individual might rehearse using such self-statements as, "I'm getting angry. Time to relax," or "Don't let anger lead to more anger. Anger is a signal to try a new approach," or "One step at a time. Don't get overwhelmed."

Even if our efforts to cope are not completely successful, cognitive self-statements can be used to help control feelings of disappointment and to reinforce trying and success: "Aggravating situations do not last forever," or "I handled that pretty well" (Novaco, 1975).

The point is that an individual can learn new and more effective cognitive reactions that can become routine reactions to stressful situations. Rather than relying on defense mechanisms and becoming confused and ineffective, an individual can learn to react with cognitive self-statements that are more likely to lead to effective coping behavior (see Insight, p. 155 for additional self-statements that are useful in stress inoculation training).

In the final phase of stress inoculation training, the application phase, attitudes and skills learned in the education and rehearsal phases are utilized. The individual is first trained to use these new skills in relatively low stress situations. The outcome is evaluated and if necessary the self-statements are modified or new statements are developed. As the person builds a set of effective self-statements, the new skills are applied to increasingly stressful situations until the person is able to respond to even the most stressful situations with adaptive and effective cognitive reactions.

Apart from stress inoculation training, recent research suggests another useful cognitive strategy for coping with stress: if there is something you would rather not think about, think about something else instead. Daniel Wegner and his colleagues at Trinity University in Texas instructed the subjects in their experiments not to think of "a white bear" during a five-minute period. They found that their subjects were never able totally to banish the thought of white bears from their minds; moreover, after the five minutes were up they became preoccupied with thoughts of white bears! In a follow-up experiment, they told a different group of subjects, ". . . if you do happen to think of a white bear [during the five-minute period], please try to think of a red Volkswagen instead." They found that these subjects also had trouble avoiding thoughts of white bears during the five-minute test period, but after the five minutes were up they showed no particular preoccupation with thoughts of white bears. This suggests that if you want to avoid thinking about something—a worry, a bothersome mistake, or an embarrassing moment—simply trying not to think of it is likely to backfire; you may end up thinking about it more than ever. A better strategy might be to substitute thoughts about something else: whenever you are reminded of your worry, immediately shift your thoughts to a distractor of some sort. This doesn't guarantee that you will never think about the suppressed topic, but it does suggest that you will not become preoccupied with or obsessed by it.

To this point we have been discussing ways to cope more effectively with the *reactions* to stressful events. As we have noted, often the first step in coping more effectively with stress is to bring the physiological, emotional and cognitive stress reactions under greater control. An important second step is to change the stressful event itself, to reduce or eliminate the *source* of stress. In the next section we turn to this aspect of effective coping.

## COPING EFFECTIVELY WITH STRESSORS

As we saw in Chapter 1, human beings have only a few built-in mechanisms for adapting. Most of our strategies for coping with stressful events are learned either through operant conditioning or through observational learning (see Chapter 2, pp. 52–57). For example, as a young child you may have turned to adults for help in coping with stressful situations; to the extent that the adults were successful in

# *Insight*

reducing your stress, this coping strategy was reinforced and you were therefore more likely to use it in future stressful situations. Similarly, on those occasions when you did something wrong and began to feel guilty, you might have tried to block out your memory of the event; to the extent that this reduced your guilt feelings, then this defensive coping response (repression) was also reinforced and you were more likely to use it in future stressful situations. In both cases, coping strategies were learned through operant conditioning.

Other coping strategies are learned by observing the people around us. For example, in some families adults keep a "stiff upper lip" in the face of stress; children in those families are likely to learn to respond in the same way through observational learning. In other families, people may deal with stress by discussing it and enlisting the support of others in the family; children in those families may learn that coping strategy through observation.

In this portion of the chapter, we will examine some of the methods that researchers have developed to help people deal effectively with stressors. Our approach will involve a general problem-solving strategy developed by D'Zurilla and Goldfried (1971). As described by these psychologists, a problem-solving strategy not only helps solve the problem at hand, but gives an individual an experience at

Often the way in which you perceive a situation determines whether it is stressful or not. For example, are you practicing music for the joy of improving, or from the fear of not being good enough?

success and an increased feeling of self-efficacy. For our purposes, the problem-solving strategy will consist of four general steps: (1) evaluating the stress situation, including available resources for coping with it; (2) formulating alternatives and deciding on a course of action; (3) taking action; and (4) utilizing feedback and correcting possible problems.

## Evaluating the Stress Situation

We are continually scanning our environment to see what opportunities or difficulties may be present. When we become aware of a new adjustive demand, our first task is to define it and evaluate its degree of threat. Here it is important that we make an accurate evaluation of the problem, for an incomplete or distorted picture would place us at a disadvantage in coping with it.

**Defining the situation accurately.** One of the first and most important things to do when faced with a new demand for adjustment is to define the situation accurately. If you inaccurately assess the situation and then make plans for dealing with it based on your inaccurate assessment, you are likely to find that your behavior increases, rather than decreases, the stress. For example, a loved one may express a need for time to be alone or to be with close friends. If we define the situation accurately—"she needs to have some time for herself"—we can then plan an appropriate course of action. However, if our definition of the situation is inaccurate—"she hates me and wants to get away from me"—our inaccurate assessment just increases the stressfulness of the situation.

**Categorizing the experience.**    Once we have appropriately assessed the situation, we can then categorize it so that we know how to begin to deal with it. By comparing the present situation to similar stressful situations in the past, we may get some ideas about which stress management techniques are most likely to succeed. For example, if we classify a situation as "a confrontation," we can use stress management techniques that have proved effective in previous confrontations. If we classify the situation as "a challenge to my authority" or "an exciting adventure," we would presumably use somewhat different stress management techniques.

However, at times this tendency to categorize situations may actually make matters worse for us. If we categorize the situation incorrectly, or if we overlook the ways in which the present situation is quite unique, we may respond incorrectly and in ways that actually increase the stress we experience. If we interpret someone's helpful advice as "just more criticism," and respond with anger and hostility rather than with gratitude and receptiveness, then we have compounded our problems.

In a similar way, at times the natural tendency to categorize situations can lead to oversimplification. As Miller (1962) has suggested: "It makes the world a great deal simpler when the good guys are always smart, honest, beautiful, and brave, while the bad guys are always stupid, crooked, ugly cowards" (p. 274). Although we are not usually this naive, it is often easy for us to see things in black and white while ignoring the many shades of gray. Psychologist George Kelly (1955) has stated that such oversimplification is often the cause of personal unhappiness and distress. The solution, he said, is to increase both the accuracy and complexity of our views of the world. For example, if an individual is asked to undertake more responsibility at work or to take difficult courses in school, the first reaction might be panic or anger. "I don't see how I could possibly take on this new responsibility." "How dare they require me to take another foreign language or chemistry course!" These responses may be based on oversimplified views: that the extra responsibility at work could never be successfully handled, and that taking a chemistry course or an advanced foreign language course is guaranteed to result in failure.

A more accurate view of the demand might result in a less stressful or threatening evaluation: "I could probably handle the responsibility for supervising another person, but I might have some trouble learning how to fill out all of these forms." "Taking an advanced chemistry course may not be the most enjoyable thing I'll ever do, but I have successfully taken chemistry courses before, and if I study effectively, I'll probably do well."

We have seen that the first step in dealing with stressors is to accurately perceive and categorize the demands being placed upon us. When our categorizing is too simple or inaccurate, we will be handicapped when we attempt to deal with the course of our stress. On the other hand, if our assessments are reasonably accurate and realistic, we have taken the first step toward coping effectively with the stressor.

### Identifying Alternative Courses of Action

Having identified the adjustive demand and accurately evaluated the challenge it presents to us, next we must decide what to do about it. This involves formulating alternative courses of action that might solve the problem and selecting the most promising one.

The process of formulating alternatives involves generating courses of action that might be used to deal with the stress-inducing problem. Sometimes, the whole process of definition, formulation of alternatives, and choice of action occurs almost instantaneously, with little or no conscious thought. An example of this would be our immediate reaction to a car stopping suddenly ahead of us on a freeway. In this situation, our reactions occur quickly, with little thought. This is an adaptive way of coping in situations where the demands are intense and must be managed immediately.

However, many stress situations do not require immediate categorization and action. In these situations, we have the opportunity to make an objective appraisal of the stress situation and to decide consciously and rationally on a constructive course of action. Such carefully worked-out, constructive solutions are more likely to be effective than impulsive and poorly planned reactions. Generally speaking, in a stressful situation there are three basic ways of coping with the source of stress: one can *attack* the problem, *withdraw* from it, or attempt to arrange a workable *compromise* (Roth & Cohen, 1986).

**Attack.**    A hero in a western seeing the "bad guy" start to draw his gun may handle the situation by beating him to the draw. This is a simple attack response, and it is the prototype of many coping responses. Most of us size up the requirements of the situation and try to meet them by direct action.

Attack responses can take somewhat different forms, depending on the nature of the stress, the situation, and the individual's resources. If you believe you have a good case for getting a higher grade in an important course, but are met with a blunt refusal from the instructor, you are likely to become angry. A possible response is, of course, physical assault on the instructor, but in this case physical attack would simply make the situation worse. Consequently you are likely to resort to more subtle and effective ways of attacking the problem, such as going beyond the instructor to the department head or dean. In other situations, however, you might choose a very different way of attacking the problem—perhaps resorting to long-range planning, increased effort, or restructuring your view of the situation. Properly focused attack responses are among the most effective methods for dealing with stress (see Psychology in Action, p. 159).

**Withdrawal.**    A second way of coping with stress is to withdraw from the situation. For example, after an emotional injury it often helps to get away, to retreat and think things through. A thoughtful review of the stressful situation often gives us new insights into the sources of the stress, allows us to evaluate our responses, and may suggest different ways of dealing more effectively with the situation. By withdrawing, we give ourselves the opportunity to evaluate the actual significance of the event and to review our assumptions about ourselves and the stressful situation.

# *Psychology in Action*

## Time Management

One of the most common sources of stress in everyday life is pressure: having too many things to do and too little time in which to do them. Yet there is a surprisingly simple way to reduce pressure. First, make a list of everything you think you should be doing in the next week or two.

Once you have a reasonably complete list, categorize the items according to how soon they must be finished. Some items probably must be completed within twenty-four hours; others should be done in the next few days; still others can be done any time within a week; others can be done in a month or two.

Now go back over the items and put a check mark beside those things that *must* be done and that *you* must do. These are the things that should receive highest priority on your time. Give lower priority to things that are not absolutely essential (it would be nice to do them, but it won't be the end of the world if they don't get done) and to things that could be done by someone else if necessary. You can attend to some of these lower priority demands as time permits.

The next step is to create time wherever possible. In the course of a day, an amazing amount of time is devoted to nonessential activities. Reading the newspaper or a magazine, watching a favorite TV program, going to a movie or a concert, buying clothes, entertaining—these are all enjoyable activities, all of them have a place in life, but for a short while (at least) some of them can be postponed to make time for more pressing demands.

The next step is to start at the top of your list and start *doing* the things that need to be done. Begin with those things that must be done within the next day, then move on to the things that can be done in the next several days. As you complete items on the list, cross them off. If you find that you have some free time, attend to some of the lower priority items. As new demands arise, add them to the list and give them their proper priority ranking. As you begin to see the light at the end of the tunnel, reinstate some of the "fun things" that you denied yourself in order to make time for the high priority items on your list.

This simple technique can be very effective in reducing pressure. First, just having a list of things to do means you don't have to worry about forgetting to do something really important. Second, seeing everything listed on a single piece of paper has a way of reminding us that the demands on our time are not infinite. "I have so many things to do" becomes instead "I have only these things to do, and some of them aren't terribly important, if push comes to shove." Third, you will probably be surprised that many of the things on your list really don't *have* to be done if time is short; and if necessary many of the things that do have to be done could be delegated to someone else. Finally, there is a great sense of satisfaction that comes from realizing that you are doing everything humanly possible to cope with the pressure you are facing: you are putting every available minute into the things that are most important to do right away. If something lower in priority doesn't get done, so be it—you've used your time as effectively as possible, and nobody (not even yourself) can ask for more from you.

**vacillation:** wavering or hesitating in making a choice

Another way of withdrawing partially from a stressful situation involves **vacillation.** People in stressful situations tend to vacillate, that is, they are indecisive and attempt to avoid making difficult decisions and choices. For example, a woman trying to choose between two careers, one of which is exciting but very demanding and the other of which is dependable but a bit dull, may find herself unable to reach a decision. When a choice involves serious consequences, many of us delay making a decision indefinitely. These delays allow for at least partial withdrawal from the stressful situation while keeping our options open until we are better prepared to make a decision.

**substitution:** acceptance of alternative goals or satisfactions in place of those originally sought after or desired

**accommodation:** settlement for a portion of that which was originally desired

**Compromise.**   Most often, attempts to cope with stressful situations will involve some kind of compromise. While we may be able to change some aspects of the situation or to withdraw from it for a while, we usually have to live with what cannot be changed and what cannot be avoided. This means we must compromise.

One way in which compromise works is through **substitution.** In a situation of sustained or seemingly inescapable frustration, we can often reduce the stress by accepting whatever goals and satisfactions we can get. For example, a person who is consistently turned down by medical schools may decide instead to pursue a career in biological research. The sexually frustrated person may find some satisfaction in sexual fantasies.

A second method of compromise is **accommodation,** in which we settle for part of what we wanted. Because the resolution of so many of our problems is dependent on the action of others, we often need mutual accommodation, in which both parties give a little and get a little.

Negotiating, bargaining, and making concessions are compromise behaviors in which the participants accommodate their requirements and get part but not all of what they wanted. We see such patterns in labor-management disputes, student-faculty conflicts, and relationships between nations, as well as in our relationships with friends and family members. If a compromise reaction succeeds in meeting the essential requirements of a situation, the stress problem is satisfactorily resolved and a person's energies can be devoted to other matters.

In any situation, there are likely to be dozens of possible ways of attacking the problem, of withdrawing, or of arriving at a compromise. Although we will discuss

*In dealing with stress, whether you are alone or involved with others, compromise is often a necessary—and productive—strategy.*

attack, withdrawal, and compromise strategies separately, it is often possible to use all three responses in coping with a stressful situation. For example, a student experiencing an unusually difficult semester might adopt new study methods (attack), drop one or more especially difficult courses (withdrawal), and settle for a slightly lower level of performance for that semester (compromise).

**brainstorming:** generation of many potential solutions to a problem while postponing criticism or evaluation of the suggestions

**Brainstorming.**    One of the best ways of discovering a variety of possible responses is to "brainstorm" a variety of options (Osborne, 1953). In **brainstorming,** an individual attempts to generate as many solutions to a problem as possible regardless of how silly or impractical the solutions might seem. For example, a person in debt might reasonably conclude that one way to solve the problem is to earn more money. Brainstorming might lead to the following list of possibilities:

- Work evenings or weekends at a fast-food restaurant.
- Rent my car to someone who can use it while I am at work each day.
- Write short stories or poems and have them published in magazines.
- Deliver morning newspapers before work.
- Do yard work for other people in the evenings or on weekends.
- Teach other people something at which I am skilled (perhaps oil painting, car repair, typing, golf, bowling, skiing, computer programming, playing bridge or poker).
- Ask for a raise.
- Start a mailorder business.
- Give blood.
- Tutor a high school or college student in a subject I know well (such as English, math, history, chemistry, statistics, humanities).
- Rent my garage to someone who needs a place to keep or work on his or her car.

Some of these ideas are more realistic than others. However, during brainstorming, all criticism and evaluation is postponed, and "killer" phrases that stop the flow of ideas are firmly suppressed. Some examples of "killer" phrases are:

- Yes, but . . .
- It won't work . . .
- I've never done it that way before . . .
- Let me think it over and see what happens . . .

To remember all the ideas generated during this phase of problem-solving, jot down the ideas as they occur to you, no matter how unworkable or silly they may seem. The objective is to generate as many potential solutions as possible. You may find it useful also to brainstorm separately in each of the three categories: ways to attack the problem, ways to withdraw partially or fully, and ways to compromise.

**Balancing probability, desirability, and cost.**    Once we have formulated a number of alternative ways of coping with a stressful situation, the task remains of assessing the relative merits of these alternatives and making a choice. In so doing, we weigh the probabilities of success, the degree of satisfaction we will accept, and the cost we are willing to pay.

1. *Weighing the odds.* Each of the alternatives formulated in the earlier steps of the problem-solving process contains a probability of success. Some alternatives have a very high likelihood of success, while others are quite likely to end in failure. In figuring the odds, we must examine the relevant information at our disposal, decide whether we need more information, and make some decision. It is important in this step to separate the probability of success from the desirability of the outcome. In the earlier examples of brainstorming, asking for a raise would probably be the simplest solution, but it also might be the least likely to succeed. In contrast, working evenings and weekends at various jobs (yard work, restaurant, tutoring) is virtually certain to increase income, though it is probably not as desirable as some of the other alternatives.

2. *Deciding on an acceptable level of satisfaction.* Each of the alternative solutions formulated also contains a level of satisfaction. Some alternatives will produce great satisfaction, while others will produce only modest amounts of satisfaction. There need not be any relationship between the probability of success, which was calculated earlier, and the satisfaction the alternative will probably produce. For example, one alternative may have a low probability of success but may also be associated with a bigger potential gain. On the other hand, an equally unlikely event may be associated with a relatively low level of satisfaction. In the earlier examples, starting a mailorder business might be an exciting prospect with potentially great payoff, even though the probability of success is small. Conversely, doing yard work is likely to be successful, though it may not be very satisfying or produce large amounts of income.

All other things being equal, we tend to select the course of action that seems to offer the greatest probability of success and the highest level of satisfaction. Naturally, what is satisfying and successful to one individual may not be to another. For example, one person may be willing to accept a good job offer rather than wait for a better one, while another would take the opposite course of action.

3. *Weighing the costs.* All behavior has its costs in effort, material resources, time, and the surrender of other possibilities. Some behavior also exacts costs in unpleasantness or loss. Thus, staying in school may require such long hours of study that a student must give up hobbies or social life, but dropping out of school might cost future opportunities for more advanced training.

In choosing between alternative courses of action, most of us balance the risks and the costs—the amount of effort or other costs—against the possible satisfactions. For high stakes and good odds we may be willing to work hard and undergo considerable sacrifice. However, if the returns look small and the risk of losing is considerable, we are usually reluctant to exert much effort. Although we often weigh the factors differently, we all look for what we regard as the best balance of probable gains and costs.

Thus, we must take each alternative, determine the benefits and costs associated with it, estimate its probability of success, and come to some reasonable conclusion about whether or not to act upon the alternative. It is apparent that since we are dealing with probabilities and not certainties, we cannot expect to win every time, as Overstreet and Overstreet (1956) have stated:

> . . . we live by batting averages, not by perfect scores. . . . We live by making plans and by making efforts that are, so far as we can see, in line with the results we want; by improving our plans and efforts as experience dictates; and by believing that a fair batting average constitutes enough success to justify our staying on the job. (p. 24)

### Taking Positive Action

Once a decision has been made, the next step is to implement it—to put the chosen alternative into action. However, implementation is not always a simple matter, particularly if we lack confidence in ourselves or in our decision. As a consequence, we may experience fear, anxiety, apprehension, and related feelings which can interfere with the effective implementation of our decision.

Often such emotions impair actual performance, whether it be intellectual or physical. Most of us have probably had the experience of speaking or performing before a group. When the time for action arrived, we may have been so fearful and anxious that our actual thought processes were partially blocked and our performance was impaired. Many trial lawyers experience excruciating stress the first few times they address a jury. Typically, however, they discipline themselves to function effectively despite their inner feelings. I could cite similar experiences of many athletes before and during the first few minutes of an important contest.

Perhaps of more importance for effective coping is the delay in action that may result from such feelings. Often in dealing with serious conflicts, for example, people vacillate, attempt to stall for time, and even get sick—despite that they have already decided on the best probable course of action. Kaufman (1973) has referred to this as "decidophobia." When time permits, such diversionary tactics may prove constructive, since postponing the action allows people to gather more information, reconsider alternatives, and feel more confident about the final decision. In other instances, however, delay may be disastrous. Often, the timing of an action is of crucial importance. What might have been an effective response today may not be so tomorrow.

In some situations, the issue is not fear or anxiety, but poor or incomplete knowledge about how to carry out a chosen course of action. For example, we may have decided upon the appropriate way to handle a troublesome acquaintance but do not know how to carry out the course of action. When our knowledge is poor or lacking, consultation with friends, family, or professionals can prove invaluable. For example, we may wish to end a relationship with as little distress as possible. We might never have done this before, however, and we might seek the advice of a more knowledgeable friend to learn how to end the relationship while preserving the integrity and self-esteem of the other individual.

### Utilizing Feedback

Whatever course of action we take, even the most carefully developed efforts to reduce stress can fail. Even when we choose well and act with skill, factors beyond our control may tip the balance in preventing our action from solving the problem. As Robert Burns put it so succinctly:

> The best-laid schemes o' mice an' men,
>    Gang aft a-gley,*
> An' lea'e us nought but grief an' pain,
>    For promis'd joy!

\* Often go awry.

**feedback**: knowledge of the results of one's behavior, used in judging the appropriateness of one's responses and making corrections where indicated

Therefore we must use available feedback to gauge the wisdom of our decision and the effectiveness with which we are carrying it out. **Feedback** enables us to make corrections in our actions when such corrections are indicated and feasible. In some cases, feedback may indicate that we are making satisfactory progress toward our goal or that the goal has been achieved. Consequently, this may reduce anxiety, build our self-confidence, and lead to increased effort, for it is a signal that the stress will be resolved and our needs met. In other cases, feedback may indicate that we are not progressing toward our goal as well as we might, perhaps because of unforeseen complications or a wrong choice of action. This kind of feedback signals the need to modify our behavior and to develop new strategies for reducing the stress.

In some situations, feedback is relatively complete and immediate. For example, a football player receives a great deal of feedback, both during and after a game, and can improve both immediate and later performance. Programmed instruction is based on the demonstrated principle that learning is most efficient and improvement most rapid when precise feedback is given immediately (Skinner, 1958). In general, immediate and complete feedback contributes to improved performance and increased confidence.

In other situations feedback may be delayed. For example, students may not be given any grades on lab reports until several reports have been submitted. In general, the delay of feedback until after the completion of an important action tends to cause worry and anxiety; it also hinders learning and results in less improvement over time.

In still other situations feedback may be prompt but limited. A student receiving a low grade on a test may have little information about why he or she received such a low rating or what he or she is doing wrong. People may notice that others seem to be avoiding or reacting negatively to them but not have any clues about the reason. Limited feedback is often ambiguous and difficult to interpret; it makes some people anxious and uncertain, especially in important situations.

Unlike its inanimate counterpart, the human "computer" uses feedback not only to monitor its progress in carrying out a course of action but also to check on the validity of its goal and the wisdom of its current "program." If the situation changes or if feedback tells us that our goal is going to be too expensive or not worth achieving, we can abandon one course of action in midstream and embark on another. For this reason, human beings are self-correcting systems. If we are to use feedback effectively, we must remain flexible in our approach to solving problems. It is all too easy to become "weighted down" by rigid beliefs and coping styles that lack the flexibility

# Psychology in Action

### Commercial Stress Management Programs

Stress has become the catchword of the 1980s. People are increasingly aware of the existence of stress and of the effects that stress can have over a long period of time. As a result, there is a growing demand for stress management programs and workshops. Stress is rapidly becoming a multi-billion dollar industry.

However, there are no generally accepted guidelines for stress management programs: some are offered as weekend workshops, others as lectures, and still others as individual training sessions. Programs are offered through people's homes, in community centers, at the office, in health spas, in self-help books, on videotapes, even on cruise ships. The techniques vary from one program to another, but they include such things as relaxation training, biofeedback, cognitive change, massage, and exercise. One intriguing program that can be installed on your home or office computer provides a tutorial to help you gain insight into the causes of your stress; it also includes a sensor to teach you to control muscle tension.

While some of the techniques taught in stress management programs can be effective, the value of other techniques is unknown. Moreover, there are no licensing standards that govern the providers of stress management training. Thus it makes sense to be cautious before spending any significant amount of time or money on stress management programs. Promises of miraculous or instantaneous cures should always be cause for concern. However, in the absence of such claims, it still makes sense to check into the training of the people running the program and the techniques they use. It is always a good idea to ask whether reliable data exist that demonstrate the effectiveness of the program, and if possible talk with some people who have completed the program. Finally, examine the extent to which the stress management program teaches you how to reduce the stressfulness of your environment, as opposed to training you simply to control your *reactions* to stress.

essential for dealing with changing conditions in a changing world (see Psychology in Action, p. 165). The importance of flexibility has been well expressed by tennis professional Pancho Gonzales, who was still competing successfully in his early forties—a feat considered virtuallly impossible in the fast-paced world of professional tennis: "Vary your game to the conditions. Shorten your strokes on a fast court, play more steadily on a slow court; hit harder when you are playing against the wind and softer when you are playing with it" (1972).

## USING STRESS FOR PERSONAL GROWTH

Stress is an inevitable fact of life. Faced with this inevitability, we can respond in one of two ways. We can simply react to stress, allowing the events of life to push us aimlessly from one difficult situation to another. Alternatively, we can take advantage of stress and make it work for us. While stress can exact a high toll in lowering adaptive resources and exhausting the human system, it can also produce stronger and more mature individuals forged by the demands and challenges of severe stress situations.

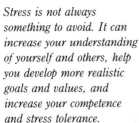

*Stress is not always something to avoid. It can increase your understanding of yourself and others, help you develop more realistic goals and values, and increase your competence and stress tolerance.*

Our task in this section is to show how stress situations can be utilized for personal growth. We shall assume that stress is an inevitable part of normal life and that individuals can plan for and utilize stress situations for personal growth. Specifically, we shall focus on: (1) increasing our understanding of ourselves and our world, (2) working out more realistic goals and values, and (3) developing increased competence and stress tolerance.

### Increasing Self-understanding

At the age of fifty-seven, a world renowned woman looked back at her life and wrote:

> Somewhere along the line of development we discover what we really are and then we make our real decision for which we are responsible. Make this decision primarily for yourself because you can never really live anyone else's life, not even your own child's. The influence you exert is through your own life and what you become yourself. (Lash, 1971)

The woman was Eleanor Roosevelt. A crucial decision point in her life was apparently precipitated by a painful event during her mid-thirties—her husband's infidelity. It led her to the realization that people cannot aspire to self-fulfillment through someone else—that each of us must shape his or her own life. As a result, she left an indelible imprint on over four of the most significant decades in our country's history.

Through our experiences in stressful situations, we often gain a clearer view of who and what we are. For example, successfully completing a difficult course is not only a source of satisfaction in its own right, but also evidence that our abilities and competencies are much greater than we had assumed them to be.

## Increasing Understanding of Others

A traumatic experience may help an individual to learn more about the nature of the world. In a divorce, for example, an individual may gain for the first time a realistic view of the former spouse, and may also learn to better understand the hurtful experiences that other people undergo. Unless a person has "been there" or had a similar experience, it is often impossible to understand and empathize with another person's experiences or to help, even though someone sincerely desires to do so. It is perhaps for this reason that people who have undergone highly stressful experiences are often effective in helping others with similar problems. Members of Alcoholics Anonymous, former heroin addicts, and ex-convicts may be more effective therapists than trained mental health workers who have never undergone such experiences themselves.

In this general context, Bovet (1973) has summarized the improved understanding of self and others that may stem from our reactions to stress—even highly negative experiences—as follows: "It is a curious fact . . . that such loss and such pain frequently enlarge a person's vision and feeling. It can lead to an enlargement of the understanding of the suffering of others . . . " (p. 6). Such experiences are not without their costs, of course. However, when they are used constructively, they can be a "creative suffering," the outcome of which can be personal growth (see Table 5.1, p. 167).

---

**TABLE 5.1　Personality Characteristics Associated with Effective Coping**

Another approach to assessing coping and adjustment is in terms of those personality characteristics that appear to foster personal effectiveness.

| | |
|---|---|
| **Attitudes toward self** | ▪ Emphasizing self-acceptance, adequate self-identity, realistic appraisal of one's assets and liabilities |
| **Perception of reality** | ▪ A realistic view of oneself and the surrounding world of people and things |
| **Integration** | ▪ Unity of personality, freedom from disabling inner conflicts, good stress tolerance |
| **Competencies** | ▪ Development of essential physical, intellectual, emotional, and social competencies for coping with life problems |
| **Autonomy** | ▪ Adequate self-reliance, responsibility, and self-direction—together with sufficient independence of social influences |
| **Growth, self-actualization** | ▪ Emphasizing trends toward increasing maturity, development of potentialities, and self-fulfillment as a person |

Source: Jahoda, 1958

### Developing More Realistic Goals and Values

*God grant me the serenity to accept the things I cannot change,*
*Courage to change the things I can*
*And wisdom to know the difference.*

Serenity Prayer (Attributed to Reinhold Niebuhr)

If we fail to achieve difficult goals which are unrealistic in terms of our coping resources, we may utilize feedback constructively and lower our aspirations to a more realistic level. On the other hand, our successes may encourage us to raise our aspirations in line with our abilities. In essence, the problem is not to avoid challenge and stress, but to pick the right kind.

Unfortunately, this is not always an easy task. Because of parental pressures and self-expectations, for example, some students pursue educational and career goals which are inappropriate to their own interests and resources. In one instance, a mother and father—both of whom were physicians—had high hopes that their only son would also become a physician. As a result, the son dutifully embarked on a premedical major at a large university. The results were failing grades, feelings that he had let himself and his parents down, and depression. Three weeks before final exams, he attempted suicide.

Later, he obtained professional counseling concerning his interests and capabilities and changed his college major. Had he received such assistance earlier, he could have avoided a highly traumatic situation. When we are emotionally involved in stress situations, however, we often fail to see the available alternatives. However, awareness that we can usually exercise some measure of control over the stresses to which we expose ourselves can be helpful.

In another situation, the student involved had set her aspirations too low. Taught from birth that females from her ethnic and racial background only were expected to become educated homemakers and mothers, the student was surprised to find that she was challenged and stimulated by her college courses. Responding to the challenge, she studied hard and received excellent grades. Perhaps more importantly, she learned that her skills and abilities were greater than she had been taught to believe or had imagined them to be, and her self-esteem improved as a result. For this student, working out more realistic goals and values involved raising her aspirations.

When our goals prove unrewarding and unsatisfying, we must take a hard look at our aspirations and values and, perhaps, modify our assumptions and goals. If our aspirations are unrealistically high, we may need to modify them. If we are unstimulated, bored, and unchallenged, our values and goals may need reappraisal.

### Increasing Competence and Stress Tolerance

In the process of dealing with life's problems, we usually learn through experience to deal more effectively with various stress situations. When we fail in these situations, we need not see the failure as unmitigated disaster, but rather as a cue to alert us to the need for improving our competencies in given areas.

Severe stress may "sensitize" us to certain types of stressful situations or it may "immunize" us, increasing our feelings of self-confidence and our coping ability. As West (1958) has stated:

> . . . an experience may be both frightening and painful, yet its repetition may be less stressful because it is now familiar, because its limits have been perceived, because the memory and imagination of the individual enable him to equate it with other known experiences, and because defenses have been developed through fantasized reexperiences during the interval. (p. 332)

He might have added that we may also go about improving our competence systematically if we feel we are likely to encounter the same type of stress situation in the future.

Improving our competence and stress tolerance appears to involve two basic tasks: (1) the acquisition of essential knowledge and (2) the inner control over such knowledge (Anderson, 1982; Hammond & Summers, 1972). A study of parachutists, for example, found that while all were anxious, the anxiety of trained parachutists peaked some time before the actual jump. For the untrained parachutists, intense anxiety continued right up to the jump and interfered with performance (Fenz & Epstein, 1969). A number of other investigators have made comparable findings with trained astronauts and concluded that they had learned some method of controlling anxiety during stressful situations. In essence, as an individual becomes increasingly capable of functioning in a stressful situation, any emotional distress he or she may experience tends to occur before or after the stress is over—thus permitting the adaptive capabilities to work best when they are most needed.

This section on utilizing stress for personal growth applies beyond the problem of learning to cope with simple adjustive demands to the problem of learning to cope constructively with severe and sustained stress situations. This is a never ending process for most of us whereby we learn to understand more about ourselves and others, to modify our goals and expectations in keeping with our skills and with reality, and to increase our competence and stress tolerance. Thus while adaptation to severe stress can be unpleasant, it can also serve as a constructive experience through which we become wiser, stronger, and more mature persons.

## SUMMARY

Psychologists and others have developed a variety of techniques that an individual can use to cope effectively with stress. Often the first step is to bring the physiological, cognitive, and emotional reactions to stress under control. *Built-in coping mechanisms* such as crying, talking about the problems, laughing, and sleeping are

often helpful in bringing stress reactions under control, but by themselves they are rarely effective in relieving all the effects of stress. Thus, it is almost always necessary to supplement these built-in reactions with other, learned coping techniques.

Relaxation and exercise are both effective techniques for relieving some of the physiological reactions to stressful events. Relaxation is a skill that is of great value. Although there are many ways of relaxing, a technique called *relaxation training* that uses muscle tension and relaxation has proved to be especially effective for many people. Regular and vigorous exercise can also help to relieve some physiological responses to stress. Additional steps can be taken specifically to deal with stress-related ulcers, headaches, and hypertension.

The most important step in coping with emotional stress reactions is to realize that emotions are a normal and appropriate response to stress and that they should be recognized and understood, rather than denied or hidden. Social support is also a valuable buffer against emotional reactions to stress. Other people can provide support and reassurance, help to assess the situation accurately and to identify effective ways of coping with it, and allow those under stress to express their emotions. At times, however, the presence of other people may add to the stressfulness of a situation.

There are a number of techniques for dealing with specific emotions when they are either extreme or inappropriate. Fear and anxiety are likely to be lessened if the individual can anticipate the stressful situation and develop some competencies for dealing with it. It also helps to take almost any kind of action in a fear-provoking situation. In coping with anger and hostility, fantasy can be helpful as can developing incompatible responses, empathy, and keeping the situation in perspective. Guilt can often be relieved through confession, reparation, and a willingness to accept forgiveness. Depression often arises from feelings of *learned helplessness;* thus one effective way of coping with depression is to realize that the situation can be dealt with effectively, that most people always have some degree of control over what happens to them.

*Stress inoculation* is a particularly effective way to counteract the cognitive effects of stress. Stress inoculation usually involves three stages: an educational phase, a rehearsal phase, and an application phase. During the educational phase, the person is given a framework for understanding their stress reactions. During the rehearsal phase the person learns to use *cognitive self-statements* to bring stress reactions under greater control. During the application phase, these self-statements are tested and modified in situations of increasing stressfulness.

Eventually, people need to deal directly with the source of stress. Since human beings have very few built-in mechanisms for adapting, most techniques for dealing with stress are learned through operant conditioning or observation. One effective approach to stress management is to adopt a general problem-solving strategy. First, it is important to define and categorize the stress situation without oversimplifying it. Next, an appropriate course of action must be selected; this usually involves formulating alternatives, then weighing costs and benefits of each alternative. In general there are three courses of action available in a stressful situation: attack the source of stress, withdraw, or compromise. Each has advantages, and each also has costs. The choice among them depends on the situation and on an individual's competencies and resources. Once action has been taken, *feedback* can be used to assess the effectiveness of the action and to suggest changes in strategy if the initial tactic is apparently working ineffectively.

Although it is always desirable to avoid excessive amounts of stress, some stress is an inevitable fact of life and may actually lead to personal growth by increasing our understanding of ourselves and our world, by helping us to establish more realistic goals and values, and by improving our competence and stress tolerance.

## KEY TERMS

built-in coping mechanisms (141)

relaxation training (143)

grief work (151)

ambivalent feelings (151)

learned helplessness (151)

stress inoculation (153)

cognitive self-statements (153)

vacillation (159)

substitution (160)

accommodation (160)

brainstorming (161)

feedback (164)

# CHAPTER SIX

# Maladaptive Behavior

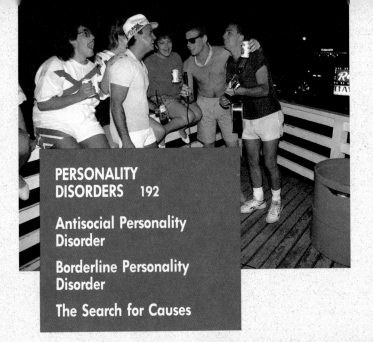

## PERSONALITY DISORDERS 192

**Antisocial Personality Disorder**

**Borderline Personality Disorder**

**The Search for Causes**

## SUBSTANCE USE DISORDERS 197

**Frequently Abused Substances**
    Alcohol
    Heroin
    Barbiturates
    Amphetamines
    Cocaine
    Marijuana
    LSD

**The Search for Causes**

## SCHIZOPHRENIC DISORDERS 204

**Clinical Symptoms**

**Types of Schizophrenia**
    Paranoid schizophrenia
    Catatonic schizophrenia
    Disorganized schizophrenia
    Undifferentiated
      schizophrenia

**The Search for Causes**

**Summary** 209
**Key Terms** 213

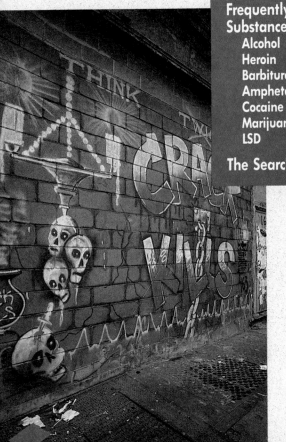

*The mind is its own place, and in itself
Can make a heaven of hell, a hell of heaven.*

John Milton

*I*N Chapter 1, we discussed at some length that not all efforts at adjustment are equally effective. If coping behavior meets the demands of the situation, meets our own needs, and contributes to the well-being of others, then it is considered to be *adaptive* behavior. The last several chapters explored various ways people under stress can cope adaptively. Unfortunately, some people find it difficult or impossible to cope effectively with stress. In some cases, their attempts to cope do not meet the immediate or long-range demands of the situation and may make the situation worse; in other cases their own immediate and long-term needs are not satisfied; in still others the needs of others are adversely affected. Such cases are known as *maladaptive* coping behavior. The following are examples of several different maladaptive coping responses.

A 37-year-old computer operator walks into an office building, enters the office of the president of the company, takes a gun from under his jacket, and kills the executive before taking his own life. One week earlier, the gunman had been fired from the company for excessive absenteeism.

The joy and happiness of a young couple is shattered when their newborn daughter is kidnapped from the hospital nursery. Two days later the police arrest a middle-aged couple and recover the infant. Upon questioning, the couple explains that their own baby had died suddenly six months earlier for no known reason. They were devastated by the loss and overcome with guilt that they might somehow have been responsible for the death. The husband explained, "We didn't mean any harm; we just miss our own baby so much."

A student at a highly competitive college begins to experience feelings of panic when he sits down to take an exam or to write a paper. At first he thinks he is just working too hard, but as time passes he begins to believe that someone is putting mind-altering drugs in his food to keep him from doing well. He comes to the attention of college officials when he slips a note under the door of a student across the hall that says "I know what you are doing. STOP—or else!"

A city bus driver in New York suddenly pulls out of rush hour traffic and drives his fully loaded bus onto an interstate highway heading south. An hour later, when state troopers finally bring the bus to a stop, the driver explains, "I've had it with all that craziness. I'm going to Florida."

Why are some people unable to cope adaptively with stress? In a few cases, the stress is so overwhelming that hardly anyone could be expected to deal with it effectively, but situations such as these are rare. Even faced with an airplane hi-

*Letting painful feelings loose is part of the healing process of post-traumatic stress disorder and helps veterans resume normal life.*

**diathesis-stress model** *(dy-ath-a-sis):* view that some people are predisposed to develop particular disorders when exposed to certain kinds of stressors

jacking, a kidnapping, or combat, some people are able to cope adaptively while others cannot. What accounts for the difference?

Psychologists usually answer this question in terms of a **diathesis-stress model.** In medicine, "diathesis" refers to a predisposition to develop a particular disease. In the same way, some people are more likely than others to develop various kinds of maladaptive behaviors or disorders when exposed to stress. As you will see throughout this chapter, in some cases the diathesis appears to be hereditary, while in other cases it seems to reflect prior experiences. Whatever the cause, these people have an "Achilles heel" or weak spot that leaves them more likely than others to respond to stress with certain kinds of maladaptive behaviors. This doesn't mean that everyone with such a diathesis will develop a particular kind of psychological disorder under stress. Rather, they are simply more *likely* to display the disorder than are most others faced with the same stressful situation.

**psychopathologies:** psychlogical disorders or abnormalities

**DSM-III-R:** *Diagnostic and Statistical Manual of Mental Disorders* (Third Edition, Revised), the current standard for diagnosing psychological disorders

In this chapter, we will examine a variety of psychological disorders, or **psychopathologies.** The diagnostic labels we will use in classifying these disorders come from the revised third edition of the *Diagnostic and Statistical Manual of Mental Disorders* (DSM-III-R) published by the American Psychiatric Association (APA, 1987). **DSM-III-R** is a widely used, comprehensive list of psychological disorders categorizing groups of disorders based on their characteristic symptoms. For each disorder, DSM-III-R describes (1) the symptoms likely to be present, (2) the typical age of onset, and (3) the likely course or outcome of the disorder including possible impairments and complications. In addition, DSM-III-R provides information concerning the characteristics of high-risk individuals, the prevalence of the disorder among men and women, the likelihood that other family members will also have the disorder, and the features that distinguish one disorder from another (see the Insight, p. 177).

Before proceeding further in our study of maladaptive behavior, a few cautions are in order. First, note that many maladaptive behaviors do not fall into neat diagnostic categories. Second, the same symptoms often have quite different meanings for different people. For example, one person may become depressed because of a biological disorder; another person may become depressed because he or she has lost a job; still another person may be depressed because the individual believes that he or she is worthless. Simply to classify all three people as suffering from "mood disorder" can obscure the important differences between them. Third, although DSM-III-R provides diagnostic labels for psychological disorders, with few exceptions these disorders are not medical diseases; rather, they represent ineffective ways of coping with stress (Smith & Kraft, 1983). As long as these cautions are kept in mind, DSM-III-R is a useful device for classifying psychological disorders.

One final caution. As you read this chapter, you may worry that you have many of the disorders being discussed. Rest assured that this is a common experience, often called the "medical students' syndrome." Characteristically, medical students often overinterpret every twinge and pain that they experience as a clear sign that they are suffering from whatever disease they are studying at the moment. The same can happen to readers of psychology texts. Everyone has moments of apprehension, depression, or guilt, but they are usually not intense and they typically pass in a short time. While reading about maladaptive behavior, some students overinterpret such minor worries or personal idiosyncrasies as signs of psychopathology. Having one or more characteristics of a disorder is usually not evidence that you have a problem. Nonetheless, if you find yourself worrying that you may have one or more of these disorders, you may find it useful to seek a professional opinion and, if necessary, obtain professional help. Chapter 7 provides some helpful advice on ways to get professional help of various sorts.

## STRESS AND ADJUSTMENT DISORDERS

**adjustment disorder:**
abnormal, unreasonable reaction to a common stressful event

The diagnosis **adjustment disorder** is made when a person uncharacteristically overreacts to a relatively common stressful experience. Unlike other, more serious forms of psychopathology, adjustment disorders are clearly linked to specific stressful experiences such as unemployment, bereavement, getting married, becoming a parent, going through divorce or separation, moving to a new community, and retirement. These are all challenging life events that require substantial coping efforts. However, when a normally well-adjusted person overreacts to such stressful experiences—showing unusual signs of depression, anxiety, irrational fears, social withdrawal, vandalism, reckless driving, fighting, physical complaints, or problems in school or work performance—then the diagnosis "adjustment disorder" is appropriate.

# *Insight*

## Adjustment Disorder

The following case (Carson, Butcher, & Coleman, 1988) illustrates some of the essential features of adjustment disorder.

Nadine, a 66-year-old former high school teacher, lived with Charles, age 67, her husband of 40 years (also a retired teacher). The couple had been nearly inseparable since they met—they even taught at the same schools during most of their teaching careers. They lived in a semirural community where they had taught and had raised their three children, all of whom had married and moved to a large metropolitan area about a hundred miles away. For years, they had planned their retirement and had hoped to be able to travel around the country visiting friends. A week before their fortieth anniversary, Charles had a heart attack and, after five days in the intensive care unit, had a second heart attack and died.

Nadine took Charles's death quite hard. Even though she had a great deal of emotional support from her many friends and her children, she had great difficulty adjusting. Elaine, one of her daughters, came and stayed a few days and encouraged her to come to the city for a while. Nadine declined the persistent invitation even though she had little to do at home. Friends called on her frequently, but she seemed almost to resent their presence. In the months following the funeral, Nadine's reclusive behavior persisted. Several well-wishers reported to Elaine that her mother was not doing well and was not even leaving the house to go shopping. They reported that Nadine sat alone in a darkened house—not answering the phone and showing reluctance to come to the door. She had lost interest in activities she had once enjoyed.

Greatly worried about her mother's welfare, Elaine organized a campaign to get her mother out of the house and back to doing the things she had formerly done. Each of the children and their families took turns at visiting, spending time with her, and taking her places until she finally began to show interest in living again. In time, Nadine agreed to come to each of their homes for visits. This proved to be a very therapeutic step since Nadine had always been very fond of children and took pleasure in the time spent with her eight grandchildren. She actually extended the visits longer than she had planned. (p. 155)

In some cases, adjustment disorders arise when an unusually large number of stressors occur at the same time. For example, an otherwise well-adjusted individual facing marital and financial difficulties and then fired from a job may find the combination of stressors overwhelming and be unable to cope effectively for a short while. In other cases, adjustment disorders arise when previous experiences have left a person especially vulnerable to a particular kind of stressful event. For example, one woman who came to see a therapist complained that she was completely unable to concentrate at work following a breakup with her boyfriend. Previous experience revealed that her father had died when she was eight years old, and the loss of her boyfriend had triggered many of the old feelings about her father's death.

The outlook in cases of adjustment disorders is usually very favorable: the cause of the disorder is identifiable, the symptoms appear relatively soon after the event, and the person is otherwise effective at coping with stress. Most often, adjustment disorders are simply "temporary setbacks" that last for a few weeks or months and then disappear. Nonetheless, some people require professional assistance to help them come to terms with the stress, put the event into perspective, and bring their normal coping mechanisms into play.

## Post-traumatic Stress Disorder

**post-traumatic stress disorder:** extreme reaction to an unusually stressful event such as assault, a natural disaster, or combat

In contrast to adjustment disorder, **post-traumatic stress disorder** refers to extreme reactions to truly extraordinary events such as sudden destruction of one's home or community in a natural disaster, witnessing a major accident, experiencing combat, being the victim of a terrorist attack, or being raped, assaulted, tortured or taken hostage.

Horrifying events such as these make massive demands on anyone's ability to cope; but some victims find the experience particularly overwhelming. Despite their best efforts to put the experience out of their minds, they reexperience the event over and over again (sometimes called "flashbacks"). If they find themselves in situations resembling the original event, they may even reenact the event as if it were happening all over again. Their traumatic experience may intrude into their dreams, and they may wake up repeatedly during the night suffering from nightmares. Often the victims say they feel cut off or distant from people around them; that is, they are unable to feel normal emotions such as love or affection, though they may feel overwhelming guilt or anxiety about the event itself. They may have difficulty concentrating on tasks; they may explode in anger for no apparent reason; or they may disappear for hours or days without explanation.

Most people are familiar with post-traumatic stress disorder through newspaper and television accounts of war veterans, most recently veterans of the Vietnam War (Brende & Parson, 1985). "Shell shock," "combat fatigue," and "combat stress" are all terms that have been used to describe post-traumatic stress reactions among soldiers. However, post-traumatic stress disorder is not limited to combat veterans. The following case describes the reactions of a 42-year-old police officer who responded to the scene of an especially gruesome airplane accident in California which took the lives of 144 people.

> Don had been a model police officer during his 14 years on the force. He was highly evaluated by his superiors, had a masters degree in social work, and had attained the rank of sergeant. While patrolling in a squad car, he heard that there had been an accident, and he quickly drove to the scene to give aid to any survivors. When he arrived he wandered around "in a daze," looking for someone to help—but there was only destruction. He later remembered the next few days as a bad dream.
>
> He was quite depressed for several days after the cleanup, had no appetite, couldn't sleep, and was impotent. Images and recollections of the accident would come to him "out of nowhere." He reported having a recurring dream in which he would come upon an airplane crash while driving a car or flying a plane. In his dream, he would rush to the wreckage and help some passengers to safety.
>
> Don decided that he needed help and sought counseling. Because of his deteriorating mood and physical condition, he was placed on medical leave from the police force. Eight months after the accident he was still in therapy and had not returned to work. During therapy it became apparent that Don had been experiencing a great deal of personal dissatisfaction and anger prior to the crash. His prolonged psychological disorder was not only a result of his anguish over the air crash but also a vehicle for expressing other problems. (Davidson, 1979: reproduced from Carson et al., 1988, p. 163)

By its very nature, post-traumatic stress disorder occurs in response to situations that "would be markedly distressing to almost anyone" (APA, 1987, p. 247). Each of the symptoms of post-traumatic stress reactions reflects an effort to cope with the overwhelming crisis. By thinking about and reexperiencing the event, the victim tries to gain control over it. In an attempt to shut down painful or intolerable feelings, even normal feelings and emotions are likely to be muted. However, preoccupation with the event makes concentrating on other things difficult and leads to feelings of detachment from the real world.

The passage of time, reassurance and support from friends and family, the opportunity to talk about and work through the crisis—for many post-traumatic stress victims, these are necessary factors for overcoming the stress reaction and resuming normal lives. Others, like Don, seek professional assistance to regain control of their lives. Still others never experience full-blown post-traumatic stress reactions because they receive immediate support and assistance from specially trained **crisis intervention** teams rushed to the scene to provide help. These teams are usually composed of physicians, nurses, psychologists, and social workers

**crisis intervention:** immediate, short-term assistance provided during or after a particularly traumatic event or crisis

who are specially trained to identify signs of stress reactions and to provide assistance in the hours and days immediately following a tragedy.

In our discussion so far, we have considered maladaptive reactions to events that all of us would consider stressful to some degree. In the next portion of the chapter, we will consider some more puzzling disorders in which people experience persistent feelings of threat and anxiety in the absence of any obvious stressor.

## ANXIETY-BASED DISORDERS

Mild anxiety is a common event. New and unfamiliar work and social situations often produce mild anxiety. Demands placed upon us to perform can produce anxiety, as well. We may, for example, feel anxious in a social situation in which we know few people (Jones, Cheek, & Briggs, 1986). Speaking in front of a large group also produces anxiety for many people (McCroskey & Beatty, 1986). Also, failing to meet our own or other people's expectations can be anxiety-evoking. In these situations, most of us are able to move ahead despite the anxiety, and we are not prevented from accomplishing the task at hand.

### Panic Disorder

However, some people experience excessive, persistent, unrealistic and irrational fears and anxieties that profoundly disrupt their lives. Consider the following case (Leon, 1977).

> During the time when Richard Benson, age 38, was experiencing intense anxiety, it often seemed as if he were having a heart seizure. He experienced chest pains and heart palpitations, numbness, shortness of breath, and he felt a strong need to breathe in air. He reported that in the midst of the anxiety attack, he developed a feeling of tightness over his eyes and he could only see objects directly in front of him. He further stated that he feared that he would not be able to swallow. The intensity of the anxiety symptoms was very frightening to him and on two occasions his wife had rushed him to a local hospital because he was in a state of panic, sure that his heart was going to stop beating and he would die. (p. 113)

**panic disorder:** intense anxiety accompanied by various worrisome physiological symptoms

Richard Benson was experiencing **panic disorder.** In cases such as his, panic attacks occur unexpectedly and are accompanied by shortness of breath, dizziness, rapid heart beat, trembling, sweating, choking, nausea, numbness, flushes or chills, chest pains, fear of dying, fear of going crazy, and fear of doing something uncontrolled.

**agoraphobia** (ag-or-a-pho-bia): irrational fear of public places and crowds

Panic attacks may last only a matter of minutes, but they are so unpleasant that they can have profound effects lasting long after the attack itself is over. Quite often, for example, the victims of panic attacks fear situations from which it would be difficult to escape or where help might not be readily available, and so they restrict travel and remain at home for days and weeks at a time. This fear, called **agoraphobia,** often leads to avoidance of travel in cars, buses, subways, and airplanes, and to avoidance of crowds and long lines.

## Simple Phobias

Agoraphobia, which can also occur in the absence of panic attacks, is just one way in which extreme anxiety can become focussed on a particular situation or object. For example, it is relatively common for people to report persistent, irrational fears of high places, spiders, snakes, enclosed spaces, darkness, animals, storms, germs, crowds, and being alone. Whenever a person experiences an intense, irrational fear of a relatively harmless situation or object and that fear interferes with normal living, psychologists speak of a **simple phobia.** Although people with phobias realize that their fears are irrational, this does not prevent them from experiencing intense anxiety when in the presence of the object. The following case (Spitzer et al., 1981) illustrates some common features of phobic disorders.

**simple phobia:** irrational fear of a specific situation or object

> This 28-year-old housewife sought psychiatric treatment for a fear of storms that had become progressively more disturbing to her. Although frightened of storms since she was a child, the fear seemed to abate somewhat during adolescence, but had been increasing in severity over the past few years. This gradual exacerbation of her anxiety, plus the fear that she might pass it on to her children, led her to seek treatment.
>
> She is most frightened of lightning, but is uncertain about the reason for this. She is only vaguely aware of a fear of being struck by lightning, and recognizes that this is an unlikely occurrence. When asked to elaborate on her fears, she imagines that lightning could strike a tree in her yard; the tree might fall and block her driveway, thus trapping her at home. This frightens her, but she is quite aware that her fear is irrational. She also recognizes the irrational nature of her fear of thunder. She begins to feel anxiety long before a storm arrives. A weather report predicting a storm later in the week can cause her anxiety to increase to the point that she worries for days before the storm. Although she does not express a fear of rain, her anxiety increases even when the weather becomes overcast because of the increased likelihood of a storm.
>
> During a storm, she does several things to reduce her anxiety. Since being with another person reduces her fear, she often tries to make plans to visit friends or relatives or go to a store when a storm is threatening. Sometimes when her husband is away on business she stays overnight with a close relative if a storm is forecast. During a storm she covers her eyes or moves to a part of the house far from windows, where she cannot see lightning should it occur. (p. 90)

## Obsessions and Compulsions

In other people, anxiety is expressed in the form of obsessions or compulsions. **Obsessions** are persistent irrational thoughts, ideas, or impulses that are distressful to the person. Most often obsessive thoughts concern dying, becoming ill, becoming contaminated, or doing something terrible. For example, a young parent might become obsessed with the possibility that his or her child might become ill or die, or that he or she might poison the child.

**obsessions:** persistent irrational thoughts or impulses

**Compulsions** are irrational, repetitive, ritualistic acts that the individual feels compelled to perform. Just as obsessions are associated with unpleasant thoughts, compulsions are experienced as irresistible impulses to act in irrational ways. Compulsions can have many forms: washing one's hands every few minutes; checking

**compulsions:** irrational and repetitive behaviors that people feel compelled to perform

*Irrational and persistent anxiety is the basis of many disorders and phobias, which can restrict everyday activities such as traveling in cars, working, or interacting with others.*

and rechecking such things as windows, doors, and gas flames prior to going to bed at night or leaving the house during the day; avoiding or counting all the cracks in the sidewalk while walking; touching every chair in a room before sitting down; setting up rigid, unvarying procedures for doing things. An important feature of compulsive behavior is that the person realizes the behavior is strange or irrational, prefers not to do it, but feels compelled to continue. The following case (Carson et al., 1988) illustrates some common features of obsessive-compulsive disorder.

> A 32-year-old high-school cooking teacher developed marked feelings of guilt and uneasiness, accompanied by obsessive fears of hurting others by touching them or by their handling something she had touched. She dreaded to have anyone eat anything she had prepared, and if students in her cooking class were absent, she was certain they had been poisoned by her cooking. In addition, she developed the obsessive notion that a rash at the base of her scalp was a manifestation of syphilis, which would gnaw at her brain and make a "drooling idiot" of her.
>
> Accompanying the obsessive fears were compulsions consisting primarily of repeated hand-washings and frequent returns to some act already performed to reassure herself that the act had been done right, such as turning off the gas or water. (p. 191)

### Somatoform Disorders

**somatoform disorders:**
unsubstantiated physical complaints

Still other people express anxiety in the form of **somatoform disorders:** complaints of physical ailments for which there is no physical cause. Some such complaints can be quite striking: a soldier experiences total blindness just prior to entering battle;

a carpenter experiences complete loss of feeling in an arm from the elbow to the fingertips; a writer suffers paralysis of the hands; an actor becomes unable to speak. In other cases the complaints may be less specific: multiple but vague aches and pains; a preoccupation with minor health problems; unrealistic fears of disease. People with complaints such as these are sometimes known as **hypochondriacs.** Consider the following case by Menninger (1945).

**hypochrondriacs:** people who have many vague medical complaints for which there are no physical causes

> Dear Mother and Husband:
>
> I have suffered terrible today with drawing in throat. My nerves are terrible. My head feels queer. But my stomach hasn't cramped quite so hard. I've been on the verge of a nervous chill all day, but I have been fighting it hard. It's night and bedtime, but, Oh, how I hate to go to bed. Nobody knows or realizes how badly I feel because I fight to stay up and outdoors if possible. . . .
>
> These long afternoons and nights are awful. There are plenty of patients well enough to visit with but I'm in too much pain.
>
> The nurses ignore any complaining. They just laugh or scold.
>
> Eating has been awful hard. They expect me to eat like a harvest hand. Every bite of solid food is agony to get down, for my throat aches so and feels so closed up. . . .
>
> My eyes are bothering me more.
>
> Come up as soon as you can. My nose runs terribly every time I eat.
>
> The trains and ducks and water pipes are noisy at night.
>
> Annie
> (pp. 139–40)

In somatoform disorders, although the complaint is without any physical cause, the symptoms are very real to the individual. Surprisingly, many people with these disorders show little outward anxiety or concern about their symptoms; indeed, the indifference of these patients toward their symptoms may be striking. The major difference between somatoform disorders and psychophysiological reactions (see Chapter 4) is that in the latter case there is a real, physiological basis for the person's complaints: ulcers, migraine headaches, and hypertension are real physical disorders brought on by stress. However, in somatoform disorders, there is no apparent physical cause for the person's complaints.

## Other Anxiety-based Disorders

**dissociative disorders:** alterations of consciousness or identity as a result of severe stress

Another way anxiety manifests itself is through **dissociative disorders,** in which a person experiences a sudden loss of memory or alteration of personal identity. Some people forget significant parts of their lives. They may wander from familiar surroundings, occasionally developing a new identity in a setting far removed from their homes. In the most severe cases, individuals may even take on multiple personalities. Dissociative disorders are a dramatic reaction to stress. Often the stress is very severe and sudden, and the individual has no adaptive resources with which to handle the demands placed upon him or her.

**generalized anxiety disorder:** persistent excessive worry, uneasiness, or apprehensiveness

Finally, there are some cases in which anxiety never focuses on a particular object or situation. In these cases psychologists speak of **generalized anxiety disorder.** The individual lives in a constant state of tension or worry without knowing why, feels apprehensive and anxious even when things are going well, worries about the past and the future, and feels upset and on edge most of the time. The following description (Carson et al., 1988) captures some of the common features of generalized anxiety disorders.

> Dr. H. J., a second-year resident in internal medicine in a major university medical center, referred himself for therapy in connection with his growing problems in coping with anxiety.
>
> On initial assessment, Dr. J., who is manifestly tense, complains of never being entirely free of a sense of impending disaster, although he cannot further specify the nature of this anticipated catastrophe. The thought of being involuntarily terminated from his envied position on the cardiology team, earlier a source of intense anxiety, has "on one or two occasions lately," he acknowledges, provided him momentary feelings of relief. He notes a number of signs of autonomic hyperarousal that he experiences on virtually a daily basis, emphasizing in particular excessive sweating, which has become a source of embarrassment. He is medicating himself for persistent attacks of diarrhea. He complains of an inability to attain a refreshing level of sleep even on those rare occasions when he can count on a few uninterrupted off-duty hours, and his very few waking "leisure" hours are filled with restless irritability. He is greatly concerned about his wife's growing complaints of loneliness and his inattentiveness to her and is fearful she may leave him; however, he expresses a sense of helplessness about being able to alter the situation.
>
> Dr. J.'s request for therapy was precipitated by three additional concerns of more recent origin: (1) He experienced his first panic attack several evenings ago and fled from an intensive care unit for which he was the sole responsible physician, an understanding nurse having to "cover" for his absence. (2) He has noticed that the "requirement" (actually, a team expectancy) of remembering without recourse to notes the details of the case of every patient under the team's care, never easy, has lately become impossible. (3) He is concerned that his ever-increasing use of antianxiety medication (Valium) will be noticed and/or will lead to drug dependency. (p. 195)

The common element running through all these disorders—panic disorders, phobias, generalized anxiety disorders, obsessive-compulsive disorders, somatoform disorders, and dissociative disorders—is overwhelming anxiety. In each case, the symptoms serve a definite purpose: by focussing anxiety in some way (perhaps on a specific object or situation, or on a physical ailment), a person under stress can develop some techniques for reducing or avoiding the threat and anxiety. While such protective measures can indeed help to control anxiety and panic at least for a while, they also can seriously disrupt normal activities such as working, eating, and sleeping. In one case, for example, a woman with agoraphobia left her home only three times in seventeen years. Each of the three occasions involved a trip to the hospital to give birth to one of her children. Moreover, while the symptoms in anxiety-based disorders are irrational and inappropriate, they usually reduce the flexibility of the person's behavior and may interfere with more effective coping efforts. For these reasons, they are considered to be maladaptive ways of coping with stress.

## The Search for Causes

Why do some people experience great anxiety when they are under stress, while other people faced with the same stressors experience little or no anxiety? Why do some anxious people develop one kind of disorder while others develop another?

There are several answers to these important questions. Consistent with the diathesis-stress model, some psychologists believe that at least some people suffering from anxiety disorders inherit a tendency to overreact emotionally to threatening situations (Wilson, 1977, 1978). Recent evidence also suggests that at least some people are genetically predisposed to develop specific anxiety disorders when they are under stress: for example, Turner et al. (1985) discovered substantial evidence of a hereditary tendency to develop obsessive-compulsive disorder, and Noyes et al. (1986) have presented similar evidence with respect to panic disorder and agoraphobia.

However, not everyone with a hereditary predisposition to develop an anxiety-based disorder actually develops one when under stress, and not everyone who develops an anxiety-based disorder has a hereditary predisposition to do so. In an effort to account for these individual differences, some psychologists emphasize life experiences as the basis for many cases of anxiety-based disorders. According to this view, some people learn to react irrationally to stressful situations through conditioning or observational learning (we discussed these basic learning processes in Chapter 2). A person who is afraid of elevators, for example, may have learned from experience to associate elevators with fear; avoiding elevators leads to a reduction in anxiety, so the avoidance behavior is reinforced. This explanation of phobias is compelling, though it doesn't explain why phobias are so likely to develop toward some objects and situations (such as spiders and snakes) and virtually never develop toward other objects. As Martin Seligman points out: "Only rarely, if ever, do we have pajama phobias, grass phobias, electric-outlet phobias, hammer phobias, even though these things are likely to be associated with trauma in our world" (Seligman, 1972, p. 455).

Somatoform disorders may also be learned and maintained through experience. Victims of these disorders are likely to receive a great deal of attention and sympathy; moreover, somatic disorders often give the victims a great deal of influence over the lives of other people around them. Such reinforcements may account for the persistence of somatic complaints in the absence of any physical disorder. Of course, it is not necessary for the victim to discover first-hand the rewarding nature of such symptoms: observing another family member or a friend who has a similar disorder can also be a source of learning.

Still other psychologists explain anxiety-based disorders from the perspective of psychoanalytic theory (see Chapter 2). According to this view, anxiety is a signal that an unacceptable id impulse (usually sexual or aggressive in nature) has been activated and is in conflict with the ego and superego. The visible symptoms are just a sign of the unconscious conflict that is raging within the person. For example, a person who unconsciously fears losing control may express that fear outwardly in the form of an elevator or airplane phobia: an irrational fear that an elevator or airplane might suddenly go out of control and crash. In contrast, a somatoform disorder permits the person to "convert" anxiety into physical complaints that bear a resemblance to the underlying source of anxiety: the actor unconsciously fearing that he is losing his acting skill may instead lose his voice; this allows him to avoid or escape from the stressful situation (having to perform in public) without having to take responsibility for doing so.

## MOOD DISORDERS

All of us at one time or another experience the "blues," feel sad, disappointed, or feel a sense of hopelessness. So, too, all of us at times feel excited or elated, "on cloud nine." For most of us, these mood changes are normal and reasonable reactions to events in our lives which do not interfere unduly with the rest of our lives and are largely under our control. For the most part, we can put aside our normal doubts and worries, and control our excitement and enthusiasm if necessary.

Some people, however, experience extreme moods that are not proportionate to the events in their lives and that are out of their control. In these cases psychologists speak of **mood disorders:** prolonged, abnormal disturbances of mood or emotion that significantly interfere with working or social relationships or that endanger the welfare of the person experiencing them. In this section of the chapter, we will look more closely at various mood disorders and consider some of the explanations that have been proposed for them.

**mood disorders:** disorders characterized by extreme and inappropriate depression or elation

### Mild to Moderate Mood Disorders

**dysthymia** *(dis-thy-mia):* mood disorder marked by chronic, inappropriate feelings of depression

**Dysthymia** is a mild mood disorder in which a person predominantly feels dejected or depressed for a period of at least two years. Often the individual experiences loss of appetite, markedly lowered sex drive, difficulty in concentrating and making decisions, and impaired personal effectiveness. Tasks that could be handled ordinarily with ease require Herculean effort or seem impossible. Sharing leisure-time pursuits or other activities with loved ones and friends is no longer rewarding. In essence, the joy has gone out of living, to be replaced by an uncomplimentary and unflattering view of oneself and one's world. The following case (Spitzer et al., 1981) illustrates some of these features of dysthymia.

> The patient is a 32-year-old man who admitted himself to a mental hospital after attempting suicide by taking sleeping pills. He said nothing in particular had prompted this attempt, but that he had been this depressed, with only minor fluctuations, for the last ten years, ever since he returned from Vietnam.
>
> He loathed the violence there; but on one occasion, evidently swept away by group spirit, he killed a civilian "for the fun of it." This seems to him totally out of keeping with his character. The memory of this incident continues to haunt him, and he is wracked with guilt. He was honorably discharged from the army, and has never worked since, except for three weeks when an uncle hired him. He has been living on various forms of government assistance.
>
> He presents as a very sad, thoughtful, introspective man with a dignified bearing, and in informal conversation appears to be of at least normal intelligence. He is not interested in anything and confides that when he sees others enjoying themselves, he is so jealous he wants to hit them; this urge is never evident from his unfailingly courteous behavior. His appetite is normal, as is his sex drive, "but I don't enjoy it." He has trouble falling asleep or staying asleep without medication. He complains of "absentmindedness," and immediate and short-term memory are grossly impaired. After two weeks, he still has trouble finding his way around the ward. (p. 114)

Other people experience extreme mood variations for no apparent reason, swinging abruptly from periods of deep depression to periods of extreme elation and excitement and back again. When depressed, their symptoms are similar to those of persons suffering from dysthymia. When elated, however, they express feelings of extreme well-being and optimism, and make exciting but grandiose plans for the future. During these periods of elation, they are likely to be highly distractible, overly talkative, and incapable of following through on proposed projects. They are also likely to need little sleep, have trouble maintaining their thoughts, and become agitated. In cases such as this where a person has experienced such extreme variations in mood for a period of several years, the appropriate diagnosis is **cyclothymia**. The following case (Spitzer et al., 1981) captures some of the common features of cyclothymia.

**cyclothymia** *(cycl-o-thy-mia):* chronic mood disorder in which periods of inappropriate depression alternate with periods of inappropriate elation

> A 29-year-old car salesman was referred by his current girlfriend, a psychiatric nurse, who suspected he had an Affective Disorder; even though the patient was reluctant to admit that he might be a "moody" person. According to him, since the age of 14 he has experienced repeated alternating cycles that he terms "good times and bad times." During a "bad" period, usually lasting four to seven days, he oversleeps 10-14 hours daily, lacks energy, confidence, and motivation—"just vegetating," as he puts it. Often he abruptly shifts, characteristically upon waking up in the morning, to a three-to-four-day stretch of overconfidence, heightened social awareness, promiscuity, and sharpened thinking—"things would flash in my mind." At such times he indulges in alcohol to enhance the experience, but also to help him sleep. Occasionally the "good" periods last seven to ten days, but culminate in irritable and hostile outbursts, which often herald the transition back to another period of "bad" days. He admits to frequent use of marijuana, which he claims helps him "adjust" to daily routines.
>
> In school, A's and B's alternated with C's and D's, with the result that the patient was considered a bright student whose performance was mediocre overall because of "unstable motivation." As a car salesman his performance has also been uneven, with "good days" canceling out the "bad days"; yet even during his "good days" he is sometimes perilously argumentative with customers and loses sales that appeared sure. Although considered a charming man in many social circles, he alienates friends when he is hostile and irritable. He typically accumulates social obligations during the "bad" days and takes care of them all at once on the first day of a "good" period. (pp. 31-32)

## Severe Mood Disorders

Although dysthymia and cyclothymia are both maladaptive and disruptive disorders, many people suffering from them can function reasonably well from day to day. However, this is seldom possible for people experiencing more extreme forms of mood disorders. For example, some people become so profoundly depressed that they find it difficult or impossible to function at all. In some cases, they cannot even get out of bed in the morning. They may feel deeply depressed for months or years at a time and lose all interest in their lives. In extreme cases, they may lapse into a depressive stupor with an almost complete lack of response. They may also lose their appetite, have difficulty getting to sleep (or else sleep most of the time), feel

**major depressive disorder:** a severe form of chronic depression in which the person's ability to function is seriously affected

**delusions:** false beliefs an individual defends despite logical evidence

**hallucinations:** perceptual experiences that are not based in reality

**bipolar disorder (manic depression):** mood disorder characterized by periods of extreme excitement and overactivity (mania) which alternate with periods of profound depression

constantly fatigued, and suffer from profound feelings of failure, worthlessness, guilt, hopelessness, apprehensiveness, and anxiety. Recurring thoughts of death and suicide are not uncommon. In cases such as this, the proper diagnosis is **major depressive disorder.**

**Bipolar disorders.**    For other people, periods of major depression alternate with periods of extreme excitement or elation in which they may talk constantly, become extremely distractible, and experience rapid shifts of thought. **delusions** and **hallucinations** may occur. Delusions are false beliefs with little or no basis in fact. For example, a person may become convinced that he has invented a perpetual motion machine and that the FBI is trying to steal his invention. Hallucinations are sensory experiences occurring in the absence of any external stimulus. For example, a person may hear voices or see objects that do not in fact exist. During such periods of excitement or elation, an individual may also suffer from impaired judgment and lowered ethical restraints, which may lead to unwise financial investments, promiscuous sexual acts, and other illegal or immoral behavior. In extreme form, the manic reaction may result in delerium and disorientation. In these cases, the proper diagnosis is **bipolar disorder** (sometimes also called manic depressive disorder).

**The problem of suicide.**    The greatest risk with mood disorders, of course, is suicide. Depression and suicide, though distinct phenomena, are closely related: depressed persons are a high-risk group with respect to suicide, and nearly 90 percent of the individuals who attempt or commit suicide do so when they are experiencing some form of depression. According to official statistics, more than 200,000 people attempt suicide each year in the United States, and over 25,000 succeed. However, since many self-inflicted deaths are officially attributed to other, more "respectable" causes than suicide, experts have estimated that the actual number of suicides in our society may be two to five times higher than the number officially reported. Of the "successes" each year, roughly 1,000 are college students; in addition, the number of suicides among teen-agers and young adults has more than doubled during the last decade (see Psychology in Action, pp. 189, 191). In our society, someone attempts suicide every twenty minutes and well over 7 million living Americans have attempted at least once to take their lives.

## The Search for Causes

The close relationship between suicide and severe mood disorders makes the search for the causes of mood disorder especially important. As you might expect, research shows that psychological stress plays a key role: typically, people suffering from mood disorders have experienced an unusually high level of life stress over a period of weeks, months, and sometimes years (Hirschfeld & Cross, 1982). Among the most frequent antecedents of mood disorders are events that lower self-esteem or threaten personal identity (such as failure on the job, failure to live up to one's responsibilities), crises in important personal relationships, health problems, increased responsibilities, death of a friend or relative, and facing difficult or impossible problems (Leff et al., 1970; Paykel, 1982).

## Suicide Among College Students

### Incidence and Methods

Ten thousand students in the United States attempt suicide each year, and more than 1000 succeed. The incidence of suicide is twice as high among college students as it is among young people in the same age range who are not in college. The greatest incidence of suicidal behavior occurs at the beginning and the end of the school quarter or semester. Approximately three times more female than male students attempt suicide, but the incidence of fatal attempts is considerably higher among males. More than half of those attempting suicide take pills, about one third cut themselves, and the remainder—mostly males—use other methods, such as hanging or gunshot.

### Warning Signs and Threats

A change in a student's mood and behavior is a most significant warning that he or she may be planning suicide. Characteristically, the student becomes depressed and withdrawn, undergoes a marked decline in self-esteem, and shows deterioration in habits of personal hygiene. This is accompanied by a profound loss of interest in his or her studies. Often the student stops attending classes and remains in his or her room most of the day. Usually the student communicates his or her distress to at least one other person, often in the form of a veiled suicide warning. A significant number of students who attempt suicide leave suicide notes.

### Precipitating Factors

When a college student attempts suicide, one of the first explanations to occur to friends and family is that he or she may have been doing poorly in school. However, students who manifest suicidal behavior are, as a group, superior students; they tend to expect a great deal of themselves in terms of academic achievement and to exhibit scholastic anxieties. Grades, academic competition, and pressure over examinations are not significant precipitating stresses. Also, while many lose interest in their studies and their grades get lower prior to the onset of suicidal behavior, the loss of interest appears to be associated with depression and withdrawal caused by problems other than academic ones.

Often, the problems are loss of self-esteem and failure to live up to parental expectations, rather than the academic failure itself. For most suicidal students, both male and female, the major precipitating stress appears to be either the failure to establish a close interpersonal relationship or the loss of one. The breakup of a romance can be a key precipitating factor. There are also significantly more suicide attempts and suicides by students from families that have gone through separation, divorce, or the death of a parent. A particularly important precipitating factor among male college students appears to involve close emotional bonds with his parents. Those bonds are threatened when the student becomes involved with another person in college and tries to break this "parental knot."

### Need for Assistance

Although most colleges and universities have mental health facilities to assist distressed students, few suicidal students seek professional help. Thus, it is of vital importance for those around a suicidal student to notice the warning signs and to try to obtain assistance.

**Biological factors.** However, not everyone experiencing severe life stress develops mood disorders. Why should this be so? In keeping with the diathesis-stress model, growing evidence shows that some people are biologically vulnerable to developing mood disorders under stress. First, a good deal of research evidence suggests that the tendency to develop mood disorders is at least partially inherited. For example, Wender et al. (1986) studied seventy-one adoptees who developed mood disorders and an equal number of adoptees who did not develop mood disorders. If heredity plays a role in predisposing people to mood disorders, the biological relatives of the disordered adoptees should have been more likely to suffer from mood disorders than were the biological relatives of those adoptees who did not develop mood disorders. The researchers found that indeed major mood disorders occurred eight times more often and suicide was fifteen times more likely among the biological relatives of those people with mood disorders.

More recently, Egeland et al. (1987) studied thirty-two cases of bipolar disorder in a small town in Pennsylvania. In every instance, the researchers found evidence of bipolar disorder throughout several previous generations. Moreover, the researchers were able to trace the disorder to a particular genetic marker: 63 percent of the people in the community carrying this marker showed signs of bipolar disorder.

Other evidence indicates that at least some cases of mood disorder are associated with changes in the levels of certain chemicals in the brain and with abnormalities in the structure of the nervous sytem (McNeal & Cimbolic, 1986). Moreover, as

*There is hope for those who suffer from bipolar disorders. Recent research has shown that at least some types have biological or biochemical bases.*

# Psychology in Action

## "Lethality Scale" to Assess Suicide Potential

In assessing "suicide potential," or the probability that a person might carry out a threat to take his or her life, the Los Angeles Suicide Prevention Center uses a "lethality scale" consisting of ten categories:

1. *Age and sex.* The potential is greater if the individual is male rather than female, and is over fifty years of age.

2. *Symptoms.* The potential is greater if the individual manifests such symptoms as sleep disturbances, depression, feelings of hopelessness, or alcoholism.

3. *Stress.* The potential is greater if the individual is subject to such stress as the loss of a loved one through death or divorce, the loss of employment, increased responsibilities, or serious illness.

4. *Acute versus chronic aspects.* The potential is greater when there is a sudden onset of specific symptoms, a recurrent outbreak of similar symptoms, or a recent increase in long-standing maladaptive traits.

5. *Suicidal plan.* The potential is greater when there is an increase in the lethality of the proposed method and the organizational clarity and detail of the plan.

6. *Resources.* The potential is greater if the person has no family or friends, or if his family and friends are unwilling to help.

7. *Prior suicidal behavior.* The potential is greater if the individual has attempted suicide in the past or has a history of repeated threats and depression.

8. *Medical status.* The potential is greater when there is chronic, debilitating illness or the individual has had many unsuccessful experiences with physicians.

9. *Communication aspects.* The potential is greater if communication between the individual and his or her relatives has been broken off, and they reject efforts to reestablish communication.

10. *Reaction of significant others.* The potential is greater if a significant other such as the husband or wife, has a defensive, rejecting, or punishing attitude, and denies that the individual needs help.

The final suicide potential rating is a composite score based on the weighting of each of the ten individual items.

Source: Based on information supplied by the Los Angeles Suicide Prevention Center

---

we will see in Chapter 7, certain drugs have proved to be remarkably effective in counteracting mood disorders; this finding further reinforces the notion that, at least in part, the cause of mood disorders is to be found in some kind of chemical imbalance in the nervous system.

Finally, some mood disorders seem to be related to seasonal patterns. For example, some people tend to become depressed in the fall and winter and return to normal moods or even manic moods in the spring and summer. Interestingly, many people suffering from such "seasonal affective disorders" respond favorably to increased light in the environment (Wehr et al., 1986).

**Life experiences.** Other psychologists look to life experiences in an effort to explain why some people, but not others, experience mood disorders when under stress. Psychoanalytic theorists have suggested that some people who are fixated at the oral stage of development are, as a result, overly dependent upon other people for psychological support and maintaining their sense of self-esteem. If a loved one dies or is otherwise lost, the effect is likely to be devastating. In less extreme cases, rejection, failure, and criticism are likely to be over-interpreted by such people as evidence of personal worthlessness and loss of love. The result is that a stressful situation that would simply cause disappointment or sadness in most people triggers deep depression in these individuals. The manic attacks that characterize cyclothymia and bipolar disorder are interpreted as extreme attempts to defend against or to overcome deep feelings of depression.

Other psychologists interpret depression in terms of basic learning processes. One theory (Lazarus, 1968; Eastman, 1976) suggests that depression is likely to occur when the person has received few positive reinforcements for more adaptive behavior. As a result, adaptive behavior tends to decrease and this leads to still further reduction in reinforcement. At the same time, many people discover that depressed behavior leads others to react with sympathy, affection, concern, and attention. These reinforcers strengthen the depressed behavior pattern and incline the person to respond to future stress with maladaptive, depressed behavior.

**Cognitive factors.**    A number of psychologists have also suggested that depression arises from faulty ways of interpreting life events. Aaron Beck (1967, 1976), for example, suggests that depressed people tend to distort and misinterpret facts in the most negative, pessimistic, and hopeless ways possible. Whenever something goes wrong, they exaggerate the problem, ignore any positive aspects of the situation, focus on the negative, and then blame themselves for everything that has gone wrong. Even casual encounters with other people become an opportunity to confirm their suspicions that they are not as good, as talented, or as worthwhile as other people. In Chapter 3, we explored some of the cognitive self-statements of such people who almost certainly will experience life as a disappointment. In a similar way, Martin Seligman (1975) has concluded that depression occurs when people come to believe that they cannot control reinforcements in their environment; regardless of what they do, the result will be a disaster and it is their fault that this is the case.

## PERSONALITY DISORDERS

Throughout this book, I have emphasized the importance of flexibility as one important component of adaptive behavior. In order to respond effectively to new adjustive demands, people must be able to change their behaviors and adopt new ways of dealing with the environment. However, some people become locked into inflexible and maladaptive ways of dealing with the environment. As a result, they are consistently unable to cope effectively with normal life challenges and cannot change their behavior to correspond more closely to the expectations of others. In such cases psychologists speak of **personality disorders:** inflexible and maladaptive behavior patterns that pervade a person's functioning and significantly impair his or her ability to function effectively. There are many kinds of personality disorders (see the listing in the Insight, p. 193). We shall focus on two: antisocial personality disorder and borderline personality disorder.

**personality disorders:**
inflexible, maladaptive behavior patterns that impair functioning

# Insight

## The DSM-III-R Clusters of Personality Disorders

### CLUSTER 1

**Disorders of Odd or Eccentric Reactions**

**Paranoid personality disorder:** an extreme sensitivity, suspiciousness, envy, and mistrust of others; the attitude of suspicion is not justified; shows a restricted range of emotional reactivity and avoidance of intimacy; rarely seeks help.

**Schizoid personality disorder:** an inability to form interpersonal relationships; little involvement in social affairs; tends to be a loner; appears cold and aloof; often involves excessive daydreaming.

**Schizotypal personality disorder:** experiences oddities or eccentricities in thought, perception, speech, or behavior of long-standing; tends to be very egocentric; although a basic contact with reality is maintained, there are occasional exceptions (e.g., strong belief in ESP, clairvoyance, or fantasy); extreme social isolation; a sense of being separated from one's own body, etc.

### CLUSTER 2

**Disorders of Dramatic, Emotional, or Erratic Reactions**

**Histrionic personality disorder:** overly dramatic, reactive, and intensely expressed behavior; very lively, tending to draw attention to one's self; tends to overreact to matters of small consequence; seeking of excitement and avoiding of routine; a tendency for dependency on others with otherwise poor interpersonal relations.

**Narcissistic personality disorder:** a grandiose exaggeration of self-importance; displays a need for attention if not admiration; tendency to set unrealistic goals; maintains few lasting relationships with others; in many ways, a childish level of behavior.

Source: Gerow, 1986, p. 514

**Antisocial personality disorder:** a history of continuous disregard for the rights and property of others; early signs include lying, truancy, stealing, fighting, and resisting authority; an inability to maintain a job is common; demonstrates poor parenting skills; a strong tendency toward impulsive behaviors with little regard for the consequences of that behavior.

**Borderline personality disorder:** (as its name suggests, there is no dominant pattern of deviance here) sometimes there is impulsivity; sometimes instability of mood; a pattern of extensive uncertainty about many important life issues; temper tantruming is not uncommon, and often appears unprovoked.

### CLUSTER 3

**Disorders Involving Anxiety and Fearfulness**

**Avoidant personality disorder:** oversensitive to the possibility of being rejected by others; an unwillingness to enter into relationships for fear of rejection; devastated by disapproval; there remains, however, a desire for social relations (i.e., does not enjoy being alone).

**Dependent personality disorder:** individual allows, and seeks, others to dominate and assume responsibility for actions; poor self-image and a lack of confidence; sees self as stupid and helpless, deferring to others.

**Compulsive personality disorder:** a restricted ability to show love, warmth, or tender emotions; an overconcern for rules and regulations and doing things in a prescribed way; becomes anxious about getting the job done, but not about being compulsive in doing so; rigid and stiff.

**Passive-aggressive personality disorder:** resistance to the demands of others is passive and indirect; tendency toward procrastination, dawdling, stubbornness, inefficiency, and forgetfulness; often tend to be whiners, moaners, and complainers.

## Antisocial Personality Disorder

*Donald S., 30 years old, has just completed a three-year prison term for fraud, bigamy, false pretenses, and escaping lawful custody. The circumstances leading up to these offenses are interesting and consistent with his past behavior. With less than a month left to serve on an earlier 18-month term for fraud, he faked illness and escaped from the prison hospital. During the ten months of freedom that followed he engaged in a variety of illegal enterprises; the activity that resulted in his recapture was typical of his method of operation. By passing himself off as the "field executive" of an international philanthropic foundation, he was able to enlist the aid of several religious organizations in a fund-raising campaign. The campaign moved slowly at first, and in an attempt to speed things up, he arranged an interview with the local TV station. His performance during the interview was so impressive that funds started to pour in. However, unfortunately for Donald, the interview was also carried on a national news network. He was recognized and quickly arrested. During the ensuing trial it became evident that he experienced no sense of wrongdoing for his activities.*

*Psychopathy: Theory and Research* (Hare, 1970, pp. 1–2)

**antisocial personality disorder:** disorder characterized by lack of moral development and inability to feel guilt or anxiety

**Antisocial personality disorder** involves a pattern of behavior that shows little or no sense of personal distress and little regard for the rights of others. The most outstanding characteristics of this disorder are a lack of ethical or moral development and an inability to follow desirable models of behavior. In the past, such individuals have been called "psychopaths" or "sociopaths." The following characteristics are often found in cases of antisocial personality disorder, though not all the traits will be found in every case.

1. *Amoral, unreliable, angry, irresponsible.* May deceive others by verbal endorsement of high standards, but does not understand or adhere to accepted moral values. Pathological lying, deceitfulness, and a callous disregard for the rights of others. Often a marked discrepancy between intellectual ability and conscience development. Often a tendency to be distrustful, angry, and self-hating.

2. *Compulsive, hedonistic, unrealistic.* Prone to thrill seeking, deviant sexual patterns, and unconventional behavior. Lives in present with primary concern for immediate pleasures and no long-range goals. Shows poor judgment and often engages in impulsive acts detrimental to personal well-being and that of others. Dislikes routine work and frequently changes jobs, moves from place to place, lives by his or her wits, or depends on others for support. Abusive of alcohol and other drugs.

*Serious health hazards including cirrhosis of the liver, heart and brain damage, and hypertension are associated with alcohol abuse. Nevertheless, many Americans persist in using this drug.*

3. *Charismatic and exploitive.* Often a charming individual with a good sense of humor and a generally optimistic outlook. Easily wins the liking and friendship of others but ruthlessly exploits these interpersonal relationships. Often shows contempt for those taken advantage of—the "marks." Unable to give or receive love.

4. *Anxiety-free and guiltless.* Little or no sense of guilt. Lack of anxiety combined with false sincerity often enables the individual to lie his or her way out of difficulties. Undeterred by punishment.

5. *Maladaptive early.* Maladaptive patterns usually emerge in adolescence and continue throughout most of adult life. Violence and aggressive behavior easily provoked.

Although antisocial personalities make up only 1 percent of the population (approximately 2.5 million people), their impact on society is far greater than their numbers would suggest. Their disregard for the rights of others and lack of guilt and remorse leads to serious problems with other people around them and usually brings them into conflict with society at large. Despite the tendency for their behavior to lead to problems with the law, the great majority of these people manage to stay out of jails and prisons. Of course, not all crimes are committed by people with antisocial personality disorder, but antisocial personalities account for a large percentage of the crimes we read about each day in the newspaper and occasionally witness first-hand.

## Borderline Personality Disorder

*A 26-year-old unemployed woman was referred for admission to a hospital by her therapist because of intense suicidal preoccupation and urges to mutilate herself by cutting herself with a razor.*

*The patient was apparently well until her junior year in high school, when she became preoccupied with religion and philosophy, avoided friends, and was filled with doubt about who she was. Academically she did well, but later, during college, her performance declined. In college she began to use a variety of drugs, abandoned the religion of her family, and seemed to be searching for a charismatic religious figure with whom to identify. At times massive anxiety swept over her and she found it would suddenly vanish if she cut her forearm with a razor blade. Three years ago she began psychotherapy, and initially rapidly idealized her therapist as being incredibly intuitive and empathic. Later she became hostile and demanding of him, requiring more and more sessions, sometimes two in one day. Her life centered on her therapist, by this time to the exclusion of everyone else. Although her hostility toward her therapist was obvious, she could neither see it nor control it. Her difficulties with her therapist culminated in many episodes of her forearm cutting and suicidal threats, which led to the referral for admission.*

*DSM-III Case Book* (Spitzer, Skodol, Gibbon, & Williams, 1981, pp. 111–12)

**borderline personality disorder:** personality disorder characterized by impulsivity, identity confusion, rage, and inability to control emotions

This woman is exhibiting symptoms of **borderline personality disorder.** She had interpersonal problems reflected in her relationship with her therapist, problems with impulsivity, substance abuse, identity confusion, and anxiety. Like many people with borderline disorder, she is a person of extremes who has difficulty preventing her emotions from spiraling out of control. When something goes wrong, the world suddenly seems all black and borderline personalities will often become suicidal. They tend to be extremely hostile and alternately to idealize and despise significant people in their lives. Individuals with this disorder are often suspicious and expect the worst from people. They are also self-loathing, so that they frequently set themselves up for abuse, which they then blame on others.

### The Search for Causes

What causes personality disorders such as these? Psychologists have only begun to develop answers to this question, partly because personality disorders are a relatively recent diagnostic category and partly because many people suffering from personality disorders do not seek treatment. It appears that genetic factors are involved in at least some of the personality disorders. For example, there is some evidence of a hereditary predisposition to develop antisocial, paranoid, and borderline disorders, but this does not appear to be true of other kinds of personality disorders (Carson et al., 1988). Evidence also suggests that biological abnormalities may account for some aspects of personality disorders. For instance, people with antisocial personality disorder tend to have a lower level of physiological arousal than normal individuals (Hare, 1970). This lowered level of arousal may leave people with antisocial personality less prone to fear and anxiety, which may account for their failure to learn from punishment.

Most psychologists, however, believe that life experiences are the most important determinants of personality disorders. For example, an extremely high percentage of antisocial personalities come from severely disturbed families; in many cases they lost a parent at an early age (often due to separation or divorce). Their lack of consideration for others and their tendency toward violence appear partly to be a reaction to their chaotic childhood and adolescence. It has also been suggested that abusive or indifferent parenting in the first two or three years of life lays the foundation for the hostility, expectations of abuse, and self-loathing that often characterize borderline personality disorders.

## SUBSTANCE USE DISORDERS

**psychoactive substances:** any substances that significantly alter normal psychological processes

Throughout history, people have used drugs to cope with stress, relieve pain, and enhance pleasure. In the United States, prior to the 1960s the drug of choice for most people was alcohol. However, starting in the 1960s, drug use expanded greatly to include psychedelics, marijuana, amphetamines, barbiturates, heroin, cocaine, and a host of other "street drugs." All of these are **psychoactive substances:** they have a marked effect on mental processes.

*Crack is the latest in a series of psychoactive drugs, substances which significantly alter normal psychological processes.*

**substance use disorder:** pathological use of a psychoactive substance despite resulting problems or threat to safety

**substance abuse:** use of a psychoactive substance to the extent that it interferes with adjustment or represents a hazard

**substance dependence:** physiological need for a psychoactive substance marked by tolerance and withdrawal symptoms; addiction

**drug tolerance:** need for increased dosage of a drug to obtain the same effects; a sign of substance dependence

**withdrawal symptoms:** unpleasant effects observed when use of a psychoactive substance is stopped; a sign of substance dependence

Along with the rapid expansion in drug usage has come a marked increase in **substance use disorders:** maladaptive, undesirable behavioral changes associated with the use of psychoactive drugs. There are two kinds of substance use disorders. **substance abuse** refers to cases in which a person continues to use a psychoactive drug despite knowledge that it causes or contributes to problems (social, occupational, psychological, or physical) or uses the drug in situations where its use is potentially hazardous. A person drinking heavily every few weekends and then missing a day or two of work or classes is abusing alcohol, as is a person driving a car while intoxicated or a person continuing to drink despite knowing that the alcohol aggravates a medical disorder such as an ulcer.

**Substance dependence** refers to more severe forms of substance abuse in which there is also evidence of **drug tolerance** (need for larger and larger doses of a drug over time to achieve the same effect) or **withdrawal symptoms** if the drug is discontinued. The key feature that distinguishes drug dependence from drug abuse is that in the case of drug dependence the user is physiologically dependent upon, or addicted, to the drug. People dependent upon a drug are likely to take more of the drug than they initially expect to take (for example, taking "just one drink" and then having many more). Despite a desire to reduce dependence on the drug, they either have never tried to be free of the drug or have been unable to remain so for any length of time. They spend a good deal of time and effort obtaining the drug, taking it, and then recovering from its effects, often at the cost of work, social activities, or recreation. They may be intoxicated or experience withdrawal symptoms when they are supposed to be working or going to classes, taking care of children, or operating machinery.

### Frequently Abused Substances

As we will see, psychoactive drugs differ greatly in their likelihood of leading to abuse and dependence. In this section, we shall begin by discussing alcohol and then turn to a description of several other commonly abused drugs: marijuana, cocaine, LSD, heroin, barbiturates, and amphetamines.

**Alcohol.**   Contrary to popular belief, alcohol is not a stimulant but a depressant that numbs the higher brain centers. Some people find that small doses of alcohol provide a sense of well-being in which unpleasant realities are minimized and stress and tension are replaced by feelings of warmth and relaxation. Alcohol can also lead to an increased sense of adequacy and a loosening of inhibitions, with the result that drinkers may say or do things they would not normally say or do.

However, in larger doses the effects of alcohol can be profound. When the alcohol content of the blood reaches 0.1 percent, motor coordination, vision, speech, and balance become impaired and the individual is considered to be in a state of intoxication. When the alcoholic content of the blood reaches 0.5 percent, the neurophysiological balance is severely disturbed and the drinker passes out. Continued abuse of alcohol over a long period of time causes severe damage to the body including cirrhosis of the liver, hypertension, and heart and brain damage.

*Substance dependence is a more severe disorder than substance abuse. The user is physiologically dependent upon the drug, and is unable or unwilling to break free of the substance.*

**alcoholism:** physiological dependence on (addiction to) alcohol

Because **alcoholism** often progresses slowly and by subtle degrees, the line that separates social drinking from alcoholism is not always readily observable. According to the Japanese proverb, "First the man takes a drink, then the drink takes a drink, and then the drink takes the man." The social drinker may increasingly rely on alcohol for relief of tension, despite signs of growing abuse and dependence. As criticism from family and friends begins to mount, many drinkers begin to rationalize and make alibis for their drinking. If alcohol abuse continues, the drinkers' control over drinking completely breaks down and alcohol plays an increasingly dominant role in everyday activities. At the same time, tolerance for alcohol begins to decrease so that the drinker becomes intoxicated on far less alcohol than previously. Tremors and other withdrawal symptoms may begin to appear while the drinker is sober, which leads to further drinking to control such symptoms. At this point, the alcoholic's life situation usually undergoes serious deterioration (see Psychology in Action, p. 200).

**Heroin.** Like alcohol, heroin is a nervous system depressant. It is an opium derivative that produces an immediate "rush" of extreme pleasure followed by euphoria and contentment combined with pleasant reverie or daydreaming. It is highly addictive, and there are now an estimated 400,000 Americans using heroin daily. The

# Psychology in Action

### Early Warning Signs of Approaching Alcoholism

1. *Frequent desire.* An early warning sign of potential alcoholism is an increase in desire, often evidenced by eager anticipation of drinking after work and careful attention to maintaining a supply of alcohol.

2. *Increased consumption.* Another early warning sign is increasing consumption of alcohol. This increase may seem gradual, but a marked change takes place from month to month. Often the individual will begin to worry about his or her drinking at this point and begin to lie about the amount actually consumed.

3. *Extreme behavior.* When the individual, under the influence of alcohol, commits various acts that cause guilt and embarrassment the next day, it is an indication that the person's drinking is getting out of control.

4. *Blackouts.* When the individual cannot remember what happened during an alcoholic bout, his or her indulgence is becoming excessive.

5. *Morning drinking.* An important sign that a frequent drinker may be becoming an alcoholic appears when he or she begins to drink in the morning—either as a means of reducing a hangover or as a "bracer" to help start the day.

A person who exhibits the preceding pattern of behavior is well on the road to becoming an alcoholic. Often an additional indication is persistent absenteeism from work, especially on Mondays.

use of heroin, its derivatives, and their synthetic counterparts (such as methadone) leads to physiological craving for and dependence on the drug. In addition, users of heroin gradually build a tolerance to the drug so that ever larger amounts are needed to achieve the desired effect. This increases the cost of the habit, and as a result addicts often turn to criminal activities such as theft, burglary, or prostitution to finance their habit.

When persons addicted to heroin do not receive a dose of the drug within approximately eight hours, they begin to experience withdrawal symptoms such as shaking, chills, and abdominal cramps. Contrary to popular opinion, these symptoms are not always painful or even dangerous. For individuals who use heavy dosages and have neglected their health, however, withdrawal can be a perilous experience. Withdrawal symptoms usually reach a peak in about forty hours, and they begin to decline by the third or fourth day.

**Barbiturates.**    Medically, these drugs are used to calm patients and induce sleep. Like alcohol and heroin, they act as nervous system depressants. Barbiturates are highly dangerous drugs, and their excessive use over a period of time leads to drug tolerance and physiological dependence. Especially prone to abuse are the short-acting barbiturates, such as Seconal ("red devils") and Tuinal ("rainbows"). There are an estimated 1 million or more barbiturate addicts in the United States, most of them between thirty and fifty years of age.

Excessive use of barbiturates causes a number of undesirable effects, including general sluggishness, poor comprehension, impaired memory, confusion, irritability, and depression. Barbiturates are often prescribed as sleep medications, but their continued use can actually increase sleep disturbances (Julien, 1981). Barbiturates are also associated with more suicides than any other drug.

An overdose of barbiturates can be lethal and the withdrawal symptoms are also very dangerous. In fact, they are more severe and last longer than those resulting from heroin addiction. In severe cases, an acute, delirious **psychosis** develops in which the individual loses contact with reality and behavior becomes grossly distorted.

**psychosis:** severe psychological disorder marked by loss of contact with reality

**Amphetamines.**    In contrast to alcohol, heroin, and barbiturates, amphetamines are "pep pills"—nervous system stimulants—sometimes used by truck drivers and students to stay awake and continue to function. The most potent and dangerous of the amphetamines is methedrine, or "speed;" other amphetamines include benzedrine and dexedrine. To get high on amphetamines, habitual users may ingest very large doses, or they may maintain a constant high for several days by taking more pills as soon as they start "coming down." Excessive use of amphetamines leads to a rapid increase in tolerance.

For the person using large doses of amphetamines, the results can be highly detrimental. Psychosis, suicide, homicide, and other acts of violence have been linked to the abuse of these drugs. Withdrawal from the drug is relatively uncomplicated, but the person's dependence on the drug may still have to be conquered.

**Cocaine.**    Cocaine, like amphetamines, is a nervous system stimulant that has been used since ancient times. According to Jarvik (1967): "The Indians of Peru have chewed cocoa leaves for centuries and still do, to relieve hunger, fatigue, and the general burdens of a miserable life," (p. 52). In America, the use of cocaine has increased dramatically over the last fifteen years, with a particularly rapid rise since the mid-1980s when the crystalline form of cocaine ("crack") became widely available. Because cocaine is so expensive, it used to be considered a drug of the very rich; however, it is now being used among a much wider spectrum of society. An estimated one third of American youth have used cocaine (National Institute of Drug Abuse, 1981) and the numbers are growing rapidly.

In its powdered form, cocaine is usually sniffed or injected and leads to a euphoric state which may last from a few minutes to as long as four to six hours (Resnick, Kestenbaum & Schwartz, 1977). Its effects are so pleasurable that rats in laboratory experiments will press a lever a thousand times for one dose of cocaine. "Crack" or "freebase" cocaine can be smoked, causing a sudden burst of the drug that reaches the brain very quickly. The result is an immediate and extremely intense high accompanied by feelings of energy, alertness, and excitement. However, this effect fades quickly (usually after about fifteen minutes) and is replaced by feelings of depression and anxiety which often lead the user to take another dose. Chronic use of cocaine can have very different results: it can lead to a state of acute intoxication in which the individual experiences frightening visual, auditory, and tactual hallucinations, such as the "cocaine bug."

Crack cocaine is generally considered to be the most dangerous psychoactive substance available today. Because it is a highly concentrated form of cocaine, it is

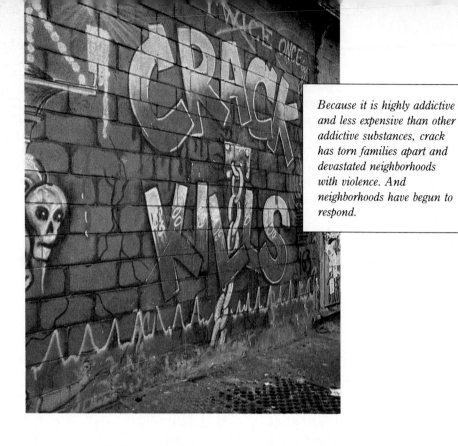

*Because it is highly addictive and less expensive than other addictive substances, crack has torn families apart and devastated neighborhoods with violence. And neighborhoods have begun to respond.*

very easy to overdose unintentionally on crack. Crack cocaine is also more addictive than any other psychoactive drug; some users report that they became addicted the first time they used the drug, though for most people addiction develops over a period of a few months (compared to years for such drugs as alcohol and heroin). Most users also report that it is almost impossible to stop using crack once they have started. In the inner cities and among the lower classes, where crack cocaine has now replaced heroin as the drug of choice, families are being torn apart and violence has escalated directly as a result of the introduction of crack.

**psychedelic drugs:** "mind expanding" drugs that produce changes in sensory experiences, moods, and thought processes

**Marijuana.**   Marijuana is one of several **psychedelic drugs** or "consciousness expanding" drugs. In the last several decades, marijuana has become one of the most commonly used psychoactive drugs in America. It is estimated that 10-15 percent of Americans are active users of marijuana. This drug is usually smoked, although it may also be ingested orally in baked goods. Its effects include mild changes in sensation, giddiness, relaxation, and drowsiness. Sensation is enhanced, so that pleasure associated with music, food, or other sensory experiences is increased. Larger doses can cause rapid mood shifts, interference with thinking processes, and some loss of memory. Very large doses can cause hallucinations and other extreme thought disorders. To some extent its effects are dependent on personality and mood; for example, if a person smokes marijuana while angry or depressed, those feelings are also likely to be intensified.

While at one time marijuana was believed to have serious side effects, recent research on this issue has been inconclusive. Occasional social use of the drug has not been shown to produce any permanent damage to the body. Long-term daily use, however, has detrimental effects on memory, the lungs and heart, the body's immune system, and sex hormones and fertility in males. Even with long-term use, however, the negative effects of marijuana use are far less severe than the effects of alcohol (Project Dawn, 1977).

**LSD.** Lysergic acid diethylamide (LSD), a chemically synthesized substance, was first discovered in 1938. Although odorless, colorless, and tasteless, it is an extremely potent **hallucinogen.** In fact, a dosage of LSD smaller than a grain of salt can produce intoxication.

**hallucinogen:** psychoactive substance capable of producing hallucinations

While the effects of taking LSD depend to a great extent on the user's expectations and mood, one of the most widely reported effects of LSD is a tremendous intensification of sensory perception. Objects seem to become brighter, more colorful, and endowed with dimensions the individual has never noticed before. Thus, the individual may become absorbed in the contemplation of a flower or some other object. Often he or she has the feeling of being tuned in to all humankind in experiencing such universal emotions as love, loneliness, or grief.

The LSD experience, or "trip," however, is not always pleasant. It can be an extremely traumatic experience in which everyday objects take on a bizarre and terrifying appearance, or in which the individual sees monsters which seem to be after him or her. It has been estimated that about 20 percent of LSD users experience "flashbacks," recurring, intrusive thoughts of a negative or frightening nature that occur weeks or months after the use of the drug. It has also been estimated that a small percentage of LSD users experience psychosis, a break with reality, sometimes on the first trip. However, unlike most other psychoactive drugs, there is no evidence that LSD causes physiological dependence or addiction.

## The Search for Causes

When considering the reasons for substance use disorders, it is important to distinguish between the factors that encourage someone to start using drugs and the factors that encourage continued use. Virtually every drug abuser describes being introduced to drugs by "friends." Moreover, we live in a pill-oriented society in which we are led to believe that almost any problem can be eased or solved by taking some sort of drug, and young children can often observe parents and other models acting on this conviction. Faced with peer group pressure or with chronic stress, it is understandable that some people will turn to drugs as a crutch in trying to cope with life's problems.

Once a person has begun to use drugs, however, a different set of forces is brought into play. Since most drugs tend to result in lowered anxiety and tension, their use is highly reinforcing; thus, with each use they are more likely to be used again in the future. In this sense, drug abuse is a learned maladaptive response that is reinforced and maintained by the brief release of tensions or the sense of euphoria that accompanies the use of most drugs. Moreover, as we have seen, many drugs are physiologically addictive; in the case of alcohol, evidence suggests that some individuals—perhaps as a result of genetic factors—develop a physiological addiction to and craving for alcohol more readily than others (Miller, 1976). Thus, while most drug users initially turn to drugs for temporary relief from life stress, the reinforcing and addictive properties of drugs make abuse and dependence a likely outcome.

## SCHIZOPHRENIC DISORDERS

*To Dr. H.G.*

*If you have the time I would appreciate some information concerning mind reading. I believe its possible for a person to be able to read another persons mind and be able to let that person communicate with him. Can a person with these extraordinary powers be capable of doing the following things below, I have read somewhere before where this can happen. (The X's before the numbers are of great importance to me.)*

*X   1. Burning sensations. Are these feelings a generation of some kind, an electromanatic energy.*

*2. headaches, feeling of an energy, wave of some kind in brain, head.*

*X   3. When writing something down or speaking you write something else down you did not intend on writing down or saying? How?*

*X   4. Sex.*

*5. crying—emotional stress*

*6. stirring into mirror and seeing an hallucination of your face changing*

*7. vibrations of hands, face, other parts of body*

*X   8. Loss of concentration*

  *a. when a person is talking out loud you can't concentrate on what they are saying.*

*I read a book once about these strange happenings and found them interesting, but I wanted to know more information of the subject of mind reading. These things can happen, quickly, very frequently, seldom, come fast and be over with quickly. This I know. I hope you will be able to help me in my research concerning this type of communication between two people. Thank you for your time.*

*Sincerely, D.S.*

**schizophrenia:** severe psychotic disorder characterized by profound disturbances of thought and emotion

This letter, with its patterns of disorganized and confused thoughts, was written by a schizophrenic woman. The term **schizophrenia** refers to a split between thought and emotion accompanied by a loss of contact with reality. The schizophrenic person does not have a dual or "split personality." Rather, schizophrenic behavior is characterized by gross distortions of reality, social withdrawal, and severely disturbed and disorganized thoughts and emotions such as those in the letter from D.S. Schizophrenia is a worldwide problem affecting approximately 1 percent of the population. It accounts for about 50 percent of all hospitalized mental patients in the United States.

## Clinical Symptoms

The clinical picture of schizophrenia differs from one person to another, but the following symptoms are typical:

1. *Thought disturbances.* Changes in the cognitive processes of the schizophrenic individual are so marked that schizophrenia is often termed a thought disorder. Schizophrenic thought processes and language are typically bizarre and disorganized. The schizophrenic individual will make up words and jumble ideas around in a confusing, unfathomable pattern.

2. *Delusions.* These are false beliefs that the schizophrenic individual defends despite their logical absurdity and despite all other contrary evidence. The most common types of delusions are (1) delusions of grandeur, in which individuals believe they are exalted and important beings, (2) delusions of reference, in which individuals interpret chance happenings as having special meaning for them, and (3) delusions of persecution, in which individuals feel that "enemies" are plotting against them.

3. *Hallucinations.* Schizophrenic individuals may have hallucinations. They may hear voices, see things, smell peculiar odors, or report other false sensory phenomena.

4. *Affective changes.* These alterations of mood may take many forms. In some cases, the individual is apathetic and emotionally unresponsive. Some may be violently active; others may appear to be depressed. Still others may have inappropriate emotional states, such as laughing when informed that a spouse or a child has been killed.

5. *Withdrawal, isolation, and disorganization.* Many schizophrenic persons withdraw from reality and lose interest in people and events. Their social skills may be limited, and they may be unable to provide even the simplest information about the current time, where they are, or even their names and identities. Often they neglect personal hygiene.

6. *Motor disturbances.* Schizophrenic individuals may engage in a variety of repetitious, stereotyped muscular activities. In some cases, they engage in virtually no motor activity, and they may allow their arms, legs, and other parts of the body to be placed into unusual positions. The schizophrenic person with this waxy flexibility will hold these seemingly uncomfortable positions for hours at a time.

## Types of Schizophrenia

Four somewhat different patterns of schizophrenia are distinguished in DSM-III-R: paranoid schizophrenia, catatonic schizophrenia, disorganized (or hebephrenic) schizophrenia, and undifferentiated schizophrenia. Identifying the particular pattern of each type of schizophrenia is a difficult task that requires an accurate assessment and understanding of each individual's clinical picture. However, the general features of each sub-type can be described briefly.

**Paranoid schizophrenia.** **Paranoid schizophrenia** is characterized by delusions, typically those of persecution and grandeur. This type of schizophrenia is the most commonly diagnosed, accounting for about half of all cases (Lahey & Ciminero, 1980). The typical individual with paranoid schizophrenia is often a male in his late twenties. Prior to his (or her) hospitalization, there were no markedly unusual aspects of his or her behavior. Often this person has functioned effectively up to the point of hospitalization and may have had an adequate work and personal history. Issues of control and sexual identity and activity are characteristic of the paranoid schizophrenic individual. They may believe that "impure" sexual thoughts are being "placed" in their brains by electronic devices. The following conversation between a therapist and a paranoid patient is fairly typical:

THERAPIST: Could you tell me a little bit about your fear of dying and is this something you have felt in the past?

PATIENT: I have felt this for almost a year.

THERAPIST: Could you tell me a little more about your fear of dying and have you any thoughts about how it is going to happen and whether anyone wants to hurt you?

PATIENT: I will end up in the sea and the Hell's Angels will do it.

THERAPIST: Could you tell me a little bit about the kinds of contact you have had with the Hell's Angels in the past?

PATIENT: I have known some of their dealers and pushers.

THERAPIST: Could you say a little more about the circumstances in which you have known some of their dealers and pushers?

PATIENT: They were members of my community when I got out of the service. They had been my friends for so long.

THERAPIST: Did you deal with them yourself and have you been on drugs or narcotics either now or in the past?

PATIENT: Yes, I have in the past been on marijuana reds bennies LSD.

THERAPIST: Could you tell me how long you have been in the hospital and something about the circumstances that brought you here?

PATIENT: Close to a year and paranoia brought me here.

THERAPIST: Could you say something about your paranoid feelings both at the time of admission and do you have similar feelings now and if so how do they affect you?

PATIENT: At the time of admission I thought the Mafia was after me and now it's the Hell's Angels.

THERAPIST: Do you have any thought as to why these two groups were after you?

PATIENT: Because I stopped some of their drug supply. (adapted from Colby, 1975, pp. 84-88)

**Catatonic schizophrenia.** Disturbances in motor activity are the characteristic feature of **catatonic schizophrenia,** a relatively uncommon form of schizophrenia. The individual with this disorder is typically inactive and passive, although bursts of hyperactivity may occur. Stereotyped movements are also sometimes evident. Perhaps the most striking feature of this disorder is that some catatonic people remain motionless in odd positions for long periods of time, as if frozen in place.

**Disorganized schizophrenia.**    Inappropriate emotions and disorganization are the hallmarks of **disorganized schizophrenia** (sometimes also called hebephrenic schizophrenia). Episodes of laughter and silliness with no apparent cause punctuate the day of such afflicted persons. Emotional blunting, bizarre and obscene behavior, and peculiar mannerisms often typify those suffering from this disorder. Disorganized schizophrenia is uncommon, accounting for about 5 percent of schizophrenia diagnoses. The following case (Carson et al., 1988) demonstrates some of the features of disorganized schizophrenia:

**disorganized (hebephrenic) schizophrenia:** type of schizophrenia characterized by inappropriate emotions and bizarre behavior

> The patient was a divorcee, 32 years of age, who had come to the hospital with bizarre delusions, hallucinations, and severe personality disintegration and with a record of alcoholism, promiscuity, and possible incestuous relations with a brother. The following conversation shows typical hebephrenic responses to questioning.
>
> DOCTOR: How do you feel today?
> PATIENT: Fine.
> DOCTOR: When did you come here?
> PATIENT: 1416, you remember, doctor (silly giggle).
> DOCTOR: Do you know why you are here?
> PATIENT: Well, in 1951 I changed into two men. President Truman was judge at my trial. I was convicted and hung (silly giggle). My brother and I were given back our normal bodies 5 years ago. I am a policewoman. I keep a dictaphone concealed on my person.
> DOCTOR: Can you tell me the name of this place?
> PATIENT: I have not been a drinker for 16 years. I am taking a mental rest after a "carter" assignment or "quill." You know, a "penwrap." I had contracts with Warner Brothers Studios and Eugene broke phonograph records but Mike protested. I have been with the police department for 35 years. I am made of flesh and blood—see doctor (pulling up her dress).
> DOCTOR: Are you married?
> PATIENT: No, I am not attracted to men (silly giggle). I have a companionship arrangement with my brother. I am a "looner". . . a bachelor. (pp. 336-37)

**Undifferentiated schizophrenia.**    Many psychotic individuals do not present clear-cut symptoms of the three types discussed above. In these cases, the symptoms overlap, and the diagnostician is unable to say with certainty that a particular diagnostic category is applicable. For these "mixed" cases, a diagnosis of **undifferentiated schizophrenia** is assigned. The following case (Carson et al., 1988) is illustrative:

**undifferentiated schizophrenia:** type of schizophrenia in which symptoms do not permit a more precise diagnosis

> Rich Wheeler, 26 years old, neatly groomed, and friendly and cheerful in disposition, was removed from an airplane by airport police because he was creating a disturbance—from his own account probably because he was "on another dimension." On arrest, he was oriented to the extent of knowing where he was, his name, and the current date, but his report of these facts was embedded in a peculiar and circumstantial context involving science fiction themes. Investigation revealed he had been discharged from a nearby state mental hospital three days earlier. He was brought to another hospital by police.
>     On admission, physical examination and laboratory studies were normal, but Rick claimed he was Jesus Christ and that he could move mountains. His speech was extremely

difficult to follow because of incoherence and derailment. For example, he explained his wish to leave the city "because things happen here I don't approve of. I approve of other things but I don't approve of the other things. And believe me it's worse for them in the end." He complained that the Devil wants to kill him and that his food contains "ground-up corpses." He was born, he claimed, from his father's sexual organs. (adapted from Spitzer et al., 1983, pp. 153-55)

## The Search for Causes

Despite a great deal of research, the causes of schizophrenic reactions remain largely unknown. In part, the problem seems to be that "schizophrenia" is not a single disorder but rather a catch-all term that draws together a number of disorders that are in many respects quite different from each other (Lander, 1988). Thus, efforts to find a common cause for these disparate disorders are doomed from the start.

Nonetheless, there is growing evidence that genetic factors create a vulnerability toward developing at least some forms of schizophrenia (Kennedy et al., 1988). For example, numerous studies have provided evidence that children with schizophrenic parents are more likely than the general population to be diagnosed as schizophrenic at some point in their lives, even when these children are adopted shortly after birth and raised by normal parents (Wender, Rosenthal, Kety, Schulsinger, & Welner, 1974).

A very recent study by Sherrington et al. published in *Nature* (1988) provides the first concrete evidence of a genetic predisposition toward schizophrenia. These

*Breaks between thought and emotion, combined with loss of contact with reality, characterize many schizophrenics. They may suffer from delusions, hallucinations, withdrawal, isolation, and lack of motor control.*

researchers identified seven families in England and Iceland in which schizophrenia was unusually common. They identified 104 living family members whose descendants or ancestors had been diagnosed as schizophrenic. They then interviewed all 104 people and, on the basis of the interview and extensive medical records, they discovered that 39 of these people suffered from some form of schizophrenia. An additional 15 people were diagnosed as having other psychological disorders. Analysis of blood samples revealed that most of the 39 schizophrenics shared a defect on a particular gene on a particular chromosome; interestingly, most of the 15 people with other maladaptive disorders shared that same genetic defect. The great majority of the family members without diagnosed disorders did not have this defect.

The preceding study provides some of the strongest evidence yet obtained for determining whether there is a genetic predisposition toward at least some forms of schizophrenia. However, the role of heredity in schizophrenia is not a simple one. For example, the same issue of *Nature* that carried the Sherrington report also contained an article by Kennedy et al. (1988) who found no evidence for the same genetic defect in a different group of schizophrenics drawn from three Swedish families. However, the researchers suggested that other defective genes yet to be discovered might predispose to the disorder in the Swedish families.

Despite the recent evidence, there is general agreement that genetic vulnerability is not the whole story behind schizophrenic disorders (Sherrington et al., 1988; Kennedy et al., 1988; Lander, 1988). Psychological, interpersonal, and family interaction patterns have also been linked to schizophrenia (Harrow, Grossman, Silverstein, & Meltzer, 1982; Parnas, Schulsinger, Schulsinger, Mednick, & Teasdale, 1982). Schizophrenics show alterations of thinking, feeling, and relating to the external world which are unique to this disorder. In fact, the schizophrenic individual may behave in apparently bizarre ways as a "special sort of strategy that a person invents in order to live in an unlivable world" (Laing, 1967, p. 56). Disturbed communication patterns in the family and unusually high levels of conflict between parents of schizophrenics have also been shown to increase the likelihood of schizophrenia (Bateson, Jackson, Haley, & Weakland, 1956).

Although the search for a simple cause of schizophrenia has proved frustrating, the evidence obtained so far is consistent with the diathesis-stress model that has been used throughout this chapter: it is likely that genetic predisposition and psychological and interpersonal factors interact to produce schizophrenic reactions. In some individuals, the genetic predisposition may be strong, and only moderate levels of stress are needed to cause the disorder. In others, the genetic predisposition may be slight, but the stress that an individual experiences is so extraordinarily severe that a schizophrenic reaction becomes likely (Zubin & Spring, 1977).

## SUMMARY

Behavior is maladaptive when it prevents a person from meeting adaptive demands, disturbs the well-being of the individual, or adversely affects the needs of others. According to the *diathesis-stress* model, some people—whether because of heredity or past experience—are more vulnerable to stress and are therefore more likely to develop various stress-related disorders, or *psychopathologies*. The revised third edition of the Diagnostic and Statistical Manual of Mental Disorders *(DSM-III-R)* is a widely used standard for classifying these various psychological disorders.

When a person uncharacteristically overreacts to a relatively common stressful experience, psychologists refer to *adjustment disorder.* Sometimes adjustment disorders arise because many stressors are present simultaneously. In other cases, previous experience has left the person especially vulnerable to a certain stressor. In contrast, *post-traumatic stress disorder* refers to extreme maladaptive reactions to extraordinarily stressful events such as natural disasters and war. Symptoms often include flashbacks, reenacting the situation, nightmares, inability to experience normal emotions and to relate to people, and difficulty in concentration. *Crisis intervention* teams can help to reduce the likelihood of post-traumatic stress disorder, while the passage of time, support from friends, and sometimes professional assistance help others to cope with this disorder.

In a number of other psychological disorders, the common element seems to be excessive, persistent, irrational fears and anxieties that prevent a person from coping effectively. In some people, the anxiety shows up as constant tension, worry, or apprehension, even when things are going well; such cases are referred to as *generalized anxiety disorder.* In other people, the anxiety becomes focussed on particular objects or situations. For example, in *panic disorder* a person experiences overwhelming panic accompanied by shortness of breath, dizziness, trembling, nausea, and various irrational fears. In other cases, anxiety or fear becomes focussed on a particular situation or object such as high places, spiders, snakes, and animals; in these cases psychologists speak of *simple phobias.*

Anxiety can also be expressed in the form of persistent irrational thoughts, ideas, or impulses *(obsessions)* or as irresistible impulses to perform irrational, repetitive, ritualistic acts *(compulsions).* Still other people express anxiety in the form of physical complaints for which there is no known physical cause; examples of such *somatoform disorders* include symptoms of blindness, loss of sensation, or paralysis without medical causes. *Hypochondriacs* having vague medical complaints or preoccupied by minor health problems are also considered to be suffering from somatoform disorder. Finally, in some cases anxiety results in a sudden loss of memory or an alteration of personal identity; in such cases of *dissociative disorder,* people may develop amnesia or take on several different personalities.

Some people suffering from anxiety-based disorders have inherited a predisposition to overreact emotionally to threatening situations or a predisposition to develop a specific disorder. However, life experiences are also important in explaining the development of anxiety-based disorders. Some psychoanalytic theorists interpret these disorders as signals that an unacceptable unconscious impulse (usually sexual or aggressive) has been aroused and is in conflict with the ego and superego. Other psychologists suggest that people learn their symptoms through conditioning or by observing others who react irrationally to stressful situations. Whatever the source of the symptoms, to the extent that they help to reduce anxiety they are likely to persist.

Other people respond to stress by experiencing *mood disorders* that interfere significantly with the normal business of living or that endanger their welfare. In cases of *dysthymia,* for example, the person feels dejected or depressed for several years and experiences no joy in living; if these feelings alternate with periods of extreme excitement, elation, and agitation, the diagnosis is *cyclothymia.* In both dysthymia and cyclothymia, although the symptoms are maladaptive and disruptive, most victims are able to continue functioning reasonably well. In cases of *major depression,* however, the victims are often so depressed that they find it difficult or impossible to function at all. They may lose interest in everything around them, have difficulty sleeping, feel profoundly depressed, and even contemplate suicide. In cases of *bipolar disorder,* feelings of profound depression alternate with periods of extreme excitement or elation that may be accompanied by *delusions, hallucinations,* delirium and disorientation. In all forms of mood disorder, the greatest risk is suicide: the vast majority of the approximately 200,000 people who attempt suicide each year are experiencing some form of severe depression.

Research evidence suggests that some people inherit the tendency to develop mood disorders when exposed to prolonged or severe stress. Moreover, there is growing evidence that mood disorders may be related to abnormalities in the nervous system. Psychoanalytically oriented psychologists have suggested that mood disorders are best understood as the results of fixation at the oral stage of development. Other psychologists point to the role of reinforcement and observational learning in the development of mood disorders. Recently, increased attention has been given to the possibility that mood disorders reflect distortions in the way that some people view and interpret the world around them.

*Personality disorders* are characterized by inflexible and pervasive personality traits that are maladaptive. *Antisocial personalities* feel no remorse for their violent and antisocial acts. Although the number of people who can be diagnosed as having antisocial personalities is small, the fear of crime and violence that these and other individuals produce in society at large is considerable. People with *borderline personality disorders* are people of extremes who are often impulsive and who have difficulty regulating emotions, problems with interpersonal relations, identity confusion, and substance abuse. Evidence suggests that there may be a hereditary predisposition to develop antisocial, paranoid, and borderline personality disorders, but heredity does not appear to be a factor in other personality disorders. In many cases, life experiences seem to be the most important determinant of the disorder.

*Substance use disorders* involve the abuse of *psychoactive substances,* chemicals that alter mental processes. In cases of *substance abuse,* the person either continues to use a psychoactive substance despite knowing that it has undesirable effects or uses the substance in situations where its use is hazardous. *Substance dependence* refers to a more severe form of substance abuse in which there is also evidence of physiological addiction to the substance as shown by *drug tolerance* or *withdrawal symptoms.*

Alcohol is the most widely abused psychoactive substance. When abuse of alcohol leads to dependence (physiological addiction), the individual is suffering from *alcoholism.* Like alcohol, heroin is a nervous system depressant though many people find heroin more addictive than alcohol. Barbiturates are extremely dangerous depressant drugs whose use and abuse may result in *psychosis* or even death. Other drugs stimulate the nervous system: amphetamines, for example, are "pep pills" whose abuse can lead to psychosis, suicide, and acts of violence. Cocaine is another

*Societal pressure to discontinue drug use may be one of the most effective ways to combat drug dealing.*

stimulant whose use results in brief feelings of euphoria; in its crystalline form, "crack" or "freebase" cocaine leads to a sudden and intense high followed within a short time by feelings of depression and anxiety. Chronic abuse of cocaine can result in severe mental disorder including terrifying hallucinations. Crack cocaine is widely considered to be the most addictive psychoactive drug available today. In contrast, marijuana and LSD are *psychedelic drugs* that produce changes in sensory experiences, moods, and thinking processes but neither of these drugs is known to be addictive. In large doses, marijuana has been shown to have significant negative effects on thinking, while even normal use of LSD can on occasion result in terrifying hallucinations (as a *hallucinogen*), flashbacks, and psychotic episodes. Though most people begin to use drugs in response to peer pressure or as a way of coping with stress, continued drug use reflects the fact that many psychoactive drugs are highly reinforcing as well as physiologically addictive.

*Schizophrenic disorders* involve a split between thought and emotion accompanied by a loss of contact with reality. Thought disturbances, delusions, hallucinations, mood changes, withdrawal, and motor disturbances are frequently reported. There are four major types of schizophrenic disorder. *Paranoid schizophrenia,* which accounts for about half of all cases of schizophrenia, is marked by delusions or persecution or grandeur. *Catatonic schizophrenia* is marked by disturbance in motor activity; for example, some people suffering from this disorder assume positions that they will maintain for long periods of time without moving. *Disorganized schizophrenia* is marked by inappropriate emotions such as episodes of laughter or silliness or emotional blunting. *Undifferentiated schizophrenia* refers to cases in which individuals display clearly schizophrenic symptoms but do not clearly match any of the other three types. The causes of schizophrenia are not well understood. As with many other disorders, some recent evidence suggests that in some people the disorder is related to a genetic defect, though disturbed family relations and communication patterns also appear to play a role in setting the stage for schizophrenia.

## KEY TERMS

diathesis-stress model (175)
psychopathologies (175)
DSM-III-R (175)
adjustment disorder (176)
post-traumatic stress disorder (178)
crisis intervention (179)
panic disorder (180)
agoraphobia (180)
simple phobia (181)
obsessions (181)
compulsions (181)
somatoform disorders (182)
hypochondriacs (183)
dissociative disorders (183)
generalized anxiety disorder (183)
mood disorders (186)
dysthymia (186)
cyclothymia (187)
major depressive disorder (188)
delusions (188)
hallucinations (188)

bipolar disorder (manic
    depression) (188)
personality disorders (192)
antisocial personality disorder (194)
borderline personality disorder (196)
psychoactive substances (197)
substance use disorder (198)
substance abuse (198)
substance dependence (198)
drug tolerance (198)
withdrawal symptoms (198)
alcoholism (199)
psychosis (201)
psychedelic drugs (202)
hallucinogen (203)
schizophrenia (204)
paranoid schizophrenia (206)
catatonic schizophrenia (206)
disorganized schizophrenia (207)
undifferentiated schizophrenia (207)

# Psychotherapy and Counseling

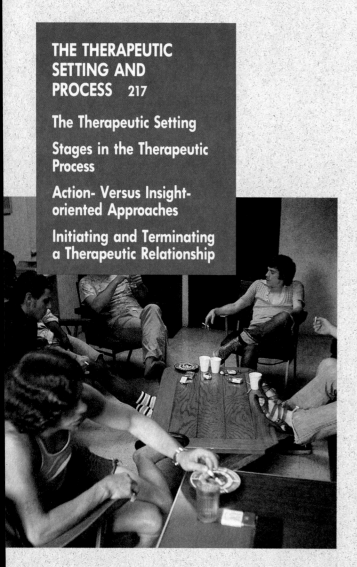

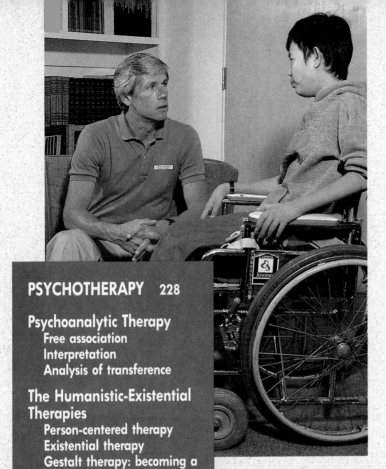

*To be listened to*
*& to be heard . . .*
*to be supported*
*while you gather your*
*forces & get your bearings.*
*A fresh look at alternatives—*
*& some new insights;*
*learning some needed skills.*
*To face your lion—your fears.*
*To come to a decision—& the courage to act on it.*
*& to take the risks*
*that living demands.*

(David Palmer, The Student Counseling Center,
University of California, Los Angeles)

*P*EOPLE consult mental health professionals for a variety of reasons: an individual feels guilty, anxious, or depressed; a relationship is troubled; a child may be difficult to manage; people may feel vaguely dissatisfied with their lives. In other words, people may seek assistance for virtually any type of behavioral or emotional difficulty.

Seeking professional assistance for personal problems is always a difficult task. Much of our training and experience has taught us to be as self-reliant as possible. Despite our enlightened views about psychological disorders, there is nonetheless a stigma attached to consulting a mental health professional. While most of us do not hesitate to consult a physician about a health problem and we do not hesitate to discuss a troublesome issue with a close friend or family member, we feel uncomfortable about seeing a counselor or psychotherapist.

This hesitancy is unfortunate. Counselors and psychotherapists are well trained and have many skills to offer people seeking assistance. Problems ranging from career planning, marital and family relationships, and various maladaptive behaviors can be competently handled by mental health professionals (Landman & Dawes, 1982; Smith, 1982; Wright, 1982).

This chapter introduces you to some of the techniques and procedures used by professionals trained in assisting those who have problems in daily living. After describing the therapeutic setting and process, I will focus on two aspects of the therapeutic process: assessment and therapy. The assessment section covers the general strategies and resources that a therapist invokes in assessing problems. The therapy section discusses the three major approaches to individual psychological

*Therapeutic encounter groups—often made-up of people sharing similar experiences—can encourage individuals to confront problems they previously considered unspeakable.*

therapy and some approaches that attempt to solve interpersonal relationships or family problems. The chapter closes with a look at self-help groups. We begin with a discussion of therapeutic settings and processes.

## THE THERAPEUTIC SETTING AND PROCESS

Entering into a therapeutic or counseling setting for the first time can be an anxiety-evoking experience. To the first-time client, the setting poses many questions: "What will the therapist or counselor be like?" "Will I like him or her?" "What will she or he think of me?" "Can he or she help me?" These are, of course, important questions, and they are generally answered within the first few meetings.

Nonetheless, the therapeutic setting remains a mystery to many people. Without direct experience, most of us rely on the few sources of information available to us. Some of these include impressions of psychologists, counselors, and other therapists from television, from "media psychologists," and from friends and acquaintances who have participated in the experience. While these pieces of information are valuable, they do not fully represent the range of settings in which psychotherapists work, and they do not fully represent the range of activities of psychologists and counselors (see Table 7.1, p. 218).

### The Therapeutic Setting

Typically, psychotherapists and counselors work in one of two general settings—an institution or a private office. The institutions can vary including community health centers, schools and universities, general medical centers, industrial settings and

**TABLE 7.1   Personnel in Counseling and Psychotherapy**

| | Professional Requirements | Type of Therapy |
|---|---|---|
| **Clinical psychologist** | Ph.D. in clinical psychology plus internship training in psychological assessment and therapy | Wide range of individual and group procedures |
| **Counseling psychologist** | Essentially same as for clinical psychologist but with emphasis on assisting less maladaptive individuals and relationships | Counseling with personal, educational, marital, and family problems |
| **Psychiatrist** | M.D. degree plus specialized training in mental hospitals or clinics | Medical therapy (drugs, shock, etc.) and/or psychotherapy |
| **Psychoanalyst** | M.D. or Ph.D. degree plus extensive training in theory and practice of psychoanalysis | Intensive system of psychotherapy based largely upon Freudian theory |
| **Social worker** | M.A. degree in social work plus supervised experience in clinics or social service agencies | May work with spouses or other family members of clients, with groups in community, and with individuals |
| **Guidance counselor** | M.A. or Ph.D. in counseling psychology | Counseling with educational and career problems |
| **Occupational therapist** | B.S. plus clinical internship | Therapy with children and adults suffering from physical handicaps, helping them to make the most of their resources |
| **Speech therapist** | M.A. in speech pathology plus internship training | Procedures appropriate to treatment of stuttering and other speech disorders |
| **Paraprofessional** | Limited but intensive training in helping approaches with supervised field experience | May utilize wide range of procedures under supervision of professional in field |
| **Interdisciplinary team** | Often programs in psychotherapy include personnel from several disciplines including clinical psychologists, psychiatrists, social workers, and other professional or paraprofessional personnel. This approach is more likely to take place in a clinic setting than in private practice. | |

psychiatric hospitals. Private offices can vary as well. Some private offices are located within large medical buildings, while others are located in general office buildings or even in private homes.

In the institutional setting, the individual psychotherapist generally is part of a psychiatric or psychological clinic. Members of the staff are generally individuals who have completed their training, although a portion of the staff may still be in training under the supervision of the more experienced members. In a private setting, the therapist may work independently or may be part of a multiperson private practice.

Most settings consist of a reception area and one or more individual or group meeting rooms. Sitting in a waiting room of a clinic can be worrisome and embarrassing. Often, the first-time visitor examines the other people waiting in the room: "Maybe he thinks I'm crazy." "I wonder what her problem is." "I'm only waiting for my friends; I don't really belong here." Many of these fears disappear rapidly, since the people in the waiting rooms of psychologists are as ordinary and unremarkable as people in the waiting rooms of other professionals.

## Stages in the Therapeutic Process

Most people enter therapy with some anxiety and uncertainty. However, feelings of trust, confidence, respect, and understanding are important to the success of therapy. Thus, at an early point all therapists try to establish rapport so that the client feels free to respond honestly and openly and feels comfortable that he or she will be understood, accepted, and helped by the therapist.

**assessment phase:** first phase of the therapeutic process in which an individual's current concerns, history, and present circumstances are identified

While establishing rapport, all therapists will also attempt to gain an understanding of the problem, get a general sense of the person's current life circumstances, and determine how the problem might be treated. This is usually referred to as the **assessment phase** of the therapy. While the assessment is underway, the client may find that his or her anxieties about discussing these personal matters decreases somewhat. The client may also find it easier to discuss feelings and attitudes that are not always socially acceptable. For example, a woman may find that her strong negative feelings about her husband and children are easier to discuss in a therapeutic situation. Also, a skillful therapist may discover problem areas and attitudes of which the client is unaware. A man may find, for example, that he has aesthetic and artistic interests that he has repressed and ignored because a "real man" would not admit interests in these "non-macho" activities.

**feedback phase:** second phase of the therapeutic process in which assessment information is used to help establish therapeutic goals

Once the assessment is completed, the second or **feedback phase** begins. In this stage, the therapist not only provides feedback on the assessment but also often reframes the problem in a way that may help the person see it from a different perspective. For example, if a person is bothered by severe headaches, the therapist may point out that the headaches appear to be connected in some way to problems the person is encountering at work. The two of them might then spend some time talking together about the client's feelings about work, beliefs about the importance of success, and concerns about his or her ability to do the job well.

**implementation phase:** third phase of the therapeutic process in which client and therapist attempt to achieve therapeutic goals

As the person begins to see his or her problems in a somewhat different light, the way is paved for a discussion of how the problems might be solved and how treatment might prove helpful. This leads to the third and final stage of therapy, the **implementation phase**. This is the part of the process normally associated with psychotherapy or counseling. Like the first two parts, the third part can last various lengths of time. The client works with the therapist in resolving the problems identified earlier in such a way that the client minimizes his or her discomfort and maximizes progress toward the final goal.

### Action- Versus Insight-oriented Approaches

Although virtually all therapists follow the three stages we just described, the overall style and involvement of the therapist can vary greatly. Some therapists take an **action-oriented approach** in which they work actively and purposefully with the client to solve the client's problems. In the action-oriented approach, the emphasis is on activity and on accomplishing tasks. Therapists using this approach tend to use **directive therapy.** In other words, they may give advice, suggest courses of action, help determine a solution, and even assign homework.

In contrast, therapists using the **insight-oriented approach** believe that a thorough appreciation of the background and development of a problem is the most important step toward resolution. An insight-oriented therapist is likely to use **nondirective therapy,** rarely giving advice but instead helping the person to gain a deeper understanding of the problem and to work out his or her own solutions.

Both approaches can be effective but both have also been the subject of criticism. Critics argue that action-oriented approaches are often superficial, tend to focus only on solvable problems that are identified by the client, and tend to ignore the reasons why the person developed the problems in the first place. Critics also argue that these approaches ignore the context in which the problems arose: the ways in which the person characteristically thinks, feels, and deals with emotions.

Critics of insight-oriented approaches, on the other hand, argue that although people come to therapists for guidance and constructive advice, insight-oriented therapists offer instead an understanding of the origins of their problems and provide

**action-oriented approach:** style of therapy emphasizing active involvement of the therapist in helping solve problems

**directive therapy:** therapy in which the therapist offers advice and suggests problem-solving strategies

**insight-oriented approach:** style of therapy emphasizing understanding of the client's problems

**nondirective therapy:** therapy in which the therapist helps the client to achieve self-understanding and avoids providing advice

*Many people prefer a one-to-one therapeutic relationship, which is shaped largely by the levels of involvement the therapist and the client bring to the process.*

little or no guidance on how best to solve them. Moreover, critics contend that insight-oriented approaches take far too long and are not cost-effective.

In actual practice, few therapists are entirely directive or nondirective, action- or insight-oriented. Some therapists will take a more active role with some clients and a more insight-oriented role with others. For example, a therapist might use directive techniques with a person who "freezes up" during an exam while using nondirective methods with a person who is uncertain whether he or she should remain in school. Also, therapists will often use both directive and nondirective techniques with the same person. For example, a therapist might use nondirective methods to help establish rapport and to assess the client, and then shift to more directive techniques during the implementation phase.

In general, the most effective therapists are those who, regardless of their general orientation, use their clients' resources to the fullest extent. Effective therapists also modify their own approach to ensure that the therapeutic contact will be maximally beneficial to the person, and they structure the therapeutic process so that their clients will feel more competent and more self-reliant and will experience personal growth (see Insight, p. 222).

While the therapeutic process is usually conducted on a one-to-one basis, it is possible for couples and families to enter therapy as well. Finally, it should be noted that conversations between a client and a therapist are private and confidential; people who have fears that a therapist will "tell all" to strangers should be reassured that such behavior on the part of the therapist is considered extremely unethical.

## Initiating and Terminating a Therapeutic Relationship

Although the settings and procedures that psychotherapists and counselors use are not mysterious, many people deny themselves competent professional help because of their unfounded fears and concerns about consulting a psychologist, while a small number of people seek assistance for each minor problem or stumbling block that crosses their lives.

Many people find that consulting friends, family, or religious leaders is a useful and inexpensive way to deal with some problems. Of course, most friends and relatives do not have professional expertise, and the ways in which they can help may be correspondingly limited. Also, asking the advice of friends, relatives, and religious leaders is sometimes more difficult than seeing a psychologist; it is not always easy to speak freely and openly to people who know us personally. In some cases, family members and friends are either part of the problem or too close to the problem to give impartial advice.

When confiding in close friends and relatives is not possible or desirable, seeking a counselor or a therapist is the next appropriate step. Individuals who have received professional help before may be invaluable sources of information. People who have already participated in counseling or psychotherapy are often good sources of information on professionals whose assistance was particularly helpful (or not helpful at all). Other good sources of information include college and university counseling centers and psychology clinics, hospital programs, and independent referral sources. This latter source can be found in the yellow pages of many telephone directories.

# *Insight*

## How Effective Is Psychotherapy?

In recent years many have questioned the value of psychotherapy. Despite the fact that hundreds of thousands of people undergo some form of psychotherapy each year, there is surprisingly little scientific data to show how often such therapeutic intervention is successful. While attempts have been made to assess and compare the outcomes of various forms of therapy, the wide variations among therapists, clients, goals, procedures, and definitions of success have made it difficult to reach any valid conclusions.

Attempts at evaluation have usually depended on one or more of the following sources of information: (1) the therapist's impression of changes that have occurred, (2) the client's report of change, (3) comparison of pre- and post-treatment personality test scores, and (4) measure of change in selected overt behaviors. Unfortunately, each source has serious limitations.

Since a therapist usually wants to see himself or herself as competent, therapists are not the best judges of their own effectiveness. They can also inflate their improvement rate by encouraging difficult clients to discontinue therapy. It has also been facetiously remarked that the therapist often thinks the client is getting better, just because the therapist is getting used to the client's symptoms. Clients are another unreliable source concerning the outcome of therapy, since they too may want to think they are improving. Psychological tests may show change but are not necessarily valid indicators of how the client will behave in real-life situations. Neither psychological tests nor measures of change in overt behaviors indicate whether such change is likely to be enduring. Finally, many emotionally disturbed people show improvement over time without psychotherapy. Thus, the question is often raised whether the client improved because of or despite psychotherapy.

Nonetheless, the available evidence suggests that counseling and psychotherapy are generally better than no treatment at all. One "meta-analysis" of psychotherapy outcome studies (Smith & Glass, 1977) found that the typical therapy client is better adjusted than 75 percent of untreated control patients. It is less clear whether therapy clients improve because they *believe* they will get better or because of the therapeutic treatment they receive. A more recent re-analysis of the Smith and Glass data (Landman & Dawes, 1982) concludes that simply believing one will get better "may contribute to some degree to successful outcomes of psychotherapy" but constitutes "only a small fraction of the overall effect" (p. 511). In short, psychotherapy does have an effect.

This raises another question: is any particular form of therapy better than the others? At this point, there is no evidence to suggest that one particular type of therapy is better than another (Garfield, 1983; Michelson, 1985). However, as knowledge and understanding of the complex process of psychotherapy improves, it is likely that psychotherapists will become increasingly selective in their use of psychological treatment techniques. Rather than give all people the same treatment, psychotherapists in the future will use a particular set of techniques for one unique person/problem combination and an entirely different set of techniques for another person/problem combination. For example, it appears that insight-oriented therapies are likely to be most effective for individuals who are relatively intelligent, seeking a greater sense of self-understanding, and seeking relief from feelings of unhappiness or anxiety or moderate depression. Behavioral therapies are probably most effective where a specific behavioral problem exists such as a phobia or well-defined fear, maladaptive habits, problems with impulse control, and sexual dysfunctions.

If the potential client becomes reasonably confident that the counselor or therapist can help with the problem, then a therapeutic relationship can be established. If not, he or she should seek another therapist. Also, if the client loses confidence in the ability of the therapist during the assessment or treatment program, the client should seek other professional assistance. It is important to keep in mind that the client is paying for a service and should feel that he or she is receiving something of value for the money and time that is spent. However, it is also important to realize that there are times when therapy may unavoidably trigger uncomfortable or anxiety-provoking thoughts and memories. Thus, a person should discuss feelings of discomfort or discontent with the therapist before deciding whether it is appropriate to terminate treatment.

Therapy usually ends when the client is reasonably satisfied with the outcome. In action-oriented therapies this point is reached when the maladaptive behavior has been changed and the problem that led to therapy has been solved. In insight-oriented therapies the proper termination point is less clear, but usually therapy ends when the client and therapist agree that the person can function effectively without further treatment.

Ending a therapeutic relationship can be a sad and upsetting experience, but it can also be a joyous one, signaling the client's new-found skills and his or her ability to lead a more meaningful and satisfying life. Some people continue to see their therapists occasionally, but most people find that they can cope effectively and live fulfilling, useful lives without continuing assistance.

In this section of the chapter, we have discussed the nature of the therapeutic process in general terms. In the remainder of the chapter we will look more closely at the assessment process and then at specific therapeutic techniques used by different therapists.

## PSYCHOLOGICAL ASSESSMENT

**psychological assessment:** use of psychological tests and other methods for the diagnosis of maladaptive behavior

**Psychological assessment** represents a systematic attempt to collect, organize, and interpret relevant information about a person and his or her life situation. This information is then used as a starting point in planning whatever help is needed.

### Types of Assessment Information

Although the information obtained in psychological assessment may vary considerably, depending on the specific goals in a particular case, the assessment usually covers most or all of the following areas:

1. *Major complaint*—information concerning the problem or problems that bring the individual to a counselor or psychotherapist.

2. *Medical and psychiatric information*—information concerning current and past medical illnesses and injuries and information concerning current or past encounters with psychotherapists.

3. *Personal and family history information*—information concerning individual history, interpersonal relationships and group memberships, educational and occupational experiences, and family relationships.

4. *Current social stresses*—information concerning stresses in the person's life situation that may contribute to the problems described in the major complaint.

5. *Strengths and resources*—information concerning environmental and personal resources and supports, skills and abilities, and prior successes at coping.

6. *Frame of reference*—information concerning reality and value assumptions, including the way clients view themselves and their world.

Naturally, the emphasis placed on these six areas will differ from individual to individual and from problem to problem. For example, an individual whose major complaint is social unease will be assessed more thoroughly in those areas concerned with interpersonal history and skills than an individual whose major complaint concerns stress-related headaches. Similarly, an individual who complains of test anxiety will be assessed more carefully in those areas dealing with prior educational experiences and study skills than an individual who fears a personal inability to control drug use.

## Methods of Assessment

In gathering information about people and their life situations, psychologists may select from a wide range of assessment methods. These various procedures can be divided into three general categories: interviews, tests, and direct observation (Bernstein & Nietzel, 1980).

**Interviewing.**    This is probably the oldest and most widely used method for gathering information and making judgments about others. The interview is usually defined as a conversation with a specific purpose, conducted so that one person can obtain information from another, or can evaluate that person. This definition, however, belies the wide range and complexity of interview situations. For example, the interview may vary from the simple interview in which a specific set of questions is asked (as in a job interview); to the stress interview, designed to see how an individual functions intellectually and emotionally in a difficult situation; to the technically complex therapeutic interview, which may involve both assessment and therapy.

Although the interview is of undoubted value for obtaining certain kinds of information, it is not always a completely reliable technique. The biases, values, motives, and limited range of experience of interviewers (and interviewees) may distort the process. Factors such as age, sex, race, socioeconomic status, and language variables can reduce the quality and usefulness of information gathered during an interview (Pope, 1979).

**Psychological testing.**    Although the assessment goals of interviews and psychological tests may be similar, a psychological test differs from an interview in its systematic and standardized observation and collection of information about an individual (Cronbach, 1970). While interviews may deal with virtually any issue, the purposes to which psychological tests are put are typically more limited. Nonetheless, there are a wide range of psychological tests designed to yield information about virtually any aspect of an individual. Some of the more common psychological tests include intelligence tests, personality inventories, projective tests, aptitude and ability tests, and tests of attitudes and values.

The intelligence test is the oldest type of psychological test. In the typical intelligence test, an individual is asked to answer questions and complete tasks designed to assess complex intellectual functions. For example, an individual's short-term memory can be assessed by asking him or her to repeat increasingly longer

*Psychological tests help systematize the process of collecting information. The skill of the therapist interpreting the data and the degree of cooperation of the subject can significantly affect the results of such tests.*

strings of numbers. In a test of abstract abilities, an individual may be asked to describe the common attributes of an apple and an orange. Other tasks that are typically found on intelligence tests involve defining the meaning of certain words, using colored blocks to reproduce a printed pattern, and successfully solving simple arithmetic problems. While intelligence tests are easily scored, the proper interpretation of the results depends on the full cooperation and motivation of the subject.

**personality inventory:** psychological test used to assess specific aspects of an individual's personality

The **personality inventory** is usually made up of a series of direct questions to which the individual is asked to respond "true" or "false" (or "yes" or "no"). (Some inventories allow for intermediate "don't know" or "cannot say" responses.) Examples of possible inventory items are:

1. I often feel as if things were unreal.                          Yes    No
2. When I am disappointed, I like to talk with someone else.       Yes    No
3. I have engaged in deviant sexual behavior about which           Yes    No
   I feel guilty.

Personality inventories may be designed to assess severe psychopathology, or they may assess normal interests, attitudes, abilities, and the like. Perhaps the best known personality inventory is the Minnesota Multiphasic Personality Inventory (MMPI). The MMPI is typically used to assess the extent to which an individual has psychological problems. In contrast, the California Psychological Inventory (CPI), another widely employed inventory, is used to assess normal psychological functioning.

**projective test:** psychological assessment technique using relatively unstructured stimuli

The **projective test** consists of an unstructured or ambiguous stimulus to which the subject is asked to respond. For example, in the well-known Rorschach technique, an individual is shown an inkblot and asked to tell what he or she sees in it. In other types of projective tests, an individual may be shown a picture and asked to make up a story about it or be given an incomplete sentence and asked to complete it. Since the stimulus is ambiguous, the creators of projective tests felt that the individual's cognitive patterns, conflicts, and defenses would be revealed in their responses (Exner, 1974). The purpose of projective tests is to discover aspects of the client's personality that may be unconscious. On the Rorschach test, for example, the person may see many aggressive images such as people fighting or patches of red blood; these images may reflect unconscious anger or fears of violence.

Self-report tests, such as the questionnaires you have filled out in the self-discovery exercises that correspond to each chapter of this book rely on your conscious or preconscious knowledge of yourself. They are limited by the fact that you may not know (or want to know) certain things about yourself. In contrast, the primary problem with projective tests is that they require a great deal of skill and training to interpret, and different psychologists may conclude quite different things from the same test responses.

Aptitude and ability tests are typically used to assess specific potentials and skills. An example you may be familiar with is the Scholastic Aptitude Test (SAT) or the American College Test (ACT); both of these tests are often employed in admissions at colleges and universities. Individuals seeking information about occupations may be asked to take the Strong Interest Inventory or the Career Assessment Inventory. More specialized skills can also be assessed. The Minnesota Clerical Test might be used to assess office skills prior to employment, and musical aptitude can be assessed with the Seashore Measures of Musical Talents.

**rating scales:** continuum for evaluating specific characteristics of individuals

Tests of attitudes and values are also available. These devices can be used to measure political orientation, honesty, anxiety, and other traits that are difficult to measure by performance on set tasks. These tests often use **rating scales,** and a rating scale item for aggressiveness, for example, might be as follows:

| Not aggressive | Moderately aggressive | Very aggressive |

**social desirability:** tendency of a person to respond in a socially correct manner

Although these scales are easy to complete and easy to score, they are subject to many sources of error. One important source of error, **social desirability,** deals with the tendency of people to respond in an expected or socially correct manner. However, tests of attitudes and values are rarely used alone, and the information received from multiple sources helps yield accurate and useful assessment data.

**Direct observation.**     Most psychological tests attempt to identify consistencies in individuals. However, clinicians are also aware that situational factors can markedly affect the ways in which people behave (Hancock, 1982). If a child behaves poorly in school but behaves well at home, we would want to know more about the school setting and the home setting. A psychologist would, with the permission of those involved, observe the child in the classroom (and, perhaps, at home as well) to try to identify the factors that seem to encourage the poor behavior in school.

Direct observation also occurs when a psychologist sets up a simulated situation. A young man, for example, who complains that he has difficulty talking to women might be asked to act as though he were calling a female acquaintance. The psychologist would then observe the young man's performance and later suggest some ways the man might decrease his anxiety and improve his conversational skills.

Finally, direct observation occurs whenever a psychologist interacts with another person. In talking with someone during an interview, the psychologist may notice subtle nonverbal signs that are clues to the person's emotional state. During an individually administered psychological test, the psychologist may observe the individual's problem-solving strategies and thereby gain further insight into the person.

Reprinted courtesy *Omni Magazine* © 1982.

## Evaluation and Integration of Assessment Data

**validity:** extent to which a measuring instrument actually measures what it is designed to measure

In evaluating the significance of assessment data, psychologists are vitally concerned with the **validity, reliability,** and **standardization** of their tools. An intelligence test, for example, is valid if it actually measures intelligence and is reliable if it gives consistent results at different times. If it has been standardized, the individual's score can be compared with the scores of a representative group of subjects, and the psychologist can determine whether the score is high, low, or intermediate.

**reliability:** degree to which a psychological test produces the same result each time it is used on the same person

It is risky to draw conclusions from single items of information. The psychologist feels more confident if there is interlocking evidence from independent sources. Even when the reliability of single scores is limited, as in the case of projective test scores, the probability that a conclusion is accurate is increased if several independent sources of information point in the same direction. Since the overall goal of psychological assessment is to formulate an accurate "working model" of the client in relation to his or her life situation, it is essential that the assessment data not only be carefully evaluated but also be integrated into a coherent picture.

**standardization:** characteristics of a psychological test allowing comparison of an individual score with those of a reference group

## PSYCHOTHERAPY

**counseling:** brief, action-oriented therapy focused on a single problem

Once an assessment is completed, the therapist and client may decide that a continuing relationship is appropriate. This continuing contact forms the basis for counseling and psychotherapy. **Counseling** refers to relatively short-term, action-oriented intervention focused on a particular problem. In contrast, **psychotherapy** is typically more prolonged and often deals with problems in greater depth than counseling. Psychotherapy can be either action-oriented or insight-oriented.

**psychotherapy:** longer-term therapy intended to help people cope more effectively in a wide range of situations

Psychotherapies generally fall into three major categories, which correspond to the models of human nature described in Chapter 2: psychoanalytic, humanistic-existential, and behavioral approaches. Within each of the major categories there are sub-areas as well. Our coverage will concentrate on the major areas, and will be relatively brief. We begin our discussion with the first of the psychotherapies to be developed, psychoanalytic psychotherapy.

### Psychoanalytic Therapy

As developed by Sigmund Freud, psychoanalytic therapy emphasizes three basic ideas. First is the important role of irrational and unconscious processes—such as repressed memories, motives, and conflicts—in self-defeating and maladaptive behavior. Second is that such difficulties originate in early childhood experiences and in the conflict between social prohibitions and basic instinctual drives. Third is the importance of bringing these unconscious and irrational processes to consciousness. A basic assumption of psychoanalytic psychotherapy is that much adult behavior—the ways in which people see the world, deal with other people, cope with stress and emotion—is shaped by childhood experiences and may no longer be adaptive. Moreover, many of the beliefs, feelings, conflicts, and defenses that result from childhood experiences and that shape adult behavior are unconscious. In psychotherapy, the client must become aware of these unconscious determinants of behavior and replace them with more conscious, deliberate decisions that are more adaptive and appropriate to the situation. Psychoanalytic therapy is a complex and long-term procedure. Perhaps the simplest way to describe it is to note the three basic techniques utilized in this approach.

**free association:** psychoanalytic procedure in which an individual gives a running account of every thought and feeling

**Free association.**    The technique of **free association** is the "basic rule" of psychoanalytic therapy. The client tells the therapist whatever comes into his or her mind, regardless of how personal, painful, or seemingly irrelevant it may be.

Free association is important for two reasons. First, according to psychoanalytic theory consciousness is just the tip of the iceberg that influences behavior. Often conscious thoughts do not adequately explain why people behave as they do. For example, people with phobias are often unaware of the reasons for their fears. By exploring their associations to dogs, heights, or whatever, both the client and the therapist may get a hint of what these feared objects mean to the client, and thus see what is causing the fear. Second, many thoughts and feelings that lead to maladaptive behavior are repressed because they make people feel guilty or anxious. Free association forces the client to let down his or her guard, so that ideas come to mind that would otherwise be repressed (see Psychology in Action, p. 230).

**interpretation:** psychoanalytic technique in which the therapist suggests unconscious motives, thoughts, or wishes that appear to account for behavior

**Interpretation.**    The second technique, **interpretation,** follows from the first. A central task of the psychoanalytic therapist is to help the client reframe his or her problems in a less defensive, less uncomfortable, and more adaptive way. To do this, the therapist will often interpret what the person does or says to suggest a meaning or a motive of which the person was not aware. For example, one client complained that his wife saw him as manipulative. While he was describing an incident in which he felt wrongly accused, the therapist noted that he was smiling smugly. When the therapist pointed this out and suggested that perhaps the person did feel manipulative, the person initially became angry but eventually came to understand that his smile betrayed the fact that indeed he had been feeling manipulative when the incident occurred and that he was trying to deny it to himself.

**Analysis of transference.**    During the course of psychoanalysis, people usually "transfer" their feelings about some significant individual from the past, such as their mother or father, to their therapists. An important part of therapy is helping people deal with this irrational **transference** and see past relationships as well as their present life situations in a more realistic light. The advantage to examining the relationship between the client and therapist is that it allows both participants to see how the client actually behaves toward other people without simply relying on the person's self-report.

**transference:** process whereby the client projects attitudes and emotions applicable to another significant person onto the therapist

Sometimes analysis of transference can be critical in dealing with a problem. The man who was manipulative with his wife, for example, continued to deny his manipulativeness until he was "caught in the act" trying to manipulate his therapist into giving him special favors. This was painful for the client to admit, but when he was unable to avoid facing his manipulativeness, he then recalled that as a child he felt he had to manipulate his mother in order to get her to respond to his needs. He was able to see, in examining his relationship with the therapist, how this once

## Myths and Realities in Hypnosis

One of the earliest therapeutic tools used by Sigmund Freud was hypnosis. In working with patients who today would receive a diagnosis of somatoform disorder (see Chapter 6), Freud found that this technique enabled him to reduce or eliminate the physical complaints presented by a substantial proportion of his patients. Freud eventually abandoned hypnosis, finding it less reliable and satisfactory than free association.

Today, hypnosis is used in a variety of settings for a variety of purposes. Probably most common is the use of hypnosis in psychotherapy to instill a sense of relaxation, to control pain, or to allow repressed memories to enter conscious awareness.

Unfortunately, many people's beliefs about hypnosis are based on incorrect impressions and stereotypes. In movies, hypnotists are often portrayed as distinctly evil characters, while hypnotists who perform on stage reinforce the impression that hypnosis is nothing more than an amusing parlor game.

Below are listed some myths and realities concerning hypnosis. In reviewing this list, you may wish to see how well your conceptualization of hypnosis corresponds to current research findings.

### Myths

1. *A hypnotized person is under the control of the hypnotist.* In fact, a hypnotized person remains under his or her own control at all times.

2. *A hypnotized person can be made to do things he or she normally wouldn't do.* In fact, a person's values are no different under hypnosis than at any other time.

3. *A hypnotized person can perform superhuman acts.* In fact, physical strength is not altered under hypnosis.

4. *A person can learn more rapidly and retain more of what is learned under hypnosis.* In fact, mental abilities are unaffected by hypnosis.

5. *The characteristics of a hypnotized person are easy to spot.* In fact, most trained observers cannot tell the difference between a hypnotized person and a nonhypnotized person asked to fake being hypnotized.

### Realities

1. *No physiological measures, including brain wave patterns, can distinguish a hypnotized from a nonhypnotized person.* The only reliable cue to whether a person is hypnotized is the individual's self-report.

2. *Hypnosis can be induced by a variety of means.* Virtually any stimulus, including suggestions of falling asleep, pedaling an exercise bike, or watching a pendulum swing back and forth, can be used to induce hypnosis.

3. *Hypnosis can be used to induce anesthesia.* Some hypnotic subjects can control surgical pain to such a degree that anesthetics are unnecessary during surgery.

4. *Expectations are important.* Some of the earliest hypnotic subjects believed they would and did have convulsions while hypnotized. Today, we expect that hypnotic subjects will appear limply relaxed.

5. *The ability to be hypnotized is unrelated to an individual's "willpower."* People easily hypnotized are no different in willpower than people who have difficulty becoming hypnotized.

Source: Barber, 1969; Hilgard, 1973; Hilgard & Hilgard 1975; Wadden & Anderton, 1982

adaptive strategy was no longer necessary or useful in relating to other people. In fact, it was costing him friends and ruining his marriage.

Classical psychoanalysis is a very lengthy and expensive process. As proposed by Freud, psychoanalysis involves three to five therapy sessions per week over the course of three to five (or more) years. These requirements obviously place severe restrictions on the number of individuals who might benefit from psychoanalysis.

To deal with these limitations, contemporary therapists have modified Freud's original approach. Many psychoanalytic psychotherapists see clients once or twice a week instead of three to five times a week. In addition, some therapists have begun to apply psychoanalytic principles to short-term psychotherapies that last less than a year (Strupp & Binder, 1984). Other therapists, such as Judd Marmor (1980), emphasize a flexible approach to psychotherapy utilizing elements of psychoanalytic, behavioristic, and humanistic therapy as the needs of the client dictate.

## The Humanistic-Existential Therapies

*A person-centered approach is based on the premise that the human being is basically a trustworthy organism, capable of evaluating the outer and inner situation, understanding herself in its context, making constructive choices as to the next steps in life, and acting on those choices.*

*Carl Rogers on Personal Power* (Rogers, 1977, p. 15)

Humanistic-existential therapies focus on creating a "psychological climate," or client-therapist relationship, that releases the person's capacity for understanding and managing his or her life. We shall confine ourselves to a brief review of the most prominent of these therapies.

**Person-centered therapy.**    This therapeutic approach is most closely associated with Carl Rogers (1951, 1961). You will recall from Chapter 2 that Rogers believed people are basically rational, are aware of what they are doing and why they are doing it, and are not helpless victims of past experiences. According to Rogers, maladaptive behavior arises when people learn to distrust their own experience and instead live their lives as others suggest. The task of the therapist is to give the client unconditional positive regard—to demonstrate that the person is prized and valued, regardless of their behavior. By expressing an attitude of caring and of unconditional acceptance, the therapist allows the client to become more open to experience, to re-discover his or her true potential, and ultimately to become a more fully-functioning person.

**person-centered therapy:** nondirective approach to psychotherapy developed by Carl Rogers; also called client-centered therapy

In **person-centered therapy** (also known as client-centered therapy), the primary responsibility rests on the client. The therapist plays a relatively passive role, since it is assumed that the client is inherently able to solve his or her problems. The therapist approaches the person with as few preconceived notions as possible and works with the material presented by the individual, repeating or reflecting the client's feelings and thoughts and helping to clarify them. In this process, the therapist avoids interpreting what the person is saying or attempting to force insight on the individual.

The following excerpt (Rogers, 1951) from a therapy session demonstrates the person-centered approach.

ALICE: I was thinking about this business of standards. I somehow developed a sort of a knack, I guess, of—well—habit—of trying to make people feel at ease around me, or to make things go along smoothly. . . .

COUNSELOR: In other words, what you did was always in the direction of trying to keep things smooth and to make other people feel better and to smooth the situation.

ALICE: Yes. I think that's what it was. Now the reason why I did it probably was—I mean, not that I was a good little Samaritan going around making other people happy, but that was probably the role that felt easiest for me to play. I'd been doing it around home so much. I just didn't stand up for my own convictions, until I don't know whether I have any convictions to stand up for.

COUNSELOR: You feel that for a long time you've been playing the role of kind of smoothing out the frictions or differences or what not. . . .

ALICE: M-hm.

COUNSELOR: Rather than having any opinion or reaction of your own in the situation. Is that it?

ALICE: That's it. Or that I haven't been really honestly being myself, or actually knowing what my real self is, and that I've been just playing a sort of false role. Whatever role no one else was playing, and that needed to be played at the time, I'd try to fill it in. (pp. 152–53)

Rogers has found that person-centered therapy follows an orderly and predictable sequence: (1) the creation of the therapeutic climate, (2) the client's expression of feelings and thoughts that had formerly been denied or distorted, including many negative feelings, (3) insight and increased self-understanding, (4) positive steps toward resolving conflicts and achieving more positive feelings about one's self and others, and (5) termination of therapy. The last step is initiated by the client who arrives at a point where he or she no longer needs the support of the therapeutic relationship.

**Existential therapy.**   As we saw in Chapter 2, existential psychologists are very much concerned about the predicament of humankind today. They emphasize the breakdown of traditional faith, alienation and depersonalization of the individual in today's mass society, and loss of meaning in human existence. Despite their predicament, however, humans are viewed as essentially free. Unlike other living creatures, humans have the ability to be self-aware, reflect on their own existence, and do something about their problems through their choices and actions.

**existential therapy:** form of psychotherapy that attempts to develop a sense of self-direction and meaning in one's existence

Thus, the primary concern of **existential therapy** is helping the person to clarify his or her values and to work out a meaningful way of "being-in-the-world." Since each individual is unique, each must find the pattern of values capable of giving meaning to his or her life. As Nietzsche has expressed it, "He who has a why to live can bear with almost any how." However, to find values and meaning, the individual must have the courage to break away from old views and defenses, make choices, and take responsibility for his or her life.

Existential therapists do not follow any prescribed procedures but believe that a flexible approach is necessary in therapy (Havens, 1974; Frankl, 1971; May, 1969). However, they do stress the importance of directly challenging the individual with questions concerning the meaning and purpose of his or her existence; they also stress the importance of the relationship established between the two human beings in a therapeutic situation. The focus is on the here and now—on what the individual is choosing to do, and therefore be, at this moment. This sense of immediacy, of the urgency of experience, is the touchstone of existential therapy and sets the stage for clarifying and choosing among alternative ways of being. Existential therapists also emphasize the individual's responsibility to others. Each person's life can only be meaningful and fulfilling if it involves socially constructive values and choices.

Existential psychotherapy is similar in many ways to person-centered psychotherapy: both approaches view psychotherapy as growth of the self. However, the existential approach places less emphasis on discovering the true self behind the facade and more emphasis on taking the responsibility for one human life—for shaping oneself into the kind of person one wants to be and living in a socially constructive and meaningful way. The Greek oracle said "Know thyself"; the poet Emerson said "Trust thyself"; and, to paraphrase Kierkegaard, the existentialists have said "Choose thyself."

**Gestalt therapy:** type of psychotherapy emphasizing the wholeness of the client and the integration of thoughts, feelings, and action

**Gestalt therapy: becoming a "whole" person.**    As developed by Fritz Perls (1969), **Gestalt therapy** is typically used in a group setting, but the emphasis is on the individual. Working intensively with one person at a time, the therapist helps people perceive those aspects of themselves and their world that are "blocked out," correct inaccuracies in their views, and achieve greater competence in coping with the problems of living.

*Gestalt therapy targets unresolved problems in an effort to help the individual finish with past business and more effectively cope with future challenges.*

Gestalt therapy utilizes a number of specific techniques including "awareness training," the "hot seat," and dream interpretation. "Awareness training" aims to help people become more perceptive and experience life more fully and richly. The "hot seat" helps people perceive themselves more clearly. Here one person occupies the "hot seat" while the others provide feedback about their reactions to the client and his or her behavior—with the proviso that the feedback be sincere. As a result, clients develop somewhat different impressions of themselves than they had before. In "dreamwork," the therapist helps the client interpret the meaning of dreams and perceive their application to real-life situations.

These various techniques are referred to as "taking care of unfinished business." According to Perls, people experience blind spots, unresolved conflicts, and traumas. This unfinished business can be carried over into new situations and relationships, often with detrimental results. Consequently, completing this unfinished business should help people achieve a more realistic awareness of themselves and their world, reduce their level of anxiety and tension, and achieve greater effectiveness in coping.

## Behavioral Therapies

As we noted in Chapter 2, psychologists adopting the behavioral model view maladjusted individuals as having learned maladaptive, rather than adaptive, behavior patterns. The goal in **behavioral therapies,** therefore, is to teach the client more adaptive and effective ways of behaving—not by providing insight into past events or unconscious conflicts or by finding meaning in life, but rather by directly modifying maladaptive behavior.

**behavioral therapies:** forms of psychotherapy that emphasize learning of adaptive patterns and modification of maladaptive patterns of behavior

Behavioral approaches tend to be more directive, action-oriented, and focussed on particular problems than either psychoanalytic or humanistic approaches. Behavior therapists usually begin by determining the maladaptive behaviors that need to be modified, identifying a set of more adaptive behaviors to be learned, and then determining a procedure for teaching the person those new behaviors. In the following portion of the chapter, we will examine a sample of behavioral techniques that have been found to be highly effective for particular problems.

**Systematic desensitization.**    A number of behavior therapies focus on anxiety management, particularly the elimination of irrational fears or phobias. One particularly successful behavioral procedure for reducing anxiety is **systematic desensitization.** Systematic desensitization was developed by Joseph Wolpe (1958, 1969, 1981) as a means to eliminate fears and phobias. Wolpe believed that phobic reactions could be reduced or eliminated if the victims could be taught a more appropriate but incompatible response to the anxiety-eliciting stimulus. Wolpe believed that, since it is not possible to be relaxed and anxious at the same time, if a person could be trained to relax in the presence of a fear-producing stimulus, fear and anxiety should gradually disappear.

**systematic desensitization:** technique used by some behavior therapists to eliminate clients' fears and phobias

Systematic desensitization occurs in several stages. First, the client and therapist put together a list of objects or situations that produce a fear reaction or an anxiety reaction. This list is then arranged into a **hierarchy** ranging from situations that

**hierarchy:** ranked list of fear-producing situations, used in systematic desensitization

produce only slight fear or anxiety to situations that trigger extreme fear or anxiety. For example, a college student who fears giving a speech in class might construct the following hierarchy of fear-producing situations:

Step  1. I am reading about speeches alone in my room. It is about a week or two before the time I have to give the speech.

Step  2. It is one week before the speech. I am discussing the speech with someone after class.

Step  3. It is one week before my speech, and I am sitting in class listening to another person give a speech.

Step  4. I am writing my speech in a study area.

Step  5. I am practicing the speech in a study area.

Step  6. I am getting dressed on the morning of the speech.

Step  7. I am carrying out some activities prior to leaving to give the speech.

Step  8. It is the day of the speech, and I am walking to class.

Step  9. I am entering the classroom.

Step 10. I am waiting while another person gives a speech.

Step 11. It is time for me to give the speech. I am walking up before the audience.

Step 12. I am giving the speech, and I am noticing the faces in the audience and seeing their reactions. (Adapted from Paul, 1966)

Once the hierarchy of situations has been constructed, the next step is for the person to learn to relax in each of the situations. As we noted in Chapter 5, most people do not know how to relax effectively, so it is usually necessary first to teach the client how to relax. Then, the therapist establishes the relaxation response for each of the situations on the hierarchy, beginning with the least anxiety-provoking one (Step 1 on the list above). The client is asked to relax, and then to imagine the least anxiety-evoking situation while trying to remain relaxed. If thinking of the scene disturbs relaxation, the person is told to stop thinking about it and to concentrate fully on regaining a state of complete relaxation. When relaxation has returned, the person again thinks about the anxiety-provoking situation. This process continues until the person can imagine the least stressful situation without becoming anxious or fearful. Then training proceeds to the next step in the hierarchy (Step 2 on the list) until it too can be imagined without causing anxiety or fear. This process continues until the person can imagine the most anxiety-evoking situation on the list (Step 12) without becoming fearful or anxious.

Interestingly, in most cases the ability to *imagine* these scenes without anxiety transfers to real life so that the person actually *is* less anxious or fearful when the situation actually arises. That is, if the person is able to imagine a scene without anxiety, it is probable that the person will respond with little or no anxiety in the actual situation. However, if necessary desensitization can also be carried out in the real world. For example, an individual who fears entering an elevator could construct a hierarchy in which he or she actually enters a building with an elevator, approaches the elevator, enters the car, takes the car up one floor, and so forth. It is often more difficult for people to relax under these real-life conditions and the therapist must go to the scene with the client, but desensitization can be achieved nonetheless (Emmelkamp, 1986).

*Both quiet inhibition and overzealous, extreme self-expression may point to a person having problems with self-assertion.*

**Assertiveness training.** A business executive who is able to express her feelings and beliefs directly, honestly, and openly with friends and acquaintances encounters serious difficulties when communicating her wants and needs to her business associates. A college student who is able to express his thoughts and feelings freely to other students feels seriously inhibited when communicating with professors. Both of these individuals are unable to be assertive in situations where assertiveness is appropriate. They are prevented from speaking out for what they consider to be appropriate and right, and as a result they may experience considerable inner turmoil and other people may take advantage of them or maneuver them into uncomfortable situations.

People vary greatly in the extent to which they are able to behave assertively. At one extreme, certain people have difficulty asking for the correct change from a salesperson in a department store, are unable to speak out when others cut into a long line ahead of them despite feeling furious, or even have difficulty expressing positive emotions toward others. At the other extreme, others are aggressive, unreasonable, demanding, uncooperative, and only concerned about themselves. Between these two extremes are assertive people who are able to express thoughts, feelings, and beliefs in direct, honest, and appropriate ways without abusing the rights and privileges of others.

**Assertiveness training** can be effective in teaching unassertive people to behave more assertively in appropriate situations. Typically the person first learns to identify various situations in which he or she is nonassertive. Then the therapist helps to identify more appropriate and adaptive behaviors in those situations; often

**assertiveness training:**
behavioral technique for helping individuals express their feelings and gain their rights without being uncooperative or overbearing

this involves asking the client to observe the way other people respond in those same situations. When a set of new, assertive behaviors have been identified, they are usually practiced in the safety of the therapeutic setting by role-playing. Eventually the client is given the opportunity to practice the new assertive behaviors in real-life situations beginning with the least threatening situations and slowly progressing to more challenging situations.

**Contingency management and behavioral contracting.**    American society is oriented toward punishment. Our laws and customs operate under the thesis that "In order to avoid punishment, you must behave in a certain way." Behavior therapists feel that a punishment-oriented approach is ineffective in teaching appropriate ways to behave. Punishment, they feel, only teaches the individual what not to do; it does not teach desirable alternatives.

**contingency management:** behavioral technique that relies on positive reinforcement to teach more adaptive behaviors

To help individuals respond more effectively, some behavior therapists use contingency management and behavioral contracting. **Contingency management** uses positive reinforcement. This reward-oriented approach operates under the rule that "In order to receive a reward, you must behave in a certain way." The reinforcer can be material, as in money or food, access to desired behaviors (child is allowed to play when homework is completed), "tokens" that can be exchanged for desired objects or activities, or the reinforcer can be intangible, as in praise, a smile, or a pat on the back. Whatever the reinforcer that is used, desired behavior is reinforced as soon as possible after it occurs.

Contingency management can be effective when the intent is to teach a person a specific new behavior. However, when attempts are made to deal with a broad spectrum of behaviors, or when the desired behavior is complex, behavior therapists are more likely to use **behavioral contracting.** In behavioral contracting, a written or oral agreement is made between individuals. This agreement specifies the rules, behaviors, and changes that must occur before reinforcers can be earned. In marital therapy, for example, a couple may, with the assistance of the therapist, set up a behavioral contract. The husband may agree to baby-sit with the children in exchange for an afternoon of watching sports on television. At the same time, the wife may agree to manage the family finances in exchange for two evenings of accounting classes at the local college.

**behavioral contracting:** behavioral technique in which contracts are developed that specify the behaviors necessary to receive reinforcement

**Cognitive behavior therapy.**    So far in our discussion of behavior therapies, we have focussed on approaches that ignore inner thoughts and try instead to reshape behavior directly. However, as seen repeatedly in previous chapters, a growing number of behaviorally-oriented psychologists now believe that cognitive events—such as thoughts, expectations, and self-statements—are often important determinants of maladaptive behavior. In Chapter 3, for example, we discussed a variety of irrational beliefs and expectations that some people carry around with them and that add to the stress that they experience. In Chapter 5, we examined Meichenbaum's stress-inoculation training in which people are taught to use cognitive self-statements to cope more effectively with stress.

Many behavior oriented therapists attempt to change maladaptive behavior by changing the underlying cognitive patterns. One of the earliest examples of such

**Rational-Emotive Therapy (RET):** form of psychotherapy which encourages the client to substitute rational for irrational assumptions in his or her inner dialogues

cognitive behavior therapy was **Rational-Emotive Therapy** (RET). RET stems from the work of Albert Ellis (1973). As you will recall from Chapter 3, Ellis theorized that ineffective and self-defeating behaviors stem from irrational, unrealistic beliefs that are maintained by a process of "self-talk," a sort of internal dialogue in which a person continually reaffirms his or her own faulty assumptions. For example, a person may continually remind him- or herself that it is essential to be approved by everyone, or that it is a disaster not to be competent at everything. Such irrational self-statements lead to self-defeating behaviors which then further increase the person's feelings of distress, incompetence and inadequacy. As long as this cycle continues, the person is likely to behave ineffectively and maladaptively and to experience a great deal of distress.

The primary goal of rational-emotional therapy is to help the person identify and change inaccurate assumptions. The therapist might draw attention to unrealistic self-statements, and challenge the validity of those beliefs; or the therapist might dispute the person's evaluation of events. "You seem to think that you must succeed at everything. Who says so?" "Will it really be a major catastrophe if you don't get an A+ on the exam?" "Who says everyone must like you?" The intent is to help the person to see that beliefs, like actions, have consequences, and that irrational beliefs, like irrational actions, usually lead to frustration, disappointment, and emotional pain. With the help of the rational-emotive therapist, the person should be able to identify and change irrational beliefs and adopt more appropriate ones.

A variation of this approach has been used by Aaron Beck in the treatment of depression (Beck, 1976). Instead of debating and directly challenging irrational and self-defeating beliefs as a rational-emotive therapist might, Beck guides his clients to a discovery of their beliefs and expectations, and then helps them learn how to test their beliefs and discover for themselves that many of them are unreasonable. For example, a person who believes "I never succeed at anything" might be told to keep a diary of daily events and to write down at the end of each day the successes and the failures; the person's spouse might be asked to do the same, so the two diaries can be compared. It is highly likely that the person indeed *does* succeed at some things, but chooses to ignore them and to concentrate instead on the inevitable failures in life.

By designing small experiments of this sort, the therapist attempts to lead the person to a more reasonable, balanced view of events in the world and their own competences: "It isn't necessary for me to succeed at everything I do; it's all right to have some failures in the course of a day, as long as I have successes too." As therapy progresses, the person gradually assumes greater responsibility for monitoring his or her own beliefs and expectations and for testing them against the real world to discover which ones are reasonable and which ones are unreasonable or irrational.

Some recent research sheds light on the reasons why cognitive behavior therapies are often especially effective in relieving depression. Richard Wenzlaff and his colleagues (Wenzlaff, Wegner, & Roper, 1988) noted that all of us from time to time have negative thoughts—doubts, worries, misgivings—but most people are able to avoid dwelling on such thoughts by substituting more positive thoughts. These researchers wondered whether depression might arise because some people, for one reason or another, are less effective at replacing negative thoughts with more positive thoughts.

In the first of three related experiments, subjects were asked to imagine being involved in a fatal car accident for which they were at fault. They were then instructed to try to avoid thinking about the accident while writing down all their thoughts during a nine minute period.

The researchers discovered that depressed subjects had a great deal of trouble suppressing thoughts about the accident because they tried to do so by thinking about other distressing thoughts. Since unpleasant thoughts tend to trigger other unpleasant thoughts, it was only a matter of time until thoughts about the accident returned. Non-depressed subjects, in contrast, tended to rely on positive thoughts as distractors, and as a result they were far more successful at avoiding unpleasant thoughts about the accident.

In two follow-up experiments, Wenzlaff et al. discovered that their depressed subjects knew that they would be more effective at suppressing unpleasant thoughts by focussing on positive thoughts instead, but they were relatively ineffective at doing so in part because they didn't have many positive thoughts to use as distractors. When the experimenters provided lists of positive, negative, and neutral distractor topics, depressed subjects made greater use of positive distractors, but they still tended to rely heavily on the less effective negative distractors.

This research suggests that depressed individuals become entangled in a downward spiral of negative thinking that is very difficult to break. They have many negative and unpleasant thoughts, and they dwell on those thoughts because they have few positive thoughts to use as distractors. To make matters worse, depressed people tend to remain in distressing situations and to surround themselves with other people who are unhappy or disapproving (Wenzlaff et al., 1988). Cognitive behavior therapy interrupts this downward spiral not only by providing positive self-statements that can be used as distractors but also by encouraging the person to get involved in satisfying and pleasant activities.

**Self-control.**    Most of the behavioral procedures reviewed so far lend themselves to self-administration. Thus, they can also be used to achieve a greater degree of self-control. We shall briefly review two behavioral techniques that are commonly used to help people become more effective at the self-regulation and control of behavior: biofeedback and environmental planning.

You may recall that we discussed biofeedback briefly in Chapter 4. The concept of biofeedback is relatively simple. Sensitive recording devices are used to record brain waves, blood pressure, and other bodily functions and this information is then fed back to the subject by means of auditory signals or visual displays so that the subject knows what a given part of his or her body is doing. In turn this enables the individual to gain some measure of self-control over bodily functions that were once thought automatic and hence not subject to learned control. As yet the full potentials of biofeedback are not known, but it has been used to enable patients to control brain waves associated with epileptic seizures and to reduce the number of attacks, reduce the frequency and duration of migraine headaches, lower heart rate and blood pressure, and exercise some measure of control over a wide range of other bodily functions (Blanchard & Epstein, 1978). Despite initial successes in dealing with a number of stress-related disorders, many questions remain concerning the range of use and long-range effectiveness of biofeedback training. Certainly it is no "miracle cure" (Andrasik & Holroyd, 1980; Roberts, 1985). However, when used in comprehensive treatment programs for dealing with maladaptive behaviors, it can be highly beneficial.

**environmental planning:**
self-control procedure in which an individual structures his or her environment to achieve positive goals

The self-control procedure of **environmental planning** focuses on changing the environmental cues that elicit specific maladaptive behaviors. For example, overeating is often influenced by a variety of physical and social cues that prompt eating even when the person is not hungry. Many people overeat to avoid wasting food. In social situations, they often eat high calorie desserts because other people are eating and enjoying them. An individual may develop a habit of eating and/or drinking while watching television. Stuart and Davis (1972) have shown that people trained to detect and avoid or alter maladaptive eating "cues" can reduce unnecessary food intake and weight gain.

Using a similar approach, Upper and Meredith (1970) reduced the smoking behavior of excessive smokers. Initially, people were asked to record their daily smoking rate. They then computed the average time between cigarettes—about fifteen minutes—and asked the clients to wear a small portable timer. The timer was set to buzz when the smoker's average time between cigarettes had elapsed,

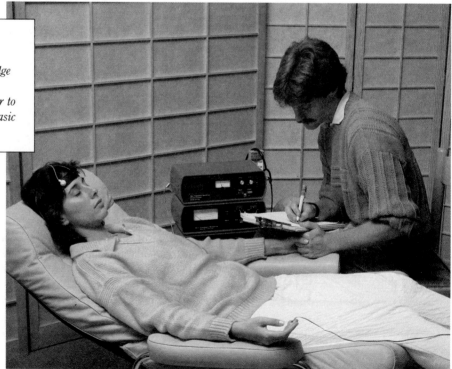

*Biofeedback helps the individual acquire physiological self-knowledge and, along with proper training, helps him or her to exert some control over basic physical functions.*

and the clients were instructed to smoke only after the timer had buzzed. With use, the buzzer replaced previous cues that had elicited smoking, such as the conclusion of a meal, conversation with a friend, or some tension-arousing experience. The interval on the timer was then gradually increased until smoking behavior was markedly reduced.

In closing the discussion of the behavioral approaches, it is important to note that combinations of these techniques are often used in therapy. It is a rare individual whose only problem is a phobic reaction or unassertive behavior. Sensitive assessment helps pinpoint the areas of maladaptive functioning; and the behavioral therapist uses the techniques that are best suited to the treatment of these various problems.

## Sex, Marital, Family, and Group Therapy

The therapies described thus far are directed at individuals. However, there are some forms of therapy that are directed at problems in interpersonal relationships, that treat a couple or family as a unit, or that deal with individuals in a group setting. In this section, we will concentrate first on three areas in which troubled relationships are at the center of maladaptive problems: sex therapy, marital therapy, and family therapy. We will then discuss individual therapy in a group setting.

**sex therapy:** therapy focusing on the treatment of sexual dysfunction

**Sex therapy.**    Masters and Johnson (1975) have concluded from their extensive research that some 50 percent of American married couples suffer from sexual dysfunctions. They consider such problems largely responsible for the high rates of marital dissatisfaction and divorce. **Sex therapy** refers to treatment for various forms of sexual dysfunction, such as impotence, orgasmic dysfunction, and premature ejaculation.

Although there are various approaches to sex therapy, the best known and most widely used is based on the pioneering work of Masters and Johnson (1970, 1975, 1976). Fundamental to this approach are the assumptions that (1) the sexual response is a natural function, (2) it is ordinarily possible to identify and remove the obstacles that are interfering with effective sexual functioning, and (3) the sexual partners should work together to eliminate the dysfunction. A thorough medical examination is required at the beginning of therapy to rule out the possibility that the dysfunction results from organic causes.

In actual therapy, the preceding assumptions can be roughly translated into the following steps and procedures. An initial period focuses on an analysis of the problem, an understanding of the therapy goals of the partners, and basic sex education, including information concerning the anatomy, physiology, and psychology of the sexual response. This initial period blends into a second stage focusing on sensual pleasure and improved communication between the partners. Prominent here is the use of sensate focus. This involves learning to experience sensual pleasure in caressing each other's bodies and genitals while temporarily refraining from intercourse. Sensate focus serves to remove stereotypes of what sexual interaction "should be," to foster nonverbal communication and natural sexual responsiveness, and to alleviate anxiety. Emphasis is also placed on techniques for improving verbal communication between the partners, which leads to better understanding and greater intimacy between the couple. This, in turn, helps to release their sexual feelings toward one another.

This second period overlaps with and blends into the final period of therapy, which focuses on maintaining and improving open communication between the partners and utilizes a series of sexual exercises that emphasize pleasure and intimacy. In this last part of therapy, specific techniques may be used to deal with the sexual dysfunction. The data reported by Masters and Johnson suggest that their treatment of sexual dysfunctions is highly effective.

**marital therapy:** therapy focusing on the marital relationship

**Marital therapy.**    The large number of people seeking assistance with problems centering around their marriage have made **marital therapy** an important field of counseling. Typically, the marital partners are seen together, and therapy focuses on clarifying and improving their interactions and relationships.

Attempts to achieve this goal include a wide range of concepts and procedures. Most therapists emphasize mutual need gratification, social role expectations, communication patterns, and similar interpersonal factors. Not surprisingly, happily married couples tend to differ from unhappily married couples in that they talk more to each other, keep channels of communication open, make more use of nonverbal techniques of communication, and show more sensitivity to each other's feelings, expectations, and needs.

Often faulty communication and role problems play havoc with marital relationships. The following example from Satir (1967) is instructive:

HUSBAND: She never comes up to me and kisses me. I am always the one to make the overtures.
THERAPIST: Is this the way you see yourself behaving with your husband?
WIFE: Yes, I would say he is the demonstrative one. I didn't know he wanted me to make the overtures.
THERAPIST: Have you told your wife that you would like this from her—more open demonstration of affection?
HUSBAND: Well, no, you'd think she'd know.
WIFE: No, how would I know? You always said you didn't like aggressive women.
HUSBAND: I don't, I don't like *dominating women.*
WIFE: Well, I thought you meant women who make the overtures. How am I to know what you want?
THERAPIST: You'd have a better idea if he had been able to tell you. (pp. 72–73).

One of the difficulties in marital therapy is the intense emotional involvement of the marital partners, which makes it difficult for them to perceive and accept the realities of their relationship. Often, wives can see clearly what is "wrong" with their husbands but not with themselves, while husbands usually have remarkable "insight" into their wives' flaws but not their own. To help correct this problem, videotape recordings have been used increasingly to recapture crucial moments of intense interaction between the marital partners. Watching these tapes helps the couple become more aware of the nature of their interactions. Thus, the husband may realize for the first time that he tries to dominate rather than listen to his wife and consider her needs and expectations. A wife may realize that she is continually nagging and undermining her husband's feelings of worth and esteem.

*Frequently, members of a family share a problem, of which each person is one part. In such cases, group therapy may provide the necessary catalyst for resolving the interpersonal conflicts.*

**family therapy:** form of therapy focusing on relationships within the family

**Family therapy.**    **Family therapy** closely parallels the pattern of marital therapy but involves a larger and more complex group system. A pioneer in the field of family therapy (Haley, 1962) has described the problem.

> Psychopathology in the individual is a product of the way he deals with his intimate relations, the way they deal with him, and the way other family members involve him in their relations with each other. Further, the appearance of symptomatic behavior in an individual is necessary for the continued function of a particular family system. Therefore changes in the individual can occur only if the family system changes. (p. 70)

This viewpoint led to an important concept in the field of psychotherapy, namely, that the problem of the "identified patient" is often only a symptom of a larger family problem. A careful study of the family of a disturbed child may reveal that the child is merely reflecting the pathology of the family. If the child is seen alone in therapy, he or she may be able to work out some of the problems. However, when the child goes back home, it will be to the same pathological circumstances that led to the problems in the first place. As a result, most family therapists share the view that the family—and not simply the designated person—should be directly involved in therapy. The family, in this view, is a system—a set of actors whose behaviors are interdependent, so that if any person changes there is a "ripple effect" throughout the entire system.

**problematic alliances:** close bonds between some family members that are disruptive to the family as a whole

Family therapists have noted several ways in which family dynamics can lead to psychological problems. The first is **problematic alliances.** An alliance in a family is a special bond. People who are allies "stick up for" each other, much as international allies do. Family alliances can be a problem when they disrupt the orderly functioning of the family system. For example, if father and daughter have a stronger alliance than father and mother, then the parents will not be able to function as a unit to make decisions about the daughter. A family therapist in this case might try to strengthen the parental alliance.

A second problem frequently encountered by family therapists is **problematic role relationships.** Just as in a play, a role is a part a person plays in a social system. In traditional American families, for example, the mother plays the role of nurturant caregiver while the father plays the role of wage earner. In some families, a child may play the role of scapegoat. The scapegoat is the person who "gets the heat" for all the family's problems. Unfortunately, this can lead to problems for the scapegoat, who may accept and even foster this role as the only way to get attention or to avoid other, more threatening problems that might erupt in the family.

**problematic role relationships:** roles played by family members that are disruptive or maladaptive for the family as a whole

A final problem is **conflicting system demands.** In this situation, family members are subject to the pushes and pulls of more than one family system. When one family demands one thing and another family demands another, the individual experiences stress and a conflict of loyalty that may lead to the development of maladaptive behavior. A married couple, for example, may find themselves torn between the expectations of grandparents, parents, in-laws, and their own children. Children of divorce may find themselves torn between their parents; if one (or both) parents remarry, the children may have to cope with conflicting demands from stepfamilies, as well.

**conflicting system demands:** incompatible requirements arising from two or more family systems that cause significant stress

When faced with problems such as these, family therapists will involve the entire family in the therapeutic process. Typically, family members attend therapy sessions together. Almost all individual therapies can be adapted for use with families. For example, some family therapists believe that the most effective way to help a family deal with a problem is to help the members gain insight into problems in the family system. These therapists will try to help family members become aware of such problems as scapegoating and inappropriate alliances so that they can choose more effective ways of dealing with conflicts and problems in the family. Other family therapists take a more directive and action-oriented approach. They are likely to point out maladaptive behaviors that occur during the therapy sessions, suggest ways in which family members can more effectively relate to one another, and sometimes even assign "homework" exercises.

In addition, some forms of therapy have been developed specifically for use with families. One of the best known of these is conjoint family therapy developed by Virginia Satir (1967, 1972). This form of therapy emphasizes improving faulty communications, interactions, and relationships among family members, and fostering a family system that better meets the needs of family members. You will find an example of Satir's therapeutic approach in the preceding section on marital therapy.

**Group therapy.**  We have seen that when members of a group have problems relating to each other, the most effective approach to therapy may be to treat the entire group as a unit. However, **group therapy** can also be used effectively as a supplement to individual therapy: on some days clients meet individually with the therapist, and on other days they meet with the therapist in a small group. Individual

**group therapy:** psychotherapy with two or more individuals at the same time

# Insight

problems such as manipulativeness, shyness, and excessive competitiveness will often become evident in the group setting. By exploring these behaviors as they occur, the therapist together with the other group members can more effectively help the person change.

Quite often, a therapist will convene a group of individuals sharing the same problem. For example, alcoholics, victims of physical or sexual abuse, people with eating disorders, and people grieving over the loss of a loved one can often be helped more effectively in a group setting with others sharing their problem. Sometimes it is valuable to discover that you are not the only one with your problem and to learn that others have developed more effective ways of coping with the same problem. Moreover, it is sometimes easier to see maladaptive behavior in others than in ourselves, and so therapy group members can sensitize us to our ineffective ways of coping.

Another form of group therapy is the **encounter group.** Encounter groups are of two distinct types, depending on their focus: (1) treating maladaptive behavior, such as encounter groups for juvenile delinquents, and (2) helping normal persons learn more about themselves, develop more satisfying interpersonal relationships, and open pathways to personal growth (see Insight, p. 245).

Usually an encounter group consists of six to twelve members, including the group leader who is also a participant. Encounter groups emphasize the open and honest communication of feelings and the constructive resolution of confrontations. This requires prompt and sincere feedback from other group members. Leaders serve as models by expressing their own feelings openly and honestly and accepting

**encounter group:** small group designed to provide an intensive interpersonal experience focusing on feelings and group interactions

hostility or other negative feelings directed toward them without becoming defensive. It is their responsibility to see that confrontations among group members are resolved in a constructive way. In general, the group leader serves as a resource person when the group needs guidance or comes to an impasse.

The most important function of the group leader is that of establishing a climate of "psychological safety" in which the members feel free to lower their defenses, express their feelings, and try out new ways of interacting with others. When such a psychological climate is coupled with the intensive give-and-take of group interaction, the possibilities for increased awareness, understanding, and personal growth are greatly enhanced. In order to foster a climate of psychological safety, the group leader encourages members to respond with descriptive rather than evaluative feedback. An example of a descriptive response would be, "When you said that, it made me feel uncomfortable and a little bit nervous," rather than the evaluative response, "Only a real jerk would make a statement like that." In group interaction the emphasis is upon present feelings and interactions—not on the past or future. Rogers (1970) has described the actual sequence of events which typically occur in encounter groups (see Insight, p. 247).

## SELF-HELP GROUPS

To this point in our discussion, we have focussed on counseling and psychotherapy provided by trained professionals. However, mental health resources are simply not adequate to provide treatment for everyone who needs or wants it. For example, in Chapter 6 we saw that in any given month 15 percent of adult Americans (approximately 30 million people) suffer from one or more psychological disorders. Almost half of those people are suffering from an anxiety-based disorder, while 10 million suffer from some form of depression and 5 million suffer from alcoholism.

Increasingly, self-help mutual support groups are being formed to provide a source of support and help for people faced with life crises. According to recent estimates, there are presently more than 500,000 self-help groups with more than 15 million members, and the Department of Health and Human Services predicts that these numbers will double in the next decade (Riordan & Beggs, 1987).

What are self-help groups, and how do they differ from traditional therapy groups? Self-help groups are small voluntary groups typically composed of people sharing a common problem and providing mutual assistance for each other (Katz, 1981). One of the most famous self-help groups is Alcoholics Anonymous, but there are also self-help groups for parents whose children have died or are chronically ill, divorced persons, adolescents, older people, overeaters, AIDS victims, former mental patients, people suffering from depression or anxiety—the list goes on and on. These groups provide two extremely important resources to their members: social support (through the creation of a caring community) and increased coping skills (by providing information and by sharing solutions to common problems).

Unlike therapy groups, self-help groups often reach individuals who are still able to cope effectively with life stress but who feel that their resources are being strained. Moreover, self-help groups usually focus on one specific problem such as addiction, bereavement, or chronic illness. While therapy groups rely upon counseling, self-

# Insight

---

## Events in Encounter Groups

Just what is it that goes on in an encounter group? On the basis of his work with such groups, Rogers (1970) has delineated a typical pattern of events.

1. *Milling around.* As the group leader makes it clear that group members have unusual freedom but also responsibility for the direction of the group, there tends to be an initial period of confusion, frustration, awkward silences, and "cocktail-party talk"—polite talk intermixed with questions about the group.

2. *Resistance to personal expression or exploration.* Initially, members tend to portray only their "public selves"; only fearfully and gradually do they begin to reveal aspects of the private self.

3. *Description of negative feelings.* The first expression of feelings concerning the here-and-now interaction in the group tends to involve negative feelings directed toward the group leader or other group members.

4. *Expression and exploration of personally meaningful material.* The event most likely to occur next is for some member to take the gamble of revealing some intimate information—perhaps a seemingly hopeless problem of communication with a spouse. Apparently this member has come to realize that this is "his" or "her" group, and he or she can help shape its direction; apparently also the fact that negative feelings have been expressed without catastrophic results tends to foster a climate of trust.

5. *The expression of immediate interpersonal feelings.* This may occur at any point. It involves the explicit expression of feelings, positive or negative, experienced at the moment by one member toward another. Each of these immediate expressions of feeling is usually explored in the increasing climate of trust developing in the group.

6. *Development of a healing capacity and the beginning of change.* Some group members show a spontaneous ability to respond to the pain and suffering of others in a therapeutic way—thus paving the way for change. This healing capacity may extend beyond the regular group sessions, as when a few members remain after the session to offer support and therapeutic aid to another member who they sense is experiencing serious difficulties.

7. *Dropping of facades, confrontations, and feedback.* As time goes on, the group finds it increasingly unacceptable for any member to hide behind a mask or facade, refusing to reveal the self to the group. In a general sense, the group demands that each individual be his or her true self. This may result in a direct confrontation, often negative in tone, between two group members. In this type of basic encounter, individuals come into more direct, honest, and closer contact than is customary in ordinary life. This is likely to provide individuals with a good deal of totally new feedback concerning themselves and their effects on others.

8. *Expression of positive feelings and behavior change.* Rogers states that "an inevitable part of the group process seems to be that when feelings are expressed and can be accepted in a relationship, then a great deal of closeness and positive feelings results. Thus as the sessions proceed, an increasing feeling of warmth and group spirit and trust is built up, not out of positive attitudes only but out of a realness which includes both positive and negative feeling" (pp. 34–35). He concludes that, while there are certain risks, there is also great therapeutic potential.

help groups rely primarily on sharing information and advice and providing support. Finally, therapy groups are almost always led by trained professionals, while self-help groups are usually organized and led by nonprofessionals.

Are self-help groups effective? Some certainly are: Alcoholics Anonymous is generally considered to be the treatment of choice for alcoholics. The sheer number

*Discussion groups amongst children and adolescents can offer valuable opportunities to explore confusions and fears before the children become overwhelmed.*

of self-help groups certainly attests to their appeal. Research studies that rely on self-reports by members also typically support these groups (Riordan & Beggs, 1987). Although only a few studies have used more objective measures of effectiveness, these studies too have found that self-help groups can be effective (Galanter, 1984; Videka-Sherman, 1982). However, much more research is needed before it will be possible to determine with confidence the role that self-help groups can play in fostering mental health.

It is worth noting that for the most part professionals' distrust and skepticism of self-help groups has disappeared; attention is now being given to ways in which the self-help movement can be used effectively as one part of a more comprehensive mental health care delivery system. Toward that end, former Surgeon General Koop (who himself benefitted from a self-help group after his son died in a mountain-climbing accident) stated that he would foster "a smooth relationship between the orthodox, formal, well-recognized health care delivery system" and self-help mutual aid groups (Riessman & Gartner, 1987).

## SUMMARY

Many people consult mental health professionals for help in coping more effectively with a wide variety of problems. Although the decision to seek psychological assistance is sometimes difficult, counseling and psychotherapy can indeed be helpful. In this chapter we have explored some of the most successful techniques and procedures used by mental health professionals as well as the more recent growth of self-help groups.

Psychologists and counselors most often work either in an institutional setting (usually as part of a psychiatric or psychological clinic) or in a private office (either independently or as part of a group practice). Although therapists use a variety of specific procedures, in general there are three phases in the therapeutic process. During the *assessment phase* the therapist tries to assess the problem as well as the person's life circumstances. During the *feedback phase* the therapist reframes the problem in a more productive way. During the *implementation phase* the therapist and client work together to solve the problem.

Some therapists take an *action-oriented approach* to therapy, working actively with their clients to solve problems. Such therapists also frequently use *directive therapy*, giving advice, suggesting solutions, and even assigning homework exercises. Other therapists prefer a more *insight-oriented approach* in which a good deal of time is devoted to understanding the person's background and the way that the maladaptive behavior developed. These therapists often use *nondirective therapy*, rarely giving advice or suggestions but instead helping their clients to work out their own solutions to problems. *Counseling* refers to relatively short-term, action-oriented intervention focussed on a particular problem. *Psychotherapy* is usually more prolonged and more wide-ranging. Many therapists take different approaches with different clients, and some take different approaches at different stages of the therapeutic process.

One major *psychological assessment* technique is the interview. However, interviewer biases, values, motives, and inexperience can distort the results of an interview and so many mental health professionals supplement the interview with additional assessment techniques such as psychological tests and direct observation.

Psychological tests include intelligence tests, *personality inventories* (such as the MMPI or the CPI), *projective tests* (such as the Rorschach inkblot test), aptitude and ability tests, and tests of attitudes and values. The effectiveness of many of these tests, however, depends on the extent to which the person is aware of his or her own thoughts and behavior. Moreover, some of them are open to distortion from such things as *social desirability*. All of them emphasize consistencies in behavior across time and situations.

Direct observation of people in different settings (real or simulated) allows the mental health professional to observe behavior directly and to note the extent to which behavior changes from one setting to another. By pooling this information with the results of interviews and tests, it is often possible to arrive at an integrated picture of the way a person copes with stress in his or her life.

There are three major approaches to psychotherapy. Psychoanalytic therapy derives primarily from the theories of Sigmund Freud. It utilizes the techniques of *free association, interpretation,* and analysis of *transference.* Free association provides insight into the unconscious meaning of ideas and objects and also increases the likelihood that repressed material will become conscious. The therapist can then interpret what the person says or does in order to suggest new ways of understanding the client's thoughts or actions. To the extent that the client transfers feelings about other people onto the therapist, it is possible to explore the ways in which this irrational behavior contributes to other problems in the person's life. Though classical psychoanalysis is a complex, time-consuming and expensive procedure, contemporary psychoanalytic therapists often use briefer versions of analysis.

Humanistic-existential therapies focus on people's perception of the world and experience. In Rogers' *person-centered therapy,* the therapist tries to demonstrate by an attitude of caring and unconditional acceptance that the client is a prized and valued individual regardless of his or her behavior. In this way, the therapist attempts to create an environment in which the client feels safe in exploring and talking about feelings and thoughts that are normally suppressed. With gains in self-understanding and self-trust, the individual is likely to become a more fully-functioning person.

*Existential therapy* is directed toward helping people find a pattern of values that will give meaning to their lives and to work out more effective ways of "being-in-the-world." Most such therapists challenge their clients with questions about the meaning and purpose of their lives, and also emphasize the importance of what their clients are choosing to do and to be in the immediate moment. The emphasis in existential therapy is on making choices and taking responsibility for one's life.

*Gestalt therapy* is often used in group settings, though the emphasis is on the individual. The goal is to help people to become more perceptive and to enrich their experiences. As a result, clients are helped to become more aware of aspects of themselves and their world that they had blocked out; with these new insights, and by correcting inaccuracies in their views of themselves and others, people are better able to cope effectively with problems of living.

Most behavioral therapies are devoted to directly modifying maladaptive behaviors; thus behavior therapies tend to be directive, action-oriented, and focussed on a narrow set of maladaptive behaviors. *Systematic desensitization* is a procedure that is often used to reduce fears and phobias. The client is taught how to relax and then learns to respond with relaxation in a set (or *hierarchy)* of situations that previously aroused fear or anxiety. *Assertiveness training* requires that the client identify those situations in which he or she is unable to be assertive, to identify more appropriate behaviors for those situations, to practice those behaviors in the therapeutic setting and then to transfer the new learning to real-life situations. *Contingency management* uses positive reinforcers (such as money, food, tokens, praise) to strengthen adaptive behavior. *Behavioral contracting* is a useful behavioral technique for situations where the objective is to change a wide spectrum of behaviors or where the desired behavior is complex. A written or oral agreement spells out the behaviors that must occur before the person can earn reinforcers.

Recently, many behaviorally-oriented psychologists have begun emphasizing the importance of cognitive events and self-control in their approaches to treatment. *Rational-Emotive Therapy* (RET), for example, attempts to change irrational and unreasonable beliefs that lead to ineffective and self-defeating behaviors. By drawing attention to such beliefs and challenging their validity, the therapist tries to help the client to adopt more appropriate beliefs that will lead to more effective and adaptive behaviors. Aaron Beck's approach to depression is similar, though here the client is helped to discover for himself or herself the degree to which his or her beliefs and expectations are irrational and self-defeating. Recent research indicates that such cognitive therapies can be effective in breaking the vicious circle in which

*Not everyone who wants or needs counseling or therapy is able to get it. In response to this excess need, in recent years thousands of self-help groups have developed that provide caring and supportive environments for the group members.*

depressed people find themselves. These techniques, together with biofeedback and *environmental planning,* can dramatically increase the extent to which behavior is brought under self-control.

Some treatment approaches deal with more than one person at a time. *Sex therapy* often involves both partners simultaneously working together to increase communication, pleasure, and intimacy. *Marital therapy* also typically involves both husband and wife meeting together with a therapist in an effort to improve their interactions and their relationship. *Family therapy* takes this approach one step farther by involving all members of a family in therapy sessions where it is possible to examine *problematic alliances, problematic role relationships,* and *conflicting system demands.* Quite often therapists working with individuals will supplement individual therapy with *group therapy;* this is particularly useful where the individuals share a particular problem or where the problem involves relationships with other people. *Encounter groups* are a particular form of therapy group in which the emphasis is on present feelings and interactions; such groups have been used to treat maladaptive behavior and to contribute to the psychological and personal growth of persons without behavior disorders as well.

All of these approaches to therapy are part of the professional mental health care delivery system. However, the incidence of maladaptive behavior is so great that not everyone who wants or needs counseling or therapy is able to get it. To fill the gap, thousands of self-help groups have arisen in which lay people provide a caring and supportive environment and helpful information to people who share a particular problem. Though research data are modest, the evidence suggests that such groups can indeed be helpful, and efforts are now underway to integrate such groups into a more comprehensive health care delivery system.

## KEY TERMS

assessment phase (219)
feedback phase (219)
implementation phase (219)
action-oriented approach (220)
directive therapy (220)
insight-oriented approach (220)
nondirective therapy (220)
psychological assessment (223)
personality inventory (225)
projective test (226)
rating scales (226)
social desirability (226)
validity (228)
reliability (228)
standardization (228)
counseling (228)
psychotherapy (228)
free association (229)
interpretation (229)
transference (229)

person-centered therapy (231)
existential therapy (232)
Gestalt therapy (233)
behavioral therapies (234)
systematic desensitization (234)
hierarchy (234)
assertiveness training (236)
contingency management (237)
behavioral contracting (237)
Rational-Emotive Therapy (RET) (238)
environmental planning (240)
sex therapy (241)
marital therapy (242)
family therapy (243)
problematic alliances (243)
problematic role relationships (244)
conflicting system demands (244)
group therapy (244)
encounter group (245)

# Adjusting to Challenges Over a Lifetime

# CHAPTER EIGHT

# Development and Adjustment in Childhood and Adolescence

*How did it come about that a man born poor, losing his mother at birth and soon deserted by his father, afflicted with a painful and humiliating disease, left to wander for twelve years among alien cities and conflicting faiths, repudiated by society . . . and driven from place to place as a dangerous rebel, suspected of crime and insanity, and seeing, in his last months, the apotheosis of his greatest enemy—how did it come about that this man, after his death . . . transformed education . . . inspired the Romantic movement and the French Revolution, influenced the philosophy of Kant and Schopenhauer, the poems of Wordsworth, Byron and Shelley, the socialism of Marx, the ethics of Tolstoi, and, altogether, had more effect on posterity than any other writer or thinker of that eighteenth century in which writers were more influential than they had ever been before?*

*Rousseau and Revolution* (Durant & Durant, 1967, p. 3)

THIS puzzling question is posed by Will and Ariel Durant as an introduction to their book describing the life and influence of the eighteenth-century philosopher Jean Jacques Rousseau. Although not all historians would evaluate the influence of Rousseau quite so highly, there is no question that his impact has been immense. Yet, it seems that the conditions of Rousseau's life would have prevented him from having such a major effect on history. How was he able to adjust so effectively to the circumstances in which he found himself—not only to adapt but to thrive as a human being?

Although the challenges Rousseau faced were far greater than you or I are likely to encounter, nonetheless each of us also has to adjust and adapt to the world in which we find ourselves. Though each of us must cope with some unique adjustive demands in the course of our lives, other adjustive demands are quite common at certain points in the life cycle. All human infants must cope with a common set of adjustive demands, just as all adolescents must come to terms with a somewhat different set of demands. In this chapter and the next, we will explore the kinds of adjustments that typically are required of all human beings at different points in the life cycle. In the process, we will discuss the ways we develop the uniquely human ability to use self-direction to adapt and cope with these and other adjustive demands. We will also see how it is that some people, by virtue of their life experiences, are better able than others to cope effectively with the stress that they encounter.

We begin by looking at the overall process of development and the changes that occur as each of us grows toward personal maturity. Then we will look more closely at healthy as opposed to faulty development and consider the family conditions that tend to foster and hinder healthy development. The remainder of the chapter is

As youngsters we identify with adults and try to be like them. Even within this role-playing, children reveal some unique characteristics that point to their future self-direction and independence.

devoted to an examination of the most important adjustive challenges that occur and the coping skills that develop during infancy, the preschool years, the school years and adolescence. In the next chapter we will explore development, adjustment, and adaptation during the years from young adulthood to old age. Although we cannot as yet provide a complete answer to the Durants' question, "How did it come about . . . ?", we can go a long way toward understanding how most human beings learn to adjust and adapt effectively throughout the course of their lives.

## THE PROCESS OF DEVELOPMENT

**development:** the predictable process of growth and change throughout the lifespan

In contrast to other animals who have "built-in" patterns of behavior and who mature rapidly, the human infant begins life as a helpless creature with few built-in coping mechanisms. A key characteristic of the human life cycle is the relatively long period of infancy and childhood, during which the body grows toward maturity and the individual begins to acquire the information and competencies needed to cope effectively with the world. This process of growth and change throughout the life span is called **development.** As we will see, the process of development not only prepares human beings to cope more effectively with adjustive demands, but in itself it also requires an extraordinary amount of adjustment and adaptation.

## Developmental Tasks

**developmental tasks:**
competencies to be mastered
during a particular stage of
development

Although the process of development continues throughout the entire life span, at each stage of development each of us must master certain **developmental tasks** or competencies if we are to become competent, effective, and well-adjusted. For example, learning to walk and talk are major tasks of infancy, while establishing a mature sense of identity and acquiring the intellectual, emotional, and social competencies needed for adulthood are key tasks of adolescence (see Table 8.1 p. 259).

If these tasks are not mastered at the appropriate stage, the individual will find it more difficult to master later developmental tasks. For example, a young child who is overly dependent on his or her parents will be at a disadvantage when entering nursery school or kindergarten. The school age child who does not form any close friendships will miss an important opportunity to acquire experience and skill in interpersonal relations. While there is opportunity to overcome these liabilities at later points in life, it is important to note that until these developmental tasks are satisfactorily resolved, the child will have greater difficulty in coping with new adjustive demands and new developmental tasks than would otherwise be the case.

## Trends Toward Personal Maturity

Throughout the course of human development, as each individual confronts and deals with the various developmental tasks, the trend is toward increasing personal maturity, responsible self-direction, and the ability to participate in and contribute to society. Though the details of these changes differ from one society to another and from one person to another, certain characteristic trends toward personal maturity appear to be universal; in one form or another, they can be seen in any society, primitive or advanced and in the life of every person.

**Dependence to self-direction.**   One of the most obvious progressions toward maturity is from dependence in infancy and childhood to independence and self-direction during adulthood. Associated with greater self-direction is the development of a clear sense of personal identity and the acquisition of information, competencies, and values. In our society, this includes enough freedom from family and other social groups to be individuals in our own right.

**Impulsiveness to self-control.**   Infants are interested primarily in obtaining immediate gratification for their wants. Over time they must learn to control impulses and desires, delay immediate gratification in the interest of long-range goals, and learn to cope effectively with the inevitable hurts, disappointments, and frustrations of living. In other words, they must begin to exercise self-control and become less impulsive.

**Ignorance to knowledge.**   Although infants are born in an apparent state of ignorance, they rapidly begin to acquire information about themselves and their world. With time, this information is organized into a stable frame of reference for guiding behavior. To be adequate, this frame of reference must be realistic, relevant to the

**TABLE 8.1   Developmental Tasks of Childhood and Adolescence**

| Developmental tasks in | Physical development | Cognitive development | Personality and social development |
|---|---|---|---|
| **Infancy** | Learning to sit up, stand, walk, and run. | Learning to differentiate oneself from the rest of the world. Learning to distinguish thoughts from reality. Becoming aware that objects continue to exist when they are out of sight. | Forming a secure attachment to a care-giver. Developing a sense of trust and security. Beginning to develop a sense of autonomy, independence, and self-reliance. |
| **The preschool years** | Gaining greater mastery over gross physical and motor skills. | Becoming skilled at symbolic thinking and the use of language. Beginning to develop a sense of morality. | Continuing to develop a mature feeling of autonomy. Developing a sense of initiative. Developing and expanding relationships with peers. |
| **The school years** | Refining and perfecting fine motor skills. | Becoming less egocentric and more effective at logical thinking. Increasing mastery over symbolic thought including acquisition of basic verbal and mathematical skills (reading, writing, arithmetic). | Adjusting to the school environment. Developing more complex social skills and more mature friendships. Developing a sense of industry, adequacy, and competence in the adult world. |
| **Adolescence** | Adapting to rapid and extreme body changes (growth, puberty). | Learning to use abstract ideas and developing a set of ethical principles. | Achieving a measure of independence from the family and from peer groups. Developing opposite-sex friendships and more intimate friendships. Developing a sense of personal identity. |

kinds of problems the individual will face, and one in which the individual has faith. Also, this knowledge base needs to be flexible, so that it can be modified by new experiences.

**Incompetence to competence.**   The entire pre-adult period from infancy through adolescence is directed toward the mastery of the intellectual, emotional, and social competencies needed for adulthood. The individual acquires skills in problem solving and decision making, and learns to control and use his or her emotions, deal with others, and establish satisfying relationships. These competencies help prepare the individual for the various sexual, marital, occupational, and parental roles of adulthood.

**Self-centered to other-centered.**   Infants are concerned almost exclusively with their own needs and wants. However, with time, they normally develop an expanding understanding and concern for the needs of others as well. This includes the ability to give love to significant others and to be concerned about and involved with people in their community and society.

**Amoral to moral.**    The newborn infant is amoral, in the sense that he or she has no concept of "right" or "wrong." Very early, however, the infant learns that certain forms of behavior are approved or "good," while others are disapproved or "bad." With time, the growing individual gradually learns a pattern of value assumptions that operate as inner guides of behavior—the conscience or superego. Initially, the individual may accept these values blindly but, with increasing maturity, he or she learns to appraise them and work out a personalized set of values.

## Maturation and Learning

maturation: growth of an organism that occurs primarily due to the passage of time

It is perhaps tempting to think that all these developments toward maturity occur solely as a result of **maturation;** that is, the child becomes more like an adult simply as a result of some preprogrammed genetic plan that unfolds over time. However, psychologists now know that a child's development toward maturity is affected greatly by learning and experience; that is, as we watch a child become more like an adult, we see the results of a continual process of adjustment and adaptation. In that sense, it is fair to say that human development is a prolonged adjustment to the world in which we find ourselves, an adjustment that does not proceed automatically over time but rather proceeds as we learn about and gain experience with the world (Seefeldt, 1984).

Since development toward maturity is not automatic but rather depends on learning and experience, it follows that some individuals are likely to adjust and adapt more effectively than others. In the next section of the chapter, we will look more closely at healthy and faulty development and at the family conditions that tend to favor healthy development.

## HEALTHY AND FAULTY DEVELOPMENT

In studying differences in development, questions arise concerning (1) the problem of defining "healthy" development, (2) the nature or forms of "faulty" development, and (3) the conditions conducive to healthy development.

## The Problem of Defining Healthy Development

Defining and describing healthy development is a more difficult task than it might initially appear. We can describe three general approaches that researchers have employed in trying to solve the problem of defining healthy development.

**"Normal" as healthy.**    This view considers development as healthy when there is no apparent physical or psychological pathology and no marked deviation from the group average. In essence, healthy development is development that does not deviate from the norm. In terms of the trends toward personal maturity, a healthy person would be about average in self-direction and ability to exercise self-control, have an adequate frame of reference for viewing the world, be as competent as most other people, show a reasonable amount of concern for others, and be as moral as most other people.

This approach, however, is not always adequate in dealing with personality development. Consider the case of an adolescent, for example, who is making passing grades at school, getting along reasonably well with classmates and teachers, and, while showing no indications of delinquency or maladjustment, is just drifting along, using only a fraction of a superior intellectual ability. This may not be "sick" but is it healthy?

**"Optimal" as healthy.**    According to this perspective, healthy development can be defined as a process leading to complete physical, mental, and social well-being. Thus, healthy development goes beyond the average or norm to the maximal utilization of talents and the fulfillment of potentials. From this perspective, a healthy person should be fully independent, self-directed, and self-controlled; extremely knowledgeable yet open to new experiences; intellectually, emotionally, and socially competent; and both other-centered and moral.

The concept of optimal development is a meaningful one, but since it defines "healthy" as "ideal," it follows that virtually no one can be considered to have experienced healthy development. Moreover, although you have just read about basic trends toward personal maturity that should mark healthy development, those things that people regard as desirable and optimal inevitably reflect the customs, demands, beliefs, and values of the larger society as well as the personal beliefs and values of the person making the judgment. The quiet, polite little boy never expressing anger was admired in the Victorian era. Today, he might be regarded as inhibited. Similarly, as educational procedures improve, the intellectual development that is normal for a six-year-old today might be considered inadequate fifty years from now. Thus, we will need much more information about human potentials and needs before we can use "optimal development" as a measure of whether an individual's psychological development is indeed "healthy."

**"Effective" as healthy.**    A third approach to defining healthy development, and the one we will adopt in this book, builds on the principles of psychological adjustment and adaptation that were developed in earlier chapters. From this perspective, healthy development is that which allows the individual to cope with and adapt effectively to the challenges of modern living. As we have seen repeatedly, adjustment is considered to be effective if the person's behavior meets the short- and long-term demands of the situation, the action meets the individual's needs, and the action is compatible with the well-being of others. If a person is sufficiently self-directed, self-controlled, knowledgeable, competent, other-centered, and moral to be able to cope effectively with the normal adjustive demands of life, then we can say that the person's development has been "healthy."

*Whether from a brother, sister, or parent, studies indicate that to the developing child, nothing is more important than unconditional love and acceptance.*

### Psychological Conditions that Foster Healthy Development

Throughout life, people have to deal with a variety of developmental tasks. By coping with those demands, most people grow toward greater personal maturity and effectiveness. What kinds of family conditions tend to foster this kind of healthy development?

**Emotional warmth and acceptance.**   An atmosphere of love and acceptance is an important factor in healthy personality development. One of the first comprehensive studies of child-rearing practices concluded that the most crucial and pervasive of all the influences exerted in the home was the love and warmth expressed by the parents (Sears, Maccoby & Levin, 1957).

Later studies supported this conclusion, demonstrating a close relationship between parental love and acceptance and the development of such traits as self-esteem, self-reliance, independence, trust and self-control. As well, many conditions that might otherwise impair development—such as a physical handicap, poverty, or harsh discipline—may be neutralized if the child feels loved and accepted. In short, children who experience a warm and accepting home environment not only enjoy a less stressful childhood but are better equipped to cope effectively with stress when it arises later in life.

**Effective structure and discipline.**   A clearly structured environment—which is orderly and consistent and provides the child with knowledge of what is expected, and acceptable, and what will cause disapproval or punishment—appears to foster healthy development and effective adjustment later in life. Three elements of structuring seem particularly important: (1) clearly defined standards and limits, so that children understand what goals, procedures, and conduct are approved; (2) adequately defined roles for both older and younger members of the family, so that children know what is expected of both themselves and others; and (3) established methods of handling children that encourage desired behavior, discourage misbehavior, and deal with infractions when they occur. Of course the kind and amount of structure in the environment must be tailored to each child's age, needs, and abilities. An environment that helps one child develop and maintain desirable behavior patterns may make another child resentful and rebellious and still another insecure and withdrawn.

Lack of structure and discipline and too much permissiveness tend to produce a spoiled, demanding, and inconsiderate child—and often an insecure and unhappy one. Overly severe restraints and punishment, on the other hand, tend to foster fear of the punisher, reduced initiative and spontaneity, and a lack of trust in authority figures. In either case, children raised under these conditions not only experience greater stress while they are growing up but also are likely to be less well equipped for coping with other kinds of stress.

**Encouragement of competence and self-confidence.**    Usually we take it for granted that a child needs help in learning to read, but we may not realize that a child also needs guidance in learning what is worth striving for, what is true and real, and what is right. At the same time, children need help in acquiring the intellectual, emotional, and social competencies needed to anticipate and meet the demands that will be made upon them.

Children also need to succeed and to have their successes recognized. One need only observe a child's eager request to "Watch me!" as he or she demonstrates some new achievement to understand the importance of success and recognition in the development of competence and self-confidence.

**Helping children meet challenges.**    While parents strive to protect their children from unnecessary hurt and trauma, they may handicap their children if they keep them from seeking out and coping with new experiences. In studies of infant, child, and adolescent development, Lois Murphy (1962) and her associates (for example, Murphy & Moriarty, 1976) have emphasized the need for such experiences.

> Over and over again we saw how the impact of a new challenge intensified the child's awareness of himself; his capacity to meet such a challenge enhances his pleasure, his sense of adequacy, and his pride. Through the successive experiences of spontaneous mastery of new demands and utilizing new opportunities for gratification the child extends and verifies his identity as one who can manage certain aspects of the environment. Through his coping experiences the child discovers and measures himself, and develops his own perception of who and what he is and in time may become. We can say that the child creates his identity through his efforts in coming to terms with the environment in his own personal way. (Murphy, 1962, p. 374)

In other words, facing and coping with challenges is essential to healthy development. It contributes to a sense of self-awareness, competence, and personal identity. Inevitably, learning to cope with new experiences leads to occasional failures. However, with few exceptions, Murphy and her colleagues found that parental support and encouragement help the child to cope with those failures and to maintain healthy development.

**Appropriate role models.**    As we saw in Chapter 2, research has shown that much human learning occurs through the observation of models. In their efforts at explicit instruction, parents often fail to realize how much guidance they are unwittingly providing as a model through their own behavior. Thus, children are likely to adopt through imitation and identification many beliefs, feelings, and coping patterns simply by observing the behavior of those around them. The presence of a parent providing a model of appropriate, adaptive behavior can make a positive contribution to the child's healthy development. Unfortunately, children may also learn maladaptive behavior by imitating and identifying with parents who are seriously maladjusted. For example, children and teenagers who become alcoholics have often grown up with at least one parent who drinks excessively. Similarly, studies of delinquent youths reveal a disproportionate number of parents who are antisocial or criminal. Also, adults who abuse children have often been themselves the victims of parental abuse.

**A stimulating and responsive environment.**    Infants do not have to learn to be curious. They are constantly exploring—touching, tasting, listening, smelling, and looking. As nerves and muscles mature and mental capacities develop, the scope of their explorations widens. Soon they learn to talk and ask questions. Good parents will provide an environment conducive to new but not overwhelming experiences, making learning a pleasurable experience. Even though the infant's tendencies toward curiosity, exploration, and learning are built-in, they can be blocked either by lack of opportunity and stimulation or by early experiences that teach the child that curiosity is dangerous and unrewarding.

Children not only need a stimulating environment but also a responsive one in which they receive immediate and adequate feedback. Their inevitable questions of "who," "what," "where," "why," and "how" must be answered and encouraged, because children need to acquire a vast amount of information about themselves and their world. (see Psychology in Action, pp. 266–67 for information regarding the development of gender roles in childhood). That knowledge will enable them to assess problems accurately and learn to predict the results of their actions. Like adults, children experience feelings and encounter problems that they need to talk about and explore. Thus, they need parents who are willing to listen and communicate in meaningful ways—rather than parents who answer their questions with "Can't you see I'm busy?"

## Forms of Faulty Development

Unfortunately, healthy development is not guaranteed. Three common types of unhealthy psychological development have been identified: arrested development, special vulnerability, and distorted development. These may appear singly or in combination. In one way or another, each impairs the individual's ability to cope and adapt (See Insight, p. 268 for a summary of maladaptive family patterns).

**Arrested development.**   In speaking of arrested development, we are concerned with immaturities that seriously impair an individual's ability to adapt effectively. For example, adolescents who remain emotionally dependent on their parents and avoid interaction with their peers show arrested development. People who never learn to delay gratification of their impulses or who are self-centered also lack a prerequisite for mature planning and choice.

Immaturities may be pervasive or limited to certain aspects of a person's life. In rare cases immaturities affect virtually every aspect of an individual's development: in terms of the trends toward maturity we have been using in this chapter, such people remain largely dependent, impulsive, ignorant, incompetent, self-centered and immoral. Far more often, otherwise mature people show immature attitudes and behavior patterns in just a portion of their lives. For example, a person may show a high degree of intellectual and moral development yet be self-centered and impulsive about spending money. A young adult who throws temper tantrums when frustrated or a middle-aged Don Juan who is unable to form a stable or meaningful intimate relationship also display signs of immaturity or arrested development in those portions of their lives.

**Special vulnerabilities.**   As we saw in Chapter 6, life experiences, especially during early stages of development, sometimes leave a lowered resistance or "diathesis" to certain types of stress. On a biological level, a severe case of influenza may lead to increased vulnerability to other respiratory disorders. On a psychological level, early traumatic experiences may create "psychic wounds" or "weak spots" which never completely heal, leaving the individual vulnerable to certain types of stressful situations. For example, an individual who has been deserted by his or her parents may have unusual difficulty in coping with rejection by others in later life. Similarly, a child whose parents experience a difficult divorce may be particularly stressed later when his or her own marriage is threatened. Most of us have some kind of vulnerability as a result of some earlier experience, and in that sense most of us have experienced faulty development.

**Distorted development.**   Sometimes development proceeds in grossly undesirable forms or directions. We examined many of these distortions in our discussion of psychopathology in Chapter 6. Distorted development can be seen in the individual murdering for "kicks," the adult abusing children, and the adolescent refusing to cope with day-to-day living by turning to heavy and consistent drug use. In all these cases and many others as well, development has proceeded in a fashion that is not conducive to the individual's or society's well-being and growth.

Fortunately, there is nothing inevitable in the effects of an undesirable childhood environment. While such settings reduce the likelihood of healthy development, nonetheless some children emerge from the most horrendous home situations relatively healthy and are able to cope effectively with life crises. In some such cases, the pathology of one parent evidently was offset by the wisdom and concern of the

# Psychology in Action

## Gender Roles

Our sex, or the biological aspects of being male or female, is determined in the prenatal stage of development. In contrast, our *gender,* or the social, cultural, and psychological aspects of our sex (Unger, 1979), develops and changes throughout life. Our internal sense of gender is one of the most fundamental parts of our self-concept. For example, one of the first things most people would list in answer to the question "What are you?" would be that they are a male or a female.

Similarly, for most people, knowing a person's sex is an important, and perhaps the most important, bit of information to have about that person. Thus, the first question we ask after a baby is born, usually before we ask about the baby's health, is "What is it?", of course referring to whether the baby is a boy or a girl. At every stage of life, knowledge of our own and the other person's gender may affect our interactions with them.

Knowing whether a person is male or female is so important to most people because people in every society share common gender role expectations. *Gender role* refers to the set of expectations that society in general shares about the behavior and traits of a woman or girl because she is female and about a man or boy because he is male. Every society appears to have at least some different expectations for men and women, although the nature of these expectations differs from culture to culture. In Western culture, we tend to see men and women as very different from each other—opposites, perhaps. Research has identified at least forty-one personality traits that are seen as differentiating men and women. For example, men are perceived as being more aggressive, independent, and self-confident and women are perceived as being more emotional, passive, sneaky, and easily influenced (Broverman, Vogel, Broverman, Clarkson, & Rosenkrantz, 1972).

How are gender roles acquired? Theories about how we acquire gender roles are based on biological and/or psychosocial arguments. Arguments for a biological basis to gender roles point to differences in the brains and in the sex hormones of males and females. However, most psychologists agree that, even if there is a biological component to gender roles (and it is not clear whether there is), our experiences and the expectations of parents and society have the greatest impact on how children behave and develop. That is, we learn to behave as boys or girls, men or women, as a result of learning and socialization experiences.

There is ample evidence that the perceptions and, consequently, the socialization of boys and girls differ from birth. For example, in one study parents of infants were asked to rate one-day old babies on several personality traits. The parents perceived the babies differently depending on whether they believed the baby to be a boy or a girl not on whether the baby was actually a boy or a girl. In keeping with gender role stereotypes, babies whom the parents thought were girls were more often described as delicate and pretty, while babies whom the parents thought were boys were more often described as coordinated and hardy (Shepherd-Look, 1982). Other research has demonstrated that parents tend to react differently to boys and girls, tolerate and expect different types of behaviors from boys and girls, and reinforce behaviors that conform to traditional gender roles and punish or discourage behaviors that do not conform. Further, these differences in expectations and socialization tend to be mirrored by peers and by other important people in the child's life, for example teachers. These socialization practices teach boys and girls to adopt traditional gender roles.

Children also learn appropriate gender role behaviors through identification and modeling. By about age two, children have a clear *gender identity* or internal sense whether they are a boy or a girl. This sense of gender identity most often results in children being motivated to behave in ways that they perceive as appropriate for girls or boys—for example, little girls want to be just

## Gender Roles   (continued)

like Mom and little boys want to be just like Dad. Since, due to their own socialization, most parents behave in many gender stereotyped ways, their children will tend to model or copy these behaviors.

Even if the parents themselves do not conform to traditional gender role stereotypes, children are likely to model the traditional behavior of other people in their lives who do act in stereotypical ways, since traditional behavior is more common than nontraditional behavior. The media also conveys strong implicit messages about appropriate roles and occupations for males and females. For example, television programs, cartoons and commercials, the lyrics of popular songs, as well as children's textbooks and readers all tend to portray males and females in stereotypical ways (Greenglass, 1982).

There are three aspects of traditional gender role socialization that are particularly problematic for adjustment. First, the traits which are seen to characterize men but not women are viewed as more positive and healthy in our society (Broverman et al., 1972). Thus, a hidden message for women in gender role socialization is that they are not as good or as healthy as men. Second, traditional gender role socialization limits people's options, since neither men nor women are likely to adopt behaviors or enter occupational roles that are defined by society as inappropriate for their gender. Third, people tend to draw conclusions about men's and women's competence to fill certain roles based on these stereotypes. For example, the stereotypes that men are more logical and that women are more nurturant may lead to the conclusion that men make better engineers and women make better nurses and therefore women should not be engineers and men should not be nurses. Since stereotypes are not accurate for many individuals, this view would limit the opportunities of individuals who would be well suited to nontraditional careers.

Most psychologists believe that the two gender roles are not mutually exclusive; that is, being masculine does

not necessarily mean not being feminine and vice versa. Rather, a person can be *androgynous* or have both characteristics typically associated with males and those typically associated with females. Thus, for example, a male or a female can be assertive and self-confident (typical masculine traits) in the workplace or on the tennis court, as well as warm, caring, and emotional (typical feminine traits) with friends and family. Other (non-androgynous) individuals will have only mostly masculine traits or only mostly feminine traits. Research suggests that there are many positive consequences to androgyny including the finding that androgynous individuals are effective in a greater variety of situations since they are more flexible in the ways that they can respond (for example, Bem, 1975).

Are males and females really that different? In general, research has not substantiated consistent gender differences on many of the traits and characteristics that people believe differentiate men and women. That is, despite our perceptions and stereotypes, there appear to be relatively few real differences between males and females. There are many more gender similarities than there are gender differences (Hyde, 1985). Even on those traits for which research has consistently found gender differences such as aggression, most of the differences are rather small, and not very meaningful for making predictions about how any given individual is likely to act or how well he or she will do a job.

Gender roles develop and change throughout life. Most psychologists believe that, at every stage of life, it is important that people can choose to act in the ways that are best for themselves whether or not these conform to traditional gender roles. The more we treat each person as an individual rather than making assumptions about them based on their gender, the more likely that they will be happy, fulfilled, and adjusted.

# *Insight*

## Maladaptive Family Patterns

A child's maladaptive behavior may be fostered by the general family environment as well as by the child's relationships with one or both parents. Although we have no model of the "ideal" family, four family patterns have been distinguished which typically have a detrimental effect on child development.

1. *The inadequate family.* This type of family is characterized by an inability to cope with the ordinary problems of living. It lacks the resources, physical and/or psychological, for meeting demands with which most families can cope satisfactorily. Such a family cannot provide its children with needed feelings of safety and security, nor can it guide the children in the development of essential competencies.

2. *The disturbed family.* Disturbed homes may involve many pathological patterns, but such homes appear to have certain characteristics in common: (1) the presence of parents who are fighting to maintain their own equilibrium and who are unable to give the child needed love and guidance; (2) the child's involvement in the emotional problems of the parents to the detriment of his or her development; and (3) the child's exposure to constant emotional turmoil, irrationality, and faulty parental models.

3. *The antisocial family.* Here the family holds values that are not accepted by the wider community. In some families, the parents are overtly or covertly engaged in behavior that violates the standards and interests of society and may be chronically in trouble with the law. Antisocial values, such as dishonesty, deceit, and lack of concern for others, provide undesirable behavioral models for the child.

4. *The disrupted family.* The most common form of disrupted family is the family without one parent. Due to a number of circumstances, including divorce, separation, and desertion, more and more children are being reared in homes with only one parent present. The departure of one parent often causes severe stress and economic hardship for the remaining family members. If the family cannot be reorganized into an effectively functioning group, the result may be an undesirable environment for the children.

It may be emphasized, however, that the long-range effects of family disruption can vary greatly. In some cases, a relatively peaceful home with one caring parent can be better than a two-parent home filled with marital conflict and tension.

other. In other cases, a pathological parent served as a "negative model," showing the child what he or she did not want to be like. In *Cradles of Eminence,* Victor and Mildred Goertzel (1962) studied the lives of 400 famous people and found that only 58 had come from warm, supportive, and relatively untroubled homes. The remainder, including Rousseau, had come from homes that demonstrated considerable pathology.

In an attempt to understand children who apparently thrive despite pathogenic family and environmental conditions, Norman Garmezy (1976) and his associates began the study of a group of children they called the *invulnerables.* An example is Todd, age eleven. His mother died when he was three and he lives with an alcoholic father, who is usually unemployed, in an environment of poverty and unrelieved grimness. Yet Todd is bright, cheerful, a good student, a natural leader, and well liked by peers and school officials. Preliminary findings indicate that these "invulnerables" tend to find solutions rather than blame others, make the best of very little, and show an unusual capacity to "bounce back" after severe setbacks and traumas. In addition, these investigators suspected the children had a desirable role model somewhere in their lives.

Let us pause to review where we have been and consider where we are going in our discussion. We have seen that human development is a relatively lengthy process of growth toward personal maturity and adult functioning. We have seen that healthy development is more likely when a child receives warmth and acceptance, effective structure and discipline, opportunities and challenges, as well as support and encouragement when coping efforts fail; it is also more likely when appropriate role models are available and when the environment is both stimulating and responsive. In the remainder of the chapter, we will look closely at the many challenges that arise during childhood and adolescence as each person grows toward personal maturity. Our intent will not be to survey every aspect of development. In our discussion, rather, we will focus particularly on the most important developmental tasks or adjustive demands that commonly arise in the early years of life and on the skills and competencies that children and adolescents must acquire in their efforts to cope with and adjust to those developmental challenges.

## DEVELOPMENTAL TASKS IN INFANCY

The first two years of life are usually referred to as the period of *infancy*. During these two years, human beings change more rapidly and dramatically than during any other two-year period in life. For example, during the first year of life infants triple their weight and increase 50 percent in height. Imagine the effect of such changes on your life if they were to occur in a single year!

Apart from physical growth, most human infants must confront and cope with the following major developmental tasks during the first two years of life:

1. Learning to sit up, stand, walk, and run.
2. Differentiating themselves from the rest of the world.
3. Distinguishing thoughts from reality and realizing that objects continue to exist when they are out of sight.
4. Forming a secure attachment to a care-giver.
5. Developing a sense of trust and security.
6. Beginning to develop a sense of autonomy, independence and self-reliance.

In this section of the chapter, we will look closely at each of these developmental tasks, at the kinds of adjustment and adaptation they require, and at the way in which their successful mastery prepares the growing child to cope more effectively with future adjustive demands.

### Development of Motor Skills

Newborn infants are poorly prepared to survive on their own. Though they are equipped with a few inborn reflexes such as breathing, sucking, crying, sneezing, coughing, and grasping, nonetheless they are totally dependent upon others to feed

For infants, learning to walk opens a very large door, and their exploration of the world and understanding of their place within it drastically expand.

them, keep them warm, protect them, and provide an environment in which they can survive, flourish and grow.

Within a few months, however, the situation begins to change: by the age of five months, most infants can roll over by themselves; in another two months, they can push themselves into a sitting position and sit alone without support for brief periods of time; and by nine months, they can creep and crawl. Shortly after their first birthday, most infants can stand alone without support and may be able to walk alone. By about 18 months of age, most infants are beginning to run around (more or less!). In two years, their range of motor skills is truly impressive. They can walk, run, jump, carry and push and pull objects, go up and down stairs, bang objects—the list is endless.

These basic motor skills are essential to effective adjustment and adaptation throughout life. However, the development of these skills also leads to new adjustive challenges with which the infant must cope. As if to make up for lost time, two-year-olds are in constant motion, exploring every nook and cranny of the world around them, going where they want to go and doing what they want to do. The result is that the world expands enormously and infants are exposed to a much greater variety of experiences. At the same time, infants also begin to exert control over the world around them, to explore those parts of the world that interest them. Each of these changes has a profound impact on the growing child.

## Development of Cognitive Skills

The Swiss psychologist Jean Piaget (1952, 1970) has been especially influential in describing the way that children's thinking or cognition changes over time as a result of their experiences (see Table 8.2, p. 271). According to Piaget, in the first two

**TABLE 8.2  Piaget's Stages of Cognitive Development**

| Approximate Age Range (years) | Stage | Cognitive Achievements |
|---|---|---|
| 0-2 | Sensorimotor | Distinction between self and other objects<br>Object permanence<br>Ability to think about things<br>Planned and purposeful behavior<br>Mental trial-and-error |
| 2-7 | Preoperational | Use of mental images, symbols, language<br>Imagination, symbolic thought, self-awareness<br>Understanding of simple rules |
| 7-11 | Concrete operations | Reduction in egocentrism<br>More logical and less intuitive thinking<br>Clear distinction between fantasy and reality<br>Strategies for problem solving, remembering, concentrating<br>Understanding of relation between time, distance, and speed<br>Understanding that rules are arbitrary and changeable |
| 11-Adult | Formal operations | Ability to deal with abstract ideas<br>Understanding of general ethical principles<br>Self-reflective thought<br>Ability to reason about rules and regulations |

**sensorimotor stage:**
according to Piaget, first stage of cognitive development in which infants understand the world by sensing it and acting on it

years of life infants understand the world by sensing it and acting on it. Therefore Piaget (1952) calls these years the **sensorimotor stage** in cognitive development. For newborn infants, no distinction exists between "me" and the rest of the world. Therefore, objects don't exist apart from their experiencing them. When infants can see or touch something, it exists; when they look away from it or drop it, it no longer exists. When they close their eyes, the world disappears entirely; when they open their eyes, the world is re-created. Objects that are out of sight are not only out of mind—they cease to exist entirely!

It is not until eight to twelve months of age, when children can crawl and reach and grasp objects, that they begin to understand that objects exist even when out of sight or touch. This is an extraordinarily important development because once infants understand that objects exist in a world apart from themselves, they will soon be able to hold images of those objects in their minds and to begin to use words to refer to objects that are out of sight. In short, toward the end of the second year of life, for the first time infants begin to be capable of *thinking about* things.

In addition, during the first two years of life infants begin to be capable of planned and purposeful behavior. For the most part, newborns and very young infants simply react to events that happen around them. When they reach about six months of age, infants show the first signs of intentional behavior: for example, they will repeat behaviors over and over again apparently simply to enjoy the results. In another six to twelve months, infants engage in trial-and-error behavior: they do something, observe the results, and then try a new behavior to obtain a different result, and on and on endlessly! In the process, each infant makes another remarkable discovery: "I cause events to occur; my behavior causes predictable things to happen. If I shake a rattle, I will hear noise; if I drop a block, it will fall; if I scream, someone will come to help me." In other words, the world is a predictable place and the child can cause things to happen in it. Moreover, as the child becomes able to think about things that are not present, mental trial-and-error activity becomes possible: "If I were to do this, then that would be likely to happen."

The cognitive skills developed during infancy have a profound lifelong impact on the way the developing child can adjust to and cope with the world. By the end of infancy, a child can imagine different ways of behaving and begin to imagine the consequences of their behavior, understand the appropriate use of various objects, make things happen and observe the consequences, and make plans and carry them out. As we have seen in previous chapters, all of these skills are essential to self-direction and to effective human adjustment throughout life.

## Development of Attachment

**attachment**: emotional tie or bond between an infant and others

The most important social event during infancy is the development of **attachment** in the first year of life. Attachment proceeds in several stages (Ainsworth, 1973; Ainsworth, et al., 1979). During the first two or three months of life, the infant responds by smiling and gazing at everyone, showing little preference for anyone in particular. During the next three months, the infant increasingly becomes attached to the primary caregivers. By about six to eight months of age, the attachment to the primary caregivers is usually well established: the infant smiles broadly at caregivers, watches them as they move about, crawls after them, and reaches out to them when they approach.

At about nine months of age, most infants show signs of *separation anxiety:* when separated from their caregivers, infants cling desperately, cry and reach out, and generally do everything possible to keep the caregivers from leaving. Remember that for infants of this age, "out of sight" means "out of existence"; there is no reason to believe that a caregiver who leaves will ever return. Thus, separation from caregivers can seem to be a matter of life and death for the infant! In addition, most infants at this age begin to show *stranger anxiety:* the same infant who smiled and cooed at everyone indiscriminately a few weeks earlier now stares at strangers or bursts into tears when they approach (particularly when caregivers are not present to serve as a base of security).

The development of secure attachment in infancy is important for healthy development later in childhood (Sroufe, 1978; Joffe & Vaughn, 1982; Damon, 1983). Infants who form strong, secure attachments at this age are more likely subsequently to become playful, sociable, curious, resourceful, self-directed, persistent, cooperative, and confident. Infants who do not form secure attachments are subsequently more likely to become withdrawn, insecure, apathetic, lacking in confidence, and unaware of their surroundings (Arend, Gove, & Sroufe, 1979). As Damon (1983) states, it is important not to overinterpret these general observations.

> The quality of a child's early attachment behavior, therefore, does indeed have important long-range developmental implications. This does not mean, however, that all aspects of the child's future life are determined once and for all by the caregiver-child relation. Some aspects of future life—future social behavior, certain personality characteristics— seem more tied to the quality of early attachment than are other aspects of later life. Even more importantly, there is increasing evidence that certain deleterious effects of early caregiver deprivation—particularly cognitive effects—may still be corrected by later intervention. Indeed, some psychologists have argued forcefully that a child's potential for development remains intact surprisingly late in life, whatever the adverse blows of early experience. Although we would certainly hope this is true, there is by now no question that poor early care places children at risk personally and socially for years after infancy. (p. 47)

## Development of Basic Trust

Also during infancy, each child develops a basic sense of whether the world is trustworthy and reliable or whether it is untrustworthy and unpredictable. According to Erikson (1963), during the first year of life when the child is helpless and totally dependent, if a parent or other care-giver is responsive to the infant's needs, provides attention and affection, and if there is a consistency and continuity to the infant's experience, then the infant is likely to develop a sense of trust and security. The infant learns that the world is consistent and predictable, that it is an interesting, secure place, and that to a certain extent events can be anticipated. In turn, this sense of basic trust provides a major safeguard against fear and anxiety, giving the infant the feeling of security needed to explore the environment and master developmental tasks.

However, if children are not provided with warmth and affection, if their care is inconsistent or unpredictable or deficient, or if their first year is unusually stressful or threatening, then they are likely to learn that they cannot trust the world to respond to their needs. In turn, they are likely to experience life with a sense of deprivation and abandonment; not surprisingly, such children tend to be pessimistic and suspicious of others and to become withdrawn and anxious.

## Development of Independence and Autonomy

During the second year of life, when infants have become more mobile and have discovered that they can cause events to occur, they begin to assert their independence from caregivers. Paradoxically, infants who are most strongly and securely attached to a caregiver are also best prepared to become independent and autonomous because the caregiver becomes a safe "base of operations" from which the infant can go forth and explore the world. As time passes, these infants range farther and farther from their caregivers, often playing happily by themselves with only occasional glances to be sure that safety and security are still nearby. Of course, most infants appear to have somewhat mixed feelings about all this: they seem at times to be caught between their desire to be independent and their need for safety and security. They may need a push to encourage them to go off on their own, but as long as the infant's attachment is strong and secure, the push need only be gentle.

Though the infant's struggle for independence is not always a joyful event for parents and other caregivers, it is an extremely important part of the infant's adjustment and adaptation to the world during the second, third, and fourth years of life. Erikson suggests that successful attempts to establish one's independence during these years contribute to a sense of *autonomy,* of being able to do things on one's own, and to feelings of self-confidence, self-reliance and competence. This is most likely to occur when parents provide a safe, stimulating environment and then allow the child to explore and to learn within that environment. By gently encouraging independence, by not immediately responding to every request from the child, and by respecting the fact that the infant is an active and inquisitive human being, parents can set the stage for the infant's development of a sense of autonomy and independence. In contrast, a harsh or severe environment, and early failure at attempts to become independent, can lead to feelings of *shame and doubt,* dependency, a lack of confidence and the expectation of failure, and self-consciousness.

All in all, in the first two years of life all human infants face several major adjustive demands and their responses to these demands lay the foundation for adjustment and coping later in life. Infants must acquire basic motor skills, learn to differentiate themselves from the rest of the world, and learn that thoughts are not the same as reality. Developing a strong and secure attachment with a care-giver, a sense of basic trust, and feelings of independence and autonomy are also important tasks during the first two years of life. In terms of the trends toward personal maturity discussed earlier in this chapter, most two-year-olds make substantial progress toward greater self-direction, knowledge, and competence, but they remain quite impulsive, self-centered, and amoral.

## DEVELOPMENTAL TASKS IN THE PRESCHOOL YEARS

The years from two to six are usually referred to as the *preschool years.* These are the years before formal schooling begins, though, as we shall see, the developing child is learning a great deal without formal instruction. In comparison with the explosive changes that occur during infancy, changes in the preschool years are more subtle and gradual, but their effects on the child are no less profound. The primary developmental tasks during the preschool years are:

1. Gaining greater mastery over physical and motor skills.
2. Becoming skilled at symbolic thinking and the use of language.
3. Beginning to develop a sense of morality and reflective self-evaluation.
4. Dealing with any residual mistrust from infancy and continuing to develop a mature feeling of autonomy.
5. Developing a sense of initiative.
6. Developing and expanding relationships with peers.

## Development of Motor Skills

The most noticeable characteristic of preschoolers is that they never stay still! They are constantly on the go—dumping, loading, pulling, pushing, pouring, hammering, scribbling, and stacking in an endless stream of activity. At times it might appear that they are simply enjoying the new experiences made possible by their developing motor skills. On closer examination however, you are likely to discover that they are refining the basic motor skills they developed in infancy, gaining control over more precise motor skills that allow them to become increasingly independent, and developing a new sense of mastery and competence. They try things to see if they can do them, practice to become more skillful, and in the process begin to develop a sense of their ability to master the world around them. Preschoolers who jump down a step, only to climb back up and jump over and over again, are not only having fun and enjoying the experience of "flying" but are also becoming more skilled at jumping and gaining a sense of competence or mastery from the fact that they can jump without falling down.

*While more subtle developments than learning to walk, learning to dress and groom oneself are profound indications of a preschooler's increasing independence and initiative.*

## Development of Cognitive Skills

Toward the end of infancy, the child's thinking changes dramatically. Piaget called this the **preoperational stage** of cognitive development. A preschool child no longer understands the world only by sensing it and acting on it. Instead, for the first time the child becomes capable of using mental images, symbols, and language in the process of thinking; that is, the child can think about, talk about, imitate, and even draw pictures of things that are not present or things that may not even exist. Imagination takes flight as the world of pretend opens to the child. In the space of a few moments, the preschooler can pretend to be a bird, a tiger, an invisible person, a car, or even a mommy or a daddy. It is now possible for the child to imagine something happening, imagine the consequences, then change the scenario and imagine the changes in outcomes. It is also possible for the child to be aware of the past and to have expectations for the future. Toward the end of the preschool years, children also become capable of taking different points of view and of becoming aware of the feelings of others. In short, the preschooler is becoming capable of symbolic thought and reflective self-awareness—qualities that, as we have seen in previous chapters, are fundamental to our uniquely human ability to adapt through self-direction (see Insight, p. 277).

Of course preschoolers have a long way to go before they can think like an adult. Their thought is **egocentric:** they assume that everybody sees things, thinks about things, and reacts to things as they do; they do not understand that other people may see things differently or have feelings or needs of their own. They assume that anything that moves (such as the sun and the moon, cars and buses) is alive. They are also greatly influenced by appearances: big is better, bigger is best! For example, they tend to believe that a nickle is worth more than a dime because it is bigger. They can count to ten, but they haven't any idea what the numbers mean; they know they are "three years old," but they don't understand what that means either.

One other cognitive change occurs during the preschool years that has a significant impact on the child's ability to adapt to adjustive demands. At about age three, the child begins to develop a sense of *morality.* For the first time, the child begins to understand that there are rules about how things should be done, that there is a right (and a wrong) way to behave, and that their own behavior can be evaluated in terms of social rules and expectations. Nonetheless, preschoolers still have no real understanding of why such rules exist or how they can be changed. That remains as a task for the next portion of childhood.

## Development of Autonomy and Initiative

As we have seen, toward the end of infancy most children begin to develop a sense of *autonomy,* independence, and self-reliance. This process continues into the first few years of the preschool period as well, but while resolving that task preschoolers increasingly turn their attention to yet another important developmental task: developing a sense of *initiative.* As Erikson (1963) put it: "Being firmly convinced that he is a person on his own, the child must now find out what kind of person he may

# Insight

## Imaginary Playmates

Binker—what I call him—is a secret of my own,
And Binker is the reason why I never feel alone.
Playing in the nursery, sitting on the stair,
Whatever I am busy at, Binker will be there.

Binker's always talking, 'cos I'm teaching him to
    speak:
He sometimes likes to do it in a funny sort of
    squeak,
And he sometimes likes to do it in a hoodling sort of
    roar . . .
And I have to do it for him 'cos his throat is rather
    sore.

Binker's brave as lions when we're running in the
    park;
Binker's brave as tigers when we're lying in the
    dark;
Binker's brave as elephants. He never, never
    cries . . .
Except (like other people) when the soap gets in his
    eyes.

Binker isn't greedy, but he does like things to eat,
So I have to say to people when they're giving me a
    sweet,
Oh, Binker wants a chocolate, so could you give me
    two?
And then I eat it for him 'cos his teeth are rather
    new.

Well, I'm very fond of Daddy, but he hasn't time to
    play,
And I'm very fond of Mummy, but she sometimes goes
    away,
And I'm often cross with Nanny when she wants to
    brush my hair . . .
But Binker's always Binker, and is certain to be
    there.

*(excerpted from Milne, 1927, pp. 17-20)*

Binker, like most imaginary playmates, is about as real as he can be! He gets a sore throat, he cries, he has likes and dislikes, he even has his own ways of doing things. In fact, he's so real that grownups give him chocolates!

Imaginary playmates like Binker are a normal part of growing up during the preschool period (Schaefer, 1969). In fact, it has been estimated that as many as 50 percent of preschool children have imaginary friends at one time or another (Stone & Church, 1968). Far from being a cause for alarm, imaginary playmates actually can play a very useful role in helping a child to adjust and cope with the difficulties of growing up. The very fact that a two- or three-year-old child can create an imaginary playmate is a sign that the child not only understands the difference between "me" and "not me" but also feels confident about keeping the two separate. Moreover, imaginary playmates can at least partially fill the gap when real playmates aren't readily available. It is interesting in this regard that imaginary playmates are especially prevalent among firstborn and only children (Papalia & Olds, 1978).

Imaginary playmates like Binker are always available to listen as the child talks about a problem. Like a good therapist, imaginary playmates are often endowed with infinite patience, understanding, and compassion; they seldom if ever criticize; and they often provide models of what the child would like to be (Binker, of course, was always brave, was never greedy, and rarely cried). Even better, they are always available for blame if the child does something bad ("Binker did it, even though I told him he shouldn't, but he did it anyway."). This is a useful mechanism for a young child who knows the difference between right—and wrong, very much wants to do what is right, but sometimes has trouble keeping his or her own behavior under control—what an extraordinarily creative device to have an imaginary friend who can take the blame when there is an occasional, unintentional slip!

become" (p. 115). Preschool children are able to plan, initiate activities, think for themselves, act with a purpose, explore, and indulge their curiosity.

On the other hand, they are increasingly aware that there are rules about what is (and what is not) permitted, what will (and will not) be tolerated. There are limits and boundaries beyond which they must not go; there are questions they should not ask. Thus, along with initiative comes the potential for feeling guilt—guilt about going too far, about overstepping boundaries, about intruding where one is not welcome, about becoming the "wrong" kind of person. Ideally, during this stage of life the preschooler will develop a sense of personal strength and purpose, a capacity for self-control, confidence that he or she can manage emotions and impulses, and initiative without being crippled by doubt and hesitation. Success in these areas lays the foundation for effective coping throughout life, while failure to develop a sense of initiative increases the likelihood of maladaptive behavior when the person is faced with stress in the future.

## Mature Independence and Relations with Peers

During the preschool years, parents, caregivers, and other adults continue to play an important role in the child's development (Damon, 1983; Hartup, 1979). However, relationships with adults also begin to change during these years. The clinging at-

*Perfecting fine motor skills and exercising imagination help young children develop early competencies in the adult world.*

tachment of infancy begins to give way to a more mature independence. The child roams farther away, spends more time playing alone, shows less distress when separated from caregivers, and becomes more interested in interacting with strangers. These changes in part reflect development of autonomy and initiative, but they also reflect the cognitive changes that have occurred since infancy. The preschooler can communicate verbally with adults, and thus physical clinging and touching are no longer the only way of feeling close to and protected by caregivers. Also, as we have seen, the preschooler has developed the ability to think about things that are not physically present; this means that the child can think about parents and caregivers when they are out of sight.

Another important adjustment in the preschool years is the gradual increase in the importance of peers. During infancy, peers are relatively unimportant to the developing child. With the advent of walking and talking near the end of infancy, the child's world expands tremendously and peers become an increasingly important part of that world. To be sure, early in the preschool years "friendship" has a very limited meaning; most early preschoolers equate "friend" with "playmate" (Rubin, 1980). There is no sense of intimacy, of sharing, of loyalty and trust, or of mutual support that older children consider essential to friendship because, as mentioned earlier, the thinking of preschoolers is very egocentric and tied closely to appearances; concepts such as loyalty and trust won't have meaning until the child is considerably older. Thus, to a preschooler "friend" means "a person who is playing with me right now." You make friends by simply asking someone to play with you! Nonetheless, preschool friendships have a lasting effect on the growing child.

By the age of six most children have moved considerably farther toward self-direction, knowledge, and competence. Although they have also begun to be less impulsive and increasingly self-controlled, other-centered, and moral, these are still areas requiring considerable development before the child will be able to cope effectively in the adult world.

## DEVELOPMENTAL TASKS IN THE SCHOOL YEARS

In comparison to the first six years of life, the years from six to about twelve, referred to as the *school years,* are relatively calm. Physical changes and the development of motor skills are less dramatic than in previous years and pose less of an adjustive demand on the growing child. However, a number of significant cognitive and social changes during this period of life have an effect on the child's developing ability to cope and adjust through self-direction. The major developmental tasks for the school years are the following:

1. Refining and perfecting fine motor skills.
2. Becoming less egocentric and more effective at logical thinking.
3. Increasing mastery over symbolic thought including acquisition of basic verbal and mathematical skills (reading, writing, arithmetic).
4. Adjusting to the school environment.
5. Developing more complex social skills and more mature friendships.
6. Developing a sense of industry, adequacy, and competence in the adult world.

## Development of Motor Skills

During the school years, the child spends less time acquiring new motor skills and more time perfecting existing skills. For example, writing and drawing become much more refined during the early school years; the school-age child not only can capture thoughts and feelings in words or pictures but also can share those thoughts and feelings more fully with others as a result. Creating objects from wood or clay, learning to play a musical instrument, learning to ski, swim, play tennis, or ride a skateboard—all these accomplishments have an effect on the child's growing sense of mastery, of competence, and of becoming more like an adult. The school-age child also becomes stronger, builds endurance, and becomes better coordinated. As a result, for the first time the child becomes physically able to participate fully in sports such as baseball, soccer, gymnastics, and volleyball. Participation in these sports has profound effects on the child's social skills, understanding of rules, and ability to strike a balance between cooperation and competition.

## Development of Cognitive Skills

Between the ages of six and twelve, cognitive changes continue at a rapid pace. There is a marked reduction in the egocentrism that characterized thinking during the preschool years: the child finally realizes that other people have their own thoughts, feelings, and wishes, and that they may view things differently. In addition, cognition during the early school years becomes much more logical and less intuitive; the child begins to draw inferences and to make logical decisions. Words and language are applied more extensively in problem solving and remembering. For example, the school-age child can imagine reversing a sequence of actions; as a result, what has been taken apart can now be put back together again. Fantasy becomes clearly separated from reality: the child now understands that dreams are not real and that other people can't see or hear the subjects of his or her dreams. For the first time, children have little difficulty comprehending beyond immediate appearances and begin to think meaningfully about the past and the future as well as the present. Also, for the first time children realize that there is usually more than one way to solve a problem, and that the most obvious solution may not be the best. As a result, they begin to understand the importance of strategies in problem solving and in remembering and concentrating more effectively.

Also, during the school years children learn to read. This opens an entirely new world of ideas, thoughts, and experiences. In addition, through reading children are exposed to new and often more effective ways of coping with common problems. They can observe others balancing their own needs against the needs of others, storybook characters coping with rules and regulations that do not always correspond to their own wishes, as well as their coping with such things as illness, conflict, stress, and peer pressure. In all these ways, children become exposed to a much wider range of models.

**concrete operational stage:** according to Piaget, third stage of cognitive development characterized by reduced egocentrism and an understanding of multiple viewpoints

Piaget (1952) referred to the early school years as the **concrete operational stage** in cognitive development: children of this age have begun to think in symbols ("operations"), although their thought processes are still tied to concrete objects

As school-age children grow more into themselves, they become less self-centered, physically stronger, and more adept at social skills. They also begin to develop friendships based upon both competition and cooperation.

and actions. They cannot yet think abstractly about such intangibles as justice, destiny, a light year, or love. "Career" means "what a person works at"; "family" means "the people who live in our house"; "science" means "what we study in fourth period." Consider, for example, their thinking about rules. Preschoolers consider rules to be fixed by adults, beyond question, and not subject to change. In contrast, the early school-age child learns that rules are arbitrary, that there is no absolute right or wrong way to do things, and that rules can be changed. Most six- or seven-year-olds (still somewhat egocentric) also conclude that anyone can unilaterally change the rules any time they want! Playing a game with such a child can be an interesting, if somewhat confusing, experience!

By age eight or nine, most children have overcome their egocentrism and have begun to appreciate the fact that different people may have different ideas about things or view things in different ways. At this point, they also begin to understand that changes in rules require consultation and that all the players have to agree to the changes. For example, if you ask these children why rules should be obeyed, you discover the concrete nature of their thinking: according to nine-year-olds, rules are to be obeyed in order to avoid punishment and among somewhat older children rules are obeyed to please others and receive their approval. The abstract ideas of fairness, equality, honesty, and duty will not appear for several more years.

## Adjusting to the School Environment

The school years also usher in major changes in the child's social life. From the very first day that the child enters school, there are new rules and regulations to learn: how and when to enter the school building in the morning, where to hang up your coat, where to sit, how to ask permission to get a drink of water or go to the bathroom, what to do during a fire drill, and so on. For the school-age child who has not spent any appreciable amount of time outside of the home, these new rules and regulations require a tremendous amount of adjustment.

The school-age child must change in other ways as well—no longer are parents or caregivers nearby to offer help and assitance when things go badly; instead, the child must learn to trust and depend on strangers (such as teachers). Moreover, since the teacher must attend simultaneously to the needs of many children, the child must learn to wait in line for help until the more urgent needs of other students are met. This in turn requires a new degree of insight and cooperation: "What kinds of things can the teacher help me with and what kinds of things will I have to learn to do all by myself? How do I know when the teacher will be available to help me? How do I know if someone else has a more important problem for the teacher? When is it all right to interrupt even if the teacher is helping someone else?" These all represent major challenges of adjustment for school-age children, but learning to cope with them is essential if they are to develop into mature and well-adjusted adults.

There are other sources of stress in the school environment (Humphrey, 1984; Humphrey & Humphrey, 1985). When several hundred fifth and sixth grade children were asked "What is the one thing that worries you most in school?", one general theme seemed to run through many of the answers: the emphasis that teachers put on competitiveness. Many of the children feared that they would not be able to respond adequately to the competitive demands placed on them. This concern surfaced especially with respect to mathematics, where the combination of time pressure, possible humiliation, and emphasis on a single right answer is often extremely stressful for students. "Test anxiety" is a related source of stress for many school children. Weaker students and those who most desire to do well are especially likely to experience severe test anxiety (see Psychology in Action, pp. 284–85).

## Developing Friendships

While children are adjusting to life in school, relationships with friends change dramatically. In the early school years, children tend to form informal cliques whose membership changes from day to day and week to week as people drift in and out of the group. Much of the children's time is spent with these friends playing formal games such as hide-and-seek, kick ball or blindman's bluff. These games require not only that children understand and obey fairly complex rules but also that they learn to balance competition and cooperation, leadership and followership, dominance and submission—all important skills for coping effectively later in life.

However, around age ten or eleven the nature of friendship groups changes. The boundaries between cliques become sharply drawn—children belong to specific cliques and are not welcome in other cliques. The members of each clique construct their own rules about how to behave and dress, where to hang out, what kinds of behavior are acceptable and unacceptable, and who is "cool" and who is not. These common expectations serve to bind group members together and to set them apart from other cliques. However, since nonconformity to the customs of the clique threatens the very existence of the group, peer pressure to conform can be intense; not surprisingly, many school-age children choose to conform totally to the rules and customs of their particular peer group (Berndt, 1979). In turn, this often leads to considerable stress: group customs and expectations may conflict with family rules and values, and it is often difficult to resolve these conflicts. Quite often people who have been friends eventually enter different cliques with quite different expectations, and discover that it is difficult to maintain their friendship in the face of strong group pressures to associate only with other members of the clique. These experiences, while painful at the time, provide important lessons about balancing personal needs

*Group friendships often promote specific rules and behavior. Individual members must weigh the goals of the group against their personal and family values.*

## Sources of Stress for School-age Children

How well can you predict the kinds of experiences that school-age children say cause them the most distress? To find out, rate the stressfulness of the following events for ten- to twelve-year-old childen on a scale from 1 (least upsetting experience) to 7 (most upsetting experience):

Receiving a poor report card     \_\_\_\_\_
Losing in any game or sport     \_\_\_\_\_
Wetting pants in class     \_\_\_\_\_
Having a new baby sister or brother     \_\_\_\_\_
Having an operation     \_\_\_\_\_
Getting lost in some strange place     \_\_\_\_\_
Going blind     \_\_\_\_\_
Having a scary dream     \_\_\_\_\_
Being caught stealing something     \_\_\_\_\_
Hearing their parents quarrel and fight     \_\_\_\_\_
Being picked last on a team     \_\_\_\_\_
Going to a dentist     \_\_\_\_\_
Telling the truth but no one believing them     \_\_\_\_\_
Losing their mother or father     \_\_\_\_\_
Getting up in front of class to give a report     \_\_\_\_\_
Moving to a new school     \_\_\_\_\_
Being kept in the same grade next year     \_\_\_\_\_
Being sent to the principal's office     \_\_\_\_\_
Not making a perfect score (100) on a test     \_\_\_\_\_
Being laughed at in front of class     \_\_\_\_\_

Kaoru Yamamoto and his colleagues have conducted a series of research projects over the past decade in an effort to determine the stressfulness of childhood events as reported by children and as estimated by adults (Yamamoto, 1979; Yamamoto & Felsenthal, 1982; Yamamoto, Soliman, Parsons, & Davies, 1987). They have found that there is remarkable agreement among children around the world (United States, Phillipines, Japan, Australia, Canada, and Egypt) regarding the relative stressfulness of the various experiences on the list above. However, to their surprise, they have also found that adults (even experienced professionals who work with children) are not very good at assessing the stressfulness of these same experiences. In the table on the next page, for example, you can compare the ratings given by two separate groups of American children with the ratings given by a group of nearly 200 adults (nurses, social workers, school psychologists, speech pathologists, special education teachers, classroom teachers, and teachers in training).

The adults tended to underestimate the stressfulness of such things as hearing parents quarrel and fight, being caught stealing, being kept in the same grade for another year, getting a poor report card, and failing to make a perfect score on a test. On the other hand, the adults tended to overestimate the stressfulness of getting lost, being ridiculed in class, being picked last on a team, having a scary dream, going to the dentist, having a new baby in the family, and getting up to give a class report. The discrepancies between the children and the

and the needs and expectations of others which, as we have seen in previous chapters, is a common source of stress during adulthood.

So far we have focused primarily on group relationships during the school years. However, as we have mentioned, true individual friendships also make their first appearance during these years. We noted earlier in this chapter that during the preschool years "friend" usually means "the person I play with." Selman and Selman (1979) call this "playmateship" as opposed to true "friendship." As the child enters school, "friend" begins to mean "a person who does things for me." This form of friendship is called "one-way assistance." Around age eight, a new pattern of friend-

## Sources of Stress for School-age Children   (continued)

adults are more striking when it is recalled that children from totally different countries agreed closely on their ratings of the stressfulness of these various experiences. In other words, there are some life experiences that are uniformly experienced as quite upsetting by school-age children around the world, yet in many cases the stressfulness of these events is not apparent to adults who could provide valuable support.

How well did you predict the stressfulness of these events for the children?

| Stressful Events | Stress Ratings | | |
| --- | --- | --- | --- |
| | Children | | Adults |
| Losing mother or father | 6.90 | 6.76 | 6.93 |
| Going blind | 6.86 | 6.58 | 6.88 |
| Being kept in the same grade | 6.82 | 6.30 | 5.51 |
| Wetting pants in class | 6.74 | 5.78 | 6.51 |
| Hearing parents quarrel and fight | 6.71 | 6.54 | 5.67 |
| Being caught stealing something | 6.63 | 5.20 | 5.65 |
| Telling truth but not believed | 6.53 | 5.86 | 5.58 |
| Receiving a poor report card | 6.23 | 5.52 | 4.36 |
| Being sent to the principal | 5.75 | 4.68 | 4.51 |
| Having an operation | 5.51 | 4.80 | 5.79 |
| Getting lost in some strange place | 5.49 | 4.42 | 6.23 |
| Being laughed at in front of class | 5.28 | 4.65 | 5.95 |
| Moving to a new school | 4.60 | 4.09 | 4.89 |
| Having a scary dream | 4.08 | 4.06 | 4.80 |
| Not making 100 on a test | 3.75 | 4.05 | 2.39 |
| Being picked last on a team | 3.30 | 3.30 | 5.17 |
| Losing in any game or sport | 3.16 | 2.75 | 3.86 |
| Going to a dentist | 2.73 | 2.54 | 4.36 |
| Giving a report in class | 2.58 | 2.79 | 4.00 |
| Having a baby sister or brother | 1.27 | 1.46 | 4.01 |

ship appears: "friends" help each other, they cooperate, they trust each other. This is called "two-way fair-weather cooperation" to capture not only the reciprocal nature of such friendships but also the fact that they last only as long as the friends continue to help each other, that is, only during "fair weather." When the relationship is strained, such friendships tend to dissolve and be replaced by new friendships.

Harry Stack Sullivan (1953) noted a similar change in friendships in the preadolescent years. He suggested that beginning at about nine or ten years of age, most children develop a special relationship with someone of the same sex, a "chum," to use Sullivan's term. For the first time, the child is able to become truly aware of and concerned about the needs and feelings of another person. No longer is friendship simply a way to get what you want; rather, it involves doing things to "contribute to the happiness or to support the prestige and feeling of worth-whileness of my chum" (p. 245). Robert White (1976) commented on the importance of this relationship.

> Having a chum is clearly more than a cognitive achievement; the importance assumed by the other person and the wish to enhance his self-esteem show that love is involved, a love that is free from the unequal and dependent implications of love in the family circle. It is not too much to say that in this type of relation children have their first experiences of something like love in the adult form. (p. 332)

Such a relationship clearly can have profound effects on the developing child and provide a model for other close and intimate relationships throughout adolescence and adulthood. This relationship also allows the child for the first time to open up to someone outside of the family, to disclose to another person his or her innermost thoughts and feelings and perhaps discover that they are not that different from the thoughts and feelings of the chum. Sullivan also believed strongly that such intimate relationships can do a great deal to remedy any shortcomings of the previous years, to "round off any rough edges" left from childhood. Thus, "chumship" can serve an important readjustment function as the child begins the transition period to adolescence and then to adulthood.

## Development of a Sense of Industry

Underlying all the particular changes that occur during the school years, there is yet another change taking place: the child is developing a *sense of industry* as opposed to a *sense of inferiority*. These are years during which children learn to make, produce, work, learn by doing, persevere, use skillfully the tools that society provides—in short, to demonstrate their competence outside their immediate family, to develop and demonstrate skills that will provide a place in adult society. Some of the skills may be academic, some may be athletic, and some may be practical. All are related to valued adult skills. Success in these tasks leads to a sense of industry, a sense that the child is competent and will be able to find a place in the adult world. However, failure can result instead in a sense of inferiority—feelings of inadequacy, discouragement, and incompetency.

By the age of twelve or so, most children have made major strides toward personal maturity. To a great extent they are self-directed, self-controlled, knowledgeable, competent, other-centered, and moral. Their independence is tempered by their reliance on peer groups, and in many respects their thinking still differs from that of mature adults, but to a great extent pre-adolescent children are able to cope effectively with a wide variety of stressors and to survive for considerable periods of time without adult intervention.

## DEVELOPMENTAL TASKS IN ADOLESCENCE

Although there are no firm boundaries to mark the beginning and end of adolescence, it is generally agreed that adolescence starts around age eleven or twelve and ends

*During adolescence, the degree of change—physical, intellectual, emotional, and social—is equaled only by that which occurs during infancy.*

about eight years later. In contrast to the relatively quiet school years, by any measure adolescence is a time of major readjustment, as you can see from the following list of developmental tasks:

1. Adapting to rapid and extreme body changes (growth, puberty).
2. Learning to use abstract ideas and developing a set of ethical principles.
3. Achieving a measure of independence from the family and from peer groups.
4. Developing opposite-sex friendships and more intimate friendships.
5. Developing a sense of personal identity.

All these changes make significant demands on the adolescent's ability to cope and adapt, and so it should come as no surprise that researchers have found that stress is higher during adolescence than during any other developmental period (Coddington, 1984).

## Physical and Motor Development

The physical changes that occur in adolescence are equaled only by the changes that occur during the first two years of life. "But, unlike infants, adolescents have the pain and pleasure of observing the whole process; they watch themselves with alternating feelings of fascination, charm, and horror as the biological changes occur" (Craig, 1989, p. 372).

One aspect of adolescent physical change is the *growth spurt.* Beginning at about age ten or eleven in girls and age twelve or thirteen in boys, the body undergoes a sudden increase in rate of growth. It is not unusual for children to grow four or five inches in a year and to add twenty or thirty pounds in weight at the same time. The growth spurt is followed almost immediately by *puberty,* the onset of sexual maturity. In girls, puberty occurs on average at about age twelve or thirteen; boys enter puberty on average at about fourteen or fifteen.

Together, all these physical changes require major readjustment and adaptation on the part of every adolescent, but the challenges are greatest for those boys who mature later than their peers. For boys, early maturation is actually something of an advantage. The added height, weight, and strength make it easier for early maturers to excel in sports; moreover, early maturers are more likely to be admired and respected and to be treated like mature adults (Jones & Bayley, 1950; Carron & Bailey, 1974). In contrast, the late-maturing boy is likely to be treated as a child longer and find it more difficult to gain the respect of others. It is perhaps not surprising, then, that late-maturing boys are more likely to be tense, more self-conscious, less self-confident, and less popular than early maturers throughout adolescence and into early adulthood.

Girls seem to be less affected psychologically by early or late maturing (Siegel, 1982; Weatherley, 1964). Nonetheless, early maturing may initially be a disadvantage for girls. The early-maturing girl is likely to be even taller than boys her own age, at least for a while, and her early maturing may be cause for some embarrassment. Late-maturing girls can experience more anxiety, but here the data are mixed. The effect maturation has on girls, in contrast to boys, appears to be more dependent on the type of social supports available from parents and peers (Conger & Petersen, 1984).

## Cognitive Development

While adolescents are attempting to cope with massive physical changes, their way of thinking also changes. Beginning in mid-adolescence, individuals enter Piaget's fourth stage of cognitive development, the **formal operations stage,** in which they become increasingly able to understand and deal with abstract ideas and possibilities. Not only can they begin to successfully manage abstract ideas about the physical world—as seen in the ability to understand and apply the laws of physics, for example—but they can also understand social and interpersonal ideas.

In one test of formal operational thought in adolescents, Peel (1971) gave a group of children and adolescents of above-average intelligence the following problem.

> Only brave pilots are allowed to fly over high mountains. This summer a fighter pilot flying over the Alps collided with an aerial cable railway, and cut a main cable causing some cars to fall to the glacier below. Several people were killed and many others had to spend the night suspended above the glacier. Was the pilot a careful airman? Why do you think so? (p. 32)

**formal operations stage:** according to Piaget, fourth stage of cognitive development characterized by the ability to think and reason abstractly

Children under the ages of fourteen or fifteen provided responses that were either irrelevant ("No, he was a show-off") or were concerned only with the situation described in the problem ("No, because if he were careful he would not have cut the cable"). However, the older group was able to give much more imaginative answers, considering a variety of possibilities that were not directly presented in the problem. For example, some mentioned bad weather, a mechanical problem in the plane, and so forth.

The opening of the "world of the possible" can lead to some difficulties, however. The application of general ethical principles such as fairness and justice to an imperfect world may provoke strong feelings of distress or uneasiness in the adolescent. Taught that all should be treated fairly, the adolescent may become very upset when adults or others in authority act in an arbitrary fashion.

Of course, these adolescent emotions may become less intense as a person learns additional abstract possibilities. In later years, the arbitrary act may be evaluated differently as other considerations, such as group effectiveness or efficiency, become factors.

Thus, the attainment of formal operations marks the beginning of adult patterns of thought in an individual. Reality and possibility are now separate, and abstract ideas can be employed in dealing with the physical world, the social world, and the emotional world. In essence, a person can become self-reflective (see Insight, p. 291).

## Developing Greater Independence

Adolescence is also a time for major changes in social relationships. Most adolescents continue to be strongly attached to their families who continue to provide support and advice. However, the relationship between adolescents and their parents also changes in important ways. As we have seen, the adolescent is capable of independent thought, can reason about things such as rules and regulations, and is less inclined to tolerate arbitrary authority. As a result, the adolescent is likely to take an active role shaping the relationship with his or her parents—to expect a greater degree of equality in the relationship, be heard and listened to, and receive explanations for rules and regulations. In turn, these changes require adjustment and adaptation on the part of both the adolescent and the parents as roles shift, expectations change, and the adolescent exercises greater autonomy and assumes greater responsibility. Although this transition period can be fraught with difficulties for everyone involved, it need not be a crisis of epic proportions! There is a good deal of evidence that the image of adolescents and parents engaged in near-warfare is simply not accurate for the majority of families (Damon, 1983).

During this period, friendships outside the family also undergo change. This further complicates adolescent adjustment. The single-sex cliques formed during the later school years give way to coed groups of various kinds. These groups provide a casual opportunity for the adolescent to explore opposite-sex relationships, begin to form beliefs and values about sexual behavior, participate in group dates, and develop social skills useful in heterosexual relationships, all without losing the security of the group situation. These groups can greatly ease the adolescent's transition into the world of heterosexual relationships. As pointed out by Siegel (1982), "Peers provide security and a sense of belonging at a time when familial ties are loosening. The peer group thus provides a setting within which the adolescent may practice and experiment with new interests and skills" (p. 544).

## Developing Intimate Friendships

Individual friendships also provide valuable support during the adolescent years. The close, "fair-weather," single-sex friendships of the school years are replaced by longer-lasting and more intimate single-sex friendships that are characterized by true loyalty and commitment as well as by intimacy, mutual sharing, and mutual understanding (Selman, 1980; Youniss, 1980). Having trustworthy, intimate friends certainly makes it somewhat easier for adolescents to begin breaking free from their families. These friendships also provide a forum in which the adolescent can gain self-understanding, learn to cope with strong feelings, resolve difficult problems of adjustment, and begin to develop self-confidence. Being liked, accepted, and valued by another person adds immeasurably to feelings of being a worthwhile, competent human being. Berndt (1982) summarized these various benefits of friendship.

> Intimate conversations with friends can contribute to adolescents' self-esteem . . . by showing adolescents that another person respects their ideas and wants their advice. In addition, intimate adolescent friendships can contribute to the development of the social skills and the sense of security that are necessary for intimate relationships later in life. Finally, intimate conversations with friends may reduce adolescents' fears and anxieties about the physical and emotional changes that occur during early adolescence and, therefore, improve their actual adjustment. (p. 1450)

*For most, adolescence is a time of many questions and few quick answers. It's a time to develop one's identity with both patience and increasing discipline.*

# *Insight*

## Development of a Sense of Identity

**identity:** our sense of ourselves as unique individuals

Finally, adolescence is a time to develop a sense of one's own identity. To have an **identity** means to have a coherent image of yourself through time, a set of ideals to which you are committed, and a recognized place in society (Westen, 1985). You not only know where you belong, who you are, and who you want to be, but also you have some idea about how you might get from where you are to where you would like to be. You have a sense of being whole and unitary, rather than chaotic and fragmented, despite a dazzling variety of experiences. Identity also allows you to maintain some connection with and understanding of past experiences. In other words, we seek a sense of continuity with the past and with past experiences. A good analogy of this aspect of identity is to consider the events in our lives as frames of a motion piccture. As individual frames, they may have no meaning. However, when they are projected onto a screen, we get a sense of flow and meaning as each frame blends imperceptibly with another.

**identity crisis:** point during adolescence at which individuals are confronted with the difficulty of developing a personal sense of self (identity)

Psychologist Erik Erikson (1963, 1968) introduced the concept of identity into both the professional literature and the popular culture. According to Erikson, during infancy and childhood individuals are so restricted by their families and other people's images of who they are and who they should be that they don't form their own, stable identities. As a result, during adolescence an **identity crisis** is likely to arise. Adolescents often begin to see themselves as a jumble of contradictions, striving for conflicting ideals, without any sense of direction and without any idea of how to fit all the pieces together. They cannot see the connections that tie past to present and present to future: life seems like a series of disconnected, insignificant experiences, leading nowhere. They look back at their own behavior years, months, or even days later and ask "Was that really me?"

One possible response to this crisis of identity is to make a commitment to adult goals and values and, thus, to attain a coherent adult identity (see Figure 8.1, p. 292). However, not all people make a commitment to the issues that are important to adult identity (Marcia, 1966). Some people instead declare a **moratorium** in which they "try on" a variety of identities. In a sense, the individual is in the midst of a crisis but has not yet resolved it. This trying on of identities can be very helpful and useful, particularly since our society presents an almost unlimited series of choices and possibilities for achieving identity. Higher education and military service are two of the ways in which a moratorium can be declared. A moratorium may be beneficial as it allows a person some "breathing room" to experiment. However, when it lasts too long, it becomes destructive, as in the individual who has not "made adult commitments, such as choosing an ideology, a life style, a vocation, or a spouse" (Berger, 1980, p. 508). A failure to commit one's self fully to the task of developing an identity only prolongs the period of psychological adolescence.

Still other people temporarily avoid confronting the identity crisis by prematurely adopting an identity that is not of their own making. This process, called **foreclosure,** is exemplified by the individual who decides to become a physician or a teacher or a lawyer because that is what other people want him or her to be. Often, the consequence of failing to be "your own person" is that the task of establishing an identity is simply delayed until a later point in life.

Another way of temporarily avoiding an identity crisis is what Erikson calls **identity diffusion.** In cases of identity diffusion, people have no motivation to develop an identity, and no commitment to larger goals and values. They drift

**moratorium:** a "pause" in identity formation in which an individual explores alternatives

**foreclosure:** premature attainment of identity, typically not preceded by a crisis

**identity diffusion:** a lack of a sense of self; role confusion

**FIGURE 8.1**

The Development of Identity

The only way to resolve the identity crisis of adolescence is through identity achievement: a commitment to yourself as an independent and unique adult, sometimes in spite of the image of you held by significant people in your life.

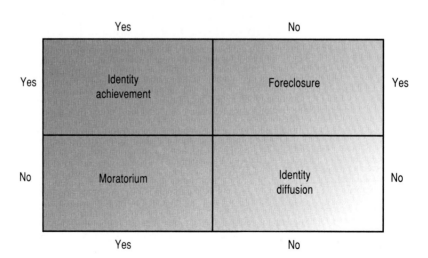

aimlessly, adopting whatever role they think is suited to the particular setting in which they find themselves. The apathetic and uninvolved adult "dropout" may exemplify identity diffusion.

We have come a long way in our efforts to understand how the newborn infant is transformed into a mature adult. In most cases, the person becomes more self-directed than dependent, more self-controlled than impulsive, more knowledgeable than ignorant, more competent than incompetent, more other-centered than self-centered, and more moral than amoral. To the extent that the outcome is healthy, the young adult is well equipped to cope effectively with adjustive demands throughout the rest of the life cycle, as we will see in the next chapter.

## SUMMARY

The process of development proceeds in a series of stages or tasks, each of which must be successfully completed if subsequent development is to proceed smoothly. As development takes place, the individual moves from immaturity to maturity largely as a result of learning rather than of simple maturation.

*Development* is a process of continual adjustment and adaptation. Although the process of development continues throughout the entire life span, at each stage of development certain tasks or competencies must be mastered if the individual is to become competent, effective, and well-adjusted.

Throughout the course of human development, as each individual confronts and deals with the various *developmental tasks,* the trend is toward developing greater personal maturity. Dependency must give way to a greater degree of self-direction, impulsiveness must be replaced with self-control, ignorance must be replaced with knowledge, incompetence must lead to greater competence, self-centeredness must be replaced by greater other-centeredness, and amorality must yield to the development of morality. Together these changes permit the human being to exercise responsible self-direction and to cope with and adapt more effectively to adjustive demands throughout the course of life.

These changes occur not simply as a result of *maturation* but rather as a result of learning and experience. It follows that some individuals learn to adjust and adapt more effectively than others. Healthy development does not mean normal or average development, nor does it mean optimal development. Rather, development is healthy to the extent that it allows the individual to cope with and adapt effectively to the challenges of modern living.

Development is more likely to be healthy if a child experiences emotional warmth and acceptance, effective structure and discipline, encouragement of competence and self-confidence, support and encouragement while facing the inevitable challenges of growing up, appropriate role models who can demonstrate effective ways of adapting and coping, and a stimulating and responsive environment. If the child's environment is not supportive, the result may be arrested development and immaturities and special vulnerabilities; in extreme cases, development can be massively distorted. On the other hand, a few children (called "invulnerables") manage to thrive despite an unhealthy environment.

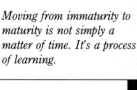

*Moving from immaturity to maturity is not simply a matter of time. It's a process of learning.*

The first two years of life (infancy) involve rapid and dramatic changes. Infants acquire basic motor skills such as walking and running that not only contribute to effective adjustment later in life but also lead to new adjustive challenges which have a profound impact on the infant. Cognitively, infants who are in the *sensorimotor stage* of development must learn to think about objects that are not present, to plan, and to understand the relationship between simple causes and their effects. They must also learn to differentiate themselves from the rest of the world and to distinguish thoughts from reality. They must also form a strong, secure *attachment* to a care-giver, a sense of basic trust in the consistency and reliability of the world, and begin to develop a sense of autonomy and independence. All of these changes have profound implications for the infant's ability to cope effectively in later stages of the life cycle.

During the preschool years (roughly from age two to age six), children spend a great deal of time refining the basic motor skills they developed in infancy, gaining control over more precise motor skills that allow them to become increasingly independent, and developing a new sense of mastery and competence. As they enter the *preoperational stage* of cognitive development, they become more skilled in the use of language and learn to think symbolically; in turn these changes permit them to engage in imagination, to be aware of the past and to have expectations for the future, and to show signs of reflective self-awareness. However, their thinking remains *egocentric*. Preschool children also begin to develop a sense of morality, continue to develop a sense of autonomy and independence, and then develop a sense of initiative. Peers become extremely important after the child has learned to walk and talk; though preschoolers do not have a mature understanding of friendship, nonetheless preschool friendships have a lasting effect.

The years from about six to twelve see a slowing of physical and motor development. Attention is given to refining and perfecting existing motor skills. At the same time, the child (who is now in the *concrete operational stage*) becomes capable of thinking more logically, of solving reasonably complex problems, and of understanding that different people may have different needs and see things differently. The ability to read exposes school-age children to new and more effective ways of coping with common problems. School requires a major readjustment, particularly for those children who have spent little time outside of the home. And friendship groups become increasingly important, often developing into exclusive cliques as the beginning of adolescence nears. A special intimate relationship with a "chum" is also a significant part of these years. During this period, children also develop a sense of industry, adequacy, and competence in the adult world.

Adolescence brings massive changes in almost every area of life. The growth spurt and puberty cause dramatic physical changes that require significant readjustment and adaptation. Boys who mature later are especially likely to experience stress. Adolescents also enter the *formal operations stage* during which they must learn to think abstractly and more like an adult and also develop a set of ethical principles. Social relationships also change dramatically. There is a gradual moving away from family, friendship groups become extremely important, truly mutual and intimate friendships appear for the first time. Most adolescents develop a firm sense of individual *identity* when faced with an *identity crisis,* but others declare a *moratorium,* or adopt prematurely an identity that is not of their own making, or simply avoid the issue altogether and suffer a diffuse identity. All these changes make significant demands on the adolescent's ability to cope and adapt, while at the same time their successful resolution contributes immensely to the person's ability to cope and adjust effectively throughout the remainder of the life cycle.

## KEY TERMS

development (257)

developmental tasks (258)

maturation (260)

sensorimotor stage (271)

attachment (272)

preoperational stage (276)

egocentric (276)

concrete operational stage (280)

formal operations stage (288)

identity (291)

identity crisis (291)

moratorium (292)

foreclosure (292)

identity diffusion (292)

# Development and Adjustment in Adulthood

*To every thing there is a season, a time to every purpose under the
    heaven:*
*A time to be born, and a time to die; a time to plant, and a time to
    pluck up that which is planted;*
*A time to kill, and a time to heal; a time to break down and a time to
    build up;*
*A time to weep, and a time to laugh; a time to mourn, and a time to
    dance;*
*A time to cast away stones, and a time to gather stones together; a time
    to embrace, and a time to refrain from embracing;*
*A time to get, and a time to lose; a time to keep, and a time to cast
    away;*
*A time to rend, and a time to sew; a time to keep silence, and a time to
    speak;*
*A time to love, and a time to hate; a time of war and a time of peace.*

                                                    (Ecclesiastes 3:1–9)

*Y*OU are sitting in a class on the psychology of adult development. One of the students in the class, Mary, a twenty-year-old sophomore, is sharing her thoughts about becoming an adult:

> My parents want me to be a teacher but I would rather go into business, maybe marketing or management. The problem is that I just can't bring myself to tell my folks how I really feel, what I want to do with my life. Sometimes I wonder if they're right: maybe I'm not cut out for business, and maybe I should become a teacher after all. Other times I think "This is *my* life, I have to do it *my* way even if I'm wrong, even if I make mistakes."

Susan, a thirty-two-year-old lawyer, comments:

> I had those same feelings six or eight years ago when I first started out in my career. Now I've settled in to a fairly independent and successful life style, but I still have my doubts. I wonder whether practicing law is really worthwhile and important; sometimes I think about running away and living an entirely different life. It's pretty depressing: I mean, I'm doing the right things but the payoff isn't as great as I thought it would be. I'm not as satisfied or as happy as I thought I would be.

Terri, a forty-six-year-old insurance agent, responds:

> I felt that way too ten or fifteen years ago, but I stayed in insurance and I'm glad I did. But now that the children are grown and I don't need as much income, I'm thinking about doing something else with my life. I'm not sure that hard work and just doing my part will make me satisfied or happy anymore. I think I'd like to help solve some important social problem, like drug abuse or poverty or pollution. I've even considered the possibility of running for public office or joining a political action group, but I need to learn more and develop some new skills before I do that.

*Independence grows from the ability to choose well among a variety of options.*

These comments capture an important fact about adulthood: it is a time of continuing change, readjustment, and adaptation. Human development does not end at age seven or seventeen; growth, change, readjustment, and adaptation are lifelong processes (see Figure 9.1). Moreover, the particular kinds of adjustments each person must make are different from one age to the next. In early adulthood, for most people the greatest adjustive challenges arise from developing self-reliance and intimacy, establishing a family, choosing a career, and creating a life plan or "dream." Typically, in middle adulthood the most important sources of adjustive demands are physical changes due to aging, the so-called "mid-life crisis" or "mid-life transition," the need to develop a firm sense of having had a lasting impact on future generations, and changes in important interpersonal relationships. Finally, in late adulthood, the most frequent sources of stress arise from aging and society's reactions to aging, retiring, losing friends and loved ones, and having to face our own eventual death.

In this chapter, we will examine all of these adjustive demands as well as others that frequently arise during the course of adulthood. (Before we begin our exploration, please take a few minutes to answer the questions in the Psychology in Action, p. 301.)

**FIGURE 9.1   Levinson Stages of Life**

*Note.* This is an expanded adaptation of an earlier version that appeared in *The Seasons of a Man's Life* (p. 57) by D. J. Levinson with C. N. Darrow, E. B. Klein, M. H. Levinson, and B. McKee, 1978, New York: Alfred A. Knopf, Inc. Copyright 1978 by Alfred A. Knopf, Inc. Adapted by permission.

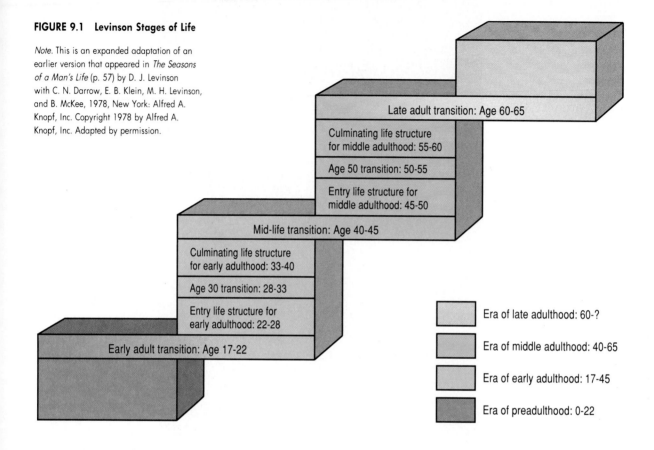

## DEVELOPMENTAL TASKS IN EARLY ADULTHOOD

In our society, the transition from adolescence to adulthood begins about the time individuals graduate from high school. The next twenty years (roughly from age eighteen to age forty) are usually referred to as "young adulthood" or "early adulthood."

For most people, the major adjustive demands of early adulthood do not come from physical changes or limitations. The dramatic physical changes of the adolescent years have usually subsided and the young adult enters a period that is in many ways the biological prime of life: strength and agility are at their peaks, the cardiovascular and respiratory systems are strong, perceptual abilities are keen, and both fertility and sexual activity are higher than at any other point in life (Hunt, 1974).

Cognitive changes during young adulthood are also not a source of major adjustive demands. Scores on standard IQ tests reach a peak in early adulthood and then remain relatively stable. Some cognitive abilities—such as verbal and numerical ability, vocabulary, general information, reasoning, and judgment—continue to improve gradually during early adulthood (Denney, 1982).

## Attitudes Toward the Elderly

Before we continue, please take a few minutes to answer the following informational questions by circling either T (true) or F (false). After you have read the chapter, the self-discovery exercise that corresponds to this chapter will show you how your answers to these questions allow you to learn more about yourself.

T  F  1. The majority of old people (age sixty-five or older) are senile (i.e., have defective memory or are disoriented or demented).

T  F  2. All five senses tend to decline in old age.

T  F  3. Most people have no interest in, or capacity for, sexual relations.

T  F  4. Most old people have poor lung capacity.

T  F  5. The majority of old people feel miserable most of the time.

T  F  6. Physical strength tends to decline in old age.

T  F  7. At least one-tenth of the aged are living in long-stay institutions (i.e., nursing homes, mental hospitals, homes for the aged, etc.).

T  F  8. Aged drivers have fewer accidents per person than drivers under age sixty-five.

T  F  9. Most older workers cannot work as effectively as younger workers.

T  F  10. About 80 percent of the aged are healthy enough to carry out their normal activities.

T  F  11. Most old people are set in their ways and unable to change.

T  F  12. Old people usually take longer to learn something new.

T  F  13. It is almost impossible for most old people to learn something new.

T  F  14. The reaction time of most old people tends to be slower than the reaction time of younger people.

T  F  15. In general, most old people are pretty much alike.

T  F  16. The majority of old people are seldom bored.

T  F  17. The majority of old people are socially isolated and lonely.

T  F  18. Older workers have fewer accidents than younger workers.

T  F  19. Over 15 percent of the United States population is now age sixty-five or older.

T  F  20. Most medical practitioners tend to give low priority to the aged.

T  F  21. The majority of older people have incomes below the poverty level (as defined by the federal government).

T  F  22. The majority of old people are working or would like to have some kind of work to do (including housework and volunteer work).

T  F  23. Older people tend to become more religious as they age.

T  F  24. The majority of old people are seldom irritated or angry.

T  F  25. The health and socioeconomic status of older people (compared with that of younger people) in the year 2000 will probably be about the same as now.

Source: Palmore, E. (1977). *The Gerontologist, 17,* 315–320.

There has been considerable debate among psychologists about whether new cognitive processes develop during adulthood as they did during childhood and adolescence. Piaget thought that the stage of formal operational thought was the final stage of cognitive development. Initially, Piaget believed this stage was completed during adolescence. More recently, however, he suggested that the development of formal operational thought may extend into early adulthood (Piaget, 1972). According to this view, adults expand upon and perfect the cognitive skills that developed during childhood and adolescence, although they may those skills more flexibly and effectively (Fakouri, 1976; Schaie & Willis, 1986).

Other psychologists, however, have proposed that a still higher level of cognitive functioning develops in early adulthood (Arlin, 1975, 1977; Riegel, 1973, 1976). Although the characteristics of such a "fifth stage" of cognitive development are not well-defined, some suggest that this stage may consist of **problem-finding**—an ability to discover new and important questions about the world or to view the world in new and different ways. Thus, rather than simply solving problems posed by others, young adults may increasingly identify new problems that need solutions. Another suggestion is that adult cognitive development involves greater autonomy in making decisions and increased tolerance for contradictions and ambiguities (Labouvie-Vief, 1980; Labouvie-Vief & Schell, 1982; Kramer, 1983).

**problem-finding:** proposed fifth stage of cognitive development, characterized by the tendency to discover questions rather than solve problems

For our purposes, however, it is sufficient to note that both physical and cognitive development proceed gradually during early adulthood, and the changes do not usually require major readjustment. However, in other respects early adulthood can be a time of major readjustment and adaptation. Even a quick glance at the Social Readjustment Rating Scale and the Life Experiences Survey in Chapter 3 shows how many potentially stressful life events are likely to arise for the first time during early adulthood: marriage, separation and divorce, pregnancy, starting a new job, experiencing changes or problems at work, and foreclosure on a mortgage or loan—all of these are highly stressful events for many people and all are most likely to arise for the first time during early adulthood.

The stressfulness of early adulthood was confirmed by Daniel Levinson who studied more than one hundred American men and women and closely examined more than one hundred biographies and autobiographies of men and women around the world. Consider Levinson's comments (1986) about early adulthood:

> This can be a time of rich satisfaction in terms of love, sexuality, family life, occupational advancement, creativity, and realization of major life goals. But there can also be crushing stresses. Most of us simultaneously undertake the burdens of parenthood and of forming an occupation. We incur heavy financial obligations when our earning power is still relatively low. We must make crucially important choices regarding marriage, family, work, and life-style before we have the maturity or life experience to choose wisely. Early adulthood is the era in which we are most buffeted by our own passions and ambitions from within and by the demands of family, community, and society from without. Under reasonably favorable conditions, the rewards of living in this era are enormous, but the costs often equal or even exceed the benefits. (p. 5)

This view of early adulthood as a time of considerable stress is shared by Havighurst (1974) who noted that young adults are under tremendous pressure to find a place for themselves in the world, yet they are provided with virtually no support or training for doing so. As a result, according to Havighurst, early adulthood can be both the most fulfilling and the loneliest period of life for many people.

Both Levinson and Havighurst were concerned with the stress that arises from fairly predictable life events during the early adulthood years, the common problems that almost everyone must address and resolve. In the next several pages, we will look at four of the most challenging developmental tasks that arise during early adulthood:

1. Becoming self-reliant and independent.
2. Developing a sense of intimacy and close, lasting relationships with others.
3. Exploring work and career alternatives and establishing a preliminary occupational identity.
4. Developing a life plan or "dream."

We begin our discussion with one of the first and most persistent adjustive demands at this stage of life: the need to become self-reliant and independent.

## Achieving Self-reliance and Independence

With the achievement of identity toward the end of adolescence, the stage is set for the development of greater psychological independence and an increasing confidence in the ability to think and plan. However, research by psychiatrist Roger Gould (1978, 1980) indicates that moving toward mature independence is extremely difficult for many young adults. After studying and analyzing questionnaires from more than 500 American men and women between the ages of 16 and 50, Gould concluded that most Americans develop a set of false assumptions or "protective illusions" that help maintain a sense of safety during childhood and adolescence. Faced with the prospect of helplessness in a confusing and sometimes threatening world, children come to believe that "I'll always live with my parents and be their child. They'll always be there to help when I can't do something on my own. Their simplified version of my complicated inner reality is correct. There is no real death or evil in the world." These illusions provide a soothing and reassuring message: "Everything will be all right; the world is a safe place and, even if it's not, my parents will protect me."

By the time most people enter early adulthood, they realize that these illusions are irrational and unrealistic. Nonetheless, Gould found that people continue to cling to these false assumptions for a sense of security, safety, support and stability. When adult life becomes overwhelming, people let themselves believe that they still live in the safe, protected, secure world of their childhood. This provides some short-term relief from stress, but in the long run, according to Gould, these childhood illusions are maladaptive. They give rise to the kinds of irrational self-statements that we examined in Chapter 3: "Everyone must love me and approve of me at all times. I must be competent and successful at everything I do. It is disastrous if everything doesn't go the way I want it to." Moreover, childhood illusions force people into restricted ways of living: they impose a set of invisible, rigid rules on people's lives that are seldom realistic or appropriate and make it almost impossible to lead an effective, creative adult life. As Gould (1978) suggests:

> If we cling too tenaciously to the childhood illusion of absolute safety . . . we will have to live at the command of others, as if we were still children. . . . We are stuck with a view of ourself that has to be replayed over and over again. We are afraid of our natural impulses, frozen in childhood morality, with our parents' visions of good and bad. We can't trust our intuition, so we lose certain nuances in life and impoverish our interpersonal relationships. We can't trust our own assessments of reality, because we constantly need endorsement from someone who is bigger. In short, if we tie ourselves too closely to the illusion of absolute safety and do not take the risks necessary to emancipate ourselves from childhood consciousness, we live a dull life without full adult consciousness. (pp. 41–42)

Therefore, during early adulthood each of us must discard the protective illusions that were developed during childhood. We must fully accept that we have the right and the responsibility to become independent adults. Profoundly important decisions about such things as marriage, pregnancy, and career *cannot* be made for us by anybody else. While we can turn to others for help, nobody else can take control of our lives. We must assume control over our own lives, accept the risks that come with true independence, learn to trust our own adult thinking and judgment, and also accept the fact that we may make mistakes. As noted by Gould (1978) one young adult commented:

> Somehow, it had never occurred to me that the freedom to straighten out your life was also the freedom to mess it up . . . there are still times when I'd like to hand the reins of my life over to someone else and say, "Here, you drive for a while." (p. 71)

## The Development of Intimacy

intimacy: establishment of a deep, caring relationship with another person

Another major adjustive challenge during young adulthood is the establishment of a deep, caring relationship with at least one other person outside the family—the establishment of **intimacy** and the avoidance of *isolation* (Levinson, Darrow, Klein, Levinson, & McKee, 1978). Orlofsky, Marcia, and Lesser (1973) described five levels of intimacy that can exist in interpersonal relationships:

1. *Intimate relationships.* These relationships are characterized by full sharing and mutuality. A person who is involved in truly intimate relationships typically will have several close friends as well as at least one, more intense intimate relationship with another person.

2. *Pre-intimate relationships.* Pre-intimate relationships are close friendships in which the participants do not have a deep mutual involvement with each other.

3. *Stereotyped relationships.* Stereotyped relationships include acquaintanceships that lack depth and meaning. Such relationships have the appearance of intimate relationships, but they lack commitment, mutuality, and sharing. The stereotype of a "playboy" corresponds closely to this type of relationship.

4. *Pseudointimate relationships.* These relationships are shallow and are usually established for convenience, rather than for mutuality of interests and values.

5. *Isolation.* This describes the absence of close relationships with others.

During young adulthood, it becomes possible for the first time for a person to engage in a truly intimate relationship with another person, to love another person for their real qualities and not just for the personal satisfactions that can be obtained from the relationship. According to Erikson (1963, 1968), such a relationship cannot occur earlier in life because a person cannot establish true intimacy without first developing a strong sense of identity. A person with a weak sense of self cannot easily tolerate the full and open sharing that is required in an intimate relationship. Moreover, without a strong sense of identity, an individual may seek praise and adulation from the other—a condition that interferes with the shared commitment and honest communication that are so necessary for an intimate relationship to develop and to be sustained.

There is some research that supports Erikson's contention that a strong sense of identity is a prerequisite to the formation of intimacy (Marcia, 1976, 1980; Waterman, 1982). For example, Orlofsky et al. (1973) found that individuals who had established a firm sense of identity were more likely to be involved in intimate and pre-intimate relationships, while people who had not achieved a sense of identity were more likely to be involved in stereotyped and pseudointimate relationships. In other words, people who have "found" themselves through the formation of an identity in late adolescence are then free to "find" others with whom to share their adulthood, as you can see in the following case study (Brodzinsky, Gormly & Ambron, 1986):

> To most people who knew him, 26-year-old Peter was a very eligible bachelor. He was attractive, got along well with people, and kept himself in good physical condition by running and playing racquetball regularly. Although he dated several different women, he was not interested in making a commitment to any one person.
>
> Just last spring, he and Jeannie had broken off their steady dating relationship when they realized each was interested in different goals. While Jeannie wanted to get married and start a family, Peter was more interested in establishing his career in computer software before making a commitment to a wife and children. So they parted as friends and saw each other only on an occasional basis.
>
> For Peter, commitment to another person seemed premature. How could he take on that responsibility, he thought, when he was not even sure who he was or what he wanted out of life. The fact that Peter also questioned occasionally whether he was really an adult yet—as his age implied—only reinforced the idea that he was not ready for a serious commitment to someone else. By settling into a career path and developing a career identity, Peter hoped to become more secure about himself—to feel more responsible and adultlike. Intuitively, he knew this decision was necessary before he could commit himself to marriage and a family. (p. 343)

As we will see throughout the remainder of this chapter and in the next three chapters, the development of intimacy does not occur all at once, nor is the quest for intimacy ever complete. Intimacy, like identity, is a process that shifts and changes over time and that requires constant readjustment and adaptation to changing conditions. In the later sections of this chapter, we will explore some of the most common changes that occur in intimate relationships throughout the life cycle. Then, in Chapters 10, 11, and 12 we will look more closely at the kinds of adjustments

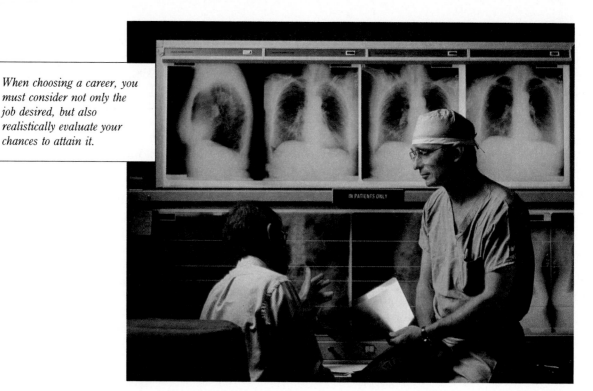

*When choosing a career, you must consider not only the job desired, but also realistically evaluate your chances to attain it.*

required in interpersonal relationships, marriage and other especially intimate relationships, and in sexual relationships.

## Establishing an Occupational Identity

The process of establishing an occupational identity is another aspect of early adulthood that can be a source of considerable stress and readjustment. Establishing an occupational identity involves more than simply finding a job and collecting a paycheck. According to Van Maanen and Schein (1977), the first steps in establishing an occupational identity are "exploration" and "establishment." **Exploration** involves getting advice from friends, counselors, and parents regarding various occupations. Prior work experiences, training received in high school and college or universities, and military service can also provide valuable guidance as each person attempts to identify potentially satisfactory careers. All of this information is compared with the individual's skills, abilities, and interests, as well as the personal and financial resources available for pursuing various occupations. For example, the possibility of pursuing a career in medicine must be tested against the person's performance in biology and chemistry courses, performance on admissions tests, and the financial resources available to pay the costs of attending medical school.

**exploration:** first stage in the development of an occupational identity, characterized by tentative first steps in the selection of an occupation

**establishment:** second stage in the development of an occupational identity, occurring in the first months and years of employment in a chosen occupation

During the process of exploration, each person typically identifies a small number of careers that seem especially promising and appropriate. The next step is the **establishment** of an initial or preliminary occupational identity. In some ways, this process is quite direct: the person takes a job, receives some orientation and training, and begins to work. However, beneath the surface, the process is usually more complex. Many people find that embarking on a career causes a major change in the way they see themselves; for the first time in their lives, they are functioning as adults, and it may take some time to adjust to that change in status. Many other people experience "reality shock" as some of the realities of the work world clash with their expectations. Most young adults also have to cope with at least some feelings of fear, anxiety, and insecurity: Will I be able to keep up? Will I be fired? What if I make a mistake? These are some of the issues that all young adults must consider during the initial phases of career exploration and establishment.

The issue of occupational identity is not resolved completely at the beginning of young adulthood. For example, according to Levinson et al. (1978), around the age of thirty most men go through a transition period in which they reassess their initial career choices (see Figure 9.1). Those whose careers no longer provide a good match with their abilities, interests, and goals are likely either to seek another career that better meets their needs or to adjust their interests and goals to better fit their existing job (Havighurst, 1982). Some recent evidence suggests that women also experience a transition at thirty that differs somewhat from the transition for men: for women, the reevaluation is more likely to center on the relative priority given to marriage and family as opposed to professional careers outside the family. Those women embarking on a career at the start of early adulthood often consider shifting to emphasis on marriage and family, while those whose primary orientation is toward the family tend to consider shifting to emphasis on a career outside the family (Craig, 1989).

### Developing a Life Theme or "Dream"

**dream:** idealized life plan developed during the early adult years

Another issue that must be addressed by both men and women during the early adult years is the development of a life theme, or dream (Levinson et al., 1978). The **dream** is an idealized life plan in which each of us specifies, to a greater or lesser extent, our goals for the future. The dream can consist of occupational achievement, personal achievement, family goals, or emotional goals. For example, one person may develop a dream of becoming a warm and loving parent, another person may have a dream of becoming an inspiring teacher, while yet another person may have a dream of becoming President or of winning the Nobel Prize.

Whatever their nature, life plans or dreams are not just idle fantasies. Whether realistic or unrealistic, simple or grandiose, the life dream becomes the focal point around which a person structures much of his or her life. The dream shapes a person's behavior and goals, and it is, in turn, shaped by that person's experiences. Someone who desires to become President may decide that a more realistic goal is to become Mayor or perhaps a state Representative. Someone who dreams of being an inspiring teacher may settle for inspiring only *some* students *some* of the time.

*As we extend ourselves, we may fulfill our dreams.*

We have seen that a number of significant developmental changes occur during early adulthood: people become more mature, self-reliant, and independent; learn to develop lasting intimate relationships with others; explore work and career alternatives and establish an occupational identity; and develop a life plan or "dream." Many of the changes initiated during these years have a profound effect on the course of middle adulthood.

## DEVELOPMENTAL TASKS IN MIDDLE ADULTHOOD

*Thou has nor youth nor age.*

(Shakespeare)

The middle adult years typically range from about age forty to sixty. Surprisingly little is known about this period. For many years, developmental psychologists focused their attention on the early years of life, including infancy, childhood, and adolescence. In the past decade or so, psychologists have shifted attention to understanding the later adult years. In the meantime, middle adulthood has remained relatively ignored.

This lack of inquiry is not surprising given the stereotype of middle adulthood as a quiet period of life in which people simply live out the patterns that were established during childhood and adolescence. In fact, this stereotype does seem to apply fairly well to cognitive development during middle adulthood: cognitive abilities remain essentially unchanged for about half of all middle-aged adults (Schaie, 1982; Schaie & Hertzog, 1983). Ten to fifteen percent of adults actually experience an increase in cognitive abilities during middle adulthood. The remaining one-third experience a decline in one or more cognitive abilities during middle adulthood, though these changes are rarely "of sufficient magnitude to be practically important" (Schaie & Hertzog, 1983).

Thus, changes in cognitive abilities do not represent significant adjustive demands for most people during middle adulthood. In other respects, however, the current picture of middle adulthood is one of continued challenge, change, readjustment, and growth. In fact, as we will see, recent evidence suggests that "the years between forty and sixty may be second only to the teenage years in degree of biological, psychological, and social change experienced by most individuals" (Stevens-Long, 1984, p. 255).

Our discussion of adjustment and adaptation during middle adulthood will be organized around four major developmental tasks or "predictable crises" of life that typically arise between the ages of forty and sixty:

1. Coping with noticeable physiological changes.
2. Adapting to changes in social relationships.
3. Achieving a sense of generativity and life satisfaction.
4. Coping with mid-life transitions.

## Adjusting to Physiological Changes

During middle adulthood, the first sure signs of aging usually appear. The skin starts to wrinkle and hair turns gray and begins to thin out. Eyesight and hearing may deteriorate noticeably. Reaction time becomes slower, and both physical endurance and strength decrease somewhat (Troll, 1975, 1982). The svelte shape of early adult life gradually gives way to body proportions that emphasize the middle part of the body. At the same time, middle-aged people are very likely to weigh more during these years than at any other time in their lives (Kent, 1976). The combination of weight gain and redistribution gives men "beer bellies" and women a thicker appearance around the waist.

Chronic illness also becomes a bigger factor in the lives of some middle-aged adults. Prior to the age of forty-four, the greatest cause of death is accidents; from age forty-five onward, the most frequent cause of death is disease (NCHS, 1987). For men in particular, one of the most significant biological changes during the middle years is the increased likelihood of cardiovascular disease. During adulthood, fatty materials called *plaques* collect in the arteries. Additionally, the walls of the arteries become less flexible and elastic. These changes, which can also be associated with high blood pressure or hypertension, high levels of fatty acids in the blood, and disturbances in the kidneys, are significantly associated with "premature" death in the middle years. Since many of these biological changes are subtle, it sometimes becomes necessary in middle adulthood to begin monitoring blood pressure, cholesterol levels, and other physiological indices in order to identify potential problems early enough to do something about them.

For many women, the most significant biological change in middle adulthood is **menopause,** the cessation of reproductive functioning marked by the end of menstrual periods typically between the ages of forty-five and fifty-five. Most women experiencing menopause report only mild symptoms—often in the form of hot flashes, insomnia, increased irritability, and headaches—which appear to be due to changes in their hormonal balance. As sociologist Bernice Neugarten and her colleagues have shown, most adult women do not anticipate or experience menopause in any "special" way (Neugarten, Wood, Kraines, & Loomis, 1963). Three quarters of the women in Neugarten's study perceived menopause as simply another life event of no overwhelming importance; they reported greater fears of cancer and of losing their husbands than of menopause. About half of the women did not find menopause unpleasant. Very few women found that the symptoms prevented them from going about their regular daily activities, and most women did not find that menopause altered their sexual desires. Some women even feel a sense of relief at the arrival of menopause.

> I felt physically in better shape—in my prime—unencumbered by the cycle of pain, swelling, discomfort, nuisance, etc.
>
> I felt better and freer since menopause. I threw that diaphragm away. I love being free of possible pregnancy and birth control. It makes my sex life better. (Boston Women's Health Book Collective, 1976, p. 328)

Unless a person is employed in a setting requiring peak physical condition, most of these physical changes should require only a small amount of adjustment and adaptation. Unfortunately, our culture puts such a premium on youth that some middle-aged adults find the first signs of aging extremely stressful. Some try to cover up or even reverse the changes with hair coloring, hair transplants and wigs, plastic surgery, and other short-term "cures." Most middle-aged adults accept the inevitable biological changes as a sign of increasing age and adjust their lives accordingly by paying more attention to regular exercise and a good diet, reducing unnecessary or excessive stress, and relying more on their accumulated experience and knowledge than on speed and physical endurance (Peck, 1968). With changes and readjustments of this sort, (see Psychology in Action, p. 311) it is possible for virtually everyone to continue living an active, vital, and fully satisfying life throughout middle adulthood (Siegler & Costa, 1985).

## Adapting to Changes in Social Relationships

Middle age typically brings many significant changes in important social relationships. These changes may be dramatic and may also result in considerable stress. To adapt to these changes, it is usually necessary for middle-aged adults to "let go" of some

**menopause:** cessation of menstrual functioning during middle adulthood

# Psychology in Action

## Maintaining Vitality Throughout Life: Slowing the Biological Clock

An issue of concern to most people is how to slow or prevent the degenerative changes of aging. Almost everyone would like to keep their cardiovascular systems as young as possible, and would like to lead an active and productive life throughout adulthood. Although the desire for a useful and healthy life is virtually universal, the evidence on how to structure one's activities to insure this type of life is controversial.

Part of the reason for the controversy is that there is little agreement on the causes of aging. Some researchers believe that aging is a consequence of wear and tear on the biological system (Stevens-Long, 1984). Others (Bierman & Hazzard, 1973) believe that aging is a consequence of "disease" brought on by air pollution, poor diet, alcohol, and other factors that ultimately result in death. Another set of theories (Sinclair, 1969; Timiras, 1972) explains the process of aging at the cellular level. Since human cells seem to have a limit to their abilities to divide, aging may reflect the fact that some cells reach the end of their ability to reproduce normally; after this point, abnormal growth and mutation occur, causing aging.

Another theory (Comfort, 1963) suggests that aging is the result of the body's turning against itself. That is, aging may be due to a self-destructive autoimmune response in which bodily defenses do not recognize tissues as part of the body but regard them as foreign substances to be destroyed. Other approaches (Hershey, 1974) have emphasized the lack of flexible proteins in the body and the availability of "free-radical" molecules as potential sources of aging.

Unfortunately, none of these explanations of the aging process offers much useful advice for maintaining health and vitality throughout adulthood. Moreover, people differ greatly in the extent to which they age and the ways in which aging appears. For example, some people show very little deterioration of the cardiovascular system well into old age, while some persons in their thirties and forties are extremely "old" as measured by cardiovascular status.

Some of these individual differences in aging are due to genetic factors. Some are also due to differences in life styles. We know, for example, that those who spend a great deal of time in the sun will show much greater aging of the skin than those who minimize exposure to the sun. In other respects as well some steps can be taken to alter one's life style to control the effects of aging—to push back the biological clock of decay and degeneration. Many of the approaches that have been suggested for slowing the biological clock are also related to suggestions for maintaining health. Some of the methods suggested for maintaining health and vitality are:

1. Eat a balanced diet
2. Maintain weight within normal limits
3. Exercise often and vigorously
4. Limit alcohol, caffeine, and nicotine intake
5. Develop a wide circle of friends
6. Stay involved in everyday affairs
7. Develop interesting and absorbing hobbies

There is no guarantee that adoption of a healthier life style will significantly increase longevity. However, research evidence is clear on one point: individuals who live their lives in ways that do not correspond to these guidelines reduce their life expectancy significantly. Thus, living a healthy and productive life helps to assure that you will live out the full span of your life, whatever that may be (Hancock, 1982).

relationships and to reinvest themselves in new ones (Peck, 1968). For example, parents must alter their relationships with older and increasingly independent children who may live some distance away and only visit home occasionally. Since parents no longer need to tend to scraped knees and broken toys, they have to learn to relate to their offspring as mature, independent adolescents and young adults who can still benefit from guidance but who also need to make their own decisions (Hess & Waring, 1978). As their children establish intimate relationships with others, it is necessary for parents to adjust to sharing their lives and their children with a widening circle of new family members. The sudden demand for intimacy with people who are total strangers can be unsettling at first, and sometimes complicated by resentment and jealousy over having to share children's time and affection with others.

Further readjustment is usually necessary when the last child leaves home, giving rise to what has come to be called the *empty nest syndrome.* Women who have devoted themselves to child-rearing and older fathers with few children and troubled marriages are among those who are most likely to experience the sudden absence of children as stressful (Lewis, Frenau, & Roberts, 1979). However, not all parents find the departure of the last child unpleasant or difficult. Harkins (1978) found that many parents welcome this time with a sense of satisfaction and relief. Working mothers are especially likely to welcome the change, as reflected in this comment by a fifty-two-year-old female executive: "I love my children, but God, how glad I am that they are out on their own. Suddenly I feel free. . . . It's just me and my husband now. . . . The funny thing is that the kids and I get along better now . . ." (Brodzinsky et al., 1986, p. 453).

Just as relationships with children change during the mid-life years, most middle-aged adults find that they must also change their relationships with their own parents.

*The roles between a parent and child may change with time, as the adult becomes increasingly dependent and the child must adjust to nurturing, supporting, and advising.*

In some cases, the change may amount to an almost complete reversal of roles: many middle-aged adults find themselves in the unusual and sometimes awkward position of acting in a protective, parental role toward their own parents who may be increasingly dependent on them for financial or emotional support. In turn, this role reversal can reactivate old conflicts over dependence and independence and other problems that were not fully resolved during adolescence and early adulthood. Many middle-aged adults are also reminded that the time may soon arrive when they will be dependent on their own children. Caring for parents also takes time and often requires significant changes in lifestyle and activities. Finally, it is usually during middle adulthood that most people must cope with the death of one or both of their parents. For all these reasons, relationships with aging parents can make significant adjustive demands on middle-aged adults.

The middle-aged adult may also need to adjust to the role of "grandparent." Many adults find this role a source of great satisfaction: at a time when their relationships with their own children are changing, becoming grandparents allows them to share with a new generation their favorite stories and activities and fun "things to do" (Bengtson & Robertson, 1985). At the same time, as grandparents they are spared both the full responsibility for raising the grandchildren and the conflict and stress that often accompanies parenthood. Satisfaction is drawn from the ability to step in and help out when your children need help with their children. Also, it is gratifying and rewarding when your own children turn to you for advice and counsel on the best way to raise their own children. In many ways, then, being a grandparent can be a wonderfully satisfying experience in which the pleasures outweigh the readjustment that is required (Neugarten & Weinstein, 1964).

Intimate relationships may also change during middle adulthood. In Chapter 11 we will see that for most married couples, the childrearing years (which usually span early and middle adulthood) are the most stressful years of the marriage. While many couples cope effectively with the inevitable stresses of married life in middle adulthood, others find it impossible to do so and either separate or divorce.

Friendships also change during middle adulthood. For example, Lowenthal, Thurnher, and Chiriboga (1975) found that in early adulthood, most people are so involved with work and family that they have relatively little time to devote to friendships. However, during middle adulthood, most people begin to develop close friendships with several other people and these relationships tend to persist for years. Thus, during middle adulthood intimacy is shared widely with people outside the family, and friendships become a rich and rewarding part of life for many people (Peck, 1968).

## Achieving a Sense of Generativity and Life Satisfaction

During middle adulthood, one important task is the achievement of a work role that is interesting, productive, and rewarding (Havighurst, 1982). Quite often people reappraise their work and its relationship to other areas of their lives and discover that, despite appropriate readjustments during early adulthood, their career achievements still do not match their goals. In some cases, this requires further revising the goals and self-image to coincide with reality (Levinson et al., 1978). On occasion it may also require retraining or development of new job skills. In at least a few cases, it may result in a mid-life career change to a career that promises a closer match with a person's interests and skills.

Another major developmental task of the middle adult years is the resolution of the crisis of **generativity** versus **stagnation** (Erikson, 1963). Generativity involves an expansion of interests with a view to the future. In essence, people who achieve generativity structure their lives around tasks and attitudes that will leave a lasting mark on future generations. Failure to achieve generativity, according to Erikson, results in stagnation—self-indulgence, boredom, inactivity, absorption in personal wishes and desires, and a lack of personal growth.

**generativity:** involvement in activities that will have a lasting effect on future generations

**stagnation:** the self-indulgence, inactivity, and lack of personal growth characteristic of the individual who has not successfully resolved the generativity versus stagnation crisis

Generativity is sometimes achieved by teaching, guiding, training, or directing younger generations. This may occur by providing children and grandchildren a sense of family history and an appreciation for society and values. It may occur through increased involvement in youth organizations or schools. In still other cases, generativity is achieved by actively participating in groups concerned with such crucial social problems as pollution, poverty, and nuclear war. Despite their apparent differences, the common element that runs through all these activities is that the person leaves behind some kind of lasting legacy for future generations.

Many adults also achieve a sense of generativity through their work. Working productively and skillfully at a job that has a lasting influence on the lives of other people can foster a strong sense of generativity and an enduring sense of pleasure and satisfaction. In fact, for this reason people in middle adulthood often change careers in an effort to find a job that provides a greater sense of generativity and lasting satisfaction. Consider the following case by Brodzinsky et al. (1986) of a middle-aged adult.

> I had the feeling I was getting nowhere. I struggled all my life to make money and be a successful business executive. But when I got there I realized it wasn't at all what I wanted. It became boring and meaningless, and that's when I decided to get out. I sold my business and got a master's degree in social work. Now I'm working in a counseling center for college kids and have never been happier. (p. 469)

A sense of generativity can also be achieved by teaching younger workers the "tricks of the trade." Initially, the appearance of ambitious and capable younger co-workers may be a source of concern and anxiety. Many middle-aged workers solve this problem effectively by establishing a mentor relationship with a younger co-worker. A **mentor** is an older worker who guides the occupational development of a younger worker, and helps a younger adult establish an occupational identity (Levinson et al., 1978). In a business setting, the mentor may be an immediate supervisor or an executive. To the young teacher in a school, the mentor may be an older teacher who helps the younger teacher to "learn the ropes."

**mentor:** an older individual who helps guide the occupational development of a younger person

## Coping with Mid-life Transitions

For most people, middle adulthood is a time of contradictions (Chiriboga, 1981; Sherman, 1987). Many middle-aged adults feel satisfied, self-confident, and in the prime of their lives (Hunt & Hunt, 1975). Yet, there is a growing realization that

*Developing new skills is one way to ease a mid-life transition and reassess the future.*

**mid-life transition:** an identity crisis during middle adulthood created by recognition of one's aging and mortality; sometimes called "mid-life crisis"

time is not unlimited: the first signs of aging have appeared, a few friends and acquaintances have died. These events provide a new sense of urgency to life, a feeling that "Whatever we do must be done now" (Gould, 1978). These and other concerns can result in what has come to be called the **mid-life transition:** a shift in self-perceptions and identity that usually occurs around the age of forty (Gould, 1972, 1978; Vaillant & Milofsky, 1980; Levinson, 1986; Levinson et al., 1978).

The heart of the mid-life transition is a conflict between self-perception and reality. The first gray hairs begin to eliminate a sense of youth. Failure to achieve all that we had hoped for in our jobs conflicts with the goals and dreams that were developed during early adulthood. Our hopes for our families may be shattered by divorce or separation. The bright, charming, achieving, and loving children of our dreams may in fact be more human and fallible than we would like. Perhaps for the first time, we become fully aware that we will die. For many of the men in the Levinson et al. (1978) study, these realities triggered a major "mid-life crisis" accompanied by emotional turmoil and considerable stress. However, other researchers have found that for most men and women, the mid-life transition is not an event of crisis proportions (Vaillant, 1977; Baruch, Barnett, & Rivers, 1983; Clausen, 1981).

Whether or not the mid-life transition becomes a crisis, each individual's self-perception must change to correspond more closely with reality (Sheehy, 1976). This typically requires some readjustment in the personal sense of identity that was established during adolescence and young adulthood. In other words, middle-aged adults, like their adolescent counterparts, must struggle with and resolve once again the problem of identity, as expressed in one case (Brodzinsky et al., 1986) of a fifty-year-old schoolteacher.

> As I watched my father go through middle age, I saw a person I loved begin to fall apart. He lost interest in everything, became preoccupied with his health and what he saw as a "looming death." He was no fun to be around. Now I'm at the point in my life that he once was and I still can't understand his reaction. Sure, it's no fun to get old. But I'm finding new interests all the time—new things to do. My job has become somewhat less important as I discover these interests. Many I can share with my husband; others are just for me. I don't feel that old and I just don't worry about getting older . . . life is just too short to be preoccupied with those kinds of thoughts. I'm middle-aged, I guess, but I feel good about where I'm at. (p. 441).

## DEVELOPMENTAL TASKS IN LATE ADULTHOOD

*Grow old along with me!*
*The best is yet to be,*
*The last of life, for which the first was made.*

(Robert Browning)

Late adulthood usually refers to the portion of life that begins around age sixty. More people than ever before are reaching late adulthood. In 1920, the average life expectancy was fifty-four; remarkably, a child born in the mid-1980s could expect to live about seventy-five years. While more people today reach the age of sixty, they also live longer after reaching that milestone: for example, the average sixty-year-old today can expect to live for another twenty years, and many will live for thirty or more years.

These facts have some important implications for understanding adjustment during late adulthood. First, because late adulthood covers such a wide age range (from age sixty to more than one hundred), it cannot be considered a homogeneous period of life: the full-time employee of age sixty faces vastly different adjustive demands than the seventy-year-old retiree or the eighty-year-old widow.

Second, in our culture the normal adjustive demands of late adulthood are compounded by the predominantly negative view that most people have of old age. Our youth-oriented society views late adulthood as the least exciting and least valued part of life. People commonly believe that late adulthood inevitably means declining health, income, self-esteem, productivity, and sexuality as well as a time of senility, unhappiness, loneliness, inactivity, and disability. (Tuckman & Lorge, 1953; Kastenbaum & Durkee, 1964; Lane, 1964; Schonfield, 1982; Babladelis, 1987; Crockett & Hummert, 1987).

# Insight

## Some Myths About Old Age

1. *The myth of senility.* There is a common stereotype that old people eventually become what is popularly called "senile": out of touch with reality, confused, unable to remember things, groom themselves, or keep themselves clean. In fact, "senility" is a symptom not of old age but of brain damage caused by such things as Alzheimer's disease and strokes. These organic disorders affect only a small percentage of older adults: about 3-4 percent of all people over the age of sixty-five and only 15-30 percent of those over the age of eighty-five (Craig, 1989).

2. *The myth of unproductivity.* Another common stereotype is that a person's work efficiency declines rapidly after the age of sixty-five. There is no evidence that this is the case. As the text points out, while physical strength and endurance do decline in late adulthood, and speed of response also declines somewhat, these changes interfere with work productivity in only a very few professions. The vast majority of older adults can continue to be efficient and productive workers well past the "normal" retirement age of sixty-five or seventy.

3. *The myth of available jobs for the elderly.* Despite overwhelming odds, about a third of the elderly are able to find substitute jobs after retirement, but these are usually of a menial nature far below their level of education and prior work experience and paying a minimum wage. The fact is that most elderly adults who would like to continue working productively at some kind of challenging job are simply unable to do so.

4. *The myth of adequate Social Security.* Although Social Security is a great help for many older people, it falls far short of providing an adequate income for living in a semblance of comfort and dignity. In and of itself, it often fails even to keep people above the officially defined poverty line.

5. *The myth of serenity.* Although there are adults of all ages in our society who do find serenity, it is no more characteristic of old age than of any other period in life. As pointed out in the text, the later adult years have their share of stresses—and in many instances more than their share (Butler, 1975).

In fact, none of these stereotypes is accurate. Most older adults are healthy, productive, happy, self-supporting, sexually active, intelligent, knowledgeable, vigorous, involved, and independent. For many, late adulthood actually provides a sense of satisfaction that was not present earlier in life (see Insight, p. 317).

The stereotypes and myths about old age are especially unfortunate for two reasons. First, many older adults are discriminated against because of the stereotypes. This has sometimes been called *ageism* to suggest similarity to racism and sexism. Second, many older adults have been raised to believe the misconceptions about late adulthood. As a result, they find themselves entering a phase of life that they have perceived as unpleasant, grim, and bleak. The result is a self-fulfilling prophecy: people who enter late adulthood with fear, misgiving, and resignation and who are discriminated against because of their age are, in fact, more likely to experience late adulthood as an unsatisfactory and unfulfilling time of life. In contrast, people overlooking the misconceptions and eagerly accepting late adulthood positively and productively are more likely to experience this period of life as fulfilling, satisfying, and challenging.

Our discussion will focus on several developmental tasks that are especially important in late adulthoood:

1. Adapting to physical changes that accompany aging.
2. Adapting to cognitive changes.
3. Coping with changes in interpersonal relationships.
4. Coping with retirement.
5. Maintaining identity and generativity, and achieving a sense of integrity.

We begin our discussion with a consideration of the readjustments that are required by physical changes that occur during the later years of life.

## Adjusting to Physiological Changes

Late adulthood is a time of gradual physical decline. The surface signs of aging that first appeared in middle adulthood continue: the hair gets grayer and thinner; wrinkles become deeper and more numerous; and physical strength and endurance decline. Bones become brittle and more vulnerable to fractures. The heart becomes less efficient, as do the lungs and kidneys. The body's immune system becomes less effective, leaving the older adult more vulnerable to infections and diseases (LaRue & Jarvik, 1982).

As we saw earlier in the chapter (see Psychology in Action, p. 311), to a great extent these physical changes can be minimized by leading a healthy and active life during early and middle adulthood. However, in any event, the great majority of older adults adapt readily to these physical changes with only modest readjustments in their normal patterns of activity: walking more slowly and for shorter distances, resting more often while mowing the lawn or vacuuming the house, eating more carefully, and taking extra care to avoid falls and minimize exposure to illness.

Most older adults also experience a decline in the senses (Perlmutter & Hall, 1985). It often becomes harder to focus visually, more difficult to perceive distance and depth accurately, and harder to see fine details and small print than it had been previously. For most people, these changes in vision can be overcome with glasses and other visual aids, while for others it may be necessary to make some changes in behavior patterns: perhaps driving less often at night, or becoming more willing to ask others to "read the fine print" on labels.

Many older adults also experience changes in hearing, particularly in the ability to hear sounds in high frequency ranges. Since so much social interaction is dependent on the ability to hear and understand what other people are saying, the loss of some hearing abilities can present an adjustive challenge. For example, an older adult who asks a younger person to repeat what he or she just said may be met with exasperation, impatience, or irritation: "Weren't you listening? Why don't you pay attention when I'm talking?" As a result of experiences like these, the older person may not make such requests in the future; in turn this excludes an important source of information and further isolates the older person from younger people.

Of course, the significance of these and other biological changes depends greatly on their effect on the individual's day-to-day functioning. Decline in muscular strength

*Exercise can invigorate the young and old, renewing both physical and emotional energy.*

and agility may represent a major adjustive demand for the person who has been very active in athletics or whose work involves heavy manual labor, while the same changes may have little or no effect on a person whose work and hobbies have been more sedentary. A modest decline in vision may require considerable readjustment for someone whose leisure time is devoted to hunting or painting or precision handicrafts, while the same decline might have little or no effect on someone else.

Physical changes can also require some readjustment in sexual behavior during late adulthood. Most older males take longer to develop an erection, and most older females do not produce as much vaginal lubrication. Moreover, many older adults find it takes longer to resume sexual activity following a period of inactivity (for example, due to illness or the death of a spouse). However, many older males are better able to control their orgasms than younger men and many older adults do not have as great a need or desire to experience orgasm with each sexual contact.

As long as both partners are aware of these possible changes, feel comfortable and not threatened by them, and adjust their sexual behavior accordingly these changes can be accommodated with ease by most older couples. As many older adults have discovered, the maintenance of sexual activity into old age is both possible and desirable. The need to be held and caressed does not diminish with age, nor does age reduce the pleasure that older adults derive from sexual activity.

## Adapting to Cognitive Changes

According to the stereotype, older adults are slower to learn, more forgetful, less rational, not as alert, and not as intelligent as younger people. In fact, however, there is very little decline in most cognitive abilities during late adulthood, and most older adults are able to adapt to the changes that do occur so that their intellectual functioning is not adversely affected (Perlmutter, 1987).

In fact, older adults take longer to perform some mental tasks such as processing new information and retrieving information from memory (Hoyer & Plude, 1980; Birren, 1974; Salthouse, 1985). However, the explanation of this fact is less clear. The change may be due in part to biological changes in the nervous system during adulthood. Alternatively, older people may be more concerned about being accurate than being fast or they may be unfamiliar with the kinds of tasks that are typically used to assess speed of mental processing (Hulicka, 1967). Note that most older adults have not been practicing quizzes and tests for school and developing optimal test-taking strategies for working under time pressure.

Older adults also have somewhat greater difficulty on tasks that require dividing their attention between two things occurring simultaneously (Craik, 1977). There is also some evidence that older adults have slightly greater difficulty retrieving recent information from memory, particularly if it is relatively meaningless information such as random lists of words that must be recalled precisely. Interestingly, there is little or no decline in most adults' ability to remember meaningful information from the distant past. Again, it is not known whether these changes reflect underlying biological changes of some sort, or whether they reflect such things as less efficient strategies for storing and retrieving test-type materials due to lack of practice, lack of interest in the tasks, and less motivation to score well on the experimental tasks.

Whatever the underlying causes of these various cognitive changes, most older adults adapt by developing strategies that allow them to compensate (Salthouse, 1985). For example, one study found that older adults tend to focus more on understanding and remembering the *meaning* of information rather than recalling the exact wording of the information (Labouvie-Vief & Schell, 1982). Also, they perform better on tasks that require remembering practical information rather than meaningless lists of words, in part because they can use their accumulated experience and their expertise to offset modest losses in memory and speed of processing new information (Salthouse, 1987).

Up to this point, we have been discussing cognitive changes as though they applied equally to all people. In fact, however, there are important individual differences in the extent to which cognitive abilities change in late adulthood (Flavell, 1970; Schaie, 1982). People whose lives provide a great deal of stimulation and intellectual challenge, who try to stay informed and keep up with daily events, whose hobbies require regular use of cognitive skills, and who remain actively involved with others are likely to experience little or no decline in cognitive abilities during late adulthood (Baltes & Schaie, 1976). In addition, specific cognitive abilities that are well-practiced and used regularly in daily life are especially likely to be maintained throughout late adulthood (Botwinick, 1977; Horn & Donaldson, 1980; Denney, 1982). Since most adults spend relatively little time solving IQ-test type problems, it is understandable that this skill tends to decline with disuse. However, many adults spend a good deal of time acquiring information, using verbal skills, and solving practical problems. These cognitive skills tend to remain stable during adulthood.

## Coping with Changes in Social Relationships

People continue to seek and enjoy intimacy during late adulthood. For example, Reedy, Birren and Schaie (1981) asked young adults, middle-aged adults, and older adults to characterize their love relationships. As you can see from Figure 9.2, there were some changes over time in several aspects of these relationships: sexual intimacy is less important in love relationships between older adults, while emotional security and loyalty become more important. Equally striking are the similarities between the three groups: at all ages, emotional security and respect are the two most important characteristics of love relationships; communication and helping and play behaviors are next in importance at all ages, followed by sexual intimacy and

**FIGURE 9.2  Importance of Various Characteristics of a Love Relationship at Different Points in Life**

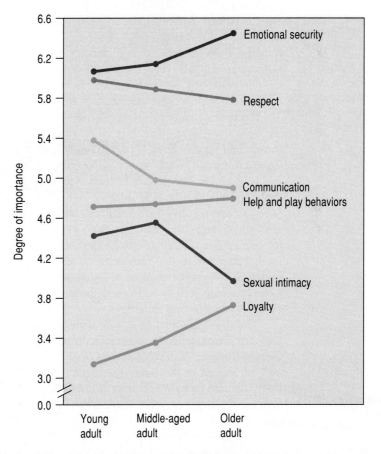

Source: Brodzinsky, Gormly & Ambron, 1986, p. 515; based on data reported by Reedy, Birren & Schaie, 1981

loyalty. As the authors point out: ". . . there is considerably more to love than sex . . . at any age, emotional security—feelings of concern, caring, trust, comfort, and being able to depend on one another—is the most important dimension in the bond of love" (Reedy, Birren, & Schaie, 1981, p. 62).

During late adulthood, family and friends may actually become more important than at any other time in the older person's life. As we will see in Chapter 11, those individuals who have maintained their marriages into late adulthood often report that these years are the happiest years of their marriage (Stinnett, Carter & Montgomery, 1972). In fact, such long-term marriages often become the center of people's lives, especially in the years following retirement. The availability of a supportive network of friends and family can also be of great assistance to the older adult (Hess, 1972). Relationships with children and grandchildren continue to bring great satisfaction to most older adults (Troll, Miller & Atchley, 1979; Troll, 1982, 1983).

However, often intimacy is not as easy to achieve during these years as it is during earlier periods of life. First of all, societal stereotypes work against the expression of intimacy between older adults. An older couple walking through a park hand-in-hand are likely to be seen as "cute" and somewhat laughable—as though older adults do not deserve and should not derive pleasure from intimate contact with others. Frequently, adult children are upset when a widowed parent wishes to remarry, thinking that love and intimacy are the sole province of the young and that remarriage is a betrayal of the parent who died. Also, some older single adults share this misconception, and consequently feel guilty about wanting to have a close intimate relationship with another person later in life.

Moreover, many older people move to a new location when they retire. While the new retirement home may be in a better location, it also may be far from old friends and family. Even a person staying in the same general location is likely to experience loss through death of close friends and relatives.

Eventually, one person in each marriage will experience the loss of the other through death. Those older adults who find themselves living alone for the first time have to cope not only with loneliness but also with the stress that results from big and little changes that must be made in everyday life (Morgan, 1976). People who for years relied on a spouse to handle financial matters, home maintenance, cooking, or shopping realize that they must do all those things themselves. Simple things—such as setting only one place at the dinner table, watching a favorite television show alone, opening letters addressed to one's spouse—can add immeasurably to the sense of isolation and aloneness.

The stress of adjusting to a life alone is great for both men and women. However, men are far more likely to establish a new intimate relationship. According to the Census Bureau, 77 percent of men over the age of 65 are married compared to only 40% of women in the same age range. In part this discrepancy is due to the fact that there are many more older women than men of the same age (men die on the average about seven years earlier than women); thus there are simply not enough older men to marry all the women who might want to remarry. In addition, in our society men of all ages are encouraged to associate with younger women. Therefore, unmarried or widowed older women are especially likely to spend their later years alone, whether or not that is their preference.

## Adjusting to Retirement

It has been said that next to dying, the recognition that we are aging may be the most profound shock of our lifetimes. Each day this shock is brought home to the nearly 2,000 persons who cross the invisible barrier of age and enter retirement.

Although retirement is often a matter of choice, in many cases it is forced on people who are both able and eager to continue working and playing a productive role in society. Not only does retirement deprive these older adults of a feeling of being needed and useful, but it tends to provide them with an image of being outmoded, outdated, and in the way. While leading to major changes in lifelong patterns of daily activity, retirement disrupts social relationships with co-workers and often leads to financial problems and loss of independence during a highly stressful transition period in life. As Robert Butler (1975) has expressed it: "The right to work is basic to the right to survive. Work, denied to older people by practice and by attitudes, is often needed to earn a living and provide personal satisfaction" (p. 64).

The stress of retirement is greatest for those enjoying their work and having no choice about when they retire. It is also likely to be high for people whose retirement income is not sufficient to meet their needs. However, the stress can be lessened through effective pre-retirement planning: attending counseling sessions that provide specific advice on preparing for retirement, gradually shifting one's major responsibilities to others, and making plans for new activities that will fill the void when retirement finally arrives. To the extent that it is possible, phased retirement can also greatly reduce the stress: this involves cutting back to part-time employment for a period of weeks or even months in anticipation of full retirement. This allows for gradual retirement, more gradual changes in lifestyle, and in some cases more realistic planning for the post-retirement years.

Quite often, the first reaction to retirement among those who have been looking forward to it and planning for it is enthusiasm, excitement, and optimism (Atchley, 1977). For some people, this outlook on retirement continues indefinitely. For others, the initial euphoria is followed by a period of disenchantment when retired life is not as satisfying as expected, or some post-retirement plans are unrealistic. The normal response at this point is one of being "let down" or depressed. Most people cope with this reaction by reorienting themselves, reassessing their goals and needs, and revising their plans.

## Maintaining Identity and Generativity, and Achieving a Sense of Integrity

The quest for a successful identity does not stop in early or middle adulthood. For the older adult, the major identity issue is the accommodation to an altered biological and social status. Looking in the mirror provides insistent information confirming age for the older adult when compared to the youthful individuals of photo albums and memories. Yet, as we noted earlier, one of the major tasks of identity is the development of a sense of continuity with the past. For the older individual, this may not be easy. Moreover, social changes also provide challenges to identity.

*Older adults, often treated as a burden in our society, can provide insight, wisdom, and guidance for younger people.*

Retirement signifies a loss of a major definition of the self. Society, to a great extent, views older adults not as potentially productive individuals but as a drain on health, housing, and governmental resources. Fixed retirement incomes reduce the standard of living, and inflation brings worries about the adequacy of financial resources. There is also the fear that independence will be taken away, retirement incomes will dwindle into poverty, and health will deteriorate. All these concerns may contribute to an identity crisis in later years and require considerable readjustment in people's sense of identity and continuity with the past.

The attainment of generativity can also pose challenges for the older adult. Our youth-oriented society is eager for older workers to step aside and let younger, more "knowledgeable" workers take over. Thus, older workers cannot give others the wisdom and skills they have developed over the years. Our emphasis on mobile, nuclear families also deprives some older adults of the time they could spend providing guidance and assistance to their children and grandchildren. Thus, in later adulthood it may become necessary to seek out new ways in which to contribute to the next generation: perhaps through work with youth groups and community agencies, service on boards and committees dealing with important social problems, or volunteer work for social action groups.

**ego integrity:** sense of satisfaction with and acceptance of the course of one's life

**despair:** despondency over the course of one's life

In addition to maintaining identity and a sense of generativity, according to Erikson (1963) the older adult must master the crisis of **ego integrity** versus **despair.** Ego integrity refers to a sense of satisfaction with and acceptance of the course of our lives and a belief that all that transpired over the course of our lives was useful, valuable, and meaningful. We cannot go back and relive parts of our lives; we cannot return and make corrections. The major part of life has been lived, and the crisis of integrity involves an examination of that life and our evaluation of whether that life, with all its triumphs and errors, its pleasures and pains, was valuable. In contrast, despair involves bitter feelings of opportunities lost, errors made, and the sense that life has been meaningless and empty.

**disengagement:** controversial idea that older adults increasingly withdraw from the external world and focus instead on inner thoughts and feelings

Some theorists have proposed that the life review that older adults undergo in their attempt to resolve the integrity versus despair crisis is part of a more general process of **disengagement.** Disengagement theory (Cumming & Henry, 1961) is based on the assumption that people become more focused on inner thoughts and feelings as they grow older. As people become more involved in internal processes and less involved in external, social events, their investment in others and in the external world decreases.

However, disengagement is not the only model of aging that has been developed. For example, successful aging can be accomplished by the individual who is deeply involved in the world. Successful aging can also occur when the person is moderately active and concentrates on a few role areas, such as the older adult who focuses his or her energies on grandchildren, a spouse, or church (Havighurst, 1969). In essence, those who make the best transition to old age are those whose personality integration was successful earlier in life (Neugarten & Hagestad, 1977). The active, engaged individual of middle age is likely to be the active, engaged individual of the later years; young adults with high self-esteem are likely to have high self-esteem in later years. For example, rather than focus on what cannot be done, these individuals may focus on the possible and attainable. If a woman's identity was that of a mother, she can now turn her energies to other activities outside the home or emphasize other skills. When spouses or friends die, individuals who have maintained strong social ties do not withdraw from intimate contact with others but seek the comfort and company of new friends. When they are unable to transmit their knowledge and skills to younger co-workers and family, they become involved in programs such as Foster Grandparents. In essence, the attainment of late adult status does not end the quest for a satisfying and fulfilling life.

## DEATH AND DYING

Each of us during our lifetimes will experience the death of others, and each of us will experience our own death. Although death for many is a terrifying prospect, it is also an occasion for learning and personal growth. Thus, Lipton (1979) has emphasized that death, as the final stage of growth, can both illuminate and illustrate the continuity of life. In this final section of the chapter, we will explore the views of death in our culture, the process of dying, and the effects of death on those who continue to live.

## Death and Dying in Contemporary American Society

*We make the dead look as if they were asleep, we ship children off to protect them from the anxiety and turmoil [telling them] . . . "Mother has gone on a long trip." . . . We don't allow children to visit their dying parents in the hospital, we have long and controversial discussions about whether patients should be told the truth. . . . Dying nowadays is more gruesome in many ways, namely, more lonely, mechanical, and dehumanized.*

*On Death and Dying* (Kübler-Ross, 1969, pp. 6–7)

Death is undeniably a frightening experience both to those who die and to those who continue to live. However, in our culture, death and dying are feared and denied to a much greater extent than in many other parts of the world. Elisabeth Kübler-Ross (1969) has made an intensive study of death and the process of dying in our society. She and a number of other social scientists (for example, Robertson, 1981) have suggested several reasons for our refusal as a society to deal with death.

In part, apparently the reason is the extraordinary emphasis our society places on youth and youthful living. Advertisements in newspapers, magazines, and television inform us about the joys of young life. Should a dreaded wrinkle appear on our skin, or, even worse, a gray hair appear on our heads, a variety of products is ready and available to help us recapture that important, elusive characteristic of youth. Except for some insurance advertisements, very little in our culture addresses the issue of dying (see Psychology in Action, p. 327).

In addition, religion has decreased in importance in our society during this century. In many religions, death is regarded as the beginning of an afterlife in which suffering and pain no longer exist. From this perspective, death is not something to be feared, but an event to be welcomed. Today, however, fewer Americans believe (or they believe less strongly) in the idea that there are rewards after death for an individual's suffering on earth. So death is seen by more people in our society as an ending, rather than a beginning.

A third reason for the greater fear of death today is the extent to which death has been separated from the mainstream of life and experience. In the past, death was a normal part of living, and people developed ways of coping with it and with the process of dying. The extended family structure characteristic of our society earlier in this century provided an excellent background for learning about death. Grandparents often shared the same house with their children and grandchildren, life expectancies were shorter, and the death rate at all ages was much higher than today. As a result, children and adults learned first-hand about death and dying by experiencing the deaths of grandparents, parents, siblings, and children. In essence, people treated death as a natural part of life.

# Psychology in Action

In contrast, in our society death has become almost unreal. As described in the quote at the beginning of this section, people are sent to hospitals to die privately and invisibly. News reports of the latest catastrophes, disasters, murders, and accidents desensitize us to death even as they depict in detail the process of dying. Movies and television almost always depict death in an artificial, sanitized way: the meaning of death for the victims is virtually never portrayed, and the deaths often have only the smallest effects on other people who continue their lives as if nothing of much importance had happened. The average college-age person has never witnessed the death of a single real person, but he or she has seen thousands of people "die" on television. All these conditions combine to make death seem unreal. Since we have no real understanding about death, the idea of our own eventual death can be alien and frightening.

There are, however, some signs that death and dying are beginning to be treated differently in our society. Both the hospice movement and the enactment of "death with dignity" laws hold the promise of increasing people's abilities to deal with death in a more accepting fashion.

**hospice:** center for the care of the terminally ill

A **hospice** is a center for the care of the terminally ill. When medical science can offer no hope for cure or remission, a hospice offers a reasonable alternative to further treatment care by attempting to keep a patient as comfortable as possible without undue sedation or drug-induced mental cloudiness. At the same time, hospices typically try to achieve a very homelike atmosphere in which patients are encouraged to surround themselves with meaningful possessions and in which visitors, including young children, are welcomed.

The specially trained staffs of hospice centers are able to deal with the emotional aspects of caring for the dying. Additionally, hospice centers may try to aid families overcoming the death of loved ones.

"Death with dignity" laws have also begun to reduce the institutional and impersonal aspects of death. Typically, death with dignity laws allow an individual to establish a "living will" giving a particular family member or physician permission to discontinue extraordinary medical treatment when hope for recovery diminishes. In this way, a person can be spared the dehumanizing experience of having life sustained only by machines and can reduce the financial burden on the family for costly medical care.

## Coping with the Prospect of One's Own Death

In her extraordinary study of dying patients, Kübler-Ross (1969) described five stages through which many dying individuals seem to pass. As she observed, these stages need not occur in a fixed, one-after-another sequence. Not all dying patients experience all stages, and some stages can be experienced simultaneously. Although there is some controversy regarding the stages of dying (Kastenbaum, 1977), these five stages are worth reviewing, for this analysis reveals the ways some individuals cope with the prospect of their own death.

**Denial.**    Often the first reaction of the person who learns that he or she is dying is denial: "No, it can't be me. It isn't true." Second opinions are sought from other physicians. There is the faint hope that the medical tests were somehow mixed up, that the X-rays were done incorrectly, or that the pathologist made a mistake.

All of these reactions reflect an unwillingness to accept the likelihood of death. In fact, these kinds of denial can be valuable to a person coping with what would otherwise be overwhelming stress. By initially denying the imminence of death, an individual can distribute the full realization of death over a longer period of time, absorbed in smaller and more manageable doses none of which results in overwhelming, terrifying anxiety or fear. Thus, when a person is faced with death, denial can be a valuable coping device.

**Anger.**    At some point, the reaction of, "This can't be me," usually gives way to the painful realization, "It is me. It wasn't a mistake." With the understanding that life is indeed about to end comes anger, rage, and envy. "Why me?" an individual may ask. Other people may seem more "deserving" than the person who is dying—the old, incapacitated man, the abusive alcoholic woman of personal acquaintance. The fact of one's own death doesn't seem fair while others will live.

In this stage, people often wonder why this "punishment" has been inflicted upon them. They may regard their lives as exemplary and feel that death is inappropriate for them. Often they have unfinished plans to accomplish. There are dreams yet to be fulfilled. The imminence of death, the frustration of knowing that they will

The death of a loved one creates grief and self-reflection, but also new strength and understanding after the grief passes.

die without the opportunity to accomplish all that they want to, the growing realization that control over their lives will transfer to the disease and to the physicians and hospitals—all these combine to produce great anger.

Because there is usually no way to express the anger productively or appropriately, it is often expressed inappropriately, indiscriminately, and without warning. It may be directed at loved ones, at medical personnel, and at friends and co-workers—none of whom is responsible for the fact that we are going to die, and all of whom are only trying to be understanding and helpful. However, they are available and convenient targets for anger that simply cannot be contained any longer. This, too, is adaptive, though it adds to the stress experienced by those around us. As we saw in Chapter 5, competence in dealing with anger and hostility starts with understanding those feelings and accepting them.

**Bargaining.**    Many people who are dying also seek to cope with this by bargaining with physicians, themselves, their families, and God. When denial and anger have not worked, they seem to hope that a more conciliatory approach may succeed: "If you let me live, I will lead a better life. I will be a better person than I have been in the past. I will devote myself to good deeds. Therefore, I simply can't die just yet." The promise of good behavior is made in exchange for longer life. In the following excerpt by Kübler-Ross (1969), you can see clearly how this kind of bargaining can be used effectively to cope with the prospect of imminent death.

> Another patient was in utmost pain and discomfort, unable to go home because of her dependence on injections for pain relief. She had a son who proceeded with his plans to get married, as the patient had wished. She was very sad to think that she would be unable to attend this big day, for he was her oldest and favorite child. With combined efforts, we were able to teach her self-hypnosis which enabled her to be quite comfortable for several hours. She had made all sorts of promises if she could only live long enough to attend this marriage. The day preceding the wedding she left the hospital as an elegant lady. Nobody would have believed her real condition. She was "the happiest person in the whole world" and looked radiant. I wondered what her reaction would be when the time was up for which she had bargained.
>
> I will never forget the moment when she returned to the hospital. She looked tired and somewhat exhausted and—before I could say hello—said, "Now don't forget I have another son!" (p. 73)

**Depression.**   As death looms closer and is more difficult to deny, many people experience depression. Weakness and disability can no longer be ignored. Often great sums of money have been spent on treatments that, in the final analysis, have only prolonged life, not saved it. The normal functioning of the family may have been disrupted or destroyed. There is a deep sense of loss of things we love and that are dear to us: we may never see the colorful leaves of autumn again, wrongs may never be righted, we will be separated from loved ones forever. The bright promise of tomorrow will never be experienced. Understandably, when these realizations first arise a reasonable response is depression.

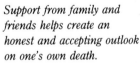

*Support from family and friends helps create an honest and accepting outlook on one's own death.*

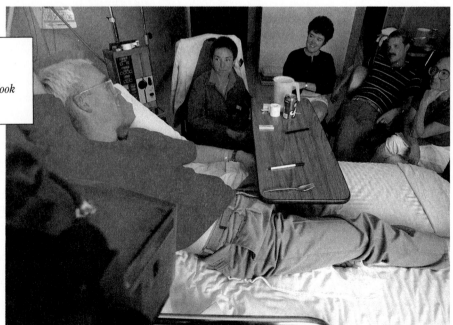

**Acceptance.**    Finally, assuming that death has not come quickly and that the person has had an opportunity to express denial, anger, bargaining, and depression in constructive forms, acceptance may occur. Acceptance does not mean that the person cheerily wishes to die. Rather, it refers to the fact that the person has finally come to terms with the reality of impending death, has said goodbye to the world and to family and loved ones, and is now prepared to die. In many cases, the person is so weak and fatigued that death offers a welcome relief.

It is important to emphasize that the sequence of reactions proposed by Kübler-Ross is not fixed, nor do all people experience all these various reactions. Rather, her model simply provides a convenient description of the various ways in which individuals often try to cope with the prospect of death.

## Coping with the Impending Death of a Loved One

Dealing with the impending death of a loved one is no less difficult than coping with one's own imminent death. You may recall from Chapter 3 that death of a spouse appeared at the top of the Social Readjustment Rating Scale: according to Holmes & Rahe's (1970) research, it requires more readjustment than any other single life event. It is also an undeniable fact of living: one partner in a marriage or other intimate relationships will inevitably witness the death of the other.

Although the death of a loved one is extremely stressful and virtually unavoidable, most people are unprepared to cope with it. In Chapter 5, we discussed a number of effective ways of coping with reactions to stress and for using unavoidable stress for personal growth. Those suggestions are also useful in coping with the death of loved ones. There are also some specific steps for dealing with the deaths of those close to us that can help to reduce, though not eliminate, the stressfulness of the event:

1. *Treat a person, not a disease.* Dying people are typically treated in hospitals, and the dying person may have little control over the care he or she receives. As Kastenbaum (1979) notes:

> In taking away the responsibility, credibility and control of the old person himself, we also set up a situation in which much of his life has become the property of others long before the process of dying begins. The terminally ill old person deserves to live and die as he himself would choose. Simple though it may seem, this concept runs counter to much in our social and health care network. It is easier to treat "diseases" and to look after "geriatric patients" than to work intimately with each person's individual needs as a person. (p. 110)

2. *Be open with the dying person.* Dying people have the right to know what is happening to them. Being "protected" from the knowledge of one's condition does not help the person—but it does protect family members and friends from discussing the issue of death with the dying individual. Acknowledging the impending death of the person can help both the sick and the well cope more readily.

3. *Ask what is needed.* Dying people often feel a need to "put their affairs in order." It is possible to aid this process by asking what they need and by following their instructions and wishes. Some of their requests can be very structured: "I

want Jean to get my jewelry after I'm gone." Some may be interpersonal: "Take care of your Uncle Rick. He needs to be looked after." And some may be more general: "Come sit with me." In carrying out these tasks, we can more effectively aid the dying person while confronting directly our own, often mixed, emotions about death and dying.

The death of a loved one is accompanied typically by intense grief even if we believe that the death was "for the best." Grief is often mixed with feelings of guilt, distress, and perhaps even some hostility. If the death was unexpected, feelings of shock and horror may be present. We discussed many of these emotions, and effective ways of coping with them, in Chapters 4 and 5. An additional point deserves to be made here: grief should not be denied. Although it can be an unpleasant experience, the expression of grief is part of the healing process. In time, feelings of grief will begin to dissipate, and it will be possible to resume at least part of the normal pattern of our lives. Of course most of us will never completely return to our "old selves," since loss and grief change us. However, we can become stronger, better able to understand and to help others because of our experience (Caplan, 1981). We can, in other words, use the experience of death, loss, and grief to help us to grow as individuals.

## A Closing Note

Learning and talking about aging, loss, and death is a sobering experience. We greatly value life, and we wonder what the future holds for us. As young children, we wondered what life would be like as young adults, and we feared the future, thinking of all the unpleasant things that could happen to us. When we reach adulthood, we discover that life is not as bad as we presumed, that most of the terrible things that could happen never do, and that there are many more rewarding and satisfying parts of life than we ever imagined. So, too, adults sometimes worry about their later years, again imagining all the unpleasant events that may befall lie ahead of them. However, just as our current years hold fewer negatives than we imagined as children, so too will our future years be more positive and hopeful than our fears suggest. As Robert Kastenbaum (1979) describes it:

> There was a time in my own life when I wondered about the value of growing and being old. No more. I do not want to miss my old age any more than I would choose to have skipped childhood or adolescence. But I do feel an increased sense of responsibility to this future self and to all those whose lives may cross my path. What kind of old man will I be, given the chance? The answer to that question largely depends on the kind of person I am right now. For growing old is an ongoing project of self-actualization through the life-span. (p. 121)

## SUMMARY

Adulthood is a time of continuing change, readjustment, and adaptation, although the particular kinds of adjustments that must be made differ from one age to another. In early adulthood (from about the age of eighteen to forty) the greatest adjustive demands come from the need to become independent from one's parents, to establish an intimate relationship with at least one other person, to make a preliminary career choice, and to create a life theme or "dream." Together these various adjustive demands can cause extremely high levels of stress at a time when the young adult is still relatively immature and inexperienced in coping effectively with stress.

According to Gould, becoming independent and self-reliant during early adulthood is more difficult because many young adults still believe in several protective illusions developed during childhood. These illusions provide a sense of safety and security, but in the long run they are maladaptive. Thus they must be discarded during early adulthood and new, more realistic and appropriate beliefs must take their place.

With the establishment of a sense of identity late in adolescence, the stage is also set for the development of more genuinely intimate relationships with others characterized by full and open sharing, commitment, and honest communication between the partners. The alternative is a growing sense of isolation. However, the development of *intimacy* does not occur all at once, nor is it completed during young adulthood. Like identity, the process of achieving intimacy is a lifelong endeavor that requires constant readjustment and adaptation as conditions change.

Early adulthood is also a time for *exploration* and *establishment* of a preliminary occupational identity. Information about possible careers must be gathered and then matched to the individual's skills, abilities, interests, and resources. Once a choice is made, an initial career choice is made. Some people experience "reality shock" when the realities of the work world do not match their expectations. Many young adults also experience feelings of fear, anxiety, and insecurity as they enter their first job. Starting to work can have a significant effect on the way young adults see themselves.

Around age thirty both men and women go through a transition period in which their initial occupational and career choices are reassessed. People who find that their jobs do not provide a good match with their talents and interests are likely to change to other careers. Women are especially likely to reevaluate the balance between marriage and family and a career outside the home.

Another developmental task of early adulthood is the creation of a life *dream* or plan. The dream captures a person's goals for the future and becomes the focal point around which each person structures much of his or her life. The dream shapes each person's behavior and is shaped by the person's experiences.

In middle adulthood (ages forty to sixty), the greatest adjustive demands typically come from the need to adapt to noticeable physiological changes and changes in important social relationships, to achieve a sense of generativity and life satisfaction, and to cope with mid-life transitions. During middle adulthood the first noticeable signs of aging usually appear in the form of such things as wrinkles, gray and thinning hair, increase in weight, slower reaction time, and a reduction in physical strength and endurance. More significant changes include the increased likelihood of disease, particularly cardiovascular disease among middle-aged men, the arrival of *menopause* in women. For some adults who are preoccupied with remaining youthful, these changes can be a source of great stress. For most adults the physiological changes of middle adulthood require only a modest amount of readjustment in life style and patterns of living.

Social relationships also change during middle adulthood, and those changes can represent adjustive demands for some people. Many marriages are enhanced during

middle adulthood. Parents have to "let go" of growing children and at the same time adapt to a widening family circle as children form intimate relationships with others. Further readjustment may be needed when the last child leaves home. Relationships with parents also change during these years; in some cases the change may amount to a complete reversal of roles that reactivates old conflicts and unresolved issues. Many middle-aged adults also become grandparents for the first time, which provides new challenges and opportunities, and close friendships usually assume a new importance during the middle adult years.

Another adjustive challenge during middle adulthood is assuring that one's career is interesting, productive, and rewarding. This may require revision in one's life goals or self-image, retraining and development of new job skills, or even a mid-life career change to a more rewarding career.

Also during the middle adult years, people must acknowledge the conflict between *generativity* and *stagnation*. By teaching younger generations (in some cases by serving as a *mentor* for younger co-workers), or by participating actively in groups concerned with important social problems, middle adults can leave behind a legacy that will have a lasting effect on future generations. Alternatively, one can spend middle adulthood in self-indulgence, inactivity, and preoccupation with one's own personal wishes and needs.

Finally, during middle adulthood there is usually a growing realization that time is growing short and that one's self-image and life plan do not correspond exactly with reality. This often leads to a *mid-life transition* in which self-preceptions are changed and self identity is readjusted to more closely correspond to reality.

In late adulthood (the years after age sixty) the most frequent sources of adjustive demands are physical and cognitive changes, changes in interpersonal relationships, life changes that occur because of retirement, and the need to maintain a sense of identity and generativity while establishing a clear sense of ego integrity. Unfortunately, in our society these normal adjustive demands are complicated by the unwarranted, negative stereotypes that many people have of old age. Because of the stereotypes, older adults experience age discrimination or "ageism"; in addition, many older adults come to expect that late adulthood will be an unsatisfactory and unfulfilling time of life, and they act accordingly, thus virtually assuring that the prophecy will be fulfilled.

To a great extent the physiological changes that accompany late adulthood can be minimized if a person leads a healthy and active life before reaching age sixty. Moreover, even though there is a gradual physical decline in strength and endurance, sensory acuity, and vulnerability to illness during the later years of life, most adults adapt readily to these changes with only modest readjustments in behavior patterns. Many couples also continue to enjoy sexual intimacy throughout later adulthood, though here too some modest readjustments in sexual behavior may be appropriate to assure a mutually satisfactory sexual relationship.

Some changes in cognitive abilities also occur during late adulthood, though these are seldom as dramatic or significant as most people expect. Moreover, people whose lives are intellectually stimulating and challenging and who remain actively involved with others are likely to experience little or no decline in cognitive abilities during late adulthood. On the whole, older adults often do take somewhat longer to process new information and to retrieve information from memory, and they are likely to have greater difficulty on tasks that require divided attention. These changes are usually modest and most older adults are able to develop strategies that allow them to compensate for the changes.

Intimacy continues to be important during later adulthood, though it is often more difficult for people to establish and maintain intimate relationships with others and to express their feelings in a society where stereotypes work against the expression of intimacy between older adults. Family and friends often become more important during late adulthood than previously, although it may be more difficult to maintain these relationships as people move from one place to another and as people die.

Retirement also requires readjustment and adaptation, particularly on the part of those older adults who are forced to retire despite their enjoyment of their work and their wish to continue working and playing a productive role in society. To some extent the stressfulness of retirement can be lessened by pre-retirement planning and by phased (or gradual) retirement. However, some people who greet retirement with enthusiasm and optimism become disenchanted when they discover that everything is not as satisfying as they had hoped; this may require further readjustment and adaptation to bring goals and needs and expectations more into line with reality.

The various changes that take place during later adulthood can represent a threat to a person's sense of identity, and as a result the older adult may have to readjust their sense of identity and their sense of continuity with the past. Achieving a sense of generativity can also become more difficult during late adulthood, and it may be necessary to change the activities that allow one to continue to have an influence on future generations. Finally, it is necessary to come to terms with one's life, the meaningfulness of one's existence, and an acceptance of what has transpired. In some cases this life review leads to a sense of *ego integrity* while in other cases the result is a feeling of *despair* and a sense of meaninglessness. It is not necessarily the case, however, that this process of life review is a sign of *disengagement* or withdrawal, or that it is "the beginning of the end." Most older adults—particularly those who have been active in previous years—continue to be actively engaged in the world around them throughout late adulthood.

Death is an inevitable, natural part of living. However, in contemporary American society, death and dying are a source of fear and denial. This may reflect the extraordinary emphasis on youth in American culture, or the decline in the importance of religion, or the extent to which death and dying have been removed from the mainstream of everyday living and converted into meaningless events that occur only to anonymous people on a television or movie screen. Whatever the cause, many Americans fear death and dying though the *hospice* movement and the "death with dignity" debate have begun to make death and dying less fearsome and more personal.

Coping with the prospect of one's own death is difficult for almost everybody. Some people respond by denying the imminence of death; others become angry; still others try to strike bargains in exchange for a longer life; and yet others become depressed. These are all normal reactions to the prospect of dying, and if they are allowed to be expressed and to take their course, the usual result is acceptance and a preparedness for the inevitable.

Coping with the impending death of a loved one is also a major source of stress during late adulthood. The same techniques that were described in earlier chapters for dealing with stressful events can be helpful in coping with this challenge as well. In addition, openness, helpfulness, and continuing to treat the dying person as an individual with needs and desires can help to reduce the stressfulness of the experience. When the death does occur, it is important to express the normal feelings of grief that arise and to realize that the grief will eventually dissipate though we will forever be changed by the experience.

## KEY TERMS

problem-finding (302)

intimacy (304)

exploration (306)

establishment (307)

dream (307)

menopause (310)

generativity (314)

stagnation (314)

mentor (314)

mid-life transition (315)

ego integrity (325)

despair (325)

disengagement (325)

hospice (327)

# *Interpersonal and Social Aspects of Adjustment*

# Interpersonal Patterns and Relationships

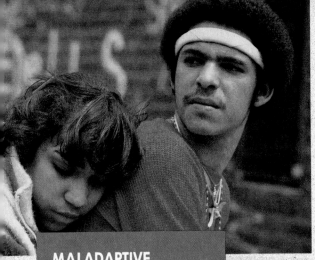

*No more fiendish punishment could be devised . . . than that one should be turned loose in society and remain absolutely unnoticed by all the members thereof. If no one turned around when we entered, answered when we spoke, or minded what we did, but if every person we met "cut us dead," and acted as if we were non-existing things, a kind of rage and impotent despair would ere long well up in us, from which the cruelest bodily tortures would be a relief. . . .*

*The Principles of Psychology* (James, 1890, pp. 293–94)

*P*ROBABLY no aspect of experience is more loaded with emotions or has a greater impact on our lives than our one-to-one relationships with other people. Relationships with friends, lovers, parents, and children are virtually always mentioned first when people are asked "What is it that makes your life meaningful?" (Klinger, 1977; Berscheid & Peplau, 1983; Berscheid, 1985). National surveys have repeatedly found that marriage, family life, and friendships do indeed contribute more to life satisfaction and happiness than do financial success, material possessions, and career achievements (Campbell, Converse & Rogers, 1976). However, interpersonal relationships can also be a major source of life stress: for example, even a quick glance back at the Social Readjustment Rating Scale in Chapter 3 (page 84) will demonstrate that many of the most stressful life events on that list involve relationships with other people.

Although interpersonal relationships are extremely important to virtually everyone, it is often difficult to understand them. Each of us approaches interpersonal relationships with a unique set of perceptions, needs, goals, feelings, and assumptions about ourselves and our world. When we add another unique individual to the mixture, it is apparent that the interaction that follows is likely to be very complex. To understand what happens in such relationships, we need to understand the nature of the interactions involved, the type of relationship which develops, and the effects of the relationship on each person involved.

In this chapter, we shall focus on four topics that are particularly important to gaining greater insight into and understanding of interpersonal relationships: (1) alternative ways of viewing interpersonal relationships, (2) ways of relating to significant others, (3) maladaptive interpersonal patterns, and (4) the foundations for building satisfying interpersonal relationships. While we will deal with these topics separately, you will see that in reality they are closely interwoven. Then in Chapter 11, we will use what you have learned in this chapter to examine intimate interpersonal relationships such as love, marriage, and alternatives to marriage.

*Although no two relationships are exactly the same, recognizing common desires—such as the desire to belong—may make complex relationships easier to understand.*

## WAYS OF VIEWING INTERPERSONAL RELATIONSHIPS

Psychologists use several different models or perspectives in their efforts to better understand relationships between people. We will also use those models in this chapter and the next. Specifically, we shall focus on the social exchange model, the social role model, and the games model.

### Social Exchange Model

**social exchange model:** view that interpersonal relationships are governed by the rewards and costs to each of the persons involved

According to the **social exchange model,** interpersonal relationships are formed for the purpose of meeting people's needs. From this perspective, each person in a relationship is concerned primarily with "What can I get out of this relationship and what will it cost me?" The resulting exchange is governed by economic principles. Thibaut and Kelley (1959, 1978), who have been influential in the development of this model, stated the matter this way: "The basic assumption running throughout our analysis is that every individual voluntarily enters and stays in a relationship only as long as it is adequately satisfactory in terms of his rewards and costs" (1959, p. 37). The social exchange model can be summarized in terms of three key concepts— (1) rewards and costs, (2) outcomes and profit, and (3) comparison level.

**Rewards and costs.** Any positively valued consequence which a person gains from a relationship is a *reward*. Rewards may include money and material possessions, but even more important in most personal relationships are social rewards such as affection, approval, support, respect, and acceptance.

A *cost* is any negatively valued consequence incurred by a person in a relationship. Costs may take a variety of forms, including time, effort, conflict, anxiety, self-devaluation, or any other conditions that deplete the individual's adaptive resources or have averse consequences. Of course, what is highly rewarding for one person may have little or no reward value for another, and what one person considers a high cost may be viewed differently by another.

**outcome:** the difference between rewards and costs in an interpersonal relationship (profit)

**Outcomes and profit.**    A key factor in the social exchange model is **outcome** or profit, which is simply the difference between rewards and costs. In most relationships, the participants expect rewards to be roughly equal to costs. Normally, people do not enter into interpersonal relationships to make the largest possible profit or to suffer a great loss (though later in this chapter we will examine some relationships of this sort). In a "just" exchange, the participants expect to receive about what they give, to just about "balance their books" (see Insight, p. 344).

**Comparison level.**    According to the social exchange theory, when we try to determine how satisfied we are with a particular relationship, we compare the outcome of that relationship with various standards. (1) We might compare it to similar relationships we have had in the past. If the outcomes of those relationships were more favorable, we're likely to feel dissatisfied with the present one; in contrast, if the outcome of the present relationship is more favorable, then we are likely to be relatively satisfied with it. (2) We might also compare a relationship to others that are available to us. If none of the alternatives seem to offer more favorable outcomes, we are likely to be more satisfied with the existing relationship than if we have many alternatives which promise greater rewards compared to costs. (3) We might also compare the outcome of the relationship to the experiences of others who are involved in similar situations. If other people seem to get more favorable outcomes from similar relationships, then we are likely to feel somewhat dissatisfied with our own. (4) Finally, we may evaluate the outcome of the relationship in terms of our resources and our ability to control our choices. If we feel that we have a great deal to offer and have control over our choices, we may expect a highly favorable outcome. On the other hand, if we feel that we have little to offer and little control over our choices, we are likely to settle for a much less favorable outcome.

According to social exchange theory, if we evaluate a relationship favorably, we are likely to continue it. If we evaluate it unfavorably, we are likely to seek other relationships that promise more favorable outcomes. Consider, for example, the following statement by a woman who sought counseling for marital problems.

> I don't want to keep trying to make the marriage work any more. Bill is a good husband, a good father to our children, he is understanding, and he supports my career. But we spend more and more time arguing, and I'm spending too much time trying to help him overcome his feelings of depression about his career, his excessive drinking, and his feeling that his life is going down the drain. I just can't keep this up much longer. It's just not worth it. My friends don't have to put up with these kinds of problems, and I didn't have to either until four or five years ago. I'd rather separate than go on living this way. Sure it would be hard to break up the marriage, but I think living apart would be more satisfying and less of a strain for everyone.

In the social exchange model, the exchange of anything of value between two people is the foundation of an interpersonal relationship. What emerges in the relationship is a compromise involving mutual concessions as well as mutual giving (Blau, 1967; Rand, 1965). In a sense, it is a compromise between what we might like to have (fantasy) and what we have to settle for (reality). As a consequence, each of us will presumably end up with the person and the relationship which we "deserve," in terms of what we have to offer and what we are willing (or forced) to accept as a compromise.

The social exchange model may seem somewhat cynical in its emphasis on the individual's "value" on the "open market" of interpersonal relationships. However, it also draws attention to some of the conditions that are likely to be important in relationships that are satisfying and enduring.

## Social Role Model

*All the world's a stage*
*And all the men and women merely players.*

(Shakespeare)

**social role model:** view that relationships between people are governed by certain agreed-upon roles

**role:** socially expected behavior pattern

A second way to gain insight into relationships between people is the **social role model.** The term **role** is borrowed from the theater and refers to the words and actions that accompany a specified part in a play. The behavior of the person playing the part is specified by the script and remains essentially the same regardless of who plays the part. While an individual may lend his or her own interpretation to the role, there are limits to the extent to which an actor can deviate from the script. Interpersonal relationships also involve roles or "parts" that are played by the participants. For example, most of us know what kinds of behavior to expect from a friend, a lover, a spouse, an advisor, a banker, and so on. We expect people to act in certain ways depending on the social role they have adopted, and violations of these expectations and demands are likely to lead to conflict, stress, and possibly the termination of the relationship.

Harold Garfinkel (1963) provided some entertaining and illustrative examples of the importance of roles in interpersonal relationships. He asked his students to violate normal, expected behavior in some simple way and to record the results. One student reported that she had been watching television with her husband when he remarked that he was tired.

STUDENT: How are you tired? Physically, mentally, or just bored?
HUSBAND: I don't know, I guess physically, mainly.
STUDENT: You mean that your muscles ache, or your bones?
HUSBAND: I guess so. Don't be so technical.

# *Insight*

## The "Prisoner's Dilemma"

A variety of two-person situations for studying interpersonal relationships have been devised. One is called the "Prisoner's Dilemma," in which the two subjects are asked to role play being accomplices in a crime who have been arrested and placed in separate cells. Each is urged by the "District Attorney" to confess and testify against the other, with the promise that he or she will receive only a light sentence in return. If the subject refuses, he or she is threatened with a trumped-up conviction on some minor charge.

The dilemma is this: If neither prisoner confesses, both will get off with relatively light sentences due to the lack of evidence. If one remains silent but the other does not, the "silent" one is likely to receive the maximum sentence. If both confess, both will probably receive fairly severe sentences. If you were one of the prisoners, would you confess to avoid the maximum sentence, or remain silent and trust that your accomplice would do the same?

This simple situation can be used in a laboratory setting to explore many aspects of interpersonal interactions. In the prisoner's dilemma, for example, the investigator can change the possible outcomes, specifying the payoffs, losses, and outcomes preferred by a player. Similarly, the investigator can manipulate the level of risk or uncertainty involved and can attempt to identify the strategy employed by the players or see whether the strategy changes during the course of the interaction. Through these laboratory analogues, originally designed to explore aspects of international relations, we can learn about caution, suspicion, trust, vengefulness, and other characteristics of behavior relevant to interpersonal relationships.

HUSBAND: *(after more watching)* All these old movies have the same kind of old iron bedstead in them.

STUDENT: What do you mean? Do you mean all old movies, or some of them, or just the ones you have seen?

HUSBAND: What's the matter with you? You know what I mean.

STUDENT: I wish you would be more specific.

HUSBAND: You know what I mean! Drop dead! (p. 221)

Another student reported:

My friend said to me, "Hurry or we will be late." I asked him what did he mean by late and from what point of view did it have reference. There was a look of perplexity and cynicism on his face. "Why are you asking me such silly questions? Surely I don't have to explain such a statement. What is wrong with you today? Why should I have to stop to analyze such a statement. Everyone understands my statements and you should be no exception." (p. 222)

Let's take a closer look at the social role model and the ways in which it sheds light on interpersonal relationships.

**Role expectations.** Certain obligations, duties, and rights go with any given role in a relationship. For example, a "close friend" is expected to be caring, supportive, helpful, and understanding. A "spouse" is not expected to have sexual relationships with other people. A "salesperson" is expected to be well-informed, helpful, obtain the item we decide to purchase, make correct change, and so on.

**role expectations:** obligations associated with a particular interpersonal role

When these **role expectations** are not fulfilled, the result is stress. For example, imagine a couple who have agreed that the wife will handle the family's finances and taxes while the husband handles the maintenance of the house and yard. If the wife suddenly announces that she doesn't intend to prepare the annual tax return, or the husband announces that he will no longer mow the lawn, then their shared role expectations are violated and they are likely to experience stress.

In cases such as these, pressures are likely to be exerted in an effort to force the individual to fulfill role expectations. If a more serious breach in role behavior occurs—such as a salesperson who deliberately misinforms us about a product, or a person who drives the wrong way on a one-way street—social or legal sanctions are likely to be imposed to reduce or eliminate the likelihood that the inappropriate behavior will recur.

**role conflict:** condition arising when an individual must play incompatible roles

**Role conflict.**    Another source of stress in interpersonal relationships is **role conflict.** This occurs when a person feels uncomfortable playing a particular role or is unable to reconcile apparently contradictory role demands. For example, a lawyer may find it difficult to be aggressive when cross-examining witnesses in court. A person may take on the roles of spouse, lawyer, and parent only to discover that those roles make conflicting demands that are difficult or impossible to reconcile.

If the social exchange model seems "materialistic," the role model seems to carry a connotation of "phoniness," of "not being one's true self." However, note that when people really believe in their roles and are committed to playing them, they are acting sincerely and are not being phony. "Phonies" are people who play a role in which they do not believe and to which they are not committed, or who play a role that arouses expectations in others that they have no intention of meeting, as in the case of a con artist.

## Games Model

*Oh, the games people play now,*
*Ev'ry night and ev'ry day now,*
*Never meanin' what they say now*
*Never sayin' what they mean.*

"Games People Play" (South, 1968)

**games model:** view that interpersonal relationships are controlled or heavily influenced by games

Another way of viewing interpersonal relationships is in terms of the **games model.** We shall deal here with psychiatrist Eric Berne's concept of games, which is described in *Games People Play* (1964). To understand interpersonal transactions in terms of this model, it is useful to review several underlying concepts.

**Child, Parent, Adult.**    Berne (1964, 1972) believed that an individual's personality is comprised of three parts or ego states: the Child—innocent, spontaneous, and fun-loving; the Parent—authoritative and conditioned to behave in "correct" ways; and the Adult—mature and reality oriented.

Berne then analyzed interpersonal relationships in terms of the ego states that are actually exercised when two people interact. For example, we may observe a woman berating her husband for failing to take out the garbage. However, said Berne, the ego states that may be operating in this example are the Parent state of the woman ("How many times have I asked you to take out the garbage, you bad boy?") and the Child state of the man ("Aw, mom"). Thus, while we see an interaction between two adults, the underlying process is better understood through reference to the Parent and Child ego states of the woman and man. Berne hypothesized that all interpersonal relationships could be analyzed in terms of these three ego states.

**games:** interpersonal strategies used to exert influence over others

**Games.**    Berne suggested that most people are constantly playing **games** in their relationships with others; that is, they utilize strategies which have a payoff. Berne labeled the most common game played by spouses as "If It Weren't For You." This game (Berne, 1964) illustrates the general characteristics of games and the purposes they serve.

> Mrs. White complained that her husband severely restricted her social activities, so that she had never learned to dance. Due to changes brought about by psychiatric treat-ment . . . her husband became more indulgent. Mrs. White was then free to enlarge the scope of her activities. She signed up for dancing classes, and then discovered to her despair that she had a morbid fear of dance floors and had to abandon this project.
>
> This unfortunate adventure, along with similar ones, laid bare some important aspects of the structure of her marriage. Out of her many suitors she had picked a domineering man for a husband. She was then in a position to complain that she could do all sorts of things "if it weren't for you." (p. 50)

The "payoff" for Mrs. White was that her husband was protecting her from doing something she was deeply afraid of and permitting her to take the stance "It's not that I'm afraid, it's that he won't let me" or "I'm trying, but he holds me back." The payoff for the husband was presumably the boost he received from playing a domineering role. (See the Psychology in Action, p. 347 for a look at some more "games people play.")

**Function of games.**    Games are played because they serve two functions. First, they are substitutes for true intimacy in daily life—intimacy for which there is presumably little opportunity and for which many people are unprepared. Second, they serve as strategies to maintain interpersonal relationships, as in the "If it weren't for you" game played by the Whites. It is important to note that these games are not consciously planned. Rather, the participants may be only partially aware or even entirely unaware of the games they are playing.

Games can be both constructive and destructive. Some games, for example, may add a touch of excitement and romance to an intimate relationship. However, most of the games described by Berne are rarely played for fun. In fact, many of

# Psychology in Action

## Some Games People Play

Here are a few of the more common games delineated by Berne (1964).

**TAC *(Try and Collect)*.** I go into debt to you. You try to collect and I keep putting off repaying. Finally, you take stern measures and I point out how greedy and ruthless you are.

**WAHM *(Why Does This Always Happen to Me?)*.** I continually provoke people into mistreating and rejecting me; then I whine, "Why does this always happen to me?" This is the game of those who are perennially the jilted, the fired, the scorned.

**NIGYSOB *(Now I've Got You, You Son of a Bitch)*.** I allow you to take advantage of me until you are quite vulnerable; then I rise in righteous indignation.

**AIA *(Ain't It Awful?)*.** I constantly invite mistreatment, then complain to others that I am mistreated.

**SWYMD *(See What You Made Me Do)*.** I am nervous or upset and drop or break something. I turn angrily to whoever is closest and say, "See what you made me do."

**YDYB *(Why Don't You—Yes But)*.** I invite you to give me advice, then find a good reason for rejecting everything you suggest—thus putting you down.

**GYWP *(Gee, You're Wonderful, Professor!)*.** This is a way of getting the professor to act the way I want, and, if he or she doesn't, I can be disappointed in my fallen idol. It works especially well if the professor responds with *YUP*, "*You're uncommonly perceptive.*"

---

them are serious and have highly destructive effects. While games may help maintain a relationship, they may exact a high cost in terms of blocked personal growth. In our discussion of maladaptive interpersonal patterns, we shall see how truly destructive some games can become.

In the remainder of this chapter, as well as in the chapters that follow, we shall have occasion to see the importance of these three models for understanding interpersonal relationships. Let's start by looking at the ways in which relationships with other people develop.

## DEVELOPMENT OF RELATIONSHIPS WITH SIGNIFICANT OTHERS

**significant others:** people especially important to an individual

**Significant others** are people who are important to us and to our lives. In childhood, significant others can include parents, teachers, and friends. In adulthood, significant others may be spouses, friends, children, and co-workers. Our discussion will focus on five key processes involved in the development and course of relationships with significant others: (1) the encounter, (2) interpersonal attraction, (3) interpersonal communication, (4) interpersonal accommodation, and (5) self-disclosure. As we shall see, level of involvement increases and commitment to the other person deepens as we move from the superficial level of the encounter to the level of self-disclosure.

In the next chapter, we will look more closely at intimate relationships, which represent the highest level of involvement and commitment between two people.

## The Initial Encounter

The first step in relating to others is the initial encounter or interaction with another person. Many people find such encounters exciting and rewarding, particularly if the other person is perceived as attractive and nonthreatening. If, on the other hand, we perceive others as unattractive and threatening, we may avoid these encounters. Similarly, our fears of rejection may cause us to avoid others. Despite the potential risks in encounters, however, we usually make ourselves accessible to selected people (see the Psychology in Action, p. 349).

**Initiating the encounter.**   An encounter begins with some sort of communicative act that invites a response from another person. Such an act may involve a smile, a gaze, or a pleasant remark. If the other person responds positively, the encounter is underway.

In the early stages of an encounter, there tends to be a good deal of uncertainty, and people usually engage in rather tentative and safe interactions until their respective roles become clear. Lalljee and Cook (1973), for example, found a great deal of uncertainty in verbal expressions during the initial phase of the encounter. This gradually decreased as the encounter progressed and each person received feedback from the other person.

*Initial encounters are usually filled with uncertainty even when we perceive others as attractive and nonthreatening. Many people find such encounters exciting and rewarding, however, and make themselves accessible to selected people.*

# Psychology in Action

## Shyness

*I'm not a person who starts conversations. It's especially hard for me to talk to strangers, like when I'm standing in a long line or sitting next to someone on a bus. At parties I depend on others to keep the jokes and stories going and to get some life into the party if it's dull. If I see someone who looks interesting, I don't introduce myself; instead I wait for them to talk to me first or to show some sign of interest. In groups, I'm rarely the leader; I let others take charge and get people introduced. I guess I just don't have much confidence in social situations where I don't already know people: I feel awkward and uncomfortable. I find it hard to relax, I feel really inhibited, I get nervous, and I worry about saying something dumb.*

Does this sound familiar? Have you ever felt this way? If so, welcome to the crowd! These feelings are the hallmarks of shyness, and virtually everybody has been shy at some point in their lives (Morris, 1983; Zimbardo, 1977). In fact, psychologist Philip Zimbardo has discovered that approximately 40 percent of college students consider themselves to be shy at any given moment and more than 90 percent say they have been shy at some point in their lives. Fully 25 percent of college students say that they have always been shy. Shyness is very nearly a universal experience.

If you look again at the preceeding description of the shy person, you will notice that a common theme emerges: the shy person doesn't take the initiative in social encounters. As a result, it should come as no surprise that shy people are often lonely and dissatisfied with their social relationships (Jones & Carpenter, 1986). However, the costs of shyness go beyond loneliness and dissatisfaction. Zimbardo (1986) suggests that shyness

*"prevents people from making and maintaining the human connection. At the same time, it also alienates the individual from an acceptance and full appreciation of the self. The shy person is voluntarily surrendering basic freedoms of action, opinion, and association in exchange for an illusion of security" (p. 18).*

Zimbardo (1977) elaborates on this idea.

*In deciding whether or not to connect with another person, we all look at the anticipated social rewards and balance them with the potential costs of being embarrassed, ridiculed, or rejected and found boring, unworthy, or inadequate. We compute the effort required, the time, money cost, distance, and the other opportunities that must be given up once we decide on full-steam-ahead. . . . For many people the answer is, "It's not worth the hurt to get some good strokes." . . . Shy people . . . choose the security of isolation over the risk of being rejected. But we must all take this risk to establish the important relationships in our lives. (pp. 111–12)*

To facilitate interpersonal interactions, many societies provide guidelines for structuring initial encounters. In Japan, for example, when two strangers meet they usually first exchange name cards so that the appropriate roles (style of language, depth of bowing, and so on) may be enacted. In the United States, most encounters are initiated on a much less formal basis. Structure usually develops as the encounter progresses and each person learns more about the position, status, and other relevant characteristics of the other. Nevertheless, there are often unwritten "rules" for encounters, even though such rules may be vague and subject to different interpretations. For example, in this country when two people meet casually it is customary to say something like "How are you?" to which the normal response is "Fine, thanks." Garfinkel (1963) studied one of his students who decided to violate these rules.

> *The victim waved his hand cheerily.*
> VICTIM: How are you?
> STUDENT: How am I with regard to what? My health, my finances, my school work, my peace of mind, my . . . .
> VICTIM: (Red in the face and suddenly out of control) Look! I was just trying to be polite. Frankly, I don't give a damn how you are. (p. 222)

**"Rules" for encounters.**    Encounters may take many different forms and involve diverse roles, interactions, and settings. Roles for a job interview are quite different from the roles and interactions of a family dinner; roles for talking with another student before the start of class are quite different from the roles and interactions with an instructor after class. A physician who asks "How are you?" when you are in a hospital bed recovering from surgery is likely to expect and receive responses very different from the a person who meets you on the street and is simply "trying to be polite."

In general, the setting in which the encounter occurs tends to establish certain guidelines. For example, an encounter that begins in a church will be different from an encounter that begins at a race track. Similarly, most of us use the actions of others as a means of guiding our own behavior. If we are uncertain how to behave at a party, we can use the principles of observational learning and watch others as a way to structure our own behavior.

Once an encounter is underway, an unwritten agreement usually develops about the expected roles and interactions. If one person suddenly changes roles or otherwise breaks the agreement, that individual is likely to be resented. An example would be the person who encourages another person to reveal intimate and potentially embarrassing confidences, only to ridicule that person when he or she does "open up."

**Termination of the encounter.**    Most initial encounters end with ritualistic role behavior in which each participant is assured that the encounter will be resumed. For example, telephone numbers may be exchanged or promises made to "get together as soon as possible."

Most encounters between people do not progress past this stage. Although these encounters can be satisfying, they are also superficial. Those that progress and deepen beyond the initial phase often involve interpersonal attraction.

## Interpersonal Attraction

"What does she see in him?" or "What does he see in her?" are questions commonly asked about relationships that apparently succeed for reasons that are unclear. Of course, we are usually ready with some "common-sense" explanation. When two people are very different in terms of background and personality, we may point out that "Opposites attract." When two people who are very much alike get along well together, we may decide, "Birds of a feather flock together."

In this section we shall examine the factors that influence the attraction between two people and thus the likelihood that they will seek a more enduring relationship.

**How we perceive others.**     Our **interpersonal perceptions** are strongly affected by our use of **stereotypes** and by first impressions. For example, someone may believe that college professors are absent-minded idealists and that all homeless people are simply too lazy to get a job. These stereotypes strongly influence the ways in which that person will initially respond to professors and to street people. When meeting a professor, their initial response may be one of bemused appreciation, while their response to a street person may be outright hostility and contempt.

**interpersonal perceptions:** ways in which we perceive other people

**stereotypes:** characteristics presumed to be shared by all members of a social category

Initial interactions with others are then used as a means to confirm the stereotypes. If the professor mentions misplacing his or her keys, this information confirms the stereotype that all professors are forgetful. If a street person is lying down and resting, this can be understood as evidence of laziness. It is important to note that information that contradicts stereotypes is often ignored, forgotten, or misinterpreted. For example, the professor may demonstrate a remarkable memory, but because of the stereotype the person is more likely to remember the keys that were misplaced. A street person may stand in line at an employment office, but this behavior may be reinterpreted simply as a way to find a warm place to waste time for a while. In both cases, information that contradicts the stereotypes is rendered ineffective.

First impressions often help determine whether we are attracted to another individual. Our first impressions of a person have a great impact on our perception of him or her, even though the initial encounter may be very brief. Thus, the effort we expend to make a good impression has a worthwhile "payoff."

Our perceptions of other people are subject to numerous sources of error. Although most people seem to be interested in other people's positive or favorable characteristics, in fact negative information is usually weighed so heavily that it overrules all the positive information that is available about the person (Hamilton & Zanna, 1972). You may find yourself initially attracted to another individual who is both pleasant and charming. However, when you discover that he or she holds political beliefs that are directly opposite to your own, your overall perception of the individual is likely to become negative.

**halo effect:** tendency to assess a person on the basis of one or two easily perceived traits, such as seeing attractive persons as being friendly

The **halo effect** (Nisbett & Wilson, 1977) can also influence our perceptions of others. Due to the halo effect, our overall impression of a person may transfer to the evaluation of specific attributes. Consider the case of a woman regarded positively by one individual and negatively by another. When asked to comment on a specific attribute, her speech accent for example, the first person may find it appealing, while the second may judge it irritating.

Another source of error in interpersonal perception is the fact that some people are deliberately misleading, they put on a "good front." As we get to know them better, we may have an opportunity to observe many additional characteristics that were not apparent during the initial encounter. This enables us to make corrections in our original perceptions and assessments.

**What makes another person attractive?**     Researchers have identified four factors that are important in determining whether we are likely to find another person

Attraction may seem to be a mysterious process, but researchers have determined that physical attractiveness, proximity, availability, and similarity of interests and beliefs are factors likely to affect whether or not two people will be drawn to each other.

attractive. These are physical attractiveness, proximity, availability, and similarity and complementarity of interest and beliefs.

1. *Physical attractiveness.* Physical attractiveness is the most important factor in the early stages of interpersonal relationships. As Krebs and Adinolfi (1975) have stated "there is a growing body of evidence which shows that the average person drastically underestimates the influence of physical attractiveness . . ." (p. 245). In general, people prefer to interact with people who are physically attractive. Although this factor is highly important in affecting initial attraction, the importance of physical attractiveness tends to diminish over time and be replaced by other personality characteristics as a relationship matures.

2. *Proximity.* Physical closeness or proximity is another important factor in interpersonal attraction. Although the process may seem quite obvious, its effects on our behavior can be significant. In one study reported by Festinger, Schachter, and Back (1950), residents of a housing complex reported the greatest number of friendships with the next-door neighbors and almost no friendships with neighbors who lived four or five doors away. In an experimental setting, Saegert, Swap, and Zajonc (1973) found that as the number of contacts between strangers increased, their evaluations of each other became more positive as well.

These findings suggest that initial attraction is most likely to develop between individuals who have frequent contact with one another. Although proximity need not be limited to the "boy or girl next door," other sources of physical closeness and social contact may prove important in initial attraction. Thus, students taking the same classes, workers in an office or factory, members of the same club, or people routinely taking the same bus together may find themselves attracted to one another.

3. *Availability.* A third factor in initial attraction is the accessibility or availability of the partner. Although we may enjoy the fantasy of a tumultuous love affair with a famous television, sports, or music personality, we are most likely to turn our attentions to the individual available for a date on the weekend.

Interestingly, too much availability may have negative effects. Research reported by Hatfield and Walster (1978), for example, found that men were most strongly attracted to women who were accessible to them, but not on an exclusive basis.

4. *Similarity and complementarity.* We are most attracted to, and become more deeply involved with, individuals sharing similar backgrounds, educational levels, beliefs, values, and purposes, and we tend to expect that they will like us as well (Gonzales et al., 1983; Buss, 1985). For example, college students are most likely to become involved with someone who also has had some college experiences than with someone who has only completed the eighth grade.

Similarity, then, is a powerful determinant of attractiveness. Birds of a feather *do* tend to flock together, and they also tend to stay together longer. But what about the idea that "opposites attract"? This is called the principle of **complementarity**, and it is well illustrated by the belief that very sociable and outgoing individuals are often attracted to people who are shy and reserved. Interestingly, a large number of research studies have failed to find support for the principle of complementarity. While it is possible that complementarity plays a small role in the early stages of a relationship when it seems exciting to meet and relate to someone "different," in long-term relationships people overwhelmingly prefer to associate with other people who are similar to them (Buss, 1985).

**complementarity:** principle that people are attracted to others whose traits or characteristics supplement or contrast with their own

We have seen so far that people tend to be attracted to others who are physically attractive, physically accessible and socially available, and similar in terms of purposes, backgrounds, beliefs, and needs. However, the continuation and progression of an interpersonal relationship requires interpersonal communication and accommodation as well as interpersonal attraction. In the next portion of the chapter, we turn our attention to those important processes.

## Interpersonal Communication

*We are living in a world saturated with communication, on the verge of perishing for lack of it; a world smothered with words, hungry for one meaningful word; a world bombarded with data, rarely capable of sorting out the truth; and a world in which we can flash messages across the ocean by way of space, but one in which we find it difficult to get through to each other face to face.*

"Telecommunication Policy and the Information Society" (Schinn, 1976, p. 2)

For interpersonal relationships to grow and move toward mutual goals, it is essential that people communicate with each other. Thus, communication lies at the center of all human relationships. Without communication, social life as we know it

*Even when we are not communicating verbally, gestures, body posture, and facial expressions may communicate what we are thinking or feeling.*

**verbal communication:**
communication through written words and the use of language

**nonverbal communication:**
communication through gestures, facial expressions, and body posture

**affective information:**
information concerning feelings, emotions, and attitudes

would come to a complete halt. While some other species also use limited forms of communication to regulate at least some aspects of their social lives, human communication is infinitely more subtle and complex. However, as we will see, the complexity and subtlety of human communication are not without drawbacks.

There are two primary ways of communicating information: **verbal communication,** which relies on spoken or written words, and **nonverbal communication,** which relies on such things as voice inflection, facial expressions, gestures, body movements, and even moments of silence. People tend to use these two forms of communication for somewhat different kinds of messages. Verbal communication is used most often to convey *factual* information, thoughts, ideas, plans, and so on. When we tell another person our name and address, our remembrances of childhood, or our opinions of a book or movie, we are conveying factual information. Human language is remarkably appropriate for this kind of communication: it allows us to communicate even the most complex factual information precisely and accurately.

Most interpersonal relationships also require the communication of emotions and feelings, or **affective information.** When we express tenderness, love, anger, or gratitude toward others, we are providing affective information. Information about feelings and emotions is usually conveyed by nonverbal communication. It may be that human language is inadequate for effectively communicating affective information, or it may be that human beings simply prefer not to put their emotions and feelings into words very often—whatever the reason, people do not often rely on verbal communication to convey affective information.

**Verbal communication.**  At first glance, verbal communication might seem relatively straightforward: people decide what they want to say to another person and then simply say it! Actually, verbal communication is surprisingly complex. For example, individuals must decide not only *what* to say but also *how* to say it to another person. If you need help and are speaking to your small child, it might be appropriate to say, "Come help Daddy." The same underlying message to a stranger on the street might be rephrased, "Excuse me, but could you please help me for just a minute?" In a tight-knit work group, you might get away with, "Don't just stand there—lend a hand!"

In other words, most of us reformulate our verbal messages to fit the intended receiver. As a result, most verbal communication contains several messages. In all the examples given in the preceding paragraph, there is certainly the literal message "I need your help." However, there are also hidden or implicit messages such as, "I am treating you like my child," "I'm aware I'm intruding and I apologize," and "We're supposed to be helping each other and you're not doing your share."

These hidden verbal messages are often helpful in establishing and maintaining interpersonal relationships. Using the word "sir," for example, is one way of showing continuing respect for a male. "Dear" and "sweetheart" suggest not only that you care a great deal about the other person, but also that the rest of your message should be interpreted in that context. However, hidden messages can also be a source of difficulty in interpersonal relationships. For example, imagine that one person says to another, "How many times do I have to ask you to clean your room?" There are several hidden messages here: one message is "I have a right to tell you what to do"; another hidden message is "You are expected to obey me"; a third is "I am permitted to criticize you"; yet another is "Don't get smart and answer my question—just clean the room!" Now, if I were to tell you that the comment was made by a husband to his wife rather than by a father to his son, you can see the potential for serious problems!

We have seen that interpersonal communication is more complex than it at first appears. Even a fairly simple verbal message can convey all sorts of hidden or implicit meanings depending on the words used by the speaker. When nonverbal aspects of communication are considered, the complexity and subtlety of interpersonal communication become even greater.

**Nonverbal communication.**  Even a verbal message has nonverbal characteristics: it is spoken in a certain tone of voice, some words are emphasized more than others, it is spoken loudly or softly, slowly or quickly, and so on. These nonverbal aspects of the message communicate additional meaning. For example, consider the changes in meaning when the simple comment "It's so nice to see you again" is spoken with the emphasis on different words: "It's SO nice to see you again," "It's so nice to SEE you again," "It's so nice to see YOU again," "It's so nice to see you AGAIN." I think you will agree that the different emphases communicate somewhat different messages.

However, emphasis is only one way to use nonverbal cues to modify a verbal message. Using the same sentence, think for a moment how you might change your voice to convey the message that it really *isn't* nice to see the person again—perhaps you're greeting someone you've always disliked intensely or someone who has spread rumors about you. Then imagine that you are greeting someone especially dear to you whom you haven't seen for years. Finally, imagine that you are at a family funeral greeting "a friend of a friend." Even this simple message takes on quite different meanings as you change the way in which it is spoken.

*Facial expressions* are another source of nonverbal communication. Psychologist Paul Ekman and his colleagues (Ekman & Friesen, 1975; Ekman, Friesen, & Ellsworth, 1972) have found that facial expressions of our primary emotions—anger, fear, disgust, surprise, sadness, and happiness—are recognized and given the same labels in cultures throughout the world. Preliterate New Guinea tribesmen, for example, and American Japanese students express and interpret these emotions in comparable ways. As Ekman (1975) has noted: "If you meet a native in New Guinea or your old boss in a Manhattan bar, you will be able to interpret their facial expressions easily, knowing how they feel—or how they want you to think they feel" (p. 35).

Most people are reasonably skillful at controlling their facial expressions, at "putting on a face" when necessary (Zuckerman, DePaulo, & Rosenthal, 1981). They learn to exaggerate their expressions or minimize them, "keep a straight face" or a "poker face," and even mask their emotions by showing the opposite facial expressions (Ekman & Friesen, 1975). Thus, facial expressions sometimes tell us more about what the person wants us to *think* they are feeling than what they are *actually* feeling. Other nonverbal cues, however, are not as easily controlled, and thus they are more likely to reveal accurately the person's emotions.

*Body movements* provide fairly reliable emotional cues that are difficult for most people to control and manipulate without training. In some cases, the message can be quite precise: for example, you nod your head for "yes," raise your eyebrows to show skepticism, cross your fingers for good luck, shrug to indicate "I don't know" or "It doesn't matter," give the thumbs-up sign for "Everything's fine," and so on. Most body cues do not correspond precisely to the emotions you are feeling, and most are much less precise than facial expressions (Feldman, 1985). Crossing your arms or legs, sitting back or leaning forward, clenching your fist or letting your hands hang loosely—all of these are examples of what Fast (1970) called *body language*. Body language provides general information about your emotional state and about your relationship to the person with whom you are communicating. For example, crossing your arms and legs communicates reservedness, inaccessibility, and distance from the other person; standing with your feet close together, holding your arms close to your body, and nodding and smiling communicates lower status (Penrod, 1986).

Even the *distance* between you and another person communicates a message, according to the anthropologist Edward Hall (1966). In middle-class American culture, relationships with complete strangers, formal meetings, speeches, and relationships with important public figures are usually conducted at a distance of more than twelve feet. However, most of our interpersonal relationships—with co-workers, casual friends, new acquaintances, and business associates—are conducted at a distance of four to twelve feet. Typically, once you are within four feet of another person, you are inside their "personal space," an invisible boundary that separates casual friends and acquaintances (who are kept "at arm's length") from close friends and acquaintances (who can legitimately come within our four-foot zone). Even within our personal space, there are boundaries: for example, the space within 18 inches of us is reserved for our most intimate relationships with children, spouses, lovers, and the closest of friends.

You can see, then, how the distance between you and another person communicates a message. If you move to within four feet of another person, you are sending a message that you consider them a close friend or acquaintance. If you touch them, you are treating them as an intimate friend. Similarly, if you back away from a close friend, he or she may perceive that something is wrong with your relationship and that you are trying to keep him or her at arm's length.

Although it may sound as if interpersonal messages are sent back and forth only through one channel at a time, every interpersonal communication involves multiple channels. A verbal message has nonverbal characteristics and, as you speak, you are simultaneously communicating messages with body language and the distance you maintain between yourself and the listener. These messages are not always consistent (see Insight, p. 359). For example, you may be verbally expressing calmness while your voice and your body communicate extreme tension or anxiety; you may be verbally respectful to a superior while standing just two or three feet from him. How do we decide which is the real message?

Research reported by Ekman et al. (1980) suggests the answer

> . . . depends on what characteristic is being judged as well as on the interpersonal situation in which the judged behavior occurs. The claims in the literature that the face is most important or that the nonverbal-visual channel is more important than the verbal-auditory channel have not been supported. (p. 276)

In other words, we consider the situation in which the communication is taking place and the characteristic we are trying to judge (for example, the person's calmness, honesty, dominance, or outgoingness) before we decide which message we will weigh most heavily.

**Improving communication.**    We have seen that interpersonal communication is complex and thus open to all kinds of errors and misinterpretations. How can we improve communication skills so that there are fewer errors and thus fewer misunderstandings? We will discuss various ways to build more satisfying interpersonal relationships later in this chapter, but some preliminary observations may be helpful here. Obviously, we must pay attention to both the verbal and nonverbal components if communication is to be interpreted accurately. For example, the phrase "How exciting" accompanied by rolled, upturned eyes conveys a sardonic quality very different from the message conveyed when the same phrase is accompanied by a bright smile.

Effective communication is not synonymous with verbosity. People can spend hours talking to one another and not communicate any information. Whether the partners in a relationship spend twenty minutes or twenty hours speaking to each other, it seems crucial that they understand one another, feel understood, and be able to express clearly their feelings on important issues.

Clarity of communication accompanied by a sensitivity to the other person's feelings and point of view is usually an effective method of communication. For example, when we are dissatisfied with some aspect of the relationship, it is probably better to express our feelings directly than to express them indirectly through shortened tempers and bad moods or by picking a fight on an unrelated topic. Thus, if you are distressed by your partner's abuse of alcohol in social situations, you can more effectively communicate your feelings by expressing them directly than by acting distant and aloof or by complaining about your partner's taste in clothes.

Similarly, interpersonal sensitivity and tact are also useful skills for improving communication. In the example described above, you could express your concern by saying, "You're a drunk and a lush," or you can express your feelings in an equally clear but less destructive fashion, "I get very upset when you drink too much at parties."

## Self-disclosure

*. . . all relations which people have to one another are based on their knowing something about one another.*
          *The Sociology of Georg Simmel* (Simmel, 1964, p. 307)

As a relationship develops and people communicate more openly with each other, the question inevitably arises "How much of myself should I disclose to this other person? What is best kept secret and what is best disclosed?" While the answers to these questions depend in part on the type and intimacy of the relationship and on the persons involved, we can consider some aspects of the problem that may help you make decisions about self-disclosure in your own relationships.

**self-disclosure:** disclosure of information about oneself to another person

**The nature and course of self-disclosure.**    **Self-disclosure** may be defined as any information we communicate about ourselves to another person. The basic dimensions of self-disclosure include (1) the amount and breadth of information disclosed, (2) the intimacy and depth of information disclosed, (3) the positive or negative nature of the information disclosed, and (4) the timing of the information disclosed (Cozby, 1973; Gilbert, 1976).

During the initial stage of a friendship, medium amounts of self-disclosure tend to be interpreted as indications of a person's truthfulness and desire for a closer relationship. Low self-disclosers revealing little or nothing about themselves are likely to experience difficulty in establishing a relationship. High self-disclosers, on the other hand, are often perceived as overly preoccupied with themselves and maladjusted (Strassberg, Robak, D'Antonio, & Gabel, 1977; Wortman, Adesman, Herman & Greenberg, 1976).

# *Insight*

As a relationship progresses, the amount and intimacy of self-disclosure usually increase. Each person tends to reveal about the same amount of information as he or she receives. However, the eventual amount and intimacy of self-disclosure may vary greatly, depending on the characteristics of the persons involved, the nature of the relationship, and the specific information involved. Interestingly enough, low disclosers as compared with high disclosers tend to mask or "gild" information they do not wish to reveal and sometimes resort to outright falsification (Gitter & Black, 1976).

**Secrets: to tell or not to tell?**   Unfortunately, the decision to tell or not to tell "secrets" about oneself is not always simple; sometimes, even deciding how much information to disclose can be difficult. For example, as a relationship progresses, it is normal for one or both partners to want to know more about the other's past. The question of what to disclose may then become important. Should a person reveal past sexual experiences to a prospective spouse? An abortion? A criminal record? Should the person be governed by honesty and openness and so reveal all? Or should one consider the possible cost in damage to the relationship? How does one realistically weigh the risk of self-disclosure against the risk of later disclosure by a third party?

Here it is interesting to note Cozby's (1973) finding that highly intimate levels of self-disclosure tend to be rewarding at first. Eventually, however, the costs outweigh the rewards. The most apparent cost is anxiety about upsetting the other person, demeaning oneself in the other person's eyes, and damaging the relationship. This conclusion applies both to "past" and "now" secrets. In fact, "now" secrets—

such as dissatisfaction with some aspect of the relationship or confessions of infidelity—are often more difficult to reveal than "past" secrets.

Although we may be convinced and proud that we are making an effort to be more open and honest in our interpersonal relationships, we should also consider the consequences of unrestrained self-disclosure. In fact, Altman and Taylor (1973) have expressed concern about a "tyranny of openness," in which persons are denied privacy and perhaps even mystery because others demand full self-disclosure in interpersonal encounters and relationships. At this point, it seems most sensible to view self-disclosure as a problem which can best be resolved by the individual in relation to his or her beliefs, feelings, perception of the other person in the relationship, and the nature of the relationship itself.

## Interpersonal Accommodation

*Persons are decidely the hardest things we have to deal with.*
    *Schizophrenia as a Human Process* (Sullivan, 1962, p. 246)

So far in this chapter, we have seen that interpersonal relationships begin with attraction and progress to communication and greater self-disclosure. In the process, each person learns a great deal about the other person's wishes, wants, preferences, expectations, and so on. As relationships grow and develop, inevitably the partners will encounter a variety of problems that require mutual adjustment and adaptation. Some of these problems arise from within the relationship, as we will see in the following portion of this chapter. Others arise from external or environmental sources. An example of the latter would be an elderly couple whose retirement income is ravaged by inflation or a couple whose parents disapprove of their relationship.

**interpersonal accommodation:** process of adjusting to problems that arise in interpersonal relationships

**Interpersonal accommodation** is the term psychologists use for the process by which two people adjust and adapt to attain common goals, meet mutual needs, and build and maintain a satisfying relationship. There are two primary processes that are involved in accommodating to adjustive demands that arise from within the relationship: (1) structuring the relationship and (2) resolving disagreements and conflicts.

**Structuring the relationship.**    Once the encounter is underway and channels of communication have been opened, the partners begin the process of structuring the relationship—defining roles, responsibilities, norms, and the other dimensions of the emerging relationship.

1. *Roles and responsibilities.* For a relationship to be successful, it is important that each individual know what is expected and in turn clarify what he or she expects of the other person. In our discussion of the role model, we noted the emphasis

placed on role expectations and demands in interpersonal relationships. Suppose a couple is contemplating marriage, and the man expects that his partner will be affectionate, be an interesting companion, and earn a reasonable income. The woman may also expect that her partner will be affectionate, be an interesting companion, and earn a reasonable income. If each person is able to enact the expected role to the satisfaction of the other, the relationship is likely to flourish.

Where role expectations and responsibilities are not mutually satisfactory, some adjustments must be made to arrive at an agreed-upon structure. If readjustments are not made, the relationship is likely to be plagued with misunderstandings and conflicts—and may even end.

2. *Standards of satisfaction.* When attending a movie, most of us expect it to meet certain standards of plot, character portrayal, and cinematography, and we usually avoid movies that seem unlikely to meet our standards. Similarly, we establish standards of satisfaction in interpersonal relationships. For example, standards are established with respect to honesty, dependability, faithfulness, and other aspects of the relationship. As we saw earlier in our discussion of the social exchange model, these standards are used to evaluate the relationship in terms of its reward-cost value.

**Resolving disagreements and conflicts.**    This process may take a variety of forms. It may involve one-sided compromise and concession or an exchange of some kind. Through barter, compromise, and concession, there may be a continual structuring and restructuring of the relationship as the partners attempt to deal with problems and resolve disagreements.

Although bargaining and compromise are basic methods of resolving disagreements and conflicts, other techniques may also be used. A person who does not like his in-laws may simply have to accept them as part of the "package deal." A woman who dislikes her husband's occupation because it is hazardous or keeps him away from home a great deal may force herself to adapt to it. Finally, in those cases where no techniques seem to be successful at resolving disagreements and conflicts, the couple may find professional counseling helpful.

**Some unpredictable outcomes.**    Some relationships continue despite a lack of affection or the obvious presence of hostility. In such relationships certain basic needs are apparently being met, or perhaps neither partner sees the possibility of finding a better relationship with anyone else, so they let matters drift along.

Conversely, there is no guarantee that a stable and mutually fulfilling relationship will endure. Demands on interpersonal relationships change over time. Thus, the problems faced by a young married couple will be quite different from those they will face twenty years later. While they may have accommodated to the original demands, they may not be able to cope with the new demands, and the relationship may end.

Similarly, friends must adapt to the changes that occur both as the friendship grows and as the individuals in the friendship develop. Sometimes we "outgrow" friendships in the course of our personal development. Attending college, for example, may ultimately result in the end of friendships with people who do not share our experiences. Although the end of a relationship can be a sad event, it can also serve as a sign that our needs and requirements in an interpersonal relationship are undergoing a normal process of change.

## MALADAPTIVE INTERPERSONAL PATTERNS

In Edward Albee's 1962 award-winning play, *Who's Afraid of Virginia Woolf?*, the main characters, George and Martha, find themselves hopelessly embroiled in a stagnant, unfulfilling marriage. They argue all the time. They overlook no opportunity to use the other's vulnerability as a target. They are preoccupied with revenge. Both are chronically unhappy and drink excessively, hoping to numb their feelings enough to continue their essentially "academic" relationship. Neither will do anything to make the marriage better; both appear unwilling to leave for a better life.

Albee's characters dramatically illustrate that the partners in an interpersonal relationship create their own unique patterns of interaction and determine the climate and quality of the relationship. The outcome—as in the marriage of George and Martha—may be destructive and maladaptive for one or both partners.

At one time or another, nearly all of us have probably been involved in a maladaptive interpersonal relationship. Also, we have probably all wondered what went wrong and whose fault it was. Unfortunately, it is often difficult or impossible to ascertain exactly what did go wrong, but in many instances we may have a good idea. It may be helpful to examine some of the ways in which interpersonal relationships can go seriously wrong.

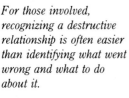

*For those involved, recognizing a destructive relationship is often easier than identifying what went wrong and what to do about it.*

Here our focus will be on three types of maladaptive interpersonal patterns: (1) fraudulent interpersonal contracts, (2) collusion in interpersonal contracts, and (3) discordant interpersonal patterns.

## Fraudulent Interpersonal Contracts

We have noted that, as a relationship progresses beyond the initial encounter, the partners enter into an arrangement, usually of informal nature, in which the "terms" of the relationship are agreed upon. In this "contract" the partners stipulate the type of relationship they hope to achieve and what each expects to contribute and receive from the relationship. Mutual acceptance of the contract usually indicates that each partner believes he or she is receiving a fair return on the investment. Here we are, of course, using the social exchange model.

**fraudulent interpersonal contract:** violation of the rules or norms governing a satisfying interpersonal relationship in a way that exploits one of the participants

In a **fraudulent interpersonal contract,** the terms of the contract are violated by one partner in a way that exploits the other. Such fraudulent patterns may develop in a variety of ways, but Carson (1969) has described a common sequence of events:

1. *A* implicitly offers *B* a type of relationship in which *B* has a high degree of interest because it seems to offer favorable possibilities for satisfaction.

2. *B* indicates acceptance of the contract and proceeds with activities appropriate to the terms of the contract.

3. *A* then assumes a stance that makes it seem "justified" to alter the terms of the contract.

4. *B* is forced to accept the new terms, thus enabling *A* to achieve the type of relationship that *A* wanted from the beginning.

Such an approach is fraudulent in that *A* presumably could not have achieved his or her objectives by an honest and straightforward approach, but only by deceit and fraud. An example of this type of interpersonal contract might involve a man planning to get married who has told his bride that he agrees with her commitment to pursue her own career. However, some years into the marriage, the husband insists that his wife quit her job so she can properly maintain their home and care for their two children, who have been in day care up until this time. The woman infers that the relationship will last only if she accedes to her husband's wishes.

In fraudulent relationships of this sort, *B* is likely to sense that he or she has been "had," and the new contractual terms are likely to prove highly frustrating to *B* and may damage the relationship. Over time *B* may feel so dissatisfied that he or she will terminate the relationship. In this case, *A* is also the loser providing he or she really did want to make the relationship work, albeit on selfish terms. Surprisingly, many fraudulent interpersonal contracts endure, in marriage and in other interpersonal settings.

## Collusion

**collusion:** agreement of partners to a relationship based on maladaptive, deviant rules and norms

In **collusion,** an interpersonal relationship is established and maintained only because the partners agree that their deviant rules and norms will be substituted for established social rules and norms. Of course there are many permissible life styles and types of interpersonal relationships in our society, and many of these do not conform strictly with established social rules and norms. Here, however, we are referring to deviant relationships that are maladaptive and destructive, usually for both partners.

One person usually takes the initiative in establishing the terms of the contract that the other must meet. Typically these terms require the partners to jointly deny or falsify some aspect of reality. For example, *A,* who drinks excessively, may agree to an intimate relationship with *B* only if *B* accepts the excessive drinking as normal. While *B* may not wish to do so, he or she may be forced to do this to complete the contract. Of course, *B* may anticipate rewards from the relationship that will outweigh this particular cost.

However, the ensuing relationship is likely to be maladaptive because the rewards in such relationships rarely justify the costs. The excessive drinking of *A,* for example, may seriously interfere with his or her occupational adjustment, the couple's social life, their sexual relationship, and many other aspects of their relationship. If the excessive drinking increases and hospitalization is required, tremendous stress may then be placed on the other partner—particularly in marital relationships. In nonmarital as well as marital relationships, the result of collusion is likely to be highly detrimental to the relationship as well as to the persons involved, and it may lead to termination of the relationship.

## Discordant Interpersonal Patterns

Some degree of friction is inevitable in interpersonal relationships, but serious and continued disagreements and conflicts hurt both the people involved as well as the quality of their relationship. These **discordant interpersonal patterns** may involve a number of areas in the relationship, or they may center on some enduring conflict. Nye (1973) has identified five particularly common sources of conflict:

**discordant interpersonal patterns:** relationships that involve serious and continuous disagreements and conflicts detrimental to the quality of the relationship

1. *Competition*—one partner gains something at the expense of the other. For example, one person may establish superiority in some area in such a way that the other feels belittled.

2. *Domination*—one partner attempts to control the other person, who then feels that his or her rights and integrity are being violated.

3. *Failure*—both partners resort to blaming each other when things go wrong in their efforts to achieve agreed-upon goals.

4. *Provocation*—one partner consistently and knowingly does things to annoy the other, and in the process, receives satisfaction from keeping things stirred up.

5. *Value differerences*—both partners seriously disagree about a variety of topics from spending money to sexual behavior to the use of leisure time.

Closely related to the preceding sources of discordance are the problems produced by conflicting communications in which the sender codes a message in such a way that it has two opposite meanings. Such a conflict between verbal and nonverbal components of a message is likely to leave the other person baffled. It may, of course, also leave a person feeling foolish and hostile.

A variation on this theme is the double-bind, those cases where we are "damned if we do and damned if we don't." For example, a husband may complain that his wife never takes the initiative in matters of affection, but when she does, he finds some excuse to reject her advances. In short, she cannot win in such a double-bind situation and is likely to end up feeling confused, devalued, and discouraged.

We have seen that some interpersonal relationships become maladaptive or even destructive over time. Nonetheless, most people are able to build and maintain satisfying relationships with others. Also, many people who find themselves caught in an unsatisfactory relationship are able to improve that relationship. In the next section of the chapter, we will look at effective ways of building and maintaining satisfying interpersonal relationships.

## FOUNDATIONS FOR BUILDING SATISFYING INTERPERSONAL RELATIONSHIPS

Despite the importance of achieving constructive and satisfying interpersonal relationships, little research has been done on this issue. Most of the popular literature on interpersonal relationships tends to offer oversimplified advice that emphasizes influencing and exploiting others. The well-publicized tactic of praising others, for example, is likely to backfire if the praise is insincere. Many people who use such simplistic techniques are shocked when realizing they have reaped a harvest of suspicion, dislike, and hostility. In contrast, the discussion that follows avoids oversimplification and is based on the well-established principles of interpersonal relationships described earlier in this chapter.

### Recognition of Mutual Rights and Purposes

In beginning our discussion, it is important to emphasize the importance of mutual rights in building healthy interpersonal relationships. This principle is illustrated in the Golden Rule—"Do unto others as you would have them do unto you." Respect for the rights of others is essential not only from an ethical standpoint but from a practical one as well. We have noted, for example, the destructive effects on a relationship when one person attempts to infringe on the rights and integrity of the other. Violating these rights almost always destroys any common ground for mutually satisfying interaction.

Through our relationships with others, we try to meet certain basic needs—perhaps for love and affection, self-esteem and worth, social approval, or maybe just feeling related to a significant other. When the relationship meets one person's needs but fails to meet those of the other person, it is likely to be difficult or impossible to maintain. Even the most generous and devoted friend may become tired of a relationship in which he or she is continually giving and never receiving.

To meet the needs of both persons, a relationship must have a common purpose. Without a shared purpose, the individuals may no longer need each other in the relationship. Two members of a college swimming team, for example, may become close friends. However, after graduation, when they pursue different careers and ways of life, the bonds that once held them together will dissolve. Similarly, a romantic relationship may be ended when one person wishes to get married and the other does not.

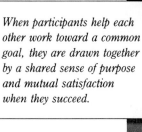

*When participants help each other work toward a common goal, they are drawn together by a shared sense of purpose and mutual satisfaction when they succeed.*

Therefore, a common purpose and mutual gratification are basic essentials for establishing and maintaining a lasting interpersonal relationship. Again we come face to face with the social exchange model and the relation of cost to satisfaction in an enduring relationship.

## Adequate Structure and Communication

In some cases, structure and communication patterns are specified by social norms. For example, there is general agreement about the type of structure and communication between teacher and student, employer and employee, bishop and parish priest, general and lieutenant. However, in most of our more personal relationships—such as those involving husband and wife, parent and child, or friend and friend—the structure and communication patterns are determined by the parties involved. This places considerable responsibility on each person in the relationship, if he or she wishes to make it a satisfying one.

**Adequate structure.**    As we saw earlier in our discussion of interpersonal accommodation, all interpersonal relationships become structured over time. It is important that the participants in a relationship assume responsibility for establishing a particular type of structure that will assure mutual satisfaction. For example, a young married couple may establish norms and expectations about visiting relatives, mutually acceptable and satisfying sexual behaviors, responsibility for various household chores,

# Insight

courtesy and honesty in dealing with each other, and so on. If they don't take active steps to set up such a structure for their relationship, one will eventually develop by itself: whatever they *usually* do will become what they *expect* to do, whether or not it is satisfactory to the individuals involved. Once such patterns and expectations have been established, it is quite difficult to change the structure.

**Effective communication.**    In the earlier discussion of interpersonal communication, we saw that meaningful communication does not occur automatically in interpersonal relationships. Often we hear people complain, "You misunderstood what I was trying to say." There are a number of ways to foster more effective communication (see Insight, p. 367 for details of some factors that can complicate communication between two people).

1. *Be a good communicator.* Know in advance what you are trying to communicate, and code the message in such a way that it is likely to be interpreted accurately. If you are unclear about the message you are trying to convey or fail to code the message appropriately, the message will probably not be understood correctly.

2. *Be a good listener.* Listen actively and make a sincere effort to understand what the other person is trying to communicate. From time to time, you have probably had the experience of talking to someone who appeared not to be listening. Perhaps they were too busy to take time to listen, did not want to hear what you had to say, or were busy thinking about what they would say next. While you may not be able to help others to listen more effectively, you can take a number of steps to assure that *you* are a good listener (see Psychology in Action, p. 368).

## Being an Effective Listener

Listening is an important skill, but not an easy one to learn. How does one become a better listener? There are a number of ways to listen more effectively.

Be alert for nonverbal cues in the speaker. Nonverbal cues convey a great deal of information about the person speaking. Be alert to their facial expression, posture, and vocal intonation. Try to understand the feeling behind the person's words, what the other person wants to say rather than what he or she is saying. Try also to understand the person's emotional state: is the person relaxed and comfortable, anxious and tense, depressed, friendly, fearful, hostile?

Ask questions about the feelings you sense may lie behind the person's words. This not only provides an opportunity to confirm the impressions you have formed on the basis of nonverbal cues, it gives the other person an opportunity to express his or her feelings and may help that person realize that their feelings do matter.

Mirror or reflect the feelings that the other person seems to be expressing. If you sense that the person is upset or anxious about the conversation, for example, share that feeling in a non-threatening way, perhaps by saying something like "It's hard for you to talk about this" or "This seems to worry you a lot." In this way, you can show empathy and concern for the other person, a sensitivity to their feelings, and at the same time help the other person bring his or her feelings into the open where you both can examine them for what they are.

Be alert to your own nonverbal cues. What message are you conveying to the speaker by the way you are sitting or standing, by your facial expressions? Are you attending to what the other person is saying, maintaining eye contact, and trying to be sure you hear accurately? Or are you thinking of other things, bored, being judgmental, or just plain uninterested? Be as honest about expressing your own feelings as you hope the other person will be about expressing his or hers: "I'm really busy right now, but I'm eager to hear what you have to say. How about if I finish what I'm doing and I'll get right back to you. It shouldn't be more than five or ten minutes." "I'm getting angry, and it's making it harder for me to hear what you are trying to say. Let's take a break and come back to this later when I'll be able to do a better job of hearing what you're trying to say."

Suspend judgment. Try to avoid making judgments about what the person is saying—whether what they are saying is correct or logical, whether their ideas make sense or are reasonable. Your task as a listener is first and foremost to listen, to understand fully the verbal and nonverbal messages the other person is sending. Making judgments as you are listening or prematurely jumping to conclusions about what the person appears to be saying not only will distract you from attending fully to what the person is actually communicating, but it will also make them less likely to communicate openly and fully with you. When you think you understand what the other person is saying, try to summarize what you are hearing and see if the person agrees that you have captured the most important points. Once you are sure you fully understand what is being said, there will be time to form an opinion or to make an evaluation if that is appropriate.

Listen actively. If there is a common thread running throughout these suggestions, it is that you be an active listener who is trying to understand everything the other person is communicating. Staring off into the distance, fiddling with your shoelaces, tapping a pencil on your desk, reading the newspaper, opening mail, or watching a television show during a conversation—all of these activities not only interfere with your ability to listen effectively, but they communicate to the other person that you're not very interested in the conversation. If that is the case, try to find some aspect of what the person is saying that you would find more interesting, and steer the conversation in that direction. If that is not possible, then it is probably better to bring the conversation to a graceful close or to change the topic to something else that interests you more.

3. *Examine metacommunication.* One approach to fostering better communication involves **metacommunication**—examining and discussing the ways in which we typically communicate with another person in a relationship. For example, who does most of the talking and who does most of the listening? What areas or problems seem to elicit particular difficulties in communicating and understanding? How much communication involves relevant information and how much is uninformative "noise"? What kind of emotional climate is created by talking together about problems? Such information can be used as a basis for readjusting communication patterns in more beneficial ways.

**metacommunication:** communication about the way in which two people typically communicate

We have seen so far that satisfactory interpersonal relationships arise out of shared purposes, mutual need satisfaction, effective structure, and good communication. Another factor is a sense of awareness of ourselves, our partners, and the relationship that exists between us, as we will see in the next section.

## Awareness

Carl Rogers (1968, 1977) and a number of other psychologists have emphasized the importance of being aware of the key ingredients in our significant interpersonal relationships. At first glance, this may seem like belaboring the obvious, but the processes involved are considerably more subtle than it initially appears. Awareness comes in many forms, but three forms are particularly relevant to building satisfactory interpersonal relationships: a realistic view of one's self, a realistic view of the other person, and an accurate view of the relationship.

**A realistic view of oneself.** As a starting point, this involves an accurate view of our own "stimulus value"—of how the other person sees us. We may view ourselves as generous, while the other person sees us as stingy; we may view ourselves as flexible, while the other person views us as rigid; we may view ourselves as cooperative and undemanding, while the other person views us as competitive and highly demanding. While the other person's view of us may be inaccurate, it is an important source of feedback about how we are perceived.

**interpersonal style:** characteristic manner in which an individual interacts with others

It is also important for each of us to become aware of our unique **interpersonal style.** Everyone has a distinctive style or way of relating to other people. For example, some people are open and honest in their relationships, while others wear a mask and are manipulative. It is useful to become aware not only of our interpersonal style, but also of the motives, assumptions, and coping patterns on which it is based, and the type of relationships it will tend to foster.

**An accurate view of the other person.** An accurate view of the other person is equally important if we are to establish a satisfying interpersonal relationship. One common error that can be avoided, particularly during the period of getting acquainted, is the "halo effect" described earlier. For example, when some of us know a person is superior in some important respect, we may tend to put a "halo" over his or her head and, through a process of generalization, overrate his or her qualities in other areas. As we have noted, we often tend to see others as we would like them to be rather than as they really are—a tendency which is readily apparent in romantic infatuations.

**An accurate view of the relationship.** When an individual is emotionally involved in an intimate relationship, it is often difficult to perceive the situation objectively. It is not only important to understand our own needs and motives in the relationship but also those of the other person—and this is not always an easy task. Drawing from social exchange theory, we can ask ourselves what we are "paying" in exchange for the satisfactions we are receiving. Are we deceiving ourselves about what we are receiving from the relationship? Are the costs actually greater than the rewards?

Furthermore, if we consider the relationship a satisfying one, then it is important that we be alert for possible indications of trouble, such as signs of dissatisfaction from the other person. Building a satisfying interpersonal relationship requires effort on the part of both persons and the early detection and correction of misunderstandings, communication problems, conflicting purposes, or other possible difficulties. Unfortunately, many relationships that were once satisfying are allowed to deteriorate eventually and to end, simply because one or both partners failed to realize that vigilance and effort are required to assure the continuation of a rewarding relationship.

## Helping Each Other Grow as Persons

*I love you,*
*Not only for what you are,*
*But for what I am*
*When I am with you.*

*I love you*
*For the part of me*
*That you bring out.*

*The Family Book of Best Loved Poems* (Roy Croft, 1952)

As we have seen, close interpersonal relationships have a profound influence upon people—whether for better or for worse. Relationships with others can diminish us (as we saw earlier in the case in maladaptive interpersonal relationships) or they can help us to grow as persons, as we will see in this final section of the chapter.

**Openness and empathy.** *Openness* means more than lowering defenses and dropping masks. It also includes a willingness to share beliefs, hopes, feelings, defeats, achievements, and despair with another. As you saw in our earlier discussion of self-

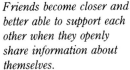

*Friends become closer and better able to support each other when they openly share information about themselves.*

disclosure, however, openness does not necessarily mean completely baring one's soul to the other person. However, it does mean being open and willing to exchange information that will contribute to better understanding and greater security in the relationship. As Rogers (1968) has expressed it, "We shall discover that security resides not in hiding oneself but in being more fully known, and consequently in coming to know the other more fully" (p. 269).

The other side of the coin is *empathy,* the ability to put oneself in another person's place. In interpersonal relationships, empathy means that each person understands what the other has experienced, is experiencing, and is trying to communicate.

**Acceptance.**   Acceptance is essential if each person in a relationship is to feel free to share his or her private world with the other. This does not mean that one has to agree with everything the other person believes or does. Rather, acceptance means that neither person takes a judgmental attitude toward the other; when two people disagree, they do not reject each other as persons. In some instances, acceptance means "agreeing to disagree"—accepting the other person's right to entertain his or her own convictions while retaining the same freedom for oneself.

**Caring.**   Caring is an elusive concept that means many things, but perhaps its central theme is concern about and commitment to the well-being of the other person. Caring may be expressed in words, as when we tell the other person "I love you"; or it may be expressed in actions ranging from simple courtesy to support in times of severe stress or crisis.

Caring may take the form of expressing sincere appreciation of the good qualities of the other person, thus confirming his or her worth as a human being. Each of us has good qualities which merit appreciation, but all too often these qualities are taken for granted. Instead of appreciation, we are subjected to nagging criticism for real or alleged shortcomings or mistakes.

## Putting It All Together

In this chapter, a number of recurring themes have emerged that are directly relevant to building satisfying interpersonal relationships: (1) the need to balance rewards and costs, (2) the central importance of communicating effectively, (3) the need for an adequate structure that assures mutual satisfaction for everyone involved in the relationship, (4) the necessity of interpersonal accommodation, and (5) the need to create conditions that foster constructive and satisfying interpersonal relationships.

By attending to these concerns, people can make interpersonal relationships far more satisfying than they would otherwise be. As Carl Rogers (1968) stated:

> There can be more of intimacy, less of loneliness, an infusion of emotional and intellectual learning in our relationships, better ways of resolving conflicts openly, man-woman relationships which are enriching, family relationships which are real, a sense of community which enables us to face the unknown. All this is possible if as a people we choose to move into the new mode of living openly as a continually changing process. (pp. 279-80)

## SUMMARY

Interpersonal relationships have a tremendous impact on most people's lives. They can be a source of great satisfaction, but they can also be the cause of much stress.

In an effort to better understand interpersonal relationships, psychologists use several different models or perspectives. The *social exchange model* emphasizes the "economic" nature of an interpersonal relationship. According to this model, each person in a relationship is concerned primarily with "What can I get out of this relationship, and what will it cost me?" The *outcome* or profit from the relationship is determined by the ratio of rewards to costs. Satisfaction with a relationship is determined by comparing the outcome of the relationship to past relationships of a similar sort, other alternative relationships, the outcomes other people are receiving from similar relationships, and the extent to which an individual has a lot to offer and a great deal of control over personal choices.

A second perspective for viewing interpersonal relationships is the *social role model*. All social relationships involve *roles* or parts that people play. Associated with each role are a set of *role expectations*—obligations or duties or rights that go along with the role. If people behave in ways that conflict with their role expectations, the result is likely to be stress and discord. Another source of stress in interpersonal relationships is *role conflict* in which a person either feels uncomfortable in a role or finds that the expectations for several roles are incompatible with each other.

The third model is the *games model*. According to this view, relationships between people frequently involve *games* that often occur with the participants' awareness. Games provide payoffs to the players, substitute for intimacy between people, sometimes add a touch of excitement to a relationship, but very often have destructive outcomes.

Relationships with *significant others* usually begin with an initial encounter: an attempt to initiate tentative and safe communication that is appropriate to the setting. During the encounter we form an initial impression of the other person. Often we start out with a *stereotype* of what the person is likely to be like, and then use the initial encounter to confirm or revise that view. Unfortunately *interpersonal perceptions* are open to numerous kinds of errors. Many people either give too much weight to negative information about others or allow their general impression of the person to cloud their judgment (the *halo effect*). Of course, some people set out deliberately to mislead others during initial encounters.

Though many encounters do not continue beyond the initial stage, in some cases the participants will find each other sufficiently attractive to continue the relationship. There are several major determinants of interpersonal attraction: in general, people prefer others who are physically attractive, physically nearby (proximity), accessible or available, and similar to them in attitudes, beliefs, educational level, and so on. There is very little evidence that people tend to be attracted to others whose personal qualities differ from but complement their own *(complementarity)*.

*Relationships that grow and endure continually present new challenges and heightened levels of uncertainty, as well as increased levels of satisfaction.*

If a relationship between two people is to persist and thrive, both people must communicate effectively. Both verbal and nonverbal communication are important in most interpersonal relationships. *Verbal communication* is most effective for conveying factual information with another person. Most verbal communications contain hidden messages. At times these hidden messages can be helpful in establishing and maintaining relationships with other people, but at other times, they can become a source of stress.

*Nonverbal communication* relies on emphasis, facial expressions, and body language to convey feelings and emotions. Nonverbal communication is used most often to communicate *affective information.* Not infrequently, the nonverbal message being communicated by someone differs from their verbal message, in which case it becomes necessary to decide which communication is most accurate.

It follows that effective communication requires attention to both verbal and nonverbal messages, clarity and consistency of communication, sensitivity to the feelings and point of view of the other person, and tact.

Inevitably, as a personal relationship develops and intensifies between two people, questions arise about *self-disclosure:* how much personal information each person should share with the other, how intimate that information should be, whether it is appropriate to share both positive and negative information, and when to make disclosures. Early in a relationship a medium amount of disclosure is usually appropriate, but as a relationship matures the amount and intimacy of self-disclosure usually intensify. However, it does not follow that complete self-disclosure is either appropriate or necessary in close personal relationships: often, the costs of total openness and unrestrained self-disclosure come to outweigh the rewards.

Eventually in all personal relationships, it becomes necessary to adjust and adapt to each other. In part, this process of *interpersonal accommodation* involves structuring the relationship: defining appropriate roles and responsibilities, and establishing standards of satisfaction. In part, it also involves resolving disagreements and conflicts through bargaining, compromise, acceptance, adaptation, or counseling.

Sometimes relationships develop in ways that are maladaptive for the participants. *Fraudulent interpersonal contracts* arise when one person violates the terms of the relationship in a way that exploits the other person. In cases of *collusion,* the partners have agreed upon a deviant, maladaptive, and destructive life style in which the eventual costs far outweigh the rewards. In still other cases, the partners become entangled in a pattern of disagreements and conflicts; such *discordant interpersonal patterns* often center on competition, domination, failure, provocation, value differences, or conflict-filled communications.

Building a satisfying interpersonal relationship requires having a common purpose and assuring that the relationship meets the needs of both participants. However, it also requires adequate structure; effective communication and *metacommunication;* a realistic view of oneself, the other person, and the relationship; and a willingness to help each other grow as persons through openness and empathy, acceptance, and caring. In attempting to respond to these needs, each person develops a distinctive *interpersonal style* for relating to other people.

## KEY TERMS

social exchange model (341)
outcome (342)
social role model (343)
role (343)
role expectations (345)
role conflict (345)
games model (345)
games (346)
significant others (347)
interpersonal perceptions (351)
stereotypes (351)
halo effect (351)

complementarity (353)
verbal communication (354)
nonverbal communication (354)
affective information (354)
self-disclosure (358)
interpersonal accommodation (360)
fraudulent interpersonal contract (363)
collusion (363)
discordant interpersonal patterns (364)
metacommunication (369)
interpersonal style (369)

# Love, Marriage, and Intimacy

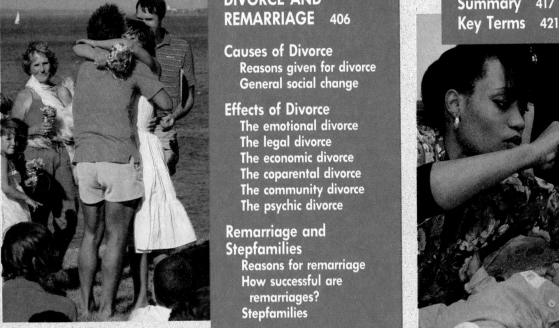

*Love alone is capable of uniting living beings in such a way as to complete and fulfill them, for it alone takes them and joins them by what is deepest in themselves.*

The Phenomenon of Man (Teilhard de Chardin, 1961, p. 265)

*One day a stranger entered my domain and my solitude was transformed into love.*

Love Is an Attitude (Rinder, 1970)

OF all the endeavors that influence people's lives, the quest for intimate relationships must be the most sought after, longed for, dreamed about, sung about, joked about, and cursed at. Few human experiences inspire the pangs, joys, ecstasies, fears, cheers, and tears that accompany the growth and development of intimacy.

As we saw in Chapter 9, for most people, achieving an intimate relationship with at least one other person is a major goal of life, marking maturity and adulthood as well as personal fulfillment and achievement. Many also expect an intimate relationship to serve as a medium for personal growth.

Often the need for love and affiliation is thought of simply as a need to receive love and affection from others, but the need to give love is as great. People need to relate to and care about other people if they are to grow and function properly as human beings. Although most people ordinarily meet their needs for love in marriage, family, and other intimate relationships, they are also capable of "brotherly love" which goes beyond the love of family and particular individuals to a basic concern for other human beings and an eagerness to form close bonds with them. As Fromm (1956) stated, "If a person loves only one other person and is indifferent to the rest of his fellow men, his love is not love but symbiotic attachment, or an enlarged egotism" (p. 46).

Both loving and being loved appear to be crucial for healthy functioning and normal personality development. Human beings need and strive to achieve warm, loving relationships with others. Our longing to be with others remains with us throughout our lives, and separation from or loss of loved ones usually presents a difficult adjustment problem. In fact, after a review of the medical evidence, Lynch (1977) has concluded that there is a direct connection between loss of love, loneliness, and premature death. In essence, we must learn to love and live together or we shall die, prematurely and alone.

Every individual differs in his or her ability to love and to maintain a durable intimate relationship with another person. The ability to achieve intimacy depends on a number of factors, including early experiences with parents, ability to trust

*Although the behavior of men and women in long-term relationships continues to change, intimate relationships are still the most common means of fulfilling the needs for love and companionship.*

others, strength of one's own identity, degree of personal maturity and self-acceptance, and freedom from exaggerated self-defenses. At least a minimally favorable emotional climate in childhood seems essential if the individual is to give and receive love in later years. However, love is a powerful force, and long-held patterns of distrust, self-doubt, and defensiveness may be dissipated by the experience of genuinely loving and being loved by another human being.

Intimate relationships also differ considerably from one society to another and within subgroups of a given society. In our culture, both the typical form and the expected content of intimate man-woman relationships have changed significantly in recent years. The reasons for making long-term commitments and for entering legally sanctioned relationships, and the behavior of both men and women within such relationships, have changed and continue to change.

In this chapter, we will attempt to describe and understand the nature of love. We will also explore the nature of intimate relationships, particularly the institution of marriage, which is the most intimate relationship most people establish. We will consider the satisfactions that marriage can bring as well as the obstacles to "living happily ever after." We will discuss the causes and effects of divorce and remarriage and, finally, we will examine some intimate relationships that are alternatives to marriage.

## LOVE

*That he sings, and he sings; and for ever sings he—*
*I love my Love, and my Love loves me!*

(Samuel Taylor Coleridge)

*Heigh-ho! sing, heigh-ho! unto the green holly:*
*Most friendship is feigning, most loving mere folly.*

(Shakespeare)

*He loves me, he loves me not.*
*He loves me, he loves me not.*

(Children's rhyme)

Liking and loving have interested poets, playwrights, and people in all walks of life for generations. As the above quotations suggest, love may take different forms and have different meanings for different people. For example, we can love humanity; parents can love and be loved by their children; we can experience love in its erotic, exciting, and romantic form; we can experience less passionate but usually more enduring companionate love; and we can experience love as a union with a supreme being (Fromm, 1956; Mathes, 1980; Hatfield & Walster, 1978).

**agape** *(ah-gah-pay):* selfless, nonsexual form of love

John Lee (1974, 1977) has systematically distinguished between these different kinds of love. For example, one style of loving he calls **agape.** Agapic love is altruistic, based on an unselfish desire to nurture and care for the other person without regard to personal gain. This is a major component in the love parents have for their children and in a life devoted to serving humanity. A second style of loving, according to Lee, is **storge.** Storgic love exists between intimate friends or very close companions who care deeply for each other and enjoy being together; it characterizes the relationships between many family members. Unlike agapic love, storgic love is a two-way street: we assume that our acts of friendship and affection will be returned in kind. **Eros** refers to erotic or passionate love that is intensely emotional and sexual, and is often related to physical attractiveness of the loved one.

**storge** *(store-gay):* love based on deep affection and companionship

**eros:** reciprocal, sexual form of love

### Romantic Love

Of course, a particular relationship may combine several of these styles of loving, and the combination may change with age and time. For example, in adolescence and early adulthood, **romantic love** is especially prevalent. This concept developed in the Middle Ages, when knights would idealize their ladies and perform many difficult tasks to "prove" or test their love. For example, these knights would demonstrate the purity of their love by sleeping in the same bed as the woman and making sexual advances toward her, but stopping short of sexual intercourse (McCary, 1980).

**romantic love:** type of love characterized by intense, passionate feelings

Today, romantic, or passionate, love is often stereotyped in books, magazines, and movies: men are strong and tender, and women develop a radiant bloom that they and their friends notice. This stereotype hints at the ecstasies and agonies of romantic love. People in its throes have strong feelings of attraction and affection for their partners. They are concerned for the other's well-being and are eager to make more of themselves for the sake of the loved one. They want to contribute to their partner's happiness and personal growth. Romantic love may have an exclusive and possessive nature. Finally, romantic love can express itself as a sexual attraction to the other person.

Romantic love has its negative side as well. People in romantic love may feel fear and anxiety when they are near the loved one. Often, their desire to make a good impression results in so much anxiety that their fantasies of acting in a suave, sophisticated fashion dissolve into cold sweats, social ineptness, and tongue-tied fear. People in romantic love may also develop intense jealousy of their loved one's thoughts and actions. They may become jealous of the "other man" or the "other woman," even if they exist as only a theroetical possibility. Such feelings may turn into anger, hostility and even physical violence. Finally, people in romantic love may be unsure of their feelings. While their positive feelings toward the partner may be strong, they may also experience some that are negative (Hatfield & Walster, 1978).

## Companionate Love

companionate love: love for one's partner accompanied by strong feelings of liking for the partner

The fires of passionate love eventually become less intense, and many partners discover **companionate love.** Where passionate love is intense and unpredictable, companionate love is friendlier and more stable. The partners feel affectionate toward and attached to each other. In many ways, companionate love has the characteristics of an excellent friendship.

Many couples start out with passionate love. For example, one study measured the passionate love scores of couples married up to three years and found that they averaged over ninety-eight points. However, couples who had been married more than ten years reported passionate love scores of eighty-four. Interestingly, there were no differences in the liking scores between newly married and long-married couples. For both kinds of couples, liking scores remained uniformly high (Cimbalo, Faling, & Mousaw, 1976).

These data suggest that both liking and passionate love are important in a long-term relationship. Passionate love may be more significant in the early phases of the relationship, but it by no means disappears in marriage only to be replaced by companionate love, as one woman mentioned to Hatfield and Walster (1978).

> When I fell in love I felt fantastic! I glowed, people said they never saw me look prettier or happier. I felt this way, I think, because of the new self-confidence Ted gave me, and because of the feeling of just being needed and desired. . . . As it turned out, I married Ted. We're still very happy and very much in love, but there is a definite difference between the first passionate feelings of love and the now-mellowed-out feelings.
>
> Don't get me wrong, though, there are still plenty of passionate times. It's just that when you live together, the passion is not as urgent a thing. You're more loving friends. (p. 4)

*Passion is only one of the many forms love takes on in the course of a long-term loving relationship.*

So, there are many different types of love, ranging from the nonsexual to the passionate. Our feelings for our partners can be both passionate and companionate in nature, and the degree to which we experience these different types of love is often related to the length of the relationship. Central to all forms of love, however, is an attitude of care, concern, and responsibility for the loved one and a desire to promote his or her growth, well-being, and interests.

Genuine love also allows both partners to grow as individuals (Branden, 1980). This latter point is particularly important, for a love that feeds on dependency or domination tends to destroy itself. Love in whatever form nurtures individual growth. In discussing his pioneering study of self-actualizing people, Maslow (1954) spoke about this aspect of loving and being loved.

> One of the deepest satisfactions coming from the healthy love relationship reported by my subjects is that such a relationship permits the greatest spontaneity, the greatest naturalness, the greatest dropping of defenses and protection against threat. In such a relationship it is not necessary to be guarded, to conceal, to try to impress, to feel tense, to watch one's words or actions, to suppress or repress. My people reported that they can be themselves without feeling that there are demands or expectations upon them; they can feel psychologically (as well as physically) naked and still feel loved and wanted and secure. (pp. 239–40)

Love, in its many different forms, can find expression in a variety of intimate relationships. In the next section of the chapter, we will examine one of them—the institution of marriage.

## MARRIAGE

*With all the variations among American families, it is apparent that they are all in greater or lesser degree in a process of change toward an emerging type of family that is perhaps most aptly described as the "companionship form". . . . The essential bonds in the family are now found more and more in the interpersonal relationships of its members, as compared with those of law, custom, public opinion, and duty in the older institutional forms of the family.*

"The Family in a Changing Society" (Burgess, 1964, p. 196)

More than 90 percent of all American men and women will marry at some time in their lives (Knox, 1985; Lamanna & Riedmann, 1985). This figure is remarkably stable: although marriage rates have declined slightly in recent years, people are waiting longer to get married, and traditional assumptions about marriage and marriage practices have been challenged, the vast majority of Americans still choose marriage as a way of meeting their needs and achieving psychological satisfaction (see Insight, p. 384).

In the following pages, we will look first at the reasons people give for marrying and the way in which marriage partners are selected. We will then examine in some detail the adjustive demands that can threaten marriages, as well as some effective ways of coping with those demands.

### Reasons for Marrying

For many, marriage is assumed to be such an integral part of their lives that they cannot verbalize their reasons for marrying. Others, if asked, may cite a variety of reasons ranging from love and companionship to financial security and pregnancy. Here we shall comment on four reasons which are most often given for marrying: love; companionship, fulfillment, and escape from loneliness; sexuality, reproduction, and child rearing; and economic security.

**Love.** The most common reason given by both men and women for marrying is love. In fact, according to Judith Stevens-Long, "most Americans claim that love is the only acceptable reason for marriage" (1984, p. 153). In an analysis of the replies of 75,000 wives to a *Redbook* questionnaire on marriage, for example, psychologist Carol Tavris and researcher Toby Jayaratne reported that love is "the key word—in the decision to marry, in marriage itself, in an evaluation of the success of marriage. . . . Eight out of ten women rated love more important than any other consideration in their marriage" (Tavris & Jayaratne, 1976, p. 90). In addition, women who married primarily for love reported themselves as more satisfied with their

## Myths About Marriage

As might be expected, there are a number of common misconceptions concerning the emotionally involved topic of marriage. Listed here are some popularly held myths about marriage.

1. Love can guarantee a happy marriage.
2. Children tend to stabilize an unhappy marriage.
3. Marriages among younger people are likely to be happier than those among older people.
4. Wives who are strongly religious usually experience less sexual satisfaction and happiness in marriage.
5. Arranged marriages are much less happy than those based on love.
6. People who seek counseling or psychotherapy rarely do so for marital problems.

marriages than women who married primarily for other reasons—such as sex, to avoid loneliness, or for financial security (see Insight, p. 386).

While love may be rather "romantic," it is by no means "impractical." As Tavris and Jayaratne (1976) expressed it:

Perhaps the reason love turns out to be a sound foundation for marrying, rather than the shaky one the experts fear it to be, is that among these respondents love means more than sunshine and champagne. The women who are most satisfied with their marriages describe a relationship that is not the starry-eyed, adolescent, heaven-made version of marriage. In fact, couples who have the best relationships do admit to hashing over problems and worries and disagreeing with each other—but they disagree more or less agreeably. (p. 92)

In essence, then, available research points to a marked tendency among Americans to put love at the center of the "marital stage."

**Companionship, fulfillment, and escape from loneliness.** Regardless of the type of partnership they choose, most people seek companionship and fulfillment in their marriage. The *Redbook* survey found that companionship and fulfillment ranked just behind love as main reasons for marrying. As David Knox (1985) points out:

Although marriage does not ensure it, companionship is the greatest expected benefit of marriage. Companionship is talking and doing things with someone you love; it is creating a history with someone. "Only my husband and I know the things we've shared," said one wife. "The shrimp dinner at Ocean City, the walk down Bourbon Street, and the chipmunk in our backyard are part of our joint memory bank." (p. 134)

Companionship and fulfillment involve a mutual sharing of thoughts, feelings, interests, tasks, decision making, and personal growth. They also require the couple to have a high number of shared interests in which both actively participate together.

Mutual love and giving are other important aspects of companionship and fulfillment. Intimate relationships offer a buffer as well—especially in times of trouble—against the fear that accompanies the awareness of one's separateness from everyone else. Thus, it is not surprising that more than half of the women in the *Redbook* survey said that avoiding loneliness was a matter of some, if not primary, importance in marrying.

**Sexuality, reproduction, and child rearing.**   For many people, marriage provides the only legal and moral basis for engaging in sexual relations. For example, in the past, it was generally expected that couples (particularly the women) would remain virgins until their marriage. Although this is not generally the case in our society today, most people find that marriage provides a highly stable and satisfying outlet for sexual urges.

Marriage also provides a legally sanctioned structure for bearing and rearing children, although a greater number of married couples are choosing to remain "childfree" than in former times (Elvenstar, 1982; Veevers, 1980, 1983). Until recent times, marriage was the only acceptable means through which children could be conceived, born, and reared. In fact, a woman who bore a child out of wedlock was likely to be stigmatized by society. Today, the situation has changed dramatically, with a substantial proportion of pregnancies occurring among unmarried teenagers. Also, a small number of women are actually choosing—either through the use of

*A show of affection can symbolize different aspects of the relationship, from appreciation for companionship to the desire for sexual contact.*

# *Insight*

## How Important to Your Marriage Is Each Item?

The *Redbook* survey asked 75,000 married women, "How important to your marriage is each of the following items?" They answered as shown in the figure below. Their answers led researchers to this conclusion: "A large majority of wives felt that love, respect, and friendship were the most important elements in their relationship. They rated sexual compatibility desirable but not essential" (Tavris & Jayaratne, 1976, p. 91).

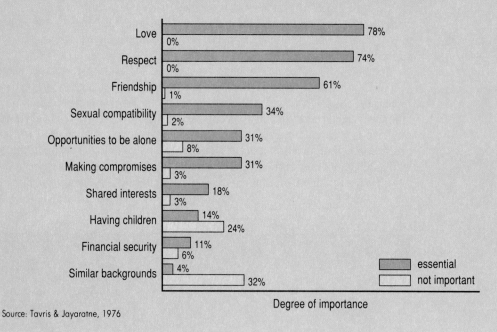

Source: Tavris & Jayaratne, 1976

sperm banks or other arrangements—to have children without any involvement on the part of the father. Nonetheless, the majority of children are the product of marriage.

Marriage also provides a means to rear children and guide their development. Children need food, shelter, and clothing. Adults must also take time to guide the child's social and emotional development. Finally, adults must find a means to educate their children both in academic and in ethical and moral areas. All of these activities require a tremendous amount of energy. Not only are these tasks difficult for one parent to accomplish, but, as we will see later in this chapter, they create adjustive demands that strain the financial and emotional resources of many parents. The presence of a partner can help lighten these responsibilities and can also provide some "time out" so that one parent can attend to his or her own needs for growth and development.

**Economic security.**    In earlier times, marriage provided a way to ensure the economic survival of the individual and the family. Women were not expected to be financially independent; marriage or spinsterhood were their only options. Similarly, the lack of retirement programs for the elderly often meant utter poverty for the couple as they grew older and became less able to work. For these couples, the only solution was to bear many children who could then help support them.

Today, the increasing independence of women and social welfare programs such as Social Security make economic security a less important reason for marriage. Two cannot live "as cheaply as one," but sharing financial resources can help couples attain economic goals—such as the purchase of a house—that each individually would find very difficult.

## Choosing a Mate

Romantic myth is that "marriages are made in heaven," that couples are "destined to marry." The fact is, however, that the origins of most partnerships are more mundane than heavenly, and they are often influenced more by social expectations than by romantic ideals or rational decision making.

Mate selection is essentially a *filtering process* in which the field of "acceptable" candidates is successively narrowed until a choice is made. In some non-Western societies, the filtering may be made by family members, as in arranged marriages. In contrast, members of Western societies normally select mates in an individual fashion and without the direct intervention of families.

Janda and Klenke-Hamel (1980) have described one way in which this filtering process works (see Figure 11.1, p. 388). In theory at least, for each of us there exist literally millions of people in the world who could be our marriage partners. Of course, we encounter only a tiny fraction of these people, and so the pool of actual candidates is quite limited from the start. From this initial pool (or *proximate field*), we tend to develop closer relationships with those whom we find attractive, with whom we can communicate effectively, and who are similar to us in some ways and complementary to us in other ways. At each point in this sequence, we filter out unacceptable partners and thus further reduce the pool of eligible candidates. If this process sounds very familiar, you are not mistaken: it is exactly the same process we described in Chapter 10 when we examined the development of interpersonal relationships in general. Marriage is, after all, just one example of an interpersonal relationship; therefore, up to a point at least, it follows the same developmental course as do other interpersonal relationships.

At some point, the process of selecting a marriage partner differs in important ways from the selection of close friends or other intimate acquaintances. Most of us have close and satisfying relationships with many people of the opposite sex whom we find attractive and with whom we can communicate effectively. However, we also realize that most of these close friends would not be suitable as marriage partners. How do we make this additional judgment, this next step in the filtering process?

In part the answer is love. Earlier in this chapter, we saw that most Americans consider romantic love to be an essential ingredient in marriage. Thus, the pool of

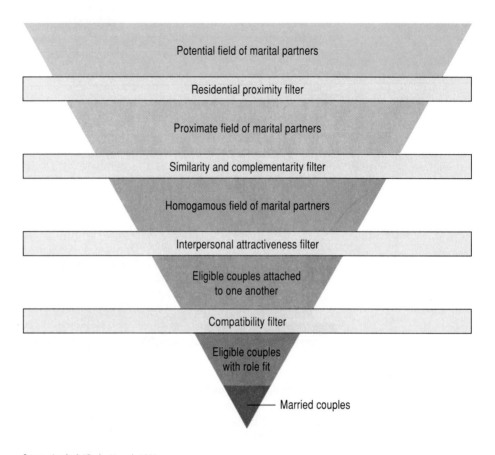

Source: Janda & Klenke-Hamel, 1980.

eligible marriage partners is further reduced to those for whom we feel romantic love. For some people, this is the end of the mate selection process. Often such people believe that there is only one person in the world who could be "right for them," and in their eagerness to believe that they have found that person, any candidate who survives the early stages of the filtering process and for whom they feel romantic love is chosen as a marriage partner. Unfortunately, most marriage counselors and many married couples agree that love alone is not enough to ensure a satisfactory marriage. As one divorced man commented, "I was so much in love with her, I knew we could work out any differences we might have. I was wrong" (Knox, 1985, p. 208).

Most people take additional steps in evaluating potential marriage partners, as illustrated in some intriguing new research by David Buss and his colleagues. Buss and Barnes (1986) asked nearly 200 married people to rate the extent to which various characteristics were desirable in a potential marriage partner. The results for the group as a whole are shown in Table 11.1. They found that the most desirable characteristics are kindness and considerateness, fondness for children, and being

**TABLE 11.1    Preferences in Human Mate Selection**

The data below show the average rating given by ninety-two married couples when asked to rate the desirability of various characteristics in a marriage partner. The ratings were made on a scale that varied from 5 (Very desirable) to 1 (Very undesirable).

Kind-considerate . . . . . . . . . . . . . . . . . . . . . . . . . . . . . . . . . . . . . . . . . . . . . . . . . . . . . . . . . . .4.56
    Kind, understanding, loyal, considerate, honest

Likes children . . . . . . . . . . . . . . . . . . . . . . . . . . . . . . . . . . . . . . . . . . . . . . . . . . . . . . . . . . . . . .4.41
    Fond of children, likes children

Easygoing-adaptable . . . . . . . . . . . . . . . . . . . . . . . . . . . . . . . . . . . . . . . . . . . . . . . . . . . . . . . .4.23
    Easygoing, able to plan ahead, well-liked by others, open-minded on questions of
    morals and ethics, adaptable

Socially exciting . . . . . . . . . . . . . . . . . . . . . . . . . . . . . . . . . . . . . . . . . . . . . . . . . . . . . . . . . . . .3.94
    Exciting personality, excellent social skills, charming, sociable, stylish appearance

Artistic-intelligent . . . . . . . . . . . . . . . . . . . . . . . . . . . . . . . . . . . . . . . . . . . . . . . . . . . . . . . . . . .3.83
    Creative, artistic, intellectually stimulating, courageous, idealistic, interesting to talk to,
    intelligent, witty

Domestic . . . . . . . . . . . . . . . . . . . . . . . . . . . . . . . . . . . . . . . . . . . . . . . . . . . . . . . . . . . . . . . . . .3.73
    Good housekeeper, good cook, frugal

Professional status . . . . . . . . . . . . . . . . . . . . . . . . . . . . . . . . . . . . . . . . . . . . . . . . . . . . . . . . . .3.59
    College graduate, professional degree, good family background, good earning capacity

Religious . . . . . . . . . . . . . . . . . . . . . . . . . . . . . . . . . . . . . . . . . . . . . . . . . . . . . . . . . . . . . . . . . .2.11
    Church-goer, not agnostic in religion, religious point of view

Politically conservative . . . . . . . . . . . . . . . . . . . . . . . . . . . . . . . . . . . . . . . . . . . . . . . . . . . . . . .1.93
    Politically conservative, not politically liberal

Source: Buss and Barnes (1986).

easygoing and adaptable. It is less important, but nonetheless desirable, for a marriage partner to be socially exciting, artistic or intelligent, domestic, well-educated and from a good family. Finally, it is somewhat undesirable for a marriage partner to be religious or politically conservative.

Buss and Barnes also analyzed differences in the ways men and women ranked the desirability of various characteristics. In particular, men put significance on such spouse characteristics as physical attractiveness, cooking ability, and frugality. In contrast, women tended to value a spouse who is considerate, kind, honest, dependable, understanding, fond of children, well-liked by others, financially stable, ambitious and career oriented, from a good family, and tall.

In a follow-up study, Buss and Barnes asked 100 unmarried undergraduates to rank the desirability of 13 spouse characteristics from most to least desirable. The results of this study are shown in Table 11.2. You can see that the results correspond generally to those of the first study. Interestingly, in this study men also weighed physical attractiveness more heavily than women did (on the average, for men it was the fourth most desirable characteristic in a spouse while for women it was

**TABLE 11.2   Ranking of Spouse Characteristics by Males and Females**

The following table shows rankings of thirteen spouse characteristics made by 100 male and female undergraduates. Characteristics were ranked from 1 (Most desirable) to 13 (Least desirable). Items are arranged in decreasing order of desirability for the group as a whole. Items in italics are those on which the rankings given by men and women differed significantly.

| Spouse Characteristic | Average Desirability Ranking | |
| --- | --- | --- |
|  | Male | Female |
| Kind and understanding | 2.43 | 2.08 |
| Exciting personality | 3.62 | 3.28 |
| Intelligent | 3.78 | 3.44 |
| Physically attractive | 4.04 | 6.26 |
| Healthy | 5.49 | 5.84 |
| Easygoing | 5.67 | 5.72 |
| Creative | 8.33 | 7.56 |
| Wants children | 8.01 | 8.82 |
| *College graduate* | 9.41 | 7.94 |
| *Good earning capacity* | 9.92 | 8.04 |
| Good heredity | 9.71 | 10.34 |
| Good housekeeper | 10.22 | 10.56 |
| Religious | 10.24 | 11.12 |

Source: Buss and Barnes, 1986, p. 568.

sixth); in contrast, women valued a college graduate and a good earning capacity (both averaged about eighth on women's lists, but ninth or tenth on men's lists).

Why do people have these preferences? One frequent explanation is *compatibility:* people who are kind, understanding, intelligent, and easygoing should be fairly easy to get along with, especially with regard to important matters. Thus, by selecting a mate with these characteristics, a person increases the likelihood that the marriage will survive and be satisfying. (In the next section we will see how important compatibility can be to the success of a marriage.)

It is difficult to account for the sex differences in the ratings between the men and women. One possible explanation cited by Buss and Barnes is that men and women have been socialized or brought up to value different things in a spouse: men have been taught to value physical beauty in their wives, while women have been taught to value the earning capacity and career-orientation of their husbands. Buss (1987) also offers a second, and far more controversial, explanation: these preferences are inborn as a result of evolution. According to this hypothesis, women who preferred males with access to resources such as food, shelter, territory, and protection were more likely to survive; correspondingly, men who preferred physically attractive women would tend to be drawn toward younger, and thus more fertile, women. Whatever the final explanation, it is interesting to note that Buss (1989) found the same sex differences in data collected from more than 10,000 people in 33 countries located on six continents.

## ADJUSTIVE DEMANDS IN MARRIAGE

Most people who marry today do so with the expectation that their relationship will be permanent. These expectations are widely shared: many religions consider marriage to be a permanent bond, and there is usually strong social pressure from family and friends for a couple to remain married and work out their problems. In fact, marriage is the only interpersonal relationship that cannot be terminated without consent from a court and, in some cases, from a religious body (Lamanna & Riedmann, 1985).

It may come as a surprise that, even in today's world, the majority of married couples remain married "for better, for worse, for richer, for poorer, in sickness and in health." However, to make a marriage last a lifetime is no small accomplishment, and it is virtually certain that in every marriage some incompatibilities and problems between partners will be discovered. Moreover, as average life expectancy continues to climb into the late seventies, many newly married couples can expect to live together for more than fifty years; many of those years will come after children have grown and left home, and some of them will be spent in declining health. In addition, as we saw in Chapter 3, the extent and rate of change in society is now greater than at any time in history. Thus, a long-lasting marriage must endure massive changes in social values, life styles, job opportunities, sexual patterns, and even leisure-time pursuits. Finally, the mobility of our population and the enormous variety of models and life styles with which we come into contact can add to the challenge of maintaining a stable marriage and make it more difficult for a husband and wife to grow together over the years (see Figure 11.2, p. 393).

In this section, we will look more closely at some of the most important challenges that are likely to arise during the course of a marriage and that represent major adjustive demands. These challenges include posthoneymoon disillusionment, communication problems, conflict, sexual compatibility, infidelity, jealousy, problems of power and control, children, and changes in marital sex roles.

### "The Bloom Is Off the Rose"

During courtship, when couples are exploring the extent of their compatibility, it is understandable that people present themselves in the most favorable light possible. They give extra attention to behaviors and appearances that might impress or delight the other in the hope of winning love and approval. Undesirable qualities are hidden, ignored, or simply diminished in the warm glow of romance and the promise of a beautiful future. In the excitement that often accompanies the establishment of a partnership, the couple is likely to experience optimism about any possible future problems, and to expect the dramatic and tingling qualities of the relationship to continue evermore.

Unfortunately, this rosy bloom does not last forever. As we noted earlier, most successful marriages experience a lessening of romantic love but sustain a less passionate and satisfying companionate form of love. Friendship, mutual respect, tolerance, and acceptance must be developed in the posthoneymoon phase of the marriage. Without the compromise and accommodation that accompany companionate love, the relationship may collapse. Given the numbers of marriages that end within a few years, it is clear that many couples either fail to make such adjustments or decide that their expectations and hopes for the relationship cannot be met.

## Ineffective Communication

Throughout the discussion of interpersonal relationships, I repeatedly stressed the importance of communication. Accommodation in marriage also depends heavily on effective communication—open communication lines and the ability and willingness to use them. Without good communication, partners cannot exchange information, coordinate efforts, or understand the other person's feelings and reactions. According to Knox (1985), minor misunderstandings can become major sources of resentment, and accommodation will not take place.

> Good communication not only helps to get the 'hidden agenda' up front but also helps to negotiate differences so that each partner continues to benefit from the relationship. Where most couples drift into trouble is when their needs are not expressed, go underground, and later resurface in a negative way. (p. 212)

In a study of communication patterns in marriage, Navran (1967) found that these distinctions characterize happily married couples as opposed to unhappily married couples: (1) they talk to each other more; (2) they convey the feeling that they understand what is being said to them; (3) they communicate about a wider range of subjects; (4) they preserve communication channels and keep them open; (5) they show more sensitivity to each other's feelings; (6) they personalize their language symbols; and (7) they make more use of supplementary nonverbal techniques of communication. The feeling that it is safe to be open and honest about personal feelings, both positive and negative, is apparently essential if such open communication is to take place between marital partners (Honeycutt, Wilson, & Parker, 1982; Montgomery, 1981). Here it is worthwhile to refer to the findings of Tavris and Jayaratne (1976).

> The most happily married wives are those who say that both they and their husbands tell each other when they are displeased and thus try to work out their displeasure together by communicating in a calm and rational way. They also say that they and their husbands rarely or never fight in any of the different ways we listed; that is, they seldom resort either to the active-aggressive fighting (swearing, shouting, hitting, crying or breaking things) or to passive-aggressive fighting (leaving the room, sulking or staying silent). (p. 92)

Conversely it was found that the most unhappily married wives believed they could not talk to their husbands about what was bothering them without causing a fight or other misunderstanding. In short, they were caught in a vicious circle of misunderstanding.

## Marital Conflict

During courtship, partners may find that there is no cause for disagreement. In the glow of romantic love, any minor disputes that may occur are rapidly and lovingly resolved, and the partners may assume that the ease with which they now deal with problems will characterize their married life as well.

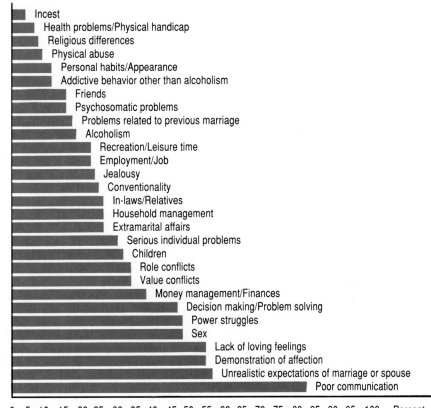

**FIGURE 11.2  Estimates of Marital Problems**

Source: *Social Psychology,* Brigham, J.C. (1966). Scott, Foresman and Company.

This soft-focused view of conflict resolution during courtship often surrenders to the hard-edged realities of married life. In their day-to-day accommodations to each other, the partners may find that they are in disagreement on both minor issues, such as who takes out the garbage, and on major issues, such as how many children they should have. They will also learn that conflict resolution is not always as easy as it was during courtship.

**Areas of conflict.**    Although researchers disagree on which areas are the most common sources of conflict, the following eight issues are more frequently mentioned (Knox, 1979): (1) Money—too little, who spends it, how it is spent, debt; (2) Sex—how much, when, contraceptive use, dysfunctions; (3) In-laws—meddling, when to visit or have visit, rejection by in-laws; (4) Recreation—what kind, solitary versus family, how much time, cost; (5) Friends—shared versus individual friends, resentment of time spent with friends; (6) Drug use—who drinks or smokes what, how much, concern over health; (7) Religion—little versus major involvement, role in children's lives; and (8) Children—how many, when to have, type of discipline.

In each of these areas, our backgrounds and values will influence our position on these issues. To the highly religious person, it may seem self-evident that children

*Different areas of conflict are likely to arise as a relationship matures. A couple's ability to communicate effectively will be a major factor in their ability to resolve conflicts.*

should be taught strong religious values. If, however, our partner belongs to a different faith or is opposed to formal religious training, significant conflicts can occur. The areas in which conflicts are likely to occur will depend on individual differences and perspectives, and it is likely that the areas of conflict will change as the spouses change.

**Resolving conflict.** Effective conflict resolution depends on effective communication. Here are some of the skills that have been suggested (Bach & Wyden, 1968; Knox, 1979) for resolving conflicts:

1. *Listening effectively.* Although you may feel threatened by your partner's complaints, the first step in resolving conflicts is to listen to the complaint and acknowledge its existence. If your partner complains that you do not share in managing the family finances, your first response should not be, "I do too help with the finances!" but, "Apparently, we disagree about our finances."

2. *Giving nondefensive feedback.* Rogers (1951) has shown that rephrasing the content of your partner's complaints can indicate that you are listening and paying attention. Additionally, your feedback can clarify and limit the area of conflict. Knox (1979) gives the following example of nondefensive feedback.

> A wife told her husband, "I get upset when you go out with Ben." Her husband's feedback (what he heard) was, "You don't want me to see Ben anymore." And the wife replied, "No, I didn't say that. Saturday night is our time, and I would like you two to play handball sometime other than Saturday night." (p. 327)

Not only can the facts of the conflict be clarified with nondefensive feedback, but the emotional tone of the conflict can be acknowledged as well. In the example above, the husband might have said, "You got angry when I went out with Ben on Saturday night" (Knox, 1979, p. 327). Using nondefensive feedback can thus define and limit the area of disagreement.

3. *Staying on target.* Once an area of conflict has been identified, it is helpful for the partners to keep their focus on that subject and not drift into others. If a husband, for example, remarks that he dislikes his wife's best friend and wishes that she would not see that person anymore, it is more likely that this conflict can be successfully resolved if the partners focus on the wife's friendship than if the husband adds, "And, by the way, I also don't like the way you're wearing your hair these days." Straying from the topic invites the partner to retaliate and lessens the chances that the immediate conflict can be resolved.

4. *Specifying behaviors to change.* Providing a partner with specific, clear suggestions for behavioral change is very helpful in resolving conflicts. Vague, ambiguous, or general requests are difficult to fulfill. For example, the request to "be more considerate" is subject to a number of interpretations. However, if the partner makes the request specific—"When you fix yourself a snack at night, I want you to ask me if I would like a snack, too" (Knox, 1979)—the request can be fulfilled.

Some marital partners believe that their spouses should be mind readers. "I shouldn't have to tell her. She should be able to figure it out." This belief places the partner in the awkward position of knowing that the other is unhappy, of knowing that change is desired, but not knowing what areas to change. Again, specific suggestions can allow the individual to accomplish the desired acts.

5. *Not expecting immediate solutions or immediate results.* Some difficult problems will need more than a few minutes to resolve, and some solutions will need a long time to become effective. If we insist on immediate resolution of problems and equally rapid implementation of the solution, we will likely be disappointed. Often, issues of values and goals will be among those that are most difficult to resolve.

As I have suggested, there is a middle ground between the brooding, destructive effects of excessive niceness and the outbursts of uncontrolled anger. However, not all conflicts will be resolved. Depending on the depth of conflict, these unresolved issues can produce very little disturbance to the relationship or they can ultimately lead to separation and divorce.

## Sexual Incompatibility and Infidelity

It is commonly assumed that both partners in a marriage will find satisfaction in their sexual relationship. We saw earlier that sexuality is one of the primary reasons for getting married. Moreover, the Tavris and Jayaratne (1976) survey, which we presented earlier, found that only love, respect, and friendship were more important than sexual compatibility in marriage. Nonetheless, sexual incompatibility among marriage partners is often a source of distress, recrimination, and self-blame. We will have a great deal more to say about sexuality in the next chapter, but a few points are worth making here.

One source of incompatibility can be a change in the frequency of sexual intercourse during the married years. As we will see in Chapter 12, for most couples the frequency of sexual intercourse tends to decline over the years due to such things as boredom, the press of other activities, and the demands and presence of children (Greenblatt, 1983; Masters, Johnson, & Kolodny, 1982). Moreover, among men, sexual need peaks in late adolescence and early adulthood and declines thereafter; among women, sexual need peaks somewhat later, usually in the thirties or early forties, and then declines. As the frequency of intercourse changes and sexual needs of the partners also change, it is almost certain that some degree of incompatibility will arise.

Another potential source of incompatibility is different sexual preferences and expectations. As noted earlier, during courtship people present themselves in the best possible light, and romantic love causes an individual to see the potential marriage partner ideally. Moreover, sexuality is a difficult topic for many adolescents and young adults to discuss frankly and openly. Thus, it is not unusual, once married, for partners to discover that they have somewhat different sexual preferences and expectations. In addition, a number of married couples experiment sexually in an effort to keep their sexual relationship stimulating and varied; as couples explore their sexuality, it is not unusual for them to discover that their tastes and preferences are not totally compatible.

Finally, there are both psychological and physical changes in sexuality as people age, and during the course of life a number of sexual problems can arise that make sexual relations difficult or impossible to sustain. These changes may contribute to sexual incompatibilities. In addition, sexual compatibility and satisfaction cannot be divorced from other aspects of a couple's relationship. Satisfying marital relationships may both foster and be enhanced by sexual satisfaction, while unsatisfying marital relationships may decrease both the frequency and enjoyment of sexual activity (Edwards & Booth, 1976).

To compound these problems, statistics indicate that about 40 to 70 percent of married persons have engaged in extramarital sexual activities (Hite, 1981; Wolfe, 1981). Shere Hite (1981) reported that the majority of men in her study were not monogamous. In fact, 72 percent of "men married two years or more had had sex outside of marriage; the overwhelming majority did not tell their wives, at least at the time" (p. 142). One response to these data has been the suggestion that marital partners consider developing an **open marriage** (O'Neill & O'Neill, 1972). In an open marriage, the partners agree beforehand that extramarital sexual activity may occur, and they agree to respond to extramarital activity in a permissive, nonpossessive fashion. In its ideal form, open marriage would allow for extramarital activity without feelings of jealousy, resentment, or competition. Presumably, an open marriage would ultimately produce a stronger, more secure, more growth-oriented relationship between the partners. However, even as advocates of open marriage have noted (O'Neill, 1978), it is difficult to give a spouse permission for extramarital activity and not feel jealousy or discomfort at the same time. It thus appears that marital fidelity still remains a cherished goal for many, but it is a goal that many will find difficult to attain.

**open marriage:** marriage in which both partners are free to take other sexual partners

## Jealousy and Possessiveness

*In a world where we are so at the mercy of rapid change and capricious chance, it is little wonder that we seek stability and certainty in intimate relationships, especially with the one we love most. Anything that seems likely to upset or interfere with that becomes a threat. Jealousy, most psychologists agree, is one understandable response to this situation.*

"Taming the Green-eyed Monster" (Lobsenz, 1975, p. 77)

The related problems of jealousy and possessiveness are common sources of conflict in marriage (Adams, 1980; Pines & Aronson, 1983). Whatever draws the partner's attentions and energies away—whether it be attraction to another person, an absorbing hobby, the person's job, or even the children—may arouse jealousy. Since jealous partners are often dissatisfied with other aspects of the marriage relationship, jealousy and possessiveness may both indicate and complicate an already troubled marriage.

Jealousy and possessiveness are commonly based on feelings of dependency and insecurity in the relationship. In some instances, as suggested by Butler (1976), feelings of insecurity arise suddenly in a seemingly stable relationship and catch the person off guard.

Wendy's marital breakup affected me very deeply. I've been married for almost seven years to a man I adore. I'd never allowed myself to consider the possibility of our ever breaking up. We were so perfectly matched. Divorce was as unreal to me as the planet earth shifting out of its orbit around the sun.

Then, during dinner one evening, my husband in a rather whimsical way and with an enigmatic grin asked me whether I thought I could survive "if something happened to us." Sheer whimsy—sure, how sure? It got me thinking and it was disturbing. What upset me most was my emotional instability at just the thought of parting from him. It dawned on me that my entire world revolved around my marriage. If it fell to pieces, I would crumble along with it. (p. 23)

In the long run, however, moderate feelings of jealousy may actually be beneficial to a relationship. They communicate the fact that one's partner "still cares," help to define the boundaries of acceptable and unacceptable behavior in the marriage, and may be an early warning sign that the marriage is in need of some revitalization (Knox, 1985). Efforts to improve the quality and stability of the relationship, which may entail an analysis of the basis of the jealous feelings, can lead to constructive results and a more satisfying marriage. Intense feelings of jealousy, however, are likely to be destructive. The jealous partner may become even more possessive, dependent, or insecure. Alcoholism, depression, assaults, divorce, suicide, and murder have been traced in some cases to extreme jealousy (Knox, 1985).

## Children and Child-rearing

*From reading popular magazines, watching TV, or listening to people
"who should know," it is easy to assume that rearing children is fun;
that children are "cute"; that good parent-child relationships are
automatic; that all married couples should have children; and that child
rearing is easier today because of modern medicine, modern appliances,
child psychology, and so forth.*

*Marriages and Families: Making Choices Throughout the Life Cycle*
(Lamanna & Riedmann, 1985, p. 280)

Lamanna and Riedmann are describing some of the great myths of marriage:
that raising children comes naturally, the presence of children will improve every
marriage, and children are a constant source of happiness. Actually, data do indicate
that the likelihood of divorce is lower in families with children (A. Thornton, 1977),
but the data also indicate that on the average couples with children are less happy
than couples who are child-free (Glenn & McLanahan, 1982b). Moreover, studies
also show that even in good marriages, the level of marital satisfaction tends to
decrease during child-rearing years and to improve when the children are grown
(Glenn & McLanahan, 1982a; Waldron & Routh, 1981). Apparently, it is less fun to
be raising a family than to have raised a family.

Virtually every couple considers the arrival of their first child a major turning
point in their marriage. At the very least, their lives are forever and unalterably
changed; in many cases, however, the arrival of children turns into a full-fledged
crisis (Dyer, 1963; Hobbs & Cole, 1977). In the face of these facts, it has become
popular to write articles proclaiming that the family is on its way out, dying, or dead.
Like Mark Twain, who stated that reports of his death had been "greatly exaggerated," those of us who were raised in families and plan families of our own may
find such claims excessive. Giving birth and raising children to be competent, healthy
persons is a notable achievement and can be a source of pride and fulfillment. A
majority of married couples today appear to want children and most do have children.
Nonetheless, few married couples would deny that child-bearing is a significant
adjustive challenge to the strongest marriage. In this section, we will examine the
satisfactions that arise from child-rearing as well as the adjustments that are often
required with the arrival of children. We will also consider some techniques for coping
more effectively with the stresses that children can cause in a marriage.

**The joys of child-rearing.**    There is no question that child-rearing can be a source
of satisfaction. Children can be great fun: they are full of energy, add a sense of
newness and freshness to living, are fun to play with, and their sense of wonderment
and discovery can be a source of pure joy. There is also the obvious sense of pride,

accomplishment, and achievement that parents feel as a child passes the various milestones of development. As with other intimate interpersonal relationships, there is a sense of fulfillment in loving and being loved by another person. Children can draw parents together into a closer relationship and deepen their sense of love and common purpose. Being needed by one's own child, and providing nurturance, guidance, and care for that child from the very moment of birth—these satisfactions are totally unique to the relationship between parent and child, and they can give an added meaning and sense of purpose to one's life.

**On the other hand . . .** Children also represent a major adjustive challenge. The advent of a child is sudden, and it launches the married couple on a new career—parenthood—for which they have little or no preparation. Most new parents are frightened at the prospect of making a mistake or being unable to cope with situations that may arise, such as What if I drop my baby? What if my baby chokes? What if my baby doesn't like me? What should I do if my baby won't stop crying?

Children also impose a financial burden on their parents, not only through direct costs for such things as medical care, food, clothing, and education, but also through lost income if one or both parents reduce their employment to care for the children. Faced with a new twenty-four-hour-a-day job, parents lose sleep, free time disappears, workload increases tremendously, and worries multiply. Routines must be changed, new schedules must be established, and time, attention, and affection must be spread among more people. As if to make things worse, there is a sudden realization that parenthood lasts forever: children can't be unborn; a couple can't decide after a week or two that they won't be parents anymore! There's simply no turning back if things don't go well. As Judith Stevens-Long (1984) puts it: "Parenting has the quality of 'alwaysness'" (p. 218).

In the midst of all this, just when it is most important for new parents to spend time reassuring and supporting each other, they discover that they are able to see each other less often and for briefer periods of time, they have fewer outside activities, go places less often, and do fewer things together. Even on those rare occasions when they can find an hour or two to get away together, plans must be made far enough in advance to assure the availability of a babysitter. As a result, fatigue builds, tension increases, and signs of severe stress begin to appear in the marriage. At this point, feelings of hostility, anxiety, and depression are normal as new parents try to cope with what seem to be impossible adjustive demands.

In sum, children can be a source of tremendous pleasure and fulfillment, but they can also be the source of severe stress. Therefore, once the first child arrives, the partners in a marriage must learn to cope as effectively as possible with the stress while at the same time enjoying the unique satisfactions of raising a child. In earlier chapters, we discussed various ways of coping with stress, and those discussions apply here as well. However, there are some additional steps available for parents for coping specifically with the stresses of child-rearing (Harris, 1986).

**Coping with the stress of parenthood.**  For coping with the stress of child-rearing the first step is to realize that periods of stress are normal, and are not a sign that you are a poor parent or spouse. Expect that, like all other parents, you will make mistakes, but also understand that it is extremely unlikely you will cause any serious or permanent damage if you simply use good common sense in dealing with your children. If you expect to be a "Supermom" or "Superdad," you are almost certain to be disappointed, and the normal stress of child-rearing is likely to be greater than is necessary.

Knowing that stress is inevitable, you can be alert for signs of stress in yourself and others in the family and then attempt to deal directly with problems as they arise. Anger, anxiety, and depression are normal responses to stress, but they are also early warning signals that more serious problems may appear if the underlying problem is not resolved. Be alert for signs that your marriage partner or children in the family need additional reassurance or extra help, or are feeling left out and neglected. Urge them to be alert for these signs from you as well. Do everything possible to respond to these early warning signs before the stress becomes greater. This may require additional time to organize new routines to minimize disruptions to yourself and your marriage. It may require setting priorities that differ somewhat from the norm: perhaps housecleaning, yard work, hobbies, or entertaining visitors will have to be neglected for a while to leave time for you and your family to cope with more important problems.

**extended family:** relatives other than parents and their children, all of whom maintain contact with one another

When necessary, relying on resources outside the immediate family can help minimize the stress of child-rearing. One such resource is the **extended family**—

**nuclear family:** parents and
their children

aunts, uncles, cousins, and grandparents—who can often supplement the physical and emotional resources of the **nuclear family**—a wife, husband, and their children. If your relatives are available, willing, and likely to be helpful, you can plan ways to draw on their resources *before* a crisis develops. Find several good babysitters and rely on them regularly to give you and your spouse the time you need to be together. Locate two or three people whose judgment you trust and to whom you can turn for advice and encouragement when you are unsure what to do; these might be experienced parents, close friends, or professionals. As we saw in Chapter 3, social support can be very effective in helping reduce the impact of stress.

## Changes in Marital Sex Roles

**sex roles:** expected behavior
patterns based solely on
gender

**Traditional marriages.**    Another major potential source of stress in marriage is changing marital **sex roles.** Traditionally, the expected roles that husbands and wives will play in a marriage have been quite different, not necessarily because of differences in skills, abilities, or preferences but simply because "that's the way it's supposed to be." For the most part, husbands have been expected to provide for the family's economic security and to be disciplinarians with the children; these marital roles correspond to the more general expectation that males are dominant, successful, self-reliant, and assertive. In contrast, wives have been expected to stay at home and perform household and child-care duties, as well as provide emotional support for the husband; these roles, too, correspond to the more general expectation that females are submissive, dependent, and supportive (see Insight, p. 402).

This form of marriage was widely accepted in this country until recently. For example, in 1940 only 14 percent of married women were in the labor force. As recently as the 1970s, more than 90 percent of married couples agreed that the husband should be the primary wage earner in the family (Lamanna & Riedmann, 1985). The legal system, also, tends to support this model of marriage: for example, in divorce proceedings it is usually the case that the husband is required to provide continuing financial support for his family while the wife is given custody of their children.

When both the husband and wife prefer the traditional roles and choose to structure their marrriage this way, a traditional marriage can be very satisfying. In fact, according to a 1977 survey, fully 43 percent of Americans preferred the traditional marriage structure with husband as exclusive wage earner and wife as full-time homemaker (Lamanna & Riedmann, 1985).

However, this kind of marriage is not without its drawbacks. The sharp separation of roles in traditional marriages can result in major power differences between husband and wife. Traditionally, the husband and wife do not share equally in important decisions. They do not have equal opportunities to develop their potentials, and they do not share equally in the various responsibilities in the family—in short, they are rarely equal partners in the marital relationship (Scanzoni, 1972). This can lead, in turn, to marital conflict. Jay Haley (1963), psychotherapist and theorist in family relations, remarked that " . . . the major conflicts in a marriage center in the problem of who is to tell whom what to do under what circumstances. . . ." It is to be expected that when two people enter an intimate relationship in which there are

# Insight

## Cultural Differences in Sex Roles

The strikingly different sex roles that develop in different societies have been described by Margaret Mead (1939) in her studies of New Guinea tribes. The contrasts she found among the three tribes she studied highlight the extremes that are possible—and the extent to which the "human nature" a child will develop is dependent on his or her early experiences.

1. *The Arapesh.* In this tribe both sexes showed characteristics and behavior that would be considered feminine in our own society. Both men and women were encouraged to be unaggressive, mild, cooperative, and responsive to the needs of others. Neither sex took an aggressive role in courtship. The ideal marriage consisted of a mild, responsive man married to a mild, responsive woman.

2. *The Mundungumor.* In this tribe both sexes would be characterized as masculine by our traditional standards. Both men and women were encouraged to be aggressive, violent, and ruthless; gentleness and tender behavior were at a minimum. The ideal marriage was that of a violent, aggressive male married to a violent, aggressive female.

3. *The Tchambuli.* While neither the Arapesh nor the Mundungumor had clearly defined roles which distinguished the behavior of the sexes, the Tchambuli did have such roles, but they were reversed by our standards. The women were characteristically dominant, impersonal, and businesslike and took the initiative in courtship and sexual behavior. By contrast, the men were irresponsible, emotionally dependent on the women, relatively passive, concerned about their physical appearance, and interested in arts and home activities.

In this study, then, we see three societies in which sex roles differ considerably from our own. In two, the roles are social rather than specifically sexual; there is very little distinction between the norms for the two sexes but a striking difference between the norms of the two societies. In the third, there is a reversal of sex roles as compared with ours.

During the past decade, there has been a trend in our society toward the convergence of conventional sex roles. That is, behaviors which were formerly considered either masculine or feminine—such as knitting, running for political office, and military service—are now considered appropriate for both sexes. Many men are now taking an active part in caring for children and performing household duties, while women are taking on responsibilities and duties in the business world that were once considered exclusively "men's work."

One interesting indication of this trend is the toys that are given to children. At one time, little boys got fire trucks and erector sets and doctor's kits, while little girls were given dolls and toy kitchens and nurse's kits. Some parents who were not following traditional sex roles objected. As a result, some companies began designing toys that do not observe traditional sex roles. Many parents are quite determined that their male and female children will both grow up with the idea that they can be whatever they want to be, regardless of traditional sex roles.

clear power differences, the two are likely to encounter some difficulties in making decisions about the roles and functions of each—and about which partner decides which issues. Unfortunately, some couples actually engage in power struggles, sometimes open and sometimes hidden. The couple who fight over whose turn it is to empty the trash may actually be battling about a more fundamental issue in their relationship.

In addition, in some traditional marriages the needs and preferences of the husband and wife do not correspond to their preassigned roles. Wives may feel resentment and anger that they have few personal choices, are unable to fulfill their desires for professional achievement, are cast in a submissive role that they do not want, and find their marriages have lost the quality of intimacy. One wife said, "My single friends don't call me anymore because they assume I have a built-in companion. I live in the same house with Rex, but *companion* isn't the word I would use to describe him. I'm terribly lonely" (Knox, 1985, p.142). In turn, some husbands in traditional marriages feel isolated from their families, anxious and fearful because they are the sole source of financial security for their families, and stifled in an exclusive relationship that has lost its vitality. One husband remarked, "As a husband, I am expected to be economically responsible for everything, eat breakfast and dinner with my wife, stay in the house from six at night until morning, have sex only with my wife, and enjoy weekends with a two-year-old" (Knox, 1985, pp. 141–42).

It is worth repeating that traditional marriages can be happy and satisfying if the partners choose their roles voluntarily and if they are alert to early warning signs of the kinds of problems that can arise. However, some couples are choosing a very different form of marriage, as we will now see.

**Modern marriages.**   As many observers have noted, there are no compelling reasons why women should be the primary child-care providers or why men should be the primary economic providers. Except for reproduction, most of the observed differences between the sexes in terms of dress, habits, behavior, and opportunity are to a large extent related to our learning experiences and to cultural stereotypes and models. Moreover, as we will see in Chapter 13, financial necessity, increased longevity, improved birth control, and better education for women have combined to encourage more women to enter the work force; and with the resulting feelings of achievement, competence, and independence, fewer women today find the traditional housewife role appealing (Hughes & Noppe, 1985).

As society has grappled with the recognition that marital sex roles are a matter of choice and custom, and not a necessary reflection of innate differences between men and women, and as women have explored options other than the traditional role of housewife, the goals and expectations of marital partners have changed. The result has been a move toward much greater flexibility in the allocation of various marital and family responsibilities to husbands and wives. It is not that wives must work or that husbands must take care of the children; rather, in a modern marriage the abilities and preferences of the partners determine who will work, who will take care of the children, who will do the grocery shopping, and so on. In some cases, husbands and wives may completely switch roles, but this is rare. Much more often, the various marital roles are simply shared more equitably: husbands acquire some of the responsibilities that would otherwise fall exclusively to their wives, and wives acquire some of their husbands' responsibilities.

This "modern" model of marriage has become increasingly popular in recent years. For example, 90 percent of the high school students in a survey said they believed that wives should be wage earners (Blumstein & Schwartz, 1983), although the 1980 census showed that only 61 percent of American households actually have two wage earners (Knox, 1985). More than half of the married couples in a 1980 survey indicated that child care was shared between husband and wife; just a decade

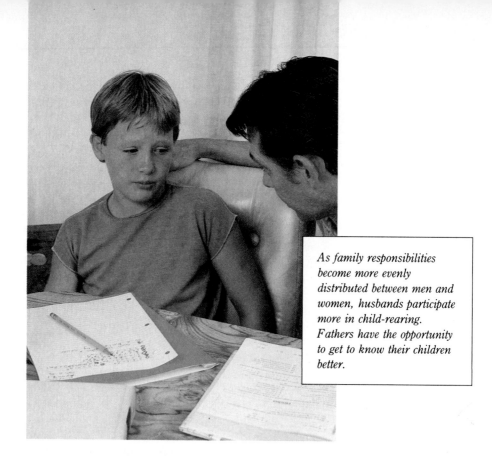

*As family responsibilities become more evenly distributed between men and women, husbands participate more in child-rearing. Fathers have the opportunity to get to know their children better.*

earlier, the same figure was 33 percent (Yankelovich, 1981). To a lesser extent, husbands have also assumed a greater responsibility for doing housework. In the majority of marriages, decision making is now shared more or less equally between husband and wife.

However, recent research data indicate that generally couples in modern marriages are neither happier nor unhappier than couples in more traditional marriages (Knox, 1985; Lamanna & Riedmann, 1985; Hoffman, 1989). Certainly the potential exists for couples in modern marriages to allocate family responsibilities in ways that better suit their unique needs and preferences. Sharing responsibilities can also make a marriage less vulnerable to stress and pressure from outside life events (Doherty & Jacobson, 1982). Work can be a morale booster for women who want to work outside the home and provide a valuable buffer for women who are experiencing stress at home (Baruch, Biener, & Barnett, 1987; Hoffman, 1989). More equitable distribution of power can also lead to greater intimacy, companionship, and fewer power struggles. Wives who want to pursue a career should be able to gain a great deal of personal satisfaction outside the home, while husbands who want to be closer to their children should be able to participate more fully in child-rearing.

At the same time, in modern marriages leisure time and shared time together are often scarce. Some working wives experience additional stress from trying to balance the dual demands of work and family, particularly if their decision to work was not a matter of choice. Moreover, most working wives are employed in "pink-collar jobs": low-paying and low-status jobs that are not particularly challenging or fulfilling. To make matters worse, most husbands are reluctant to share equally in housework, so in most modern marriages that chore continues to fall primarily on the wife. For example, John Robinson (1988) compared the extent to which married men and women spent time doing housework in 1965, 1975, and 1985. He found a steady decline in hours spent on household chores by women (from 27 hours per week in 1965 to 19.5 hours per week in 1985). At the same time men have been spending more time doing household chores: from 4.6 hours a week in 1965 to 9.8 hours a week in 1985. Nonetheless, women still spend twice as much time on household chores as do men. A *New York Times* nationwide survey in the fall of 1987 found that among women with full-time jobs, 90 percent said that they did the primary shopping for the family and 86 percent said they did most or all of the family's cooking (Burros, 1988). Finally, the very fact of breaking new ground can be a source of additional stress: there is no "conventional wisdom" to rely on, parents and grandparents are less likely to provide helpful models to imitate, and the need to decide who will do what can lead to conflict and indecision.

What, then, are we to conclude about the relative merits of modern and traditional marriages? First, an arrangement that works for one couple may be a disaster for another couple. Just as the traditional marriage is not optimal for all, neither is modern marriage likely to suit everyone. Each couple must develop an arrangement that fits their unique needs and preferences. If either partner does not support the arrangement fully, it is unlikely to be successful (Houseknecht & Macke, 1981). Second, couples who enter a nontraditional marriage with the expectation that automatically it will be more satisfying than a traditional marriage are heading for trouble. The adjustive demands of modern marriages are at least as great as the adjustive demands of traditional marriages. Being alert for early signs of stress and using the techniques for coping with stress that we have described in this and earlier chapters can go a long way toward assuring that a marriage (whether modern or traditional) is successful.

Unfortunately, not all marriages are successful despite the best efforts of the partners to make them so. Like any other relationship, the husband-wife relationship is subject to constant change—both short-term and long-term. Periods of intimacy may follow periods of emotional distance, excitement may follow calm, and growth may follow stagnation. These short-term changes occur in the context of long-term change and its effects on the nature and stability of the marriage.

A crucial problem here is the challenge both partners face in adjusting to change and growth in the other. Since one partner does not ordinarily change and grow at the same time or in the same areas as the other, this poses a difficult challenge—that of being supportive and maintaining closeness while experiencing change both in oneself and one's partner.

In our complex and rapidly changing world, marital happiness is not something that, once achieved, can be counted on to continue indefinitely. Rather, couples must be willing to work to continue achieving happiness. The alternative is the gradual deterioration of the marriage and, in some cases, the prospect of separation or divorce.

## DIVORCE AND REMARRIAGE

*For every two couples who will take the big step to the altar this year,
there will be a man and woman somewhere else in the U.S. who have
found marriage to be one of life's most painful and wrenching
experiences. They will be getting divorced.*

"Today's Marriages," (1975, p. 35)

The divorce rate in the United States increased dramatically through the mid-1970s. One in seven marriages ended in divorce in 1920, compared with one in four in 1960 and one in three in 1974. These figures do not include the substantial number of married couples who separate without bothering to get a divorce. According to the National Center for Health Statistics, there is some sign that since the late-1970s the number of new divorces each year has finally begun to drop, but it is too early to tell whether this trend will continue.

Of course, divorce and separation statistics do not tell the whole story about the incidence of unhappiness and maladjustment in marriages. Many unhappily married couples stay together because of religious or financial considerations, reluctance to disrupt the lives of their children, fear of not being able to do any better on a second try, or simply habit or lethargy. Thus, many of the marriages that end in divorce may have been as happy as or even happier than some of those that endure.

### Causes of Divorce

Many factors undoubtedly combine to account for our high divorce rate. These factors include characteristics of the two people involved, the pattern of interaction between them, and the conditions in the social setting.

**Reasons given for divorce.** In one of the few large-scale studies available, Levinger (1966) examined the counseling records of 600 couples applying for divorce and compared the complaints of husbands and wives of middle-class and lower-class couples. Husbands complained of mental cruelty, neglect of home and children, infidelity, and sexual incompatibility. Complaints most often made by the wives were of physical and mental cruelty, financial problems, and drinking. In general, the middle-class couples were more concerned with psychological and emotional aspects while the lower-class couples were more concerned with financial problems and the physical actions of their partners.

In a more recent study, Albrecht (1979) asked 500 remarried people why their first marriages failed. The results are shown in Table 11.3. Dissatisfaction with the emotional relationship between partners is high on this list, followed by the usual assortment of financial, alcohol, sexual, and in-law problems. The results suggest that if we were to delve more deeply, it is likely that unrealistic expectations and failure to invest the effort necessary to make the marriage work were basic underlying factors leading to divorce.

**General social change.**    As we have seen, most of our traditional values and social structures have been challenged in recent years. Mobility, instability, and change appear to be both commonplace and expected—both in our society and in our personal lives. Our high standard of living has raised our expectations for satisfactions of all kinds, including those by which we measure the acceptability of a marital relationship. It is also possible that marriages based on fulfilling love and emotional needs are inherently more hazardous than those based on economic and other pragmatic considerations, where the conditions that give rise to the marriage help to maintain it.

Modern urbanization and the rise of the nuclear family have removed many of the supports and the help that tend to be available to the extended family living in a less hurried, less impersonal, more stable social network. At the same time, occupational opportunities for women have provided an alternative to continuing unhappy marriages. Better opportunities for remarriage may also influence their decision. Also, with less stringent divorce laws and less stigma attached to divorced people, there is wider acceptance of divorce as a means to resolve all unsatisfactory marital situation. All these factors make stable, satisfying marriages more difficult and separation more attractive when expectations are not met.

Unfortunately, the rate and complexity of social change, with all its implications for mate selection and marital happiness, have not been matched by the development of realistic expectations in young people or attitudes and skills needed for a stable and satisfying marriage in this kind of society. A great deal of misery and many

**TABLE 11.3    Major Reasons for Failure of First Marriage**

|  | Listed First | | Total Number of | |
|---|---|---|---|---|
|  | (N) | (Order) | Times Listed | (Order) |
| Infidelity | 168 | (1) | 255 | (1) |
| No longer loved each other | 103 | (2) | 188 | (2) |
| Emotional problems | 53 | (3) | 185 | (3) |
| Financial problems | 30 | (4) | 135 | (4) |
| Physical abuse | 29 | (5) | 72 | (8) |
| Alcohol | 25 | (6) | 47 | (9) |
| Sexual problems | 22 | (7) | 115 | (5) |
| Problems with in-laws | 16 | (8) | 81 | (6) |
| Neglect of children | 11 | (9) | 74 | (7) |
| Communication problems | 10 | (10) | 18 | (11) |
| Married too young | 9 | (11) | 14 | (12) |
| Job conflicts | 7 | (12) | 20 | (10) |
| Other | 7 |  | 19 |  |

Source: Albrecht, 1979; p. 862.

*Because divorce is essentially the loss of a meaningful relationship, it has its own from of grief. However, when the grief subsides one can reassess one's identity, evaluate one's expectations in a relationship, and grow toward greater self-understanding.*

wasted years might be avoided by more adequately preparing young people for both choosing and living with a mate.

In any case, American marriages today are undertaken against a cultural background which places an increasingly heavy burden on the marital partners for establishing stability and meeting each other's psychological needs. As society's stake in stable families has come to be regarded as secondary to the individual's happiness — in marked contrast to the priorities established in many other cultural groups — the way appears to be paved for a continued high incidence of marital failure (see Table 11.4, p. 408).

**TABLE 11.4  Summary of Background Factors Related to Divorce**

| | |
|---|---|
| **Educational Level** | The lower the educational level, the higher the divorce rate. |
| **Occupational Status** | Divorce more common among lower socioeconomic groups than among professional groups. |
| **Family Background** | Higher divorce rate among couples raised in unhappy homes and/or by divorced parents. |
| **Racial Background** | Nonwhite marriages more divorce-prone than white marriages at all educational and occupational levels. |
| **Religion** | Higher divorce rates among nonchurchgoers. |
| **Length of Courtship** | Divorce rates higher for those with brief courtships. |
| **Age at Time of Marriage** | Divorce rates very high for those marrying in their teens. |
| **Factors Not Related to Divorce Rate** | Interracial, mixed religion, sexual experience prior to marriage, age difference between spouses. |

## Effects of Divorce

*Divorce is a disorganizing and reorganizing process in a family with children. The process extends over time, often several years. Although it has, like most life events and crises, the potential for growth and new integrations, the road is often rocky and tortuous and many people underestimate the vicissitudes and difficulties of the transition.*

"Divorce and Counseling" (Wallerstein & Kelly, 1977, p. 5)

The specific effects of divorce on the married couple depend on many factors, such as the emotional involvement of the partners, the happiness and duration of the marriage prior to divorce, the opportunities for remarriage, and the stress tolerance and other personality characteristics of both partners.

Divorce is often interpreted as a sign of failure, and divorced persons often feel that they have failed in one of life's most important tasks. Following a divorce, many people experience a sense of personal inadequacy, disillusionment, and depression. Often they are torn by self-recrimination and thoughts of what they might have done that would have made their marriage a success.

Divorced persons are likely to face difficult adjustments because of changes in their life situations. Individuals may have to cope with loss of security, guilt and self-recrimination, the cessation or disruption of sexual satisfactions, and financial problems. Feelings of alienation and loneliness may add to the stress. When the divorce was sought by the other partner, the one who was left usually feels rejected and hurt, which leads to self-devaluation. For the partner who sought the divorce, the stress of divorce and readjustment may bring more severe problems than those from which he or she was trying to escape. Thus, it may come as no surprise that in a ten-year study of sixty divorced couples, Wallerstein (1986) found that in only 10 percent of the cases both partners had succeeded in improving their lives. The women in particular showed persistent anger and widespread loneliness. The growing realization that divorce is not a cure-all for stress in marriage, coupled with the greater availability of counseling services and self-help groups, may account at least in part for the recent decline in the divorce rate noted earlier.

Bohannan (1972) has analyzed the enormously complex and overlapping experiences which divorce brings; he terms them the "six stations of divorce":

**The emotional divorce.** This occurs when spouses withhold emotion from their relationship because they dislike the intensity of ambivalence of their feelings. The couple grows mutually antagonistic. The natural response to the loss of a meaningful relationship is grief. Yet, Bohannan notes, the grief has to be handled alone.

**The legal divorce.** The couple makes a public declaration that their marriage has ended. Although "no fault" divorces and marital dissolution have made this step simpler, the parties normally consult lawyers and must often appear in court—often an emotional, humiliating, and anxiety-provoking experience.

**The economic divorce.**    This aspect of divorce involves the settling of property and the division of assets and may involve many painful aspects including loss of wealth and support.

**The coparental divorce.**    This aspect of divorce centers around the children—custody and visitation rights—and affects not only the children (who often feel that they have been divorced by one parent or the other), but also the spouses, since the family unit changes unalterably. The loss of the relationship with the children, or the prospect of raising the children alone may, of course, be very painful experiences for the parents.

**The community divorce.**    The spouses experience the loss of friends and, often, of community ties, in addition to the other losses occasioned by divorce.

**The psychic divorce.**    "Psychic divorce means the separation of self from the personality and the influence of the ex-spouse . . .." The issue of gaining new autonomy and becoming once again whole and complete may be one of the most difficult of the six aspects, but also potentially the most personally constructive.

In their five-year study of sixty divorced families, Wallerstein and Kelly (1977) not only found that divorce is an extremely disorganizing process in a family but that:

> . . . we may reasonably expect a period of several years of disequilibrium before new, more gratifying job, social, and sexual relationships can become stable enough to provide comfort and a renewed sense of continuity. . . . It is important to keep in mind that two or three years of disequilibrium in the life of a child may represent a significant proportion of his entire life experience. . . . Therefore, the parent's functioning following the divorce, especially in the instance of the young child, is of crucial importance in the child's continued development. . . . (p. 5)

Although older children and adolescents were found to be less dependent on the custodial parent, it was found that the youth's capacity to maintain his or her developmental stride was "related inversely to the (custodial) parent's need to lean heavily on the child for emotional and social sustenance and to involve the child in continuing battles and recriminations with the divorced spouse" (Wallerstein & Kelly, 1977, p. 5).

We have seen that divorce typically involves difficult adjustments for children as well as parents. The magnitude of this problem is indicated by the fact that in the United States, one child in four under the age of eighteen lives in a one-parent home. Usually the custodial parent is the mother, due to her traditional role in childrearing. The short-term effects on children may vary considerably depending on age, the effectiveness of the custodial parent, and success in alleviating feelings of rejection and insecurity—the fear of "what will happen to me?" The evidence suggests that children may benefit more from living with a single parent who loves them and with whom they have a close relationship than living with two parents whose relationship is characterized by extreme stress, anger, and conflict (Hess & Camara, 1979). However, the effects of divorce on children are less clear. One recent study of more than 8,000 adults by Nock (1982) found virtually no evidence of long-term effects of divorce on children. However, Wallerstein's (1985) review of the literature suggests that there are indeed long-lasting effects of divorce on children. Clearly, additional research must be conducted before it will be possible to reconcile these contradictory findings.

## Remarriage and Stepfamilies

*But one lives and loves, suffers and forgets, and begins again—perhaps even thinking that this time, this new time, is to be permanent.*

*Loneliness* (Clark E. Moustakas, 1961)

In colonial times, nearly all remarriages were of widowed persons, but in recent decades there has been a gradually swelling tide of remarriages of those who have been divorced. Overall about 75 percent of divorced women and 80 percent of divorced men remarry within two to five years. Remarriages occur, on the average, about two and a half years after the divorce.

**Reasons for remarriage.**   Societal pressures and individual needs steer divorced persons toward remarriage. A divorced mother may be encouraged to remarry because, she is told, the children need two parents in the home. Divorced persons often feel awkward in the company of married friends. Divorced men and women may find themselves incapable of handling all the responsibilities of maintaining a household for themselves and their children. Factors such as these, along with the need for affection, adult companionship, and sexual intimacy lead many divorced persons to seek new marital partners.

In considering remarriage, there are often new factors to be weighed: a woman who has children from a previous marriage may be concerned about how her children will accept their prospective stepfather and how he will relate to them. A man considering remarriage may have financial responsibility for children of a former marriage. If he pays alimony and child support, he may not be in a position to assume the financial responsibilities of another family. The individual may also be strongly motivated to overcome the emotional hurt and self-devaluation from the prior divorce. The possibility that one may be marrying "on the rebound" is a factor to be considered carefully.

**How successful are remarriages?**   Do second marriages have a better chance of success than first marriages? Has the divorced person's experience taught him or her how to avoid the common pitfalls in marriage, or should earlier failure be taken as a sign that the person is a poor marital risk? The research evidence is scanty and

contradictory. In general, it appears that more remarriages than first marriages end in divorce. Marriages in which one or both of the spouses have had multiple prior marriages are the least stable. However, there are many exceptions, and each marriage has to be evaluated on its own merits. Moreover, "remarriages of divorced persons which do not quickly end in divorce probably are, as a whole, almost as successful as intact first marriages" (Glenn & Weaver, 1977, p. 331). Udry (1966) has suggested several reasons for the success of many remarriages.

> The divorced person has probably learned something about marriage from the first failure. If age contributes anything to maturity, he should be able to make a more mature choice the second time. The significance of sex is transformed, since it can be more taken for granted in the approach to second marriage. Second marriages have the advantage of being compared with a marriage which recently ended in bitterness and conflict. The second time around, the first-time loser has probably readjusted his expectations of marriage and is simply easier to please than those without previous marital experience. (p. 521)

Whether or not divorced persons learn from their failure, and regardless of the odds against them, the potential rewards of the marital relationship appear to lead most divorced persons to try again. Apparently we do not easily abandon our romantic dream of "living happily ever after."

**Stepfamilies.** In many remarriages, one or both partners have children from a previous marriage. In fact, nearly 20 percent of all American families are stepfamilies, and according to the Census Bureau one of every six children under the age of eighteen lives in a stepfamily. The partners in these marriages face not only the usual adjustive challenges of parenthood but also some additional challenges that are unique to stepfamilies. For example, children in stepfamilies have to cope with the disruption of their previous family as well as the readjustment to the new family. They also may have to adjust to new and different ways of doing things in their own homes. In addition, they may be feeling abandoned and unloved by the absent parent yet they may also feel guilt if they begin to like or love their new stepparent. As the victims of one unsuccessful marriage, they are also likely to be cautious about investing themselves emotionally in the new marriage. As noted by Knox (1985), one stepchild pointed out:

> As long as my mother was alive she cooked me plain ole meatloaf and potatoes for dinner. And her potatoes always were the real kind with lumps in them. My stepmother cooks all her meats in some fancy French wine sauce and her potatoes are the instant variety. I don't like her cooking but didn't know how to tell her. And if I started to like her French cooking I might feel guilty because I would be betraying the memory of my mother. (pp. 555–56)

Stepparents also face substantial adjustive problems. It is not easy to love someone else's children, especially if they are withdrawn and seem to resent your presence. If you try to help your stepchildren cope with their feelings, it may seem that you are intruding; but if you don't help them, it may seem as if you don't care. Moreover, the way you want to do some things may differ from the accustomed ways of your stepchildren. You will have to decide between insisting that things be done your way or adapting to the old ways of doing things. Your spouse also will be coping with the stresses of readjustment and will need extra support during the transition period.

It may seem that the challenges to adjustment in stepfamilies are insurmountable, but that needn't be the case. The most important step is to realize from the start that there will be difficult challenges and that the development of the new family will not be instantaneous. Knox (1985) estimates that at least two years is needed for the partners in a remarriage to adjust to each other and another two or three years before everyone will feel completely comfortable with the new family arrangements. As with parenthood generally, it is essential for the partners to set aside time for themselves and to ensure that communication channels remain open. Finally, the children's relationships with their absent parent and their grandparents should be encouraged and supported by both partners in the remarriage. While these suggestions do not guarantee the success of the remarriage, they can help to make the adjustment less difficult for everyone involved.

## ALTERNATIVES TO MARRIAGE

Although culturally desirable and individually popular, marriage is not the only means by which people can develop satisfying interpersonal or intimate relationships. Perhaps two of the most popular alternatives to marriage are cohabitation and singlehood.

### Cohabitation

**cohabitation:** process involving emotional commitments and living arrangements similar to marriage but without a formal or legal announcement of marriage

**Cohabitation,** or living together without marriage, has been the fastest growing alternative to traditional marriage in the United States. In the mid-1960s, a female student made the front page of *The New York Times* because she shared her living quarters and bed with a man. More recent studies, however, have suggested that the incidence of cohabitation ranges from about 20 percent to 35 percent of college students (Cole, 1977; Macklin, 1980). However, cohabitation is still relatively rare in the population though it is becoming more frequent: according to Census figures,

# Psychology in Action

## "Will You Be My POSSLQ?"

When the U.S. Census Bureau developed the acronym POSSLQ, or Persons of the Opposite Sex Sharing Living Quarters, to describe people who cohabitated, newsman Charles Osgood penned this whimsical poem:

Come live with me and be my love,
And we will some new pleasures prove
Of golden sands and crystal brooks
With silken lines and silver hooks.

There's nothing that I wouldn't do
If you would be my POSSLQ.
You live with me, and I with you,
And you will be my POSSLQ.
I'll be your friend and so much more;
That's what a POSSLQ is for.
And everything we will confess;
Yes, even to the IRS.
Someday, on what we both may earn,

Perhaps we'll file a joint return.
You'll share my pad, my taxes joint.
You'll share my life—up to a point!
And that you'll be so glad to do,
Because you'll be my POSSLQ.

Come live with me and be my love,
And share the pain and pleasure of
The blessed continuity,
Official POSSLQuity.
And I will whisper in your ear
That word you love so much to hear.
And love will stay forever new,
If you will be my POSSLQ.

in 1988 there were 2.6 million unmarried couple households compared to 1.6 million in 1980 (see Psychology in Action, p. 414).

The impetus for living together stems from a number of sources. One major factor is changing sexual norms. In the past, a couple who lived together without marriage were likely to be lower-class, uneducated individuals who were "shacking up," and the woman who engaged in these activities was looked upon with disfavor. However, the replacement of the double standards with a standard of "permissiveness with affection" (Reiss, 1976) and the availability of effective contraceptive methods have removed much of the worry and stigma of living together.

Another factor that contributes to cohabitation is the rising divorce rate. Many men and women decide to live together before marrying because they want to be "certain" that they are compatible. They take to heart the old adage that "you don't really know a person until you live with them."

Many men and women also have very mixed feelings about marriage. While there are numerous reasons for getting married, marriage also entails some loss of personal freedom and individuality, brings new responsibilities, and requires constant adjustment and adaptation if it is to succeed.

Financial considerations also play a role in decisions about whether or not to cohabit. It is usually less expensive for two people to live together than for each of them to live separately. However, married couples with two sources of income suffer significant tax disadvantages compared to unmarried couples with the same income.

There is also a growing number of elderly people who are cohabiting as well. While a sexual element is typically very strong in young cohabiting couples, the major reason for cohabiting among the elderly appears to be companionship. Although many cohabiting elderly would like to marry their partners, the couple may suffer a financial loss if they do so, since some retirement plans reduce benefits to an individual if he or she marries.

Despite their aversion to official marriage, cohabiting partners share a relationship strikingly similar to that of married partners. People who live together are as affectionate toward, concerned about, and supportive of their partners as are married couples. Cohabiting couples, on the other hand, are not as sure of the future of the relationship as are married couples. While cohabiting couples believe that ending their relationship would be easier and less troublesome than dissolving a marriage, the breakup of a cohabiting relationship is probably as difficult and stressful as is divorce for married couples.

Not surprisingly, the personal characteristics of cohabiting individuals differ significantly from those of noncohabiting individuals. Cohabiting persons tend to be less involved in organized religion, have a liberal life style, and be friends of other cohabitants. On the other hand, those who live together do not differ from noncohabitants in terms of grades, the perceived happiness of their parents' marriages, or in terms of the educational or occupational status of their parents. Also, cohabitants do not differ from noncohabitants in terms of having urban or rural backgrounds. Although cohabitation is often understood by the couple as preparation for marriage, studies reveal that cohabitants who eventually married are not different from couples who did not live together prior to marriage (Hanna & Knaub, 1981; Risman, Hill, Rubin, & Peplau, 1981).

Like other aspects of intimate interpersonal relationships, the decision to live together can have both positive and negative effects. On the positive side, people can get to know their partners well and can share in their lives. On the other hand, cohabiting individuals may use the relationships to avoid long-term emotional commitments to their partners. In essence, an individual can use the relationship to satisfy his or her own needs while manipulating the feelings and emotions of the partner.

Although cohabitation is increasingly popular, the differences between married and cohabiting partners are becoming smaller. As we have seen, the personal and emotional factors in most cohabiting relationships are similar to those in marriage. Also, the successful prosecution of "palimony" suits suggests that even the legal distinctions between living together and marriage are disappearing as well. Regardless of legal status, the relationship between the partners remains a key factor in determining the quality of an intimate relationship.

## Marriage Redefined

**renewable marriage:** marriage contract that is extended only when the partners specifically agree to continue the marriage

Some investigators have suggested a middle ground between permanent marriages and alternatives to marriage. As sociologist Jessie Bernard (1973) has noted, the advocates of **renewable marriage** argue that couples who depend on the law or other institutional props to support their marriage are likely to let the conscious, voluntary supports decay. If the marriage were subject to optional renewal, the

© William Hamilton                    "More or less."

couple would presumably remain very aware of the fact that they must work to make the relationship stronger and happier.

An alternative perspective has been presented by Toffler (1971), arguing that the goal of permanence will gradually shift to a more temporary marital arrangement. In essence, Toffler (and others) are predicting that people will shift to the one-after-another pattern of **serial marriage.** Toffler's position receives support not only from the rise in divorce rates in recent years and the number of couples who elect cohabitation instead of marriage, but also from statistics showing that 80 percent of widowed and divorced people eventually remarry.

Renewable marriages, cohabitation, serial marriage, and other patterns that recognize the strong possibility of impermanance from the start may yield benefits in terms of freedom and choice, but they do not present perfect alternatives. By recognizing the fact that relationships may not last, people are likely to feel highly insecure and anxious about continuing relationships.

**serial marriage:** two or more marriages for an individual in which one marriage follows the termination of the preceding one

## Singlehood

At any one time, about one-third of adult Americans are single (Libby, 1977). The largest proportion of these have never married, followed by separated and divorced

singlehood: life style
stressing the positive aspects
of being unmarried

singles, and by widowed singles. Of the never-married, the majority eventually become married. However, an increasing number of people see **singlehood** as a legitimate life style, not as just a way station to matrimony.

For those who see singlehood as a positive alternative to marriage, singlehood offers many advantages. Some of the most commonly mentioned ones include freedom to travel, to come and go as the individual pleases, to seek friendships and sexual experiences, and to have no responsibilities to anyone else (Nadelson & Notman, 1981).

Although single people of all ages can and do engage in sexual activities, the stereotype of the "swinging single" as a sexually licentious person is inaccurate. Statistics indicate that the frequency of and the satisfaction associated with sexual activity is significantly higher among married couples than among single people (Hunt, 1974).

Of course, some people use singlehood as a means to avoid marriage. Perhaps they or their parents had a bad marriage. Perhaps they do not want to be answerable to a spouse or children. Or, perhaps, they simply do not feel ready to marry and need more time to develop their interests and careers. Finally, there may not be suitable partners available for marriage. This is especially true of elderly widows.

Many people use singlehood as a way to develop their sense of autonomy and self-worth. For these individuals the ability to "make it" on their own can be a tremendous source of pride and can lead to personal growth.

## SUMMARY

Intimate relationships play an important role in virtually everyone's life. The need to love and be loved appears to be universal among humans of all ages, though individuals differ in their ability to engage in intimate relationships. In this chapter, we have explored the nature of love, marriage, and some other especially intimate relationships that offer an alternative to marriage.

There are many different types of love which range from the nonsexual, altruistic *agape* and the familial companionship of *storge* to the passionate, sexual *eros*. Often more than one kind of love occurs in a single relationship as in *romantic* love and *companionate* love. The mix of different types of love usually changes as the relationship between two people changes and matures. However, all forms of love share a common attitude of care and concern for the loved one and a desire to contribute to his or her growth, well-being, and happiness.

More than 90 percent of Americans eventually marry. For some people, marriage offers companionship, fulfillment, and escape from loneliness. For others, it offers sexual expression, reproduction, child-rearing, and economic security. However, the most common reason people give for marrying is love, and in one survey it was found that women who married for love were more satisfied with their marriages than those who married primarily for other reasons.

People select their mates through a filtering process that, up to a point, is quite similar to the process by which friends are selected. The initial pool of mates is narrowed substantially by the fact that a person encounters only a small percentage of the people he or she might happily marry. From the remaining candidates, those who are unattractive are screened out leaving a still smaller pool of close or intimate acquaintances from which a spouse is eventually selected. In making this final selection, feelings of love play an important role but most people seek various other desirable characteristics in their mates. For many people these qualities include such things as kindness and considerateness, liking children, and being easygoing and adaptable. Throughout the world, men tend to value physical attractiveness more than women, while women tend to put greater value on having good earning capacity. The shared preferences seem to reflect a desire for a partner who will be easygoing and easy to live with, and increase the likelihood that the marriage will survive and be satisfying. It is more difficult to account for the sex differences; they may be learned, or they may reflect inborn preferences that have resulted from evolutionary processes.

Once married, couples must be prepared to cope with a number of adjustive demands. In the early years of marriage, it is necessary to cope with some disillusionment as each partner discovers or is forced to acknowledge some of the less desirable qualities of the other person. It is necessary to establish effective patterns of communication: talking to each other frequently about a wide range of subjects (including bothersome aspects of the marriage), keeping both verbal and nonverbal communication channels open, and showing sensitivity to each other. It is also necessary to deal effectively with conflict in such areas as money, sex, in-laws, recreation, friends, drug use, religion, and children. By listening effectively, giving

*For many people, a traditional marriage continues to be the most fulfilling form of romantic relationship.*

nondefensive feedback, staying on target, specifying behaviors to change, and not expecting immediate solutions, the likelihood is greater that a couple will be able to resolve their conflicts effectively.

As a marriage progresses, sexual incompatibility and infidelity are likely to become problems that require adjustment and adaptation. Some couples resolve sexual incompatibilities by developing an *open marriage* in which both partners agree that extramarital activity is acceptable; however, most couples choose to discuss their sexual preferences and expectations and adjust their sexual relationship so that it continues to be stimulating and rewarding.

Jealousy and possessiveness also can become problems in a marriage. Moderate feelings of jealousy can lead to efforts to build a more stable and satisfying relationship, intense jealousy can be destructive.

Children and child-rearing can be a source of great satisfaction, and can even serve to draw parents together in a closer relationship to each other. However, children can also represent a significant challenge to even the strongest marriage. Most parents have various fears and anxieties about their ability to cope with infants. Children represent a substantial financial burden. Parents lose sleep and must rearrange their routines, and there is less time to spend together as a couple. The first step in coping with these stressors is to realize that they are normal, and that it is not necessary to be a perfect parent. Being alert to early warning signs of unusual stress is also helpful. Drawing on the resources of people outside the *nuclear family* can also provide welcome relief; members of the *extended family* can be helpful, as can trusted babysitters, friends, and professionals.

Marital roles can also be a source of stress. Some couples find traditional *sex roles* fully satisfactory. A substantial percentage of married couples prefer to structure their relationship along traditional lines, with the husband as exclusive wage-earner and the wife as full-time homemaker. However, inequality of power, unequal opportunities to develop potentials, and unequal sharing of family responsibilities can create dissatisfaction and conflict in such marriages especially if one or both partners do not fully agree to the roles thay have assumed. Other couples prefer more flexible and equal distribution of work and family responsibilities that reflect the different abilities and preferences of the partners. Some people find such marriages satisfactory, while others find them stressful: there may be less time together as a couple, the combination of work and family responsibilities can be difficult for both husbands and wives, most working wives are employed in less challenging and fulfilling jobs, and very few husbands assume a fair share of household chores. Research data indicate that neither form of marriage is necessarily better than the other: each couple must choose the form of marriage that best fits their unique needs and preferences.

A substantial percentage of marriages are not satisfactory, though only one-third of all marriages end in divorce (there are some signs that the divorce rate may have begun declining). The reasons for divorce range from dissatisfaction with the emotional relationship, social change, physical and mental cruelty, and neglect to infidelity, sexual incompatibility, financial problems, in-law problems and excessive drinking. Underlying these specific problems seem to be unrealistic expectations and

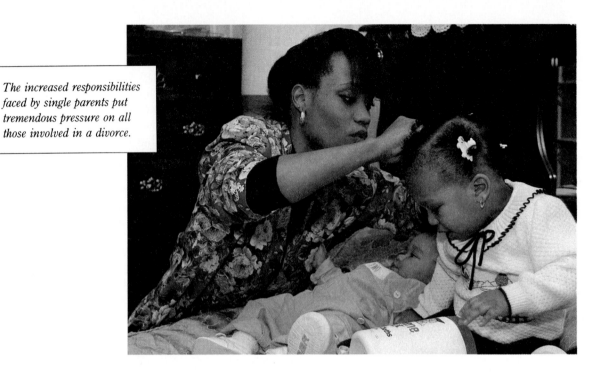

*The increased responsibilities faced by single parents put tremendous pressure on all those involved in a divorce.*

failure to invest the effort necessary to make a marriage more satisfactory, personal dissatisfactions and general social change.

For virtually every family, divorce is a painful process. Moreover, research data show that in only a small percentage of cases are both partners happier ten years after the divorce. Divorced women in particular often experience persistent anger and loneliness. Moreover, some research evidence shows that divorce can have long-lasting effects on children as well, though more research will be needed before we will know with certainty how many children suffer such long-term effects. In any event, growing realization of the fact that divorce is not a magic cure-all—together with greater availability of counseling services and self-help groups—may account in part for the reduced rate of divorce in recent years.

The great majority of divorced people eventually remarry, many successfully, although the rate of success for second marriages is lower than that for initial marriages. Remarried couples are older, hopefully wiser and more realistic, all of which contribute to greater likelihood of success "the second time around." However, stepfamilies present some unique adjustive challenges to the husband and wife and to their children that act to reduce the likelihood that the remarriage will succeed. Readjustment to a new marriage is likely to take several years, during which stress is likely to be quite high at times.

Finally, marriage is not the only means through which people develop intimate relationships. For a number of reasons, several million couples in this country (including many elderly couples) have chosen *cohabitation* as an alternative to marriage or remarriage. Other people have chosen a *renewable marriage* in which the partners periodically choose whether to renew the marriage or to dissolve it. Still another alternative is *serial marriage* in which people shift from one marriage to another throughout the course of their lives. An increasing number of people are also choosing *singlehood* as a positive alternative to marriage.

## KEY TERMS

agape (380)
storge (380)
eros (380)
romantic love (380)
companionate love (381)
open marriage (396)
extended family (400)

nuclear family (401)
sex roles (401)
cohabitation (413)
renewable marriage (415)
serial marriage (416)
singlehood (417)

# Sexual Attitudes and Behavior

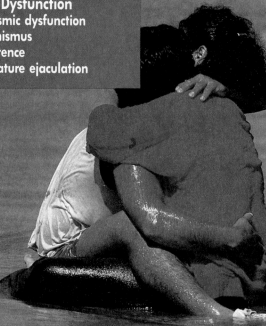

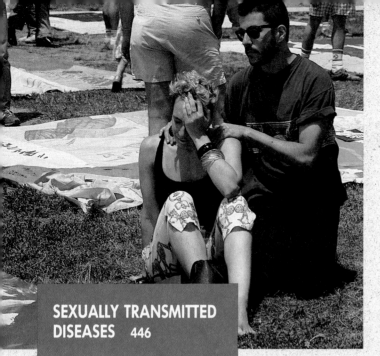

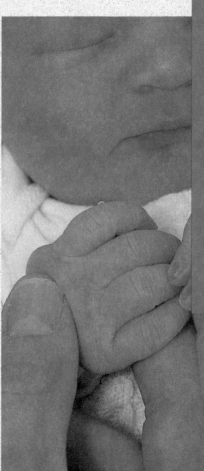

*Sex lies at the root of life, and we can never learn to reverence life until we know how to understand sex.*

*Studies in the Psychology of Sex* (Havelock Ellis, 1906)

*H*UMAN sexuality is one of the most discussed, most pleasurable, and most feared aspects of human life. Human sexuality is both a private and a shared, interpersonal activity. It can be used to help maintain and solidify a relationship with another. It can be used manipulatively, so that the sharing aspects of sexuality are forgotten in a selfish quest for personal satisfaction. Human sexuality thus exemplifies many positive aspects of the human experience and many of the negative, destructive ones as well.

In this chapter, we shall explore several aspects of human sexuality. First, we will look at the so-called sexual revolution and the corresponding changes in values, attitudes, and behaviors. Then we will examine the nature of the sexual response in relation to recent research data. Next, we will address problems of sexual dysfunction. Finally, I will provide an overall perspective from which to view human sexual behavior.

Before we continue, you may find it interesting to take stock of your knowledge about some aspects of human sexuality (see Psychology in Action. p. 425).

## CHANGES IN SEXUAL VALUES, ATTITUDES, AND BEHAVIORS

During the last several decades, some major changes have occurred regarding sexual values, attitudes, and behaviors. These changes are sometimes referred to as the "sexual revolution," but in reality the changes have not really been revolutionary. For example, probably the greatest change has been a marked increase in permissiveness: some previously taboo sexual behaviors are tolerated more widely now than used to be the case. This does not mean that previously taboo behaviors are now expected or encouraged, but that to a greater extent today than ever before the decision about what is and is not acceptable sexually is determined by the individuals involved.

In turn, human sexuality is more closely related to individual values than ever before. Greater permissiveness offers the opportunity to move away from arbitrary restriction and toward personal choice and responsibility. Each individual's personal sense of right and wrong becomes the primary guide to appropriate behavior and attitudes in sexual matters. People's beliefs and attitudes about themselves also influence the ways in which they express and experience their sexuality. Sexuality can be used to express values and to find greater joy and meaning in life.

In this section of the chapter, we shall discuss some of the more important recent changes in sexual values, attitudes, and behaviors. Specifically, we shall

## Human Sexuality

Indicate for each of the following statements whether you believe that it is true (T) or false (F):

**T  F**  1. Most men and women over the age of 65 have little or no interest in sexual behavior.

**T  F**  2. Women are more likely than men to have multiple orgasms.

**T  F**  3. Women are more likely to achieve orgasm if their partner has a large penis.

**T  F**  4. Alcohol is a stimulant that increases sexual motivation.

**T  F**  5. Masturbation has harmful effects.

**T  F**  6. Mature women are more likely to have vaginal orgasms while immature women are more likely to have clitoral orgasms.

**T  F**  7. In a successful and mature sexual relationship, the partners usually have simultaneous orgasms.

**T  F**  8. The experience of sexual orgasm is quite similar in men and women.

The second and last statements are true; all the others are false. If you answered some items incorrectly, don't worry: even people who have been married for a long time get some of these questions wrong.

discuss contemporary views of masturbation, premarital sex, marital sex, extramarital sex, and homosexuality. My intent is not to give specific directives, but to show the various ways in which personal values are reflected in contemporary sexual attitudes and behaviors.

## Masturbation

**masturbation**: deliberate stimulation of one's body to produce sexual arousal and satisfaction

**Masturbation** has been a common practice for centuries, especially among men. In the middle of this century, Kinsey et al. (1948, 1953) reported that 92 percent of males and 58 percent of females surveyed said they had masturbated. The figures have not changed greatly in recent years: Hunt (1974) reported that the figures were 94 and 63 percent, respectively, for his sample of adults, and Sarrel and Sarrel (1984) reported that about 80 percent of college men and women said they masturbated. Moreover, masturbation does not stop with marriage. Hunt found that about 70 percent of married adults reported masturbating (men masturbated twice a week on the average and women once a week). More recently, Grosskopf (1983) reported a comparable figure for masturbation among married women.

Although masturbation is commonly practiced, it is not regarded favorably by many people: more than one-third of adults surveyed say they believe that masturbation is wrong (Hunt, 1974). Many people oppose masturbation for religious reasons. Many others believe it is harmful (Ambramson & Mosher, 1975). Shame, anxiety, and guilt are commonly associated with masturbation, detailed in the Insight on the next page (Greenberg & Archambault, 1973).

## The "Evils" of Masturbation

In the past, masturbation was viewed with considerably less tolerance than today. Indulgence in masturbation was considered a sign of disease or moral laxness, and parents were urged by a variety of sources to prevent masturbation at all costs.

Below you will find a segment of a text by H.R. Stout. The text, *Our Family Physician,* was printed in 1885 and vividly illustrates how far our views of masturbation have progressed in the past hundred years.

*This is a very degrading and destructive habit, indulged in by young people of both sexes. There is probably no vice which is more injurious to both mind and body, and produces more fearful consequences than this. It is generally commenced early in life before the patient is aware of its evil influence, and it finally becomes so fastened upon him, that it is with great difficulty that he can break off the habit.*

*The symptoms produced by this vice are numerous. When the habit begins in early life, it retards the growth, impairs the mental faculties and reduces the victim to a lamentable state. The person afflicted seeks solitude, and does not wish to enjoy the society of his friends; he is troubled with headaches, wakefulness and restlessness at night, pain in various parts of the body, indolence, melancholy, loss of memory, weakness in the back and generative organs, variable appetite, cowardice, inability to look a person in the face, lack of confidence in his own abilities.*

*When the evil has been pursued for several years, there will be irritable condition of the system; sudden flushes of heat over the face; the countenance becomes pale and clammy; the eyes have a dull, sheepish look; the hair becomes dry and split at the ends; sometimes there is pain over the region of the heart; shortness of breath; palpitation of the heart. . . ; the sleep is disturbed; there is constipation; cough; irritation of the throat; finally the whole man becomes a wreck, physically, morally and mentally.*

*Some of the consequences of masturbation are epilepsy, apoplexy, paralysis, premature old age, involuntary discharge of seminal fluid, which generally occurs during sleep, or after urinating, or when evacuating the bowels. Among females, besides these other consequences, we have hysteria, menstrual derangement, catilepsy and strange nervous symptoms.*

Nonetheless, masturbation does not have any known physical or psychological ill effects, and it need not result in feelings of shame, anxiety, and guilt. In some cases, it may actually have a number of positive effects: it can be a process of exploration during which a person discovers what is, and what is not, sexually enjoyable; women who have difficulty achieving orgasm during intercourse can often achieve orgasm through masturbation; masturbation can provide sexual satisfaction when one's regular sexual partner is unavailable or would prefer not to have intercourse; masturbation has been found to be a valuable aid in sex therapy for some individuals; and in some cases masturbation as a supplement to intercourse may reduce the likelihood of extramarital sexual behavior (Knox, 1985).

However, as with other forms of sexual behavior discussed in this chapter, the ultimate decision about whether or not to engage in masturbation is intimately tied to an individual's personal attitudes and values. Even though attitudes toward masturbation have changed relatively little in the past several decades, other sexual attitudes have changed significantly, as we will now see.

## Premarital Sex

Traditional standards for sexual behavior in our society have emphasized abstinence from sexual relations prior to marriage, particularly for women. However, both attitudes and behavior concerning premarital sex have changed dramatically. A study of college students reported in 1940 showed that 6 percent of women and 15 percent of men approved of premarital sex for both men and women. In a similar survey conducted in 1971, the percentages approving jumped to 59 percent and 70 percent for women and men, respectively (Landis & Landis, 1973). Reflecting this change in attitudes, the reported incidence of premarital sex has also increased. In the 1940s, Kinsey found that more than 30 percent of women and more than 80 percent of men reported engaging in premarital intercourse by the age of 25. Hunt's (1974) survey found that by the early 1970s the incidence of premarital intercourse had increased to 81 percent and 95 percent, respectively, among young women and men under the age of 25. Thus, the frequency of premarital sex has increased significantly in the last several decades.

**double standard**: unequal standard stating that premarital intercourse is acceptable for men but unacceptable for women

At the same time, there has been a change in what is known as the **double standard.** Traditionally, premarital sex has been tolerated (if not actually approved) for males but strongly disapproved for females. The data on both attitudes and behaviors cited in the preceding paragraph support this double standard, but they also show that the double standard is disappearing: although women are still somewhat less likely than men to report engaging in premarital sex, the difference between their reports is getting smaller.

It is worth noting that the increase in premarital sex apparently is not due primarily to a significant increase in casual, promiscuous sexual relations — so-called "one night stands." Rather, the increase seems to reflect a growing belief that sexual relations are acceptable and appropriate for unmarried couples who are involved in a close, loving, intimate relationship.

Despite (or perhaps because of) the widespread changes in attitudes and behavior toward premarital sex, the choice about whether or not to engage in a premarital or nonmarital sexual relationship is a source of stress and conflict for many people. In the rush to engage in premarital intercourse, many individuals have acted in response to peer pressure rather than to their internal values. As one young woman expressed it: "My older sister says she used to lie to her friends and say she was a virgin to protect her reputation. It is just the opposite for me. I lie to my friends claiming I'm not a virgin" (Crooks & Baur, 1980, p. 397). In addition, conflict and stress can arise from fear of pregnancy, fear of contracting a sexually transmitted disease, anxiety about the disapproval of others, and guilt about violating moral values (see Psychology in Action, pp. 428–29).

As with other areas of human sexuality, today's greater freedom and permissiveness toward premarital sex allows a greater range of individual choice. To a greater degree than in the past, people must make personal decisions about premarital sex with respect to individual values and attitudes. In turn, however, this increased personal responsibility can be a source of considerable stress. Particularly since social attitudes and practices toward premarital sex no longer match traditional religious values, some individuals find that premarital sex is a source of considerable

# *Psychology in Action*

## Responsible Sexuality

Too many people often rely on hopes to prevent pregnancy. For example, some people believe that certain periods in a woman's menstrual cycle are "infertile" times. This is incorrect, as is the assumption that a woman cannot become pregnant if she does not have an orgasm or if she douches immediately after intercourse.

People may also avoid the use of contraceptives because they feel some residual guilt about their sexual activity, maintaining that the use of contraception would spoil the "spontaneity" of the moment. This is a poor reason for avoiding the use of contraceptives. People engaging in sexual intercourse must also make a decision about a possible pregnancy. Refusing to confront the bi-

ological connection between sexual activity and reproduction is not acting in a responsible fashion, particularly when contraceptives can "take the worry out of being close."

The following table lists a variety of contraceptive techniques, along with their theoretical and actual effectiveness rates, as well as the advantages and disadvantages associated with each method. Proper use of a technique reduces the risk of failure, as does the use of multiple techniques.

The pregnancy rate is expressed as the number of pregnancies per 100 women per year. Pregnancy rate data from Contraceptive Technology 1980-1981.

### Comparison Table of Contraceptive Methods

| Method | Theoretical Pregnancy Rate | Actual Pregnancy Rate | How It Works | Advantages | Disadvantages |
|---|---|---|---|---|---|
| Birth control pills (Combination pills) | 0.34 | 4-10 | prevents ovulation | extremely effective; coitus independent; reduced menstrual flow and cramping | continual cost; daily use; side effects |
| Intrauterine device (IUD) | 1-3 | 5 | prevents implantation of fertilized ovum | effective; coitus independent; no memory or motivation required for use | increased cramping and bleeding; expulsion |
| Condom | 3 | 10 | barrier to sperm | effective; only major technique available to males; protects against STD | coitus dependent; reduced sensation |
| Diaphragm and cream or jelly | 3 | 17 | barrier to and chemical destruction of sperm | effective; inexpensive, few side effects | coitus dependent; aesthetic objections |
| Spermicides | 3 | 17-22 | immobilization and destruction of sperm | easily available; no prescription required | unreliable when used improperly |

**Comparison Table of Contraceptive Methods   (continued)**

| Method | Theoretical Pregnancy Rate | Actual Pregnancy Rate | How It Works | Advantages | Disadvantages |
|---|---|---|---|---|---|
| Rhythm (cervical mucus, basal body temperature, calendar) | 2-13 | 20-25 | periodic abstinence | low cost; acceptable to Catholic Church | requires periods of abstinence; best suited for women with regular cycles |
| Withdrawal | 9 | 20-25 | external ejaculation | no cost | reduces sexual pleasure; produces spectatoring attitude; unreliable |
| Douching | ? | 40 | mechanical removal of sperm | inexpensive | unreliable |
| Lactation (breast feeding) | 15 | 40 | inhibition of ovulation | no cost | unreliable |
| Vasectomy | 0.15 | 0.15 + | mechanical barrier to sperm | permanent; extremely reliable | substantial one-time expense; should be considered irreversible |
| Tubal ligation | 0.04 | 0.04 + | mechanical barrier to sperm | permanent; extremely reliable | substantial one-time expense; should be considered irreversible |
| Abortion | 0 | 0 + | removal of fetal tissue | extremely effective | risk of miscarriage increases with repeated abortions |
| Abstinence | 0 | ? | prohibits intercourse | extremely effective | prohibits sexual intercourse |
| No method of contraception used | 90 | 90 | | | |

*Older couples tend to be less sexually active than younger couples. This may be due to their upbringing and different sexual attitudes, rather than diminishing interest.*

conflict, guilt, and anxiety. As we saw in the discussion of existentialism in Chapter 2, the problems of choice and responsibility often become an agonizing burden, for finding satisfying values is a lonely and highly individual matter.

## Marital Sex

Unlike premarital sex, sex in marriage has always been not only acceptable but also expected. As a result, this area of human sexuality has changed the least over the last several decades. Kinsey (1948) reported that in the 1940s young married couples (less than thirty five years of age) were having intercourse two to three times per week, while older couples were somewhat less active. In the early 1970s, Hunt (1974) found that each age group was slightly more active sexually: young couples were having intercourse slightly more than three times a week on average, couples in their thirties and forties were averaging slightly more than twice a week, and couples in their fifties and older were having sexual intercourse on average once a week. Thus it appears that there has been a slight, but consistent, increase in sexual activity among married couples over the past several decades.

There are, of course, significant differences in sexual activity from couple to couple. Researchers have found, on the whole, that couples who have a closer relationship and who are more satisfied with their marriages tend to have intercourse more often and also report that it is more enjoyable than couples whose relationship is not as close and less satisfactory (Hunt, 1974; B. Thornton, 1977). It is perhaps tempting to think that a good sex life leads to a happier marriage, but it could be the opposite. Consider this observation from Strong and DeVault (1986).

> Although we may tend to believe that good sex depends on good techniques, it really depends more on the quality of the marriage. . . . If the marriage is happy, then the couple is likely to have good sex; if it is unhappy, then the unhappiness is likely to be reflected in the sexual relationship. p. 219

As one married man explained "If you've got a good out-of-bed relationship, sex only makes things better. But sex can't make a bad marriage good" (Knox, 1985, p. 115).

Both the Kinsey and Hunt survey data indicated that older couples reported having sexual intercourse less often than did younger couples. This finding is more perplexing that it at first appears. It is known that sexual intercourse can be enjoyed well into old age; why should there be such a marked decline in frequency of intercourse? In part, the biological changes that occur as men and women grow older slightly alter the nature of intercourse and, as a result, some couples may find intercourse less satisfying. Also, after years of marriage, sexual behavior can become familiar and monotonous unless efforts are made to maintain spontaneity and variety (Blumstein & Schwartz, 1983). Knox (1985) refers to this as *satiation*.

In addition, as we saw in Chapter 11, many marriages shift from erotic or passionate love to companionate love, which is equally satisfying and fulfilling but which does not need to be expressed sexually. Finally, to a great extent in our culture sexuality is equated with youth. Thus the frequency of sexuality may decrease in later life because people are led to expect that it should! If sexual intercourse is widely considered to be inappropriate and ridiculous or unseemly among older people, if people think of sexually motivated older men as "dirty old men," and if people assume that it is natural for sexual interest to disappear with advancing years, then it is likely that older people will tend to curtail their sexual activities with advancing age.

One other point is worth stating before we continue. The age differences reported by Kinsey and Hunt *do not* show declining sexual activity in the same couples as they grow older. Rather, they show that younger couples are more sexually active than older couples surveyed at the same time. However, couples who were in their fifties or sixties at the time of Hunt's survey were raised in the early years of this century when sexual attitudes and values were quite different from those today. To what extent does the lower frequency of intercourse among these couples reflect not their age but rather their upbringing and the view of sexuality that was prevalent when they were married decades ago? We don't know, of course, and so it is wise to interpret the apparent age differences in sexual activity with caution.

A young couple today with a strong marriage—already more sexually active than young couples in previous generations—can understand the need for variety and spontaneity in sexual behavior. While expecting and preparing for the biological changes that come with aging, they do not expect that advancing age will necessarily put an end to sexual activity. As such, there is no reason to assume that these people will not be just as sexually active when they reach their sixties and seventies as they are today in their twenties or thirties.

## Extramarital Sex

One aspect of human sexuality has remained virtually untouched by change in the past several decades: the vast majority of people still consider marriage to be an exclusive sexual relationship and more than 80 percent consider extramarital sex to be wrong (Hunt, 1974). Moreover, there has been little or no increase in the rate of extramarital sexuality over the past few decades: as we saw in the last chapter, slightly more than 40 percent of married adults reported having had an extramarital sexual experience at one time or another (Thompson, 1983).

Why do people engage in extramarital sexual behavior? One reason often given is marital dissatisfaction: if a marriage is unstable, unsatisfying, stressful, or boring, it is sometimes tempting to find happiness outside of the marriage rather than expend the effort required to revitalize the marriage (Thompson, 1983). Other reasons for extramarital sex include a search for variety and renewed sexual vitality or an effort to prove sexual attractiveness and desirability. In some cases, partners turn to extramarital sex when their spouses are away for a prolonged period of time (such as in military service) or when their spouses become sexually inactive or uninterested for one reason or another.

Whatever the reason, the guilt, anxiety, and fear of discovery that typically accompany extramarital sex often result in an experience that is not particularly satisfying (Hunt, 1974). Moreover, if the adultery is discovered, the consequences for the marriage are often disastrous: no matter how compelling the reasons for the extramarital affair, the deceit involved undermines the basic trust that is essential for a strong and vital marriage (Thompson, 1984).

## Homosexuality

Homosexuality has been widely misunderstood throughout history. The Judeo-Christian tradition in Western thought has consistently maintained that homosexuality is unnatural and sinful (Katchadourian & Lunde, 1980). Over the years, laws and traditions have imposed severe sanctions on homosexual behavior, including imprisonment and burning at the stake. In our society, homosexuality has traditionally been considered as sinful, perverted, and abnormal. Until the early 1970s, the American Psychiatric Association classified homosexuality as a psychiatric disorder.

Like many sexual attitudes, attitudes toward homosexuality are slowly changing. The American Psychiatric Association now classifies homosexuality as a disorder— called ego-dystonic homosexuality—*only* in those cases where the individual is persistently concerned and distressed about his or her homosexual impulses. Moreover, while the great majority of Americans still consider homosexual relations as "always wrong," nearly 30 percent of Americans are tolerant of homosexuality under at least some conditions (Mahoney, 1983).

Most people think there is a clear dividing line between homosexuality and heterosexuality: a person is either one or the other. Actually, Kinsey's surveys (1948; 1953) strongly suggested a continuum of sexual behavior with exclusive homosexuality at one end and exclusive heterosexuality at the other. In between these two extremes are numerous blends of homosexuality and heterosexuality.

*American attitudes toward homosexuality are gradually changing. Homosexuality has traditionally been considered abnormal and sinful in this culture, but Americans are becoming tolerant, if not accepting, of homosexuals.*

Some people are largely heterosexual but have a history of some homosexual activity as well; others are equally heterosexual and homosexual (sometimes called *bisexual*); still others are largely homosexual but have a history of some heterosexuality as well. More recently, Bell and Weinberg (1978) have confirmed the accuracy of this view of sexual preference.

The data from various surveys suggest that about 2-4 percent of adult males and 1-2 percent of adult females are exclusively homosexual; another 5-10 percent of males and 3-5 percent of females are predominantly homosexual, and about the same percentages are bisexual. Between 20 and 40 percent of adult males and 10 to 15 percent of adult females report having at least one homosexual experience at some point in their lives (Hunt, 1974; Kinsey et al., 1948, 1953; Marmor, 1980b; Fay, Turner, Klassen, & Gagnon, 1989).

Not only does the rate of homosexuality differ among males and females, but sexual life style varies as well. The majority of male homosexuals report that they frequently have sexual relations with someone they have just met (Knox, 1985). In view of this fact, it is perhaps not surprising that homosexual males report having sexual relationships with many partners: in several studies, about half of the homosexual males reported having more than 500 sexual partners over the course of their lifetimes (Meredith, 1984). Moreover, most male homosexual relationships are transitory; long-lived intimate relationships are the exception rather than the rule (Knox, 1985). The reverse seems to be true of female homosexuals. Among lesbians,

95 percent say that they never or rarely have sexual relations with someone they have just met, and 60 percent say their sexual relationships always occur in the context of emotional intimacy (another 35 percent say this is frequently the case). Knox (1985) states: "So for gay women the formula is love first and sex second; for gay men it is sex first and the emotional relationship second. This pattern is also characteristic of heterosexual women and men" (p. 81).

Research also suggests that the differences between heterosexuals and homosexuals are not as great as had been originally thought. The sexual responses of homosexuals are no different from those of heterosexuals (Masters & Johnson, 1979). Homosexuals are, as a group, no more and no less psychologically disturbed than their heterosexual counterparts (Bell & Weinberg, 1978). As research continues, the stereotype of the homosexual as a sad and lonely individual is being replaced with the more accurate portrait that suggests that except for their sexual preference, homosexuals are no different from heterosexuals.

Because homosexuality is still regarded unfavorably by most Americans, homosexual relationships are especially likely to be accompanied by feelings of guilt, shame, anxiety, and fear. Guilt and shame derive from engaging in a relationship that is still considered deviant by most people and "vulgar and obscene" by many (Weinberg & Williams, 1974). Anxiety and fear most often derive from concern over being "discovered" by family, friends, or coworkers, though more recently the fear of AIDS has become another source of anxiety (see Chapter 4, p. 132–33). When an individual acknowledges or "works through" a homosexual identity, guilt and shame can be greatly reduced. Publicly acknowledging homosexuality can also greatly reduce the fear and anxiety of being "discovered," although the disclosure may jeopardize relationships with family and friends.

In this section, we have surveyed some of the changes in sexual attitudes, values, and behaviors that have occurred over the past few decades. In the next section, we will look at the sexual response cycle from initial excitement through the aftermath of orgasm.

## THE NATURE OF THE SEXUAL RESPONSE

Sexual motivation is probably second only to hunger in its far-reaching implications for social living. The family is based upon a sexual union as well as upon enduring emotional ties. Sex is a dominant theme in much of life, including music, art, drama, and literature.

Unlike hunger and thirst, the sexual drive in humans does not appear to be related to cyclic variations in bodily chemistry. In contrast, lower mammals show periods of sexual desire and receptivity only when particular hormones are at a high point in the body. For example, a female dog is sexually receptive only when she is in "heat," a condition caused by profound changes in the animal's hormones.

Another significant difference between humans and other mammals is that sexual activity in humans appears to be primarily a learned phenomenon, not an instinctual one. Humans can react sexually to other persons, to themselves, and to objects in the environment. Humans can also voluntarily deny or limit their sexual activities or pleasures. For example, a youngster who is indoctrinated with the view that sex is evil and dirty may develop little sexual motivation and as an adult may even find sexual intercourse unpleasant or repugnant.

As a consequence of differing cultural viewpoints and individual life experiences, there are widespread differences in the strength and perceived significance of the sex drive among adolescents and adults. Approved patterns of sexual gratification also vary considerably from one society to another although sexual codes seem generally to be becoming more liberalized. In any event, the great variety of sexual activities and preferences among human beings attests to the importance of learning in humans.

## The Sexual Response Cycle

Although a great deal is known about human physiology (see Figure 12.1) and sexual motivation, until recently little had been learned about the nature of the sexual response itself. For example, one of the earliest sex researchers, Havelock Ellis (1906), suggested that the sexual response cycle could be divided into two stages— tumescence (the building up of sexual tension) and detumescence (the release of sexual tension).

*Expressions of sexuality reflect personal values, choices, and attitudes.*

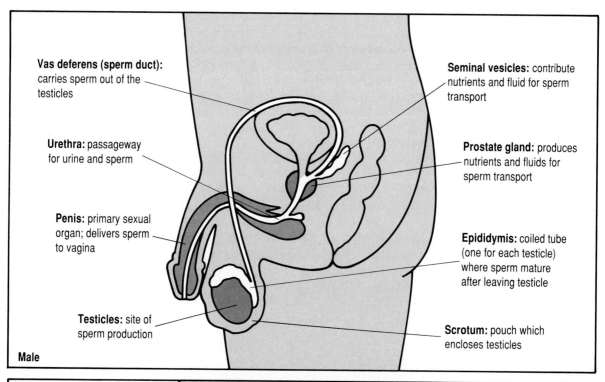

**Vas deferens (sperm duct):** carries sperm out of the testicles

**Urethra:** passageway for urine and sperm

**Penis:** primary sexual organ; delivers sperm to vagina

**Testicles:** site of sperm production

**Seminal vesicles:** contribute nutrients and fluid for sperm transport

**Prostate gland:** produces nutrients and fluids for sperm transport

**Epididymis:** coiled tube (one for each testicle) where sperm mature after leaving testicle

**Scrotum:** pouch which encloses testicles

Male

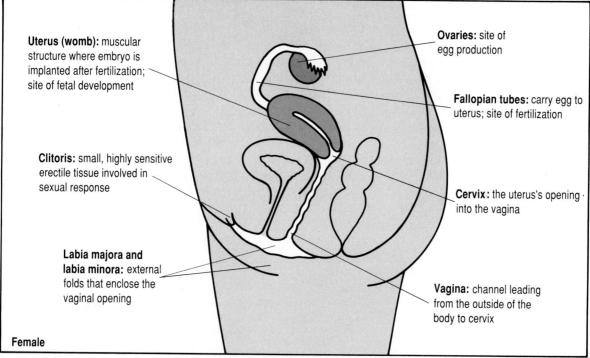

**Uterus (womb):** muscular structure where embryo is implanted after fertilization; site of fetal development

**Clitoris:** small, highly sensitive erectile tissue involved in sexual response

**Labia majora and labia minora:** external folds that enclose the vaginal opening

**Ovaries:** site of egg production

**Fallopian tubes:** carry egg to uterus; site of fertilization

**Cervix:** the uterus's opening into the vagina

**Vagina:** channel leading from the outside of the body to cervix

Female

**FIGURE 12.1 Anatomy of Sexual Organs.**

In 1966 this lack of understanding was dramatically altered with the publication of *Human Sexual Response* by researchers William Masters and Virginia E. Johnson. While earlier studies had focused primarily on self-reports, Masters and Johnson took the daring step of measuring sexual responses in a laboratory setting. The work of Masters and Johnson is important because it provided the first detailed, reliable knowledge about the nature of the sexual response. Additionally, their research clarified many areas of uncertainty and effectively eliminated a number of myths about sexual responses. For these reasons, and because their work is well known, I will use their model of the sexual response cycle to organize our discussion.

Masters and Johnson (1966) proposed that the sexual response cycle can be broken into four phases, or stages: *excitement, plateau, orgasm,* and *resolution.* The relationships between these phases are shown in Figures 12.2 and 12.3. In men, the typical sexual response cycle is for excitement to lead to a plateau, which is followed by one orgasm and resolution; occasionally, a man may experience a second orgasm after a brief resting period, but this is not typical. Among women, there is greater variability in response cycles. One pattern (*A* in Figure 12.3) is quite similar to the male response cycle: excitement builds to a plateau, which is followed by orgasm and resolution. However, in contrast to men, some women are capable of having several orgasms in close succession before resolution. A very different sexual pattern among women (*B*) starts with excitement, which builds to a prolonged plateau and then a slow resolution without any orgasm. Another pattern of sexual response among women (*C*) involves a rapid building from excitement to orgasm and then rapid resolution.

It is interesting to note that in the early study by Kinsey et al. (1948) of the male sexual response, the total time from initiation of sexual intercourse to orgasm was reported to average about two minutes; in many cases, men reported the total time to orgasm was only twenty or thirty seconds. Several decades later, Hunt (1974) found that the average time to orgasm for males had increased to ten minutes. This increase reflects some profound changes in contemporary sexual behavior: couples today devote a great deal of attention to the entire response cycle, not just to the pleasure of orgasm and release; they also report greater enjoyment of all aspects of the sexual response cycle and devote greater attention to mutual sexual satisfaction (Hunt, 1974). Thus, a full understanding of contemporary human sexual behavior requires attention to *all* phases of the sexual response cycle, not just the orgasmic phase (see Psychology in Action, p. 439).

Let's look more closely at these four phases of the sexual response cycle. However, as you read, remember that there are no sharp boundaries between the various phases of the response cycle; rather, each phase tends to blend smoothly into the next. Moreover, people differ greatly in the ways they experience each of the phases, as we will see.

**The excitement phase.**    Human sexual arousal can be triggered by a wide range of stimuli: thoughts, imagination, fantasy, sights, sounds, smells, touches, caresses, and direct genital stimulation all can be effective in starting the excitement phase of the response cycle. During the **excitement phase,** the first sign of sexual arousal in women is vaginal lubrication. In younger women, this lubrication can occur within

**excitement phase:** first stage of sexual response cycle in which physical signs of sexual arousal become evident

**FIGURE 12.2   The Male
Sexual Response Cycle.**

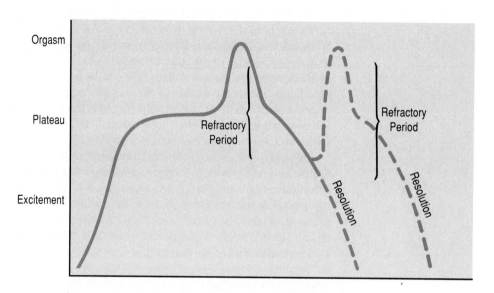

**FIGURE 12.3   The Female
Sexual Response Cycle.**

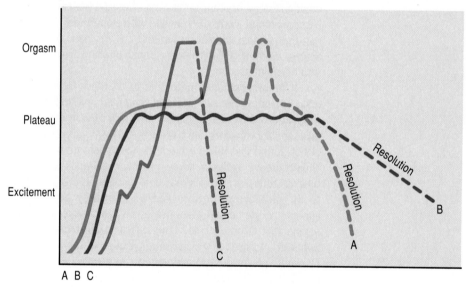

ten seconds of initial arousal. The lubrication comes directly from the "sweating" action of the vaginal walls. In addition, the vaginal lips and the clitoris tend to swell and the lips open somewhat. In men, a somewhat similar pattern of responses emerges. The first response of the male to sexual stimulation is penile erection. Erection can occur within a few seconds after the onset of sexual stimulation. In older men, erection may take longer to develop. Externally, the scrotum thickens during the excitement phase, and the testes are drawn closer to the body.

In both sexes, nipple erection may occur. Muscle tension, heart rate, and blood pressure increase. In women, some increase in breast size may be noted during this

# Psychology in Action

period. An interesting phenomenon, termed the *sex tension flush,* can also occur during the excitement phase. This flush appears as a measleslike rash, first appearing in the mid-chest region. It tends to appear more often in women than in men.

Subjectively, the excitement phase is experienced as a period of waxing and waning interest. Interruptions during the excitement phase typically lower sexual arousal, but in most cases arousal can begin again with little difficulty. This excitement phase can be prolonged as long as the couple wishes. The pleasant, though mild, stimulation occurring during this phase of the response cycle is sufficiently rewarding to encourage continued activity. Eventually, if the sexual response cycle is to continue its course, there will be a transition to what Masters and Johnson call the plateau phase.

**plateau phase:** second stage of the sexual response cycle in which physical changes initiated in the excitement phase are intensified

**The plateau phase.**   During the **plateau phase,** the changes that were initiated during the excitement phase continue and intensify. In women, vaginal lubrication continues, as does the enlargement of the vagina. The outer one third of the vagina shows marked engorgement with blood during the plateau phase. This *orgasmic platform,* as it was termed by Masters and Johnson, marks the achievement of the plateau phase in women. The clitoris appears to retract from its normal body position during the plateau phase. Although somewhat retracted, the clitoris continues to respond to sexual stimulation.

In men, some changes that were initiated during the excitement phase continue during the plateau phase. In the penis, the ridge at the base of the glans (the *coronal ridge*) increases in size and may deepen in color. Similarly, the testes continue their elevation and become enlarged by as much as 50 percent.

In both sexes, extragenital changes continue. The sex tension flush appears in increasing proportions of people and covers a larger part of the chest, shoulders, and back. In both sexes, muscle tension continues to increase, as do blood pressure, heart rate, and respiration.

The experience of the plateau phase is not markedly different from the excitement phase, but it is more intense in nature. During the plateau phase, the participant is less willing to discontinue stimulation. The individual's involvement in sexual arousal increases, pressing for the release of the orgasmic phase. If stimulation ceases at this point without the experience of orgasm, both males and females may experience discomfort and pain in the genitals resulting from the slow reduction of accumulated physical tension and arousal.

**orgasmic phase:** third stage of sexual response cycle in which a peak of sexual pleasure is experienced

**The orgasmic phase.**    In the **orgasmic phase,** the accumulated sexual tensions are discharged in a brief, but extremely pleasurable set of sensations.

In women, the orgasmic phase is marked by contractions of the orgasmic platform. These contractions typically number from three to fifteen and the first few contractions are typically spaced 0.8 seconds apart. Masters and Johnson also found that, contrary to psychoanalytic theory, a woman does not experience two different types of orgasm, the vaginal and the clitoral. Rather, orgasm is physiologically the same whether it results from sexual intercourse or masturbation.

**ejaculation:** expulsion of semen from the penis, indicating orgasm in the male

In men, orgasm is normally accompanied by **ejaculation,** the process by which semen is forced out of the body. During the orgasmic contractions, the male experiences a sense of "inevitability" where no amount of self-control could prevent an orgasm from reaching completion.

In both sexes, muscular tension is at its highest, and orgasm is often accompanied by specific contractions of muscles in the pelvic area. Heart rate and blood pressure also reach a peak, as does the sex tension flush.

Continued stimulation may result in *multiple orgasms* for some women; that is, if she desires it and the stimulation is effective, a woman can go from orgasm to orgasm without entering the resolution phase. Interestingly, some research by Robbins and Jensen (1978) have suggested that at least some men may also have the capability to experience multiple orgasms. However, after ejaculation most men

**refractory period:** in males, period after ejaculation during which further stimulation will not produce sexual arousal

enter a **refractory period** in which no type or degree of stimulation is effective in producing an erection. In younger men, the refractory period may last for only a matter of minutes, while in older men, the refractory period may be considerably longer.

Since male orgasm is typically marked by the ejaculation of semen, males have little difficulty learning when an orgasm occurs and what it feels like. On the other hand, women do not have physical evidence that an orgasm has occurred. Some women may mistake intense arousal for orgasm. Other women, thinking that all orgasms should be earth-shattering experiences, may not label a less intense orgasm in the proper manner.

There is little doubt, however, that both sexes report that orgasm is extremely pleasurable. During an orgasm, consciousness dims and perception is clouded. Awareness is typically focused on physical sensations during orgasm. Surprisingly, the facial expressions of individuals experiencing orgasm do not suggest pleasure but instead suggest pain or discomfort. No matter what the facial expressions may suggest, many people feel that the pleasure is well worth the price.

One question that has interested researchers is whether the experience of orgasm is similar in men and women. It is, of course, impossible to know precisely another individual's experience. People can look at the same sunset, eat the same apples, and look at the same paintings, but their experiences while viewing the sunset, while eating the apple, and while looking at the painting are very private and personal experiences. The same can be said of an orgasm. It would seem that there is no way of knowing whether the experience of an orgasm is basically similar or intrinsicially different between men and women.

However, two researchers (Vance & Wagner, 1976) devised an interesting strategy for resolving the question of whether orgasms are essentially similar or different between the sexes. They asked some psychology students to write a description of an orgasm and a description of a nonsexually oriented event. These latter descriptions were then examined by a group of judges who attempted to determine whether the description had been written by a male or a female. If the judges could reliably ascertain the sex of the writer, the description of orgasm prepared by the same student was eliminated from consideration. This procedure reduced the possibility that the sex of the writer of the orgasm experience could be identified by writing style alone.

From the remaining descriptions, twenty-four written by females and twenty-four written by males were randomly selected. These descriptions were then given to groups of medical students, clinical psychologists (both graduate students and faculty), and obstetrician-gynecologists. All the groups were asked to judge whether a given item was written by a male or a female. Since forty-eight items were used, a score of twenty-four would be expected by chance alone. (If you want to try judging some of these descriptions, fill in the questionnaire shown in Psychology in Action, p. 442.)

The results were surprising. No group performed at a level significantly better than chance. On average, the medical students correctly identified the source of 25.96 of the descriptions, the obstetrician-gynecologists' score was 25.03, and the psychologists' score was 24.92. In other words, none of these groups was able to distinguish between male and female descriptions of orgasm: the experience of an orgasm is relatively similar for both sexes.

**The resolution phase.**     During the **resolution phase,** many of the physiological changes rapidly disappear, often in the reverse order of their appearance. For example, the orgasmic platform rapidly dissipates following orgasm, followed by a return to the normal size of the vagina within a few minutes. Similarly, changes in the labia are rapidly reversed, as are changes in the clitoris and uterus.

In males, erection is lost in two stages. In the first stage, erection is reduced by about 50 percent within a few minutes. The remainder of the erection is reduced

**resolution phase:** fourth stage of sexual response cycle in which signs of sexual arousal subside

# Psychology in Action

## The Sex of Orgasm Questionnaire

Here are some of the descriptions used in the Sex of Orgasm Questionnaire developed by Vance and Wagner (1976). Decide whether each item was written by a male (M) or a female (F). Hint: there are unequal numbers of males and females. Match your answers against the correct answers below.

1. _____ An orgasm feels like heaven in the heat of hell; a tremendous build-up within of pleasure that makes the tremendous work of releasing that pleasure worthwhile.

2. _____ There is a building up of "tension" (poor description) to a very high stage. There is then a surging release which is exhilarating, leaving me in a totally relaxed, exhausted state.

3. _____ Spasm of the abdominal and groin area, tingling sensation in limbs, and throbbing at the temples on each side of my head.

4. _____ Experience of a build-up of tension, uncoordination of movement—to a few seconds of amazing feeling, to a release of tension and a period of satisfaction and relaxation.

5. _____ Often loss of contact with reality. All senses acute. Sight becomes patterns of color, but often very difficult to explain because words were made to fit in the real world.

6. _____ A feeling where nothing much else enters the mind other than that which relates to the present, oh sooo enjoyable and fulfilling sensation. It's like jumping into a cool swimming pool after hours of sweating turmoil. "Ahh Relief!" What a great feeling it was, so ecstatically wild and alright.

7. _____ A feeling of intense physical and mental satisfaction. The height of a sexual encounter. Words can hardly describe a feeling so great.

8. _____ Stomach muscles get "nervous" causing a thrusting movement with hips or pelvis. Muscular contraction all over the body.

9. _____ Building of tenseness to a peak where it seems as if everything is going to drain out of you. It's almost like a complete physical drain.

10. _____ Starts with hot-cold tingles up in the back of the thighs. What happens from there depends on the strength of the stimulation. Usually, shuddery contractions and the same sort of hot-cold feeling only in the genital area. Sometimes, with a really strong stimulation, there's more of a blackout of complete mental awareness of what's happening, then a gradual letting down.

11. _____ An orgasm is a heightening relief of tension wherein the muscles are flexing and a great deal of tension is relieved in an extremely short period. It's a feeling of incurring climax and enjoyment due to the acute sensual nerve feelings and consciousness (kind of two opposing dialectics).

12. _____ Building up of a good type of tension. With the release of all this build-up in one great rush that makes your whole body tingle and feel very pleasurable. Feeling is weakening and is great. Just want to stay still for a long time.

13. _____ Has a build-up of pressure in genitals with involuntary thrusting of hips and twitching of thigh muscles. Also contracting and releasing of the genital muscles. The pressure becomes quite intense—like there is something underneath the skin of the genitals pushing out. Then there is a sudden release of the tension with contraction of genitals with a feeling of release and relaxation.

14. _____ I have had orgasm at times under certain conditions. I also have had it during intercourse. It is more relaxing with less mental duress during intercourse. It is a tensing of the whole body and a bright sensual feeling of release after.

15. _____ Orgasm amounts to a build-up of muscle tension accompanied by an increase in respiration rate. A sudden release of the build-up constitutes an orgasm. All in all, a highly pleasurable physical sensation.

Answers for the Sex of Orgasm Questionnaire: 1-M, 2-M, 3-M, 4-F, 5-M, 6-M, 7-F, 8-M, 9-M, 10-F, 11-M, 12-M, 13-F, 14-M, 15-F.

more slowly. These changes are accelerated in the older male. Both the testes and scrotum return to their normal positions.

In both sexes, the extragenital changes disappear. The sex tension flush disappears rapidly, and muscle tension, blood pressure, and respiration also return to normal. A *sweating reaction* may also occur. This sweating is unrelated to the amount of physical activity that preceded the resolution phase.

## Sexual Dysfunction

*When I was overseas I was having problems with my wife—but a lot of the guys were having problems with their wives. As soon as I got back to the states I called her and first thing she said she wanted a divorce. . . . The next week I met a girl at a pool party, and it did not take much before we were in bed together. She was really a doll and really built. But when I got ready to go in her, I lost my hard. I tried again later in a little while, but the same thing happened. It happened about three more times after that. It really shook me up. . . . I had been through Vietnam and everything over there and people were getting killed all around me and I was never afraid of death. But this was something else, and it shook me up more than anything I had been through. Maybe it was the stress of Vietnam and getting out, or maybe it was guilt because I knew I was still married then, or maybe it was just everything at once like the divorce and my brother on drugs and finding out my best friend was a homosexual. But it really cracked me up when it happened.*

*Understanding Sexual Interaction* (DeLora et al., 1981, pp. 139–40)

**sexual dysfunction:** inability to fully enjoy sexual activity despite the desire to do so

For those who have experienced satisfactory and pleasurable sexual activities, the occurrence of a **sexual dysfunction** can be frightening and worrisome. For those who have never enjoyed satisfactory sexual activities, sexual dysfunctions can raise questions of their adequacy and threaten their self-esteem.

Sexual dysfunctions may arise from a variety of sources. Among the most important factors that produce sexual dysfunctions are fears and anxiety, poor communication, anger and hostility (particularly toward one's partner), and an upbringing that emphasized control, lack of physical and emotional closeness, and other negative emotions regarding sex and sexual activity. Traumatic experiences can also produce sexual dysfunctions, as can poor or incorrect information regarding sex. Finally, cultural variables that emphasize passivity in women and aggressiveness in men contribute in subtle ways to sexual dysfunction.

In this section we shall focus on four types of sexual dysfunction: *orgasmic dysfunction, vaginismus, impotence,* and *premature ejaculation.*

**orgasmic dysfunction:** in women, persistent difficulty achieving orgasm

**Orgasmic dysfunction.**     **Orgasmic dysfunction** refers to a long- or short-term difficulty of a woman to achieve sexual satisfaction through orgasm. When the problem is long-standing and the woman has never achieved orgasm or when the woman has never experienced sexual arousal, it is usual to speak of *primary sexual dysfunction.* If a woman is capable of achieving orgasm only under specific conditions, she exhibits *situational orgasmic dysfunction.* For instance, a woman may be capable of achieving orgasm with her lover but not with her husband.

Orgasmic dysfunction is probably the most common sexual problem reported by women. A woman who has never experienced orgasm may have to be taught how to relax, how to be stimulated, how to enjoy stimulation, and how to communicate her needs to her partner. In the woman with situational dysfunction, the relationship between the partners is carefully examined, and other aspects of the woman's feelings about sexual activity and her sexual history are explored.

**vaginismus:** strong contraction of the vaginal muscles, making intercourse painful or impossible

**Vaginismus.**     The involuntary spasm of the muscles surrounding the entrance to the vagina is called **vaginismus.** This relatively uncommon disorder prevents any object from being introduced into the vagina. Women with this disorder may have had some traumatic experience such as rape, may have undergone painful pelvic examinations, or they may have fears regarding men, penetration, pregnancy, or childbirth. Fortunately, treatment of this dysfunction is generally neither complicated nor expensive.

**impotence:** in men, inability to achieve or maintain an erection sufficient for sexual intercourse

**Impotence.**     **Impotence** is a sexual dysfunction in which a man is unable to achieve or maintain an erection long enough to have successful sexual relations. Although men with this disorder can frequently masturbate to orgasm, the dysfunction most often occurs in the context of a sexual encounter. As with orgasmic dysfunction, males can experience both primary and situational forms of impotence. With *primary impotence,* the male has never had an erection sufficient for sexual intercourse. In *situational impotence* (such as the example that opened this section), the man has had at least one successful sexual encounter.

Primary impotence is usually due to the same factors that lead to primary orgasmic dysfunction in women. Upbringing, relationship issues, and cultural variables serve to produce the primary form of impotence; only a small proportion of these disorders are due to medical conditions (Masters & Johnson, 1970).

Secondary or situational impotence most often arises from worries that are triggered by occasional failures to achieve an erection. Most men experience at least occasional episodes of impotence throughout their lives. Many of these occasional problems are due to excessive alcohol consumption or other drug use, fatigue, or temporary relationship difficulties. If a person regards such occasional failures as only temporary, they are not likely to recur often in the future. However, if a person becomes overly worried about occasional episodes of impotence and becomes preoccupied with the extent of his arousal when he is engaged in sexual intercourse, then the likelihood of further impotence increases. This negative process produces a self-perpetuating cycle of worry, impotence, more worry, more impotence, and so on. In such cases, therapy involves eliminating worry and reestablishing nondemanding pleasurable activity.

Sexual dysfunction, whether it occurs in a man or a woman, is a problem shared by the couple. It must be resolved by both partners working together.

**premature ejaculation:**
inability of a male to delay orgasm long enough to allow his partner an opportunity to achieve orgasm

**Premature ejaculation.** In **premature ejaculation,** the male is unable to delay his orgasm sufficiently to allow his partner to achieve orgasm at least 50 percent of the time. Premature ejaculation can occur for a variety of reasons. A male may be involved with an exciting new partner, or he may express his hostility toward his partner through premature ejaculation. Perhaps the most important factor, though, is learning. As a young man, the individual may have learned to hurry sexual activity, perhaps to prevent detection and embarrassment by parents who returned home too quickly. Or, the man (and his partner) may not be aware that voluntary control is possible and potentially desirable. Fortunately, non-medical treatment techniques to increase the time that a man can be highly sexually excited without orgasm are available and are quite effective.

Although orgasmic dysfunction and vaginismus are often regarded as "female" problems and premature ejaculation and impotence are often regarded as "male" problems, it is important to recognize that sexual difficulties do not "belong" to an individual. Rather, these are problems that are shared by the couple and, as we saw in Chapter 7, successful treatment of sexual dysfunctions virtually always requires that both partners work together to eliminate the problem. As Masters and Johnson (1970) have stated, it is the relationship that suffers when a sexual dysfunction occurs.

Some cases of sexual dysfunction arise because one or both partners are concerned about contracting a sexually transmitted disease. In the next section of the chapter, we turn our attention to several such diseases.

## SEXUALLY TRANSMITTED DISEASES

sexually transmitted
diseases: diseases that are
typically transmitted by
sexual activity

**Sexually transmitted diseases** are diseases that are transmitted primarily by sexual contact. They are also known as *venereal diseases.* I have chosen the phrase "sexually transmitted diseases" (STD) because it is a term gaining favor with researchers in sexual health and because the term does not have the negative connotations associated with "V.D."

### Types of Sexually Transmitted Diseases

In this section, we shall discuss six of the most common and most troublesome sexually transmitted diseases: gonorrhea, syphilis, genital herpes, nonspecific urethritis, pubic lice, and AIDS.

gonorrhea: common sexually
transmitted disease often
accompanied by a discharge
(especially in men)

**Gonorrhea.** **Gonorrhea** is probably second only to the common cold in frequency (Masters, Johnson, & Kolodny, 1982). Its symptoms in men include a yellowish discharge from the penis, and a burning sensation during urination. In women, symptoms may include increased vaginal discharge.

Unfortunately, 10 percent of men and 80 percent of women show no symptoms whatsoever. Also, untreated gonorrhea may spread to other parts of the body, causing arthritic-like inflammations of the joints and other symptoms. When the infection spreads in women, *pelvic inflammatory disease* may develop. PID, as it is sometimes known, is an infection of the uterus, fallopian tubes, and ovaries. The unfortunate outcome of PID in women and untreated gonorrhea in men can be sterility.

Not only do women show fewer symptoms, they are also more likely to contract the disease. Men exposed to an infected partner are likely to develop the disease about 25 percent of the time, while women exposed to infected partners may develop gonorrhea up to 90 percent of the time. If a woman is taking oral contraceptives, her chances of developing gonorrhea when exposed to infection are virtually 100 percent (Masters, Johnson, & Kolodny, 1982).

The detection of gonorrhea requires examination of the discharge or the examination of cultures. Treatment typically involves injection of large doses of penicillin. Some recent reports have, however, suggested that some strains of gonorrhea may be resistant to penicillin. In these cases, other antibiotics may be required.

syphilis: sexually transmitted
disease marked initially by
the appearance of a chancre

chancre (shan-ker): painless
ulcerated sore that is the first
sign of syphilis

**Syphilis.** **Syphilis** is caused by a corkscrewlike organism that invades the body. The first symptom of syphilis is the appearance of a **chancre,** a painless round, ulcerated sore about the size of a dime, surrounded by a red rim. It usually appears two to four weeks after exposure, and heals within three to six weeks. The chancre may appear in the vagina or on the cervix in women and may therefore not be noticed.

Once the chancre has disappeared, the disease enters the secondary phase. In this phase, which can last from three to six months, an individual may suffer from a rash, fever, sore throat, headache, and other symptoms. These symptoms may appear and reappear and not be particularly severe. However, the infected individual can still pass the disease on to sexual partners.

After the secondary phase, the disease enters the latent phase in which no obvious symptoms are present. Less than half of these untreated individuals will enter the last, tertiary phase, in which a variety of neurological and cardiovascular problems develop, including psychosis and death.

Syphilis may be diagnosed through a blood test, and the usual treatment is injections of penicillin.

**genital herpes:** painful viral infection marked by genital blisters

**Genital herpes.**    **Genital herpes** is a viral infection that is similar to the herpes infections that cause cold sores or fever blisters around the mouth. The first sign of herpes is the appearance of small, fluid-filled blisters in the genital area. These blisters then ulcerate, producing severe pain. From one to three weeks, the ulcers heal, leaving no visible damage. However, the herpes virus remains in the body, and herpes attacks can occur again at unpredictable intervals.

There is no cure for genital herpes and no specific treatment for this disease. Pregnant women may have a higher risk of miscarriage if a herpes attack occurs during pregnancy. Also, because of the serious effects of genital herpes on newborns, a woman who has an attack of genital herpes at the time of delivery is strongly urged to deliver by cesarean section. Also, women with genital herpes seem to have a higher risk of cervical cancer (Katchadourian & Lunde, 1980; Wallis, Redman, & Thompson, 1982).

**nonspecific urethritis (NSU):** infection of the urethra that causes pain and burning during urination

**Nonspecific urethritis (NSU).**    Most infections of the male urethra are not caused by gonorrhea, but by a variety of organisms that are sexually transmitted. Like gonorrhea, **nonspecific urethritis** (NSU) causes a penile discharge and a burning sensation during urination. As with gonorrhea, treatment is through antibiotics. In women, untreated NSU can cause pelvic inflammatory disease. However, NSU infections are more difficult to identify than gonorrhea.

**pubic lice:** parasites that attach themselves to pubic hairs and cause intense itching

**Pubic lice.**    **Pubic lice** or *crabs* are parasites that attach themselves to pubic hairs and feed on fresh blood. The major symptom of pubic lice is intense itching. A variety of creams, lotions, and shampoos is available to kill the lice. However, the eggs of the lice can fall into sheets and clothing and reinfest the individual. Thus, it is necessary to use fresh bed linens and clothing during treatment.

**Acquired immune deficiency syndrome (AIDS).**    In Chapter 4, we examined the ways people try to cope with the stress of having AIDS. Since 1981, when AIDS was first diagnosed, tens of thousands of cases have been identified. It is estimated that 1-2 million Americans have been exposed to the AIDS virus, of whom about 20 percent are expected to develop the disease. There is currently no cure for AIDS and it always results in death. By 1991, it is expected that 100,000 people will have died of AIDS and there will be 250,000 more people who will be suffering from the disease (Bridge, 1988a, 1988b).

AIDS appears to be caused by a virus that attacks the body's immune system leaving the victim vulnerable to a wide variety of infections. Symptoms of AIDS include a persistent fever or cough, persistent fatigue, swollen lymph glands, loss of weight, and diarrhea as well as susceptibility to infection. AIDS is spread through body fluids such as blood and semen. Sexual activity and intravenous drug use are

As a disease spreads, so usually does the social support. In the case of AIDS, support came slowly, but recent years have seen an increase in public efforts to mourn the dead and treat the sick.

the primary means by which AIDS is transferred from one person to another; effective screening techniques have virtually eliminated the possibility of transferring AIDS through blood donations and transfusions. Homosexuals, intravenous drug users, and hemophiliacs are particularly vulnerable to AIDS. For more information on reactions to the stress of AIDS, see the earlier discussion on pp. 132–33.

## Avoiding Sexually Transmitted Diseases

Since the discomfort, danger, and embarrassment of sexually transmitted diseases are fairly high, most people take steps to avoid contracting these diseases. The most useful tactic to avoid these diseases is to avoid sexual contact with an infected person. If you are unsure about your partner, the use of a condom can help reduce the chances of becoming infected. If you become infected, inform your partner or partners promptly so that they too can seek treatment. Finally, be aware that one exposure to a sexually transmitted disease does not confer immunity to the disease. It is possible to be infected, treated, and reinfected unless every individual takes steps to prevent the spread of these diseases. If you have any questions or concerns about any sexually transmitted disease, you can call a toll-free national hotline at (800) 227-8922. Your call will be kept confidential.

## CONTEMPORARY SEXUALITY IN PERSPECTIVE

At the beginning of this chapter, we saw that sexual permissiveness allows much greater room for personal attitudes and values to influence sexual behavior. In turn, people can engage in sexual activity for a variety of positive, enhancing reasons or for a variety of manipulative, interpersonally destructive reasons.

### Attitudes, Values, and Motives

On the positive side, Knox (1979) suggests that in an otherwise impersonal society, sexuality can provide an unequaled emotional and physical closeness with another person. Sexual behavior can also provide an opportunity for expressing deep feelings of love and caring in a highly enjoyable, delightful way. As Kirkendall and Anderson (1973) have stated:

> The most intimate and meaningful experiences come when [sexuality] is . . . an integral part of a relationship in which people are trying to express care and love for one another. Sex is not simply an end, but is a part of a more encompassing relationship. (p. 420)

However, on the negative side, sexuality can also be used as a means of building up a sense of self-esteem, sometimes at the expense of another person. Knox (1979) refers to this as *ego enhancement.* Moreover, in some relationships sexual activity is used to maintain the relationship or to prevent the relationship from faltering or dissolving. Sexual activity can also be used to rebel against parents, established authority, or previous partners. In some cases, sexual behavior occurs simply in response to pressure from a partner. Sexuality also can be a response to boredom and tension, result from a sense of duty, or occur as a part of a reconciliation.

In other words, in a permissive society such as ours sexual activity can occur for a variety of reasons, ranging from the positive to the negative. Moreover, it is likely that a mixture of these reasons applies to any particular sexual act. Thus, the same sexual act can have a variety of meanings depending on the attitudes and values that are brought to the situation. In making decisions about sexuality, it is also important to judge not only a particular activity but also the feelings that are brought to the activity. For example, although a person may have generally positive attitudes toward premarital intercourse, those attitudes can have a variety of meanings, depending on the person's motivations for engaging (or not engaging) in this behavior.

**The trivialization of sexuality.**     There are two other aspects of contemporary sexuality that are especially problematic. Many people contend that we have entered a phase of overt preoccupation with sex—mass-produced, slickly marketed, dehumanizing, performance-oriented sex. Some social commentators suggest that we are "doing it more and enjoying it less," that, in fact, the new freedom causes anxiety. This viewpont has been well expressed by the existential psychotherapist and author, Rollo May (1969).

> By anesthetizing feeling in order to perform better, by employing sex as a tool to prove prowess and identity, by using sensuality to hide sensitivity, we have emasculated sex,

and left it vapid and empty. The banalization of sex is well-aided and abetted by mass communication. For the plethora of books on sex and love which flood the market have one thing in common—they oversimplify love and sex, treating the topic like a combination of learning to play tennis and buying life insurance. In this process, we have robbed sex of its power by sidestepping eros; and we have ended by dehumanizing both. (pp. 64–65)

Thus, it is important not to confuse smooth sexual technique with loving concern and involvement with another. Sex is not a mechanized "touch here, stroke that" endeavor. Rather, it is a means by which loving partners can give and receive pleasure. In a society with numerous sex manuals, "experts" on sex, and sexual symbols in various media, it may be easy to forget that the most important variables are still the human ones.

**Rising expectations.**    In an atmosphere of free sexual experimentation, men and women expect themselves to act without inhibition, perform with great competence and variety, and make sexual excitement a high priority. As Lydon (1971) states:

> Rather than being revolutionary, the present sexual situation is tragic. Appearances notwithstanding, the age-old taboos against conversation about personal sexual experience still haven't broken down. This reticence has allowed the mind-manipulators of the media to create myths of sexual supermen and superwomen. So the bed becomes a competitive arena, where men and women measure themselves against these mythical rivals, while simultaneously trying to live up to the ecstasies promised them by the marriage manuals and fantasies of the media. ("If the earth doesn't move for me, I must be missing something," the reasoning goes.) Our society treats sex as a sport, with its record-breakers, its judges, its rules, and its spectators. (p. 66)

Obviously, all the expectations surrounding sexual behavior in our era of "sexual freedom" can be a painful burden. Perhaps more than ever before, people must evaluate the personal meaning of sexual relations and choose ways to satisfy their sexual needs without doing violence to other needs and values (Robinson & Jedlicka, 1982). Like all freedoms, sexual freedom exacts the heavy cost of personal choice and responsibility. Perhaps nowhere is this more clearly demonstrated than in decisions regarding contraception.

## Contraception and Sexual Attitudes

The number of teenagers and young adults engaging in sexual activity prior to marriage is probably higher than at any time in our nation's history. Teenagers and adults are enjoying sexual activity more frequently and at an earlier age than ever before. Part of the reason for this dramatic increase in premarital sexual activity is the availability of effective **contraceptive** methods.

**contraceptive:** device or technique used to allow sexual intercourse while preventing pregnancy in fertile individuals; also known as birth control

Given the ready availability of many effective contraceptives, why do so many teen-aged women become pregnant? As reported by Byrne (1977), 700,000 unwanted pregnancies occur among teenaged girls each year. Also, an estimated one out of every six teen-aged girls becomes pregnant prior to graduation from high school.

*Given the availability of effective contraceptives and a generally well-informed population, a surprising number of sexually active adults practice no reliable contraceptive methods, due, in part, to their attitudes about sex.*

These statistics are startling. Despite all parental and societal efforts to explain and control teenage sex, our efforts seem to be failing. Moreover, this failure is not due to widespread ignorance of contraceptive techniques.

**Attitudes toward sexuality.**    In a survey of some sexually active undergraduate women, Byrne (1977) found that less than a third of the women always used contraceptives, and more than a third never did. These behavior patterns persisted although half the women had had the frightening experience of thinking they had become pregnant. Byrne felt that the decision of these women not to use contraceptives reliably was in part related to their feelings about sex.

Based on their reactions toward sexually explicit materials, Byrne found that people could be placed into one of two groups. One group, the **erotophiles,** tended to rate sexually explicit materials as pleasant and arousing. Additionally, they were fairly open and accepting about sexual matters. They noted that sex was discussed in their homes, and felt that they had few problems in their sexual adjustment.

In contrast, the **erotophobes** reported much more negative attitudes toward sexual materials, rating sexually explicit materials as shocking and pornographic. Additionally, they reported that sexual matters were not often discussed in their homes. They disapproved of premarital sex and tended to be less well-informed about sexual matters. Despite their strongly negative attitudes, erotophobes did not

**erotophiles:** individuals who are comfortable with sexual materials and their sexual feelings and behaviors

**erotophobes:** people who have difficulty dealing with sexual materials and their sexual feelings and behaviors

*Individuals who are comfortable with their sexual feelings and behaviors are also more open to contraceptive use.*

refrain from premarital sex, although the frequency of their premarital sexual activity tended to be less than that of erotophiles.

When it came to contraceptive use, it was the erotophobes who intended not to use contraceptives. Despite their worries, concerns, anxieties, and negative feelings about sex, the erotophobes appeared to be more willing to risk an unwanted pregnancy by refusing to use contraceptives.

Byrne felt that four reasons accounted for this seemingly paradoxical outcome. First, the decision to use contraceptives is also an admission that sexual intercourse is likely to occur. Although erotophobes have negative feelings about premarital sex, their negative feelings are not strong enough to totally prevent sexual desires and activities. One way to deal with these sexual feelings, however anxiety-provoking they might be, is to regard sexual activity as a spontaneous event. Thus, says Byrne, the erotophobe is likely to say that "It just happened," rather than admit that sexual activity had been planned.

Second, once an individual decides that sex is likely to occur, he or she must consult a physician or clinic or purchase the necessary contraceptive supplies in a drug store. This is a difficult task initially for many people, but it is especially difficult for erotophobes. For example, Byrne sent groups of men to a drug store to purchase condoms. For the man who has never done so, the purchase of condoms for the first time can be an acutely embarrassing experience, especially if the pharmacist or salesclerk is a woman. Erotophobes who completed this task felt that the druggist was judging them as immoral persons, an evaluation they found particularly troublesome. In a real-world situation, this discomfort might reduce the probability that contraceptive devices would be procured.

The third factor involves communication. Using contraception implies at least some level of communication between the partners. Erotophiles apparently are able to discuss sex matters, including contraceptive use, more easily than erotophobes. Because erotophobes have difficulty discussing sexual matters, their unwillingness to raise the subject of sexual activity and contraceptive use decreases the chances that contraceptives will be effectively employed.

Finally, contraceptives must be used. Pills must be swallowed, diaphragms inserted, and condoms unrolled onto an erect penis. In contrast to erotophiles, erotophobes reported greater difficulty with contraceptive methods that require them to touch their genitals.

**Roles and mores.**   There are other reasons for the failure to use contraceptives. For example, contraceptive use has traditionally been defined as part of the woman's role. Some men have argued that it is the woman who gets pregnant, not the man. However, this argument ignores the implied partnership and shared responsibility that is an integral aspect of an intimate relationship. Biologically, of course, women do become pregnant, but they do not become pregnant without assistance from their partners!

Failure to use contraceptives can also be a deliberate act. Women who are trying to become pregnant will obviously not use contraceptives. However, the decision to become pregnant may not involve a shared decision between the woman and her partner. For example, a teenaged girl may decide to become pregnant to prove to herself and to her parents that she is a "woman." Or, she may become pregnant as a way of retaliating against real or imagined hurts and disappointments she has received at home or in school.

The failure to use contraceptives and the resulting pregnancy may be used by some people to help bolster a faltering relationship or as a way to help prevent a relationship from dissolving. The cost of contraceptives may be a deterrent to others.

Finally, some individuals hold strong religious beliefs in which the use of contraceptives is considered unnatural or improper. For these individuals, pregnancy is something to be desired and valued.

In essence, contraceptive use can be an integral part of responsible sexuality. Contraceptive use appears to be highest in those who readily acknowledge their sexual desires and activities, while it appears to be lowest in those who feel the greatest degree of anxiety and uncertainty regarding their sexuality. Engaging in sexual activity without the willingness to either use contraceptives or accept a probable pregnancy incurs a great price to the individuals sense of him- or herself as a thoughtful, competent individual.

*Often young partners fail to discuss and establish their sexual roles and values. The decision to become sexually active is made before the responsibility of the decision is assessed.*

## SUMMARY

Sexual values, attitudes, and behaviors have changed significantly in the past several decades. The marked increase in permissiveness has allowed sexual behavior to become more closely tied to personal values. In turn, this has resulted in greater personal choice and responsibility in matters related to sexuality.

Although *masturbation* has been a common practice for a long time, attitudes toward masturbation have changed relatively little in the recent past: it is still not favorably regarded by many people. Although masturbation can have a number of positive effects, it also can result in feelings of shame, anxiety, and guilt.

Attitudes toward other sexual behaviors have changed more dramatically in recent years. Attitudes toward premarital sex have become more favorable, and the number of people who engage in premarital sex has increased dramatically. There has also been some change in the *double standard* which tolerates premarital sexuality for males but not for females. Because engaging in premarital sex is increasingly a matter of personal choice, the decision whether to do so is a growing source of stress and conflict for many young people.

Attitudes toward marital sexuality, and the frequency of sexual behavior among married couples, have changed the least over the last several decades. The great majority of people still consider extramarital sexuality to be wrong, and there has been little increase in the incidence of extramarital sex over the past few decades. Moreover, there appears to have been only a slight increase in frequency of intercourse during this same period. Large differences continue between couples in the frequency of sexual intercourse. Older couples engage in sexual intercourse less often than younger couples. However, this difference cannot be attributed entirely to a decline in sexual activity over the life span: older couples were raised at a time when sexual attitudes and values were quite different than they are today. This undoubtedly accounts for some of the differences between those couples and younger couples who were raised in a more permissive society.

Attitudes toward homosexuality have also become more permissive, though the great majority of Americans still consider homosexuality "wrong." This attitude can give rise to feelings of guilt, shame, anxiety, and fear among people who prefer homosexual relationships. It is important to realize that there is no clear dividing line between homosexuality and heterosexuality: some people are exclusively homosexual, others are exclusively heterosexual, while many others are both. Moreover, the sexual response of homosexuals is not different from the sexual response of heterosexuals.

The sexual response cycle can be arbitrarily broken into four phases: excitement, plateau, orgasmic, and resolution. In men, excitement usually leads to a plateau which is followed by one orgasm and resolution. The pattern among women is more varied. Some women follow a pattern much like the male pattern. Others reach a prolonged plateau and then enter a prolonged resolution period without an orgasm. Still others build very rapidly to an orgasm and then rapidly resolve.

During the *excitement phase,* the first signs of sexual arousal appear. In women this is marked by vaginal lubrication and swelling of the genitals; in men, arousal is marked by penile erection, thickening of the scrotum, and elevation of the testes. In both sexes, nipple erection, increased heart rate, and elevated blood pressure are normal. Sex tension flush or rash may also appear. During the *plateau phase,* arousal is intensified. Further changes in the genitals of men and women prepare the body for the third or *orgasmic phase* of intercourse during which accumulated sexual tensions are discharged in a brief, pleasurable orgasm. In men, orgasm is usually accompanied by *ejaculation.* Both men and women report that the experience of orgasm is extremely pleasurable. Moreover, research indicates that the experience is described virtually identically by men and women. The final phase of the sexual cycle is the *resolution phase* during which the physiological changes subside.

Occasionally, the normal sexual cycle becomes disrupted. In such cases of *sexual dysfunction,* one or both partners become unable to enjoy sexual relations despite the desire to do so. In women, *orgasmic dysfunction* refers to the inability to be sexually aroused or to reach an orgasm. The problem may be long-standing (primary sexual dysfunction) or it may arise only in some situations and relationships but not in others (situational orgasmic dysfunction). *Vaginismus,* a relatively uncommon disorder, involves spasms around the entrance to the vagina that prevent penetration by any object.

In men, sexual dysfunctions most often take the form of *impotence,* or inability to achieve or maintain an erection, and *premature ejaculation,* in which the male is unable to delay orgasm long enough for his partner to achieve satisfaction. In some cases, impotence is a life-long problem, while in other cases impotence can become a problem only in certain situations or relationships.

Unfortunately, sexual activity can lead not only to pleasure and greater intimacy but also to *sexually transmitted diseases* (venereal diseases) such as *gonorrhea, syphilis, genital herpes, nonspecific urethritis, pubic lice,* and *AIDS.* Prompt diagnosis is critical in all of these diseases. However, the high death rate among AIDS patients has cast

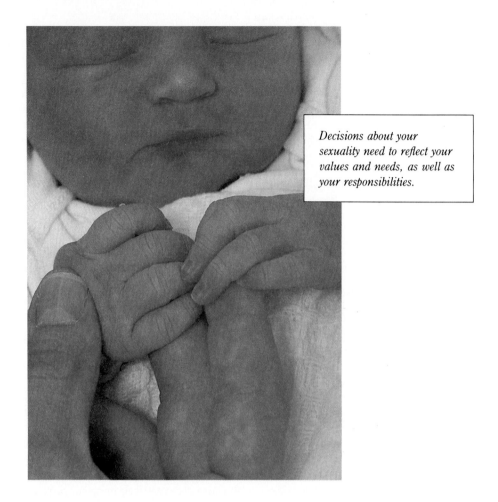

*Decisions about your sexuality need to reflect your values and needs, as well as your responsibilities.*

the spotlight on the importance of prevention as well. Avoiding sexual contact with infected partners and use of a condom are both important preventive steps.

As individual attitudes and values play a greater role in shaping sexual behavior and practices, sexuality has come to serve a wider variety of functions. Sexuality can provide unequalled closeness with another person, an opportunity for expressing deep feelings of love, and an opportunity to share an intimate and meaningful experience as part of a close relationship with another. However, sexual behavior can also be used simply to build one's self-esteem, to hold an unsatisfactory relationship together, as an avenue for rebellion, or a response to boredom or tension. Thus a single sexual act can often have many different meanings for the participants. It is important to be aware of these meanings, as well as the difference between simple sexual technique, on the one hand, and concern, caring, and intimacy on the other. Ultimately, it is essential to choose ways of meeting one's sexual needs without doing violence to the needs and values of others.

The importance of values and the burden of choice and responsibility in responsible sexuality is clearly demonstrated in decisions about pregnancy and contraception. Some people avoid using *contraceptives* for religious reasons. Other people avoid them because they feel anxious or uncertain about their sexuality. Still others avoid contraception as a way of working out other problems in their lives or in their relationships with their partners. Whatever the decision a couple makes, it must be a joint decision that reflects the attitudes and values and preferences of both partners; and both partners must then bear the burden and responsibility for their decision.

## KEY TERMS

masturbation (425)

double standard (427)

excitement phase (437)

plateau phase (439)

orgasmic phase (440)

ejaculation (440)

refractory period (440)

resolution phase (441)

sexual dysfunction (443)

orgasmic dysfunction (444)

vaginismus (444)

impotence (444)

premature ejaculation (445)

sexually transmitted diseases (446)

gonorrhea (446)

syphilis (446)

chancre (446)

genital herpes (447)

nonspecific urethritis (NSU) (447)

pubic lice (447)

contraceptive (450)

erotophiles (451)

erotophobes (451)

# Work and Leisure

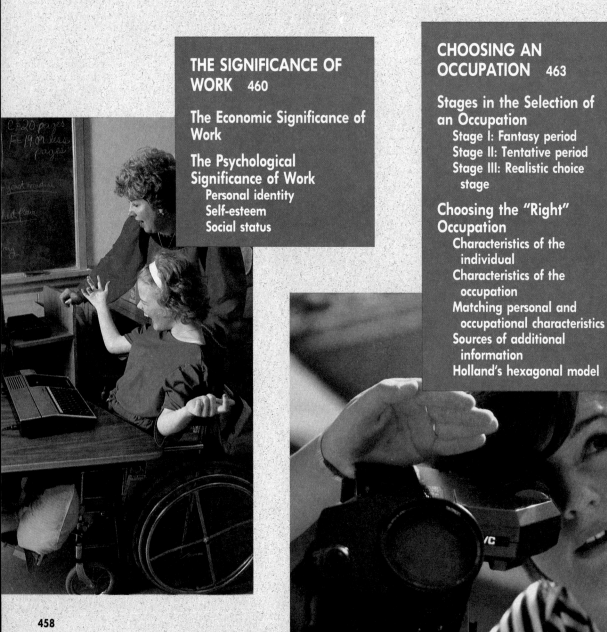

*Without work all life goes rotten. But when work is soulless, life stifles and dies.*

(Albert Camus)

$\mathcal{W}$ORK is one of the most basic of all human institutions. Its importance stems not only from the fact that it is necessary in order to survive, but also from the philosophical, moral, religious, political, and psychological significance attributed to it over the centuries.

Most adult Americans can anticipate spending about forty years of their lives working outside the home, but a fully adequate definition of "work" must include more than just "paid employment." The person who spends each day at home cooking, cleaning, laundering, marketing, and caring for children does not receive pay for his or her labors but works nonetheless. Therefore, it is more accurate to define **work** as "an activity that produces something of value for other people" (Special Task Force on Work in America, 1972).

**work:** any activity that produces something of value for other people

Traditionally, most men have worked outside the home while most women have worked in the home. As recently as 1960, for example, only 30 percent of all married women were in the labor force. However, in the last three decades, there has been a remarkably sharp increase in the number of married women working outside the home. Today, more than 50 million women and 64 million men in the United States hold jobs outside the home. More than half of all women between the ages of eighteen and sixty-four are in the work force, and studies suggest that more than 90 percent of women will work outside of the home at sometime in their lives. According to Strong and DeVault (1986), more than 15 million working women are also mothers (see Table 13.1, p. 461).

As we will see, work can be a source of great satisfaction and meaningfulness in a person's life, but it can also be a major source of stress. In this chapter, we will consider (1) the function of work in people's lives, (2) the ways in which people choose careers, (3) job-related stress, stress from unemployment, and ways of coping more effectively with such stress, and (4) the role of leisure in people's lives. We begin by examining the significance of work in people's lives.

## THE SIGNIFICANCE OF WORK

The word *work* conjures up odious images of toil, effort, and energy-sapping activity. It is usually assumed that work is something few people do willingly, that everyone would prefer other activities if it weren't for financial necessity. However, this viewpoint neglects many crucial psychological aspects of work in contemporary society. Today, many people expect more from work than economic reward.

**TABLE 13.1   Facts About the World of Work**

| | |
|---|---|
| Number of workers in U.S. labor force | Over 115 million |
| Number of women in U.S. labor force | Over 50 million |
| Number of wives who work outside home | About 50 percent |
| Number of mothers of school-age children who work outside home | Over 60 percent |
| Number of women living alone, most of whom work to support themselves | Over 9 million |
| Number of different types of jobs | Over 40 thousand |
| Number of jobs that do not require a higher degree | Over 85 percent |
| Number of so-called prestige jobs held by women, e.g., in law, medicine, engineering | About 1 in 6 |
| Number of women in service jobs, nurturing tasks (e.g., nursing), assistance roles | About 9 out of 10 |
| Women entering college who plan a career in business, engineering, law, or medicine | About 1 in 6 |

Source: Department of Labor & Census Bureau.

## The Economic Significance of Work

**extrinsic satisfaction:** satisfaction that comes from something other than work itself (such as money, fringe benefits)

**Theory X:** management theory which assumes that workers are motivated solely by extrinsic satisfactions

The economic significance of work is obvious: people do work, at least in part, to support themselves and their families. Assuming that work is unpleasant and unrewarding and that people will try to avoid it, people will work only if they receive some kind of **extrinsic satisfaction** such as money or fringe benefits. Companies that subscribe to this traditional view of work typically follow the **Theory X** approach to management. They tend to assume that workers are lazy, disinterested, and unmotivated in their jobs. They also assume that extrinsic rewards, coupled with close monitoring and strict supervision, are both necessary and sufficient to assure worker productivity (McGregor, 1960; O'Toole, 1982).

## The Psychological Significance of Work

Working is increasingly recognized as more than simply "doing a job" and "making a living." Work plays an important psychological role in people's lives.

**Personal identity.**   To a large extent, people become what they do. Asking someone, "Who are you?" almost invariably elicits occupational responses, such as "I am a lawyer," or "I work for Lockheed," or "I am a homemaker." In view of the vast amounts of time and energy devoted to working, it is not surprising that work has become one of the most salient means of identifying oneself in our society.

**Self-esteem.**   Closely related to personal identity is the effect of work on self-evaluation. Work has the capacity to assure individuals of their competence. Most work situations provide frequent feedback about people's ability to perform satisfactorily. Work can also confirm the fact that a person is valued by society, that he or she is doing something which needs to be done, and that the product, whether material or service, is valued by others. Therefore, to the degree that people take pride in the quality and significance of their work, self-esteem may be enhanced.

**Social status.**    Sociologists note that one of the major determinants of status in our society is a person's occupation. Indeed, the entire family typically assumes the status of the job held by the head of the household.

Several important conclusions follow from the fact that work is an important source of personal identity, self-esteem, and social position:

1. Being unemployed means a great deal more than loss of income. People unable to find employment or forced to retire at an arbitrary age are denied an important source of identity and worth. As we noted in Chapter 9, research confirms the fact that retirement from work does represent a major adjustive challenge for most people.

2. People employed in low-status jobs are likely to experience not just low pay but also low self-esteem since they derive their sense of identity, self-worth, and social status from their work just as everyone else does. The consequences can be devastating, as described so vividly by Studs Terkel (1974) in *Working*.

> For the many, there is a hardly concealed discontent. The blue-collar blues is more bitterly sung than the white-collar moan. "I'm a machine," says the spot welder. "I'm caged," says the bank teller, and echoes the hotel clerk. "I'm a mule," says the steelworker. "A monkey can do what I do," says the receptionist. "I'm less than a farm implement," says the migrant worker. "I'm an object," says the high-fashion model. Blue collar and white call upon the identical phrase "I'm a robot." (p. xiv)

3. Many people believe that they would feel lost and useless if they didn't have a job. As one woman in her thirties remarked: "Everyone needs to feel they have a place in the world. It would be unbearable not to. I don't like to feel superfluous. One needs to be needed. I'm saying being idle and leisured, doing nothing, is tragic and disgraceful. Everyone must have an occupation" (Terkel, 1974, p. 554). Research data confirm that occupational satisfaction is closely linked to mental health (Hornung & McCullough, 1981; Terkel, 1980).

Companies that acknowledge the psychological significance of work typically follow the **Theory Y** approach to management. They tend to emphasize the importance of the **intrinsic satisfactions** that can be found in work—its ability to satisfy people's needs for self-esteem, relatedness, meaning, and personal growth and fulfillment. Such companies spend a great deal of time trying to make people's jobs more interesting and to involve employees in decisions that affect their jobs. In one case, janitorial personnel in an office building were split into two groups. One group was asked to develop a plan to help curb absenteeism. In discussions with management, this group developed a financial bonus plan for reducing absenteeism. The plan was put into effect for both groups of janitors, but it was successful only for the group that helped develop the plan (Lawler & Hackman, 1969).

It has long been assumed that professional and executive people are highly attracted to the intrinsic satisfactions of their work while blue-collar and unskilled workers are more attracted by the extrinsic satisfactions of work. However, research suggests that both white-collar and blue-collar workers benefit from a Theory Y

**Theory Y**: management theory which assumes that workers are motivated primarily by intrinsic satisfactions

**intrinsic satisfactions:** satisfactions found in work itself (such as meaning, fulfillment, personal growth)

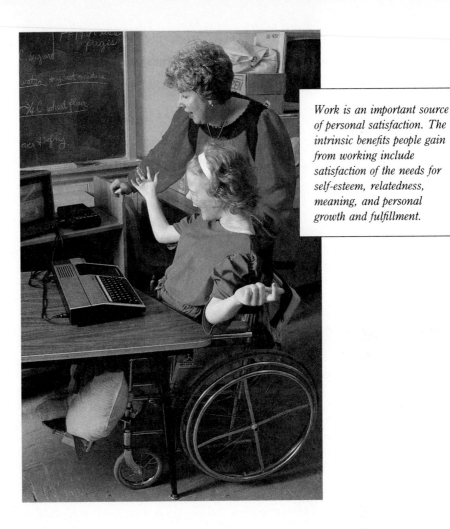

*Work is an important source of personal satisfaction. The intrinsic benefits people gain from working include satisfaction of the needs for self-esteem, relatedness, meaning, and personal growth and fulfillment.*

approach, particularly when extrinsic satisfactions such as pay and fringe benefits are above a reasonable threshold level. For example, in various research studies over the years, between 80 and 90 percent of all working men and women surveyed, blue-collar and white-collar alike, indicated that they would continue working even if they didn't have to for economic reasons (Stevens-Long, 1984; Craig, 1989). In fact, in many companies that follow the Theory Y approach to management, people actually find their jobs so interesting and meaningful that they work at them longer and harder than is required (see Insight, p. 464).

## CHOOSING AN OCCUPATION

We have seen that for most people work not only provides a source of income but also has a profound effect on the way they come to view themselves and their place in the larger world. Hence, the choice of an occupation is an important one. In the next section of the chapter, we shall consider the ways in which most people go about making this choice.

---

### Theory Z

An alternative to the Theory X and Theory Y approaches to organizational structure and management has been developed by William G. Ouchi (1981). His approach, which has been termed *Theory Z,* is a variant of the Theory Y approach.

Ouchi, drawing from the successes of Japanese business, proposed that a Theory Z organization has several characteristic features. Primary among these features is its "corporate culture." Far from being a place where people work "nine to five," the Theory Z organization is, in a sense, part of an employee's "family." One company noted by Ouchi helped develop the friendly, easy going atmosphere of a family by holding "beer busts" once a month. These beer busts were not meant solely for production-line employees but for all members of the organization, including executive and managerial personnel.

A party for employees, however, is only an outward sign of a Theory Z company. More important than parties is a company philosophy in which each person is made to feel as though he or she is important to the company and has something to contribute to the overall success of the organization. Trust and friendship are an integral part of a Theory Z company, as are an emphasis on working together and decision by consensus. Often the outcome of such a corporate culture is the creation of products in which each worker takes pride and whose quality is uniformly high.

Although Theory Z organizations are common in Japan, they may not be easily transplanted to other cultures. For one thing, people in Japan typically spend their entire working lives with a single organization. In contrast, many Americans expect to change jobs when conditions warrant. Similarly, promotions and advancement are quite slow in Japan, even for people with recognized talent and ability. In contrast, Americans expect that rapid promotion will accompany personal success. Finally, the Japanese emphasis on group consensus and long-term results contrasts markedly with the American emphasis on the "maverick" style and short-term performance.

Several American companies have adopted a Theory Z approach. Among them are the electronics giant Hewlett-Packard and the retailing company of Dayton-Hudson (probably best known for its Waldenbooks stores). Several other companies, such as General Motors, have experimented with various aspects of the Theory Z approach. Although it may not be possible to adopt fully the characteristics of successful Japanese companies, the Theory Z approach emphasizes again the importance of work to the individual and shows how an individual's sense of involvement in a group setting can aid both the worker and the company for whom he or she works.

## Stages in the Selection of an Occupation

As we saw in Chapter 9, an occupational choice usually is not made until the individual reaches late adolescence or early adulthood. Prior to this time, many decisions have been made that have led toward or away from given occupations. Long before taking their first full-time job, people develop ideas about the function of work in their lives as well as attitudes toward different kinds of work. Early work experiences, exposure to positive (or negative) models, and the training and education the individual has received also help point the way toward some kinds of work and away from others. Thus, the groundwork for a career choice is laid long before actual choice is made. Investigators have pointed to three stages in career choice (Ginzberg, 1966).

**fantasy period:** first stage of occupational selection in which choices are based on fantasy, not fact or ability

**Stage I: Fantasy period.**    For most children, this period extends until about age eleven. In the **fantasy period,** children do not relate occupational choice to their intellectual and personal qualifications or to realistic opportunities. Rather, they tend to assume that they can become whatever they want to become—whether it be a police officer, a model, an astronaut, or a nurse. Children try out many occupational roles in their play, often identifying with the occupation of their father or mother or other adults they know or have seen on television.

**tentative period:** second stage of occupational choice in which occupational preferences begin to be based on the person's strengths and weaknesses

**Stage II: Tentative period.**    From about eleven to seventeen years of age, young people begin to recognize the need to decide on a future occupation. In the **tentative period,** they make tentative choices based on whatever awareness they have of their interests, abilities, and opportunities. For most adolescents, compatible interests appear to be a primary consideration in the early stages of career choice. Later, ability and training prerequisites become more important, and still later, personal values begin to have an influence.

**realistic choice stage:** third stage of occupational choice in which preferences are tested in the world of work

**Stage III: Realistic choice stage.**    In the **realistic choice stage,** adolescents and young adults begin to recognize that their hopes and desires have to be tempered by the realities of environmental limitations and opportunities. This leads to career *exploration,* as young people acquire more information about careers and perhaps gather some preliminary work experience; *crystallization,* as they narrow their range of alternatives and prepare to make a career choice; and finally, *specification* and commitment to a preliminary occupational goal. In the next section, we will examine more closely the process by which most people determine a realistic career choice.

## Choosing the "Right" Occupation

It is worth noting that the very idea of "making a career choice" is relatively recent. In earlier times—and in many societies even today—most people had their choices made for them or were severely limited in the careers they could choose. Of necessity, most males followed what their fathers had done or entered whatever apprenticeship training was available to them in their communities. Women remained in the home.

Today, people have a much wider choice of careers and a person's choice of occupation is increasingly a matter of personal preference. Nowhere is this clearer than in the jobs that are now available to men and to women. Women can now work at jobs that were once the exclusive domain of men: as welders, construction workers, and professional athletes, for example. Similarly, men can now choose careers that traditionally have been the domain of women: as elementary school teachers, telephone operators, flight attendants, and nurses, for example. This does not mean that men and women can be found in equal numbers in these various occupations: it is still the case that more than 95 percent of all secretaries and nurses are women, and more than 95 percent of engineers are men (Craig, 1989). However, as the traditional divisions between "man's work" and "woman's work" continue to erode, self-direction is becoming increasingly important in occupational choices for both sexes.

Having a large number of careers from which to choose is a mixed blessing. While it opens the possibility that a person will find a career that is "right," it also greatly increases the difficulty of finding the "right" career. Both the characteristics of the individual and the characteristics of the occupation must be considered when making a career choice.

**Characteristics of the individual.**    In Chapter 9, we examined briefly the personal constraints that affect career choice. Answers to the following questions help to narrow considerably the field of possible careers:

1. *What does the individual want to do?* The answer to this question involves interests, motives, and values. Does the individual like to work with people? With ideas? With things? Does the person prefer a leisurely pace or thrive on pressures and deadlines? Another relevant question concerns what the individual would like the occupational experience to help him or her become.

2. *What can the individual do—or learn to do?* The answer to this question involves abilities and aptitudes. What knowledge and skills does the person possess? What is the individual's potential for acquiring further competence in particular areas? What special abilities, such as artistic, athletic, or mechanical skills, does he or she possess? Does the individual have any special physical or mental limitations that might exclude a particular occupational area?

3. *What economic pressures does the individual face?* Economic issues can have an effect on career choice. For example, the cost of a college education is a significant burden for many families, and many students must work during their college years.

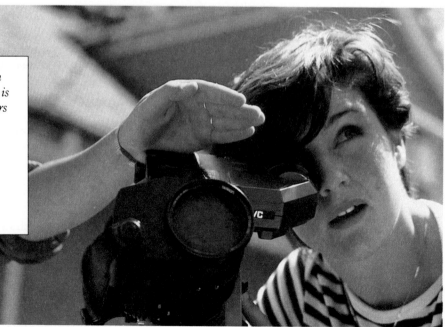

*Selecting a career to match your interests and motives is important. But other factors such as knowledge, skills, and economic needs of the individual, and characteristics of the occupation must be considered to make a satisfying career choice.*

These economic considerations cause some people to foreclose some career opportunities and seek other, less expensive routes to career preparation.

**Characteristics of the occupation.**    Characteristics of various occupations must also be considered when making career decisions. The following questions are especially relevant:

1. *What are the requirements and working conditions?* What training and skills are needed? What personal qualities—such as initiative, social competence, particular temperament, or physical endurance—are required? What would the individual be doing? In what kind of setting?

2. *What does the occupation have to offer?* What rewards and satisfactions can be expected in terms of income, social status, and opportunities for advancement and personal growth?

3. *What changes are likely to occur in the field?* Since today's college students will be working well into the twenty-first century, the question of future trends in one's chosen occupational area is relevant. With the accelerating rate of technological and social change, major shifts in many occupations are occurring in relatively short periods of time. Thus, it is important that the individual not only gain a clear view of given occupations as they presently exist but also know about probable changes in the near and distant future that might affect his or her work.

**Matching personal and occupational characteristics.**    With the answers to these six questions, the task becomes matching individual characteristics to occupational characteristics. The individual's interests, motives, values, abilities, aptitudes, and goals must be compared with the requirements, working conditions, and satisfactions provided by various occupations. How do the job requirements correspond to the individual's abilities and interests? Do the rewards and satisfactions coincide with the desires of the person? Will the individual find the work interesting and personally fulfilling? What can he or she expect to contribute? Will the job change in important ways in the foreseeable future? Are the economic costs of preparing for the career realistic and acceptable?

Although it is easy to describe the matching process as I have just done, in practice the task is a good deal more difficult. Most young people are unsure of their interests, values, goals, and career objectives. Many are also unsure of their abilities and aptitudes, and very few adolescents or young adults are well-informed about the requirements and rewards of even a small number of occupations. In the absence of good information about various careers, people are likely to rely on stereotypes about various occupations. For example, many people believe that physicians are all-knowing, calm people who diagnose rare diseases and save lives on a daily basis. Their image of lawyers is that of the trial lawyer engaged in challenging, dramatic courtroom debate. Unfortunately, these stereotypes are inaccurate and career decisions based upon them are not likely to be wise (Anastasi, 1982).

**Sources of additional information.**    Numerous resources are available to the person unsure about occupational plans. One very useful method of learning more about the match between personal and job characteristics is part-time or summer work in a setting that closely matches career plans. If, for example, an individual is interested in pursuing a law career, he or she might work in a law office as a clerk. Although this experience is not, strictly speaking, equivalent to being a lawyer, it can provide a valuable opportunity to match personal expectations against the realities of the chosen field.

Volunteer work can also be a valuable means of learning more about a profession. Volunteer work in psychology and other health-related fields is especially likely to provide realistic and useful information about the chosen field. Some occupations, such as engineering and food service, provide apprenticeships or work-study programs, both of which can be helpful.

In situations where paid or volunteer work is not possible, conversations with people already engaged in an occupation can provide useful (and often contradictory) insights. Similarly, information available from professional organizations and libraries can help to fill the information gap.

Career counseling programs are available at most colleges and universities through psychology clinics, counseling centers, or offices that provide student services. Career counselors usually provide psychological testing, career information and guidance in helping people to identify appropriate careers. Quite often career counselors will use specially developed **interest inventories** or tests that attempt to match an individual's interests and preferences to the interests of people who have been successful and are satisfied with various careers. The degree of similarity is then used as a measure of the likelihood that the individual would also be successful and happy in that career.

**interest inventories:** psychological tests that can be used to help an individual make an appropriate career choice

**Holland's hexagonal model.** The way in which interest inventories can be used to match individuals with careers is illustrated clearly in a technique developed by John Holland (Holland, 1966, 1973, 1985). On the basis of several decades of research, Holland concluded that in our culture, there are basically six personality types:

1. *Realistic.* These people prefer to manipulate real objects (tools, machines, animals). They tend to develop mechanical and technical skills and abilities.

2. *Investigative.* These people are primarily interested in understanding and controlling phenomena. They tend to develop scientific and mathematical abilities and aptitudes.

3. *Artistic.* These people prefer free, expressive manipulation of materials that produces art forms. They tend to develop artistic and expressive abilities.

4. *Social.* These people enjoy working with people—informing them, teaching them, curing them. They tend to have strong human relations abilities.

5. *Enterprising.* These people prefer to work with people to achieve organizational or monetary goals. They tend to be strong in such skills as leadership and persuasion.

6. *Conventional.* These people enjoy well-organized and structured activities such as keeping records, organizing information, and operating business machines. They tend to be strong in clerical, computational, and business skills.

Each of Holland's six types is a "pure" or ideal type. Most people, of course, do not match just one of the six types; instead, they exhibit a mixture of types. For example, a person might be very Realistic, moderately Conventional and Investigative, not very Enterprising or Artistic, and not at all Social. Someone else might be a very different mixture of types—perhaps high on Artistic, moderate on Investigative and Social, low on Realistic and Enterprising, and very low on Conventional.

**hexagonal model:** Holland's model of six personality types and six corresponding environments; according to the model, a person is most likely to be satisfied in a career where the environmental demands correspond clearly to his or her personality profile

Holland's research suggests that these six types can be arranged around the outside of a hexagon; hence, his model is sometimes called the **hexagonal model** of personality types (see Figure 13.1). The hexagon captures an important piece of information about the relationships between the six types: types that are close together are more likely to occur together in a person than are types that are far apart. Thus, someone who is Realistic might also be moderately Conventional or

**FIGURE 13.1  Holland's Hexagonal Model of Interests and Some Associated Occupations.**

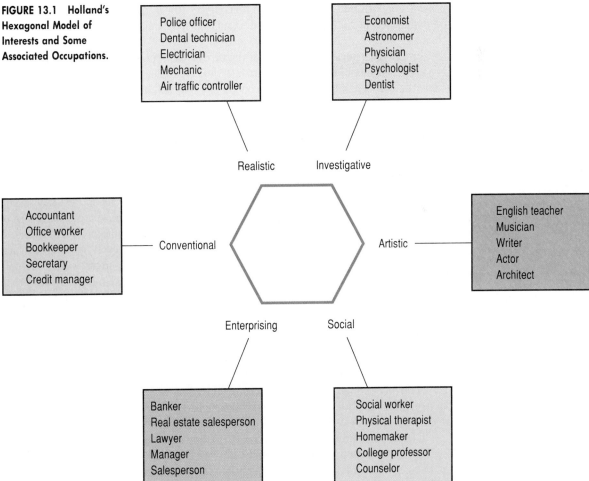

Investigative, since those two types lie quite close to Realistic in the hexagon. However, this same person is less likely to be Social, since Social is on the opposite side of the hexagon from Realistic.

A number of psychological tests are available that permit a person to identify his or her own mix of the six personality types. One of the most widely used tests, the "Strong Interest Inventory," must be administered and interpreted by trained professionals; it is often provided as part of the career counseling available through counseling centers. However, Holland also provides a brief "Self-Directed Search" in *Making Vocational Choices;* this short questionnaire can be completed and scored quite easily by anyone.

You may be asking at this point "How does this relate to occupational choice? Of what importance is learning about my own unique mix of personality types?" The answer, according to Holland, is that there are also six types of environments that correspond to each of the six personality types. A Realistic environment, for example, provides opportunities to manipulate real objects (tools, machines, animals); success or dominance in this environment depends on mechanical and technical skills and abilities.

Just as each person is a particular mixture of the six basic types, each occupation is a particular mix of the six environments. For example, as you can see from Figure 13.1, the careers of economist, astronomer, physician, geologist, and dentist are all high on the Investigative dimension: they all require, first and foremost, the observation and investigation of phenomena and they all reward scientific competence. They differ somewhat in their secondary qualities: dentistry, for example, is also quite high on Social and moderately high on Realistic demands; geologist, however, is quite high on Realistic and moderately high on Artistic.

Holland and his colleagues have compiled a comprehensive "dictionary" which identifies the characteristics of more than 12,000 occupations in relation to the hexagon (Gottfredson, Holland, & Ogawa, 1982). By comparing a person's mix of personality types with the mix of environments provided by various occupations, it is possible to identify careers that seem to provide an especially good match and deserve much closer examination. People whose personality profiles most closely match their jobs tend to remain in those jobs longer and are more satisfied than those whose personality profiles do not closely match their jobs (Holland, 1985). Thus, someone strong on the Investigative dimension, with secondary strengths in the Social and Realistic areas, would be well advised to explore the possibility of a career as a dentist, a biologist, an osteopathic physician, a chiropractor, a natural science teacher, or an optometrist. These are all careers that are very high on the Investigative dimension, high on Realistic, and moderately high on Social. In contrast, someone who is high on the Enterprising dimension with secondary strengths in the Conventional and Social areas should consider careers as a credit analyst, real estate agent, business or office manager, dispatcher, bill collector or salesperson.

Of course, neither Holland's approach nor any other single resource can magically answer the question of "What should I do with my life?" However, resources such as this can point the way toward especially promising careers that seem to be worth further investigation and, as a result, help to make the process of arriving at a career choice more manageable, less stressful, and more likely to be successful. Moreover, they can also help to break down job stereotypes: for example, according to Holland's analyses, hospital administration, college presidency, historian, history teacher, home-service director, and training instructor are all careers that are very similar in their demands, though it is doubtful that most people would have reached that conclusion.

## WORK-RELATED STRESS

Unfortunately, not everyone finds an occupation that matches his or her personal characteristics. Even people who find a satisfying occupation later discover that they, or their jobs, have changed and no longer provide a good match. In addition, some occupations, by their nature, are stressful even for people who are well suited to them. Many people experience stress because they are *not* able to work for one reason or another. In this section of the chapter, we will explore all these sources of work-related stress as well as the kinds of readjustments and adaptations they require.

### Sources of Stress in the Workplace

**Work dissatisfaction.**    Some people are able to establish themselves in an occupation with apparent ease. Although they may change jobs from time to time, they show an orderly progression of advancement in their chosen field. Other people, however, have a great deal of difficulty in finding a job that satisfies them and in "taking hold"; their job dissatisfaction is likely to be a source of stress.

Measuring job satisfaction or discontent is a complex undertaking. An individual cannot simply rely on public opinion polls for reports of attitudes toward work. Although most people who are polled report that they are "satisfied" with their jobs, they usually mean only that their pay is acceptable and their working conditions adequate. In contrast, measures that are more sensitive to worker dissatisfaction, such as absenteeism, turnover rates, inferior work, and accidents on the job, typically reveal considerable dissatisfaction at all occupational levels.

The reasons for work dissatisfaction are numerous:

1. Some people are dissatisfied with their work because they did not choose an appropriate career. In some cases people make career choices that are ill-considered or impulsive. Others simply "drift" into their occupation. Still others follow a family tradition of entering a specific occupation. For example, the children of a business-person may be expected by their parents to enter the "family business." Unless career choice is based on a realistic analysis of personal and job characteristics, the choice of a particular occupation is likely to lead ultimately to dissatisfaction.

However, even with careful selection, it is unreasonable to expect that all of an individual's needs and expectations will be satisfied in any single occupation. There-fore, some amount of dissatisfaction is inevitable in any job. The person who expects to find the "ideal job" may understandably experience chronic dissatisfaction and stress as he or she moves from one job to another in search of the nonexistent "perfect" career (see Psychology in Action on p. 473).

2. Some jobs are inherently less satisfying than others. Some jobs are boring and repetitive, while others do not allow for creativity or initiative. The very size of many organizations also helps foster job dissatisfaction. In many of today's factories and offices, a person is unlikely to appreciate how his or her efforts contribute to the overall functioning and productivity of the organization. In contrast, a craftsperson, such as a silversmith, starts with a piece of raw material and transforms it into a useful, often beautiful, finished piece in which he or she can take personal pride.

**overeducation:** education, training, knowledge, or skills that are in excess of those required by a particular job

3. **Overeducation** and rising expectations also contribute to job dissatisfaction. In the past, a college education practically guaranteed the degree holder a better job, higher status, and better pay. Today, college educations are more common, but the payoff is not as great. As a result, for many young adults the first job is a disappointment. The new employee is often overly ambitious and idealistic. However, the realities of work are realized eventually: the person who expected to become a company vice-president within a few short years instead finds that he or she is in a boring or routine job. People discover that they are overtrained for their jobs and their skills are not being utilized. In fact, some of the highest levels of job dissatisfaction are found among educated young people who hold low-paying, low-status, and generally unrewarding jobs ("Education and Job Satisfaction," 1976).

4. Many people discover that the skills they have developed outside the work situation are not fully appreciated or utilized. For example, an individual who successfully has managed a home, reared children, and handled the family finances may find that the skills required to do those things are not valued or recognized in the workplace. Not infrequently, a person who has had experience in a work setting is valued more highly than an individual who has developed similar (or superior) skills as a volunteer or at home. It can be frustrating to a talented but less experienced older worker to find that he or she does not garner the recognition that younger but more experienced workers receive.

5. In some cases, people become dissatisfied with their jobs because their interests shift, their values and goals change significantly, or they lose some skills or acquire new ones. In these cases, people often discover that they are bored and unfulfilled, disheartened and saddened by careers that once gave them pleasure and excitement. Even a change in health can cause job dissatisfaction, as when a surgeon develops arthritis, a dancer is crippled by bad knees, or a construction worker develops heart disease.

6. Just as people change over time, jobs also change as technology advances and the needs of businesses change. A job that initially requires skilled labor may become so mechanized that it is no longer satisfying to a skilled worker. A job that required simple, basic skills five or ten years ago may now require more advanced training and special aptitudes. The effect of such job changes is especially evident to people trying to return to work after being out of the work force for an extended period of time. Such people often find that the work environment has changed dramatically. For example, the person who worked as a secretary or librarian or accountant ten years ago is likely to find that a similar job today requires skills in managing word processors, spreadsheets, databases, and computer-based equipment.

## Burnout: What to Do About It

Imagine that you have acquired an extremely difficult job, but have high expectations that with tremendous effort you will succeed. Perhaps you want to help eradicate domestic violence or eliminate alcoholism or drug abuse; perhaps you want to help people who are unemployed to regain control over their lives. If you are in business, you may have taken on a weak subsidiary and plan to make it the most successful division in the company. Maybe you have started a brand new business of your own despite the failure of other, similar businesses in your community. In each of these cases, you have taken on an extraordinarily difficult challenge, yet you are fully convinced that hard work, long hours, and total dedication will assure your success.

Slowly you begin to realize that you will not be completely successful, the people you want to help do not always respond to your efforts and in fact may criticize or reject you, the problems you are trying to solve are too overwhelming, or your business undertakings may not be successful despite your dedicated efforts. You redouble your efforts until you become physically and mentally exhausted—you become tired and worn out, have trouble sleeping, develop frequent headaches; you feel frustrated, angry, trapped, helpless, depressed, and inadequate. In an effort to overcome the difficulty, you devote even more time to your project, you spend less time with your family and friends, and sink deeper into exhaustion. You are experiencing *burnout* (Chance, 1981; Maslach, 1982; Baron, 1985). You have depleted your resources and worn yourself out "by excessively striving to reach some unrealistic expectation imposed by one's self or by the values of society" (Freudenberger & Richelson, 1980, p. 17).

What can you do to cope with the situation and break the vicious circle? The first step, of course, is to acknowledge that you have a problem that deserves attention. The next step is to reevaluate your goals with emphasis toward setting more realistic objectives for yourself; acknowledge that you can't possibly do everything yourself

and that you will have to arrange for some work to be done by others. This might mean shifting some responsibility to others, or it might mean simply redirecting the flow of your work somewhat so that others can share part of the load. You might use the self-discovery exercises corresponding to Chapters 3–5 to identify other factors that contribute to burnout and begin to develop alternative ways of coping more effectively with those sources of stress as well.

These steps will help you identify and change the external sources of your stress. In addition, there are steps you can take to reduce the impact of the stress on you. Instead of worrying about the things you haven't accomplished, spend more time reflecting on your successes. What things have gone well, what changes have you been able to make, what improvements have you made, and how is the world already a better place due to your efforts? In other words, instead of worrying that your cup is half empty, think about the ways that it is half full.

In addition, and perhaps most important of all, make a deliberate effort to renew and rebuild your interpersonal relationships. As we saw in Chapter 3, social resources are valuable in reducing the impact of stress, yet interpersonal relationships are often early victims of burnout. Rebuilding social relationships will require initially that you "compartmentalize" your life (Baron, 1985). Draw a line between work and nonwork, and make a deliberate effort to keep work-related problems from intruding on nonwork time. Then use the nonwork time to rediscover outside interests and to re-establish relationships with family and friends, to "cultivate closeness," as Freudenberger and Richelson (1980) refer to it.

Finally, a message we have repeated throughout this book: be alert (and ask those close to you also to be alert) for early warning signs of burnout in the future, and then take the time to respond to those warnings before your resources are depleted and you find yourself exhausted once again.

*Stress is a standard element in some jobs. When stress cannot be avoided or its sources controlled, the ability to deal effectively with stress is critical.*

7. Discrimination in the workplace is another source of dissatisfaction and job-related stress. In spite of continuing efforts to end discrimination, race, sex, and age still limit career choices and occupational opportunities for many people. For example, it has been estimated that one in three minority workers is employed irregularly or is unemployed. Also, the annual salary of employed minority males is far below that of the average salary of white workers. While Black Americans have been subjected to the greatest discrimination in education, career choice, and occupational opportunity, Americans of Spanish-speaking, Indian, and Asian ancestry as well as women, older adults, and the handicapped have also been victims of discrimination.

Despite recent efforts to eliminate discrimination in the workplace, its effects continue to be felt. For example, women are still overrepresented in low-paying, low-status, "dead-end" jobs (Strong & DeVault, 1986). Nine out of ten women work in service jobs, nurturing tasks, and assistance roles—as waitresses, clerical workers, secretaries, phone operators, lab technicians, nurses, and teachers. On the other hand, only a very small percentage of women gain entry into so-called high-status fields, such as engineering, law, and medicine.

Moreover, women are generally paid less than men doing the same job. For example, the average income of female computer specialists in 1981 was only 72 percent of the average income of males in the same field. On the average, female attorneys earned 70 percent as much as males; female engineers earned 67 percent as much as males; female physicians earned 81 percent as much as males. This wage discrepancy exists even in traditionally female occupations: women teaching elementary school earn only 82 percent as much as men; female clerical workers earn only 67 percent as much as males; and the list continues (Stevens-Long, 1984). For skilled and highly motivated women, and for other victims of discrimination, facts such as these are a frequent source of job dissatisfaction and job stress.

**Job stressfulness.**    While job dissatisfaction is a frequent source of job-related stress, it is not the only source. Some jobs are inherently more stressful than others, even for people who are well suited to perform them. The examples that most involve stress are jobs in which competition, time pressure, work overload, responsibility without authority, and rapid and continuous change play a large role.

As we saw in Chapter 3, pressure is only one source of stress. For example, stress can also arise from frustration caused by delays, daily hassles, lack of resources, losses, failure, and conflict. Jobs that are high in these characteristics will also be experienced as stressful, even though most people may not think of them as such. For example, city bus drivers have jobs that are generally as stressful as air traffic controllers and emergency room physicians.

As we saw in Chapter 4, the costs of chronic stress from whatever source are high: frequent symptoms of work-related stress include anxiety, depression, hostility, headaches, ulcers, heart attacks, family problems, and abuse of alcohol and drugs. Clearly, it is important for people to be able to cope effectively with stress in the workplace, whatever its cause. We now turn our attention to this topic.

## Coping Effectively with Stress in the Workplace

In Chapter 5, we examined a number of techniques that permit you to deal more effectively with stress in your life. Those same techniques are just as appropriate for coping with work-related stress, as we will now see.

**Controlling reactions to stress.**    The first step in trying to deal with any major stressful event is to bring your reactions to the stress under control before trying to deal with the source of the stress itself. While built-in coping mechanisms such as those described on pp. 141–43 can be helpful, by themselves they are unlikely to be effective in relieving all the effects of job-related stress. Thus, it is usually necessary to take additional steps to bring job-related stress reactions under control.

You can relieve some of the physiological reactions to work-related stress through a regular program of relaxation and exercise; other reactions such as headaches, ulcers, and hypertension may require medical attention. To bring emotional reactions to stress such as anxiety, fear, anger, guilt, and depression under control, use some of the techniques described on pp. 148–52. Distinguishing appropriate and inappropriate emotional reactions is an important first step, in addition to accepting some emotional reactions as normal and healthy, developing "safety valves," and identifying ways to regain control of the stressful situation.

Any person regularly exposed to significant work-related stress would be well-advised to develop stress inoculation techniques such as those described on pp. 153–54. This may involve developing a framework for understanding the response to stress and learning to use cognitive self-statements to monitor and control stress reactions.

Finally, social support is a valuable buffer against stress, and so it becomes especially important for people who are experiencing high levels of job stress to reach out to others who can provide support and reassurance and on whom they can vent some of their emotions.

**Dealing with the source of stress.**     Once the reactions to work-related stress have been brought under some degree of control, you must shift your attention to reducing or eliminating the *cause* of the stress.

1. *Evaluating the stressful situation.* As we saw in Chapter 5, the first step in dealing effectively with stressors is to evaluate the stressful situation. This requires defining and categorizing the situation correctly. If you are experiencing significant job-related stress, for example, you must identify the sources of stress and then determine whether you have effective stress management techniques for dealing with those stressors.

Often the most apparent source of stress is not, in fact, the real or even the most important cause. For example, many people tend to personalize the source of job-related stress: "The problem is my manager. She is absolutely impossible to please." Defined in this way, the "problem" is another person over whom the person has little or no control, so the prospects for improving the situation seem bleak. It is probably more productive to ask: Is the manager in fact never pleased by anything, or are there some things that do meet with her approval? What are those things and how do they differ from things of which she does not approve? Is the manager critical of everyone's work, or only some people's work? Do those people actually differ in the quality of their work? By carefully exploring questions such as these, it should be possible to determine whether the problem is the poor quality of your work, inappropriate expectations on the part of the manager, some kind of problem between the two of you, or something else entirely.

Another common obstacle to effective coping is the tendency to oversimplify the cause of stress: "My job is too hard" or "People don't listen to me." Both of these may be true, but they are likely to be only part of the story: jobs are only difficult in relation to the skills and effort that people bring to them; a job that is difficult for one person may be easy for another. Thus, "my job is too hard" might better be phrased as "my job requires knowledge and skills that I don't have" or "my job requires more time and effort than I am willing to give it." Similarly, "people don't listen to me" might be analyzed more effectively as "I can't communicate my ideas clearly to others" or "people listen to and understand my ideas, but they seldom agree with me."

It is important to spend a good deal of time defining and analyzing the source of stress, since the most effective course of action will differ depending on which of these various explanations is actually correct.

2. *Deciding on an appropriate course of action.* The second step in dealing effectively with stressors is to formulate alternative courses of action that might solve the problem and then select the most promising of these possibilities. As we saw in Chapter 5, there are basically three kinds of action that one can take in any stressful situation: attacking the problem, withdrawing from the situation, or ar-

*Identifying the cause of stress is the first step in reducing or eliminating it. Dealing with the source of stress helps keep a stressful situation from becoming overwhelming.*

ranging a workable compromise of some sort. In order to identify a wide range of options within each of the three categories, it is often useful to engage in brainstorming using the techniques described in Chapter 5.

For example, *attacking* the problem of the critical manager might require changing the ways work is accomplished in order to gain the manager's approval. Another approach might involve talking directly with the manager about the reasons the work does not often meet with her approval, and discussing ways in which the job might be done better. It also might be appropriate to talk with co-workers to discover whether they have similar problems with the manager; if they do not, it would be worthwhile to try to find out how they manage to meet the manager's expectations. By discussing the problem with the manager's supervisor, the company personnel office, or a union steward, you can seek suggestions on effective ways of dealing with the source of the problem. If your work is "too hard," you might decide to acquire the skills and knowledge necessary to do the job well or ask that work assignments be rearranged to match more closely your skills and abilities. All of these actions share a common characteristic: they attack the problem directly.

An alternative set of actions involves *withdrawing* in some way from the stressful situation. This might involve taking a vacation or a brief leave of absence, or mean seeking a transfer to a new manager or a different branch of the company. It could require a change of jobs, taking a position with a new company, or even making a major career change.

Although making a major career change is difficult and usually requires great courage, the outcome in some cases can be highly beneficial, as you can see from the accounts provided by Studs Terkel (1974).

> [Fred Ringley] is forty years old. Until a year ago he had lived all his life in the environs of Chicago. He was born in one of its North Shore suburbs; he was raised, reached adulthood, and became . . . a "typical suburbanite." He had worked in advertising as a copywriter and salesman.
>
> [As Ringley put it,] We were caught up in the American Dream. You've gotta have a house. You've gotta have a country club. You've gotta have two cars. . . . I doubled my salary. I also doubled my grief. . . . We got a house in the suburbs and we got a country club membership and we got two cars and we got higher taxes. We got nervous and we started drinking more and smoking more. Finally, one day we sat down. We have everything and we are poor. (pp. 688-89)

To cope with the accumulating stresses that he had as a salesman, Ringley withdrew from the situation by moving to a small farm in Arkansas. Since the family's savings were decreasing and the farm was not yet productive, Ringley also borrowed money to purchase a small restaurant / dairy fountain. Although he was satisfied with his new life, many of his former associates were taken aback.

> People say, "You're wasting your college education." My ex-employer said to my father, "You didn't raise your son to be a hash slinger." I've lost status in the eyes of my big city friends.
>
> But where I am now I have more status than I would in the city . . . I can be a hash slinger (in Arkansas) and be just as fine as the vice president of the Continental Bank (in Chicago). My personal status with somebody else may have gone down. My personal status with myself has gone up a hundred percent. (p. 693)

Interestingly, many of the "second chancers" interviewed by Terkel switched occupations after some life crisis, often of a philosophical nature. As we saw in Chapter 9, issues of what people want to do with their lives are a major part of the transitions that most adults experience during the course of their lives. For some people, the best resolution to such a life crisis is a change in jobs.

Another individual interviewed by Terkel avoided some of the traps associated with staying in a job that was too stressful by leaving her job as a television producer and becoming a librarian. She discussed the costs of staying in an unpleasant job.

> My father was a mechanical engineer, hated every day of it. He couldn't wait forty-six years, or whatever it was, until he retired. When we were little, we knew he loathed his job. . . . He went through the motions and did it very well. But he dreaded every minute of it.
>
> I have a sister who can't wait until December, cause she's going to retire at a bank. She's just hanging on. How terrible.
>
> I don't think I could ever really retire. There's not enough time. (p. 702)

If neither attacking nor withdrawing is the most appropriate response to the source of job stress, it is possible that some *compromising* might solve the problem. It may be possible to reduce the manager's criticism quite a bit, but not eliminate it entirely. It might be possible to acquire at least some skills that will make the job seem easier, even if the solution is less than perfect. It might also be possible to increase the rewards and satisfactions in other aspects of the job, so that the job becomes less stressful and more evenly balanced even though the original problem still exists.

3. *Balancing rewards and costs and taking action.* In most stressful situations, it is likely that there will be a number of possible actions for reducing or eliminating the source of stress. Some of the actions are more likely to succeed than others. Moreover, some of the actions will greatly reduce the stressfulness of the situation while others will probably have only a small effect. Also, some of the available actions will result in substantial costs (in terms of effort, time required, resources needed) while others will be much less costly. For each alternative course of action, the likelihood of success must be determined, and the costs and benefits balanced.

Once the best solution to the problem has been identified, it must be put into action. If feedback indicates that the strategy is not working as well as expected, the strategy can be modified somewhat or another strategy put into operation until stress is at a tolerable level.

4. *Using stress for personal growth.* As we saw in Chapter 5, stress is not always something to avoid. It can be the basis for important learning about yourself and about the world. For example, if you discover that you have made a poor initial career choice, you have nonetheless learned something of great value about your strengths and weaknesses and about the work world. You can use that knowledge to your advantage in the future. Similarly, the realization that you are not willing to make the effort to do a particular job well can lead to less stress in the future if you change your goals and values accordingly. As we saw in Chapter 9, this process of readjustment is an important and continuous part of adult life.

## UNEMPLOYMENT

Just as some work situations can be a source of stress, being out of work is a source of extreme stress for most adults. It is often assumed that unemployment is simply an economic problem, that being out of work is stressful only because it leads to

*Unemployment is stressful not only because of the financial hardships it brings. Unemployed persons also face a loss of the identity, esteem, and fulfillment that comes from working.*

financial hardship. However, as we saw earlier in this chapter, work serves many purposes: in addition to being a source of income, it is also an important source of identity, esteem, and fulfillment for most adults. Therefore, the loss of employment means much more than just a loss of wages. Moreover, a person's loss of employment can be just as stressful for his or her spouse and family (Derr, 1977).

While some individuals are able to handle the stress of unemployment effectively and adaptively, for many people unemployment is a crushing experience. The following figures may help you to grasp the significance of unemployment in people's lives: it has been estimated that for every 1 percent increase in the rate of unemployment, there will be 37,000 additional deaths during the following six years. Most of those deaths will come from heart attacks, but many others will be suicides. During the same six year period, it is estimated that 7,500 unemployed people or members of their families will either commit crimes that cause them to be sent to prison or will be committed to mental hospitals. Many others will be overcome by depression, anxiety, guilt, despair, and hopelessness (Craig, 1989).

## Stages in Prolonged Unemployment

One of the first efforts to understand how people cope with unemployment was made by Powell and Driscoll (1973). These investigators found that when joblessness was prolonged, their subjects (who were all middle-class, male scientists and engineers) progressed through four well-defined stages.

**Stage I: A period of relaxation and relief.**   Most of the men in this study had seen their companies failing and had anticipated a layoff. Their mood following the layoff was one of relief and relaxation. Most of the men viewed this initial period as sort of a vacation at home, a time to be with family, read, and catch up on hobbies. There was a sense of being between jobs, and the men were confident that they could obtain another job as soon as they were ready to return to work.

**Stage II: A period of concerted effort.**   After nearly a month, most of the men began to feel bored and edgy and they started to make systematic attempts to find work. During this second stage, most of the men relied on job-finding strategies they had used in the past, such as calling friends, going back to their university placement centers, and sending resumes to potential employers. They were still optimistic and did not become anxious or depressed when they received letters of rejection or no response at all.

**Stage III: A period of vacillation and doubt.**   In the third stage, most of the men had been out of work longer than ever before and realized that their job-seeking efforts were not succeeding. Job-seeking behavior became sporadic and alternated between intense activity and none at all. Extreme moodiness characterized the men during this stage, and family and other interpersonal relationships began to deteriorate. After a month or two, most of the men stopped trying and job-hunting came to a virtual halt.

*After being out of work for a long period, unemployed persons often become apathetic, stop looking for work, and sometimes even stop thinking about returning to work at all.*

**Stage IV: A period of malaise and cynicism.** Those men who continued to look for jobs after the third stage tended to use job-seeking strategies that were oriented more toward protecting their self-esteem than obtaining employment. For example, some men refused to consider a job unless it matched their training and experience exactly. However, most of the men lost hope and became listless and apathetic. Eventually they gave up. Some even stopped thinking about work and returning to the world of work. They were defeated.

The researchers did not consider these reactions unique to the particular men in their study. Rather, Powell and Driscoll (1973) concluded that these four stages are quite typical of reactions to prolonged unemployment.

The image of competent and energetic men reduced to listless discouragement highlights the personal tragedy and the loss of valuable resources when there is substantial un-employment. . . . Perhaps more significantly, the situation of these middle-class un-employed further dramatizes the plight of the larger number of unemployed nonskilled workers whose fate is to deal with unemployment often during their lifetime. (p. 26)

## Coping with Unemployment

Strong and DeVault (1986) propose the following steps that can be taken to cope more effectively with unemployment:

**Planning Ahead**

If job loss looks imminent, take stock of your resources. Find out what community services offer assistance or counseling, what medical clinics and lawyers offer sliding-scale or free services, where to obtain public food, child care, financial advice and so on.

**Income Gathering**

Look at the entire family as an income unit. Adolescent children can contribute to the family through delivery services, child care, house cleaning. Who can work at what? Brainstorm possibilities (see p. 161 for tips on brainstorming).

**Financial Planning**

List your assets and decide which are the most expendable; reexamine your expenditures to determine which are absolutely necessary.

**Support Groups**

Find others who are unemployed and form a support group to talk about your feelings; in this way, some of the emotional consequences of unemployment may be eased.

**Communicating with Your Family**

**Take time to talk.** Come right out and let your family know what's happened. Layoff? Plant closing? Depressed economy? Business down? Explain what happened. Break down the big words so that everyone understands, especially the kids.

Fill in everyone at a family meeting or on a one-to-one basis. The important thing is don't leave anyone in the dark. If a family meeting seems out of the question, take time to talk when, for example, cleaning up after meals, cutting or raking the lawn, or taking trips to the store.

Don't "sugar-coat" the facts or tell "fairy tales." Living with less money will force your family to make hard changes. Yet, let your kids know that even though there's less money, they can still count on a loving family, maybe more loving than ever.

**Take time to listen.** Let everyone have their say about what these changes mean to them. Especially now, kids should be seen *and* heard. Listen to words *and* actions. Is someone suddenly:

1. having a lot of crying spells
2. sleeping in late all the time
3. acting angrily
4. drinking heavily
5. withdrawing
6. abusing drugs
7. complaining of stomach pains

## Reducing the Impact of Unemployment

Given the profound effects of unemployment, it is critical that individuals, businesses, and communities develop mechanisms for reducing the impact of unemployment on people. For example, we saw in Chapter 3 that sudden and unexpected change is generally more stressful than change that is gradual and expected. Therefore, one way to reduce the stressfulness of unemployment is to forewarn workers who may

## Coping with Unemployment   (continued)

**Find out who's hurting.**   Let everyone say what he or she is *really* feeling from time to time.

After someone speaks, repeat whatever you heard. Then look for a nod to see if you heard it right. Is someone feeling:

1. helpless
2. sad
3. unloved
4. confused
5. worried
6. frightened
6. angry
7. like a burden to the family

Try not to say, "you shouldn't feel that way" because someone may be in real pain. The best you can do is let your loved ones have their say and get it off their chest.

**Let your feelings out, together or alone.**   Give everyone in your family space and time to let deep feelings out. Don't bottle them up, or hide them from yourself. If you're not comfortable showing others how you feel or fear you may strike someone who's dear to you, consider:

1. getting out of the house for a run or a brisk walk
2. having a good cry, alone
3. hitting a cushion or pillow
4. going to your room, shutting the door, and screaming
5. all of the above

**Solve problems together.**   Every week, look at the changes occurring in your household and develop ways to deal with them. Working together as a team, your family can do *more* than survive. It can grow together and come through stronger. Decide together things like:

1. what we can't afford now
2. what things we can do for family fun that don't cost a lot of money
3. who will do what chores around the house
4. how we'll all get by with less

If your discussions break down, go back to Step 1.

If you have a lot of trouble going through these steps, professional help may be what you need. Call and make an appointment with the family service agency nearest you. Whether or not you have money to pay for the services, the agency will do its best to help your family. Remember, you're not alone.

Source: Strong & DeVault, 1986, pp. 344, R40, R42.

lose their jobs. Communities that are struck by unemployment can help by treating the problem as a genuine crisis and making treatment facilities known and available to the unemployed and their families.

At the individual level, a well-functioning social support network of family and friends can significantly reduce the stress associated with unemployment. Also, as described in the Psychology in Action on pp. 482–83, there are a number of specific steps an unemployed person can take to minimize the stressfulness of losing a job.

Through the utilization of all of the available resources, the unemployed individual can greatly increase his or her chances of adaptive adjustment to this major life change (Dooley & Catalano, 1980).

## LEISURE

If work has the connotation of drudgery, leisure usually evokes images of lounging around a beach or swimming pool on a warm, sunny day, sipping cool drinks. However, as we shall see, leisure is more complex than this. In this final section of the chapter, we will consider the relationship between leisure and work, and discuss some ways in which leisure can be used for personal growth.

### Nonwork, Leisure, and Maintenance

Let's start by noting that in general leisure activities occur during nonwork time. However, not all activities that occur outside of the work setting are "leisure" activities. As Kabanoff (1980) has suggested, at least a portion of everyone's nonwork time is spent in **maintenance activities** such as cleaning up after dinner, buying food, and sleeping. These activities are necessary parts of life. People need to obtain food and sleep to continue living. Similarly, social conventions require that people clean dishes after a meal, wash clothes, and take baths and showers. These various required activities are not what is meant by "leisure."

**maintenance activities:** nonwork activities that are required or expected for normal daily functioning

**leisure:** nonwork, nonmaintenance activities involving prescribed tasks that people choose for their intrinsic motivating qualities

In contrast, **leisure** is "a set of activities that individuals perform outside their work context and excludes essential maintenance functions" (Kabanoff, 1980, p. 69). As explained by Kabanoff, this definition of leisure contains five points:

1. *Nonwork context.* In general, leisure activities occur outside work situations. According to this definition, a business lunch or golf date with customers of a firm would not be considered leisure.

2. *Nonmaintenance activities.* Maintenance activities are also excluded from the definition of leisure.

3. *Element of choice.* People who engage in leisure activities do so because they choose to—they are free to engage in the activity or not, as they wish.

4. *Intrinsic motivation.* The motivation for engaging in leisure activities is primarily personal and individual. People engage in leisure activities because the activity is personally meaningful.

5. *Absence of monetary reward as a motivator.* People engage in leisure activities because they are enjoyable in their own right, not because they get paid for their activities. This part of the definition excludes professional athletes and other people whose activities may seem to involve leisure but which are actually work activities instead.

### The Relationship Between Work and Leisure

Psychologists and sociologists have developed a number of theories in an effort to explain the relationship between work and leisure. In this section, we shall discuss

*Psychologists and sociologists have different theories about the relationship between work and leisure, but most agree that key factors in leisure are a nonwork context, personally satisfying activity, and the freedom to choose whether or not to participate.*

three approaches that have been developed to help understand this relationship: the compensatory hypothesis; the alienation hypothesis; and the segmentalist hypothesis.

**The compensatory hypothesis.** The **compensatory hypothesis** suggests that people use leisure as a way to release tensions and deprivations that have accumulated at work. In essence, according to this view leisure provides a way to "blow off steam."

Some research studies provide support for this view of leisure. In one such study (Mansfield & Evans, 1975), the management and personnel of a bank were asked to rate their satisfactions at work and leisure. The researchers found that people who reported feeling dissatisfied at work attempted to compensate for their dissatisfaction through leisure activities.

**The alienation hypothesis.** The **alienation hypothesis** suggests that qualities of the job "spill over" into leisure activities. According to this view, people who are satisfied with their jobs should report more involvement in satisfying leisure activities, while those who are dissatisfied at work should also report being less satisfied in their leisure activities.

**compensatory hypothesis:** theory that leisure offsets accumulated work tensions and work dissatisfaction

**alienation hypothesis:** theory that people who are satisfied in their work will also tend to be satisfied with their leisure activities

In support of this hypothesis, Meissner (1971) found that people whose jobs required a high degree of personal involvement and social interaction were more likely to be involved in leisure activities. Conversely, people whose jobs called for little or no personal involvement, such as unskilled workers on an assembly line, were likely to report little participation in voluntary social and leisure activities. These findings have also been extended to the personal adjustment of workers: people whose jobs require individual responsibility and who have higher wages and status also tend to have better mental health.

**The segmentalist hypothesis.**    Unlike the compensatory and alienation hypotheses which propose a relationship between work and leisure, the **segmentalist hypothesis** suggests that work and leisure are psychologically independent (Dubin, 1958; Kabanoff, 1980). If the segmentalist hypothesis is correct, there should be no relationship between work and leisure satisfaction.

**segmentalist hypothesis:** theory that work satisfactions and involvement in leisure activities are independent of each other

In one examination of this hypothesis (London, Crandall, & Seals, 1977), a sample of 1,297 American workers were interviewed about aspects of their leisure, work, and quality of life. The results indicated that job satisfaction and leisure satisfaction were related to higher overall quality of life. However, job satisfaction and leisure satisfaction showed very little relationship to one another. Thus, the quality of work and leisure contribute to the quality of life, but for most American workers work and leisure activities are separate and unrelated.

With further thought, it is not surprising that there is some supporting evidence for each of the three theories of leisure. Just as people work for many different reasons—for example, money, security, and personal development—people engage in leisure activities for a variety of reasons. The relationship between work and leisure depends to a great extent on each individual person's characteristics.

In fact, a number of studies have identified several different relationships between work and leisure as well as the personal characteristics of the individuals who fit these patterns (Kabanoff & O'Brien, 1980; Kando & Summers, 1971):

1. *Passive generalization.* This pattern is characterized by low levels of satisfaction in both work and leisure activities. People who showed this pattern tended to be males with low education and low income. Additionally, these individuals typically sought extrinsic rather than intrinsic satisfactions from their work.

2. *Supplemental compensation.* This pattern describes low involvement in work but high involvement in leisure activities. People in this group tended to have low income and low intrinsic work motivation. While a large percentage were older women, a substantial proportion were fairly young men and women whose work and leisure patterns seemed to fit the compensatory theory described above: satisfaction in leisure activities tended to offset dissatisfaction in the work setting.

3. *Active generalization.* People in this category reported high involvement in both work and leisure. The individuals who best fit this pattern tended to be well-educated and well-paid. The satisfactions they derived from work were primarily intrinsic. The high level of leisure activity, however, suggests that they used leisure to fulfill additional personal needs that were not met at work (Parker, 1971).

4. *Reactive compensation.* In this category, people reported high involvement in work and low involvement in leisure. People in this category tended to be males

who were primarily extrinsically motivated in their work. These are "job-centered" individuals for whom work satisfactions are primarily economic.

These patterns illustrate some of the ways in which work and leisure can be related to one another. However, they also demonstrate that the relationship between leisure and work is complex and highly dependent on personal characteristics and satisfactions (see Psychology in Action, p. 488).

## Making the Most of Leisure Time

How can leisure time be used effectively for personal growth? Numerous studies, summarized by Kabanoff (1980), have shown that a decrease in work time does not automatically result in an equivalent increase in leisure activities. Although the historical trend is toward a shorter work week, for example, many people do not use the available nonwork time in a personally productive fashion. For example, although many people who are placed on a four-day work week initially report substantial satisfaction with their new working hours, most of them subsequently report a decrease in satisfaction over time. Apparently, the reason is that much of the time available for leisure is filled with maintenance activities rather than by leisure activities. As a result, little personal growth can occur (Linder, 1970).

To take full advantage of leisure time requires planning for personally beneficial leisure activities. Nonwork time is unstructured time, and an individual can choose

*Getting the most out of your free time requires that you plan time for both maintenance and leisure activities. More personal growth occurs when you get involved in personally satisfying leisure activities.*

# Psychology in Action

how that time will be allocated. While a certain amount of time must be allocated to maintenance activities, each of us has considerable leeway in deciding how the remaining portion of time can be spent. We can, on the one hand, use the time to meet with friends, engage in physical activities, or work on a favorite hobby. In other words, we can choose to use our leisure time for personal growth and fulfillment, or we can choose to fill our leisure time with maintenance activities and "busy work."

The need to choose and plan for leisure becomes especially evident during the retirement years. Retirees, more than any other adult group, are subject to the adjustive challenge of a sudden increase in nonwork time. As we noted earlier, at least initially this freedom is often greeted with a sense of relief and enthusiasm. However, only those who have well-developed social and familial contacts and personally rewarding activities to engage their time are likely to find that retirement represents an opportunity for personal growth (O'Brien, 1981).

## SUMMARY

*Work* is more than just "paid employment." The best definition of work seems to be "an activity that produces something of value for other people." It follows that virtually all people, both men and women, spend most of their adult lives working either inside or outside of the home, though in recent years there has been a sharp increase in the number of women who work outside the home.

Traditionally it has been assumed that work must be unpleasant and that people engage in work only for *extrinsic satisfactions* such as money. The *Theory X* approach to management follows this view of work and emphasizes the importance of extrinsic rewards and close monitoring and supervision to assure high productivity among employees.

However, it is now recognized that work also plays an important psychological role in people's lives, whether they are white-collar or blue-collar workers: it contributes to personal identity, self-esteem, and social status. It follows from this that being unemployed or being forced to retire can have profound psychological effects. Moreover, low status jobs can have negative effects on people who must work in them. Companies that acknowledge the psychological significance of work are said to endorse the *Theory Y* approach to management. They are likely to emphasize the *intrinsic satisfaction* of working, attend to making jobs interesting, and involve employees in decisions that affect them and their work.

Given the importance of work in people's lives, selecting the "right" occupation is an important decision. The groundwork for occupational choice is established long before a final decision is made. Young children go through a *fantasy period* in which they try out all kinds of occupational roles while they play. Adolescents, in the *tentative period,* begin to make preliminary career choices that reflect their abilities, interests, opportunities, and values. Young adulthood ushers in the *realistic choice stage* in which reality plays a larger role in occupational choice; during this stage, the young adult is likely to experience processes of exploration and crystallization before finally making a tentative commitment to a career.

Being able to choose a career is a relatively recent phenomenon. In earlier times, people were either forced into a career or their choices were quite limited. Today, the range of career choices is broad and to a great extent a person's choice of a career is a matter of personal preference. However the large and growing number of occupational roles increases the difficulty involved in selecting the "right" occupation.

In choosing a career, both the characteristics of the individual and the characteristics of the occupation must be considered. On the individual side, it is important to consider interests, values, attitudes, preferred style of life, skills, abilities, limitations, and economic constraints. As for the career, it is important to consider the

*One source of work dissatisfaction is a boring or repetitive job. Work dissatisfaction can, in turn, lead to job stress.*

training, skills, and personal characteristics required; the life style required; the rewards and satisfactions provided; and potential changes in the nature of the job in the near and distant future. Ideally, the individual will find at least one career that matches closely his or her characteristics.

In the process of selecting a career, experience working in the job, conversations with people who hold comparable jobs, and career counseling can all be helpful. *Interest inventories* can also be useful. For example, Holland identified six basic personality types: Realistic, Investigative, Artistic, Social, Enterprising, and Conventional. According to Holland's *hexagonal model,* each person is a mix of these six types. Moreover, each occupation is best suited to people with a particular mix of these six types: people whose careers tend to match their personal characteristics are also likely to stay in those careers longer and experience greater satisfaction than people whose careers do not closely match their personal characteristics.

Work dissatisfaction can contribute to job stress. Some people are dissatisfied with their work because they chose an inappropriate career or because they change (or their jobs change) over time. Dissatisfaction can also stem from inherently boring or repetitive jobs, from *overeducation,* from excessively high expectations, from lack of appreciation for skills developed outside the work setting, or from discrimination.

While job dissatisfaction contributes to job-related stress, some jobs are inherently more stressful than others. High pressure jobs, as well as jobs characterized by frustration and conflict, are likely to be especially stressful.

Coping effectively with job-related stress requires the same techniques as coping with any stressful situation. The first step is to control the physiological, emotional, and cognitive reactions to the stressful situation. Once these reactions are brought under control, efforts can be made to reduce or eliminate the source of the stress. This requires evaluation of the stressful situation to identify the most likely sources of stress, identifying various courses of action (perhaps attacking the problem, or withdrawing, or compromising), evaluating the various possible actions in terms of their rewards and costs, putting the best alternative into action, and using feedback to adjust and modify one's behavior subsequently. However, not all should be avoided, since stress is also a source of personal growth.

Unemployment can also be a source of great stress. While it causes financial difficulty, it also may have serious consequences in terms of self-devaluation and loss of self-esteem. One study of unemployment among middle-class male scientists and engineers found that the initial reaction of relaxation and relief was soon followed by systematic efforts to find new work. When these efforts failed, job-seeking behavior became sporadic and eventually came to a halt entirely as the men became listless and apathetic.

The stressfulness of unemployment can be reduced by providing workers with warnings that they may lose their jobs, by marshalling community resources and making them available to unemployed people. In addition, there are numerous steps that can be taken by the unemployed individuals themselves to reduce significantly the stress they experience.

At least part of everyone's nonwork time is devoted to required or expected *maintenance activities* such as eating and sleeping. For most people, some additional nonwork time is allocated to *leisure* activities that are enjoyable in their own right. As predicted by the *segmentalist hypothesis,* there is no single relationship between work and leisure that applies to everyone. For some people the *compensatory hypothesis* seems most appropriate: leisure activities are used as a way of releasing tensions that have accumulated at work and providing satisfactions that are missing from work. For other people, the *alienation hypothesis* seems most accurate: people who are quite satisfied with their work are also involved in satisfying leisure activities, while those who are dissatisfied with their work are also dissatisfied with their leisure time.

If leisure time is to be used effectively, it must be planned for and appropriately used. Otherwise, it is likely to be filled with maintenance activities. With careful planning, leisure activities can contribute to personal growth and development.

## KEY TERMS

work (460)
extrinsic satisfaction (461)
Theory X (461)
Theory Y (462)
intrinsic satisfactions (462)
Theory Z (464)
fantasy period (465)
tentative period (465)
realistic choice stage (465)

interest inventories (468)
hexagonal model (469)
overeducation (472)
burnout (473)
maintenance activities (484)
leisure (484)
compensatory hypothesis (485)
alienation hypothesis (485)
segmentalist hypothesis (486)

# Adjusting to Living in Groups

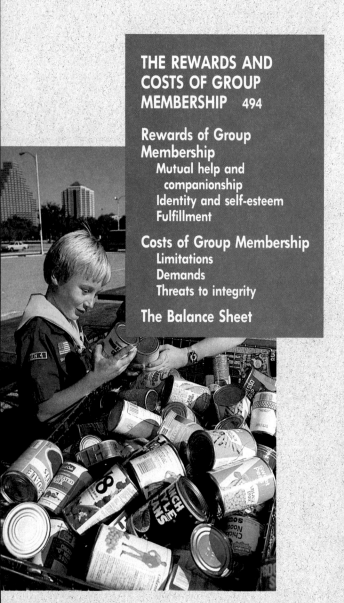

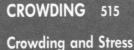

*If it were possible for the overworked hypothetical man from Mars to take a fresh view of the people of Earth, he would probably be impressed by the amount of time they spend doing things together in groups. He would note that most people cluster into relatively small groups, with the members residing together in the same dwelling, satisfying their basic biological needs within the group, depending upon the same source for economic support, rearing children, and mutually caring for the health of one another. He would observe that the education and socialization of children tend to occur in other, usually larger, groups in churches, schools, and other social institutions. He would see that much of the work of the world is carried out by people who perform their activities in close interdependence within relatively enduring associations. He would perhaps be saddened to find groups of men engaged in warfare, gaining courage and morale from pride in their unit and a knowledge that they can depend on their buddies. He might be gladdened to see groups of people enjoying themselves in recreations and sports of various kinds. Finally he might be puzzled why so many people spend so much time in little groups talking, planning, and being "in conference."*

*Group Dynamics: Research and Theory* (Cartwright & Zander, 1968, p. 3)

THROUGHOUT this book, we have seen the extent to which people interact with and depend on other people, the degree to which human beings are group creatures. Only recently, however, have psychologists systematically studied the ways in which individuals and groups mutually influence each other. In these ways, they have added greatly to our understanding of human behavior.

In this chapter, we shall concern ourselves with stress that arises in groups and other social settings. Specifically, we shall study (1) why people belong to groups; (2) social influence, and ways of coping effectively with pressures to conform, comply, and obey others; (3) fear of communicating in social situations, and ways of coping effectively with that fear; and (4) crowding, and ways of dealing effectively with the stress that results from feeling crowded. We begin by exploring briefly the reasons people belong to groups.

## THE REWARDS AND COSTS OF GROUP MEMBERSHIP

By observing people even casually, we see that much of their time is spent in groups. If we take a closer look at any individual, we will find that he or she is a member of a large number of groups. Groups evolve and persist because some important needs of individuals are best met in group settings. Among the benefits of group membership are mutual help, companionship, identity, self-esteem, and fulfillment.

*Belonging to a group has a number of benefits. Working in groups satisfies a person's need for companionship, builds a sense of identity and self-esteem, and gives life a sense of fulfillment.*

## Rewards of Group Membership

**Mutual help and companionship.**   People belong to many groups to benefit from various kinds of mutual help. For example, membership in some groups helps to provide food, shelter, and companionship. This is one of the functions of a family— or of sharing an apartment! While it is possible for individuals to provide their own food and shelter and care for themselves in other respects, it is not easy to do so even in reasonably favorable circumstances. In large cities, such self-sufficiency is virtually impossible. Moreover, an individual's needs for companionship can only be satisfied in group settings. While some people learn to live alone in relative solitude, most find the presence of other people a source of great comfort. In fact, for many people the threat of social ostracism can be a very powerful persuader.

**Identity and self-esteem.**   Group membership can also satisfy needs for identity and self-esteem. For example, we saw in Chapter 13 that work is an important source of identity and self-esteem for most individuals. Similarly, belonging to a community group or a task force can provide an important source of identity: "I am a concerned citizen. I am also a person who is willing to share my time with others who are in need of it. I have valuable ideas that are respected by others." As people participate in many group settings, their identity and self-esteem can be enhanced.

**Fulfillment.**   Moreover, many human potentials can be realized only in groups. The joys of loving and being loved, the feeling of being needed, the opportunity to make a lasting contribution to society and achieve a sense of generativity—all these and many other opportunities for personal growth and fulfillment are found only in group settings. Without groups there is also no opportunity for leadership, no continuity of values, no shared visions, and no sowing of seeds that others can harvest. Without ties to other people, there is no enlargement of the self to include a family, a nation, or a people.

As you may have noticed, even as I have described the rewards of group membership, I have also hinted at some of the costs.

## Costs of Group Membership

**Limitations.**   The first cost of group membership is the experience of limitations on your freedom. As children, everyone learns that the people who protect and care for them also restrict them. As adults, people continue to discover that membership in groups is accompanied by limitations. To be a member of a particular church we must limit our behavior. If we are active in a political party, beliefs that are contrary to the party line cannot be easily expressed. Even leisure activities are subject to limitations: there are rules for playing golf and tennis, there are a limited number of tickets to plays and concerts, and there are limitations on people's behavior when attending such events. This is nothing new: the rules for boarding house behavior in the 1800's listed such things as no chickens in a room, and emptying the spitoon before leaving. Some of the constraints on behavior make the group function smoothly, but other limits imposed by groups constrain the behavior of group members. They can lead to frustration, conflict, and pressure, and as we saw in Chapter 3, each of these contributes to stress.

**Demands.**   Groups not only set limits, they make demands on their members. Sometimes these demands can become an additional source of stress. There is, first of all, and perhaps most important, the demand of loyalty: "Are you with us or against us?" If a person feels loyal to several groups, the result can be a classic approach-approach conflict of the sort described in Chapter 3: there are several desirable goals (groups, in this case), but the demand of loyalty requires that only one can be chosen. For instance, someone who belongs to the local Chamber of Commerce and to a group dedicated to environmental protection may suddenly have to choose between the one group that expects its members to support local industries and the other group that expects its members to boycott certain local industries which contribute to environmental pollution. Not surprisingly, the person who must choose between the groups is likely to experience stress as a result of such demands for exclusive loyalty.

Most groups also demand a measure of conformity, compliance, and obedience. These demands—to behave correctly, wear the "correct" clothes, say the "right" things, take the "correct" stand on issues—can be one of the highest and most stressful costs of group membership. You will learn a great deal more in the remainder of this chapter and the next about the costs associated with demands for conformity in groups.

Finally, there are demands for responsible participation—for assuming specified roles, paying dues and taxes, voting, or supporting group leaders. For example, a neighborhood association may form to build a park for the community. However, to reap the benefits of the park, community residents may have to join the organization or pay fees to use the park. Membership in an organization opposed to a public works project that will damage the natural environment may require writing letters to public officials, speaking out against the project in public hearings or community meetings, gathering community support, and so on. These demands all require precious resources (such as time and money), and they may also conflict with demands of other groups to which a person belongs, such as a work group or the person's family. As a result, they can lead to considerable stress for even the strongest supporter of the group.

**Threats to integrity.**    The limitations and demands of group membership may also pose a threat to an individual's integrity. All group life requires compromises. However, how far can a person compromise before losing his or her soul? When is silence discreet and when is it cowardly? When is dissent irresponsible and when is it courageous? There are no easy answers here, and the struggle for integrity by people who love the group but have misgivings about its actions can be intensely painful. This price of group membership makes many people reluctant to join groups and commit themselves to group goals. This topic is also a central concern throughout the remainder of this book (see the Insight, p. 498).

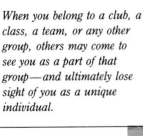

*When you belong to a club, a class, a team, or any other group, others may come to see you as a part of that group—and ultimately lose sight of you as a unique individual.*

# *Insight*

## Group or Individual: Which Is Better for Task Performance?

We have examined some of the rewards and some of the costs of group membership. If we weigh one against the other, how do they balance? Each of us will find a different answer. For some, the costs are greater than the rewards, and for others the rewards are greater than the costs. The balance is also different for each group to which we belong.

In situations in which the labor is divided and the achievement of the final goal requires the coordination of many people, groups are essential. Examples include playing a Beethoven string quartet, mass-producing automobiles, or providing mental-health services for a large community. In such instances, group action clearly represents an improvement over individual action.

When the task involves problem solving, research suggests that groups produce more and better solutions to some problems than do individuals. There are many factors that may account for this, including the integration or coordination of individual strengths; rejection of incorrect suggestions and the checking of errors; and social stimulation and the arousal of greater interest in the task. On the other hand, when time is a factor, the number of person-hours per solution is lower for the individual than for the group. Although groups may provide superior solutions in many instances, efficiency is the price that must be paid.

Shaw (1971) has summarized his finding: "Groups are more effective than individuals on tasks which require a variety of information, which can be solved by adding individual contributions, and which require a number of steps that must be correctly completed in a definite order; individuals are better on tasks that call for centralized organization of parts. Groups perform better than individuals when the process is learning or problem solving, but not necessarily when the process investigated is judgment. These conclusions are based upon measures of outcome; when the measure of effectiveness is the amount of investment per man, individuals are generally shown to be more efficient." (pp. 70-71)

In decision-making, group participation can have a number of interesting effects. At one time, it was assumed that group interaction would eliminate radical or risky alternatives, resulting in a conservative decision that was acceptable to all members (Whyte, 1956). Researchers have since found that some people are willing to make a riskier decision after they have discussed the decision in a group than if they had decided alone (Wallach, Kogan, & Bem, 1962). This phenomenon is called the risky shift.

Further research has suggested that group interaction can shift decisions either way, toward greater risk or greater caution (Fraser, 1971; Moscovici & Zavalloni, 1969). Social psychologists now believe that this is part of a more general effect called the shift toward polarization. Following a group discussion, an individual's views will become more extreme, in either the risky or cautious direction.

## The Balance Sheet

We have seen that group membership has some unique rewards, but it also incurs some costs. In Chapter 10, the social exchange model illustrated that each person has to balance rewards and costs before deciding to continue belonging to various groups. If the costs are far greater than the rewards, the decision is usually clear: leave the group. However, in cases where that action is not possible, the individual is likely to experience a great deal of stress.

On the other hand, if the rewards are far greater than the costs, it is sensible to join or to remain in the group. However, this can be stressful also, since the group continues to impose some undesirable costs. For example, even if you value working for a particular company and do not want to change jobs, you may still find the work stressful and the job may impose frustrating limitations and demands upon you.

Even when the rewards and costs of group membership are relatively balanced, when there are nearly as many reasons to leave a group as to stay in it, a person can experience stress. This is an example of an approach-avoidance conflict which, as we saw in Chapter 3, can lead to high levels of stress.

While groups add an important dimension to people's lives and to the stability and continuity of society, they can also be a source of considerable stress. In the remainder of this chapter, we will examine several common sources of stress that arise in groups. We begin with social influence.

## SOCIAL INFLUENCE

*To most of us, conformity is a dirty word evoking images of robot-like acceptance of the attitudes, opinions, and beliefs of others.*
    *The Psychology of Being Human* (McNeil, 1974, p. 410)

It was hell night. For the initiation, each of the pledges had to drink a bottle of whiskey. Allan didn't want to; he said alcohol made him sick, he couldn't stand it. The guys razzed him, told him he was a baby, he was chicken, he wasn't good enough to be in the fraternity. I don't know. . . . I was worried, 'cause he sounded pretty serious. . . . I mean, he was really upset about having to drink the stuff. I told Bob that maybe we shouldn't make him drink it, but he got angry and started calling me names. . . . He said "You're either with us or against us. Which is it going to be?" Nobody else seemed to be worried, and I didn't want to rock the boat, so I went along with the rest of the guys. I razzed Allan, too, really got on his case. Eventually, he drank the whole bottle.

Later that night, Allan was taken to the emergency room of the local hospital where he later died of alcohol poisoning. Even though several fraternity members said that they had been worried about forcing Allan to drink the alcohol, nobody did anything to stop the hazing. Why not?

### Forms of Social Influence

**social influence:** implicit or explicit pressure to become like other group members

**conformity:** yielding to social influence without being asked or instructed to do so

The answer is found in a greater understanding of social influence. **Social influence** refers to pressure of one sort or another to change an individual's behavior, opinions, beliefs, attitudes, values. In some situations, often without being asked, people change their behavior or opinions to match those of other people. This is called **conformity.** For example, most people in our culture wear dark clothes to a funeral although they are not specifically asked or instructed to do so; it is simply customary.

On the other hand, in some Asian countries the custom is to wear white, and members of those societies tend to conform to that cultural expectation. Other examples of conformity are easy to find: students on campus this year seem to have a fondness for blue jeans that are ripped in one knee; they are conforming to a current fad, in most cases without actually being asked or instructed to do so. Nearly every campus has one fast food outlet which is known as a place "where all the freshmen hang out" and indeed most of the patrons there are first year students. No one instructs the upper class students to avoid that restaurant; it is simply common knowledge that most upper level students eat elsewhere. In all of these cases, social influence is subtle but effective: people's behaviors, opinions, attitudes, and so on are relatively uniform without anyone making a request or issuing an order (see the Psychology in Action, p. 501).

In other cases, people change their behavior or their opinions because they are specifically asked to do so. This is called **compliance.** Perhaps someone asks you to sign a petition, and you do so, or a roommate asks to borrow a book, and you agree. A friend asks you to drive them home from a party, and you say, "Sure." In these and other cases of compliance, behaviors or opinions or attitudes change in response to a specific request or suggestion from someone else.

In still other cases, people do something because they are ordered or instructed to do so by someone in a position of authority. In these cases, psychologists speak of **obedience.** You file your federal tax forms by April 15 because you have been

**compliance:** yielding to social influence as a result of a specific request to do so

**obedience:** yielding to explicit orders or instructions from another person

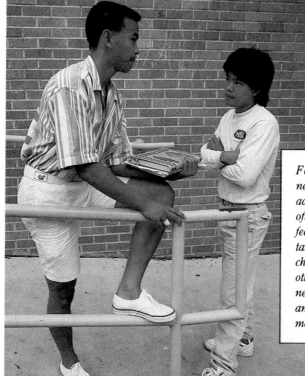

*Feeling as if you belong is necessary for healthy adjustment, but there are often costs involved. If you feel you must conform, must take on the same characteristics or beliefs as others in your group, you need to weigh the benefits and the costs of group membership very carefully.*

## Social Contagion

Sometimes social influence takes the form of *social contagion:* a form of irrational behavior that spreads rapidly throughout a group and that puzzles even the members of the group when it is over. Social contagion can include rumors and panics. One recent rumor claimed that a well-known fast-food chain was placing horsemeat into its hamburgers. This rumor became so prevalent that the firm began to lose business. Only an intensive advertising campaign stressing the "100 percent beef" content of the hamburgers prevented serious damage to the firm. Similarly, a rumor continues in many parts of the country claiming that the collection of many thousands of tax stamps from cigarette packages and their delivery to some (unknown) firm will result in the donation of a kidney dialysis machine to the National Kidney Foundation.

In large cities, the effects of a rumor can be devastating, leading to civil disobedience and violence. In an attempt to limit the effects of rumors, many cities have established rumor control "hot lines," telephone numbers that residents of a city can call to receive current and correct information. Presumably, this corrct information limits the degree to which a rumor is taken seriously.

Panic is another, more dramatic example of social contagion. The flavor of such social contagion has been well captured by humorist James Thurber (1933):

*Suddenly somebody began to run. It may be that he had simply remembered, all of a moment, an engagement to meet his wife, for which he was now frightfully late. Whatever it was, he ran east on Broad Street (probably toward the Maramor Restaurant, a favorite place for a man to meet his wife). Somebody else began to run, perhaps a newsboy in high spirits. Another man, a portly gentleman of affairs, broke into a trot. Inside of ten minutes, everybody on Broad Street, from the Union depot to the Courthouse was running. A loud mumble gradually crystallized into the dread word "dam." "The dam has broke!" Two thousand people were abruptly in full flight. "Go east!" was the cry that arose—east away from the river, east to safety. "Go east! Go east!"* . . . .

*A tall spare woman with grim eyes and a determined chin ran past me down the middle of the street. I was still uncertain as to what was the matter, in spite of all the shouting. I drew up alongside the woman with some effort, for although she was in her late fifties, she had a beautiful easy running form and seemed to be in excellent condition. "What is it?" I puffed. She gave me a quick glance and then looked ahead again, stepping up her pace a trifle. " Don't ask me, ask God!" she said. (pp. 41-42, 47)*

Unfortunately, social contagion is not usually this comical. A more serious example of social contagion has been described by Kerckhoff and Back (1968). These researchers reported on an outbreak of "hysterical contagion" in a clothing factory. In this incident, 62 workers from a total of 965 reported an illness that they presumed was caused by a bug bite. Almost all the affected workers worked in the dressmaking department. One woman reported her experience.

*I was bit by the bug and it was such a sudden and sharp bite, you really didn't know what happened. It felt like a pin sticking me. Then the pain went down and up my arm and into my neck. I walked about six steps, and my legs started getting weak, and I just passed out. (p. 8)*

There were many more "cases" reported to the factory officials and medical authorities. Some affected were hospitalized; some vomited; some had seizures. Although health officials found no insects that could cause such an extreme reaction, the building was "debugged." After one week, the "epidemic" was over.

The researchers reported that the outbreak occurred during a peak production time in a new factory in which personnel policies were not yet well formed. As a result, many workers were experiencing an extraordinary level of stress. It appeared that the "epidemic" was an expression of their common anxiety and concerns. In fact, prior to the outbreak rumors had circulated around the factory that the building was infested.

instructed to do so by the Internal Revenue Service. You hand in your term paper before the deadline set by the professor. You stop your car when a police officer instructs you to do so. You write a memo that summarizes your month's sales activity if your supervisor instructs you to do so. In all of these cases, behavior is changed as a result of explicit instructions or orders from another person.

Psychologists have been interested in all these kinds of social influence for many different reasons, two of which are especially important for our purposes:

1. *Social influence can be a source of considerable stress.* For example, you might prefer not to lend more money to a friend who already owes you $20, but you fear you will endanger the friendship if you say "No." The fraternity member described at the start of this section experienced a great deal of stress as he tried to decide whether to comply with the hazing activities.

2. *The act of conforming, complying, or obeying is an example of adaptation and adjustment.* In every case of social influence, behaviors, opinions, beliefs, or values change in response to some kind of adjustive demand. As with other kinds of adaptation and coping we have studied in this book, we will see that some ways of coping with social influence are more effective than others.

In the next section, we will first consider several classic research studies on the nature of social influence. Then we will discuss the reasons people yield to social influence and the pros and cons of social influence. Finally, we will consider a number of effective ways in which people can resist social influence in situations where that is appropriate.

## Social Influence in the Laboratory

Psychologists have conducted a number of ingenious experiments in an effort to understand how social influence works. In one particularly simple but compelling demonstration of conformity, Milgram, Bickman, and Berkowitz (1969) placed five research assistants on a sidewalk in New York City and instructed them to stand silently, staring up at a sixth-floor window in a nearby building. The researchers discovered that 70 percent of the people passing by stopped and also looked up at the window! Nobody asked them to; in fact, none of the research assistants said anything at all, but the passersby changed their behavior, nonetheless.

A more elaborate study of conformity was conducted by Solomon Asch (1952, 1955). In his classic experiment, small groups of male college students were shown three lines on a card (Figure 14.1a) and asked to determine which of the three lines was the same length as a fourth line on a different card (Figure 14.1b). On every trial, one of the three lines was the same length as the fourth line while the other two lines were either shorter or longer. Asch determined in advance that the correct choice in each case was clearly distinguishable.

In every group, all but one of the subjects were actually "stooges," research assistants who were instructed to make a unaminous wrong choice on certain trials. Moreover, most of the stooges announced their judgments before the real subject had an opportunity to announce his own judgment. Thus, on the predetermined trials the subject was faced with a conflict: if he made the clearly correct choice, he would have to disagree with all the other people in the group. If he agreed with the group,

**FIGURE 14.1a**
**Comparison Lines.**

**14.1b**
**Standard Line.**

(a)

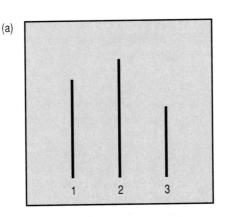

(b)

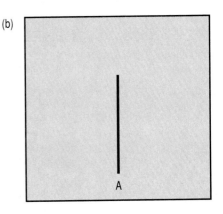

he would have to say something that clearly was not correct. In other words, the subject had to choose between lying and contradicting the judgment of the group. What do you think the subjects did?

Asch found that about a fourth of the subjects never conformed to the group when its judgments were wrong. In contrast, a few subjects yielded to the incorrect majority decision at nearly every opportunity. On average, the subjects yielded to the erroneous group about one-third of the time, although the group consensus was clearly wrong in each case and although nobody had asked them or instructed them to conform to the majority.

Why did the subjects in Asch's experiment yield to the erroneous majority as often as they did? When the subjects were interviewed after the experiment, it was found that some continued to believe the validity of their own judgments but yielded to the erroneous group out of fear of "seeming different." Others concluded that, although their own perceptions clearly seemed correct, the majority could not be wrong. In a small number of cases, it appeared that the subject really believed the group's judgment was correct and was totally unaware of having yielded to group pressure! We will return shortly to the reasons why people yield to social influence.

One of the criticisms of the Asch study was that the task—judging the length of lines on cards—was so trivial that it was not surprising that people were willing to surrender to the group. According to this view, it seems likely that people would be less willing to agree in situations where the task is more significant. In one of the most controversial studies of social influence ever conducted, psychologist Stanley Milgram (1963, 1968) tested this hypothesis. Milgram recruited volunteer subjects who were told that they would be involved in a study concerning the effect of punishment on learning. The subjects, all male, were tested in groups of two. One of the subjects was told that he would be the learner, and the other was told that he would be the teacher. Actually, the experiment was rigged so that in every case, the "learner" was an accomplice of the experimenter while the real subject was always assigned to be the teacher.

The "teacher" was seated in front of an impressive looking machine with many switches, lights, dials and buttons. He was told that the machine would deliver shocks ranging from 15 to 450 volts to the learner, who was strapped into a chair in an adjacent room. The teacher was instructed to shock the learner each time that the learner made a mistake, and to increase the level of the shock by 15 volts with each mistake. While the learner was never actually shocked, a tape recording was played on which the learner variously grunted, pounded on the table, shouted and screamed in agony to make it sound as if he was receiving the shocks and was eventually experiencing real pain. If a teacher balked at continuing to administer shocks, the experimenter would simply say "Please continue" or "The experiment requires that you continue" or "You must go on."

What would you have done in this experiment? How strong a shock would you have administered before refusing to continue? Milgram asked more than 100 people this question before he conducted the experiment. He found that no one believed they would deliver a shock stronger than 300 volts; on average, they said they would stop at about 135 volts. A group of psychiatrists, when asked to predict people's behavior in the experiment, predicted that only one person in a thousand would administer the maximum 450-volt shock.

In fact, Milgram discovered that every one of his subjects administered at least 300 volts of "shock" (labeled "INTENSE SHOCK" on the instrument and accompanied by agonized screams from the "learner"). Moreover, two-thirds of his subjects administered the maximum 450-volt "shock" even though the "learner" ceased to make any noise after he received 330 volts and screamed hysterically that his heart was bothering him. Milgram's "teachers" showed signs of extreme stress: they sweated, trembled, stuttered, and laughed nervously. However, to a remarkable degree, they obeyed the experimenter's instructions to continue with the experiment. When they were interviewed after the study, the subjects said that they had experienced tremendous pressure from the experimenter to continue administering the shocks.

These studies, and others like them, demonstrate in a dramatic way just how susceptible people are to social influence. Although we cannot generalize from these experiments to all of human behavior, the experiments show that under the proper conditions, people will behave in ways that are contrary to their beliefs and values as a result of very mild social influence. Why do people respond to social influence in this way? Why do people conform, comply, and obey?

## Why People Yield to Social Influence

According to Deutsch and Gerard (1955), there are basically two reasons that people yield to social influence: to be liked and to be right. Let's look at each of these explanations in greater detail.

**Normative influence.**    Many people yield to social influence because it is rewarding to do so; in cases of this sort, psychologists speak of **normative influence**. People who conform or comply with group norms and expectations are more likely to be liked by others and accepted into the group. On the other hand, people who refuse

**normative influence:** conforming, complying, or obeying in order to be liked or accepted by others

*Rejecting the norms of a social group is a difficult decision at any age—people want to be accepted and to feel their beliefs are correct. But there comes a time when "everyone's doing it" is not a good enough reason, when part of being a responsible person involves asserting your own beliefs.*

to yield to social influence are more likely to be rejected and ridiculed, the targets of disapproval, and considered "deviant." Most people learn these facts of life at an early age, and adjust their behavior in order to be liked and accepted. You may recall Rogers' notion of "conditional positive regard" that we discussed in Chapter 2. Conditional positive regard is an example of normative social influence.

The Asch experiment provides a clear demonstration of normative social influence at work: most of the subjects agreed with the erroneous group judgments simply to keep harmony in the group, to avoid conflict, and to be liked and accepted even though they believed the group's judgment was incorrect. You may recall another illustration of normative social influence that was discussed in Chapter 2: Victor S., the frustrated artist, explained, "I gave up part of myself because I cared about what other people thought of me. I wanted to be liked, I wanted to be loved, I wanted to be respected and accepted." Victor yielded to normative social influence in order to be liked and loved by others.

**informational influence:** conforming, complying, or obeying because of a desire to be correct or to do the correct thing

**Informational influence.**   On other occasions, however, people yield to social influence because of a desire to be right, to make the correct judgment, and to do the right thing. In these cases psychologists speak of **informational influence.** For example, in an unfamiliar situation, or when working on a difficult or ambiguous task, it is often hard to know what is right and wrong, correct and incorrect. In situations of this sort, there is a strong tendency to rely on others to indicate the right way to behave, the right thing to do. When I was first learning to fly, as I approached the airport for landing my flight instructor would call out, "Throttle back to 1500 rpm and maintain 70 knots airspeed." I did as I was told, not because I wanted him to like or accept me, but because I had no idea what I was doing, I wanted to live, and I figured (rightly) that he knew what I should do in order to land safely. You may have had a similar experience when visiting a foreign country, eating at an unfamiliar ethnic restaurant, or working on an unfamiliar task with others who have more experience and knowledge than you do. In uncertain, ambiguous, or unfamiliar situations, people tend to follow the majority in part because they believe that the majority is likely to be correct.

The Milgram et al. sidewalk study provides a demonstration of informational influence. People passing by apparently assumed that if five people had stopped to stare up at a building, there must be something important to see, and so they stopped and looked up also. The artist Victor S. also hinted at informational social influence in his life: "When so many people seemed to see me similarly, instead of holding fast to my own perceptions and trusting my experiences, I adopted other people's perceptions and conformed to their will." In other words, Victor believed that other people were better able to judge his skill and expertise than he was, and so he accepted and believed their vision of him.

## The Pros and Cons of Social Influence

Social influence serves a number of useful purposes. Normative influence helps to assure that important group and social tasks are accomplished in a smooth, coordinated fashion. Imagine what would happen, for example, if people could drive on whichever side of the road they prefer, pay only those bills they wish to pay, and do only what they feel like doing. If you are part of a work group, it is important for others to be able to depend on you to do your job, just as you must depend on them to do their jobs. Even in leisure situations, some conformity and compliance is beneficial: if you are playing tennis with a friend, for example, you are both more likely to enjoy yourselves if you play by the rules. In many situations, then, normative social influence helps to provide a measure of stability and predictability. It also helps to minimize change; and since change is a common source of stress, it follows that normative social influence serves to reduce stress in most people's lives.

Informational social influence also serves useful purposes. For example, it can increase security and safety: if you are visiting a strange country and notice that all the tourists avoid drinking the water, you might be well advised to do the same, at least until you have a chance to learn more about the water quality. If you are visiting an unfamiliar city and the desk clerk at your hotel warns you against walking alone at night in the neighborhood, you might be wise to heed that advice. If you are attending an unfamiliar religious ceremony and everyone else suddenly stands up, you can probably assume that standing is the proper and correct thing to do at that point in the ceremony. If the television weather forecaster predicts rain, or your financial adviser predicts a fall in the stock market, you probably should heed their advice unless your expertise and information is superior to theirs. In all these cases, the behavior of others provides useful information about what people ought to do in certain situations.

Aronson (1984) nicely illustrates the value of informational social influence.

> Suppose that you need to use the toilet in an unfamiliar classroom building. Under the sign "Rest Rooms" there are two doors, but, unfortunately, a vandal has removed the specific designations from the doors—that is, you cannot be certain which is the Men's room and which is the Women's room. Quite a dilemma—you are afraid to open either door for fear of being embarrassed or embarrassing others. As you stand there in dismay and discomfort, hopping from one foot to the other, the door on your left opens and out strolls a distinguished-looking gentleman. With a sigh of relief, you are now willing to forge ahead, reasonably secure in the knowledge that left is for men and right is for women. (p. 26)

We have seen that social influence serves a number of useful and important purposes, but there is also a negative side to social influence. Under some circumstances, pressures toward conformity can produce a stifling and unproductive uniformity that violates individual autonomy and can result in disaster. Although some measure of conformity is essential for coordinated group effort, some measure of nonconformity is also needed to assure the group's adaptability. If a group is to adapt effectively to changing conditions, it must be able to change appropriately. If a group's thinking and structure become rigid, if the group ceases to adapt and change, the group will cease to function effectively when faced with change (Buckley, 1968; Miller, 1977). It is essential for someone in the group to recognize new conditions, propose new approaches, and make other group members aware of the need for change. Someone in the group must have the integrity and commitment to values beyond the group to challenge the group when it is about to make mistakes. Change and effective adaptation come not from the majority but from a minority who "have a better idea."

The consequences of discouraging or ignoring minority viewpoints can be disastrous. In the hours before the space shuttle Challenger was launched, several engineers at Morton Thiokol Company expressed grave concerns about the effect of the cold temperatures on the launch vehicle. Their concerns were dismissed: the NASA official who was responsible for making the decision to launch the shuttle was never told of the engineers' concerns. Seven lives were lost when the launch vehicle exploded. In the mid-1960s, President Johnson surrounded himself with advisors who believed that escalating the war in Vietnam was the best way to achieve peace; more than 50,000 American lives were lost as a result (see Psychology in Action, p. 508).

Clearly, there are situations in which social influence must be resisted, in which nonconforming viewpoints must be expressed and heeded. In the next section of the chapter, we will explore various ways in which people can more effectively resist social influence in appropriate situations. However, resisting social influence can be extremely difficult. Even in the Asch study, where the pressures to conform were weak and the task was relatively unimportant, most of the subjects who refused to yield to the erroneous group said that they were bothered by their disagreement

# $P$sychology in $A$ction

The Characteristics of Groupthink

After analyzing a number of high-level decisions that led to historic fiascoes and blunders, such as the lack of preparedness at Pearl Harbor, the Bay of Pigs invasion, and the Vietnam War, Janis and Mann (1977) identified eight common characteristics that can lead to *groupthink*, the tendency to preserve group unity at the cost of ignoring danger signals. The following characteristics are adapted from Janis and Mann (1977):

1. An illusion of invulnerability—shared sense of invulnerability which creates excessive optimism and encourages taking extreme risks.

2. Rationalization—collective efforts to rationalize in order to discount warnings which might lead the members to reconsider their assumptions before they recommit themselves to their past policy decisions.

3. Unquestioned belief—an unquestioned belief in the group's inherent morality, inclining the members to ignore the ethical or moral consequences of their decisions.

4. Stereotyped views—rivals and enemies are perceived as too evil to warrant genuine attempts to negotiate, or as too weak or stupid to counter whatever risky attempts are made to defeat their purposes.

5. Intolerance to dissent—direct pressure on any member who expresses strong arguments against any of the group's stereotypes, illusions, or commitments, making clear that such dissent is contrary to what is expected of all loyal members.

6. Self-censoring—self-censorship of deviations from the apparent group consensus, reflecting each member's

inclination to minimize to himself the importance of his doubts and counterarguments.

7. Unanimity—a shared illusion of unanimity, partly resulting from this self-censorship and augmented by the false assumption that silence implies consent.

8. Emergence of self-appointed "mindguards"—members who protect the group from adverse information that might shatter their shared complacency about the effectiveness and morality of their decisions.

How can the tendency toward groupthink be minimized? Janis (1982) offers some suggestions:

1. The group leader should remain neutral, at least initially.

2. The leader should encourage and protect critical evaluation, the expression of objections, and concerns.

3. One group member should be appointed to play the role of critic, or "devil's advocate" whose job is to criticize and point out the drawbacks to various alternatives.

4. Outside experts should be consulted and asked to challenge the group's ideas.

5. When a preliminary decision has been reached, the group should take a break and individual members should be instructed to discuss the decision with others in an effort to identify loopholes, unanticipated problems, and so on. When the group reconvenes, members should be encouraged to report the comments made by others (perhaps by writing them anonymously rather than presenting them verbally).

with the majority. Many said that they had been seriously tempted to go along with the group in order to avoid seeming inferior or absurd.

In fact, a later study by Bogdonoff, Klein, Estis, Shaw, and Back (1961) found that students who "called them as they saw them" in the Asch situation suffered much more anxiety (as measured by physiological changes) than subjects who conformed to the erroneous group judgment. One subject who consistently disagreed with the group was dripping with perspiration by the end of the session, even though his judgments were correct in every instance.

Similarly, many of the "teachers" in the Milgram experiment experienced tremendous stress as the level of shocks went higher and higher and they tried to cope with the instructions from the experimenter on the one hand and the screams of the "learner" on the other. In situations such as these, how is it possible to resist social influence without experiencing intolerable levels of stress?

## Resisting Social Influence

When you find yourself trying to deal with a conflict between your position and that of others in a group, perhaps the most important thing to realize is that the power of a group to influence people is dramatically reduced when there is even a single dissenter. If you believe the group is wrong, voicing your dissent and holding out for what you believe is right will make it much easier for others to express their doubts as well. As Sears et al. (1988) suggest: " . . . even one deviant voice can have an important effect as long as there are other people who inwardly disagree with the majority but are afraid to speak up . . . any dissent substantially reduces conformity" (p. 363). Even if you don't succeed in convincing the majority of group members, the support you receive from one other person will greatly reduce the stressfulness of speaking out.

**Resisting normative social influence.**   When faced with the need to resist normative social influence, there are a number of things you can do to ease your task and reduce the stress that you experience:

1. *Reduce the attractiveness of others.* People experience greater stress when resisting influence from others who are attractive. Anything you can do to decrease the attractiveness of the group will reduce the stress that accompanies your taking an independent stand. For example, you might focus on the shortcomings of group members, or recall other times when the group unwisely resisted your views on important issues.

2. *Emphasize dissimilarities.* People are likely to experience greater stress when resisting the influence of others who are similar to themselves. Try to distance yourself from the other group members. Are the similarities between you and others in the group real or are they only apparent? Are you in fact very much like the other people, or are there essential differences between you and them? What are all the ways in which you differ from the people who are trying to influence you?

3. *Find alternative rewards.* Stress is greater when resisting the influence of others who control important rewards. Are there other ways to obtain some of the rewards that are presently controlled by the group? Can you reduce your involvement in the group so that acceptance by them is less important to you?

4. *Re-evaluate the costs.* People are more likely to experience stress when they expect to be punished for asserting their independence. Have you overestimated the costs of resisting the group's influence? Are your fears about what might happen realistic, or are they exaggerated? How important is it that you be accepted and liked by the group that is trying to influence you? What actually will happen if they dislike you or reject you? Does it really matter if they think you are silly, stupid, foolish, or misinformed? And is that more important than doing and saying what you believe is right?

*The most serious form of resistance comes when an individual's personal liberty and very life are at risk. Finding others who believe as you do can make such resistance less frightening, but ultimately you alone must answer for your beliefs. Nonetheless, there are those who believe that their ideals are worth the price.*

5. *Deal with the individual members.* Up to a point, the more people that try to influence you the more difficult it will be to resist. So, break the group into individuals. Then talk individually with each member, one-on-one, about your ideas. If possible, avoid getting into a large meeting in which everyone else is lined up against you at once.

6. *Identify allies.* As I noted earlier, it is far easier to voice an unpopular position when there is at least one other person who shares that position. Therefore, try to find at least one other person who believes as you do and share your thoughts with that person. Even one ally can make a tremendous difference in your ability to withstand social pressure (Morris & Miller, 1975), and an ally who is similar in many respects to the majority can also significantly increase the likelihood that your position will eventually be accepted (Sears, Peplau, Freedman & Taylor, 1988).

7. *Seek ways to ensure privacy.* Research on social influence has shown repeatedly that conformity, compliance, and obedience decrease significantly when individuals are allowed to express their thoughts anonymously or privately (Deutsch & Gerard, 1955). In Asch-type studies, for example, when subjects are allowed to write their judgments anonymously on slips of paper that are seen only by the experimenter, the amount of conformity to erroneous group judgments drops nearly to zero. If a vote must be taken, try to assure that the voting is done by secret ballot. If the group leader asks for the opinions of group members, try to assure that opinions are communicated anonymously, perhaps in writing.

8. *Make your commitment public.* Research indicates that people who have made a public commitment to their position are less easily influenced. Make your position

known publicly; tell others what you think; put it in writing, if possible, and send copies to others whose opinions matter to you. Each of these steps decreases the likelihood that you will experience conflict about whether you should succumb eventually to the majority viewpoint.

9. *Take time out.* Find an opportunity to delay making a decision. Say "Let me think about it; I'll call you back tomorrow morning and tell you what I think" or "Let's take a break and come back to this in a few days (or hours)." This not only gives you a chance to marshall your resources, it gives you an opportunity to reduce the stress you may be experiencing by using some of the techniques in Chapter 5. It also gives others a chance to think about what you have said.

**Resisting informational social influence.** In situations where you believe it is important to resist informational social influence, the following suggestions may be useful:

1. *Re-evaluate the expertise of the group members.* It is more difficult to resist being influenced by others who appear to be better informed and trustworthy. Ask yourself whether the people who are trying to influence you are better informed on the topic than you are. Are they perhaps less credible, less well-informed than they appear to be? Have their opinions and positions always been correct?

2. *Re-evaluate your own expertise.* It is difficult to resist being influenced by others when you believe you have little or no expertise on the subject (Campbell, Tesser & Fairey, 1986). To what extent is your own knowledge and ability greater than it at first appears? Do you know more than you think you do about the task? Are you at least as well informed on the topic as the others are? Have you underestimated your own expertise?

3. *Re-evaluate the familiarity of the task.* Most people find it harder to express a dissenting opinion when working on unfamiliar tasks. Ask yourself whether the task is similar to other tasks with which you are familiar. Have you had success in similar situations, even if they are not precisely identical to the present one?

4. *Define your role conservatively.* Rather than seeing yourself as someone who must overturn group opinions, consider a less dramatic role for yourself: by dissenting, you make it possible for others who also have doubts to voice their real feelings. Whether or not the group is convinced of your position, you can create an environment in which others will be more willing to express their true beliefs.

5. *Be persistent, coherent, forceful, but reasonable.* People who become highly emotional about an issue, or who become rigid, unyielding, and dogmatic not only are likely to experience more stress but also are easily dismissed by others. Express your beliefs persistently in a coherent, clear, and forceful way; be reasonable and resist the temptation to get overly emotional (Moscovici, 1980). By being persistent yet reasonable, you demonstrate not only that you continue to believe your position is correct, but also that it is very unlikely that the group will be able to achieve unanimity. In turn, that may encourage others to express dissenting opinions as well.

Inappropriate social influence is a common source of stress for virtually everybody who lives and works in social groups. For some people, however, even the need to speak out in social situations is a source of considerable stress as we will see in the next section.

## COMMUNICATION APPREHENSION

When people are asked to describe their fears, fear of speaking in public is mentioned more often than anything else (Paivio, 1965; McCroskey, 1977). Spiders, snakes, airplanes—all of these are less threatening for most people than having to stand up in front of a large group and perform or give a speech. About one out of every five college students say that they suffer from extreme "stage fright"; many more students report lesser degrees of discomfort about public speaking. Even speaking in meetings or in small groups is a source of anxiety for many people.

### The Nature of Communication Apprehension

**communication apprehension:** anxiety or concern about speaking in groups or meetings or in front of an audience

McCroskey and Beatty (1986) suggest that these various fears are simply different facets of a more general concern about speaking in social situations that they call **communication apprehension,** see the *Self-Discovery Journal* exercise that accompanies this chapter for a test of communication apprehension. Most people who are extremely apprehensive about speaking in group situations try to cope by using avoidance and withdrawal (McCroskey, 1984; McCroskey & Beatty, 1986). They tend to choose careers that require relatively little communication with others, live where they will be less likely to come into contact with others, elect large classes and then sit in the back of the lecture hall, and so on. When they are caught in group situations that normally require communication, they are likely to remain silent or speak as little as possible; they often speak only when asked a question, and even then keep their answers as short as possible (often just "Yes" or "No").

While these techniques can be effective in reducing stress in the short run, they are not the most effective ways of dealing with communication apprehension in the long run. It is impossible to avoid or withdraw from all the situations where communication with others is expected, required, or desirable. Thus, a person who is apprehensive about communicating with others will inevitably experience anxiety, fear, and emotional upset. Moreover, communication becomes increasingly important as people assume positions of greater responsibility in the workplace and in the community; people who cannot cope effectively with their fear of communication are less likely to succeed (Zimbardo, 1977).

Apart from the effect on the individual, communication apprehension can also have a detrimental effect on groups. We have seen in this chapter how important it is for groups to draw upon the opinions, knowledge, and expertise of all members. If 30 or 40 percent of the members of a group are apprehensive about communicating their opinions and beliefs, the group will be severely disadvantaged. As Zimbardo (1986) suggests:

> Sharing information-based knowledge and social-emotional support are vital to small group effectiveness. . . . When some members of the team withhold potential contributions, the team cannot fully benefit from their wisdom and skills. . . . Those not contributing fully are likely to become more bored and to feel less competent. Their self-esteem will be lowered, whereas their dependence on those to whom they defer is increased. (p. 22)

## Reducing Communication Apprehension

There are basically two ways in which people can learn to cope more effectively with communication apprehension: developing communication skills and reducing anxiety.

**Developing communication skills.**    Some people are apprehensive about communicating because they lack good communication skills. For these people, an important first step is to obtain training in those skills. There are now a number of training techniques that bolster specific communication skills such as public speaking, interviewing, or conversing informally; however, the specific program must be tailored to the particular problem (Kelly, 1984). Most counseling centers can provide training of this sort, as do most speech or communications departments in colleges and universities. A number of self-help groups are also available to provide assistance with developing communication skills (see Chapter 7 for further information on self-help groups).

However, research indicates that simply acquiring better communication skills is seldom the most effective way to reduce communication apprehension (McCroskey, Richmond, Berger, & Baldwin, 1983). Additional steps must usually be taken to reduce the anxiety that people feel when communicating with others.

*The idea of speaking in public, before an audience, is often more frightening than actually giving a speech. Running through a series of desensitization exercises before a speech can relieve some of the stress and enhance your performance.*

**Reducing communication anxiety.**    The two most effective approaches to lowering communication anxiety involve either systematic desensitization or cognitive restructuring. We discussed both of these techniques in general in Chapter 7. Here we will examine the ways in which they can be used to reduce communication apprehension.

In systematic desensitization, the first step is to establish a range of situations that vary from little anxiety to extreme anxiety. For example, the following list (Friedrich & Goss, 1984) has been used successfully for treating public speaking anxiety through systematic desensitization:

1. Lying in bed in room just before going to sleep—describe room.
2. Reading about speeches alone in room (one to two weeks before).
3. Discussing coming speech a week before (in class or after).
4. In audience while another gives speech (week before presentation).
5. Writing speech in study area (room, library).
6. Practicing speech alone in room (or in front of roommate).
7. Getting dressed the morning of the speech.
8. Activities just prior to leaving for speech (eating, practice).
9. Walking over to room on day of speech.
10. Entering room on day of speech.
11. Waiting while another person gives speech on day of presentation.
12. Walking up before the audience.
13. Presenting speech before the audience (see faces, etc.). (p. 177)

To undertake systematic desensitization, the person first becomes deeply relaxed by using techniques such as those described in Chapter 5. He or she then vividly imagines the least anxiety-provoking situation on the list; at the first sign of anxiety, attention is shifted immediately to restoring relaxation, after which the situation is imagined again. This process continues until the person is able to imagine the least threatening situation while remaining completely relaxed. Then the process is repeated for the next situation on the list, and so on until the most anxiety-provoking situation can be imagined without any noticeable increase in anxiety. In some cases, it may also be possible for the person to carry out some of the actions rather than just imagine them. For example, visiting the empty auditorium in advance of a speech and practicing total relaxation in that setting, or giving the talk in the empty auditorium before the actual speech while using relaxation techniques to minimize or eliminate anxiety.

An alternative, and equally effective, approach to reducing communication anxiety is cognitive restructuring (Fremouw & Scott, 1979; Fremouw, 1984). Here the person first learns to identify negative self-statements that interfere with his or her ability to communicate in social situations. For example, many people who suffer from communication apprehension harbor beliefs such as "People will probably think I'm stupid," "Nobody is interested in what I have to say," "They'll probably be waiting for me to make a mistake," "People will laugh at me if I do a poor job," "It will be absolutely horrible if I make a mistake," and "I always forget what I want to say." Each of these self-statements significantly increases the stress of communicating with others.

However, simply becoming aware of negative self-statements is not enough; in fact, evidence indicates that by itself this may simply *increase* communication anxiety

(Glogower, Fremouw, & McCroskey, 1978; Fremouw, 1984). Therefore, it is essential to substitute more adaptive, positive self-statements such as the following: "The audience is just like me," "The audience wants me to do well and wants to hear what I have to say," "I have something valuable and worthwhile to say," "Speak slowly," "Pause and take a deep breath to relax," "I've given the speech perfectly in practice and I can do it again," "I know this material better than the audience does," "If I make a mistake and move past it, no one will be likely to know the difference" and so on. These positive self-statements should be practiced in advance. For example, the person might give a practice speech in front of a small group of friends while using the self-statements to control anxiety. By keeping track of which statements are most effective in reducing anxiety, many people are able to bring communication apprehension completely under control and many others are able to reduce the stress and anxiety of social communication to a level that is quite tolerable (Fremouw, 1984).

We have seen that standing in front of a large audience can be a stressful experience. It can also be stressful for those in the audience, even if the speech or the performance goes quite well, as we will see in the next section.

## CROWDING

**crowding:** the feeling of being cramped, not having enough space

**density:** the number of people occupying a particular amount of space

**Crowding**, the feeling of being cramped, of having less than adequate space, is an extremely common source of stress for those who live and work in groups of one kind or another. It is important to realize that the psychological experience of crowding is not the same thing as high population **density** (the number of people per unit of space). Crowding is an uncomfortable feeling or experience; high density is a characteristic of a social situation or the environment. You may feel crowded if someone takes the seat next to you on an empty bus despite the fact that the population density is quite low; yet you may not feel at all crowded in an overflowing theater or concert hall where people are packed in like sardines. Two lovers sharing the same small restaurant booth will probably enjoy the intimacy; two strangers in the same booth would probably find the booth intolerably crowded. Members of a family sharing the same house are less likely to feel crowded than the same number of total strangers living in the same house. Crowding is a psychological experience; although it can arise in situations where many people are jammed into a small space, it can also arise in settings where there are few people and a great deal of space.

### Crowding and Stress

The distinction between density and crowding is important for understanding the link between crowding and stress. A number of studies show that high population density is not necessarily experienced as stressful (Freedman, 1975; Nogami, 1976). However, numerous studies have demonstrated that the experience of crowding is indeed stressful for most people (Epstein, 1981). For example, Karlin, Epstein and Aiello (1978) found that three students crammed into college dormitory rooms designed to hold only two people experienced greater stress, were more disappointed, and earned lower grades than two students in the same room. High-density prisons

*In part, crowding is stressful because people feel they lose their personal space when strangers come too close. Proximity triggers feelings of being threatened, often in situations over which people feel they have no control.*

have higher death rates and higher rates of psychological disorders than prisons with lower population densities (McCain, Cox, & Paulus, 1976). People in crowded environments report feeling anxious, fearful, unhappy, and angry; in crowded conditions, blood pressure is higher, heart rate increases, and more adrenaline is pumped into the bloodstream (Evans, 1979, 1980). As we saw in Chapter 4, these symptoms are all signs of stress.

There are a number of explanations for why crowding is stressful. No single explanation seems to be fully adequate by itself.

**Frustration.**    In part, crowded conditions are stressful because other people can interfere with satisfaction of needs and, as a result, create feelings of frustration. You may want to study, but perhaps your roommate prefers to talk on the phone. You may feel cold and want to turn up the heat, but your roommate may find the room too hot already. At the end of the day you may be eager to get home, but you may find yourself stalled in a traffic jam and unable to move. At a cocktail party, you may want to talk to a person on the other side of the room; when you are finally able to work your way through the crowd, you may find that they are no longer there. Frustrations of this sort are inevitable in crowded settings and, like all frustrations, they can be a source of irritation, anger, and stress.

**Constraints on behavior.**    Crowded situations often constrain behavior and reduce people's freedom to act. In a small apartment, for example, one person can live relatively as he or she pleases. However, when the apartment is crowded, people have to be careful not to bump into each other, not to use all the hot water, to keep telephone calls short so others can use the phone, to keep the stereo and TV volume low so others won't be disturbed, and so on. Each of these constraints reduces one's sense of freedom and, as a result, can give rise to stress.

**Loss of control.**    Quite often, crowded situations are accompanied by perceived loss of control. The more people there are in a space, the less control each individual person has over the situation and the less likely people are assured they will be able to cope with the situation (Baron & Rodin, 1978). As we saw in Chapter 3, loss of control, and feelings of powerlessness and helplessness, are important contributors to stress. For example, a single student in a college dormitory room has considerable control over who visits and when they visit as well as noise level, temperature, and neatness of the room; he or she determines when the room will be used for studying, when it will be used to entertain visitors, and when it will be used for sleeping. If a second student is added to the room, control must be shared and this perceived loss of control can lead to feelings of stress. A third student would increase the stressfulness of the situation still further (Baron, Mandel, Adams, & Griffen, 1976).

It is important to note that the key factor here is *perceived* loss of control; a person can sense that he or she has lost control when in fact that is not the case. In one laboratory study, for example, some of the students working in cramped conditions were given a button that they could push if they wanted to leave the room. Even though none of the students ever pushed the button, they experienced significantly less stress than students who did not have a button (Sherrod, 1974). In a crowded elevator, simply standing near the control panel has been shown to reduce significantly people's feelings of being crowded and the resulting stress, even in those people who never touched the buttons on the control panel (Rodin, Solomon, & Metcalf, 1978).

**Information overload.**    In crowded conditions, people are likely to find themselves overwhelmed with too much information (Milgram, 1970). When too many people are talking in a small space, for example, the noise level and the confusion may become absolutely overwhelming. In a crowded store, it may become impossible to distinguish customers from salespeople, it may be difficult to concentrate on making purchases, and it may be difficult to find an exit (in which case loss of control is added to confusion as a source of stress).

**territoriality:** psychological attachment to a specific area

**personal space:** psychological boundaries surrounding a person which only certain people are supposed to cross

**Invasion of personal space.**    Crowded situations are also stressful in part because they often lead to violations of **territoriality** and invasions of **personal space** by others. People tend to stake out a territory that is "theirs" and expect others to keep out of that territory. For example, in most work settings people have strong feelings about "their" desk and chair, "their" telephone, "their" parking place. When the situation becomes crowded, it is more difficult for these artificial boundaries to be sustained: people have to borrow desks and chairs, use each others' telephones, and share parking spaces. On submarines, it is not unusual for sailors to share the same bunk: one person sleeps in the bunk for part of the day, after which someone else moves in and uses the bunk.

People also prefer to keep a certain amount of space between themselves and others. The more intimate two people are, the closer they can get without feeling uncomfortable. In our society, strangers are usually kept at least two feet away, close friends are allowed to come as close as eight or ten inches, and lovers can actually be touching. In crowded settings, it is often impossible not to invade someone else's personal space.

When territorial boundaries and personal space are violated, discomfort and stress increase (Loo, 1977). For example, in a study by Felipe and Sommer (1966-67), researchers went to a library to see how students would react to the violation of personal space. When the researcher sat in the chair next to a student, 70 percent of the students got up and left within thirty minutes. In contrast, 25 percent of the students left within thirty minutes if the experimenter sat farther away or across from them, and only 15 percent left within thirty minutes if no one sat next to them.

## Reducing the Stressfulness of Crowding

**Environmental design.**    It is possible to minimize feelings of crowding through effective environmental design. In one interesting study, Baum and Valins (1977) studied the effect of living in a hall-type dormitory as opposed to a suite-type dormitory. In the hall-type design, bedrooms were aligned along a long hall, with bathrooms generally in the middle of the hall. In the suite-type dormitory, a smaller number of students shared a common bathroom and lounge area; bedrooms were arranged around the outside of the lounge area. Although the density was similar in the two dormitories, students in the suite arrangement reported feeling less crowded than students in the hall-type dormitory, apparently because the residents of the suite felt they had more control over those with whom they would come into contact.

**Retaining a sense of control.**    We have seen throughout this book that retaining a sense of control can reduce the stressfulness of many situations, even if the control is not real. Unfortunately, long-term crowding can lead to decreased desire to exert control (Rodin, 1976; Baum & Valins, 1977). Nonetheless, the stressfulness of crowding can be reduced by believing you have a measure of control, that you can change the situation if you wish, even if in fact your control is limited or nonexistent (Epstein, 1981; Langer & Saegert, 1978).

If you find yourself in a cramped apartment building or dormitory, concentrate on the fact that you can choose to spend certain times away from the building (for example, going to the library to study rather than sitting and fuming in your room for most of the evening); or think about setting up some kind of screening mechanism that allows you to regain some control over your privacy (perhaps a "Do not disturb" sign that you can put on the door when you feel you need more space for yourself). Think about putting on stereo headphones, picking up a good book, and immersing yourself in the music and the story until you feel more relaxed. If all else fails, remember that you can leave the situation entirely if it becomes totally intolerable. Whether or not you act on these various options, simply reminding yourself of them and thinking about them is likely to make the situation less stressful because you gain a sense of control over a situation that would otherwise leave you feeling helpless.

*Knowing you have an "out"—a means of escape—can help you perceive a crowded situation as less stressful. Open architectural design is one way to provide people with a greater sense of freedom of environment.*

Even remembering what you have learned in this chapter about the effects of crowding can give you a greater sense of control when you find yourself feeling closed into an area. For example, Langer and Saegert (1977) told some supermarket shoppers that "crowding sometimes causes people to feel aroused and sometimes anxious. We just wanted you to know this so that if you feel aroused or anxious you will know why." (p. 178) Other shoppers were not given this information about the effects of crowding. The researchers discovered that the shoppers who had been informed in advance about the effects of crowding were more satisfied with the crowded stores, more comfortable, and felt much less crowded than the shoppers who were not informed.

**Predictability.**  When people expect to be crowded in a given situation, they tend to find the situation less stressful. In one study, for example, subjects were told to expect either a high density situation or a low density situation (Klein & Harris, 1979). Some subjects from each group subsequently entered a room that coincided with their expectations; others found themselves in a room that did not match their expectations. The experimenters found that the population density of the room, by itself, had no consistent effect on the subjects. However, subjects whose expectations were not confirmed experienced significantly more stress. You may have had a similar experience at a party. If you expect a quiet, intimate gathering you are likely to experience more than normal stress if you walk in the door and find the room packed with people.

It follows that one way to reduce the stress that comes from crowding is to have realistic expectations about the physical characteristics of situations in which you may find yourself. A person who attends college expecting to have a single room and who then receives a double or triple is likely to find the experience more stressful than someone who expected to be in a double or triple room from the outset.

**Changing attributions.**    Worchel and Teddlie (1976) have suggested that people feel crowded when they are aroused physiologically and attribute their arousal to the presence of other people. From this viewpoint, one way to reduce the feeling of being crowded is to attribute one's arousal to something other than the closeness of other people. At a football game, for example, it is possible to attribute one's arousal to the game and not to the presence of other people. Similarly, in a high density work setting, attributing arousal to job stress, eagerness to do well, poor building design, or whatever should help to reduce the sense of being crowded (Webb, Worchel, Riechers & Wayne, 1986).

**Cooperation.**    One particularly effective response to crowding is increased cooperation. In families, for example, cooperation tends to lead to less sense of being crowded than one might otherwise expect. The effect of cooperation on crowding and stress was demonstrated dramatically in a study by MacDonald and Oden (1973). These researchers studied five couples who shared a 30-by-30 foot room for three months while training for the Peace Corps. The couples reported feeling virtually no sense of crowding and very little stress, in part because they felt that the situation was good training for what they were going to experience in the field and in part because they cooperated closely in dealing with what they perceived as a common problem. Freedman, Levy, Buchanan and Price (1972) found that in high density settings, women tended to become more cooperative while men became more aggressive and competitive; the women in these situations also experienced less stress and less sense of crowding than did the men.

In closing our discussion of the individual and the group, we note the importance of accurate perceptions and flexibility in dealing with the various aspects of our lives. Individuals and groups interact on a variety of levels, in profound and subtle ways, and in ways which either detract from our functioning as human beings or which enhance our full and active participation in and enjoyment of life. Ultimately, the quality of interaction between individuals and groups shapes our destiny as human beings.

## SUMMARY

Groups and group living are important in most people's lives. Groups provide their members with mutual help and companionship. Groups are also an important source of identity and self-esteem, and many opportunities for growth and personal fulfillment occur only in group settings. However, groups also incur costs: behavior is often constrained by limits imposed by groups; most groups make demands on their members for such things as loyalty, conformity, compliance, obedience, and participation; under some circumstances, groups can also become a threat to a person's integrity.

Each person has to weigh the costs and benefits of group membership when deciding whether to continue as a member. If the costs outweigh the rewards but it is not possible to leave the group, a great deal of stress may result. Even if the rewards outweigh the costs, there are nonetheless some costs associated with belonging to every group, and these can be a source of stress for the group member.

Finally, if the costs and benefits of group membership are about equal, the member may experience stress as a result of an approach-avoidance conflict about remaining in or joining the group. Therefore, although groups perform important functions in the lives of individuals and societies, they are also an important source of stress.

One source of stress is *social influence,* which can take several forms. Often people change their behavior, attitudes, or values to match those of other people without being asked or instructed to do so; this process is known as *conformity.* At other times, people change as a result of a specific request to do so; this is known as *compliance.* On still other occasions, people change in response to instructions or orders to do so from someone in a position of authority; this is known as *obedience.*

The topic of social influence is peculiarly appropriate in a textbook on the psychology of adjustment and adaptation. First, all forms of social influence are examples of adjustment and adaptation: in every case, a person changes in response to a perceived adjustive demand. Moreover, pressures to conform, comply, and obey are an important source of stress in many people's lives. Various laboratory studies of social influence demonstrate both of these points clearly: people will behave in ways that are contrary to their beliefs and values as a result of even very mild social influence, even though they experience considerable stress as a result.

People yield to social influence for two somewhat different reasons. In some cases, they want to be liked, respected, and accepted by others, not rejected, ridiculed, or considered "deviant." In such cases psychologists speak of *normative*

*Being part of a group provides essential feelings of acceptance and a comfortable social environment.*

*influence.* On other occasions, people yield to social influence because they wish to be right, to do the right thing, and they believe that others are likely to be correct. This is known as *informational influence.*

Both kinds of influence serve useful purposes: Normative influence helps to assure smooth, coordinated behavior between people, greater dependability and stability, and often greater satisfaction for group members; it also helps to minimize the amount of change to which group members must adjust and adapt. Informational social influence often increases security and safety as well as effectiveness of behavior in various situations. However, both kinds of influence also have disadvantages. Pressures toward uniformity can violate individual autonomy and in some cases may result in disaster, as in some cases of groupthink; groups that become rigid and inflexible are likely to be unable to cope effectively with changing conditions, as illustrated in some cases of social contagion. In these cases, it is often important for group members to resist social influence, although that can lead to considerable stress and discomfort.

There are a number of techniques that reduce the stressfulness of resisting social influence. Normative influence can be reduced by reducing the attractiveness of the other people; emphasizing the dissimilarities between oneself and others; finding alternative sources of rewards; re-evaluating the costs of resisting; dealing with individuals rather than with the group as a whole; identifying others who share one's beliefs; assuring privacy and anonymity when people express their feelings; making an irrevocable public commitment to one's position; and taking time away from the situation. Normative influence can be limited by re-evaluating personal expertise and the expertise of the others; re-evaluating the familiarity of the task; defining the individual role in a limited fashion; and being persistent, coherent, forceful yet reasonable. Perhaps the most important fact to remember is that by speaking out, even if the majority is not convinced, others in the group who have concerns and doubts will be far more likely to express them.

*Communication apprehension* is often a source of stress for people in social groups. It is possible for a while to reduce communication apprehension by avoiding or withdrawing from situations that call for social communication, but since it is virtually impossible to avoid all such situations, people who adopt this strategy are certain to experience considerable recurrent stress. Moreover, groups and society at large are disadvantaged if a significant number of people are unwilling or unable to share their thoughts, knowledge, and concerns about important issues.

In some cases, communication apprehension can be reduced through the learning of more effective communication skills. However, in most cases, additional steps must be taken to reduce the anxiety that people feel when communicating in social situations. This can be done through a program of systematic desensitization or through cognitive restructuring in which negative self-statements are replaced by more effective positive statements.

Another source of stress in social settings is *crowding,* the experience of feeling cramped and having less than adequate space. Often a sense of crowding arises when population *density* is high, but this is not always the case: Some high density situations such as concerts, sporting events, and families living together rarely lead to a sense of crowding. Some low density situations such as walking on an isolated beach can result in a sense of being crowded if only one other person is nearby. There are a number of reasons crowding is experienced as stressful: crowding often results in frustration; people's behavior in crowded conditions is likely to be constrained or restricted; there is a reduction in perceived control in crowded situations; people in crowded settings often experience information overload; and crowding can result in violations of *territoriality* and *personal space,* both of which result in an increase in stress.

Feelings of crowding can be reduced by effective environmental design. They can also be reduced by techniques that increase one's sense of personal control, by knowledge in advance that the situation is likely to be crowded, by attributing one's arousal in crowded settings to something other than the presence of other people, and by increased cooperation between people.

## KEY TERMS

social influence (499)

conformity (499)

compliance (500)

obedience (500)

social contagion (501)

normative influence (504)

informational influence (505)

groupthink (508)

communication apprehension (512)

crowding (515)

density (515)

territoriality (517)

personal space (517)

# The Quest for Values

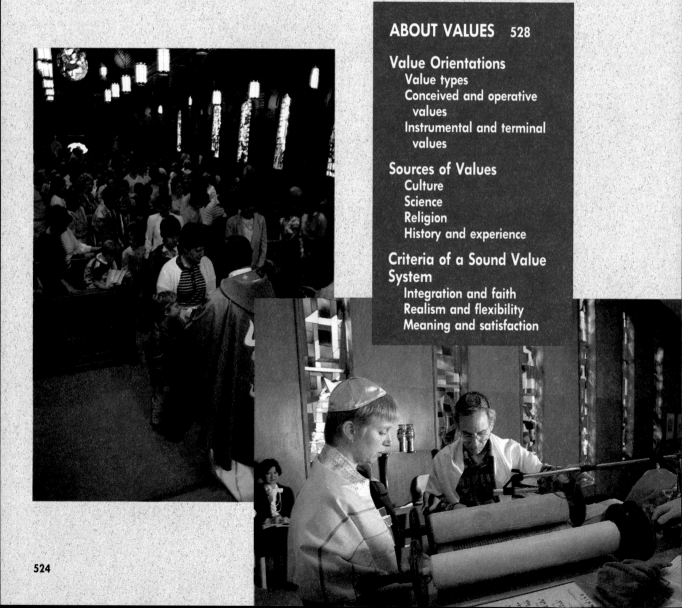

*Psychology cannot tell people how they ought to live their lives. It can, however, provide them with the means of effecting personal and social change. And it can aid them in making value choices by assessing the consequences of alternative life styles and institutional arrangements.*

*Social Learning Theory* (Bandura, 1977b, p. 213)

**values:** assumptions or beliefs concerning what is good and bad, desirable and undesirable

$\mathcal{I}$N this book, we have taken a long journey into the world of human nature and behavior. Now as we approach the end of this journey, it is fitting that we come to grips with the issue of **values** and the role that values can play in people's lives.

Throughout this book, you have seen that more effective adjustment often comes from discovering new options and being able to identify the most appropriate of those options. In Chapter 5, for example, we explored a number of different ways people can cope more effectively with stress. In Chapter 7, we discussed the great variety of therapies that are available to those who need assistance in coping with stress. In Chapters 10-12, we explored the tremendous variety of choices available to us in our relationships with others. In Chapter 13, we discussed the broad range of alternatives available in the world of work.

The availability of choices, however, presents a new dilemma—which of the options should you choose? Which options are better? What is the "good" or "right" choice? Answering these questions involves values. In Chapter 1, for example, I spoke of the need to solve the uniquely human problems of acquiring both under-standing and values. In the *Self-Discovery Journal* exercise that accompanies Chapter 1, I suggested that each person should try to find the answers to three key questions: Who am I? Where am I going? How do I get there? These questions deal with the image of the self, life plans and value patterns, and the skills necessary to achieve personal needs and goals—in essence, with the self-knowledge, goals and value judgments, and competencies involved in self-direction.

In part, the search for values involves a consideration of meaning—of what human existence is all about. This concern with meaning, so basic to thought and action, is unique to the human species. Most of us are concerned with our proper roles in life and with the meaning of our existence. We are also aware of our finite existence here on earth, an awareness which adds a crucial note of urgency to the human situation. As psychoanalyst Erich Fromm (1955) has contended: "Man is the only animal who finds his own existence a problem which he has to solve and from which he cannot escape" (pp. 23-24).

Sometimes the most troubling questions can be the most basic. This is especially true of the seemingly simple question "Why?" In the brief quote that follows, Charles

*Our values help us determine what is important in our lives and what human existence is all about. The answers we seek may not be simple to find, but pursuing them, whether through religion or other channels, leads to a more satisfying life.*

Burke and Robert Cummins (1970) describe the many problems people encounter in trying to answer this question and the problems they will encounter if they try to avoid it.

> Each of us is faced with the fact that we are here, alive in the twentieth century. We had no choice in the matter of our coming and we are not sure about exercising our right to end it all. Nor are we sure just why we are here or where we are going. Some of us have come to fear life as much as we do death because of our uncertainty with regard to both. We are amazed at our own powers as human beings, our creativity, our insight, and our adaptability. Yet we are shocked by our history of inhumanity—our cruelty, greed, and prejudice. The struggle between good and evil goes on in each of us and is a constant source of confusion for every human being.
>
> How often we wish we had some simple answer to the meaning of life. If only we could find a definite pattern to follow. In our frustration we strike out at the world around us and often hurt the ones we most love. In fear we attempt to run from our responsibilities and suffer the uneasiness of one who seeks to cut himself off from life without paying the price of death itself.
>
> The question of why each of us exists is indeed a troubling one, but we cannot afford to avoid it and still presume to live a full life. (p. 1)

Widespread feelings of disillusionment, apathy, and alienation offer eloquent testimony to the need for values and the difficulty of finding them. Often people are repulsed by what they perceive to be the superficiality, hypocrisy, and gross materialism which seem to permeate our way of life. However, finding or agreeing upon a coherent set of personal values is not always easy in view of the bewildering array of conflicting and changing values offered by contemporary society. Here one is reminded of the poignant lines of Biff in Arthur Miller's *Death of a Salesman:* "I just can't take hold, Mom. I can't take hold of some kind of a life."

Whether or not we find adequate answers, most people are searching—sometimes desperately—for information and values that will provide purpose and meaning in their lives. They do not easily accept the doctrine of despair so dramatically portrayed in the lines of Shakespeare that life "is a tale/Told by an idiot, full of sound and fury,/Signifying nothing."

In this chapter, we will not solve the problem of finding adequate values to guide your life. However, I will attempt to clarify the dimensions of the problem and point to some of the directions your solution might take. As a starting point, we shall explore some of the differences in people's value orientations. Then, we shall look at the sources of values and some criteria for identifying a sound value system. Finally, we shall examine the significance of values for personal growth and fulfillment as well as for determining the kind of world in which we and others will live.

## ABOUT VALUES

Values are implicit or explicit judgments about things, goals, and actions that are considered desirable or undesirable. In selecting goals, in choosing means for reaching them, and in resolving conflicts, people are continually influenced by their conception of the preferable, the good, and the desirable. Values thus help determine behavior, but they are not the only determinants of behavior. As we have seen throughout this book, any act reflects the interplay of a wide range of inner and

*Judgments that determine our own behavior and our reactions to the behavior of others are based, in part, on our values.*

outer determinants, including needs, goals, and various situational factors. However, key choices and decisions are based upon values which shape the kind of person each of us will become and the type of life each of us will build for ourselves.

## Value Orientations

There are various ways of describing value orientations. For our purposes, the most useful way of viewing value orientations seems to be in terms of (1) value types, (2) conceived and operative values, and (3) the distinction between values relating to goals or ends and values relating to the means for achieving these goals.

**Value types.**    Some years ago Spranger (1923/1928) contended that each person can be regarded as approaching—but rarely fitting perfectly within—one of six value types. According to Spranger, there are six main types of values that appeal to people in varying degrees and around which they build the unity of their lives:

1. *The theoretical.* The primary value of the theoretical person is the discovery of *truth*. Since this involves the use of rational, critical, and empirical processes, the theoretical type is an intellectual—often a philosopher or scientist.

2. *The economic.* The economic person values what is *useful* and is concerned with the business world or other practical affairs involving the production, marketing, or consumption of goods. Tangible wealth and material possessions are of central importance.

3. *The esthetic.* The esthetic person values *form* and *harmony*. People of this type may or may not be creative artists, but their chief interest is the artistic or esthetic experiences in life.

4. *The social.* The social person places great value on *affiliation* and *love*. The social person values other persons as individuals and tends to be kind and sympathetic.

5. *The political.* The political person greatly values *power*. Activities of persons of this value type need not be restricted to politics alone, but may involve power, influence, and active competition to maintain and expand power in personal relationships.

6. *The religious.* The highest value for the religious person may be called *unity*. Religious people are mystical and seek to comprehend and relate to the cosmos and find higher value experiences through their religious philosophy.

Spranger's classification of value types is necessarily limited. Few individuals approach the ideals described above, and some people appear to have few, if any, strong values beyond those of hedonism and sensual pleasure. Despite such limitations, however, these value orientations can help you understand the general directions in which values may lead you, as well as their influence upon the career you choose, the quality of interpersonal relationships you achieve, and the life style you develop.

**Conceived and operative values.**    People who have studied values systematically often distinguish between conceived and operative values. **Conceived values** are conceptions of the ideal. Most often, these values are taught by the culture and talked about in any discussion of morality or ethics. However, conceived values,

**conceived values:** values an individual considers valid but does not necessarily live by

even though held with a good deal of conviction, often have little practical influence on behavior. For example, people who espouse human equality, nonviolence, service to humanity, and complete honesty may not be guided by these values in their actions—even when circumstances make it fairly easy for them to do so.

**operative values:** values which actually guide the behavior of an individual, as opposed to the values he or she may profess to believe in

**Operative values,** on the other hand, are the actual value assumptions people use when making decisions and taking action. Sometimes the discrepancy between a person's conceived and operative values is alarming. The husband or wife who extols selfless love but contributes little to the relationship, and the politician who praises freedom but votes for measures that curtail the freedom of fellow citizens are examples of an all too common phenomenon. To identify a person's real values, then, it is necessary to understand not only what he or she *says* but also what he or she *does* in situations that involve an element of choice. In essence, people become and are what they do—not what they say they believe in or want to be.

It is rarely if ever possible, of course, to bring conceived and operative values into complete harmony. The person who highly values nonviolence will usually fight rather than be killed, and the person who values complete honesty may lie to protect a friend. Utopia is an ideal against which to measure our progress rather than a goal we can realistically hope to achieve because human nature and society are so complex. This does not invalidate conceptions of the ideal or strip them of their practical value. Salvador de Madariaga, a Spanish diplomat and political essayist, made this point well: "Our eyes must be idealistic and our feet realistic. We must walk in the right direction but we must walk step by step" (in Smith & Lindeman, 1951, p. 123).

**Instrumental and terminal values.** In his extensive studies of values, Rokeach (1973) has made the following distinction between instrumental and terminal values: "When we say that a person has a value, we may have in mind either his beliefs concerning desirable *modes of conduct* or desirable *end-states of existence.* We will refer to these two kinds of values as *instrumental* and *terminal* values" (p. 7).

**instrumental values:** values that concern the means used in achieving goals

**terminal values:** values that concern desirable end-states or goals

In essence, **instrumental values** represent means for achieving goals, such as being honest or dishonest, while **terminal values** represent ends or goals, such as personal security or a world of beauty. This distinction is thought-provoking since many people believe that "the end justifies the means." Thus, in the pursuit of goals that most people would consider desirable, such as social order and security, political leaders might resort to means most people would consider undesirable or unethical, such as repression and torture. Similarly, some people resort to dishonesty and deceit in the pursuit of goals, such as professional achievement, that most people would consider desirable. On both group and individual levels, the use of unethical means often defeats the achievement of ethically desirable goals (see Psychology in Action, p. 531).

## Sources of Values

When Neil Armstrong set foot on the moon and declared his first small step to be "one giant step for mankind," it may have compelled many of us to realize that we are barely on the threshold of understanding the physical, spiritual, mental, and moral forces in our universe. Although we have made remarkable progress in many areas,

# Psychology in Action

where can we find sound values? How can we arrive at a system of values that is stable and flexible enough to survive change? The complexity of this problem has been well summarized by Sinnott (1955).

> One of man's chief problems is to determine what the basis of a moral code should be, to find out what he *ought* to do. Is the right that which is the word of God given to man in the Ten Commandments? Is it what is revealed to us by conscience and intuition? Is it whatever will increase the sum of human happiness? Is it that which is the most reasonable thing to do? Is it whatever makes for the fullness and perfection of life? Above all, is there any absolute right, anything embedded, so to speak, in the nature of the universe, which should guide our actions? Or are right and wrong simply relative, dependent on time and place and culture pattern, and changing with environment and circumstance? What, in short, is the basis of our moral values? These questions are of vital importance in a day when intellectual power threatens to outrun moral control and thus destroy us. (p. 147)

While we cannot fully answer the questions raised by Sinnott, there are four key sources of values that we can use in formulating a workable value system: (1) culture, (2) science, (3) religion, and (4) experience, including our own and others' life experiences.

*Different cultures have different orientations to problems and as a result, their values are different too. The traditions and customs based on the values of one culture may seem very strange to someone of another culture.*

**Culture.**    To some extent, values are determined by culture. What might be considered normal and moral in one culture might seem strange or even bizarre in another culture. The extent to which this is true is shown in the following analysis by Robertson (1977).

> Americans eat oysters but not snails. The French eat snails but not locusts. The Zulus eat locusts but not fish. The Jews eat fish but not pork. The Hindus eat pork but not beef. The Russians eat beef but not snakes. The Chinese eat snakes but not people. The Jale of New Guinea find people delicious. (p. 61)

In a pioneering attempt to show the systematic nature of such cultural similarities and differences in values, Kluckhohn and Strodtbeck (1961) suggested that the core values of a society reflect its orientation to five basic problems:

1. *Orientation toward human nature.* Is human nature basically good, bad, or neutral? You will recall that this is an issue we discussed at some length in Chapter 2.

2. *Orientation toward the environment.* Is the environment to be preserved and regarded as crucial to our life support system or is it a resource to be conquered in the interest of our material comfort and convenience?

3. *Time orientation.* Should a person live for the present or for the future? Should customs and traditions be preserved or should they be replaced by new standards and patterns?

4. *Activity orientation.* What kind of activity is most valued? Making money? Service to others? Accomplishing things?

5. *Interpersonal orientation.* What is the dominant or desired relationship among members of the group? Is it competitive or cooperative, hostile or friendly? Are warm and loving relationships valued?

The answers given to these questions in our society determine the background against which each person develops his or her personal system of values. Depending on individual concepts of what is good and bad in human life, people tend to select certain goals over others and to pattern their behavior according to standards of what they believe to be desirable and worthwhile.

**Science.**    Psychology and other sciences have the advantage of providing information that has been checked and rechecked by objective methods. However, facts are impersonal and provide the basis for values only to the extent that people use them as a basis for deciding what is desirable or what ought to be. Albert Einstein (1949), perhaps the greatest scientist of our age, acknowledged that:

> . . . the scientific method can teach us nothing beyond how facts are related to, and conditioned by, each other.
>
> One can have the clearest knowledge of what *is,* and yet not be able to deduce from that what should be the *goal* of our human aspirations. Objective knowledge provides us with powerful instruments for the achievement of certain ends, but the ultimate goal itself and the longing to reach it must come from another source. . . . The knowledge of truth as such is wonderful, but it is so little capable of acting as a guide that it cannot prove even the justification and the value of the aspiration toward that very knowledge of truth. Here we face, therefore, the limits of the purely rational conception of our existence. (pp. 21-22)

In short, science can provide information about what is good or bad for physical, psychological, and social well-being, but it cannot make the value judgments needed to decide how to use this information. For example, science has demonstrated clearly that atomic bombs can destroy lives. However, whether we should continue to build more powerful and deadly thermonuclear weapons or whether they should ever be used must be based on value judgments.

Fortunately, modern science is increasingly concerned not only with acquiring dependable information about human beings and their world but also with how this information is actually used. The old dictum that "Science deals only with facts, not values" is increasingly questioned. Bandura (1977b) has expressed the situation in this way: "As a science concerned with the social consequences of its applications, psychology must promote understanding of psychological issues that bear on social policies to ensure that its findings are used in the service of human betterment" (p. 213). This statement applies to the physical and biological as well as the behavioral sciences.

**Religion.**    Religion, as customarily understood in its institutionalized form, is based on revelation believed to be from God as recorded in tradition and sacred literature. Typically religion involves a formal system of values that can be passed on from generation to generation, as well as a theology, a system of worship, and prescriptions for social relationships. Many of the basic values familiar to us in Christianity are found also in other religions of the world such as Confucianism, Judaism, Islam, and

# *Insight*

Buddhism. For example, the mandate "Do unto others as ye would have them do unto you" appears in one form or another in most religions (see Insight, p. 534).

Although theologians have used logic, reasoning, and historical arguments to help prove the existence of God and the validity of their beliefs, the proof of religious truth must rest finally on faith. People who have received strength and comfort from their religion may have an unshakable belief in the reality of God, but the correctness of their belief can never, by argument alone, be made convincing to anyone who has not shared a similar experience. In the well-known words of Pascal, "The heart has its reasons which reason knows nothing of."

Unfortunately, for a substantial number of people, religion consists of repeating religious beliefs but not practicing them. Thus, the religious beliefs espoused by many people often seem hypocritical. As someone has put it, "They pray in church on Sunday and they prey on their fellow human beings the rest of the week."

It has become increasingly apparent, however, that religion has not lost its essential relevance to our existential problems, particularly for those who have rediscovered and reinforced religious values in their lives. Mahs' (1973) comment on the words of one astronaut exemplifies the essential relevance of religion for some.

> "I am not the same man," Rusty Schweickart says, "none of us are." The Apollo veterans have become poets, seers, preachers, all of them evangelists for the privileged vision from space. (p. 50)

**History and experience.** In the life of the group and of the individual, many values originate from experience. Each of us experiences success or failure, satisfaction or dissatisfaction in different situations. We are regularly making judgments about what is good and bad, more desirable and less desirable, more meaningful and less meaningful. As we make these judgments about our experiences, we modify our value system accordingly.

We can also learn from the experience of others. Through libraries and museums, we can refer to the experience of individuals and nations throughout the world from the beginning of human history. We can observe the effects that the values of various civilizations have had on the well-being of their citizens. We can observe the effects of greed, selfishness, and ignorance in causing general human misery and warfare. We also can note the ultimate futility of war in solving basic problems. In the long run, most of the values that actually influence our behavior are validated by the satisfaction we have experienced in pursuing them. Hence, experience becomes a key factor in determining the values we follow and the ones we discard.

## Criteria of a Sound Value System

Although values are an individual matter based largely on experiences, the following three standards appear to be useful criteria of a sound value system: integration and faith, realism and flexibility, and meaning and satisfaction.

**Integration and faith.**   An adequate value system is internally consistent and integrated with reality. It is also something in which we can have a good deal of faith. An integrated value system implies a hierarchy of values that enables people to choose confidently between things of greater and lesser importance and to be relatively undisturbed by frustrations that temporarily interfere with the attainment of short-range goals.

Values are exercised in direct proportion to how much faith we have in them. Faith helps to close the gap between conceived and operative values and enables us to achieve a sense of wholeness in everything we feel, say, and do. This is the kind of faith illustrated in the lives of the "self-actualizing" persons studied by Maslow (1954, 1971) and discussed in Chapter 2. The kind of faith that encourages personal growth and self-actualization is quite different, however, from the type of dogmatic faith that seems to reflect fear and uncertainty more than positive understanding and conviction.

It is important to note that the integration of a value system is primarily related to a person's self-esteem. As Rokeach (1968) stated: "consistency with self-esteem is probably a more compelling consideration than consistency with logic or reality" in maintaining a value system (p. 164).

**Realism and flexibility.**   An adequate value system requires accurate assumptions concerning reality. This implies, first of all, the individual's need to be informed— to have adequate information. Socrates believed that no person knowingly chooses falsehood over truth. Similarly, Jefferson's concept of democracy is based on the belief that full information leads to right action and that right action is not possible without it. When we are fully informed about a given situation, the matter of choice or value judgment is much easier and more decisive.

A realistic value system also implies the need for a certain amount of flexibility. Of course, value systems undergo change as people go through life. Typically this change is related to one of three factors: (1) people engage in some acts that are not consistent with their value systems; (2) they are exposed to new information that may be inconsistent with other information; and (3) they perceive an inconsistency or contradiction in their values. Like other cognitive inconsistencies, inconsistencies in value systems motivate people to change their values and to re-establish a new, more appropriate, more integrated system.

Fundamental values may remain relatively stable, but they must be refined and their compass extended as the individual's understanding broadens. This is essentially the attitude expressed by Mahatma Gandhi (1957) in his autobiography.

> I am far from claiming any finality or infallibility about my conclusions. One claim I do indeed make and it is this. For me they appear to be absolutely correct, and seem for the time being to be final. For if they were not, I should base no action on them. (p. 5)

If values are to prove adequate, they must coincide with changes in the individual's understanding and knowledge, in his or her life situation, and in the physical and sociocultural environment. Such an attitude enables the individual to take forthright action based on conviction while at the same time maintaining an openness to new or fuller truth.

**Meaning and satisfaction.**    A final consideration in judging the adequacy of a value system is the amount of satisfaction that is derived from living by it—whether it gives meaning to life and a sense of fulfilling the purposes of existence. Dorothy Lee

*Value systems change as we go through life. Though the values we establish early in life may remain fundamentally the same, they must be refined and broaden as we learn.*

(1959), an anthropologist who has made intensive studies of value in other cultures, has emphasized the experience of satisfaction as a universal criterion of value.

> . . . we experience value when our activity is permeated with satisfaction, when we find meaning in our life, when we feel good, when we act not out of calculating choice and not for extraneous purpose but rather because this is the only way that we, as ourselves, deeply want to act. (p. 165)

Similarly, John Dewey (1939) has suggested that individuals derive a sense of meaning and satisfaction from their values when they carefully choose from alternative values and repeatedly act upon and prize their choices.

In short, values are subject to the pragmatic test of their consequences for the individual and for the group. As Janis and Mann (1977) contended: "Gaining utilitarian and social rewards is not enough; the person has to live with himself" (p. 9). As the existentialists have stated, one's life can be meaningful and fulfilling only if it involves socially as well as personally constructive values and choices (see Psychology in Action, p. 538).

## VALUES AND BECOMING

**becoming:** personal growth over time

**Becoming** refers to personal change over time. We all are in the process of becoming throughout our lives, for every experience of life leaves us changed. In addition, we would all hope that this continuing change is in positive directions and that we are becoming more proficient, more capable, and more attractive. However, sometimes change is in a negative direction, as in the case of people who become chronic alcoholics or who become cynical and embittered and believe that their lives have been wasted.

Opportunities, chance factors, personal resources, and many other conditions enter into our lives. It is largely through choices and actions that we shape the kind of person we will become as well as the kind of personal world in which we will live.

In this context, three aspects of becoming require special consideration: becoming an authentic person, building a favorable life for ourselves, and building a favorable life for others.

### Becoming an Authentic Person

The authentic person is an individual who lives a truthful, insightful existence. They are people who have integrity, have thought through their values, and live by them. The alternative to seeking and living the truth is to lead a wasted life, and to be phony, unauthentic, and the architect of one's destruction.

One of the first requirements for becoming an authentic person is trusting individual values. As we have seen, individuals derive some of their values from external sources, such as science, religion, culture, and the experience of others, and some from their own direct experiences of values. Ideally, people are selective in what they accept from external sources: enriching their insights by adding those of other people, weighing the value experiences of others, and choosing the particular values which have validity for them.

# *Psychology in Action*

## The Quality of Life for Americans

In a large-scale survey Flanagan (1978) asked thirty-, fifty-, and seventy-year-old Americans to rate fifteen components that had been defined as important or very important to Americans' quality of life. Health and personal safety, having and raising children, and understanding one's self were typically rated as important to quality of life. Surprisingly, the differences among the various age groups and between men and women were fairly small. Some differences that emerged from the data were relatively obvious. Older Americans, for example, rated work as less important to their quality of life than did young and middle-aged Americans.

You may identify some values in your life by completing Flanagan's questionnaire. Rate each of the components from 0 to 4, where 0 = not at all important, 1 = slightly important, 2 = moderately important, 3 = important, and 4 = very important to you.

### Physical and Material Well-being

_____ A  *Material comforts*—things like a desirable home, good food, possessions, conveniences, an increasing income, and security for the future.

_____ B  *Health and personal safety*—to be physically fit and vigorous, to be free from anxiety and distress, and to avoid bodily harm.

### Relations with Other People

_____ C  *Relationships with your parents, brothers, sisters, and other relatives*—things like communicating, visiting, understanding, doing things, and helping and being helped by them.

_____ D  *Having and raising children*—this involves being a parent and helping, teaching, and caring for your children.

_____ E  *Close relationship with a husband/wife or a person of the opposite sex.*

_____ F  *Close friends*—sharing activities, interests, and views; being accepted, visiting, giving and receiving help, love, trust, support, guidance.

### Social, Community, and Civic Activities

_____ G  *Helping and encouraging others*—this includes adults or children other than relatives or close friends. These can be our own efforts or efforts as a member of some church, club, or volunteer group.

_____ H  *Participation in activities relating to local and national government and public affairs.*

### Personal Development and Fulfillment

_____ I  *Learning,* attending school, improving your understanding, or getting additional knowledge.

_____ J  *Understanding yourself* and knowing your assets and limitations, knowing what life is all about and making decisions on major life activities. For some people, this includes religious or spiritual experiences. For others, it is an attitude toward life or a philosophy.

_____ K  *Work* in a job or at home that is interesting, rewarding, worthwhile.

_____ L  *Expressing yourself* in a creative manner in music, art, writing, photography, practical activities, or in leisure-time activities.

### Recreation

_____ M  *Socializing*—meeting other people, doing things with them, and giving or attending parties.

_____ N  *Reading, listening to music, or observing* sporting events or entertainment.

_____ O  *Participation in active recreation*—such as sports, traveling and sight-seeing, playing games or cards, singing, dancing, playing an instrument, acting, and other such activities.

When people's experiences of value contradict the value judgments of their culture or the prescriptions of science or religion, they must decide which they trust most—their own experience or that of others. As we saw in Chapter 2, Rogers (1969, 1977) has found that many of those who seek therapy have, knowingly or not, chosen to follow external value judgments, ignoring or denying their own perceptions of value. These persons have blindly accepted the values of others and find them unsatisfactory.

Assuming that people are not estranged and alienated from their inner selves and that they understand the consequences of various alternatives, they can become true to themselves—both in terms of being what they are and in terms of shaping their selves through their choices and actions. This is a basic theme underlying **authenticity.**

**authenticity:** human quality of being spontaneous and genuine, of being one's true self without a false front or facade

A second and equally important theme is concern for and commitment to others. In the humanistic-existential model, commitment to others follows almost automatically from commitment to the self. Humanistic-existential theorists believe there is a basic unity of humanity, and the task of learning to live constructively leads automatically to involvement, obligation, and commitment to fellow human beings. Rogers (1964) has dealt with this point succinctly: "I believe that when the human being is inwardly free to choose whatever he deeply values, he tends to value those objects, experiences, and goals which make for his own survival, growth, and development, and for the survival and development of others" (p. 166). Thus, the authentic person's life leads to self-fulfillment and to the well-being of others.

## Building a Favorable Life for Ourselves

Most people will, in the course of their lives, build friendships, undertake specific occupations, get married, and raise families. Their values emerge in their decision to marry, in determining the type of person that they might marry, and in the emphasis that they will place on material possessions and interpersonal relationships.

Reactions to stress and to the changes that occur throughout life are other ways in which people help build favorable lives for themselves. As we saw in Chapter 9, even the way each person approaches the end of life reflects values and can become the final stage of personal growth and development.

In essence, every person has the potential for both a growth-including or growth-retarding type of life within their grasp. Their choice will determine whether they achieve this potential (Bandura, 1982b; Furlong, 1981).

## Building a Favorable Life for Others

Positive becoming is not entirely a matter of personal change and growth. Of crucial importance, too, is the type of world each person constructs for themselves and others. Choices for a constructive or destructive life style affect others as well as ourselves. For example, a decision to speed down a highway while intoxicated has consequences for not only ourselves but also for other people.

The choices each of us makes today will also affect future generations. Our decision to pollute the air and water and to desecrate the land leaves a legacy for

*Becoming an authentic person involves understanding not only what actions to take, but also understanding how those actions will affect others.*

our descendants that will take many lifetimes to restore. For example, the radio-activity that is generated in a nuclear reactor container vessel will remain dangerous for at least 80,000 years (Norman, 1982). Similarly, our polluted environment, our self-centered concerns, and the world, the history, and the values that we give to our children will not be easy to change.

Becoming an authentic person obviously involves personal growth and development, but actions have consequences for others as well. In the search for authenticity, others must not be forgotten. As John Donne has expressed it, "No man is an island, entire of itself; every man is a piece of the continent, a part of the main."

## VALUES AND THE WORLD OF THE FUTURE

*From now on, everything in our environment, in our physical makeup and behavior, and in our future development is subject to human meddling, interference, and "control." But we lack the appropriate guiding ethic and institutions for making the momentous choices which face us.*

"The Coming Transformation" (Harman, 1977, p. 8)

While "Spaceship Earth" has an efficient life-support system, it is limited. The number of its inhabitants is increasing with frightening rapidity and overburdening its decreasing resources. While people are divided into conflicting groups often fighting and killing each other, several nations have developed thermonuclear weapons capable of killing every human being several times over.

Apparently, in the remaining years of the twentieth century, the world's peoples will be faced with three Herculean tasks: (1) to eliminate poverty and discrimination and provide equal opportunity for all; (2) to cope with new problems produced by technological advances—pollution, the population explosion, and accelerating and largely uncontrolled technological and social change; and (3) to plan and achieve a good future for all human beings.

## Exploring Alternative Futures

*The future is not a result of choices among alternative paths offered by the present, but a place that is created—created first in the mind and will, created next in activity. The future is not some place we are going to, but one we are creating. The paths to it are not found but made, and the activity of making them changes both the maker and the destination.*

*Footnotes to the Future* (Schaar, 1974, p. 1)

The problem of survival confronts all of us as an immediate concern, but a good future will not come without equal concern. In recent years a growing number of organizations and scientists have become directly involved in identifying various possible futures for our country and for the world as a whole. These groups have been established by the federal government, by major universities, and by private foundations and organizations. They are composed of interdisciplinary teams of scientists, historians, philosophers, and specialists from a diversity of fields. They devote their time to considering the range of alternatives open to us in planning a good future and the probable consequences of given alternatives.

The "futurists" point to the fact that throughout history, those organisms unable to adapt to the demands of a changing environment have perished. Human beings are not trapped by some absurd fate. Unlike other animals, human beings can choose their course in life and history. Thus, it becomes essential that we carefully explore and evaluate the options open to us, that we choose our own future. Through the advances in psychology and technology, we are no longer limited by the "givens" in ourselves and our surroundings but are increasingly capable of directing the destiny of ourselves and our world. It is our choices that will determine our destiny, and herein lies the source of our greatest strength and our greatest weakness. In theory, the options are unlimited. However, will we make the right choices? As the futurist Hubbard (1981) expressed: "We can create new worlds . . . or self-destruct" (p. 31). Thus, it is clear that having choices can be a source of anxiety and despair as well as one of hope and challenge. The question is whether these choices will be made by default or with imagination and the use of all the information potentially at our disposal.

Many behavioral scientists—and others—are seriously worried about the possibility that some elite minority may someday plan and exercise control over the rest of us, utilizing behavioral scientists primarily as tools in achieving their goals. This is the warning in such prophetic and frightening "utopias" as Aldous Huxley's *Brave New World,* and George Orwell's *1984.*

To safeguard ourselves from the possible use of science as a means to restrict rather than enrich people's lives, many psychologists and other investigators are becoming increasingly concerned with the alternative futures proposed by science and technology. The value orientations which determine a choice among these futures are also factors in these concerns (Fishman & Neigher, 1982).

## The Crucial Role of Values in Shaping the Future

*Human values, in addition to their commonly recognized significance from a personal, religious, or philosophic standpoint, can also be viewed objectively as universal determinants in all human decision making. . . . More than any other causal system with which science now concerns itself, it is variables in human value systems that will determine the future.*

"Bridging Science and Values" (Sperry, 1977, p. 237)

Science and technology have steadily increased our power not only to shape our future environment but also to control our development and behavior. Most scientists consider it inevitable that such controls will eventually be used. This has prompted several serious questions: (1) What type of controls will be used? (2) Who will exercise these controls? and (3) What values will they be based on?

The models of human nature and behavior that we discussed in Chapter 2 are value-laden and contain differing guides to the type of future people should try to construct for humankind. In an attempt to resolve such differences, Collier (1968) has suggested a basic value orientation with which most scientists and nonscientists alike would probably agree: "the consecutive concern for whatever capacity the individual has for self-regulation and self-determination" (p. 5).

Coleman (1973) has insisted that implicit in this value orientation is the concept of a participatory and anticipatory democracy

... in which the people are directly involved in establishing priorities and guiding social change—a society in which each individual has maximal opportunities for fulfilling his potentialities and living a meaningful and fulfilling life, a society in which human freedom and dignity are truly established. (p. 178)

In any event, we can, if we choose to, create a future society that will provide our descendants with richer lives and greater opportunities for self-direction and

*Though values may often lead us into conflict, they also help us to shape our future and search for new solutions that will change what needs to be changed while preserving what is essential.*

self-actualization than has ever been known. In fact, humans of the future may well be as different from us as we are from our Neanderthal ancestors (see Insight, p. 544).

As we embark upon the great adventure of shaping our own future, let us hope that we will find new solutions that will change what needs to be changed while preserving essential values that are still valid. We must constantly guard against the danger of discarding the essential for that which is new but trivial or unsound. For change in and of itself is no guarantee of progress. As Haskins (1968) has pointed out, we must be continually aware of the danger that

> . . . in embracing new and experimental courses on myriad fronts of movement with the ardor that we must, we do not at the same time discard long-tested values and long-tried adaptive courses which, if they are lost, will only have, one day, to be rewon— and probably at enormous cost.

It has taken the human race many thousands of years to achieve the imperfect level of freedom and opportunity for self-determination that has been reached. If these crucial achievements and other time-tested values are carelessly discarded, the change can bring us more loss than gain, and it may take long effort and suffering simply to regain our present position. The warning that "the price of freedom is eternal vigilance" is not one to be dismissed lightly in our age of turmoil and rapid change.

# Insight

## How Can We Contribute to a Good Future World?

Our society has frequently been accused of being a dehumanizing mass bureaucracy in which individuals are becoming increasingly alienated and believe they have little or no control over their destiny, let alone that of society. In a sense, the "average citizen" has become an alienated observer rather than an active and enthusiastic participant in the American Dream.

When citizens become aware of the problems facing society, most of them realize that their futures as well as those of their children are directly involved. And they ask "What can I do?"

Perhaps the starting point is to become familiar with the special needs and problems of one's community. Whatever the occupation—student, homemaker, teacher, lawyer, executive, trade-unionist—an interested person can find ways to contribute, such as participating in various civic organizations, serving as a part-time volunteer in a hospital or community mental health center, working for the election of particular political candidates, taking an active and responsible role as a citizen. Often, over time, many persons find themselves in leadership positions where their individual influence can be more strongly exerted. In any event, if we are to survive as a society it seems essential that we each not only "do our thing" but also "do our part."

In accepting the Nobel Prize for Literature in 1950, William Faulkner (1961) made this prophetic statement, which seems equally relevant today and a fitting conclusion for our discussion.

> I decline to accept the end of man. It is easy enough to say that man is immortal simply because he will endure: that when the last ding-dong of doom has clanged and faded from the last worthless rock hanging tideless in the last red and dying evening, that even then there will still be one more sound: that of his puny inexhaustible voice, still talking. I refuse to accept this. I believe that man will not merely endure: He will prevail. He is immortal, not because he alone among creatures has an inexhaustible voice, but because he has a soul, a spirit capable of compassion and sacrifice and endurance. (p. 4)

## SUMMARY

There continues to be a great need for *values* that can withstand the impact of scientific and technological advances. Values are essential to making effective and adaptive choices from among the alternatives that are available at any given moment. Values also contribute to a sense of meaning in life, an answer to the question of why each person exists. The absence of values can lead to disillusionment, apathy, and alienation. However, it is often difficult to settle upon a coherent and meaningful set of values given the array of conflicting and changing values offered in contemporary society.

According to one view, there are six general value types: theoretical, economic, esthetic, social, political, and religious. Moreover, it is possible to distinguish between *conceived values* (conceptions of the ideal) and *operative values* (the values

*A sound personal value system contributes to a sense of meaning in life and provides a basis for making decisions that will affect the individual and his or her role in shaping society.*

each person uses in making day-to-day decisions). It is also possible to distinguish between *instrumental values* and *terminal values:* the former concern desirable means for achieving goals, while the latter concern desirable goals to be achieved.

Culture, science, religion, and experience all contribute to the formation of values, but they cannot inform us whether the values are sound. The core values of a culture reflect its orientation to five basic problems: orientation toward human nature, orientation toward the environment, time orientation, activity orientation, and interpersonal orientation. Science also provides information that is useful in making value judgments. Religions typically have a formal system of values that is passed on from one generation to the next. Finally, experience contributes to values: people's own experiences of what is satisfying and dissatisfying, as well as the experiences of others as reflected in libraries and museums.

From whatever source, a sound personal value system must meet three criteria. It must be internally consistent and integrated with reality and be something in which the person can have faith when making decisions. It must be founded in a full understanding of reality and be flexible enough to change as a result of changing understanding and knowledge, changing situations, and changing environments. A sound value system must also provide a sense of satisfaction and meaning.

Everyone is in the process of *becoming* throughout their life, though change can occur in a positive or negative direction. Positive becoming takes three forms: becoming an authentic person and achieving a degree of *authenticity,* integrity, and commitment to others; building a favorable life for oneself; and building a favorable life for others now and in future generations.

Values also play an important role in shaping the world of the future. Eliminating poverty and discrimination, providing equal opportunity for all, coping with problems spawned by technological advances, and providing a good future for all human beings—these are the essential adaptive challenges that confront the human race at this point in history. To respond effectively to these challenges requires careful exploration and evaluation of the available options, and this in turn depends not only on information and knowledge, but also on values that will help to shape the future.

## KEY TERMS

values (526)
conceived values (529)
operative values (530)
instrumental values (530)

terminal values (530)
becoming (537)
authenticity (539)

# References

The reference list includes not only the sources from which the author has drawn material, but also the acknowledgments of the permission granted by authors and publishers to quote directly from their works.

Abramson, L. Y., Garber, J., & Seligman, M. E. P. (1980). Learned helplessness in humans: An attributional analysis. In J. Garber & M. E. P. Seligman (Eds.), *Human helplessness: Theory and application* (pp. 3-34). New York: Academic Press.

Abramson, L. Y., Seligman, M. E. P., & Teasdale, L. (1978). Learned helplessness in humans: Critique and reformulation. *Journal of Abnormal Psychology, 87,* 49-74.

Abramson, P. R., & Mosher, D. L. (1975). Development of a measure of negative attitudes toward masturbation. *Journal of Clinical and Counseling Psychology, 43,* 485-490.

Adams, V. (1980, May). Getting at the heart of jealous love. *Psychology Today,* pp. 38-47, 102-106.

Ainsworth, M. (1973). The development of infant-mother attachment. In G. Caldwell & H. Ricciuti (Eds.), *Review of child development research* (Vol. 3, pp. 1-94). Chicago: University of Chicago Press.

Ainsworth, M. D., Blehar, M. C., Waters, E., & Wall, S. (1979). *Patterns of attachment.* New York: Halstead Press.

Albee, E. (1962). *Who's afraid of Virginia Woolf?* New York: Atheneum.

Albrecht, S. L. (1979). Correlates of marital happiness among the remarried. *Journal of Marriage and the Family, 41,* 857-867. Copyrighted 1979 by the National Council on Family Relations, 1910 West County Road B, Suite 147, St. Paul, MN 55113. Reprinted by permission.

Altman, I., & Taylor, D. A. (1973). *Social penetration: The development of interpersonal relationships.* New York: Holt.

American Psychiatric Association. (1987). *Diagnostic and statistical manual of mental disorders* (3rd ed.–revised). Washington, DC: Author.

American Psychological Association. (1981). Ethical principles of psychologists. *American psychologist, 36*(6), 633-638.

Anastasi, A. (1982). *Psychological testing* (5th ed.). New York: Macmillan.

Anderson, J. R. (1982). Acquisition of cognitive skill. *Psychological Review, 89,* 369-406.

Andrasik, F. & Holroyd, K. A. (1980). A test of specific and nonspecific effects in the biofeedback treatment of tension headache. *Journal of Consulting and Clinical Psychology, 48,* 575-586.

Arend, D., Gove, F., & Sroufe, L. A. (1979). Continuity of individual adaptation from infancy to kindergarten: A predictive study of ego-resiliency and curiosity in preschoolers. *Child Development, 50,* 950-959.

Arlin, P. K. (1975). Cognitive development in adulthood: A fifth stage? *Developmental Psychology, 11,* 602-606.

Arlin, P. K. (1977). Piagetian operators in problem-finding. *Developmental Psychology, 13,* 297-298.

Aronson, E. (1984). *The social animal* (4th ed.). New York: Freeman.

Asch, S. E. (1952). *Social psychology.* New York: Prentice-Hall.

Asch, S. E. (1955, May). Opinions and social pressure. *Scientific American,* pp. 31-35.

Atchley, R. C. (1977). *The social forces in later life.* Belmont, CA: Wadsworth.

Babladelis, G. (1987). Young persons' attitudes toward aging. *Perceptual and Motor Skills, 65,* 553-554.

Bach, G., & Wyden, P. (1968). *The intimate enemy: How to fight fair in love and marriage.* New York: Avon.

Baltes, P. B., & Schaie, K. W. (1976). On the plasticity of intelligence in adulthood and old age. *American Psychologist, 31,* 720-725.

Bandura, A. (1977a). Self-efficacy: Toward a unifying theory of behavioral change. *Psychological Review, 84,* 191-215.

Bandura, A. (1977b). *Social learning theory.* Englewood Cliffs, NJ: Prentice-Hall.

Bandura, A. (1982a). The psychology of chance encounters and life paths. *American Psychologist, 37,* 747-755.

Bandura, A. (1982b). Self-efficacy mechanism in human agency. *American Psychologist, 37,* 122-147.

Barber, T. X. (1969). *Hypnosis: A scientific approach.* New York: Van Nostrand Reinhold.

Baron, R. A. (1985). *Understanding human relations: A practical guide to people at work.* Boston: Allyn and Bacon.

Baron, R. M., & Rodin, J. (1978). Perceived control and crowding stress: Processes mediating the impact of spatial and social density. In A. Baum & Y. Epstein (Eds.), *Human response to crowding.* Hillsdale, N.J.: Erlbaum.

Baron, R. M., Mandel, D. G., Adams, C. A., & Griffen, L. M. (1976). Effects of social density in university residential environments. *Journal of Personality and Social Psychology, 34,* 434-446.

Bartrop, R. W., Luckhurst, E., Lazarus, L., Kiloh, L. G., & Penny, R. (1977). Depressed lymphocyte function after bereavement. *Lancet, 1,* 834-836.

Baruch, G. K., Biener, L., & Barnett, R. C. (1987). Women and gender in research on work and family stress. *American Psychologist, 42,* 130-136.

Baruch, G., Barnett, R., & Rivers, C. (1983). *Life prints: New patterns of love and work for today's women.* New York: McGraw-Hill.

Batchelor, W. (1984). AIDS: A public health and psychological emergency. *American Psychologist, 39,* 1279-1284.

Bateson, G., Jackson, D. D., Haley, J., & Weakland, J. (1956). Toward a theory of schizophrenia. *Behavioral Science, 1,* 251-264.

Baum, A., & Valins, S. (1977). *Architecture and social behavior: Psychological studies in social density.* Hillsdale, NJ: Lawrence Erlbaum.

Beck, A. T. (1967). *Depression: Causes and treatment.* Philadelphia: University of Pennsylvania Press.

Beck, A. T. (1976). *Cognitive therapy and the emotional disorders.* New York: International Universities Press.

Bell, A. P., & Weinberg, M. S. (1978). *Homosexualities: A study of diversity among men and women.* New York: Simon & Schuster.

Bem, S. L. (1975). Sex-role adaptability: One consequence of psychological androgyny. *Journal of Personality and Social Psychology, 31,* 634-643.

Bengtson, V. L., & Robertson, J. F. (Eds.) (1985). *Grandparenthood.* Beverly Hills, CA: Sage.

Benson, H. (1975). *The relaxation response.* New York: Morrow.

Berger, K. S. (1980). *The developing person.* New York: Worth.

Bernard, J. (1973). *The future of marriage.* New York: Bantam Books.

Berndt, T. J. (1979). Developmental changes in conformity to peers and parents. *Developmental Psychology, 15,* 606-616.

Berndt, T. J. (1982). The features and effects of friendship in early adolescence. *Child Development, 53,* 1447-1460.

Berne, E. (1964). *Games people play.* New York: Grove Press.

Berne, E. (1972). *What do you say after you say hello?* New York: Grove Press.

Bernstein, D. A., & Nietzel, M. T. (1980). *Introduction to clinical psychology.* New York: Wiley.

Berscheid, E. (1985). Interpersonal attraction. In G. Lindzey & E. Aronson (Eds.), *Handbook of social psychology* (Vol. 2, 3rd ed.). New York: Random House.

Berscheid, E., & Peplau, L. A. (1983). The emerging science of relationships. In H. H. Kelley et al. (Eds.), *Close relationships.* New York: Freeman.

Bierman, E., & Hazzard, W. (1973). Biology of aging. In D. Smith & E. Bierman (Eds.), *The biologic ages of man.* Philadelphia: W. B. Saunders.

Birren, J. E. (1974). Transitions in gerontology — From lab to life: Psychophysiology and speed of response. *American Psychologist, 29,* 808-815.

Blanchard, E. B., & Epstein, L. H. (1978). *A biofeedback primer.* Reading, MA: Addison-Wesley.

Blau, P. M. (1967). *Exchange and power in social life.* New York: Wiley.

Bluestone, H., & McGahee, C. L. (1962). Reaction to extreme stress: Impending death by execution. *American Journal of Psychiatry, 119,* 393-396.

Blumstein, P., & Schwartz, P. (1983). *American couples.* New York: Morrow.

Bogdonoff, M. D., Klein, R. F., Estis, E. H., Shaw, D. M., Jr., & Back, K. W. (1961). The modifying effect of conforming behavior upon lipid responses accompanying CNS arousal. *Clinical Research, 9,* 135.

Bohannan, P. (1972). The six stations of divorce. In J. Bardwick (Ed.), *Readings on the psychology of women.* New York: Harper & Row.

Booth-Kewley, S., & Friedman, H. S. (1987). Psychological predictors of heart disease: A quantitative review. *Psychological Bulletin, 101,* 343-362.

Boston Women's Health Book Collective (1976). *Our bodies, ourselves: A book by and for women* (2nd ed.). New York: Simon & Schuster.

Botwinick, J. (1977). Intellectual abilities. In J. E. Birren & K. W. Schaie (Eds.), *Handbook of the psychology of aging* (pp. 580-605). New York: Van Nostrand Reinhold.

Bovet, T. (1973). Human attitudes toward suffering. *Humanitas, 9*(1), 5-20.

Branden, N. (1965). *Psychotherapy and the objectivist ethics.* New York: Nathaniel Branden Institute.

Branden, N. (1980). *The psychology of romantic love.* Los Angeles: J. P. Tarcher.

Brende, J. O., & Parson, E. R. (1985). *Vietnam veterans: The road to recovery.* New York: Plenum.

Bridge, T. P. (1988a). AIDS and HIV CNS disease: A neuropsychiatric disorder. In T. P. Bridge, A. F. Mirsky, & F. K. Goodwin (Eds.), *Psychological, neuropsychiatric, and substance abuse aspects of AIDS* (pp. 1-13). New York: Raven Press.

Bridge, T. P. (1988b). Legal and ethical issues in the neuropsychiatric research in AIDS. In T. P. Bridge, A. F. Mirsky, & F. K. Goodwin (Eds.), *Psychological, neuropsychiatric, and substance abuse aspects of AIDS* (pp. 241-247). New York: Raven Press.

Brigham, J. C. (1986). From John C. Brigham, *Social Psychology,* p. 225. Based on Geiss, S. K., & O'Leary, K. D. (1981), "Therapist rating of frequency and severity of marital problems: Implications for research," *Journal of Marital and Family Therapy, 7*(4): 515-520. Copyright © 1986 by John C. Brigham. Reprinted by permission of Scott, Foresman and Company.

Brim, O. G., Jr., & Ryff, C. D. (1980). On the properties of life events. In P. B. Baltes & O. G. Brim (Eds.), *Life-span development and behavior* (Vol. 3). New York: Academic Press.

Brodzinsky, D. M., Gormly, A. V., & Ambron, S. R. (1986). Chart from *Lifespan human development* (3rd ed.). Copyright © 1979 by Holt, Rinehart & Winston, Inc. Reprinted by permission of the publisher.

Broverman, I. K., Vogel, S. R., Broverman, D. M., Clarkson, F. E., & Rosenkrantz, P. S. (1972). Sex-role stereotypes: A current appraisal, *Journal of Social Issues, 28,* 59-78.

Brown, G. W., & Harris, T. O. (1978). *Social origins of depression: A study of psychiatric disorder in women.* New York: Free Press.

Brown, M. S., & Tanner, C. (1988). Type A behavior and cardiovascular responsivity in preschoolers. *Nursing Research, 37,*(3), 152-155, 191.

Buckley, W. (1968). Society as a complex adaptive system. In W. Buckley (Ed.), *Modern systems research for the behavioral scientist.* Chicago: Adline.

Burgess, E. W. (1964). The family in a changing society. In A. Etzioni & E. Etzioni (Eds.), *Social changes: Sources, patterns, and consequences.* New York: Basic Books.

Burke, C., & Cummins, R. (Eds.) (1970). *Searching for meaning.* Winona, MN: St. Mary's College Press. Copyright © 1970, St. Mary's College Press. Used by permission.

Burros, M. (1988, February 24). Women: Out of the house but not out of the kitchen. *New York Times,* pp. 1, 18.

Buss, D. M. (1985). Human mate selection. *American Scientist, 73,* 47-51.

Buss, D. M. (1987). Sex differences in human mate selection criteria: An evolutionary perspective. In C. Crawford et al. (Eds.), *Sociobiology and psychology: Issues, ideas, and findings.* Hillsdale, N.J.: Erlbaum.

Buss, D. M. (1989). Sex differences in human mate preference: Evolutionary hypotheses tested in 37 cultures. *Behavioral and Brain Sciences, 12,* 1-49.

Buss, D. M. & Barnes, M. (1986). Preferences in Human Mate Selection. *Journal of Personality and Social Psychology,* Vol. 50, No. 3, 559-570. Copyright © 1986 by the American Psychological Association. Adapted by permission.

Butler, R. N. (1975). *Why survive? Being old in America.* New York: Harper & Row.

Butler, S. (1976). Breaking dependency in marriage. *Marriage and Family Living, 58,*(8), 23-25.

Byrne, D. (1977, February). A pregnant pause in the sexual revolution. *Psychology Today,* pp. 67-68. Used by permission.

Callahan, S. (1986). *Adrift: Seventy-six days lost at sea,* pp. 74, 81, 96, 108, 113, 144, 116, 187.

Campbell, A., Converse, P. E., & Rodgers, W. L. (1976). Human mate selection. *American Scientist, 73,* 47-51.

Campbell, J. D., Tesser, A., & Fairey, P. J. (1986). Conformity and attention to the stimulus: Some temporal and contextual dynamics. *Journal of Personality and Social Psychology, 51,* 315-324.

Cantril, H. (1958). *The politics of despair.* New York: Basic Books.

Caplan, G. (1981). Mastery of stress: Psychosocial aspects. *American Journal of Psychiatry, 138,* 413-420.

Carron, A. V., & Bailey, D. A. (1974). Strength development in boys from 10 through 16 years. *Monographs of the Society for Research in Child Development, 39,* No. 4, 1-36.

Carson, R. (1969). *Interaction concepts of personality.* Chicago: Aldine.

Carson, R. C., Butcher, J. N., & Coleman, J. C. (1988). *Abnormal psychology and modern life* (8th ed.). Glenview, IL: Scott, Foresman.

Cartwright, D., & Zander, A. (Eds.). (1968). *Group dynamics: Research and theory* (3rd ed.). New York: Harper & Row.

Chance, P. (1981, January). That drained-out, used-up feeling. *Psychology Today,* pp. 88-95.

Chiriboga, D. A. (1981). The developmental psychology of middle age. In J. Howells (Ed.), *Modern perspectives in the psychiatry of middle age.* New York: Brunner/Mazel.

Cholden, L. (1954). Some psychiatric problems in the rehabilitation of the blind. *Menninger Clinic Bulletin,* 18, 107-112.

Cimbalo, R. S., Faling, V., & Mousaw, P. (1976). The course of love: A cross-sectional design. *Psychological Reports, 38,* 1292-1294.

Clausen, J. A. (1981). Men's occupational careers in the middle years. In D. H. Eichorn, J. A. Clausen, N. Haan, M. P. Honzik, & P. Mussen (Eds.), *Present and past in middle life* (pp. 299-319). New York: Academic Press.

Cobb, S., & Rose, R. M. (1973). Hypertension, peptic ulcer, and diabetes in air traffic controllers. *Journal of the American Medical Association, 224,* 489-493.

Coddington, R. D. (1984). Measuring the stressfulness of a child's environment. In J. H. Humphrey (Ed.), *Stress in childhood* (pp. 97-126). New York: AMS Press.

Cohen, L. H. (Ed.) (1988). *Life events and psychological functioning: Theoretical and methodological issues.* Newbury Park, CA: Sage Publications.

Cohen, S., & McKay, G. (1984). Social support, stress, and the buffering hypothesis: A theoretical analysis. In A. Baum, J. E. Singer, & S. E. Taylor (Eds.), *Handbook of psychology and health* (Vol. 4, pp. 253-263). Hillsdale, NJ: Erlbaum.

Colby, K. M. (1975). *Artificial paranoia: A computer simulation of paranoid processes.* New York: Pergamon Press.

Cole, C. L. (1977). Cohabitation in social context. In R. Libby & R. Whitehurst (Eds.), *Marriage and alternatives: Exploring intimate relationships.* Glenview, IL: Scott, Foresman and Co.

Coleman, J. C. (1973). Life stress and maladaptive behavior. *The American Journal of Occupational Therapy, 27,* 169-178.

Coleridge, S. T. (1802). "Answer to a child's question."

Collier, R. M. (1968). A biologically derived basic value as an initial context for behavioral science. *Journal of Humanistic Psychology, 8,* 1-15.

Comfort, A. (1963). Maturation, autoimmunity, and aging. *Lancet, 2,* 138.

Conger, J. J., & Petersen, A. C. (1984). *Adolescence and youth* (3rd ed.). New York: Harper & Row.

Corsini, R. J. (Ed.). (1977). *Current personality theories.* Itasca, IL: Peacock.

Cozby, P. C. (1973). Self-disclosure: A literature review. *Psychological Bulletin, 79,* 73-91.

Craig, G. J. (1986). *Human development* (4th ed.). Englewood Cliffs, NJ: Prentice-Hall.

Craig, G. J. (1989). *Human development* (5th ed.). Englewood Cliffs, NJ: Prentice-Hall.

Craighead, W. E., Kazdin, A. E., & Mahoney, M. J. (1981). *Behavior modification: Principles, issues, and applications* (2nd ed.). Boston: Houghton Mifflin.

Craik, F. I. M. (1977). Age differences in human memory. In J. E. Birren & K. W. Schaie (Eds.), *Handbook of the psychology of aging* (pp. 384-420). New York: Van Nostrand Reinhold.

Crockett, W. H., & Hummert, M. L. (1987). Perceptions of aging and the elderly. In K. W. Schaie & K. Eisdorfer (Eds.), *Annual review of gerontology and geriatrics* (Vol. 7) (pp. 217-241). New York: Springer.

Croft, R. (1952). From "Love" by Roy Croft. Reprinted from *The family book of best loved poems,* copyright 1952 by Doubleday & Co., Inc. by permission of Copeland & Lamm, Inc.

Cronbach, L. J. (1970). *Essentials of psychological testing* (3rd ed.). New York: Harper & Row.

Crooks, R., & Baur, K. (1980). *Our sexuality.* Menlo Park, CA: Benjamin/Cummings Publishing Co.

Cumming, E., & Henry, W. (1961). *Growing old.* New York: Basic Books.

D'Zurilla, T. J., & Goldfried, M. R. (1971). Problem solving and behavior modification. *Journal of Abnormal Psychology, 78,* 107-126.

Damon, W. (1983). *Social and personality development.* New York: W. W. Norton. Copyright © 1983 by W.W. Norton & Company, Inc. Used by permission.

Davidson, A. D. (1979). Coping with stress reactions in rescue workers: A program that worked. *Police Stress.* [Cited in Carson, Butcher, & Coleman, 1988]

Davison, G. C., Tsujimoto, R. N., & Glaros, A. G. (1973). Attribution and the maintenance of behavior change in falling asleep. *Journal of Abnormal Psychology, 82,* 124-133.

DeLora, J. S., Warren, C. A. B., & Ellison, C. R. (1981). *Understanding sexual interaction* by Joann S. DeLora,

Carol A. B. Warren and Carol Rinkleib Ellison. Copyright © 1981, 1977 by Houghton Mifflin Company. Reprinted by permission of Harper & Row, Publishers, Inc.

Dembroski, T. M., & Williams, R. B. (in press). Definition and assessment of coronary-prone behavior. In N. Schneiderman et al. (Eds.), *Handbook of research methods in cardiovascular behavioral medicine.* New York: Plenum Press.

DeNike, L. D., & Spielberger, C. D. (1963). Induced meditating states in verbal conditioning. *Journal of verbal learning and verbal behavior, 1,* 339-345.

Denney, N. W. (1982). Aging and cognitive changes. In B. B. Wolman (Ed.), *Handbook of developmental psychology* (pp. 807-827). Englewood Cliffs, NJ: Prentice-Hall.

Derr, M. (1977). Unemployment: The family crisis. *Marriage and Family Living, 59* (1), 18-20.

Deutsch, M., & Gerard, H. B. (1955). A study of normative and informational social influence upon individual judgment. *Journal of Abnormal and Social Psychology, 51,* 629-636.

Dewey, J. (1939). *Theory of valuation.* Chicago: University of Chicago Press.

Dickens, C. (1958). *A tale of two cities.* New York: Dutton. (Originally published, 1859).

Doherty, W. J., & Jacobson, N. S. (1982). Marriage and the family. In B. Wolman (Ed.), *Handbook of developmental psychology* (pp. 667-680). Englewood Cliffs, NJ: Prentice-Hall.

Dollard, J., & Miller, N. E. (1950). *Personality and psychotherapy: An analysis in terms of learning, thinking, and culture.* New York: McGraw-Hill.

Dooley, D., & Catalano, R. (1980). Economic change as a cause of behavioral disorder. *Psychological Bulletin, 87,* 450-468.

Dubin, R. (1958). *The world of work: Industrial society and human relations.* Englewood Cliffs, NJ: Prentice-Hall.

Durant, W., & Durant, A. (1967). *Rousseau and revolution.* New York: Simon & Schuster. Copyright © 1967 by Will and Ariel Durant. Reprinted by permission of Simon & Schuster, Inc.

Dyer, E. D. (1963). Parenthood as crisis: A re-study. *Marriage and Family Living, 25*(5), 196-201.

Eastman, C. (1976). Behavioral formulations of depression. *Psychological Review, 83,* 277-291.

Education and job satisfaction. (1976, May 8). *Science News,* p. 297.

Edwards, J. N., & Booth, A. (1976). Sexual behavior in and out of marriage: An assessment of correlates. *Journal of Marriage and the Family, 38,* 73-81.

Egeland, J. A., Gerhard, D. S., Pauls, D. L., Sussex, J. N., Kidd, K. K., Allen, C. R., Hostetter, A. M., & Housman, D. E. (1987). Bipolar affective disorders linked to DNA markers on chromosome 11. *Nature, 325,* 783-787.

Einstein, A. (1949). *The world as I see it.* New York: Philosophical Library.

Ekman, P. (1975, September). Face muscles talk every language. *Psychology Today,* pp. 35-36; 38-39.

Ekman, P., & Friesen, W. V. (1968). Nonverbal behavior in psychotherapy research. In J. M. Schlien (Ed.), *Research in psychotherapy.* Washington, DC: American Psychological Association.

Ekman, P., & Friesen, W. V. (1975). *Unmasking the face: A guide to recognizing emotions from facial clues.* Englewood Cliffs, NJ: Prentice-Hall.

Ekman, P., Friesen, W. V., & Ellsworth, P. (1972). *Emotion in the human face: Guidelines for research and an integration of findings.* New York: Pergamon Press.

Ekman, P., Friesen, W. V., O'Sullivan, M., & Scherer, K. (1980). Relative importance of face, body, and speech in judgments of personality and affect. *Journal of Personality and Social Psychology, 38,* 270-277.

Ellis, A. (1973). Rational-emotive therapy. In R. Corsini (Ed.), *Current psychotherapies.* Itasca, IL: F. E. Peacock.

Ellis, A., & Harper, R. A. (1961). *A guide to rational living.* Hollywood, CA: Wilshire.

Ellis, A., & Harper, R. A. (1975). *A new guide to rational living.* No. Hollywood, CA: Wilshire Book Co.

Ellis, H. (1906). *Studies in the psychology of sex.* New York: Random House.

Elvenstar, D. (1982). *A child: To have or have not?* San Francisco, CA: Harbor.

Emmelkamp, P. M. G. (1986). Behavior therapy with adults. In S. L. Garfield & A. E. Bergin (Eds.), *Handbook of psychotherapy and behavior change* (3rd ed.) (pp. 385-442). New York: Wiley.

Engler, B. (1985). *Personality theories: An introduction.* Boston: Houghton Mifflin.

Epstein, Y. M. (1981). Crowding, stress and human behavior. *Journal of Social Issues, 37*(1), 126-144.

Erickson, M. H. (1939). Experimental demonstration of the psychopathology of everyday life. *Psychoanalytic Quarterly, 8,* 338-353. Reprinted by permission.

Erikson, E. H. (1963). *Childhood and society* (Rev. ed.). New York: Norton.

Erikson, E. H. (1968). *Identity, youth, and crisis.* New York: Norton.

Evans, G. W. (1979). Crowding and human performance. *Journal of Applied Social Psychology, 9,* 27-46.

Evans, G. W. (1980). Environmental cognition. *Psychological Bulletin, 88,* 259-287.

Evans, P., & Bartolome, F. (1980). *Must success cost so much?* New York: Basic Books.

Exner, J. E. (1974). *The Rorschach: A comprehensive system.* New York: Wiley.

Fakouri, M. E. (1976). "Cognitive development in adulthood: A fifth stage?" A critique. *Developmental Psychology, 12,* 472.

Fast, J. (1970). *Body language.* New York: Penguin.

Faulkner, W. (1961). "Acceptance Speech Upon Receipt of the Nobel Prize for Literature" from the *The Faulkner reader.* New York: Random House.

Fay, R. E., Turner, C. F., Klassen, A. D., & Gagnon, J. H. (1989). Prevalence and patterns of same-gender sexual contact among men. *Science, 243,* 338-348.

Feldman, R. S. (1985). *Social psychology: Theories, research, and applications.* New York: McGraw-Hill.

Felipe, N. J., & Sommer, R. (1966-1967). Invasion of personal space. *Social Problems, 14,* 206-214.

Fenz, W. D., & Epstein, S. (1969, September). Stress: In the air. *Psychology Today,* pp. 27-28; 58-59.

Feshbach, S., & Weiner, B. (1982). *Personality.* Lexington, MA: D.C. Heath.

Festinger, L., Schachter, S., & Back, K. (1950). *Social pressures in informal groups: A study of human factors in housing.* New York: Harper & Row.

Fishman, D. B., & Neigher, W. D. (1982). American psychology in the eighties: Who will buy? *American Psychologist, 37,* 533-546.

Flanagan, J. C. From "Research approach to improving our quality of life" by John C. Flanagan in *American Psychologist,* February 1978. Copyright © 1978 by the American Psychological Association. Reprinted by permission of the author.

Flavell, J. H. (1970). Changes in adulthood. In L. R. Goulet & P. B. Baltes (Eds.), *Life-span developmental psychology: Research and theory.* New York: Academic Press.

Fox, B. (1983). Current theory of psychogenic effects on cancer incidence and prognosis. *Journal of Psychosocial Oncology, 1,* 17-32.

Frankl, V. (1971). *Man's search for meaning.* New York: Simon & Schuster.

Fraser, C. (1971). Group risk-taking and group polarization. *European Journal of Social Psychology, 1,* 493-510.

Freedman, J. L. (1975). *Crowding and behavior.* New York: Viking Press.

Freedman, J. L., Levy, A. S., Buchanan, R. W., & Price, J. (1972). Crowding and human aggressiveness. *Journal of Experimental Social Psychology, 8,* 528-548.

Fremouw, W. J. (1984). Cognitive-behavioral therapies for modification of communication apprehension. In J. A. Daly & J. C. McCroskey (Eds.), *Avoiding communication: Shyness, reticence, and communication apprehension* (pp. 209-215). Beverly Hills: Sage.

Fremouw, W. J., & Scott, M. D. (1979). Cognitive restructuring: An alternative method of the treatment of communication apprehension. *Communication Education, 28,* 129-133.

Freud, A. (1946). *The ego and the mechanisms of defense.* New York: International Universities Press.

Freud, S. (1954). *Psychopathology of everyday life* (2nd ed.). London: Ernest Benn, Ltd. (Originally published, 1901.)

Freud, S. (1955). *Civilization and its discontents.* Westport, CT: Associated Booksellers. (Originally published, 1930.)

Freud, S. (1961). Female sexuality. In S. Freud, *The standard edition of the complete psychological works of Sigmund Freud. Vol. XXI. The future of an illusion, civilization and its discontents, and other works* (pp. 225-243). London: Hogarth Press. (Originally published, 1931.)

Freudenberger, H. J., & Richelson, G. (1980). *Burnout: The high cost of high achievement.* New York: Bantam Books.

Friedman, H. S., & Booth-Kewley, S. (1988). Validity of the Type A construct: A reprise. *Psychological Bulletin, 104,* 381-384.

Friedman, M., & Rosenman, R. H. (1974). *Type A behavior and your heart.* New York: Knopf.

Friedman, M., Thoresen, C., Gill, J., Powell, L., Ulmer, D., Thompson, L., et al. (1984). Alteration of Type A behavior and reduction in cardiac occurrences in postmyocardial infarction patients. *American Heart Journal, 108,* 237-248.

Friedrich, G., & Goss, B. (1984). Systematic desensitization. In J. A. Daly & J. C. McCroskey (Eds.), *Avoiding communication: Shyness, reticence, and communication apprehension* (pp. 173-187). Beverly Hills: Sage.

Fromm, E. (1955). *The sane society.* New York: Holt.

Fromm, E. (1956). *The art of loving.* New York: Harper & Row.

Furlong, F. W. (1981). Determinism and free will: Review of the literature. *American Journal of Psychiatry, 134,* 435-439.

Galanter, M. (1984). Self-help large-group therapy for alcoholism: A controlled study. *Alcoholism: Clinical and Experimental Research, 8,* 16-23.

Gandhi, M. (1957). *An autobiography: The story of my ex-*

*periments with truth* (M. Desai, Trans.). Boston: Beacon Press.

Garfield, S. L. (Ed.) (1983). Special section: Meta-analysis and psychotherapy. *Journal of Consulting and Clinical Psychology, 51,* 3-75.

Garfinkel, H. (1963). A conception of, and experiments with, "trust" as a condition of stable concerted actions. In O. J. Harvey (Ed.), *Motivation and social interaction* (pp. 187-238). Copyright © 1963 by the Ronald Press. Reprinted by permission of John Wiley & Sons, Inc.

Garmezy, N. (1976). Vulnerable and invulnerable: Theory, research, and intervention. *Master Lectures in Developmental Psychology,* American Psychological Association. (Ms. No. 1337).

Gatchel, R. J., Schaeffer, M. A., & Baum, A. (1985). A physiological field study of stress at Three Mile Island. *Psychophysiology, 22,* 175-181.

Geer, J. H., Davison, G. C., & Gatchel, R. I. (1970). Reduction of stress in humans through nonveridical perceived control of aversive stimulation. *Journal of Personality and Social Psychology, 16,* 731-738.

Gelven, M. (1973). Guilt and human meaning. *Humanitas, 9*(1), 69-81.

Gerow, J. R. (1986). *Psychology: An introduction.* Glenview, IL: Scott, Foresman. Used with permission.

Gilbert, S. J. (1976). Self-disclosure, intimacy, and communication in families. *The Family Coordinator, 25,* 221-231.

Gillespie, P. R., & Bechtel, L. (1986). *Less stress in 30 days.* New York: NAL Penguin.

Gilligan, C. (1982). *In a different voice: Psychological theory and women's development.* Cambridge, MA: Harvard University Press.

Ginzberg, E. (1966). *The development of human resources.* New York: McGraw-Hill.

Gitter, A. G., & Black, H. (1976). Is self-disclosure self-revealing? *Journal of Counseling Psychology, 23,* 327-332.

Glaser, R., & Kiecolt-Glaser, J. (1988). Stress-associated immune suppression and Acquired Immune Deficiency Syndrome (AIDS). In T. P. Bridge, A. F. Mirsky, & F. K. Goodwin (Eds.), *Psychological, neuropsychiatric, and substance abuse aspects of AIDS* (pp. 203-215). New York: Raven Press.

Glass, D. C., & Singer, J. E. (1972). *Urban stress: Experiments on noise and social stressors.* New York: Academic Press.

Glenn, N. D., & McLanahan, S. (1982a). Children and marital happiness: A further specification of the rela-

tionship. *Journal of Marriage and the Family, 44* 63-72.

Glenn, N. D., & McLanahan, S. (1982b). The effects of offspring on the psychological well-being of older adults. *Journal of Marriage and the Family, 44,* 409-421.

Glenn, N. D., & Weaver, C. N. (1977). The marital happiness of remarried divorced persons. *Journal of Marriage and the Family, 39,* 331-337.

Glogower, F. D., Fremouw, W. J., & McCroskey, J. C. (1978). A component analysis of cognitive restructuring. *Cognitive therapy and research, 2,* 209-223.

Goertzel, V., & Goertzel, M. (1966). *Cradles of eminence.* Boston: Little, Brown.

Gold, M., & Yanof, D. S. (1985). Mothers, daughters, and girlfriends. *Journal of Personality and Social Psychology, 49,* 654-659.

Goldberger, L., & Breznitz, S. (Eds.). (1982). *Handbook of stress: Theoretical and clinical aspects.* New York: Free Press.

Goldfried, M. R., & Sobocinski, D. (1975). Effects of irrational beliefs on emotional arousal. *Journal of Counseling and Clinical Psychology, 43,* 504-510.

Gonzales, M. H., Davis, J. M., Loney, G. L., LuKens, C. K., Junghans, C. M. (1983). Interactional approach to interpersonal attraction. *Journal of Personality and Social Psychology, 44,* 1192-1197.

Gonzales, P. (1972). *Tennis,* New York: Cornerstone Library.

Gottfredson, G. D., Holland, J., & Ogawa, D. K. (1982). *Dictionary of Holland occupational codes.* Palo Alto, CA: Consulting Psychologist Press.

Gould, R. L. (1972). The phases of adult life: A study in developmental psychology. *American Journal of Psychiatry, 129,* 521-531.

Gould, R. L. (1978). *Transformations: Growth and change in adult life.* New York: Simon & Schuster.

Gould, R. L. (1980). Transformations during early and middle adult years. In N. J. Smelser & E. H. Erikson (Eds.), *Themes of work and love in adulthood.* Cambridge, MA: Harvard University Press.

Greenberg, J., & Archambault, F. (1973). Masturbation, self-esteem, and other variables. *Journal of Sex Research, 9,* 41-51.

Greenblatt, C. S. (1983). The salience of sexuality in the early years of marriage. *Journal of Marriage and the Family, 45,* 289-299.

Greenglass, E. R. (1982). *A world of difference: Gender roles in perspective.* Toronto: Wiley.

Grosskopf, D. (1983). *Sex and the married woman.* New York: Wallaby Books.

Haley, J. (1962). Whither family therapy. *Family Process, 1,* 69-100.

Haley, J. (1963). *Strategies of psychotherapy.* New York: Grune & Stratton.

Hall, C. S., & Lindzey, G. (1978). *Theories of personality* (3rd ed.). New York: Wiley.

Hall, E. T. (1966). *The hidden dimension.* Garden City, NY: Doubleday.

Hamilton, D. L., & Zanna, M. P. (1972). Differential weighting of favorable and unfavorable attributes in impressions of personality. *Journal of Experimental Research in Personality, 6,* 204-212.

Hammarskjöld, D. From *Markings,* by Dag Hammarskjöld, translated by Leif Sjoberg and W. H. Auden. Translation Copyright © 1964 by Alfred A. Knopf, Inc. and Faber and Faber, Ltd. Reprinted by permission of Alfred A. Knopf, Inc. and Faber and Faber, Ltd.

Hammond, K. R., & Summers, D. A. (1972). Cognitive control. *Psychological Review, 79,* 58-67.

Hancock, T. (1982). Beyond health care: Creating a healthy future. *The Futurist, 16,*(4), 4-18.

Hanna, S. L., & Knaub, P. K. (1981). Cohabitation before marriage: Its relationship to family strengths. *Alternative Lifestyles, 4,* 507-522.

Hare, R. D. From *Psychopathy: Theory and research* by Robert D. Hare. New York: Wiley, 1970. Copyright © 1970 by John Wiley & Sons, Inc. Reprinted by permission of John Wiley & Sons, Inc.

Harkins, E. B. (1978). Effects of empty-nest transition on self-report of psychological and physical well-being. *Journal of Marriage and the Family, 40,* 549-558.

Harman, W. W. (1976). *An incomplete guide to the future.* San Francisco: San Francisco Book Company.

Harman, W. W. (1977). The coming transformation. *The Futurist, 11,*(1), 4-12.

Harris, A. C. (1986). *Child development.* St. Paul, MN: West Publishing Co.

Harrow, M., Grossman, L. S., Silverstein, M. L., & Meltzer, H. Y. (1982). Thought pathology in manic and schizophrenic patients. *Archives of General Psychiatry, 39,* 665-671.

Hartmann, H. (1958). *Ego psychology and the problem of adaptation.* New York: International Universities Press.

Hartup, W. W. (1979). The social world of children. *American Psychologist, 34,* 944-950.

Haskins, C. P. (1968). *Report of the president, 1966-1967.* Washington, DC: Carnegie Institute of Washington.

Hatfield, E. and Walster, G. W. *A new look at love.* Lanham, MD: University Press of America, 1978.

Havens, L. I. (1974). The existential use of the self. *American Journal of Psychiatry, 131,* 1-10.

Havighurst, R. J. (1969). Research and development in social gerontology: A report of a special committee of the Gerontological Society. *The Gerontologist, 9,* 1-90.

Havighurst, R. J. (1974). *Developmental tasks and education* (3rd ed.). New York: McKay.

Havighurst, R. J. (1982). The world of work. In B. Wolman (Ed.), *Handbook of developmental psychology* (pp. 771-787). Englewood Cliffs, NJ: Prentice-Hall.

Hennigan, K. M., Del Rosario, M. L., Heath, L., Cook, T. D., Wharton, J. D., & Calder, B. J. (1982). Impact of the introduction of television on crime in the United States: Empirical findings and theoretical implications. *Journal of Personality and Social Psychology, 42,* 461-477.

Hergenhahn, B. R. (1984). *An introduction to theories of personality* (2nd ed.). Englewood Cliffs, NJ: Prentice-Hall.

Hershey, D. (1974). *Life span and factors affecting it.* Springfield, IL: Charles C. Thomas.

Hess, B. (1972). Friendship. In M. Riley, M. Johnson & A. Foner (Eds.), *Aging and society, Volume 3: A sociology of age stratification.* New York: Russell Sage Foundation.

Hess, B., & Waring, J. M. (1978). Parent and child in later life: Rethinking the relationship. In R. Lerner & G. Spanier (Eds.), *Child influences on marital and family interaction: A life-span perspective.* New York: Academic Press.

Hess, R. D., & Camara, K. A. (1979). Post-divorce family relationships as mediating factors in the consequences of divorce for children. *Journal of Social Issues, 35,* 79-96.

Hilgard, E. R. (1973). The domain of hypnosis: With some comments on alternative paradigms. *American Psychologist, 28,* 972-982.

Hilgard, E. R., & Hilgard, J. R. (1975). *Hypnosis in the relief of pain.* Los Angeles: Kaufman.

Hirschfeld, R. M. A., & Cross, C. (1982). Epidemiology of affective disorders. *Archives of General Psychiatry, 39*(1), 35-46.

Hite, S. (1981). *The Hite report on male sexuality.* New York: Alfred A. Knopf.

Hjelle, L. A., & Ziegler, D. J. (1981). *Personality theories* (2nd ed.). New York: McGraw-Hill.

Hobbs, D. F., Jr., & Cole, S. P. (1977). Transition to parenthood: A decade of replication. *Journal of Marriage and the Family, 38,* 723-731.

Hoffman, L. (1989). Effects of maternal employment in the two-parent family. *American Psychologist, 44,* 283-292.

Hohenemser, C., Kates, R. W., & Slovic, P. (1983). The

nature of technological hazard. *Science, 220,* 378-384.

Holland, J. L. (1966). *The psychology of vocational choice.* Waltham, MA: Blaisdell.

Holland, J. L. (1973). *Making vocational choices: A theory of careers.* Englewood Cliffs, NJ: Prentice-Hall.

Holland, J. L. (1985). *Making vocational choices: A theory of vocational personalities and work environments* (2nd ed.). Englewood Cliffs, NJ: Prentice-Hall.

Holmes, T. H., & Rahe, R. H. (1967). Reprinted with permission from *Journal of Psychosomatic Research, 11,* 213-218, Holmes, T. H., & Rahe, R. H., The social readjustment rating sale, Copyright 1967, Pergamon Press, Ltd.

Holmes, T. S., & Holmes, T. H. (1970). Short-term intrusions into the life-style routine. *Journal of Psychosomatic Research, 14,* 121-132. Copyright © 1970 by Pergamon Press Ltd. Reprinted by permission from Journal of Psychosomatic Research.

Honeycutt, J. M., Wilson, C., & Parker, C. (1982). Effects of sex and degrees of happiness on perceived styles of communicating in and out of the marital relationship. *Journal of Marriage and the Family, 44,* 395-406.

Horn, J. L., & Donaldson, G. (1980). Cognitive development in adulthood. In J. Kagan & O. G. Brim, Jr. (Eds.), *Constancy and change in development.* Cambridge, MA: Harvard University Press.

Hornung, C. A., & McCullough, B. C. (1981). Status relationships in dual-employment marriages: Consequences for psychological well-being. *Journal of Marriage and the Family, 43,* 125-141.

Horton, P. C., Gewirtz, H., & Kreutter, K. J. (1988). *The solace paradigm: An eclectic search for psychological immunity.* New York: International Universities Press.

House, J. S., Landis, K. R., & Umberson, D. (1988). Social relationships and health. *Science, 241,* 540-545.

Houseknecht, S. K., & Macke, A. S. (1981). Combining marriage and career: The marital adjustment of professional women. *Journal of Marriage and the Family, 43,* 651-661.

Hoyer, W. J., & Plude, D. G. (1980). Attentional and perceptual processes in the study of cognitive aging. In L. Poom (Ed.), *Aging in the 1980s: Psychological issues.* Washington, DC: American Psychological Association.

Hubbard, B. M. (1981). Critical paths to an all-win world. *The Futurist, 15*(3), 31-37.

Hudson, W. W., Murphy, G. J., & Nurius, P. S. (1983). A short-form scale to measure liberal vs. conservative orientations toward human sexual expression. *Journal of Sex Research, 19,* 258-272. Reprinted by permission of *The Journal of Sex Research,* publication of the Society for the Scientific Study of Sex.

Hughes, F. R., & Noppe, L. D. (1985). *Human development across the life span.* St. Paul, MN: West Publishing Co.

Hulicka, I. M. (1967). Age differences in retention as a function of interference. *Journal of Gerontology, 22,* 180-184.

Hull, D. (1977). Life circumstances and physical illness: A cross-disciplinary survey of research content and method for the decade 1965-1975. *Journal of Psychosomatic Research, 21,* 115-139.

Humphrey, J. H. (1984). Some general causes of stress in children. In J. H. Humphrey (Ed.), *Stress in childhood* (pp. 3-18). New York: AMS Press.

Humphrey, J. H., & Humphrey, J. N. (1985). *Controlling stress in children.* Springfield, IL: Charles C. Thomas.

Hunt, B., & Hunt, M. (1975). *Prime time: A guide to the pleasures and opportunities of the new middle age.* New York: Stein & Day.

Hunt, J. McV. (1964). The psychological basis for using preschool enrichment as an antidote for cultural deprivation. *Merrill-Palmer Quarterly, 10,* 209-248.

Hunt, M. (1974). *Sexual behavior in the 1970s.* Chicago: Playboy Press.

Hyde, J. S. (1985). *Half the human experience: The psychology of women.* (3rd ed.) Lexington, Mass.: Heath.

Ivanhoe, A. J. (1977, January/February/March). Overcoming loneliness. *Elysium,* pp. 18-19.

Jacobson, E. (1934). *You must relax.* New York: McGraw-Hill.

Jacobson, E. (1938). *Progressive relaxation.* Chicago: University of Chicago Press.

Jahoda, M. (1958). *Current concepts of positive mental health. Joint Commission on Mental Illness and Health.* New York: Basic Books.

James, W. (1890). *The principles of psychology.* New York: Holt.

Janda, L. H., & Klenke-Hamel, K. E. *Human sexuality.* New York: D. Van Nostrand, 1980. Copyright © 1980 by Litton Educational Publishing, Inc. Reprinted by permission of the publisher, Brooks/Cole Publishing Company, Monterey, California.

Janis, I. L. (1982). *Groupthink: Psychological studies of policy decisions and fiascoes* (2nd ed.). Boston: Houghton Mifflin.

Janis, I. L., & Mann, I. Reprinted with permission of The Free Press, a Division of Macmillan, Inc. from Decision making: A psychological analysis of conflict, choice, and commitment by Irving L. Janis and Leon Mann. Copyright © 1977 by The Free Press.

Jarvik, M. E. (1967, May). The psychopharmacological revolution. *Psychology Today,* pp. 51-58.

Jemott, J. B., III, & Locke, S. E. (1984). Psychosocial factors, immunologic mediation, and human susceptibility to infectious disease: How much do we know? *Psychological Bulletin, 95,* 78-108.

Joffe, L. S., & Vaughn, B. E. (1982). Infant-mother attachment: Theory, assessment, and implications for development. In B. Wolman (Ed.), *Handbook of developmental psychology* (pp. 190-207). Englewood Cliffs, NJ: Prentice-Hall.

Jones, M. C., & Bayley, N. (1950). Physical maturing among boys as related to behavior. *Journal of Educational Psychology, 41,* 129-148.

Jones, W. H., & Carpenter, B. N. (1986). Shyness, social behavior, and relationships. In W. H. Jones, J. M. Cheek, & S. R. Briggs (Eds.), *Shyness: Perspectives on research and treatment* (pp. 227-238). New York: Plenum Press.

Jones, W. H., Cheek, J. M., & Briggs, S. R. (Eds.). (1986). *Shyness: Perspectives on research and treatment.* New York: Plenum Press.

Joseph, J. G., Emmons, C., Kessler, R. C., Wortman, C. B., O'Brien, K., Hocker, W. T., & Schaefer, C. (1984). Coping with the threat of AIDS: An approach to psychosocial assessment. *American Psychologist, 39,* 1297-1302.

Julien, R. M. (1981). *A primer of drug action* (3rd ed.). San Francisco: W. H. Freeman.

Kabanoff, B. (1980). Work and nonwork: A review of models, methods, and findings. *Psychological Bulletin, 88,* 60-77.

Kabanoff, B., & O'Brien, G. E. (1980). Work and leisure: A task attributes analysis. *Journal of Applied Psychology, 65,* 596-609.

Kando, T., & Summers, W. (1971). The impact of work on leisure. *Pacific Sociological Review, 14,* 310-327.

Karlin, R. A., Epstein, Y. M., & Aiello, J. R. (1978). Strategies for the investigation of crowding. In A. Esser & B. Greenbie (Eds.), *Design for communality and privacy.* New York: Plenum Press.

Kasper, R. G. (1980). Perceptions of risk and their effects on decision making. In R. C. Schwing and W. A. Albers, Jr. (Eds.), *Societal risk management: How safe is safe enough?* (pp. 71-84). New York: Plenum.

Kastenbaum, R. (1977). *Death, society, and human experience.* St. Louis: C. V. Mosby.

Kastenbaum, R. (1979). *Growing old: Years of fulfillment.* New York: Harper & Row.

Kastenbaum, R., & Durkee, N. (1964). Young people view old age. In R. Kastenbaum (Ed.), *New thoughts on old age.* New York: Springer.

Katchadourian, H. A., & Lunde, D. T. (1980). *Fundamentals of human sexuality* (3rd ed.). New York: Holt, Rinehart & Winston.

Katz, A. H. (1981). Self-help and mutual aid: An emerging social movement? *American Review of Sociology, 7,* 129-155.

Kaufman, W. (1973). *Without guilt and justice: From decidophobia to autonomy.* New York: Wyden.

Kelley, H. H., & Thibaut, J. W. (1978). *Interpersonal relations: A theory of interdependence.* New York: Wyden.

Kelly, G. A. (1955). *The psychology of personal constructs* (Vols. 1 and 2). New York: Norton.

Kelly, L. (1984). Social skills training as a mode of treatment for social communication problems. In J. A. Daly & J. C. McCroskey (Eds.), *Avoiding communication: Shyness, reticence, and communication apprehension* (pp. 189-207). Beverly Hills: Sage.

Kempe, R. S., & Kempe, C. H. (1978). *Child abuse.* Cambridge, MA: Harvard University Press.

Kennedy, J. L., Giuffra, L. A., Moises, H. W., Cavalli-Sforza, L. L., Pakstis, A. J., Kidd, J. R., Castiglione, C. M., Sjogren, B., Wetterberg, L., & Kidd, K. K. (1988). Evidence against linkage of schizophrenia to markers on chromosome 5 in a northern Swedish pedigree. *Nature, 336,* 167-170.

Kent, S. (1976, March). How do we age? *Geriatrics,* pp. 128-134.

Kerckhoff, A. C., & Back, K. W. From Alan C. Kerckhoff/Kurt W. Back, *The June bug: A study of hysterical contagion,* © 1968, p. 8. Reprinted by permission of Prentice-Hall, Inc., Englewood Cliffs, New Jersey.

Kessler, R. C., Price, R. H., & Wortman, C. B. (1985). Social factors in psychopathology: Stress, social support, and coping processes. *Annual Review of Psychology, 36,* 531-572.

Kiecolt-Glaser, J. K., Glaser, R., Williger, D., Stout, J., Massick, G., Sheppard, S., Ricker, D., Romisher, S. C., Briner, W., Bonnell, G., & Donnerberg, R. (1985). Psychosocial enhancement of immunocompetence in a geriatric population. *Health Psychology, 4,* 25-41.

Kiecolt-Glaser, J., & Glaser, R. (1988). Major life changes, chronic stress, and immunity. In T. P. Bridge, A. F. Mirsky, & F. K. Goodwin (Eds.), *Psychological, neuropsychiatric, and substance abuse aspects of AIDS* (pp. 217-224). New York: Raven Press.

Kinsey, A. C., Pomeroy, W. B., & Martin, C. E. (1948). *Sexual behavior in the human male.* Philadelphia: W. B. Saunders.

Kinsey, A. C., Pomeroy, W. B., Martin, C. E., & Gebhard, P. H. (1953). *Sexual behavior in the human female.* Philadelphia: W. B. Saunders.

Kirkendall, L. A., & Anderson, P. B. (1973). Authentic selfhood: Basis for tomorrow's sexuality. In E. S. Morrison & V. Borosage (Eds.), *Human sexuality: Contemporary perspectives.* Palo Alto, CA: National Press Books.

Klein, K., & Harris, B. (1979). Disruptive effects of disconfirmed expectancies about crowding. *Journal of Personality and Social Psychology, 37,* 769-777.

Klinger, E. (1977). *Meaning and void: Inner experience and the incentives in people's lives.* Minneapolis, MN: University of Minnesota Press.

Kluckhohn, C., & Murray, H. A. (1953). Personality formation: The determinants. In C. Kluckhohn, H. A. Murray, & D. M. Schneider (Eds.), *Personality in nature, society, and culture* (2nd ed., pp. 53-67). New York: Knopf. Used with permission.

Kluckhohn, F. R., & Strodtbeck, F. L. (1961). *Variations in value orientation.* New York: Harper & Row.

Knox, D. (1979). *Exploring marriage and the family.* Glenview, IL: Scott, Foresman and Co.

Knox, D. (1985). *Choices in relationships: An introduction to marriage and the family.* St. Paul, MN: West. Used with permission.

Kobasa, S. C. (1979). Stressful life events, personality, and health: An inquiry into hardiness. *Journal of Personality and Social Psychology, 37,* 1-11.

Kohlberg, L. (1976). Moral stages and moralization: The cognitive-developmental approach. In T. Lickona (Ed.), *Moral development and behavior: Theory, research, and social issues.* New York: Holt, Rinehart & Winston.

Kohut, H. (1971). *The analysis of the self.* New York: International Universities Press.

Kohut, H. (1977). *The restoration of the self.* New York: International Universities Press.

Kramer, D. A. (1983). Post-formal operation? A need for further conceptualization. *Human Development, 26,* 91-105.

Krauthammer, C. (1983, August 1). The politics of a plague. *New Republic,* pp. 18-21.

Krebs, D., & Adinolfi, A. A. (1975). Physical attractiveness, social relations, and personality style. *Journal of Personality and Social Psychology, 31,* 245-263.

Kübler-Ross, E. (1969). *On death and dying.* New York: Macmillan.

Labouvie-Vief, G. (1980). Beyond formal operations: Uses and limits of pure logic in life-span development. *Human Development, 23,* 141-161.

Labouvie-Vief, G., & Schell, D. A. (1982). Learning and memory in later life. In B. Wolman (Ed.), *Handbook of developmental psychology* (pp. 828-846). Englewood Cliffs, NJ: Prentice-Hall.

Lahey, B. B., & Ciminero, A. R. (1980). *Maladaptive behavior:* An introduction to abnormal behavior. Glenview, IL: Scott, Foresman and Co.

Laing, R. D. (1967). *The politics of experience.* New York: Pantheon.

Lalljee, M., & Cook, M. (1973). Uncertainty in first encounters. *Journal of Personality and Social Psychology, 26,* 137-141.

Lamanna, M. A., & Riedmann, A. From *Marriages and families: Making choices throughout the life cycle,* 2nd ed., by Mary Ann Lamanna and Agnes Riedman © 1985, 1981 by Wadsworth, Inc. Used by permission of the publisher.

Lamott, K. (1975). *Escape from stress.* New York: G. P. Putnam's Sons.

Lander, E. S. (1988). Splitting schizophrenia. *Nature, 336,* 105-106.

Landis, J. T., & Landis, M. G. (1973). *Building a successful marriage* (6th ed.). Englewood Cliffs, NJ: Prentice-Hall.

Landman, J. T., & Dawes, R. M. (1982). Psychotherapy outcome: Smith and Glass' conclusions stand up under scrutiny. *American Psychologist, 37,* 504-516.

Lane, B. (1964). Attitudes of youth toward the aged. *Journal of Marriage and the Family, 26,* 229-231.

Langer, E. J., & Saegert, S. (1977). Crowding and cognitive control. *Journal of Personality and Social Psychology, 35,* 175-182.

LaRue, A., & Jarvik, L. F. (1982). Old age and behavioral changes. In B. Wolman (Ed.), *Handbook of developmental psychology* (pp. 791-806). Englewood Cliffs, NJ: Prentice Hall.

Lash, J. P. (1971). *Eleanor and Franklin.* New York: Norton.

Laudenslager, M. L., Ryan, S. M., Drugan, R. C., Hyson, R. L., & Maier, S. F. (1983). Coping and immunosuppression: Inescapable but not escapable shock suppresses lymphocyte proliferation. *Science, 221,* 568-570.

Lawler, E. E., & Hackman, J. R. (1969). The impact of employee participation in the development of pay incentive plans: A field experiment. *Journal of Applied Psychology, 53,* 467-471.

Lazarus, A. P. (1968). Learning theory in the treatment of depression. *Behavioral Research and Therapy, 8,* 83-89.

Lazarus, R. (1981). The stress and coping paradigm. In

C. Eisdorfer, D. Cohen, A. Kleinman, & P. Maxim (Eds.), *Models for clinical psychopathology*. New York: Spectrum.

Lazarus, R. S. (1981, July). Little hassles can be hazardous to health. *Psychology Today,* pp. 58-62. Reprinted with permission from Psychology Today Magazine. Copyright © 1981 (APA).

Lazarus, R. S., & DeLongis, A. (1983). Psychological stress and coping in aging. *American Psychologist, 38,* 245-254.

Lazarus, R. S., & Folkman, S. (1984). *Stress, appraisal, and coping.* New York: Springer.

Lazarus, R. S., DeLongis, A., Folkman, S., & Gruen, R. (1985). Stress and adaptational outcomes: The problem of confounded measures. *American Psychologist, 40,* 770-779.

Lee, D. (1959). Culture and the experience of value. In A. H. Maslow (Ed.), *New knowledge in human values.* New York: Harper & Row.

Lee, J. A. (1974, October). The styles of loving. *Psychology Today,* pp. 44-50.

Lee, J. A. (1977). A typology of styles of loving. *Personality and Social Behavior, 3,* 173-182.

Lefcourt, H. M., Miller, R. S., Ware, E. E., & Sherk, D. (1981). Locus of control as a modifier of the relationship between stressors and mood. *Journal of Personality and Social Psychology, 41,* 357-369.

Leff, M. J., Roatch, J. F., & Bunney, W. E., Jr. (1970). Environmental factors preceding the onset of severe depressions. *Psychiatry, 33,* 298-311.

Leon, G. R. (1977). *Case histories of deviant behavior: An interactional perspective.* Boston: Allyn & Bacon.

Levine, J., & Zigler, E. (1975). Denial and self-image in stroke, lung cancer, and heart disease patients. *Journal of Consulting and Clinical Psychology, 43,* 751-757.

Levinger, G. (1966). Sources of marital dissatisfaction among applicants for divorce. *American Journal of Orthopsychiatry, 36,* 803-807.

Levinson, D. J. (1986). A conception of adult development. *American Psychologist, 41,* 3-13.

Levinson, D. J., Darrow, C. N., Klein, E. B., Levinson, M. H., & McKee, B. (1978). *The seasons of a man's life.* New York: Ballantine Books.

Levy, S. M. (Ed.). (1982). *Biological mediators of behavior and disease.* Neoplasia, NY: Elsevier Biomedical.

Lewinsohn, P. M. (1974). A behavioral approach to depression. In R. J. Friedman & M. M. Katz (Eds.), *The psychology of depression: Contemporary theory and research.* New York: Halstead Press.

Lewis, R. A., Frenau, P. J., & Roberts, C. L. (1979). Fathers and the postparental transition. *The Family Coordinator, 28,* 514-520.

Libby, R. W. (1977). Creative singlehood as a sexual lifestyle. In R. W. Libby & R. N. Whitehurst (Eds.), *Marriage and alternatives: Exploring intimate relationships* (pp. 37-61). Glenview, IL: Scott, Foresman and Co.

Linder, S. B. (1970). *The harried leisure class.* New York: Columbia University Press.

Lipton, R. J. (1979). *The broken connection: On death and the continuity of life.* New York: Simon & Schuster.

Lobsenz, N. T. (1975, March). Taming the green-eyed monster. *Redbook,* pp. 74; 76-77; 188; 190.

London, M., Crandall, R., & Seals, G. W. (1977). The contribution of job and leisure satisfaction to the quality of life. *Journal of Applied Psychology, 62,* 328-334.

Loo, C. M. (1977). Beyond the effects of crowding: Situational and individual differences. In D. Stokols (Ed.), *Perspectives on environment and behavior.* New York: Plenum.

Lowenthal, M. F., Thurnher, M., & Chiriboga, D. (1975). *Four stages of life: A comparative study of women and men facing transitions.* San Francisco: Jossey-Bass.

Ludwick-Rosenthal, R., & Neufeld, R. W. J. (1988). Stress management during noxious medical procedures: An evaluative review of outcome studies. *Psychological Bulletin, 104,* 326-342.

Lydon, S. (1971). The politics of orgasm. In M. Garskof (Ed.), *Roles women play: Readings toward women's liberation.* Belmont, CA: Brooks/Cole.

Lynch, J. J. (1977). *The broken heart: The medical consequences of loneliness.* New York: Basic Books.

MacDonald, W. S., & Oden, C. W., Jr. (1973). Effects of extreme crowding on the performance of five married couples during twelve weeks of intensive training. *Proceedings of the 81st Annual Convention of the American Psychological Association,* 209-210.

Macklin, E. D. (1980). Nontraditional family forms: A decade of research. *Journal of Marriage and the Family, 42,* 905-922.

Maddi, S. R. (1989). *Personality theories: A comparative analysis* (5th ed.). Homewood, IL: Dorsey Press.

Mahl, G. H. (1968). Gestures and body movements in interviews. In J. M. Schlien (Ed.), *Research in psychotherapy.* Washington, DC: American Psychological Association.

Mahoney, E. R. (1983). *Human sexuality.* New York: McGraw-Hill.

Mahs, M. (1973, January 1). God, man and Apollo. *Time,* pp. 50-51.

Maier, S. (1987). Stress: Depression, disease, and the

Immune System. In F. Farley & C. N. Hull (Eds.), *Using psychological science: Making the public case* (pp. 13-24). Washington, DC: The Federation of Behavioral, Psychological, and Cognitive Sciences.

Maier, S. F., Davies, S., Gray, J. W., Jackson, R. L., Morrison, D. H., Moye, T., Madden, J., & Barchas, J. D. (1980). Opiate antagonists and long-term analgesic reaction induced by inescapable shock in rats. *Journal of Comparative and Psychological Psychology, 94,* 1172.

Mansfield, R., & Evans, M. G. (1975). Work and non-work in two occupational groups. *Industrial Relations, 6,* 48-54.

Marcia, J. E. (1966). Development and validation of ego-identity status. *Journal of Personality and Social Psychology, 3,* 551-558.

Marcia, J. E. (1976). Identity six years after: A follow-up study. *Journal of Youth and Adolescence, 5,* 145-160.

Marcia, J. E. (1980). Identity in adolescence. In J. Adelson (Ed.), *Handbook of adolescent psychology* (pp. 159-187). New York: Wiley.

Marmor, J. (Ed.). (1980a). Recent trends in psychotherapy. *American Journal of Psychiatry, 137,* 409-416.

Marmor, J. (Ed.). (1980b). *Homosexual behavior: A modern reappraisal.* New York: Basic Books.

Marx, M. B., Garrity, T. F., & Bowers, F. R. The influence of recent life experience on the health of college freshmen. *Journal of Psychosomatic Research, 19,* 1975, 87-89. Copyright © 1975 by Pergamon Press, Ltd. Reprinted by permission.

Maslach, C. (1982). *Burnout.* Englewood Cliffs, NJ: Prentice-Hall.

Masling, J. (Ed.) (1983). *Empirical studies of psychoanalytic theories* (Vol. 1). Hillsdale, NJ: Academic Press.

Masling, J. (Ed.) (1985). *Empirical studies of psychoanalytic theories* (Vol. 2). Hillsdale, NJ: Academic Press.

Maslow, A. H. (1954). *Motivation and personality.* New York: Harper & Row.

Maslow, A. H. (1968). *Toward a psychology of being* (2nd ed.). New York: D. Van Nostrand.

Maslow, A. H. (1969). Toward a humanistic biology. *American Psychologist, 24,* 734-735.

Maslow, A. H. (1970). *Motivation and personality* (rev. ed.). New York: Harper and Row.

Maslow, A. H. (1971). *The farther reaches of human nature.* New York: Viking.

Masters, W. H., & Johnson, V. E. (1966). *Human sexual response.* Boston: Little, Brown. Used with permission of the authors.

Masters, W. H., & Johnson, V. E. (1970). *Human sexual inadequacy.* Boston: Little, Brown.

Masters, W. H., & Johnson, V. E. (1975). *The pleasure bond.* Boston: Little, Brown.

Masters, W. H., & Johnson, V. E. (1976). Principles of the new sex therapy. *American Journal of Psychiatry, 133,* 548-554.

Masters, W. H., & Johnson, V. E. (1979). *Homosexuality in perspective.* Boston: Little, Brown.

Masters, W. H., Johnson, V. E., & Kolodny, R. C. (1982). *Human sexuality.* Boston: Little, Brown.

Mathes, E. (1980). Nine "colours" or types of romantic love. *Psychological Reports, 47,* 371-376.

Matthews, K. A. (1988). Coronary heart disease and Type A behaviors: Update on the alternative to the Booth-Kewley and Friedman (1987) quantitative review. *Psychological Bulletin, 104,* 373-380.

Matthews, K. A. (1988). Coronary heart disease and Type A behaviors: Update on and alternative to the Booth-Kewley and Freidman (1987) quantitative review. *Psychological Bulletin, 104,* 373-380.

May, R. (1969). *Love and will.* New York: Norton.

Mays, J. A. (1974, January 16). High blood pressure, soul food. *Los Angeles Times,* Part II, p. 7.

McCain, G., Cox, V. C., & Paulus, P. B. (1976). The relationship between illness, complaints and degree of crowding in a prison environment. *Environment and Behavior, 8,* 283-290.

McCann, R. "Inconsistency." Reprinted from *The Complete Cheerful Cherubs* by Rebecca McCann. Copyright 1932 by Covici-Friede, Inc. Copyright renewed © 1960 by Crown Publishers, Inc. Used by permission of Crown Publishers, Inc.

McCary, J. L. (1980). Historic development of romantic love. In C. Gordon & G. Johnson (Eds.), *Readings in human sexuality: Contemporary perspectives* (2nd ed.). New York: Harper & Row.

McCroskey, J. C. (1977). Oral communication apprehension: A summary of recent theory and research. *Human Communication Research, 4,* 78-96.

McCroskey, J. C. (1984). The communication apprehension perspective. In J. A. Daly & J. C. McCroskey (Eds.), *Avoiding communication: Shyness, reticence, and communication apprehension* (pp. 13-38). Beverly Hills: Sage.

McCroskey, J. C., & Beatty, M. J. (1986). Oral communication apprehension. In W. H. Jones, J. M. Cheek, & S. R. Briggs (Eds.), *Shyness: Perspectives on research and treatment* (pp. 279-293). New York: Plenum Press.

McCroskey, J. C., & Beatty, M. J. (1986). Oral communication apprehension. In W. H. Jones, J. M. Cheek, & S. R. Briggs (Ed.), *Shyness: Perspectives on research and treatment* (pp. 279-293). New York: Plenum.

McCroskey, J. C., Richmond, V. P., Berger, B. A., & Baldwin, H. J. (1983). How to make a good thing worse: A comparison of approaches to helping students overcome communication apprehension. *Communication: The Journal of the Communication Association of the Pacific, 12(1),* 213-220.

McGregor, D. (1960). *The human side of enterprise.* New York: McGraw-Hill.

McNeal, E. T., & Cimbolic, P. (1986). Antidepressants and biochemical theories of depression. *Psychological Bulletin, 99,* 361-374.

McNeil, E. B. (1974). *The psychology of being human.* New York: Canfield Press.

Mead, M. (1939). *From the South Seas: Studies of adolescence and sex in primitive societies.* New York: Morrow. Used with permission.

Mechanic, D. (1962). *Students under stress.* New York: The Free Press.

Meichenbaum, D. (1974). *Cognitive behavior modification.* Morristown, NJ: General Learning Press. Used by permission.

Meichenbaum, D. (1977). *Cognitive-behavior modification: An integrative approach.* New York: Plenum. Used by permission.

Meissner, M. (1971). The long arm of the job: A study of work and leisure. *Industrial Relations, 10,* 239-260.

Meredith, N. (1984, January). The gay dilemma. *Psychology Today,* pp. 56-62.

Michelson, L. (Ed.) (1985). Meta-analysis and clinical psychology. [Special issue.] *Clinical Psychology Review,* 5(1).

Michener, J. A. (1949). *The fires of spring.* New York: Random House.

Milgram, S. (1963). Behavioral study of obedience. *Journal of Abnormal and Social Psychology, 67,* 371-378.

Milgram, S. (1968). Some conditions of obedience and disobedience to authority. *International Journal of Psychiatry, 6,* 259-276.

Milgram, S. (1970). The experience of living in cities. *Science, 167,* 1461-1468.

Milgram, S., Bickman, L., & Berkowitz, L. (1969). Note on the drawing power of crowds of different size. *Journal of Personality and Social Psychology, 13,* 79-82.

Miller, G. A. (1962). *Psychology: The science of mental life.* New York: Harper & Row.

Miller, J. G. (1977). *Living systems.* New York: McGraw-Hill.

Miller, P. M. (1976). *Behavioral treatment of alcoholism.* New York: Pergamon Press.

Milne, A. A. (1927). From *Now we are six* by A. A. Milne.

Copyright 1927 by E. P. Dutton, renewed 1955 by A. A. Milne. Reprinted by permission of the publisher, Dutton Children's Books, a division of Penguin Books USA Inc. and of the Canadian publishers, McClelland and Stewart, Toronto.

Mischel, W. (1981). *Introduction to personality* (3rd ed.). New York: Holt, Rinehart & Winston.

Mischel, W., & Ebbesen, E. (1970). Attention in delay of gratification. *Journal of Personality and Social Psychology, 16,* 329-337.

Montgomery, B. M. (1981). The form and function of quality communication in marriage. *Family Relations,* 30(1), 21-30.

Morgan, L. A. (1976). A reexamination of widowhood and morale. *Journal of Gerontology, 31,* 687-695.

Morris, C. G. (1983, August). *Shyness and social anxiety.* Paper presented at the meeting of the American Psychological Association, Anaheim, CA.

Morris, C. G. (1985). *Psychology: An introduction* (5th ed.). Englewood Cliffs, NJ: Prentice-Hall.

Morris, W. N., & Miller, R. S. (1975). The effects of consensus-breaking and consensus-preempting partners on reduction in conformity. *Journal of Experimental Social Psychology, 11,* 215-223.

Moscovici, S. (1980). Toward a theory of conversion behavior. In L. Berkowitz (Ed.), *Advances in experimental social psychology* (Vol. 13), pp. 209-239. New York: Academic Press.

Moscovici, S., & Zavalloni, M. (1969). The group as a polarizer of attitudes. *Journal of Personality and Social Psychology, 12,* 125-135.

Moustakas, C. E. (1961). *Loneliness.* Englewood Cliffs, NJ: Prentice-Hall.

Murphy, H. B. M. (1978). The advent of guilt feelings as a common depressive symptom: A historical comparison of two continents. *Psychiatry, 41,* 229-242.

Murphy, L. B. (1962). *The widening world of childhood.* New York: Basic Books.

Murphy, L. B., & Moriarty, A. E. (1976). *Vulnerability, coping and growth: From infancy to adolescence.* New Haven: Yale University Press.

Myers, J. K., Weissman, M. M., Tischler, G. L., Holzer, C. E., III, Leaf, P. J., Orvaschel, H., Anthony, J. C., Boyd, J. H., Burke, J. D., Jr., Kramer, M., & Stoltzman, R. (1984). Six-month prevalence of psychiatric disorders in three communities: 1980-1982. *Archives of General Psychiatry, 41,* 959-970.

Nadelson, C. C., & Notman, M. T. (1981). To marry or not to marry: A choice. *American Journal of Psychiatry, 138,* 1352-1356.

National Center for Health Statistics (June 3, 1987). Advance report of final marriage statistics, 1984. *Monthly Vital Statistics Report, 36*(2).

National Institute of Drug Abuse. (1981). *Trend report: January 1978-September 1980.* Data from Client Oriented Data Acquisition Program (CODAP) (Series E, No. 24). Washington, DC: U.S. Department of Health and Human Services.

National Institutes of Health, Review Panel on Coronary Prone Behavior and Coronary Heart Disease. (1981). Coronary prone behavior and coronary heart disease: A critical review. *Circulation, 63,* 1199-1215.

Navran, L. (1967). Communication and adjustment in marriage. *Family Process, 6,* 173-184.

Neugarten, B. L., & Hagestad, G. O. (1977). Age and the life course. In R. H. Binstock & E. Shanas (Eds.), *Handbook of aging and the social sciences.* New York: Van Nostrand Reinhold.

Neugarten, B. L., & Weinstein, K. K. (1964). The changing American grandparent. *Journal of Marriage and the Family, 26,* 199-204.

Neugarten, B. L., Wood, V., Kraines, R. J., & Loomis, B. (1963). Women's attitudes toward the menopause. *Vita Humana, 6,* 140-151.

Neulinger, J. (1981). From J. Neulinger, *The Psychology of Leisure* (2nd ed.), 1981. Courtesy of Charles C. Thomas, Publisher, Springfield, Illinois.

Nisbett, R. E., & Wilson, T. D. (1977). The halo effect: Evidence for unconscious alteration of judgments. *Journal of Personality and Social Psychology, 35,* 250-256.

Nock, S. L. (1982). Enduring effects of marital disruption and subsequent living arrangements. *Journal of Family Issues, 3, 25-40.*

Nogami, G. Y. (1976). Crowding: Effects of group size, room size, or density? *Journal of Applied Social Psychology, 6,* 105-125.

Norman, C. (1982). A long-term problem for the nuclear industry. *Science, 215,* 376-379.

Novaco, R. (1975). *Anger control: The development and evaluation of an experimental treatment.* Lexington, MA: D. C. Heath.

Noyes, R., Jr., Crowe, R. R., Harris, E. L., Hamra, B. J., & McChesney, C. M. (1986). Relationship between panic disorder and agoraphobia: A family study. *Archives of General Psychiatry, 43,* 227-232.

Nye, R. D. (1973). *Conflict among humans.* New York: Springer.

O'Brien, G. E. (1981). Leisure attributes and retirement satisfaction. *Journal of Applied Psychology, 66,* 371-384.

O'Neill, N. (1978). *The marriage premise.* New York: Bantam Books.

O'Neill, N., & O'Neill, G. (1972). *Open marriage: A new lifestyle for couples.* New York: M. Evans and Co.

O'Toole, J. (1982). How to forecast your own working future. *The Futurist, 16*(1), 5-11.

Orlofsky, J. L., Marcia, J. E., & Lesser, I. M. (1973). Ego identity status and the intimacy versus isolation crisis of young adulthood. *Journal of Personality and Social Psychology, 27,* 211-229.

Osborne, A. F. (1953). *Applied imagination: Principles and procedures of creative thinking.* New York: Charles Scribner's Sons.

Osgood, C. From *There's nothing that I wouldn't do if you would be my POSSLQ* by Charles Osgood. Copyright © 1981 by CBS, Inc. Reprinted by permission of Henry Holt and Company.

Ouchi, W. G. (1981). *Theory Z: How American business can meet the Japanese challenge.* New York: Avon Books. William Ouchi, *Theory Z,* © 1981, Addison-Wesley Publishing Company, Inc., Reading, Massachusetts. Reprinted with permission.

Overstreet, H., & Overstreet, B. (1956). *The mind goes forth.* New York: Norton.

Paivio, A. (1965). Personality and audience influence. In B. A. Maher (Ed.), *Progress in experimental personality research* (Vol. 2) (pp. 127-173). New York: Academic Press.

Palmore, E. (1977). Facts on aging: A short quiz. *The Gerontologist, 17,* 315-320. Reprinted by permission of *The Gerontologist.*

Papalia, D. E., & Olds, S. W. (1981). *Human development* (2nd ed.) New York: McGraw-Hill.

Parker, S. R. (1971). *The future of work and leisure.* London: MacGibbon & Kee.

Parkes, C. M. (1972). Components of the reaction to loss of limb, spouse, or home. *Journal of Psychosomatic Research, 16,* 343-349.

Parnas, J., Schulsinger, F., Schulsinger, H., Mednick, S. A., & Teasdale, T. W. (1982). Behavioral precursors of schizophrenia spectrum. *Archives of General Psychiatry, 39,* 658-664.

Paul, G. L. (1966). *Insight vs. desensitization in psychotherapy.* Stanford, CA: Stanford University Press.

Paul, G. L. (1969). Physiological effects of relaxation training and hypnotic suggestion. *Journal of Abnormal Psychology, 74,* 425-437.

Paulhus, D. L. (1984). Two-component models of socially desirable responding. *Journal of Personality and Social Psychology, 46,* 598-609.

Paulhus, D. L. (1986). Self-deception and impression management in test responses. In J. Angleitner & J. S.

Wiggins (Eds.), *Personality assessment via questionnaire* (pp. 143-165). New York: Springer-Verlag.

Paykel, E. S. (Ed.) (1982). *Handbook of affective disorders.* New York: Guilford Press.

Pearlin, L. I., & Schooler, C. (1978). The structure of coping. *Journal of Health and Social Behavior, 19,* 1-21.

Peck, R. (1968). Psychological developments in the second half of life. In B. L. Neugarten (Ed.), *Middle age and aging* (pp. 88-92). Chicago: University of Chicago Press.

Peel, E. A. (1971). *The nature of adolescent judgment.* New York: Wiley.

Penrod, S. (1986). *Social psychology* (2nd ed.). Englewood Cliffs, NJ: Prentice Hall.

Perlmutter, M. (1987). Aging and memory. In K. W. Schaie & K. Eisdorfer (Eds.), *Annual review of gerontology and geriatrics* (Vol. 7). New York: Springer.

Perlmutter, M., & Hall, E. (1985). *Adult development and aging.* New York: John Wiley.

Perls, F. S. (1969). *Gestalt therapy verbatim.* Lafayette, CA: Real People Press.

Peterson, C., Schwartz, S. M., & Seligman, M. E. P. (1981). Self-blame and depressive symptoms. *Journal of Personality and Social Psychology, 41,* 253-259.

Phares, E. J. (1984). *Introduction to personality.* Columbus, OH: Charles E. Merrill.

Piaget, J. (1952). *The origins of intelligence in children.* New York: International Universities Press.

Piaget, J. (1970). *Genetic epistemology.* New York: Columbia University Press.

Piaget, J. (1972). Intellectual evolution from adolescence to adulthood. *Human development, 15,* 1-12.

Pines, A., & Aronson, E. (1983). Antecedents, correlates, and consequences of sexual jealousy. *Journal of Personality, 51,* 108-109.

Pope, B. (1979). *The mental health interview: Research and application.* New York: Pergamon Press.

Posner, M. J. (1982). Cumulative development of attentional theory. *American Psychologist, 37,* 168-179.

Powell, D. H., & Driscoll, P. F. (1973). Middle class professionals face unemployment. *Society, 10*(2), 18-26.

Project Dawn Drug Enforcement Agency (1977). *Drug abuse warning network: Project DAWN V, May 1976-April 1977.* Washington, DC: Government Printing Office.

Rahe, R. H., & Lind, E. (1971). Psychosocial factors and sudden cardiac death: A pilot study. *Journal of Psychosomatic Research, 15,* 19-24.

Ramsay, R. W. (1977). Behavioral approaches to bereavement. *Behavior Research and Therapy, 15,* 131-135.

Rand, A. (1965). *The virtue of selfishness.* New York: The New American Library.

Raskin, N. H. (1988). *Headaches.* New York: Churchill Livingstone Inc.

Reedy, M. N., Birren, J. E., & Schaie, K. W. (1981). Age and sex differences in satisfying love relationships across the adult life span. *Human Development, 24,* 52-66.

Regier, D. A., Boyd, J. H., Burke, J. D., Jr., Rae, D. S., Myers, J. K., Kramer, M., Robins, L. N., George, L. K., Karno, M., & Locke, B. Z. (1988). One-month prevalence of mental disorders in United States based on 5 epidemiologic catchment area sites. *Archives of General Psychiatry, 45,* 977-986.

Reiss, I. L. (1976). The effect of changing trends, attitudes, and values on premarital sexual behavior in the United States. In S. Gordon & R. Libby (Eds.), *Sexuality today and tomorrow.* North Scituate, MA: Duxbury.

Resnick, R. B., Kestenbaum, R. S., & Schwartz, L. K. (1977). Acute systemic effects of cocaine in man. *Science, 195,* 696-698.

Richter, C. P. (1957). On the phenomenon of sudden death in animals and man. *Psychosomatic Medicine, 19,* 191-198.

Riegel, K. F. (1973). Dialectic operations: The final period of cognitive development. *Human Development, 16,* 346-370.

Riegel, K. F. (1976). The dialectics of human development. *American Psychologist, 31,* 689-700.

Riessman, F., & Gartner, A. (1987, Fall). The Surgeon General and the self-help ethos. *Social Policy,* pp. 23-25.

Rinder, W. (1970). *Love is an attitude.* San Francisco: Celestial Arts Publishing. Copyright © 1970 by Celestial Arts. Reprinted with permission of the publisher.

Riordan, R. J., & Beggs, M. S. (1987). Counselors and self-help groups. *Journal of Counseling and Development, 65,* 427-429.

Risman, B. J., Hill, C. T., Rubin, Z., & Peplau, L. A. (1981). Living together in college: Implications for courtship. *Journal of Marriage and the Family, 43,* 77-83.

Robbins, M., & Jensen, G. D. (1978). Multiple orgasm in males. *Journal of Sex Research, 14,* 21-26.

Roberts, A. H. (1985). Biofeedback: Research, training, and clinical roles. *American Psychologist, 40,* 938-941.

Robertson, I. (1981). *Sociology* (2nd ed.). New York: Worth.

Robins, L. N., Helzer, J. E., Weissman, M. M., Orvaschel, H., Gruenberg, E., Burke, J. D., & Regier, D. A. (1984). Lifetime prevalence of specific psychiatric disorders in three sites. *Archives of General Psychiatry, 41*, 949-958.

Robinson, I. E., & Jedlicka, D. (1982). Change in sexual attitudes and behavior of college students from 1965 to 1980: A research note. *Journal of Marriage and the Family, 44*, 237-240.

Robinson, J. R. (1988). Who's doing the housework? *American Demographics, 10* (12), pp. 24-28, 63.

Rodin, J. (1976). Density, perceived choice and responses to controllable and uncontrollable outcomes. *Journal of Personality and Social Psychology, 12*, 564-578.

Rodin, J., Solomon, S., & Metcalf, J. (1978). Role of control in mediating perceptions of density. *Journal of Personality and Social Psychology, 36*, 988-999.

Rogers, C. R. (1958). *On becoming a person.* Austin: University of Texas Press.

Rogers, C. R. (1959). A theory of therapy, personality, and interpersonal relationships, as developed in the client-centered framework. In S. Koch (Ed.), *Psychology: A study of a science* (Vol. 1, pp. 184-256). New York: McGraw-Hill.

Rogers, C. R. (1961). *On becoming a person: A therapist's view of psychotherapy.* Boston: Houghton Mifflin. Used by permission.

Rogers, C. R. (1964). Toward a modern approach to values: The valuing process in the mature person. *Journal of Abnormal and Social Psychology, 68*, 160-167.

Rogers, C. R. (1968). Interpersonal relationships: U.S.A. 2000. *Journal of Applied Behavioral Science, 4*, 265-280.

Rogers, C. R. (1969). *Freedom to learn.* Columbus, OH: Charles E. Merrill.

Rogers, C. R. (1970). *Carl Rogers on encounter groups.* New York: Harper & Row.

Rogers, C. R. (1977). *Carl Rogers on personal power.* New York: Delacorte Press.

Rogers, C. R. (1980). *A way of being.* Boston: Houghton Mifflin.

Rogers, C. R. From Carl R. Rogers: *Client-centered therapy,* pp. 152-153. Copyright © 1951, renewed 1979 by Houghton Mifflin Company. Used by permission.

Rokeach, M. (1968). *Beliefs, attitudes, and values: A theory of organization and change.* San Francisco: Jossey-Bass.

Rokeach, M. Reprinted with permission of The Free Press, a Division of Macmillan, Inc. from *The nature of human values* by Milton Rokeach. Copyright © 1973 by The Free Press.

Rosenman, R. H., Brand, H. T., Jenkins, C. D., Friedman, M., Straus, R., & Wurm, M. (1975). Coronary heart disease in the Western Collaborative Group Study: Final follow-up experience of 8-1/2 years. *Journal of the American Medical Association, 233*, 872-877.

Rosenman, R., Friedman, M., Strauss, R., Wurm, M., Jenkins, D., & Messinger, H. (1966). Coro-heart disease in the Western Collaborative Study: A follow-up experience of two years. *Journal of the American Medical Association, 195*, 86-92.

Roth, S., & Cohen, L. J. (1986). Approach, avoidance, and coping with stress. *American Psychologist, 41*, 813-819.

Rubin, Z. (1980). *Children's friendships.* Cambridge, MA: Harvard University Press.

Rychlak, J. F. (1981). *Introduction to personality and psychotherapy: A theory-construction approach* (2nd ed.). Boston: Houghton Mifflin.

Saegert, S., Swap, W., & Zajonc, R. B. (1973). Exposure, context, and interpersonal attraction. *Journal of Personality and Social Psychology, 25*, 234-242.

Salthouse, T. (1985). Speed of behavior and its implications for cognition. In J. E. Birren & K. W. Schaie (Eds.), *Handbook of the psychology of aging* (2nd ed.). New York: Van Nostrand Reinhold.

Salthouse, T. (1987). The role of experience in cognitive aging. In K. W. Schaie & K. Eisdorfer (Eds.), *Annual review of gerontology and geriatrics* (Vol. 7). New York: Springer.

Sarason, I. G., Johnson, J. H., & Siegel, J. M. (1978). Assessing the impact of life changes: Development of the Life Experiences Survey. *Journal of Consulting and Clinical Psychology, 46*, 932-946. Copyright © 1978 by the American Psychological Association. Reprinted by permission.

Sarason, I. G., Sarason, B. R., Potter, E. H., & Antoni, M. H. (1985). Life events, social support, and illness. *Psychosomatic Medicine, 47*, 156-163.

Sarrel, L. J., & Sarrel, P. M. (1984). *Sexual turning points: The seven stages of adult sexuality.* New York: Macmillan.

Sasmor, R. M. (1966). Operant conditioning of a small-scale muscle response. *Journal of experimental analysis of behavior, 9*, 69-85.

Satir, V. M. (1967). *Conjoint family therapy* (Rev. ed.). Palo Alto, CA: Science and Behavior Books.

Satir, V. M. (1972). *Peoplemaking.* Palo Alto, CA: Science and Behavior Books.

Scanzoni, J. H. (1972). *Sexual bargaining: Power politics in the American marriage.* Englewood Cliffs, NJ: Prentice-Hall.

Schaar, J. (1974). In *Footnotes to the future, 4*(3), 1.

Schaefer, C. E. (1969). Imaginary companions and creative adolescents. *Developmental Psychology, 1*, 747-749.

Schaeffer, M. A., & Baum, A. (1984). Adrenal cortical response to stress at Three Mile Island. *Psychosomatic Medicine, 46,* 227-237.

Schaie, K. W. (1982). The Seattle longitudinal study: A twenty-one year exploration of psychometric intelligence in adulthood. In K. W. Schaie (Ed.), *Longitudinal studies of adult psychological development.* New York: Guilford Press.

Schaie, K. W., & Hertzog, C. (1983). Fourteen-year cohort-sequential analyses of adult intellectual development. *Developmental Psychology, 19,* 531-543.

Schaie, K. W., & Willis, S. L. (1986). *Adult development and aging* (2nd ed.). Boston: Little, Brown and Co.

Schinn, R. (1976). Telecommunication policy and the information society. *Footnotes to the Future, 6*(2), 2.

Schonfield, D. (1982). Who is stereotyping whom and why? *Gerontologist, 22,* 267-272.

Sears, D. O., Peplau, L. A., Freedman, J. L., & Taylor, S. E. (1988). *Social psychology* (6th ed.). Englewood Cliffs, NJ: Prentice Hall.

Sears, R. R., Maccoby, E. E., & Levin, H. (1957). *Patterns of child rearing.* New York: Harper & Row.

Seefeldt, C. (1984). Child growth and development—a source of stress? In J. H. Humphrey (Ed.), *Stress in childhood* (pp. 19-45). New York: AMS Press.

Seeman, J. (1984). The fully functioning person: Theory and research. In R. F. Levant & J. M. Shlien (Eds.), *Client-centered therapy and the person-centered approach: New directions in theory, research, and practice.* New York: Praeger.

Seligman, M. E. P. (1972). Phobias and preparedness. In M. E. P. Seligman & J. L. Hager (Eds.), *Biological boundaries of learning.* Englewood Cliffs, NJ: Prentice-Hall.

Seligman, M. E. P. (1975). *Helplessness: On depression, development, and death.* San Francisco: W. H. Freeman.

Selman, R. L. (1980). *The growth of interpersonal understanding.* New York: Academic Press.

Selman, R. L., & Selman, A. D. (1979, October). Children's ideas about friendship: A new theory. *Psychology Today,* pp. 71-80, 114.

Seyle, H. (1974). *Stress without distress.* Philadelphia: Lippincott.

Selye, H. (1976). *The stress of life* (Rev. ed.). New York: McGraw-Hill.

Selye, H. (1978, November). On the real benefits of eustress. *Psychology Today,* pp. 60-64.

Selye, H. (1980). The stress concept today. In I. L. Kutash, L. B. Schlesinger, & Associates (Eds.), *Handbook on stress and anxiety.* San Francisco: Jossey-Bass.

Shane, H. G. (1976). America's educational future. *The Futurist, 10*(5), 252-257.

Shaw, M. E. (1971). *Group dynamics.* New York: McGraw-Hill.

Sheehy, G. (1976). *Passages: Predictable crises of adult life.* New York: Dutton.

Shepard-Look, D. L. (1982) Sex differentiation in the development of sex roles. In Wolman, B. B. (Ed.) *Handbook of developmental psychology.* Englewood Cliffs, N. J.: Prentice-Hall.

Sherman, E. (1987). *Meaning in mid-life transitions.* Albany, NY: State University of New York Press.

Sherrington, R., Brynjolfsson, J., Petursson, H., Potter, M., Dudleston, K., Barraclough, B., Wasmuth, J., Dobbs, M., & Gurling, H. (1988). Localization of a susceptibility locus for schizophrenia on chromosome 5. *Nature, 336,* 164-167.

Sherrod, D. R. (1974). Crowding, perceived control and behavioral aftereffects. *Journal of Applied Social Psychology, 4,* 171-186.

Sherwood, G. G. (1981). Self-serving biases in person perception: A reexamination of projection as a mechanism of defense. *Psychological Bulletin, 90,* 445-466.

Sherwood, G. G. (1982). Consciousness and stress reduction in defensive projection: A reply to Holmes. *Psychological Bulletin, 91,* 372-375.

Sherwood, M. (1969). *The logic of explanation in psychoanalysis.* New York: Academic Press.

Shibutani, T. (1964).The structure of personal identity. In E. E. Sampson (Ed.), *Approaches, contexts, and problems of social psychology* (pp. 231-235). Englewood Cliffs, NJ: Prentice-Hall.

Schultz, D. (1981). *Theories of personality* (2nd ed.). Monterey, CA: Brooks/Cole.

Siegel, O. (1982). Personality development in adolescence. In B. B. Wolman (Ed.), *Handbook of developmental psychology* (pp. 537-548). Englewood Cliffs, NJ: Prentice-Hall.

Siegler, I. C., & Costa, P. T., Jr. (1985). Health behavior relationships. In J. E. Birren & K. W. Schaie (Eds.), *Handbook of the psychology of aging* (2nd ed.). New York: Van Nostrand Reinhold.

Simmel, G. (1964). The secret and the secret society. In K. Wolff (Ed.), *The sociology of Georg Simmel.* New York: The Free Press.

Sinclair, D. (1969). *Human growth after birth.* London: Oxford University Press.

Singer, J. L. (1976, July). Fantasy: The foundation of serenity. *Psychology Today,* pp. 32-34; 37.

Sinnott, E. W. (1955). *The biology of the spirit.* New York:

Viking Press.

Skinner, B.F. (1953). *Science and human behavior.* New York: Macmillan.

Skinner, B. F. (1958). Teaching machines. *Science, 128,* 969-977.

Skinner, B. F. (1971). *Beyond freedom and dignity.* New York: Knopf. Used by permission.

Skinner, B. F. (1974). *About behaviorism.* New York: Knopf.

Skinner, B. F. (1977). The force of coincidence. *The Humanist, 37*(3), 10-11.

Sklar, L. S., & Anisman, H. (1979). Stress and coping factors influence tumor growth. *Science, 205,* 513-515.

Slovic, P., Fischhoff, B., & Lichtenstein, S. (1985). Characterizing perceived risk. In R. W. Kates, C. Hohenemser, & J. X. Kasperson (Eds.), *Perilous progress: Managing the hazards of technology* (pp. 91-125). Boulder, CO: Westview Press.

Smith, B. D., & Vetter, H. J. (1982). *Theoretical approaches to personality.* Englewood Cliffs, NJ: Prentice-Hall.

Smith, D. (1982). Trends in counseling and psychotherapy. *American Psychologist, 37,* 802-809.

Smith, D., & Kraft, W. A. (1983). DSM-III: Do psychologists really want an alternative? *American Psychologist, 38,* 777-784.

Smith, M. L., & Glass, G. V. (1977). Meta-analysis of psychotherapy outcome studies. *American Psychologist, 32,* 752-760.

Smith, T. V., & Lindeman, E. C. (1951). *The democratic way of life.* New York: New American Library.

South, J. From the song *"Games people play,"* written by Joe South. Copyright © 1968 by Lowery Music Co., Inc., Atlanta, Ga. International Copyright Secured. All Rights Reserved. Used by permission.

Spanier, G. B. (1976). Measuring dyadic adjustment: New scales for assessing the quality of marriage and similar dyads. *Journal of Marriage and the Family, 38,* 15-28. Copyrighted 1976 by the National Council on Family Relations, 1910 West County Road B, Suite 147, St. Paul, Minnesota 55113. Reprinted by permission.

Special Task Force, to the Secretary of Health, Education, and Welfare (1972). *Work in America.* Cambridge, MA: MIT Press.

Sperry, R. W. (1977). Bridging science and values. *American Psychologist, 32,* 237-245.

Spielberger, C. D., Johnson, E. H., Russell, S. F., Crane, R. S., Jacobs, G. A., & Worden, T. J. (1985). The experience and expression of anger. In M. A. Chesney & R. H. Rosenman (Eds.), *Anger and hostility in car-*

*diovascular and behavioral disorders* (pp. 5-30). New York: Hemisphere/McGraw-Hill.

Spitzer, R. L., Skodol, A. E., Gibbon, M., & Williams, J. B. W. *DSM-III case book.* American Psychiatric Association, copyright 1981. Used with permission.

Spitzer, R. L., Skodol, A. E., Gibbon, M., & Williams, J. B. (1983). *Psychopathology: A case book.* New York: McGraw-Hill.

Spranger, E. (1928). [*Types of men,* 3rd ed.] (P. Pigors, Trans.). New York: Steckert. (Originally published, 1923.)

Sroufe, L. A. (1978). Attachment and the roots of competence. *Human Nature, 1,* 50-57.

Stevens-Long, J. (1984). *Adult Life: Developmental processes* (2nd ed.). Palo Alto, CA: Mayfield.

Stinnett, N., Carter, L. M., & Montgomery, J. E. (1972). Older person's perceptions of their marriages. *Journal of Marriage and the Family, 34,* 665-670.

Stone, L. J., & Church, J. (1984) *Childhood and adolescence* (5th ed.). New York: Random House.

Stout, H. R. (1885). *Our family physician.* Peoria: Henderson and Smith.

Strassberg, D., Robak, H., D'Antonio, M., & Gabel, H. (1977). Self-disclosure: A critical and selective review of the clinical literature. *Comprehensive Psychiatry, 18,* 31-40.

Strong, B., & DeVault, C. (1986). *The marriage and family experience* (3rd ed.). St. Paul, MN: West. Reprinted by permission.

Strupp, H., & Binder, J. (1984). *Psychotherapy in a new key.* New York: Basic Books.

Stuart, R. B., & Davis, B. (1972). *Slim chance in a fat world: Behavioral control of obesity.* Champaign, IL: Research Press.

Student Counseling Center at the University of California at Los Angeles. Poem by David Palmer published in *Counsel,* a publication of the Student Counseling center at the University of California Los Angeles. Reprinted by permission of the author.

Sullivan, H. S. (1953). *The interpersonal theory of psychiatry.* New York: Norton.

Sullivan, H. S. (1962). *Schizophrenia as a human process.* New York: Norton.

Tavris, C., & Jayaratne, T. E. How happy is your marriage? What 75,000 wives say about their most intimate relationship. *Redbook,* June 1976, pp. 90-92; 132; 134. Copyright © 1976 the Redbook Publishing Company. Reprinted by permission.

Taylor, S. E. (1983). Adjustment to threatening events: A theory of cognitive adaptation. *American Psychologist,*

*38,* 1161-1173.

Teilhard de Chardin, P. (1961). *The phenomenon of man.* New York: Harper & Row.

Temoshok, L. (1988). Psychoimmunology and AIDS. In T. P. Bridge, A. F. Mirsky, & F. K. Goodwin (Eds.), *Psychological, neuropsychiatric, and substance abuse aspects of AIDS* (pp. 187-197). New York: Raven Press.

Terkel, S. (1980). *American dreams: Lost and found.* New York: Pantheon Books.

Terkel, S. *Working.* New York: Pantheon, 1974. Copyright © 1972, 1974 Studs Terkel. Reprinted by permission of Pantheon Books, a division of Random House, Inc.

Thibaut, J. W., & Kelley, H. H. (1959). *The social psychology of groups.* New York: Wiley.

Thompson, A. P. (1983). Extramarital sex: A review of the research literature. *Journal of Sex Research, 19,* 1-22.

Thompson, A. P. (1984). Emotional and sexual components of extramarital relations. *Journal of Marriage and the Family, 46,* 35-42.

Thornton, A. (1977). Children and marital stability. *Journal of Marriage and the Family, 39,* 531-540.

Thornton, B. (1977). Toward a linear prediction model of marital happiness. *Personality and Social Psychology Bulletin, 3,* 674-676.

Thurber, J. (1933). The day the dam broke. Copyright © 1933, 1961 James Thurber, from *My Life and Hard Times,* published by Harper & Row. (British title: *Vintage Thurber* by James Thurber. The collection Copyright © 1963 Hamish Hamilton Ltd., London.) Originally printed in *The New Yorker.*

Timiras, P. S. (1972). *Developmental physiology and aging.* New York: Macmillan.

Today's marriages: Wrenching experience or key to happiness. (1975, October 27). *U. S. News & World Report,* pp. 35-38.

Toffler, A. (1970). *Future shock.* New York: Random House.

Toffler, A. (1971, January 26). In Kronenberger, J. Is the family obsolete? *Look,* pp. 35-36.

Toffler, A. (1980). *The third wave.* New York: William Morrow.

Troll, L. E. (1975). *Early and middle adulthood.* Monterey, CA: Brooks/Cole.

Troll, L. E. (1982). *Continuations: Adult development and aging.* Monterey, CA: Brooks/Cole.

Troll, L. E. (1983). Grandparents: The family watchdog. In T. Brubaker (Ed.), *Family relationships in later life.* Beverly Hills, CA: Sage.

Troll, L. E., Miller, S. J., & Atchley, R. C. (1979). *Families in later life.* Belmont, CA: Wadsworth.

Tuckman, J., & Lorge, I. (1953). Attitudes toward old people. *Journal of Social Psychology, 37,* 249-260.

Turner, S. M., Beidel, D. C., & Nathan, R. S. (1985). Biological factors in obsessive-compulsive disorders. *Psychological Bulletin, 97,* 430-450.

Udry, J. R. (1966). *The social context of marriage.* Philadelphia: Lippincott.

Unger, R. K. (1979). Toward a redefinition of sex and gender. *American Psychologist, 34,* 1085-1094.

United States Centers for Disease Control. (1980). *Ten leading causes of death in the United States, 1977.* Washington, DC: Government Printing Office.

United States Department of Commerce, Bureau of the Census (1980). *Statistical abstract of the United States: 1980* (101st ed.). Washington, DC: U.S. Government Printing Office.

United States Public Health Service (1980). *Public health reports.* Washington, DC: U.S. Government Printing Office.

Upper, D., & Meredith, L. (1970, August). *A stimulus control approach to the modification of smoking behavior.* Paper presented at the meeting of the American Psychological Association, Miami.

Vaillant, G. E. (1977). *Adaptation to life: How the best and brightest came of age.* Boston: Little, Brown.

Vaillant, G. E., & Milofsky, E. (1980). Natural history of male psychological health: IX, Empirical evidence for Erikson's model of the life cycle. *American Journal of Psychiatry, 137,* 1348-1359.

Van Maanen, J., & Schein, E. H. (1977). Career development. In J. R. Hackman & J. L. Suttle (Eds.), *Improving life at work.* Santa Monica, CA: Goodyear Publishing Co.

Vance, E. B., & Wagner, N. N. (1976). From "The Sex of Orgasm" questionnaire by Nathaniel N. Wagner and Ellen Bell Vance in *Archives of Sexual Behavior,* Volume 5. Copyright © 1976 by Plenum Publishing Company. Reprinted by permission.

Veevers J. E. (1980). *Childless by choice.* Toronto: Butterworth.

Veevers, J. E. (1983). Researching voluntary childlessness: A critical assessment of current strategies and findings. In E. D. Macklin & R. H. Rubin (Eds.), *Contemporary families and alternative lifestyles* (pp. 75-96). Beverly Hills, CA: Sage.

Videka-Sherman, L. (1982). Effects of participation in a self-help group for bereaved parents: Compassionate friends. *Prevention in Human Services, 1*(3), 69-77.

Wadden, T. A., & Anderton, C. H. (1982). The clinical use of hypnosis. *Psychological Bulletin, 91,* 215-243.

Waldron, H., & Routh, D. K. (1981). The effect of the first child on the marital relationship. *Journal of Marriage and the Family, 43,* 785-798.

Wallach, M. S., Kogan, N., & Bem, D. J. (1962). Group influence on individual risk taking. *Journal of Abnormal and Social Psychology, 65,* 75-86.

Wallerstein, J. S. (1985). Children of divorce: Emerging trends. *Psychiatric Clinics of North America, 8,* 837-855.

Wallerstein, J. S. (1986). Women after divorce: Preliminary report from a ten-year follow-up. *American Journal of Orthopsychiatry, 56,* 65-77.

Wallerstein, J. S., & Kelly, J. B. (1977). Divorce counseling. *American Journal of Orthopsychiatry, 47,* 4-22.

Wallis, C., Redman, C., & Thompson, D. (1982, August 2). Battling an elusive invader. *Time,* pp. 68-69.

Waterman, A. S. (1982). Identity development from adolescence to adulthood: An extension of theory and a review of research. *Developmental Psychology, 18,* 341-358.

Watson, J. B. (1919). *Psychology from the standpoint of a behaviorist.* Philadelphia: Lippincott.

Watson, J. B., & Rayner, R. (1920). Conditioned emotional reactions. *Journal of Experimental Psychology, 3,* 1-14.

Weatherley, D. (1964). Self-perceived rate of physical maturation and personality in late adolescence. *Child Development, 35,* 1197-1210.

Webb, B., Worchel, S., Riechers, L., & Wayne, W. (1986). The influence of categorization on perceptions of crowding. *Journal of Personality and Social Psychology, 12,* 539-546.

Wegner, D. M., Schneider, D. J., Carter, S. R., III, & White, T. L. (1987). Paradoxical effects of thought suppression. *Journal of Personality and Social Psychology 53,* 5-13.

Wehr, T. A., Jacobsen, F. M., Sack, D.A., Arendt, J., Tamarkin, L., & Rosenthal, N. E. (1986). Phototherapy of seasonal affective disorder. *Archives of General Psychiatry, 43,* 870-875.

Weinberg, M. S., & Williams, C. (1974). *Male homosexuals: Their problems and adaptations.* New York: Oxford University Press.

Weiss, J. M. (1968). Effects of coping responses on stress. *Journal of Comparative and Physiological Psychology, 24,* 409-414.

Wender, P. H., Kety, S. S., Rosenthal, D., Schulsinger, F., & Ortman, J. (1986). Psychiatric disorders in the biological and adoptive families of adopted individuals with affective disorders. *Archives of General Psychiatry, 43,* 923-929.

Wender, P. H., Rosenthal, R., Kety, S. S., Schulsinger, S., & Welner, J. (1974). Cross fostering: A research strategy for clarifying the role of genetic and experiential factors in the etiology of schizophrenia. *Archives of General Psychiatry, ?0,* 121-128.

Wenzlaff, R. M., Wegner, D. M., & Roper, D. W. (1988). Depression and mental control: The resurgence of unwanted negative thoughts. *Journal of Personality and Social Psychology, 55,* 882-892.

West, L. J. (1958). Psychiatric aspects of training for honorable survival as a prisoner of war. *American Journal of Psychiatry, 115,* 329-336.

Westen, D. (1985). *Self and society: narcissism, collectivism, and the development of morals.* NY: Cambridge University Press.

White, R. W. (1976). *The enterprise of living.* New York: Holt, Rinehart and Winston.

Whyte, W. H. (1956). *The organization man.* New York: Simon & Schuster.

Wildavsky, A. (1979, January-February). No risk is the highest risk of all. *American Scientist,* pp. 32-37.

Wilson, G. (1978). Introversion/Extraversion. In T. Blass (Ed.), *Personality variables in social behavior* (pp. 179-218). Hillsdale, N.J.: Erlbaum.

Wilson, G. (1977). Introversion/Extraversion. In H. London & J. E. Exner, Jr. (Eds.), *Dimensions of personality* (pp. 217-261). New York: John Wiley & Sons.

Wolf, S., & Wolff, H. G. (1947). *Human gastric functions.* New York: Oxford University Press.

Wolfe, L. (1981). *The Cosmo report.* New York: Arbor House.

Wolpe, J. (1958). *Psychotherapy by reciprocal inhibition.* Stanford, CA: Stanford University Press.

Wolpe, J. (1969). *The practice of behavior therapy.* New York: Pergamon Press.

Wolpe, J. (1981). Behavior therapy versus psychoanalysis. *American Psychologist, 36,* 159-164.

Woodward, W. B. (1982). The "discovery" of social behaviorism and social learning theory, 1870-1980. *American Psychologist, 37,* 396-410.

Worchel, S., & Teddlie, C. (1976). The experience of crowding: A two-factor theory. *Journal of Personality and Social Psychology, 34,* 30-40.

Wortman, C. B. (1984). Social support and the cancer patient: Conceptual and methodological issues. *Cancer, 53,* 2339-2360.

Wortman, C. M., Adesman, P., Herman, E., & Greenberg, R. (1976). Self-disclosure: An attributional perspective. *Journal of Personality and Social Psychology, 33,* 184-191.

Wright, L. (1982). Rethinking clinical psychology's turf. *The Clinical Psychologist, 35*(2), 3-4.

Yamamoto, K. (1979). Children's ratings of the stressfulness of experiences. *Developmental Psychology, 15,* 581-582.

Yamamoto, K., & Felsenthal, H. M. (1982). Stressful experiences of children: Professional judgments. *Psychological Reports, 50,* 1087-1093.

Yamamoto, K., Soliman, A., Parsons, J., & Davies, O. L., Jr. (1987). Voices in unison: Stressful events in the lives of children in six countries. Reprinted with permission from *Journal of Child Psychology and Psychiatry, 28,* 855-864.

Yankelovich, D. A. (1981). *New rules: Searching for self-fulfillment in a world turned upside down.* New York: Random House.

Yarnold, P. R., & Grimm, L. G. (1982). Time urgency among coronary-prone individuals. *Journal of Abnormal Psychology, 91,* 175-177.

Youniss, J. (1980). *Parents and peers in social development: A Sullivan-Piaget perspective.* Chicago: University of Chicago Press.

Zimbardo, P. G. (1977). *Shyness.* New York: Jove Publications Inc.

Zimbardo, P. G. (1986). The Stanford Shyness Project. In W. H. Jones, J. M. Cheek, & S. R. Briggs (Eds.), *Shyness: Perspectives on research and treatment* (pp. 17-25). New York: Plenum Press.

Zubin, J., & Spring, B. (1977). Vulnerability: A new view of schizophrenia. *Journal of Abnormal Psychology, 86,* 103-126.

Zuckerman, M. (1978). Sensation seeking. In H. London & J. Exner (Eds.), *Dimensions of personality* (pp. 487-559). Copyright © 1978 by John Wiley and Sons, Inc. Reprinted by permission of John Wiley and Sons, Inc.

Zuckerman, M. (1979). *Sensation seeking: Beyond the optimal level of arousal.* Hillsdale, NJ: Erlbaum.

Zuckerman, M., DePaulo, B. M., & Rosenthal, R. (1981). Verbal and nonverbal communication of deception. In L. Berkowitz (Ed.), *Advances in experimental social psychology* (Vol. 14, pp. 1-59). New York: Academic Press.

# Acknowledgments

Unless otherwise acknowledged, photographs are the property of Scott, Foresman and Company. Abbreviations for page positions are as follows: T for top; C for center; B for bottom; L for left; and R for right.

**Chapter 5**
138    David Austen, Stock Boston
139T   Kevin Vandiver, TexaStock
139B   Chuck Wyrostok, Appalight
141    Bob Daemmrich, The Image Works
144    Cary Wolinsky, Stock Boston
149    David Austen, Stock Boston
156    Kevin Vandiver, TexaStock
160    Jeffry W. Myers, Stock Boston
166    Chuck Wyrostok, Appalight
170    Joel Gordon

**Chapter 6**
172TL   Christopher Morris, Black Star
172BL   Owen Franken, Stock Boston
172 R   John Goodman
173TL   David Wells, The Image Works
173BL   Joel Gordon
173R    Topham from The Image Works
175     Christopher Morris, Black Star
182     Owen Franken, Stock Boston
190     John Goodman
195     David Wells, The Image Works
197     Joseph Rodriguez, Black Star
199     Lawrence Migdale
202     Joel Gordon
208     Topham from The Image Works
213     Joel Gordon

**Chapter 7**
214L    Mark Antman, The Image Works
214R    David R. Frazier
215T    David R. Frazier
215B    Bob Daemmrich, The Image Works
217     Mark Antman, The Image Works
220     Richard Hutchings
225     David R. Frazier
233     David R. Frazier
236     Mark Antman, The Image Works
240     Joel Gordon
243     Bob Daemmrich, Stock Boston
248     Bob Daemmrich, The Image Works
251     Martin Rogers, Stock Boston

**Chapter 8**
254L    Joan Liftin, Actuality Inc.
254R    Erika Stone
255TL   Elizabeth Crews
255CL   Carol Palmer, The Picture Cube
255BL   Willie L. Hill, Jr., Stock Boston
255R    Robert Brenner, PhotoEdit

257    Joan Liftin, Actuality Inc.
262    Erika Stone
270    Elizabeth Crews
275    Brent Jones
278    Carol Palmer, The Picture Cube
281    Willie L. Hill, Jr., Stock Boston
283    Ellis Herwig, The Picture Cube
287    Robert Brenner, PhotoEdit
290    Susan Lapides, Design Conceptions
294    Paul Light, Lightwave

**Chapter 9**
296L    Robert Brenner, PhotoEdit
296-7   Mark W. Richard, PhotoEdit
297T    Bob Daemmrich
297B    Bob Daemmrich, Stock Boston
299     Robert Brenner, PhotoEdit
306     Charles Gupton, Stock Boston
308     Richard Pasley, Stock Boston
312     Mark W. Richards, PhotoEdit
315     Bob Daemmrich, The Image Works
319     Bob Daemmrich
324     Bob Daemmrich, The Image Works
329     Bob Daemmrich, Stock Boston
330     Nubar Alexanian, Stock Boston
334     Lawrence Migdale

**Chapter 10**
338     Joseph Neumayer, Design Conceptions
338-9   Cary Wolinsky, Stock Boston
339T    Joan Liftin, Actuality Inc.
339B    Joel Gordon
341     Joseph Neumayer, Design Conceptions
348     Bob Daemmrich
352     Myrleen Ferguson, PhotoEdit
354     Cary Wolinsky, Stock Boston
362     Joan Liftin, Actuality Inc.
366     Joel Gordon
371     Jim Cronk
373     Nathaniel Antman, The Image Works

**Chapter 11**
376L    Charles Harbutt, Actuality Inc.
376R    Edward L. Miller, Stock Boston
377T    Elizabeth Crews
377BL   Ulrike Welsch
377BR   Robert Brenner, PhotoEdit
379     Erika Stone
382     Charles Harbutt, Actuality Inc.
385     Edward L. Miller, Stock Boston
394     Harriet Gans, The Image Works

399    Elizabeth Crews
404    Bob Daemmrich
408    Chuck Wyrostok, Appalight
412    Ulrike Welsch
418    Stephen McBrady, PhotoEdit
420    Robert Brenner, PhotoEdit

**Chapter 12**
422L   Charles Harbutt, Actuality Inc.
422R   Bob Daemmrich, The Image Works
423T   Dion Ogust, The Image Works
423B   Darryl Baird, Lightwave
430    Charles Gupton, Stock Boston
433    Charles Harbutt, Actuality Inc.
435    Bob Daemmrich, The Image Works
445    Topham from The Image Works
448    Dion Ogust, The Image Works
451    David R. Frazier
452    Bob Daemmrich
454    Bob Daemmrich
456    Darryl Baird, Lightwave

**Chapter 13**
458L   David E. Kennedy, TexaStock
458R   Charles Harbutt, Actuality Inc.
459TL  Jeffry W. Myers, Stock Boston
459BL  Mark W. Richards, PhotoEdit
459R   Kevin Syms from David R. Frazier Photolibrary
463    David E. Kennedy, TexaStock
466    Charles Harbutt, Actuality Inc.
474    John Running, Stock Boston
477    Jeffry W. Myers, Stock Boston
479    Mark W. Richards, PhotoEdit

481    Bob Daemmrich, The Image Works
485    Kevin Syms from David R. Frazier Photolibrary
487    Joel Gordon
490    Charles Harbutt, Actuality Inc.

**Chapter 14**
492L   Bob Daemmrich, The Image Works
492R   Kenneth Jarecke, Contact Press Images
493T   Bob Daemmrich, The Image Works
493B   Robert Brenner, PhotoEdit
495    Bob Daemmrich, The Image Works
497    Mary Kate Denny, PhotoEdit
500    Bob Daemmrich, Stock Boston
505    Darryl Baird, Lightwave
510    Kenneth Jarecke, Contact Press Images
513    Bob Daemmrich, The Image Works
516    Robert Brenner, PhotoEdit
519    Lawrence Migdale, Stock Boston
521    Joan Liftin, Actuality Inc.

**Epilogue**
524L   John Eastcott/Yva Momatiuk, The Image Works
524R   David E. Kennedy, TexaStock
525T   Joan Liftin, Actuality Inc.
525B   Alan Oddie, PhotoEdit
527    Joan Eastcott/Yva Momatiuk, The Image Works
528    Michael Kienitz, Picture Group
532    David E. Kennedy, TexaStock
536    Lawrence Migdale, Stock Boston
540    Joan Liftin, Actuality Inc.
543    Murrae Haynes, Picture Group
545    Alan Oddie, PhotoEdit

# Glossary

**accommodation** settlement for a portion of that which was originally desired

**acquired immune deficiency syndrome (AIDS)** disease that weakens the body's immune system and leaves the victim vulnerable to illnesses

**action-oriented approach** style of therapy emphasizing active involvement of the therapist in helping solve problems

**actualizing tendency** striving toward growth and fulfillment of inborn potential

**adaptive behavior** behavior that effectively meets adjustive demands, satisfies our needs, and contributes to the well-being of others

**adjustive demand** life event that requires changes in an individual's thoughts or behaviors

**adjustment** the process of meeting environmental demands and modifying the world around us to better meet our needs in the future

**adjustment disorder** abnormal, unreasonable reaction to a common stressful event

**affective information** information concerning feelings, emotions, and attitudes

**agape** (*ah-gah-pay*) selfless, nonsexual form of love

**aggression** expression of anger with the intent to harm or injure another person

**agoraphobia** (*ag-or-a-pho-bia*) irrational fear of public places and crowds

**alarm and mobilization reaction** first stage of the General Adaptation Syndrome, characterized by the mobilization of defenses to cope with stress

**alcoholism** physiological dependence on (addiction to) alcohol

**alienation hypothesis** theory that people who are satisfied in their work will also tend to be satisfied with their leisure activities

**ambivalent feelings** simultaneous existence of contradictory emotions toward the same person

**anal stage** second stage in development, during which pleasure is centered on the anus

**antisocial personality disorder** disorder characterized by lack of moral development and inability to feel guilt or anxiety

**anxiety** generalized feelings of fear and apprehension

**approach-approach conflict** conflict produced when a person must choose between two or more desirable alternatives

**approach-avoidance conflict** conflict produced when a goal has both positive and negative features

**assertiveness training** behavioral technique for helping individuals express their feelings and gain their rights without being uncooperative or overbearing

**assessment phase** first phase of the therapeutic process in which an individual's current concerns, history, and present circumstances are identified

**attachment** emotional tie or bond between an infant and others

**authenticity** human quality of being spontaneous and genuine, of being one's true self without a false front or facade

**avoidance-avoidance conflict**   conflict produced when an individual must choose between two or more undesirable alternatives

**becoming**   personal growth over time

**behavioral contracting**   behavioral technique in which contracts are developed that specify the behaviors necessary to receive reinforcement

**behavioral model**   view that most human behavior, whether adaptive or maladaptive, is learned

**behavioral therapies**   forms of psychotherapy that emphasize learning of adaptive patterns and modification of maladaptive patterns of behavior

**behaviorism**   belief that psychology, as a science, should focus on observable behavior rather than unobservable mental processes

**bipolar disorder (manic depression)**   mood disorder characterized by periods of extreme excitement and overactivity (mania) which alternate with periods of profound depression

**borderline personality disorder**   personality disorder characterized by impulsivity, identity confusion, rage, and inability to control emotions

**brainstorming**   generation of many potential solutions to a problem while postponing

criticism or evaluation of the suggestions

**built-in coping mechanisms**   predominantly unlearned patterns such as crying and laughing that can be used to relieve stress reactions

**burnout**   physical, mental, and emotional exhaustion from overworking

**catatonic schizophrenia**   type of schizophrenia marked by periods of inactivity and frozen immobility, although outbursts of excited activity may also occur

**chancre** (*shan-ker*)   painless ulcerated sore that is the first sign of syphilis

**classical (respondent, Pavlovian) conditioning**   a learning process in which a response is transferred from one stimulus to another after multiple pairings of the stimuli

**cognitive behaviorism**   contemporary version of behaviorism that acknowledges the importance of some unobservable mental processes in learning

**cognitive self-statements**   statements that can be used to recast a stressful situation in a more effective and productive way

**cohabitation**   process involving emotional commitments and living arrangements similar to marriage but without a formal or legal announcement of marriage

**collusion**   agreement of partners to a relationship

based on maladaptive, deviant rules and norms

**communication apprehension**   anxiety or concern about speaking in groups or meetings or in front of an audience

**companionate love**   love for one's partner accompanied by strong feelings of liking for the partner

**compensation**   defense mechanism in which an undesirable trait is covered up by emphasizing a desirable trait

**compensatory hypothesis**   theory that leisure offsets accumulated work tensions and work dissatisfaction

**complementarity**   principle that people are attracted to others whose traits or characteristics supplement or contrast with their own

**compliance**   yielding to social influence as a result of a specific request to do so

**compulsion**   irrational and repetitive behavior that a person feels compelled to perform

**conceived values**   values an individual feels are valid and ideal, but not necessarily the values he or she actually lives by

**concrete operational stage**   according to Piaget, third stage of cognitive development characterized by reduced egocentrism and an understanding of multiple viewpoints

**conditional positive regard**   situation in which the love and affection of others is conditional on our behaving as they wish us to behave

**conditioned response**　a new response that comes to be elicited by the conditioned stimulus after association has occurred

**conditioned stimulus**　stimulus that does not initially elicit the desired response until new learning has occurred

**conflict**　simultaneous arousal of two or more incompatible motives

**conflicting system demands**　incompatible requirements arising from two or more family systems that cause significant stress

**conformity**　yielding to social influence without being asked or instructed to do so

**congruence**　according to Rogers, condition in which one's self-concept is consistent with one's inborn nature

**contingency management**　behavioral technique that relies on positive reinforcement to teach more adaptive behaviors

**contraceptive**　device or technique used to allow sexual intercourse while preventing pregnancy in fertile individuals; also known as birth control

**counseling**　brief, action-oriented therapy focussed on a single problem

**crisis intervention**　immediate, short-term assistance provided during or after a particularly traumatic event or crisis

**crowding**　the feeling of being cramped, not having enough space

**cyclothymia** (*cycl-o-thy-mia*)　chronic mood disorder in which periods of inappropriate depression alternate with periods of inappropriate elation

**defense-oriented responses**　self-deceptive responses to stress that protect one's feelings of adequacy and worth or alleviate unpleasant emotions

**deficiency motivation**　domination of behavior by physiological and safety needs

**delusions**　false beliefs an individual defends despite logical evidence

**denial**　defense mechanism in which the individual refuses to perceive unpleasant or threatening aspects of reality

**density**　the number of people occupying a particular amount of space

**despair**　despondency over the course of one's life

**development**　the predictable process of growth and change throughout the lifespan

**developmental tasks**　competencies to be mastered during a particular stage of development

**diathesis-stress model** (*dy-ath-a-sis*)　view that some people are predisposed to develop particular disorders when exposed to certain kinds of stressors

**directive therapy**　therapy in which the therapist offers advice and suggests problem-solving strategies

**discordant interpersonal patterns**　relationships that involve serious and continuous disagreements and conflicts detrimental to the quality of the relationship

**disengagement**　controversial idea that older adults increasingly withdraw from the external world and focus instead on inner thoughts and feelings

**disorganized (hebephrenic) schizophrenia**　type of schizophrenia characterized by inappropriate emotions and bizarre behavior

**displacement**　defense mechanism for redirection of emotions to objects other than those which initially aroused the emotions

**dissociative disorder**　alteration of consciousness or identity as a result of severe stress

**distress**　negative stress; stress that has a detrimental effect

**double standard**　unequal standard stating that premarital intercourse is acceptable for men but unacceptable for women

**dream**　idealized life plan developed during the early adult years

**drug tolerance**　need for increased dosage of a drug to obtain the same effects; a sign of substance dependence

**DSM-III-R**　Diagnostic and Statistical Manual of Mental Disorders (Third Edition, Revised), the current standard for diagnosing psychological disorders

**dysthymia** (*dis-thy-mia*)　mood disorder marked by

chronic, inappropriate feelings of depression

**ego** reality-based portion of the personality that mediates between the demands of the id, the superego, and the real world

**ego integrity** sense of satisfaction with and acceptance of the course of one's life

**egocentric** preoccupied with one's own concerns or beliefs

**ejaculation** expulsion of semen from the penis, indicating orgasm in the male

**Electra complex** version of the Oedipus complex that occurs in females

**emotional insulation** defense mechanism in which the individual reduces his or her emotional involvement in potentially hurtful situations

**encounter group** small group designed to provide an intensive interpersonal experience focusing on feelings and group interactions

**environmental planning** self-control procedure in which an individual structures his or her environment to achieve positive goals

**eros** reciprocal, sexual form of love

**erotophiles** individuals who are comfortable with sexual materials and their sexual feelings and behaviors

**erotophobes** people who have difficulty dealing with sexual materials and their sexual feelings and behaviors

**establishment** second

stage in the development of an occupational identity, occurring in the first months and years of employment in a chosen occupation

**eustress** positive stress; stress that has a beneficial effect

**excitement phase** first stage of sexual response cycle in which physical signs of sexual arousal become evident

**exhaustion** final stage of the General Adaptation Syndrome, characterized by the use of extreme measures to cope with stress

**existential therapy** form of psychotherapy that attempts to develop a sense of self-direction and meaning in one's existence

**expectancies** predictions about future events based on previous experience

**exploration** first stage in the development of an occupational identity, characterized by tentative first steps in the selection of an occupation

**extended family** relatives other than parents and their children, all of whom maintain contact with one another

**extinction** gradual disappearance of a learned behavior when reinforcement is withheld

**extrinsic satisfaction** satisfaction that comes from something other than work itself (such as money, fringe benefits)

**family therapy** form of

therapy focusing on relationships within the family

**fantasy** defense mechanism in which the individual escapes from the world of reality to a world of imagination

**fantasy period** first stage of occupational selection in which choices are based on fantasy, not fact or ability

**fear** feeling of threat or danger from a specific object or event

**feedback** knowledge of the results of one's behavior, used in judging the appropriateness of one's responses and making corrections where indicated

**feedback phase** second phase of the therapeutic process in which assessment information is used to help establish therapeutic goals

**fixation** concentration of mental energy in an infantile stage of development

**foreclosure** premature attainment of identity, typically not preceded by a crisis

**formal operations stage** according to Piaget, fourth stage of cognitive development characterized by the ability to think and reason abstractly

**fraudulent interpersonal contract** violation of the rules or norms governing a satisfying interpersonal relationship in a way that exploits one of the participants

**free association** psychoanalytic procedure in which an individual gives a running account of every thought and feeling

**frustration** result of being

unable to satisfy needs or desires

**fully-functioning person** according to Rogers, a person who is well-adjusted, mature, and fully open to experience

**future shock** stress produced by rapid, accelerating technological, social, and cultural change

**game** interpersonal strategy used to exert influence over another

**games model** view that interpersonal relationships are controlled or heavily influenced by games

**General Adaptation Syndrome (GAS)** series of physical responses to both physical and psychological stress

**generalization** tendency to give a learned response when in the presence of different but similar stimuli

**generalized anxiety disorder** persistent excessive worry, uneasiness, or apprehensiveness

**generativity** involvement in activities that will have a lasting effect on future generations

**genital herpes** painful viral infection marked by genital blisters

**genital stage** fifth and last stage in development, during which adult sexuality and genuine love for others appear

**Gestalt therapy** type of psychotherapy emphasizing the wholeness of the client and the integration of thoughts, feelings, and action

**gonorrhea** common sexually transmitted disease often accompanied by a discharge (especially in men)

**grief work** the processes associated with mourning and the recovery from loss

**group therapy** psychotherapy with two or more individuals at the same time

**groupthink** tendency to make group decisions that preserve group unity at the cost of ignoring important issues or data

**growth motivation** domination of behavior by needs for love and belongingness, esteem, and self-actualization

**hallucinations** perceptual experiences that are not based in reality

**hallucinogen** psychoactive substance capable of producing hallucinations

**halo effect** tendency to assess a person on the basis of one or two easily perceived traits, such as seeing attractive persons as being friendly

**hexagonal model** Holland's model of six personality types and six corresponding environments; according to the model, a person is most likely to be satisfied in a career where the environmental demands correspond closely to his or her personality profile

**hierarchy** ranked list of fear-producing situations, used in systematic desensitization

**hierarchy of needs** Maslow's suggestion that needs can be arranged in order from the most basic deficiency needs to higher level growth needs such as self-actualization

**hospice** center for the care of the terminally ill

**humanistic model** view of human nature that emphasizes self-direction and strivings toward growth and fulfillment

**hyperstress** overstress; stress that exceeds the person's ability to handle it

**hypertension** chronically high blood pressure

**hypochondriac** person who has many vague medical complaints for which there is no physical cause

**hypostress** understress; insufficient stress resulting in boredom

**id** biologically-based portion of the personality composed of primitive needs and drives such as sex and aggression

**identity** our sense of ourselves as unique individuals

**identity crisis** point during adolescence at which individuals are confronted with the difficulty of developing a personal sense of self (identity)

**identity diffusion** a lack of a sense of self; role confusion

**immune system** complex mechanism which the body uses to protect itself against infections and diseases

**implementation phase** third phase of the therapeutic process in which client and therapist attempt to achieve therapeutic goals

**impotence** in men, inability to achieve or maintain an erection sufficient for sexual intercourse

**incongruence** according to Rogers, condition in which one's self-concept does not correspond to one's inborn nature

**informational influence** conforming, complying, or obeying because of a desire to be correct or to do the correct thing

**insight-oriented approach** style of therapy emphasizing understanding of the client's problems

**instrumental values** values that concern the means used in achieving goals

**intellectualization** defense mechanism by which the individual achieves some measure of insulation from emotional hurt by treating the situation as an abstract problem to be analyzed

**interest inventories** psychological tests that can be used to help an individual make an appropriate career choice

**intermittent (partial) reinforcement** providing reinforcement only some of the time that a desired behavior occurs

**interpersonal accommodation** process of adjusting to problems that arise in interpersonal relationships

**interpersonal perceptions** ways in which we perceive other people

**interpersonal style** characteristic manner in which an individual interacts with others

**interpretation** psychoanalytic technique in which the therapist suggests unconscious motives, thoughts, or wishes that appear to account for behavior

**intimacy** establishment of a deep, caring relationship with another person

**intrinsic satisfaction** satisfaction found in work itself (such as meaning, fulfillment, personal growth)

**latency stage** fourth stage in development, during which sexual instincts are largely missing

**learned helplessness** state in which an individual believes that he or she is helpless to cope with adjustive demands

**leisure** nonwork, nonmaintenance activities involving prescribed tasks that people choose for their intrinsic motivating qualities

**Life Change Unit** quantitative measure of the stressfulness of events on the Social Readjustment Rating Scale

**maintenance activities** nonwork activities that are required or expected for normal daily functioning

**major depressive disorder** a severe form of chronic depression in which the person's ability to function is seriously affected

**maladaptive behavior** behavior that does not meet adjustive demands, does not satisfy our needs, or does not contribute to the well-being of others

**marital therapy** therapy focusing on the marital relationship

**masturbation** deliberate stimulation of one's body to produce sexual arousal and satisfaction

**maturation** growth of an organism that occurs primarily due to the passage of time

**menopause** cessation of menstrual functioning during middle adulthood

**mentor** an older individual who helps guide the occupational development of a younger person

**metacommunication** communication about the way in which two people typically communicate

**mid-life transition** an identity crisis during middle adulthood brought on by recognition of one's aging and mortality; sometimes called "mid-life crisis"

**migraine headache** severe, intense headache, often accompanied by nausea and vomiting

**mood disorder** disorder characterized by extreme and inappropraite depression or elation

**moratorium** a "pause" in identity formation in which an individual explores alternatives

**multiple approach-avoidance conflict** conflict produced when an individual must choose between two or more goals, each of which has positive and negative features

**muscle contraction headache** most common form of headache characterized by "bands" of pain around the head

**negative reinforcer** any event whose reduction or removal increases the likelihood that a behavior will occur again in the future

**nondirective therapy** therapy in which the therapist helps the client to achieve self-understanding and avoids advice-giving

**nonspecific urethritis (NSU)** infection of the urethra that causes pain and burning during urination

**nonverbal communication** communication through gestures, facial expressions, and body posture

**normative influence** conforming, complying, or obeying in order to be liked or accepted by others

**nuclear family** parents and their children

**obedience** yielding to explicit orders or instructions from another person

**observational learning (modeling)** form of learning in which an individual learns by watching someone else

**obsession** persistent irrational thoughts or impulses

**Oedipus complex** child's desire for the opposite-sex parent and wish to replace the same-sex parent

**open marriage** marriage in which both partners are free to take other sexual partners

**operant conditioning** a learning process in which the likelihood of behavior changes as a result of the consequences of the behavior

**operative values** values which actually guide the behavior of an individual, as opposed to the values he or she may profess to believe in

**oral stage** first stage in development, during which pleasure is centered on the mouth

**organ specificity** tendency for different people to react to stress with different physical disorders

**orgasmic dysfunction** in women, persistent difficulty achieving orgasm

**orgasmic phase** third stage of sexual response cycle in which a peak of sexual pleasure is experienced

**outcome** the difference between rewards and costs in an interpersonal relationship (profit)

**overeducation** education, training, knowledge, or skills that are in excess of those required by a particular job

**panic disorder** intense anxiety accompanied by various worrisome physiological symptoms

**paranoid schizophrenia** type of schizophrenia characterized by delusions of grandeur or persecution

**peptic (gastric) ulcer** a pathological condition of the stomach brought about by excessive stomach acid

**personal space** psychological boundaries surrounding a person which only certain people are supposed to cross

**personality disorders** inflexible, maladaptive behavior patterns that impair functioning

**personality inventory** psychological test used to assess specific aspects of an individual's personality

**person-centered therapy** nondirective approach to psychotherapy developed by Carl Rogers; also called client-centered therapy

**phallic stage** third stage in development, during which pleasure is derived especially from the genitals

**plateau phase** second stage of the sexual response cycle in which physical changes initiated in the excitement phase are intensified

**pleasure principle** pursuit of immediate pleasure regardless of reality or morality

**positive reinforcer** any event whose presence increases the likelihood that a behavior will occur again in the future

**post-traumatic stress disorder** extreme reaction to an unusually stressful event such as assault, a natural disaster, or combat

**preconscious**   portion of the mind that can be brought into consciousness after a moment's reflection

**premature ejaculation**   inability of a male to delay orgasm long enough to allow his partner an opportunity to achieve orgasm

**preoperational stage**   according to Piaget, second stage of cognitive development characterized by symbolic thinking and the acquisition of language

**pressure**   adjustive demand that requires an organism to speed up, intensify, or change behavior

**primary appraisal**   judgment of the stressfulness of an event

**primary process**   gratification of an instinctual need by fantasy

**problematic alliances**   close bonds between some family members that are disruptive to the family as a whole

**problematic role relationships**   roles played by family members that are disruptive or maladaptive for the family as a whole

**problem-finding**   proposed fifth stage of cognitive development, characterized by the tendency to discover questions rather than solve problems

**projection**   defense mechanism in which the individual attributes his or her unacceptable desires and impulses to others

**projective test**   psychological assessment technique using relatively unstructured stimuli

**psychedelic drugs**   "mind expanding" drugs that produce changes in sensory experiences, moods, and thought processes

**psychoactive substance**   any substance that significantly alters normal psychological processes

**psychoanalytic model**   view that all human behavior is heavily influenced by unconscious factors such as needs, instincts, wishes, and conflicts

**psychological assessment**   use of psychological tests and other methods for the diagnosis of maladaptive behavior

**psychology**   the science of behavior and mental processes

**psychopathology**   psychological disorder or abnormality

**psychophysiological disorders**   physical disorders produced by stress

**psychosis**   severe psychological disorder marked by loss of contact with reality

**psychotherapy**   longer-term therapy intended to help people cope more effectively in a wide range of situations

**pubic lice**   parasites that attach themselves to pubic hairs and cause intense itching

**punishment**   any event whose presence reduces the likelihood that a behavior will occur again in the future

**rating scale**   continuum for evaluating an individual on a specific characteristic

**rationalization**   defense mechanism in which the individual thinks up "good" reasons to justify what he or she has done, is doing, or is going to do

**Rational-Emotive Therapy**   form of psychotherapy which encourages the client to substitute rational for irrational assumptions in his or her inner dialogues

**realistic choice stage**   third stage of occupational choice in which preferences are tested in the world of work

**reality principle**   pursuit of instinctual gratification through the real world

**reciprocal determinism**   view that individuals affect the environment and the environment in turn affects individuals

**refractory period**   in males, period after ejaculation during which further stimulation will not produce sexual arousal

**regression**   defense mechanism in which the individual retreats to the use of less mature responses in attempting to cope with stress and maintain self-integration

**reinforcer**   any consequence that strengthens or maintains a behavior that precedes it

**relaxation training**   specific learned techniques that help an individual attain a relaxed state

**reliability**   degree to which a psychological test produces the same result each time it is used on the same person

**renewable marriage**   marriage contract that is extended only when the partners specifically agree to continue the marriage

**repression**   defense mechanism in which anxiety-arousing desires or intolerable memories are kept out of consciousness

**resistance**   second stage of the General Adaptation Syndrome, in which physical and psychological resources are used to combat continued stress

**resolution phase**   fourth stage of sexual response cycle in which signs of sexual arousal subside

**role**   socially expected behavior pattern

**role conflict**   condition arising when an individual must play incompatible roles

**role expectations**   obligations associated with a particular interpersonal role

**romantic love**   type of love characterized by intense, passionate feelings

**schizophrenia**   severe psychotic disorder characterized by profound disturbances of thought and emotion

**secondary appraisal**   judgment of the most appropriate coping strategies for dealing with stress

**secondary process**   rational processes used by the ego such as planning, reasoning, decision making

**segmentalist hypothesis**   theory that work satisfactions and involvement in leisure ac-

tivities are independent of each other

**self-direction**   using one's mental abilities to devise effective methods of adjustment

**self-actualizing tendency**   striving to enhance and maintain one's self-concept

**self-concept**   image or beliefs about oneself

**self-disclosure**   disclosure of information about oneself to another person

**sensorimotor stage**   according to Piaget, first stage of cognitive development in which infants understand the world by sensing it and acting on it

**serial marriage**   two or more marriages for an individual in which one marriage follows the termination of the preceding one

**sex roles**   expected behavior patterns based solely on gender

**sex therapy**   therapy focusing on the treatment of sexual dysfunction

**sexual dysfunction**   inability to fully enjoy sexual activity despite the desire to do so

**sexually transmitted diseases**   diseases that are typically transmitted by sexual activity

**significant other**   any person who is especially important to an individual

**simple phobia**   irrational fear of a specific situation or object

**singlehood**   life-style stressing the positive aspects of being unmarried

**social contagion**   irrational

group behavior such as mobs, panics, and widespread rumors

**social desirability**   tendency of a person to respond in a socially correct manner

**social exchange model**   view that interpersonal relationships are governed by the rewards and costs to each of the persons involved

**social influence**   implicit or explicit pressure to become more like other members of a group

**social role model**   view that relationships between people are governed by certain agreed-upon roles

**somatoform disorder**   unsubstantiated physical complaint

**stagnation**   the self-indulgence, inactivity, and lack of personal growth characteristic of the individual who has not successfully resolved the generativity versus stagnation crisis

**standardization**   characteristics of a psychological test allowing comparison of an individual score with those of a reference group

**stereotypes**   characteristics presumed to be shared by all members of a social category

**storge** (*store-gay*)   love based on deep affection and companionship

**stress**   adjustive demand that requires change or adaptation

**stress inoculation**   cognitively oriented approach to coping with stress, consisting of educational, rehearsal, and application phases

**stressors**    sources of stress outside the individual such as delays, losses, job demands

**substance abuse**    use of a psychoactive substance to the extent that it interferes with adjustment or represents a hazard

**substance dependence**    physiological need for a psychoactive substance marked by tolerance and withdrawal symptoms; addiction

**substance use disorder**    pathological use of a psychoactive substance despite resulting problems or threat to safety

**substitution**    acceptance of alternative goals or satisfactions in place of those originally sought after or desired

**superego**    culturally-based portion of the personality responsible for conscience, ethics, and moral standards

**suppression**    defense mechanism in which thoughts or desires are consciously excluded from immediate awareness

**syphilis**    sexually transmitted disease marked initially by the appearance of a chancre

**systematic desensitization**    technique used by some behavior therapists to eliminate clients' fears and phobias

**tentative period**    second stage of occupational choice in which occupational preferences begin to be based on the person's strengths and weaknesses

**terminal values**    values that concern desirable end-states or goals

**territoriality**    psychological attachment to a specific area

**Theory X**    management theory which assumes that workers are motivated solely by extrinsic satisfactions

**Theory Y**    management theory which assumes that workers are motivated primarily by intrinsic satisfactions

**Theory Z**    management theory which stresses the importance of making each person feel as though he or she is important

**transference**    process whereby the client projects attitudes and emotions applicable to another significant person onto the therapist

**Type A behavior**    life style characterized by an emphasis on speed, competitiveness, and aggressiveness

**Type B behavior**    life style characterized by tolerance, relaxation, and lack of time pressure

**unconditional positive regard**    situation in which the love and affection of others is unconditional and does not depend on our behaving as they would prefer we behave

**unconditioned response**    the desired response that is elicited whenever the unconditioned stimulus occurs

**unconditioned stimulus**    stimulus that always elicits the desired response before new learning begins

**unconscious**    portion of the mind that cannot be brought to awareness under normal circumstances

**undifferentiated schizophrenia**    type of schizophrenia in which symptoms do not permit a more precise diagnosis

**undoing**    defense mechanism in which the individual performs activities designed to atone for misdeeds

**vacillation**    wavering or hesitating in making a choice

**vaginismus**    strong contraction of the vaginal muscles, making intercourse painful or impossible

**validity**    extent to which a measuring instrument actually measures what it is designed to measure

**values**    deeply-held, enduring beliefs about what is desirable and undesirable

**verbal communication**    communication through words and the use of language

**withdrawal symptoms**    unpleasant effects observed when use of a psychoactive substance is stopped; a sign of substance dependence

**work**    any activity that produces something of value for other people

**worry**    commonly used term to describe the simultaneous experiences of fear and anxiety

# Name Index

# Subject Index